Connecting with Computer Science

second edition

Greg Anderson
David Ferro
Robert Hilton
Weber State University

COURSE TECHNOLOGY
CENGAGE Learning™

Australia • Brazil • Japan • Korea • Mexico • Singapore • Spain • United Kingdom • United States

COURSE TECHNOLOGY
CENGAGE Learning

**Connecting with Computer Science,
Second Edition**

Greg Anderson, David Ferro, Robert Hilton

Executive Editor: Marie Lee

Acquisitions Editor: Amy Jollymore

Senior Product Manager: Alyssa Pratt

Development Editor: Lisa M. Lord

Editorial Assistant: Zina Kresin

Content Project Manager: Matthew Hutchinson

Art Director: Faith Brosnan

Copyeditor: Karen Annett

Proofreader: Foxxe Editorial Services

Indexer: Liz Cunningham

Photo Researcher: Abby Reip

Compositor: Pre-Press PMG

For product information and technology assistance, contact us at
Cengage Learning Customer & Sales Support, 1-800-354-9706

For permission to use material from this text or product, submit all requests online at **cengage.com/permissions**
Further permissions questions can be e-mailed to
permissionrequest@cengage.com

Library of Congress Control Number: 2009940546

ISBN-13: 978-0-538-47573-0

ISBN-10: 0-538-47573-0

Course Technology
20 Channel Center Street
Boston, MA 02210

Cengage Learning is a leading provider of customized learning solutions with office locations around the globe, including Singapore, the United Kingdom, Australia, Mexico, Brazil, and Japan. Locate your local office at: **international.cengage.com/region**

Cengage Learning products are represented in Canada by Nelson Education, Ltd.

For your lifelong learning solutions, visit **course.cengage.com**
Visit our corporate website at **cengage.com**.

Some of the product names and company names used in this book have been used for identification purposes only and may be trademarks or registered trademarks of their respective manufacturers and sellers.

Any fictional data related to persons or companies or URLs used throughout this book is intended for instructional purposes only. At the time this book was printed, any such data was fictional and not belonging to any real persons or companies.

Course Technology, a part of Cengage Learning, reserves the right to revise this publication and make changes from time to time in its content without notice.

The programs in this book are for instructional purposes only.

They have been tested with care but are not guaranteed for any particular intent beyond educational purposes. The author and the publisher do not offer any warranties or representations, nor do they accept any liabilities with respect to the programs.

Printed in Canada
2 3 4 5 6 16 15 14 13 12 11 10

brief contents

table of contents

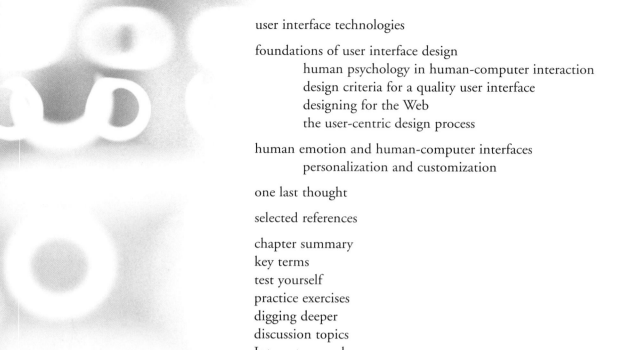

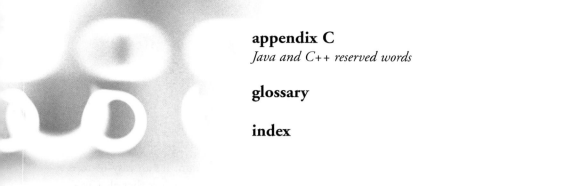

preface

The second edition of *Connecting with Computer Science* continues to have a fresh approach to learning the essentials of computer science. The style encourages students in Introduction to Computer Science (CS0) courses to actually read the assigned material, and the content enables them to learn the foundational material needed to handle the rigor of a computer science program. It's an easy-to-read yet comprehensive introductory book for computer science majors that also appeals to nonmajors who want a broad-based introduction to the field. In other words, it's a computer science book that students can connect with. The second edition continues to include the core knowledge outlined by the ACM/IEEE Joint Task Force on Computing Curricula in a context suitable for beginning students, without "dumbing down" the material or patronizing students.

As in the first edition, this edition maintains a conversational writing style, an open design, and an optimal balance of text, figures, tables, and margin features. It has been updated to reflect current and emerging technologies, and the chapter order has been altered slightly because of student and faculty feedback to create a better learning experience. Additionally, new chapters introduce students to problem solving, designing human-computer interfaces, and C++ programming.

The informal writing style, along with numerous practical examples, will continue to draw students into reading and enjoying the material, so they will be better able to learn and retain the necessary concepts. *Connecting with Computer Science, Second Edition*, is suitable for students with varying levels of knowledge and expertise and will help ensure that students moving on to a CS1 course have a consistent foundation.

what's new in the second edition

Connecting with Computer Science was first published in 2005—the same year YouTube was founded. Since then, YouTube has undergone several major changes, but there have been even more changes in the computing industry, prompting the need for an updated edition of this book.

Connecting with Computer Science has been used successfully in many computing education programs. Those using the book were solicited for ideas for improvement that could be incorporated along with other revisions.

Our goal in the second edition is to provide a current, relevant book that's written and organized in a manner that encourages students to read, enjoy, and learn. We believe we have accomplished this goal in the second edition.

The main changes in this edition are as follows:

- The material has been updated throughout to incorporate current technology and ideas. Every page was checked and edited to make sure outdated material was revised to reflect the current state of computing.
- Chapters have been reordered, based on student and faculty feedback, to give students in a first computing course a better learning experience. This sequence is designed to draw students in and lead them through the topics. The chapter mapping after this list helps those familiar with the first edition correlate old chapters with the new sequence.
- Two new chapters, "The Human-Computer Interface," and "Problem Solving and Debugging," delve into topics that were discussed only briefly in the first edition.
- The programming chapter was split into two chapters to better separate program design and programming basics from exercises in programming. In addition, coverage of C++ was added to the sections on Java programming so that the book is valuable in programs emphasizing either language.
- More emphasis was placed on Linux to reflect its growing popularity in computing.
- The chapters on emerging technologies and software tools for techies were moved to the Web so that they can be updated more easily to stay on the frontiers of computing.
- The appendix material was expanded to be more useful as a reference.

We believe this edition continues the tradition established in the first edition and will give both faculty and students an enhanced experience in a first computing course.

chapter mapping

2nd edition chapter	1st edition chapter	topic
1	1	History and Social Implications of Computing
2	13	Computing Security and Ethics
3	3	Computer Architecture
4	6	Networks
5	7	The Internet
6	8	Database Fundamentals
7	4	Numbering Systems and Data Representations
8	9	Data Structures

approach

Our approach in this book is to present the breadth of the computer science discipline in a way that's accessible, understandable, and enjoyable. The following sections outline specific elements of this approach.

draw students in at the beginning of each chapter

Each chapter begins with a humorous vignette, "the lighter side of the lab," by CS student and journalist Spencer Hilton. These vignettes capture the students' attention and provide a bridge to the chapter material. Many studies have demonstrated that humor is an effective catalyst to learning. These vignettes were written in a way that students can relate to.

explain why the material in the chapter is important

Students are more likely to read and study the material in a chapter if they understand why it will be important to them in their studies. A short section at the beginning of each chapter explains why students need to learn the material in the chapter and how they will benefit from it.

keep the pages informative and visually interesting

The chapters are filled with margin sidebars and definitions that break up the text and add interest. Photos and conceptual diagrams are also used throughout to illustrate and provide examples. We took care to not clutter the text with excessive nontext material and maintain a good balance between text and supporting material. Additionally, appropriate humorous material is interspersed to further encourage students to keep reading.

give key term definitions in the margins

Key terms are defined in the margin at the point they're first used so that students don't have to turn to the back of the chapter or book to find definitions. Each chapter has a list at the end of key terms with page references. At the end of the book, all the key terms and their definitions are compiled in a glossary for easy reference.

include ample end-of-chapter review materials

At the end of each chapter are many types of review materials to solidify students' grasp of the material, including the following:

- **test yourself questions:** At the end of the chapter are 10 to 20 questions that students can use to test their knowledge of the subject matter in the chapter. Answers to these questions are in Appendix A.
- **practice exercises:** At the end of each chapter are also 10 to 20 multiple-choice practice exercises. The answers for these questions aren't given in the book but are available with the instructor's materials. They would also work well as questions for weekly quizzes on the material to further encourage students to read and study the chapter.
- **digging deeper questions:** Five questions at the end of each chapter are designed to lead students (and the instructor) deeper into the subject matter. These questions can be assigned as topics for research papers, oral presentations, or projects to maintain the interest of more advanced students. This section encourages students to use critical thinking and reasoning skills rather than rote memorization.
- **discussion topics:** Each chapter includes five thought-provoking discussion questions. They're designed to be used in class and will encourage student participation in and engagement with topics related to the chapter. Many of these questions address ethical and societal issues, and others lead students into a "Which is better?" discussion. The questions in this section allow students to apply their understanding of the chapter's material to society in general.
- **Internet research:** An effective method of enhancing learning is to conduct research related to the material. This end-of-chapter section consists of five questions that direct students to Internet research on topics related to the chapter. The authors have researched the questions to ensure that Web materials are available for each one. This section helps students develop essential research skills and demonstrates the power of finding out information for themselves—as well as the danger of accepting everything they find on the Internet at face value.

include a companion Web site full of exciting extras and updated support materials

The chapters on emerging technologies and software tools have been moved online so that they can be updated quickly and easily. They're available for instructors at *www.cengage.com/coursetechnology*. Students, please contact your instructor for more information on online chapters and resources.

In addition, several resources to augment the material in the book, such as tutorials, labs, and other learning materials, are now available on the companion Web site for the book. Information on accessing this material is available at *www.cengage.com/computerscience/anderson/connecting2e*.

organization

This book is organized into 15 chapters, so it's suitable for use in 15-week semesters; however, it can be adaped for other schedules easily. The chapters are modular and can be covered in any order that the instructor chooses.

chapter 1, "history and social implications of computing," is a short tour through the essentials of the history of computers and computing. Key players in the computing field and their contributions are introduced, and an overview of the social implications of computing is given. This chapter's less technical content eases students into the curriculum.

chapter 2, "computing security and ethics," helps students grasp the issues in computer and network security and the ethical use of computers. Hacking, social engineering, privacy, and other topics are discussed to help students develop positions and policies on security and ethical issues.

chapter 3, "computer architecture," covers the basics of computer architecture, focusing on the Von Neumann machine, and discusses memory, CPU, I/O, and buses. This chapter also explains digital logic circuits and how they're used to build the CPU and other computer devices.

chapter 4, "networks," familiarizes students with the OSI reference model and the operation of LANs, WANs, and WLANs. Networking protocols and standards are also explained, giving students a basis for further networking courses.

chapter 5, "the Internet," expands on knowledge gained in the networking chapter by explaining TCP/IP and higher-level protocols, such as DHCP, HTTP, and FTP. Concepts such as NAT, DNS, and IP addressing are also covered. Examples of HTML coding are given, along with a basic explanation of how Web pages are created. Finally, students are introduced to using the Internet and search engines as a tool for research.

chapter 6, "database fundamentals," introduces database development and concepts and proceeds into database design, including the normalization process. This chapter also covers the basics of SQL and explains some basic SQL commands.

chapter 7, "numbering systems and data representations," is a key chapter designed to give students a strong foundation in numbering systems and conversion between number bases, with emphasis on binary, hex, and decimal conversions. Students are also introduced to forms of data representation, including signed and unsigned integers, floating-point numbers, characters, and sound and video files.

chapter 8, "data structures," discusses the importance of data structures in computing. Stacks, queues, linked lists, binary trees, and other structures are explained with examples and diagrams. Students are also taught the basics of sorting and using pointers.

chapter 9, "operating systems," explains the fundamentals of operating systems. This chapter also includes tables showing how to perform tasks in Windows and Linux to prepare students for using operating systems in later courses.

chapter 10, "file structures," gives insight into different methods of storing information on mass storage devices. This chapter also explains the basics of file systems, including FAT and NTFS. Students are introduced to the differences between sequential and random record storage and the use of hashing and indexing to retrieve stored records.

chapter 11, "the human-computer interface," is a tour through developing the parts of computer systems that people interact with: the user interface. This chapter reviews the psychological principles involved in the human-computer interface and explains the process of analysis and design of user interfaces. It's placed before the programming chapters as a reminder that people use the programs you write.

chapter 12, "problem solving and debugging," provides a strong foundation in the processes of problem solving and debugging as preparation for the programming chapters. This chapter gives an overview of problem-solving techniques and describes useful rules for ensuring success in debugging. You can return to this chapter often for guidelines when you begin writing programs.

chapter 13, "software engineering," shows how software engineering procedures are used to develop computer applications. The main software development models are discussed, and students are introduced to design documents, flowcharts, and UML diagrams. This chapter also describes the different players in a software development team and explains their roles.

chapter 14, "programming I," is an introduction to the concepts of computer programming. It gives an overview of different types of programming languages, explains developing algorithms and pseudocode as part of program design, and introduces variables, operators, and control structures. This chapter also covers the basics of object-oriented programming.

chapter 15, "programming II," delves into variables and data types and explains standard control structures with code examples in both Java and C++ that show correct coding techniques.

In addition, there are three appendixes (appendix A, "answers to test yourself questions," appendix B, "ASCII table," and appendix C, "Java and and C++ reserved words"), a glossary, and a comprehensive index.

instructor's materials

This book includes the following teaching tools to support instructors in the classroom:

Electronic Instructor's Manual. The Instructor's Manual that accompanies this book includes additional material to assist instructors in class preparation, including suggestions for lecture topics.

Solutions. Solutions to end-of-chapter practice exercises are included. (Solutions to the test yourself questions are included in Appendix A of this book.)

ExamView®. This book is accompanied by ExamView, a powerful testing software package that allows instructors to create and administer printed, computer (LAN-based), and Internet exams. ExamView includes hundreds of questions that correspond to the topics covered in this book, enabling students to generate detailed study guides that include page references for further review. The computer-based and Internet testing components allow students to take exams at their computers and save instructors time because each exam is graded automatically.

PowerPoint Presentations. This book comes with Microsoft PowerPoint slides for each chapter. They are included as a teaching aid for classroom presentations and can be made available to students on the network for chapter review or be printed for classroom distribution. Instructors can add their own slides for additional topics they introduce to the class.

Distance Learning Content. Course Technology is proud to present online test banks in WebCT and Blackboard to provide the most complete and dynamic learning experience possible. Instructors are encouraged to make the most of the course, both online and offline. For more information on how to access the online test bank, please contact your local Cengage representative.

acknowledgments

This second edition continues to be a joint effort of three authors and many other talented people. All three authors would like to thank the following people:

Amy Jollymore, the acquisitions editor, was a strong supporter of the first edition and gave us the encouragement and support to get started on the second edition. She made things happen.

Alyssa Pratt, the senior product manager, has been a motivating factor from the beginning of the first edition and continued to be a very competent taskmaster in the second edition. Without her help and support, neither edition would have become a reality.

Lisa Lord, the development editor, was instrumental in motivating us to make this edition the best book possible, as she edited and cleaned up our revisions to the first edition. She had a positive attitude throughout the process, even when we whined, complained, and kicked our feet in tantrums. Her editing skills have greatly improved the delivery of the content and kept the relaxed writing style as one that's enjoyable, entertaining, and informative.

Deb Kaufmann, the development editor of the first edition, should continue to be acknowledged for helping us transform our different writing styles into the consistent style that has been carried through into this edition.

Matthew Hutchinson, the content project manager, did a great job of shepherding the chapters through production and keeping us informed about the process.

Karen Annett, the copyeditor, polished the prose of the new chapters, and the proofreading provided by Foxxe Editorial Services helped ensure the consistency of terminology and the accuracy of details.

Spencer Hilton added a dimension to the book that kept us enthused about the book's topics. Thanks to Spencer, we got a chance to chuckle at least once during the writing of each chapter. (It's too bad readers of this book didn't get an opportunity to laugh at "the lighter side of the lab" forewords that were rejected because they were too funny!)

We would also like to thank the reviewers for their candid and constructive feedback:

Proposal reviewers:

Jerry Ross: Lane Community College

Mark Hutchenreuther: Cal Poly State University

Aaron Stevens: Boston University

Marie desJardins: University of Maryland, Baltimore County

William Duncan: Louisiana State University

Khaled Mansour: Washtenaw Community College

Johnette Moody: Arkansas Tech University

John Zamora: Modesto Junior College

Chapter reviewers:

Mark Hart: Indiana University–Purdue University Fort Wayne

Jerry Ross: Lane Community College

Rajiv Bagai: Wichita State University

Brian Kell: Wake Forest University

Because this book is a collaboration of three authors who each had the support of family, friends, and associates, each would like to acknowledge some special people separately.

Greg Anderson: I would like to thank my wife, Gina, for again giving in and consenting to me writing another book. She supports me in all my wild or painful endeavors. Thanks also to my great children: Kelsi, Kaytlen, Marissa, and Miles. A special thanks to Rob, Dave, and Spencer: You guys make writing fun! Rob, thanks for taking the lead and encouraging me to keep moving forward. Last, a special thanks to all the faculty and students who use this book. We wrote it because we wanted education to be both fun and informative. I hope this book can help lay a foundation for students to be successful in the exciting world of computers. Remember: "Code unto others as you would have others code unto you."

David Ferro: I want to thank my students for their suggestions and help during the writing of the first edition. Many became instrumental in its creation—proving that undergraduates, research, and interesting and useful projects can coexist fruitfully. Three students who went above and beyond are Matt Werney, John Linford, and Adam Christensen. I also want to thank my coauthors. The working relationship we established couldn't have been stronger or more enjoyable. Even on the darkest days, with deadlines looming, one or all of us could bring some sense of humor to the proceedings. Finally, I want to thank two very special people who gave me more support than anyone: my wife and daughter, Marjukka and Stella. I am indebted to you both.

Rob Hilton: Thanks to Alyssa and Amy for their support of this book and for encouraging us to go forward with the second edition. I'm grateful that Greg and Dave were willing to jump on board again, in spite of other heavy demands on their time, and I'm especially grateful for their continuing friendship. I also appreciate the CS students and faculty at Weber State University who gave us valuable feedback on suggested improvements to the first edition. Most of all, I'm grateful for a strongly supportive family: my wife, Renae, and my sons, Brent, Spencer, Joel, and Michael. Special thanks to my daughter Jenn for her willingness to share her time and professional expertise in helping me work through a project like this.

history and social implications of computing

the lighter side of the lab
by spencer

My first memory of computers dates back to 1984. I was 6 years old, wandering through my house, looking for my parents to ask them how to spell "sword" so that I could kill the troll in Zork.

You probably don't remember Zork, but it was the hottest computer game around at the time. It was back in the days of no mouse, no joystick, no sound, and no graphics: just blinking green text on a solid black screen. Messages appeared on the screen, such as "You are in a room with a door." If the player typed "open door," the message "The door is open" was displayed. The player might then type "go north." Screen message: "You are now in a room with a big, scary, ax-wielding troll." This is where the user *should* type "kill troll with sword," which is why I was frantically searching for my parents. There I was, trapped in a room with a troll, and the idiots who invented English decided to put a silent "w" in "sword."

This brings me to my point: Computers have come a long way since then. Not only do we have computers, but we have "super" computers. In a year or two, we'll probably have "super-duper" computers. To illustrate my point, the Pentium IV is capable of completing roughly 500,000,000 tasks per second! (That's approximately the same number of tasks my professors are capable of assigning per second.)

We're all aware of where this technology is headed because we've seen movies such as *The Matrix* and *The Terminator*—computers are eventually going to become smarter than humans and take over the world. (We could stop it from happening by destroying all the computers right now, while we're still stronger, but then how would anyone play World of Warcraft?)

It might already be too late. Not long ago, Vladimir Kramnik, the undisputed world champion of chess, was challenged to a rematch by Deep Fritz, the world's most powerful chess computer. The two first met back in 2002, and the eight-match game ended in a draw. Frans Morsch, the creator of Fritz, said, "We've learned a lot from this, and there is much we can do to increase Fritz's playing strength." Did they ever! In the rematch of human versus computer, Kramnik was defeated by Deep Fritz, 2-4, in a six-game match.

I smell trouble. My next foreword will be handwritten because I'll be destroying my computer promptly, right after a game of Zork.

why you need to know about...
the history of computing

Today, the computer has become so much more than its origins promised. With the advent of the Internet, the computer has become a communication device. With a video screen and a mouse, it has become a tool for artists, architects, and designers. With growing storage capacity and the growth of information in a digital format, the computer has become a device for archiving information of all kinds. By connecting the computer to sound and video at both the production and receiving ends, it becomes an entertainment device—potentially replacing your CD player, DVD player, television, stereo, and radio. Put four wheels on it and add a steering wheel, and the computer turns into your Honda Civic. Add some wings and a couple of jet engines, and it's a Boeing 777. You can find computers in everything from the coffeemaker on your kitchen counter that starts brewing at 6 a.m. to a North Face jacket that monitors your body temperature.

So why look at the history of computing? Associations such as the Association for Computing Machinery (ACM) and the Institute of Electrical and Electronics Engineers (IEEE) have long recognized the importance of students understanding the social, legal, and ethical issues embedded in technology development. With the ubiquity of software-driven devices today, this understanding becomes even more critical. A person listening to her iPod and flying in a 777 demands that the songs play dependably and the plane operate safely. As someone who potentially creates these devices, you need to be able to ask and answer important questions concerning their implications. In addition, joining the world of computer development doesn't require just acquiring technical expertise; it requires understanding its professional and cultural contexts. This chapter explores where the discipline has been, is, and is going. With the following stories, the messages are "Listen carefully" and then "Welcome to the club!"

ancient history

The most logical place to start when talking about the origins of computer science is ancient Assyria. Don't worry: You won't stay in Assyria forever.

At its core, the computer is basically doing math. Applied mathematics—numbers and their manipulation—allows you to play an MP3 file of the

abacus – A counting device with sliding beads, used from ancient times to the present; useful mainly for addition and subtraction

slide rule – A device that can perform complicated math by using sliding guides on a rulerlike device; popular with engineers until the advent of the cheap electronic calculator

Ketchup song, display an F22 Raptor screen saver, and calculate last year's taxes. Applied mathematics brings you back to the Assyrians. The Assyrians invented tablets with the solutions to square roots, multiplication, and trigonometry right there on the tablet—easily accessible. With the proper training, you could solve your mathematical problems easily by using these tablets.

Why did the Assyrians need to solve mathematical problems? Because math was—and still is—a handy tool for solving personal and societal problems. With the advent of civilization, humanity began to discard its nomadic ways and invent the concepts you now take for granted. Concepts such as property and ownership spurred the need for measuring that property—whether it was land or food supplies. When people settled and no longer ranged laterally, they built vertically. The Egyptian pyramids and the Greek Parthenon demanded more complex math than the construction of tents and teepees. Later, navigation across both land and water also demanded more complex mathematics.

You can thank the Greeks for some of the ideas of logic that you use in computer science. You can thank the Persians for refining or inventing algorithms, algebra, and the concept of zero. These civilizations borrowed and improved many of the ideas of previous ones. Other civilizations (in China and Central and South America) also borrowed these mathematical concepts or, in many cases, invented them independently.

Pascal and Leibniz start the wheel rolling

For a long time, paper, wood, stone, papyrus tables, and increasingly complex *abacuses* were the "computers" through which mathematical solutions emerged. In Western society, where most of the rest of this story continues, you can probably credit the 1622 invention of the *slide rule* as the beginning of solving complex mathematical problems by using mechanical devices with moving parts. In 1642, Blaise Pascal designed a mechanical calculator with gears and levers that performed addition and subtraction. Gottfried Leibniz built on Pascal's work in 1694 by creating the Leibniz Wheel, which added multiplication and division to the mechanical calculator's capabilities. The number and size of tables to solve the numerous problems society required had become unmanageable. Devices such as Pascal's and Leibniz's allowed a user to "key in" a problem's parameters and get a solution. Unfortunately, cost and complexity kept these devices from becoming widespread.

Joseph Jacquard

In 1801, a major invention allowed not only keying in the parameters of a problem, but also storing parameters and using them whenever needed. This invention freed users from having to enter parameters more than once. Interestingly, this invention addressed a problem that had nothing to do with solving issues in land speculation or navigation and is seldom noted in the history of mathematical development. The invention, in fact, created fabric.

This invention has been called the Jacquard loom (see Figure 1-1). The Frenchman Joseph Jacquard (1752–1834) invented a device attached to a loom, where a series of pins selected what threads would get woven into a fabric. If a pin was down, that thread was selected; if the pin was up, the thread wasn't used. Different patterns could be produced by changing the orientation of the sets of pins. The orientation of the pins was determined by a set of reusable cards. It worked similarly to a player piano (also an invention of the 19th century), where a paper roll with a series of holes and air blowing through those holes determined which notes played. Both the Jacquard loom and the player piano had a "stored program" and could be "programmed" by using the interface, a series of holes in wooden cards or paper rolls. To this style of programming, as you'll see, IBM owes its great success.

Figure 1-1, The Jacquard loom, using a string of punched cards that feed into the machine

Courtesy of IBM Archive

Charles Babbage

Before the story gets ahead of itself, you need to visit England's Charles Babbage. Babbage continued the work of Pascal and Leibniz by creating a prototype Difference Engine in 1823, a mechanical device that did addition, subtraction, multiplication, and division of six-digit numbers. To the dismay of the British government, which had subsidized his work, Babbage abandoned his quest to improve it. Instead, he focused on an Analytical Engine that had many characteristics of modern computers. Unfortunately, he was never able to build it because of lack of funds. Babbage died fairly poor and obscure, but by the middle of the 20th century, he was recognized as the father of the modern computer, and the British government even issued a commemorative postage stamp with his likeness.

Despite his failures, Babbage managed to design a machine that captured the key working elements of the modern electronic computer (an invention that was still more than a century away). First, he envisioned that more than human hand power would drive the machine, although steam, not electricity, would power the thousands of gears, wheels, shafts, and levers of his device. More important, his machine had the four critical components of a modern computer:

- An input device (borrowing the idea of punch cards)
- Memory (a place where numbers could be stored while they were worked on)
- A central processing device (that decides what calculations to do)
- An output device (dials that showed the output values, in this case)

This programmable device—despite never having been built—also introduced another critical figure in computing: Ada Lovelace Byron. Ada was a patron of Babbage and the daughter of the poet Lord Byron. She was also a mathematician. Through a series of letters with Babbage, she described many instructions for the Analytical Engine. The concept of the *program loop* has been attributed to her, and she has been called the first programmer. In the early 1980s the U.S. Department of Defense named its Ada programming language after her. Although research in the late 1990s showed that many of the concepts came from Babbage himself, her contributions to programming are still widely recognized.

In 1991, the Science Museum of London actually constructed a working, historically accurate Difference Engine from Babbage's designs, attempting to use only materials and techniques that would have been available at the time. It was thought that Babbage failed largely because of the difficulty in manufacturing the multiple complex and precise parts, but the success of the Science Museum team indicates that the main cause of Babbage's failure was that he simply couldn't secure adequate funding—not the last time you'll hear that story.

> **program loop** – *The capability of a program to "loop back" and repeat commands*

Herman Hollerith

One person who *did* find adequate funding to develop a "computing" machine was American Herman Hollerith, although he never intended to create a mechanical adding machine.

The Constitution of the United States states that an accounting of its people must occur every 10 years. Hollerith was working for the U.S. Census Bureau during the 1890 census when he realized that with the counting methods of the day, they wouldn't finish before the next census 10 years away. Hollerith solved this problem by introducing electromechanical counting equipment, using punch cards as input (see Figure 1-2). Hollerith created a company around this technology, and this company eventually became the International Business Machines (IBM) Corporation.

Figure 1-2, The Hollerith census counting machine

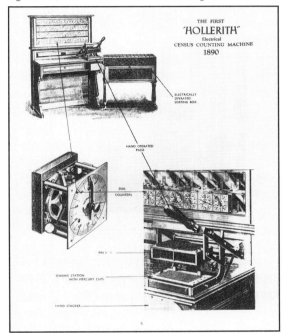

Courtesy of IBM Archive

Strangely enough, IBM didn't build the first electronic computer. Hollerith, and later IBM, sold single-purpose machines that solved routine tabulation problems. It was a huge industry in the United States and included companies such as Burroughs, Remington Rand, and National Cash Register (NCR). The machines these companies sold weren't modeled on Babbage's multipurpose engine.

IBM finally did invest in the development of a multipurpose machine in 1937: the Mark I. Howard Aiken led the Mark I project at Harvard. Only after starting did he become aware of the work of Charles Babbage, who he later claimed as his inspiration. The machine was completed in 1944. It was a single 50-foot-long drive shaft powered by a 5-horsepower electric motor synchronizing hundreds of electromechanical relays. It was said to sound like a large room full of people knitting. Despite the massive press coverage it received, by the time of its introduction, a critical technological invention had already made it obsolete. The technology that made electronic computing possible was familiar to most Americans and was sitting in their living room radios: the vacuum tube.

progression of computer electronics

Developments in computing, although ongoing since the middle of the 19th century, were mostly the product of weak or poorly funded efforts. By the 1880s, American Charles Sanders Peirce, extending the work of Charles Boole, realized that electric switches could emulate the true/false conditions of *Boolean algebra*, also known as *Boolean logic*. A complex arrangement of switches could model a complex Boolean expression, with on as "true" and off as "false." Benjamin Burack built a small logic machine that used this concept in 1936 (it was even portable) with electric relay switches. The Mark I team also adopted the approach of using a series of electric switches.

John Atanasoff of Iowa State College realized that the switches could be replaced with electronics and be much faster and less power hungry. He, along with Clifford Berry, designed and built a small limited-function prototype of the Atanasoff-Berry Computer (ABC) with *vacuum tubes* in the late 1930s. Although proving the usefulness of vacuum tubes for computers, with only $7000 in grant money, Atanasoff and Berry couldn't realize the full potential of this design, nor did they get much credit for their innovation until years later.

A momentous occasion spurred the development of the first modern electronic computer: the entry of the United States into World War II.

wartime research drives technological innovation

During World War II, the U.S. military had a huge problem: The pace of weapons development was so fast that often the men in the field were the first to truly test and learn to use the weapons. This rapid development was a particular problem with gun trajectory tables, where field-testing often led to missed targets and, worse, friendly-fire incidents. The U.S. Navy Board of Ordnance became involved in the Mark I project at Harvard to attempt to correct this deficiency. In 1943, the U.S. Army sponsored a different group at the Moore School of Engineering at the University of Pennsylvania. This team, led by John Mauchly and J. Presper Eckert, created the Electronic Numerical Integrator and Computer (ENIAC)—a machine that could run 1000 times as fast as the Mark I. As it turns out, both machines were completed too late in the war to help with the military's purpose of creating trajectory tables.

ENIAC and EDVAC

Although it was a landmark, by no stretch of the imagination could you argue that the ENIAC was portable. It was loud, even without thousands of clattering switches. It was a 30-ton collection of machines with banks of switches and switchboard-operator-style connections that filled a huge basement room (see Figure 1-3). A group of technicians ran around replacing the more than

---

Boolean algebra or Boolean logic – A logical system developed by George Boole that uses truth tables to indicate true/false output based on all possible true/false inputs; the computer owes a lot to this concept because at its most basic level, the computer is manipulating 1s and 0s—in other words, true or false

vacuum tube – A signal amplifier that preceded the transistor. Like a transistor, it can be integrated into a circuit, but it takes more power, is larger, and burns out more quickly

18,000 vacuum tubes that continually burned out. Another team of women programmers meticulously flipped the more than 6000 switches that entered the many machine instructions needed to perform a simple arithmetic operation.

Figure 1-3, The ENIAC and some of its programmers

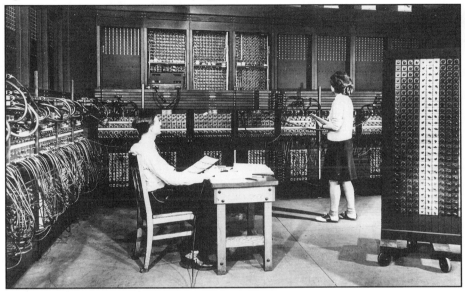

Courtesy of IBM Archive

However, ENIAC was a functioning and useful computer that could perform both arithmetic and logical operations. It could use symbols for variables and operations and, therefore, wasn't limited to a single purpose.

The architecture of the ENIAC was a model for all subsequent machines except for one critical problem: It could not modify the program's contents. In fact, its memory could hold only 20 10-digit numbers at one time and had to be programmed externally. In 1944, a number of engineers and scientists, including Mauchly and Eckert, created the Electronic Discrete Variable Automatic Computer (EDVAC). This machine, which truly is the model for current computers, became recognized as the *Von Neumann machine*, named after John Von Neumann, a mathematician who was critical to its success. Its operation was governed by a program loaded into memory. The program could even modify itself during operation and could be written to perform many different functions. Programs were entered just as data was. In fact, the programs, whether calculating logarithms or bell curves, were just more data. In addition, programs could be stored for repeated use, which became known as the *stored program concept*.

World War II spawned a few other secret computing machines. More than 20 years after the war's end, it was publicly revealed that the British had also built a computer—10 of them in fact, collectively named Colossus. Its designers

---

Von Neumann machine – *A computer architecture developed by John Von Neumann and others in the 1940s that allows for input, output, processing, and memory; it also includes the stored program concept*

stored program concept – *The idea that a computer can be operated by a program loaded into the machine's memory; also implies that programs can be stored somewhere and repeatedly loaded into memory, and the program itself, just like other data, can be modified*

John Von Neumann

During World War II, Von Neumann, a professor at Princeton, worked with J. Robert Oppenheimer on the atomic bomb. It was there, faced with the complexities of nuclear fission, that he became interested in computing machines. In 1944 he joined the team working on the ENIAC. With his influence, the team was supported in working on the EDVAC. The origin of its key feature—the stored program—has been disputed ever since. There is evidence that Eckert had written about the concept months before Von Neumann knew of the ENIAC, although Von Neumann got most of the credit after the EDVAC was completed in 1952. Von Neumann also owes a debt to Britain's Alan Turing, who created the Turing machine—a logical model that emulated the techniques of computing, later put into practice through the hardware of the ENIAC and EDVAC. Regardless of this dispute, Von Neumann is recognized for his many contributions, and modern computers are still sometimes called Von Neumann machines.

and builders returned to their prewar jobs, sworn to secrecy. All but two of those British machines were destroyed after the war, with the remaining two destroyed sometime during the 1960s.

The Colossus played a critical role in winning the war for the Allies by helping crack the German U-boat Enigma code. (Figure 1-4 shows the German Enigma encoding machine.) It turns out the Germans had been developing a computer as well—the Z1 developed by Conrad Zuse—so the time was right. Technology and need came together to spur the development of the electronic computer.

Figure 1-4, The Enigma machine was used to encode German military intelligence in World War II

Courtesy of NSA

the computer era begins: the first generation

The 1950s are generally considered the first-generation years for the development of both computer *hardware* and *software*. Vacuum tubes worked as memory for the machine. Data was written to a magnetic drum and, typically, paper tape and data cards handled input. As the decade wore on, the computer industry borrowed magnetic tape from the recording industry to use as a cost-effective storage medium. The line printer also made its first appearance, and for

hardware – *The physical device on which software runs*

software – *The instructions that operate the hardware*

the next 30 years and more, programmers read their output on wide, perforated green-barred printouts.

In the '50s, hardware and software personnel parted ways, and software development became more specialized. Computer machine instructions were, and still are, written in what's called *binary code* or *machine code*—instructions that use only 0s and 1s to mimic the on/off logic of the computer. An instruction for a machine to add a 1 to another number might be written like this: 110000000011000000100000001. Now imagine needing thousands of lines of this code to do anything useful!

Writing programs in binary is a long, tedious, and error-prone process. To remedy this problem, a programming language was developed called *assembly language*. An assembly instruction version of the preceding binary code might look something like this: "add x, y." It might still be somewhat cryptic, but it's easier to manage than straight binary. It also meant you had engineers and programmers who worked in binary and others who worked in assembly to create applications. Programmers soon split into "system engineers" (those who programmed the system) and "application engineers" (those who programmed applications—accounting programs, for example—that ran on the system).

You learn more about assembly language and other programming languages in Chapter 14, "Programming I."

During the 1950s, a major shift began in almost all disciplines of science, engineering, and business. Before this time, making scaled-down mechanical models of devices or systems—dams, airplanes, cars, electrical grids, or whatever—was the most widely used method of creating new technology. In the 1950s and 1960s, this analog model of development began to be replaced with digital electronic mathematical models. Before this, using mathematical calculations to model systems, although possible, was often far too complex and slow without a computer or many people doing calculations. In fact, the term "computer" originally described people who "computed." In some cases, as in British insurance companies, tens of thousands of people did hand calculations, later augmented with electromechanical calculators. The 1950s and 1960s changed all that. For its scientific and business needs, Western society went from mostly analog models and human computers to the electronic computer. Suddenly, a single machine could create software models of natural phenomena and technology and do the work of thousands of boring and repetitive business calculations.

UNIVAC

Mauchly and Eckert went on to build the first commercially viable computer, the UNIVAC (see Figure 1-5). First they formed a division of the old Remington Typewriter Company, then Remington Rand (later Sperry UNIVAC and then Unisys). Their first customer was the U.S. Census Bureau. The name UNIVAC became as synonymous with the computer in the 1950s as

binary code or machine code – The numeric language of the computer based on the binary number system of 1s and 0s

assembly language – A human-readable language used to represent numeric computer instructions (binary code)

Kleenex became for paper tissues or Xerox for paper copies. Between 1951 and 1954, the company installed 19 UNIVACs, including at U.S. Steel and Pacific Mutual Life Insurance. Ironically, Howard Aiken, builder of the Mark I, felt there was a need for only five or six computers like the EDVAC in the United States and recommended that the U.S. Bureau of Standards not support Eckert and Mauchly's proposal to make commercial computers.

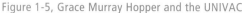

Figure 1-5, Grace Murray Hopper and the UNIVAC

Courtesy of IBM Archive

Grace Murray Hopper and the "bug"

Grace Murray Hopper made many contributions to programming. As part of the Mark I project at Harvard, she coined the term "bug" (referring to a problem in hardware or software) when she found an actual bug— a moth—in one of the Mark I's electromechanical relays and taped it to the logbook. She called the process of finding and solving these problems "debugging," and she spent much of the next 40 years doing it. She went on to work on the UNIVAC with Eckert and Mauchly. There she developed a compiler—a totally new concept—for a higher-level programming language. Later she created an even more powerful language called COBOL, one of the most widely used business programming languages.

The most celebrated use of the UNIVAC came during the 1952 presidential election. CBS News decided to include the machine's calculation of election results in its U.S. presidential election broadcast. Anchor Walter Cronkite learned that with a computer, it was definitely "garbage in—garbage out"! By 8:30 p.m. the night of the election, the UNIVAC calculated 100 to 1 odds in favor of Eisenhower. No one could believe the results, and so CBS delayed reporting an Eisenhower win. Mauchly and Max Woodbury, another mathematician from the University of Pennsylvania, reentered the data (incorrectly, as it turns out), and CBS reported at 9 p.m. that UNIVAC gave Eisenhower 8 to 7 odds over Stevenson. The final electoral vote of 438 for Eisenhower and 93 for Stevenson proved the original data was closer to correct. In the end, CBS was first to call the race, although not as soon or by the degree it could have. CBS hadn't trusted the computer's calculations. By the end of the night, it was convinced of the computer's usefulness, and four years later (and ever since), all the major U.S. television networks used computers in their election coverage.

IBM (Big Blue)

By 1955, Remington Rand's UNIVAC no longer dominated the computer marketplace. International Business Machines (IBM) took advantage of its longstanding ties to business to capture the hearts and minds of international businessmen. IBM had more than twice as many orders as Remington Rand that year. A saying developed: "You can't go wrong by buying IBM." Its salesmen's button-down shirts and blue suits became a familiar sight to anyone in the computer industry, and IBM became known as "Big Blue." It also became known as "Snow White" (as in "Snow White and the Seven Dwarfs") because by the 1960s, IBM controlled more than 70% of the market in computers. (Sperry Rand, with its UNIVAC, along with Control Data, Honeywell, Philco, Burroughs, RCA, General Electric, and NCR, were the "dwarfs.") This arrangement lasted quite a long time, until the microcomputer (PC) arrived on the scene in the 1980s. More about that later.

mainframe – A large, expensive computer, often serving many terminals and used by large organizations; all first-generation computers were mainframes

Although it's generally thought that IBM won the ***mainframe*** battle with superior salesmanship, a skill that founder Thomas Watson prided himself on, Remington Rand had many consumer products unrelated to office equipment and didn't have the focused vision of IBM in its drive to become *the* computer services company. This focus eventually led to superior products from IBM, starting with the 701 and the smaller 650 calculating machine in the mid-1950s. IBM's position grew even stronger with the introduction of the System/360 (see Figure 1-6) in the 1960s. It was a scalable system, allowing companies to continue to add components as

Figure 1-6, IBM 360 mainframe computers were the size of refrigerators and required a full staff to manage them

Courtesy of IBM Archive

their businesses and computing needs increased. IBM usually leased its systems to the customer. Often IBM could recapture its investment in manufacturing systems within a couple of years. Meanwhile, most systems stayed in place for 10 to 15 years or even longer. IBM made a lot of money during this period.

transistors in the second generation

The late 1950s and the first half of the 1960s might be considered the second-generation years. In software, higher-level languages, such as FORTRAN, COBOL, and LISP, were developed. Assembly language, although easier to use than machine code, still had a one-to-one correspondence with machine code. Each line of a high-level language could be far more powerful and might correspond to many lines of binary machine code. In one of these high-level languages, you might be able to write something like "FOR A = 1 TO 20 PRINT A," which would take numerous lines of assembly code.

transistor – A signal amplifier much smaller than a vacuum tube used to represent a 1 (on) or a 0 (off), which are the rudiments of computer calculation; often used as part of an integrated circuit (IC)

Hardware took a major leap forward as well. The *transistor* replaced the vacuum tube. It was far smaller, cooler (meaning cooler in temperature), and cheaper to produce and lasted longer. A form of random access memory (RAM) also became available with the use of magnetic cores. With tape and drum, the magnetic read head could be positioned over the information you wanted. Now information could be available instantaneously. The first magnetic disks, similar to ones in use today, also became available. Information that wasn't resident in memory could be accessed more quickly and efficiently.

circuit boards in the third generation

integrated circuit (IC) – A collection of transistors on a single piece of hardware (called a "chip") that reduces the circuit's size and physical complexity

chip – A piece of encased silicon, usually somewhere between the size of your fingernail and the palm of your hand, that holds ICs

operating system (OS) – Software that allows applications to access hardware resources, such as printers or hard drives, and provides tools for managing and administering system resources and security

With the third generation, in the second half of the 1960s, transistors were replaced with *integrated circuits (IC)* on *chips* on circuit boards. ICs are miniaturized transistors in solid silicon. They're called semiconductors because they have electronic conducting and nonconducting channels etched onto their surface. Cost and size were decreasing as speed and reliability took a leap in magnitude. Keyboards and screens were also introduced, giving users a much easier way to communicate with the computer. Software saw the first *operating system (OS)*, a program for managing all the computer's jobs.

Operating systems had a number of advantages. First, the operating system could take care of using all resources of the machine—printing or writing to files, for example, so that each separate program didn't have to perform these tasks. Second, the OS enabled the machine to have multiple users or complete multiple tasks. Up to this point, the machine did one job at a time for a single user.

Imagine what it was like in the days before operating systems: You carried your stack of IBM cards (see Figure 1-7) over to the computer center in a shoebox. You stepped gingerly over your officemate, who was picking up his stack of cards that had fallen in the parking lot, and made your way down the long hall,

Figure 1-7, A very short stack of IBM punched cards

handing your stack to the computer operator. Yes! You were "first in," which meant you would be "first out." Unfortunately, you were first only this morning; there were at least five stacks of cards ahead of you from the previous day. Fortunately, you had brought the requisite coffee and donuts, and somehow your stack ended up at the head of the line. The operator put the stack of cards in the card reader, and after about 1000 "thip-thip-thips" as the cards went through the reader, the program was input into the computer. If there was a problem in your code, you had to go back and fix the card containing the problem, put the card back in the right place in the deck, and go through the process again. You might have picked up some more donuts while you were at it because you knew it was going to be a long night.

time-sharing

time-sharing – A computer's capability to share its computing time with many users at the same time

Time-sharing solved the vicious "donut and card stack" cycle. Now a number of users could sit at terminals—screens or teletype-like consoles that used long paper rolls instead of punch cards to input instructions—and it looked like you had the computer to yourself. Of course, many times the system was very slow, even if you were doing something simple. This slowdown usually meant a lot of other people were "sharing" your time or a few people were running some resource-intensive processes. It shouldn't be any surprise that people got excited about owning their own computer a few years later.

During this period, the computer was beginning to be used by a broader population as a general-purpose machine, and many application programs were written—programs geared toward an end user rather than the programmer. Some programmers began to focus on writing code at the OS level, working on compilers and other tools that application programmers then used to create statistical or accounting programs, which were used by end users who generally knew little about programming and just wanted to use the application for a particular task. Now get out your silky shirt, disco shoes, and the suit with the wide lapels because you're heading into the '70s.

living in the '70s with the fourth generation

In computing, the period from the early 1970s to today is known as the fourth generation of hardware and software and is characterized by the continuing repackaging of circuits into smaller and smaller spaces. First came Large-Scale Integration (LSI) and then Very Large-Scale Integration (VLSI). Chips used in the '60s contained around 1000 circuits, LSI chips contained up to 15,000, and VLSI chips contained 100,000 to 1 million circuits. The number of circuits essentially doubled every 1.5 years. This process of fitting an ever increasing number of transistors and circuits on smaller and smaller chips is called miniaturization and is one of the most important trends in computer hardware.

minicomputer – Mid-sized computer introduced in the mid to late '60s; it typically cost tens of thousands of dollars versus hundreds of thousands of dollars for a mainframe

The '70s saw the growth of *minicomputer* companies, such as Digital Equipment Corporation (DEC) with its PDP and VAX machines and Data General and its Nova. Minicomputers put a lot of power in much less physical space. One of these new computers could fit into the corner of a room, and software programs blossomed in this new environment.

The UNIX operating system was created by Ken Thompson and Dennis Ritchie in 1973 as an offshoot of a joint effort by AT&T, GE, and MIT. It was originally created on a DEC PDP-7 and written in B and later C (computer languages also invented by Thompson and Ritchie). Because of market limitations resulting from AT&T's monopoly status, AT&T couldn't sell UNIX, so it distributed the software free to educational institutions. The real revolution of the '70s wasn't the minicomputer, however. By the end of the 1970s, "ordinary" people were buying software game packages at the local Radio Shack and taking them home to play on something sitting on their desk called a "microcomputer." This development changed the computer industry a great deal. A large percentage of computing no longer occurs via large companies leasing hardware with free software. Starting with microcomputers, both computers and software might be commodities that could be bought and sold separately.

the personal computer revolution

So how, in less than 10 years, did the world go from expensive, complicated machines (even minicomputers required a lot of room and expertise to operate) to the small plastic boxes that sat on desks at home entertaining kids (of all ages)? The culprits range from engineers forcing a hardware vision on their business managers, to software developers in it for the challenge, to electronics hobbyists realizing a dream, to software experts thumbing their noses at the establishment. In a few words, the time for a revolution was right. All the necessary hardware and software elements were at hand or being developed, and many different social, economic, and personal forces came together to support it. All that was needed was the will. Technically, almost everything needed was available right off the shelf.

note

David Ahl, formerly of Digital Equipment Corporation (DEC), noted "We [Digital] could have come out with a personal computer in January 1975. If we had taken that prototype, most of which was proven stuff, the PDP-8A could have been developed and put in production in that seven- or eight-month period."

Intel

One necessary element for the development of the PC came from a mid-sized company called Intel. In 1969, Intel had been creating semiconductors for electronic calculators, among other things, but had no intention of creating a computer. However, in contributing to the chip design of a calculator for a contract with the Busicom Company, Ted Hoth proposed putting more functionality on a single chip, essentially creating a *central processing unit (CPU)*. That chip was named the 4004 for the number of transistors onboard. It was the precursor to the Intel 8008, then 8080, then 8086, then the 80286, 80386, 80486, Pentium, Pentium II, and Pentium 4 chips, and so on to today.

central processing unit (CPU) – The central controlling device inside a computer that makes decisions at a very low level, such as what math functions or computer resources are to be used and when

microprocessor – A CPU on a single chip used in microcomputers

Intel, however, wasn't focused on trying to create a whole computer, never mind an industry. Even those in the company with vision mandated that the company wouldn't get into end-user products (sold directly to the customer). When the programmer who created a little operating system for the Intel *microprocessor* asked if he could sell the combined chip and OS himself, Intel management told him he could do whatever he liked. That programmer was Gary Kildall, and you'll hear about him again.

More than just the miniaturization of computing happened in the '70s and '80s. The whole computer marketplace changed. For the first time, software could be purchased as a commodity separate from computer hardware. The story of that development involves electronics hobbyists and a competition in an electronics magazine.

the Altair 8800

Hobbyists depended on magazines such as *Popular Electronics* and *Radio Electronics* to learn about the latest advances in electronics. In addition, *Popular Electronics*, edited by Les Solomon, not only reported the latest advances, but also spurred their development. The hobbyist community was small enough that many knew each other, even if indirectly through publication in the magazine. In 1973, Solomon sought out the best contributors, asking for a story on "the first desktop computer kit." He received a number of designs but didn't think they were worthy of publication. A promising design by André Thi Truong actually did get created and was sold in France that year but never made it to the pages of the magazine.

It wasn't until the January 1975 issue that Solomon published an article by Ed Roberts on the Altair 8800 (named after a planet in a *Star Trek* episode), a kit based on the Intel 8080. In 1974, Roberts faced the demise of his Albuquerque, New Mexico, MITS calculator company, with competition from big players such as Texas Instruments and Hewlett Packard. He decided to bet the farm and take up Solomon's challenge—a bold decision given that, as far as anyone knew, there was no market for the device beyond a few electronics hobbyists.

The results surprised almost everyone. Within three months of the *Popular Electronics* article, Roberts had 4000 orders for the Altair, at $397 each. Unfortunately, Roberts was a long way from fulfilling these orders. Parts were difficult to come by and they weren't always reliable. Not only that, but the machine was completely disassembled and had no screen, keyboard, card reader, tape reader, disk drive, printer, or software. When it was complete, you had a box with a front panel that had switches and lights for each binary bit. Data and program entry and the results were much like those of the original ENIAC, only in a much smaller package (see Figure 1-8).

Figure 1-8, The MITS Altair 8800—assembled

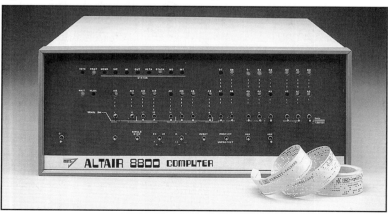

Courtesy of Microsoft Archives

Nevertheless, the orders kept pouring in. Electronics hobbyists were hungry for a relatively portable machine that they could control and didn't have to wait in line to use. In addition, Roberts's machine had the goods—the capacity for input, storage, processing, and output—or at least the promise of the goods. Knowing that all the peripherals would have to be created later, Roberts created a machine with an *open architecture*—a critical part of the microcomputer world, even today. The machine had what would eventually be called a motherboard with expansion slots so that circuit boards for a computer screen or disk drive could be added. Many hobbyists moved quickly to fill in the missing elements themselves.

open architecture – *Computer hardware that is accessible for modification and sometimes even documented*

enter Bill Gates, Paul Allen, and Microsoft

A couple of people who moved to fill the void were Paul Allen and Bill Gates. Gates and Allen were buddies living in Washington State. They were, essentially, technology hobbyists. While in high school, they created a computer-like device called a Traf-O-Data. To gain experience with computers, they worked for the automotive supplier TRW and other companies as programmers, mostly free for the fun of it. Gates was in college and Allen was working for Honeywell when Roberts's *Popular Electronics* article came out.

They called Ed Roberts, and the results of that call changed the world of hardware and software. They told Roberts they had software, a BASIC programming language, already working—a claim not quite corresponding to reality. BASIC was an easy-to-use language that had been invented in the 1970s. Nevertheless, six weeks later, Gates and Allen (see Figure 1-9) demonstrated a rudimentary

Figure 1-9, Paul Allen and Bill Gates in 1981

Courtesy of Microsoft Archives

BASIC interpreter. It would be a huge leap over the machine code programming that the Altair required. Gates and Allen sold the BASIC software of their newly formed Micro-Soft company, and Allen got the job of MITS Software Director—which meant the newly formed corporate division of MITS now had one person in it. Soon after, Bill Gates left Harvard to join the fray. By 1981, Microsoft was on its way to becoming a multibillion-dollar company.

the microcomputer begins to evolve

microcomputer – A desktop-sized computer with a microprocessor CPU designed to be used by one person at a time

After it was shown that a *microcomputer* could be created and be profitable, a number of people got into the act, also using Altair's techniques. Because the Altair bus (the mechanism through which the computer communicated with its components) wasn't patented, hobbyists borrowed it and renamed it the S100 bus, establishing a standard that any hardware/software company could use. A company called IMSAI started getting market share. Two companies, Southwest Technical Products and Sphere, began building computers based on the more powerful Motorola 6800 chip. Another company was building the z80 processor. Also on the horizon, Tandy Corporation, owner of Radio Shack, had a machine it was working on.

In general, MITS had its hand in so many efforts to correct its startup flaws and compete at many levels that it was a victim of its own success. Problems continued to plague most of the hardware components. At one point, the BASIC software had proved so much more popular than a flawed 4K memory board that MITS linked the prices to protect its hardware income. Buy the board and BASIC would cost around $150. Otherwise, you had to fork out $500 for BASIC, which in those days was a tidy sum of money. Hobbyists countered by pirating the software and going to a third party for the board—possible because the bus was now a standard. The battle against the competition proved equally troublesome. For example, MITS countered the Motorola chip by also building a 6800 Altair, but its software and hardware were totally incompatible with the 8080 version. For distribution, MITS started to insist that the growing number of computer stores carry MITS products exclusively, an anathema to the hobbyist culture, and stores balked at the idea.

By the end of 1977, MITS was sold to Pertec Corporation, the beginning of the end for the Altair. More than 50 hardware companies had introduced competing models, including the PET from Commodore and another from a company named after a fruit, Apple Computer.

an Apple a day...

Apple Computer had its origins in Sunnyvale, California's Homestead High, where Steve Jobs and Steve Wozniak met and shared a love of electronics and practical jokes. (Creating a bomblike ticking inside a friend's locker was one Wozniak "Woz" trick.) They also shared a dream—to own a computer. In truth,

Homestead High probably had several students with that dream because many were the progeny of parents in the area's electronics industry, but it was a difficult dream to realize. Their first commercial product was a game idea from Nolan Bushnell at Atari: Breakout. Jobs and Woz (then at college and working at Hewlett-Packard, respectively) finished the game in four days. In 1975 Woz began working on his high school dream and successfully created a computer. It was a hobbyist's ideal, a simple design housed in a wooden box, but nowhere near being a commercial product, nor was it ever intended to be. Jobs, however, convinced Woz the machine had a commercial future and dubbed it the Apple I. Their prankster spirits still alive, they began the company on April Fool's Day, 1976, and priced the machine at $666.

Apple might have remained a hobbyist machine, but Jobs could inspire people with his drive and enthusiasm. In 1976 they secured nearly $300,000 in funding. In 1977, Apple released the Apple II, based on the Motorola 6502 processor, and made a profit by year's end, doubling production every few months. The Apple II was compact, reliable, and "talked up" in the industry. It was also adopted by many schools and became many students' first experience with computers—making a lasting impression. What really pushed it toward broad acceptance was the ease with which programmers could write applications for it.

To a large extent, microcomputers had so far been playthings for hobbyists. The most popular programs running on these machines were games. Games such as MicroChess, Adventure, and Breakout put the machines in people's homes and introduced kids to computing. The microcomputer wasn't recognized as a business tool, however, until Dan Bricklin and Bob Frankston, working in Frankston's Boston attic office, created VisiCalc for the Apple II.

VisiCalc was the first spreadsheet program in which columns and rows that went far beyond the screen's boundaries could have data values or equations. In its release year of 1979, it sold 500 copies a month. The program was so flexible that customers used it for things it hadn't been intended for, such as word processing, and it was powerful enough to become a tool not just for home users, but also for small businesses. It drove the sales of Apple IIs to such an extent that it created a new category of software: the *killer app* (short for killer application).

killer app – *A software program that becomes so popular that it drives the popularity of the hardware it runs on*

In 1983 another killer app called Lotus 1-2-3, based on the same spreadsheet principle as VisiCalc, pushed a different company's hardware. It had a huge marketing blitz behind it, had no ties to Apple, and seemed legitimate to the inhabitants of Wall Street. More important, however, the company that made the computer fairly screamed legitimacy among corporate executive types.

IBM offers the PC

When IBM realized that the Apple II had moved beyond the hobby and toy arena, it took a long view of the future and realized that the microcomputer might play a significant part in the traditional computer marketplace. IBM decided to enter the battle, intending to dominate the microcomputer market to the same extent it dominated the mainframe marketplace. Of course, to dominate the market, it needed to build the machine, and fast.

To get to market quickly, IBM approached the problem differently than it had for other hardware. Instead of building its own chip for the new machine, IBM used a chip that was right off the shelf—the Intel 8088—similar to those used in other microcomputers. Learning from the success of the Altair and recognizing that it needed the broad talents of the micro world to build peripherals and software for its *personal computer (PC)*, IBM did a few other things that never would have occurred in the mainframe world. The IBM PC used a nonproprietary CPU, had approachable documentation, and used an open architecture similar to the Altair's. Recognizing the change in the market landscape, IBM also sold the machine through retail outlets instead of through its established commercial sales force.

personal computer (PC) – Originally an IBM microcomputer; now generally refers to any microcomputer

MS-DOS

Searching for applications for its PC, IBM contacted Microsoft and arranged a meeting with Gates and his new business manager, Steve Ballmer. Gates and Ballmer put off a meeting with Atari (another fledgling home computer development company) and signed a confidentiality agreement so that both Microsoft and IBM would be protected in future development.

IBM also needed an operating system, and Gates sent the IBM team across town to meet with Gary Kildall at Digital Research Incorporated (DRI). Kildall, who wrote the operating system for the Intel 4004, had also written CP/M, an operating system for the IMSAI and other Altair-like computers that became quite popular. Before Kildall's CP/M, the closest thing to an operating system on the microcomputer had been Microsoft BASIC. CP/M was much more powerful and could work with any application designed for the machines. However, IBM hesitated at the $10 per copy cost of CP/M. Talking again with Gates, IBM became convinced it might be better off with a new operating system because CP/M was an 8-bit OS, and the 8088 was a 16-bit CPU. So despite Microsoft not actually owning an operating system at the time, IBM chose Microsoft to develop its PC operating system.

note

A myth in the world of microcomputers persists that instead of meeting with IBM, Gary Kildall decided to go flying. The truth is that he had gone flying earlier that day for business. He did, in fact, meet with IBM.

Now all Microsoft had to do was create the operating system. Microsoft developed Microsoft Disk Operating System (MS-DOS), which IBM called PC-DOS, to run on the Intel 8088. It accomplished this by reworking a program called SCP-DOS that imitated CP/M. Kildall, getting an early version of the program and discerning how similar it was to his, threatened to sue. Instead, he reached an agreement with IBM. IBM would offer his operating system as well as the Microsoft version. Unfortunately, when the product came out, IBM offered PC-DOS at $40 and CP/M-86 at $240. Which one would you have bought?

the Apple Macintosh raises the bar

With the IBM PC and DOS, Apple faced serious competition for the first time. Jobs, however, already had a response. As an operating system, DOS adequately controlled the machine's operations, but few would call the user interface easy to learn. Users had to type commands (many of them cryptic) to get the machine to do anything. Jobs had a completely different idea for a user interface.

In late 1979, Steve Jobs had visited Xerox Palo Alto Research Center (PARC). Since the 1960s, its scientists and engineers had been at the cutting edge of computing science. He saw a machine called the Alto that had graphics, menus, icons, windows, and a mouse. He also saw a technique for linking documents called hypertext and an Ethernet network that linked machines on engineers' desks. Many of Xerox's experiments implemented the ideas of Douglas Engelbart of Stanford Research Institute (SRI), a visionary inventor who also created the mouse. Unfortunately for Xerox, it had not successfully brought any of these products to market. The cost of one Alto—almost 2000 were built and installed— was about as much as a minicomputer. It's also possible that Xerox didn't want to commit wholeheartedly to ideas that might threaten its core business of making paper copies. Jobs had no such worries and aimed to put something on everyone's desk—paper or no paper.

Steve Jobs has said of his Apple I, "We didn't do three years of research and come up with this concept. What we did was follow our own instincts and construct a computer that was what we wanted." The same could be said of Jobs's next foray into computer development, and the effort again changed the industry. After several years and at least one commercial false start, a small "skunk works" team pushed by Jobs built a computer and small screen combination in a tan box, together with keyboard and mouse: the Apple Macintosh. The operating system didn't look anything like DOS. The user moved an arrow on the screen with a mouse and clicked pictures (called icons) to get things done. To delete a file, for instance, the user dragged the file to a little icon of a trash can. The Macintosh had the first mass-produced *graphical user interface (GUI)*.

graphical user interface (GUI) – An interface to the computer that uses graphical instead of text commands; the term has come to mean windows, menus, and a mouse

The Macintosh's public unveiling was as dramatic a departure as the operating system itself. During the 1984 Super Bowl broadcast, a commercial showed gray-clothed and ashen-skinned people trudging, zombie-like, into a large, bleak room. In the front of the room, a huge television displayed a talking head of Big Brother droning on. An athletic and colorfully clothed woman chased by security forces ran into the room. She swung a sledgehammer into the television, which exploded. A message then came on the screen: "On January 24th, 1984, Apple Computer will introduce Macintosh. And you'll see why 1984 won't be like *1984*." The commercial referred to George Orwell's apocalyptic visionary novel *1984*, in which Big Brother is an omnipresent authoritarian power that tries to force everyone to do its bidding. It wasn't hard to guess who Apple was likening to Big Brother; it was probably Apple's old nemesis, Big Blue (IBM).

In reality, the Macintosh, or "Mac" as it was affectionately called, was stymied by hardware limitations and an initial lack of software, although it did sell well and changed the competitive landscape. However, in terms of competition for Apple, IBM didn't end up playing the role of Big Brother for long. In the early 1990s, that role went to the combination of Microsoft and Intel and has remained that way.

other PCs (and one serious OS competitor) begin to emerge

In the early 1980s, Gates had persuasively argued that IBM should follow the direction of open architecture it began in hardware by supporting any operating system as well. Successful third-party programs, such as VisiCalc, drove hardware sales and helped make the case. Gates also managed to convince IBM that Microsoft should be free to sell its operating system to other hardware manufacturers. With that one decision, IBM likely created the future of the PC world, in which IBM would become a minority player. Because of its open architecture, third parties could essentially clone the IBM machine's hardware, and any hardware whose workings weren't covered by IBM's documentation was "reverse-engineered" (reinvented to work exactly the same way). IBM's share of the PC market slowly declined in the mid-1980s through 1990s. Competing machines from Compaq, Dell, Gateway, Toshiba, and others, including hundreds of small shops, were first called "clones" but eventually co-opted the names "personal computer" and "PC."

In this same time frame, Microsoft rose to dominance. Every clone had the Microsoft operating system onboard. It turns out people needed a consistent user interface and operating system on which all the third-party software could run. Microsoft began to compete against Apple as well (despite writing application software for Apple machines). Microsoft worked to provide an OS that would incorporate the Mac's GUI features. In 1988, Microsoft released the first commercially viable version of its Windows operating system. It also introduced the first serious competition for the Mac GUI in 1991 with Windows 3.1, despite the fact it wasn't really a new operating system but a program that ran on top of DOS. IBM also developed a competing operating system called

OS/2—actually written by Microsoft—but with few applications or users, it went nowhere.

In the 1990s, Microsoft took advantage of its position as almost the sole supplier of operating systems to PCs. Application software companies began to lose market share. In 1990, Lotus 1-2-3 was the best-selling software package and WordPerfect was the best-selling word processor. Lotus had a gross revenue that wasn't much smaller than Microsoft's. (Only three years earlier, Lotus had been the bigger company.) By 2000, Lotus 1-2-3 and WordPerfect were blips on the software screen, replaced by Microsoft Excel and Word. Some flavor of Windows is now on more than 90% of the world's personal computers.

the latest generation (fifth)

parallel computing – The use of multiple computers or CPUs to process a single task simultaneously

From 1990 to today is generally labeled the fifth generation of hardware and software. In hardware, this period includes *parallel computing* (or parallel architectures), where a number of CPUs can be applied to the same task simultaneously.

One approach is the single instruction, multiple data (SIMD) stream, in which a single command can operate on multiple sets of data simultaneously. Another approach is the multiple instruction, multiple data (MIMD) stream (MIMD), in which different parts of a program or different programs might be worked on simultaneously. A number of computers used to control Web pages, databases, and networks have two to four parallel processors in the same machine and use these techniques. They are small enough and affordable enough that you can buy them and put them on your desk. Larger and more expensive machines, such as the Cray *supercomputer*, can be used for complex modeling and scientific research. These supercomputers are at the extreme edge of computer processing power. A third approach for parallel processing uses another signature aspect of the fifth generation of computing: the network and its most spectacular realization, the Internet.

supercomputer – The fastest and usually most expensive computer available; often used in scientific and engineering research

the Internet

You can safely date the origins of the Internet back to a memo in 1962 by J. C. R. Licklider, in which he proposed that different machines needed to communicate despite their different operating instructions. Licklider ran the Information Processing Techniques Office (IPTO) of the Advanced Research Projects Agency (ARPA; occasionally called the Defense Advanced Research Projects Agency, or DARPA) of the U.S. Department of Defense. Four years later, Bob Taylor, who had inherited the position from Licklider, looked at the three terminals in his office that connected him to three different machines in three different parts of the country and decided to resurrect Licklider's idea—to create more office space, if nothing else—and got Pentagon funding of $1 million.

Taylor argued that a communication system might help in three major ways:

- Research institutions working with the IPTO could share resources.
- Computers the government was purchasing could be better utilized because incompatibility would not be a problem.
- The system could be created so that it was robust: If one line went down, the system could rechannel through another line.

This last point led to characterizing the development of the Internet as a product of the Cold War. This characterization isn't far fetched because ARPA itself was created by Eisenhower as a direct response to the possible threat posed by the Russian launch of Sputnik. Some have written that ARPANET was created so that it could survive a limited nuclear war or sabotage by rechanneling communication dynamically.

In fact, Paul Baran of the Rand Corporation had been working on this concept since 1960 with the U.S. telephone system, and the British had begun work along similar lines as well. Baran had ideas of a distributed network, where each computer on the network decided independently how to channel to the next computer. In addition, information could be divided into blocks that were reassembled at their destination, with each block possibly following a different path. The ARPANET project did end up adopting these concepts (now called packets and packet switching), although arguably for reasons that had more to do with system unreliability than with any enemy threat.

Several months after the 1969 Apollo moon landing, ARPANET was born, consisting of four computers at four locations: UCLA, UC at Santa Barbara, Stanford Research Institute, and University of Utah. The first message was the first three letters of "LOGIN" just before the system crashed. After that startup hiccup, however, the system expanded fairly rapidly. ARPA managed the feat of linking different systems by having a computer (an Interface Message Processor, or IMP) linked to the telephone or telegraph line and each mainframe having its own IMP. In addition, as long as you knew the communication protocols, you could build your own IMP. Professors and graduate students essentially built the beginnings of the Internet as part of their research or in their spare time.

You learn more about the Internet in Chapter 5, "The Internet."

By the mid-1970s, scientists the world over were communicating by connecting their local networks via the protocols created for ARPANET. By the mid-1980s, the loose collection of networks was called "the Internet" (short for "internetwork"), and by the early '90s, thousands of research institutions, U.S. government organizations, such as the National Science Foundation, and corporations, such as AT&T and GE, made up the Internet. Agreed-on networking standards and international cooperation made the network a worldwide phenomenon. Another interesting development was that by the second year of operation, over two-thirds of the traffic on the network consisted of personal notes, similar to today's e-mail. It seems that despite the initial goal of sharing computer resources, the Internet was used mainly for communication.

LANs and WANs and other ANs

The Internet is a network of networks. It usually connects and works with local area networks (LANs) and wide area networks (WANs, which can be made up of LANs). A WAN might be the network on your campus, and a LAN connects the machines in your computer science building. They are usually controlled by a network technology called Ethernet and are physically linked by Ethernet cable. As fiber optics and wireless technologies have improved, they have become critical in adding computers to networks and have given rise to the terms wireless LAN (WLAN) and metropolitan area network (MAN) or urban area network (UAN).

When you share files with someone in the next room, use a central printer, or use a program on a different machine in your building, you probably are not using the Internet; you're most likely using a LAN, maybe even a WLAN. If the Internet is the "superhighway" of information, you might call LANs and WANs the small-town roads and freeways of information. A number of competing architectures for LANs and WANs arose in the 1970s, but by the late '70s, Ethernet was on its way to becoming the most popular standard for controlling network traffic. A company called Novell became a dominant player in networks in 1989 with its NetWare file server software.

You learn more about LANs, WANs, Ethernet, and networking standards in Chapter 4, "Networks."

super software and the Web

Paralleling the development of multiprocessors, networks, and the Internet, software also made great changes in the fifth generation. Programmers began to adopt modular approaches more widely, such as object-oriented programming (OOP), which facilitated larger and more complex software products that could be delivered more quickly and reliably.

You learn more about OOP in Chapter 13, "Software Engineering."

Another development was computer-aided software engineering (CASE) tools—tools that make software development easier and faster. Although the promise of software programs writing other software programs has yet to reach the point of replacing the programmer, a number of inroads toward automatic code generation have occurred. Today, object-oriented graphical programs, such as Visio and Rational Rose, can generate some code. In addition, word-processing programs, such as Word and WordPerfect, and Web page development environments, such as Macromedia Dreamweaver, can create Web pages almost automatically—which brings you to probably the most monumental software development of the 1990s and beyond: the World Wide Web (WWW).

hypermedia – *Different sorts of information (text, sound, pictures, video) that are linked in such a way that a user can move and see content easily from one link to another*

hypertext – *Hypermedia that is specifically text*

browser – *A program that accesses and displays files and other information or hypermedia available on a network or on the Internet*

You've seen how the Internet developed over the course of 40 years, but it didn't really begin to develop into the powerful communication and economic system it is today until someone wrote the killer app. Tim Berners-Lee (see Figure 1-10), working at the Conseil Européen pour la Recherche Nucléaire (CERN), a laboratory for particle physics in France, created two software elements that would lead to making the Internet more accessible to the general public and commercial interests: the Web page and the browser. These two elements, combined with network access through the Internet, became known as the World Wide Web (WWW). Before the WWW, computer gurus handled communication between machines. Communicating required knowing the cryptic language of machine protocols and didn't attract the casual user. The application of *hypermedia* (and *hypertext*) to the Internet and a program to read that media (called a *browser*) radically changed the equation.

Figure 1-10, Tim Berners-Lee, inventor of the World Wide Web

Donna Coveny/Courtesy of the World Wide Web Consortium (W3C)

Hypertext had its origins in a 1945 proposal by U.S. President Roosevelt's science advisor, Vannevar Bush. Bush imagined a machine that could store information and allow users to link text and illustrations, thus creating "information trails." A computer visionary in the 1960s, Ted Nelson, coined the word "hypertext" and spent years conceptualizing how it would work with the computer technology of his day.

The invention of the World Wide Web has been called a side effect of high-energy physics. A 1990 proposal by Berners-Lee to link and manage numerous documents includes the ideas of browsing links of documents kept on a server.

In 1991 a prototype was created on a NeXT computer. (NeXT is a Steve Jobs company started after he left Apple.) In the next few years, using the Berners-Lee protocols, a number of simple browsers were created, including one that had the most impact beyond the walls of academia: Mosaic. Written for the Mac and Windows systems by Marc Andreessen and released free of charge in 1993, Mosaic had an intuitive graphical interface. Now the cat was out of the bag. Although general consumers didn't know it at the time, an easy-to-use browser interface was just what they had been waiting for. The proof: In six years, between 1992 and 1998, the number of Web sites went from 50 to approximately 2.5 million. Andreessen went on to found Netscape and developed Mosaic into the Netscape browser, which dominated the marketplace in the 1990s and pushed Microsoft to develop its own browser.

Table 1-1 is an overview of generations in the development of computing. All date ranges are approximate.

Table 1-1, Generations

generation	characteristics
1. late 1940s to 1950s	• Electronic computing • Introduction of binary code and Von Neumann architecture • Vacuum tubes used in hardware • Punched cards for storing programs and data • Increased viability of mathematical/computer models of real life
2. late 1950s to mid-1960s	• Transistors used in hardware • Rotating drum storage • Magnetic core memory • Higher-level languages, such as FORTRAN and COBOL
3. second half of 1960s	• Integrated circuits—transistors on "chips" on printed circuit boards used in hardware • Rotating disk storage widely used • Introduction of operating systems for job management • Time-sharing

(continued)

Table 1-1, Generations *(continued)*

generation	characteristics
4. 1970s to 1980s	• Microprocessors—the computer on a "chip" • Minicomputers and microcomputers (PDP, Altair, IBM PC, Apple) • Connections through the Internet • The graphical user interface (GUI) • Computers and software programs as commodities
5. 1990s to today	• Parallel processing • Networks • World Wide Web • Embedded computing • Software engineering concepts, such as object-oriented programming, widely used • Cloud computing

the Microsoft era and more

By the mid-1990s, Microsoft was feeling the pressure from Netscape: Netscape had one of the most successful public stock offerings in history, and its browser was dominating the Web. Netscape was also operating system independent—meaning it didn't require a particular operating system to run. Microsoft reacted by restructuring its products to be Internet compliant and developing the Internet Explorer (IE) browser that it first gave away and then integrated into its Windows 98 OS. This integration of IE with the dominant operating system was the turning point in what came to be known as the "browser wars." In 1996, Internet Explorer's market share went from 7% to 29%—assisted by Microsoft becoming the promoted browser for AOL in exchange for an AOL icon appearing on every Windows desktop (competing with Microsoft's own MSN service). IE never stopped gaining users after that. In 1998, Netscape took a different tack, going *open source*, and released the source code for its browser.

In an antitrust suit filed against Microsoft in 1998, the U.S. government claimed that Microsoft's near monopoly in operating systems created an unfair advantage in competing against Netscape. Microsoft claimed that Internet Explorer was an integral part of the operating system and could not be separated

open source – Software with source code that's accessible—and potentially even documented—for modification

from the rest of the code easily. The 1998 sale of Netscape to AOL also muddied the legal waters.

The government case went even farther back than the browser wars. It claimed that Microsoft's control over computer manufacturers in matters such as what third-party program icons could appear on the desktop was monopolistic. Microsoft's alleged practice—going back to the original releases of DOS—of not releasing critical operating system information to third-party software vendors, such as Lotus and WordPerfect (to the advantage of Microsoft's own application software), was also claimed to be monopolistic. In the end, however, Microsoft came out of the suit fairly well. Various parties settled separately, and although a threat of breakup seemed possible, in 2001 under the Bush administration in the White House, most of the antitrust suit was dropped or lessened.

Today, one of the biggest threats to Microsoft in the personal computer market is the rise of Linux, a UNIX-based program written by Linus Torvalds while a student at the University of Helsinki. It's available, including source code, essentially free. Many hobbyists have embraced Linux as their choice of operating system because of the low cost, available source code, and reputed reliability. Although not originally written with this intention, it has been selected, and not without cost, by many corporations, large and small, as a viable operating system for servers, for these very reasons. Corporate information technology experts cite eliminating dependence on a single vendor—Microsoft, in this case—as appealing.

The threat of Linux hangs over Microsoft, but how it has played out might surprise some. In 2001 Microsoft released Windows XP, following Windows 2000, which was built on the NT platform released in 1993. Windows 98 was the last version based on DOS, which many users held on to, as it supported a number of applications that NT did not. Microsoft partially became a victim of its own success. It had many users with many needs to satisfy. When Windows Vista was announced as a replacement for Windows XP, it originally seemed to be a paradigm shift: It would be far more secure and look far different. However, after its release in 2006, it garnered much criticism. Users complained that the digital rights management was onerous and the operating system required too much in the way of resources. Microsoft claims that its projected figure of 200 million users by January 2009 has been on target, but the perception developed that many end users were reluctant to upgrade to Vista. Its successor, in 2009, is Windows 7.

Operating systems on personal computers, however, are only part of the story in computing. Although it's true that a Microsoft operating system runs on more than 90% of Intel-based computers (or Intel clones), only 10% of the software running on all the computing devices in the world comes from Microsoft—far from a monopoly. This fact puts the world of computing in perspective. For each personal computer, there are numerous mainframes, networked machines, handheld devices, and *embedded computers*, all requiring software. Where does this software come from? From large companies such as CA, Inc., Oracle, and

embedded computers –
Computers embedded into other devices: a phone, car, or thermometer, for example

Germany's SAG; small local firms and startups; and the hundreds of thousands of programmers worldwide.

In addition, one refrain heard in the 1990s (with little to back it up at the time) was "The Internet is the new operating system." This claim was one reason Microsoft pursued the browser with such vigor when it finally did. Today, however, this statement is more obviously true with the advent of "cloud computing," in which applications are not only available online, but the systems powering them are distributed internationally in numerous huge server farms. In a related development, many institutions have gone to a model that might remind you of the time-sharing used with third-generation machines. In this model, called "thin clients," machines have little storage but some local processing power and use networked applications and data.

what about the future?

A quick look at the future shows tantalizing possibilities in computer development—and the social implications of that development. You've probably already noticed the first signs of these possibilities.

For more information on cutting-edge technologies and trends, see the online chapter "Emerging Technologies."

Parallel computing, for example, can create massive computing power. In 2003, Virginia Tech created the third fastest machine in the world by writing specialized software linking a collection of networked Macintosh computers. Many organizations have followed suit and built their own parallel supercomputer. Parallel processing can work on the Internet as well. For example, you can sign up for a scientific research project where, via the Web, you loan out some of your machine's processing power. Your machine can join hundreds, thousands, or even more machines working on a single scientific problem. With millions of machines on the Internet, imagine parallel computing as a model for problem solving.

ubiquitous computing – *The possibility of computers being embedded into almost everything and potentially able to communicate*

With wireless networking, you can surf the Web without plugging into the wall. Soon, using wireless technologies such as Bluetooth in addition to embedded computing (sometimes called *ubiquitous computing*), all the appliances in your home might be "talking." The water heater might hear from the furnace that it's on vacation mode and adjust itself automatically. Who knows? Maybe your lost sock can tell you where it is! Medical equipment can be miniaturized and even implanted in your body, communicating to doctors via the Web.

What has been termed "open-source software" continues to be influential in the computer field. You might be reading this book while taking a course that uses Moodle or Sakai course management software. More than 30% of colleges and universities in the United States use this software, and the percentage is growing. The software is "free," but what that really means is that instead of purchasing the software and getting support from a single vendor, the organization decides whether to maintain the software itself or purchase support from competing support companies. It also means the organization joins a community of other organizations and people—potentially paying employees to help write the software—who discuss, build, document, and test additions and modifications to the software and, therefore, benefit from influencing the technology's direction. A program such as Sakai is actually slightly different from most open-source systems. It's sometimes called "directed source" because organizations come together to commit to designing and building an open-source system. This approach began recently with Kuali, a university administration system that might one day be the system you use to register for classes, get financial aid, and view your transcript. Open source sounds positive, especially given the high quality of programs, such as Linux, that benefit from numerous eyes viewing the code. However, it depends on the community of practitioners remaining together and not creating code bases that differ overly much (which is called "forking"). It remains to be seen what open-source development will mean for the computer industry.

Everything is going digital, it seems. Will books, film, and photographs eventually disappear? Will music lovers no longer own CDs but download what they want, when they want, from the Web? What of privacy? As increasing amounts of information about people are stored on computers, does everyone need to choose between invasion of their privacy and physical and fiscal security?

In addition, what powers all these devices? Today, more organizations are realizing the cost benefits of "going green." Even with continual cost reductions in memory and processing, coding in efficient ways—similar to the ways of early programmers—could become more important again. It's estimated that more than 5% of the electrical power consumed in the United States runs all the computers within its borders. Efficient hardware and software could have considerable economic and environmental benefits. System security and coding for robustness are increasingly important, too. With more objects controlled through software, ensuring that software has been tested fully and run through a broad series of virtual scenarios is critical. In any of these eventualities, you, as a computer professional, will have an important role to play.

What does the future have in store for you if you join the many characters (named and unnamed) in the stories you've just read? What exactly can you do in the computer field? The ACM labels four paths for computer science. The first two, devising new ways to use computers and developing effective ways to solve computing problems, tend to require a computer science degree. The second two, designing and implementing software and planning and managing infrastructure, also use computer science graduates but draw on graduates of newer programs in software engineering, information technology, and systems management. Outside computer science lies a fifth path: computer engineering, in which you design computer hardware. Typically, it requires a degree in electrical engineering.

Fields requiring computer professionals include medical imaging, mobile devices, gaming and simulations, Web applications, and online entertainment. As a computer scientist, you might devise a better search algorithm, create a more lifelike artificial intelligence for a game, or design a database for storing movies and music online. As a software engineer or computer scientist, you might build an online application for viewing movies or write the code for a new plane's aviation system. As a computer engineer, you might design a faster chip to render games or medical graphics faster. As an information technology specialist, you might keep multiple and complex networks running or devise a system for providing online search results for movies and music. Information system specialists typically work more closely with customers to ensure, for example, that doctors have the right information at the right time.

The direction you choose is up to you, but know this: Job growth in computing, despite the economy's ups and downs, has been averaging from 30% to more than 50% for decades and is expected to continue in this direction. The jobs are often fulfilling, influential, and lucrative. For example, a 2006 *CNN/Money* poll listed software engineering as the best job for salary and future opportunities.

one last thought

Underlying all the developments in computer hardware and software that you've seen in this chapter is a larger context: Societal and personal needs, wants, and desires shape the development of any technology, including computers and the programs that run them. Further, these developments have implications for the societies where they're implemented.

Perhaps there was market demand for the product because it fulfilled a physical and commercial requirement. For example, chip designers competed to cram more circuits in a smaller area so that hardware designers would choose their chips. Hardware designers then created smaller, faster, and less expensive computers that appealed to a broader market, increasing hardware sales. Perhaps the impetus behind an innovation was the drive to discover a solution to a problem—as with Babbage and his Analytical Engine—or the desire to create something new—as with Woz and the Apple I. Perhaps it was the need for control exhibited by many early hobbyists, who promoted getting away from centralized mainframes and owning their own machines. Perhaps it served a social or political need, such as winning a war. Perhaps it met an ideal of what a computer should look like—as with Engelbart and his mouse—or was an effort to stay ahead of possible competition, like Bill Gates and his drive to succeed. In any event, needs, from the highest level to the most personal, play a complex role in creating computer hardware or a computer program.

These developments have had their impact on society. The miniaturization of electronics changed the way people entertain themselves, with movies and music delivered directly to people wherever they are—in trains, planes, and automobiles. It even changed the way people communicate with each other. In the past, people roamed the grocery store with only a paper list, not a cell phone so that they could ask someone at home to look in the refrigerator to see whether they need butter. Some researchers now argue that this lickety-split culture is rewiring our brains. Computerized business practices, such as those initiated by IBM, made banking and airline transactions faster but also created customer demand for even more speed. Personal computers gave people access to computing power but also created a mountain of waste, as customers upgraded every few years. Monopolistic practices created almost universal platforms from which customers could work but limited innovative approaches. The rise of software as a commodity drove legal practices that created more intellectual property rights but might also have limited software innovations. The Macintosh version of Douglas Engelbart's interface made computers easier to use but in a one-size-fits-all way. Because the interface was more intuitive, young children found their way to the computer screen instead of outside, where some running around might have helped prevent the rise in the national rate of obesity. All these developments had their consequences, intended or otherwise.

Although an arm's-length view of history might suggest that technological development occurs in a seamlessly purposeful evolutionary direction, a closer look, as this chapter has shown, reveals the truth as being more complex. Perhaps the best idea wins, but it depends on your definition of "best." As a computer scientist, only part of your job is to program or design. You need to be aware of the complex mix of requirements and historical forces affecting you. You should also be aware of the implications of what you create. That's how you will succeed: by avoiding the mistakes of the past and emulating the triumphs. You will share and appreciate a common heritage with those around you, and you'll be able to tell a good story or two. Have fun!

chapter summary

- Understanding the evolution of computers and computer science helps you understand the broader context of the many different tasks you'll undertake throughout your education and career.

- Computers are unique tools, in that they can do different jobs depending on what software is running on them.

- Today you can find computers everywhere from your desktop to your countertop.

- At its core, every computer performs symbolic and mathematical manipulation.

- The history of mathematical tools can be traced as far back as the Assyrians and their clay mathematical tables.

- The punch card, a major development in the history of computing, owes its development to Jacquard's loom.

- Charles Babbage is considered the father of modern computing because of his development of the Analytical Engine; Ada Lovelace Byron is considered the first programmer.

- Herman Hollerith, later playing a part in what would become IBM, solved the U.S. Census problem of 1890 by use of a mechanical counting tool.

- The ENIAC, attributed mainly to John Mauchly, J. Presper Eckert, and John Von Neumann, has been called the first electronic computer; it used vacuum tubes, had thousands of switches, and weighed tons.

- Mauchly and Eckert went on to build the first commercial computer, the UNIVAC.

- IBM dominated the mainframe marketplace in the late '50s, '60s, and '70s.

- Transistors, and then integrated circuits, shrank the size of the computer, leading first to the minicomputer in the mid-1960s and then to the microcomputer in the late '70s.

- UNIX and BASIC were invented in the early 1970s.

- Hobbyists created the first microcomputers; the Altair was considered to be the very first.

- Big business officially entered the microcomputer scene with the introduction of the IBM PC.

- In the 1980s, with the microcomputer, companies began selling software directly to end users; before the microcomputer, software usually came with the machine.

- Apple Computer introduced the small business community to inexpensive computing with the Apple II and VisiCalc, the first "killer app."

- Apple's Macintosh introduced the first graphical user interface to most of the world but was built on the work of Douglas Engelbart.

- IBM lost market share in the late '80s and '90s because it had created an open system and had an agreement in which Microsoft could sell its operating system independent of IBM.

- The Internet began with ARPANET, built by the U.S. Department of Defense in the 1960s as a way to share computing resources, but the parties involved soon realized that it was more useful as a communication device.

- The World Wide Web and the browser, especially Mosaic, permitted a broader audience to use the Internet; consequently, the use of the Internet via the Web exploded.

- Wireless networks, ubiquitous and embedded computing, and parallel computing all promise to change the world you live in.

- Societal and personal needs, wants, and desires shape the development of any technology, including computers and the programs that run them, and in turn these developments shape society and its people.

key terms

abacus (*6*)

assembly language (*13*)

binary code or machine code (*13*)

Boolean logic (Boolean algebra) (*10*)

browser (*30*)

central processing unit (CPU) (*19*)

chip (*16*)

embedded computers (*33*)

graphical user interface (GUI) (*25*)

hardware (*12*)

hypermedia (*30*)

hypertext (*30*)

integrated circuit (IC) (*16*)

killer app (*23*)

mainframe (*15*)

microcomputer (*22*)

microprocessor (*19*)

minicomputer (*18*)

open architecture (*21*)

open source (*32*)

operating system (OS) (*16*)

parallel computing (*27*)

personal computer (PC) (*24*)

program loop (*8*)

slide rule (*6*)

software (*12*)

stored program concept (*11*)

supercomputer (*27*)

time-sharing (*17*)

transistor (*16*)

ubiquitous computing (*34*)

vacuum tubes (*10*)

Von Neumann machine (*11*)

test yourself

1. Name two needs of society that led to the development of more complex mathematics.

2. What was the first mechanical device used for calculation?

3. How would you compare the early electronic computer to the player piano?

4. What technology did Herman Hollerith borrow from the Jacquard loom?

5. Who has been called the first programmer?

6. Name an important concept attributed to the person named in Question 5.

7. What innovation does the ENIAC appear to borrow from the Atanasoff-Berry Computer?

8. Name at least one computer other than ENIAC that was developed independently and simultaneously during World War II.

9. What reason is given for the invention of assembly language?

10. What color can you attribute to IBM of the 1950s, and what significance did it have for IBM's eventual dominance of the marketplace?

11. Name two important developments of the second generation of hardware.

12. What long-term memory storage device that computers have today did second-generation computers often lack?

13. In what language was the first UNIX operating system written? What did Thompson and Ritchie have to create for the second version of UNIX?

14. On what kind of computer was the first UNIX operating system written?

15. Before the Altair, Ed Roberts created what?

16. What software did the Altair microcomputer get that later helped make Bill Gates rich?

17. Name the two people responsible for the first Apple computer. Name the "killer app" responsible for the Apple II's success.

18. What challenge to the IBM PC did Apple launch in 1984? What response did Microsoft launch against Apple a few years later?

19. One of the ideas used in the development of ARPANET—splitting information into blocks and reassembling them at their destination—came from the Rand Corporation. The initial concept began in relation to what system?

20. To whom, writing in the 1940s, have the origins of hypertext been attributed?

practice exercises

1. In 1642 Pascal created a mechanical device with gears and levers. This device was capable of what kind of calculation?

   a. Addition
   b. Addition and subtraction
   c. Addition, subtraction, and multiplication
   d. Addition, subtraction, multiplication, and division

2. Leibniz built on Pascal's work by creating the Leibniz Wheel. This device was capable of what kind of calculations in addition to the ones Pascal's could do?

   a. Subtraction
   b. Addition and multiplication
   c. Subtraction and multiplication
   d. Multiplication and division

3. The Jacquard loom is important in the history of computing for what innovation?

   a. It worked like a player piano.
   b. Reusable cards with holes held information.
   c. It used gears and wheels for calculation.
   d. Paper rolls with holes held information.

4. IBM has some of its origins in what 1890 event?

   a. The U.S. census
   b. The first Jacquard loom in the United States
   c. Ada Lovelace's first program loop
   d. The introduction of electricity to the United States

5. Name the four important elements of Babbage's Engine that are components of today's computer.

   a. The stored program technique, an input device, an output device, and memory
   b. Mechanical calculation equipment, human-powered mechanisms, punched cards, and an output device
   c. An input device, memory, a central processing unit, an output device
   d. An input device, the stored program technique, a central processing unit, and an output device

6. What logical elements did Charles Sanders Peirce realize electrical switches could emulate in 1880?

   a. Epistemological calculus
   b. Ontological algebra
   c. Boolean algebra
   d. Metaphysical algebra

7. The U.S. military used the ENIAC computer for its intended purpose during World War II.

   a. True
   b. False

8. What important concept is attributed to John Von Neumann?

   a. The large memory concept
   b. The stored program concept
   c. The discrete variable automation concept
   d. The virtual memory concept

9. What company controlled 70% or more of the computer marketplace in the '60s and '70s?

   a. Sperry-Univac
   b. International Business Machines
   c. Hollerith Machines
   d. Microsoft

10. What features of transistors made them superior for computers, compared with vacuum tubes?

    a. They were more expensive than tubes but lasted longer and were cooler in temperature.
    b. They didn't last as long as tubes but were less expensive.
    c. They were cheaper and smaller than tubes.
    d. They were cheaper, smaller, and cooler than tubes and lasted longer.

11. What important pastry helped move your job up in the queue in second-generation software, and what third-generation software development made that pastry unnecessary?

    a. Donuts and integrated circuits
    b. Bear claws and multitasking
    c. Donuts and time-sharing
    d. Donuts and virtual memory

12. In hardware, the next step up from the transistor was the transmitter.

    a. True
    b. False

13. What magazines can you thank for the first microcomputer?

    a. *Science* and *Wall Street Journal*
    b. *Popular Electronics* and *Radio Electronics*
    c. *Popular Electronics* and *Star Trek Monthly*
    d. *New Mexico Entrepreneur* and *Radio Electronics*

14. What important concept did the Altair use, which was borrowed by its competition, including the IBM personal computer?

    a. The computer came in kit form.
    b. The computer's price was $666.
    c. The machine had an open architecture.
    d. The machine could be used without plugging it into a wall outlet.

15. The Apple computer became very popular. What was its largest market, and what software made it interesting to that market?

    a. The education market and the educational game Shape Up
    b. The games market and the game The Big Race
    c. The business market and the program Lotus 1-2-3
    d. The business market and the program VisiCalc

16. In 1990, what software company dominated the software market, and what major product did it sell?

    a. Lotus and Lotus 1-2-3
    b. Bricklin and VisiCalc
    c. Apple and the Apple Operating System
    d. Microsoft and Word

17. Today, Microsoft considers its major competition in operating systems to be what system?

    a. Control Data Corporation OS
    b. Sega Games operating system
    c. Linux operating system
    d. Mac OS X

18. ARPA was created in response to what major event in world history?

    a. World War II
    b. The McCarthy hearings of the 1950s
    c. The launch of Sputnik
    d. The inability of computers to communicate with one another

19. Name the three most likely critical large-scale developments of the fifth generation of software development from this list of options:

    a. Parallel computing, networking, and the multiple-data-stream approach
    b. The graphical user interface, networking, and computer-aided software engineering (CASE) tools
    c. Networking, the graphical user interface, and packet switching
    d. ARPANET, the Internet, and CASE tools

20. Marc Andreessen released what application that made browsers widespread?

    a. Netscape
    b. Mosaic
    c. Explorer
    d. Hypertext

digging deeper

1. How has the idea of open-source development changed the software industry?

2. How did the microcomputer revolution change how software was distributed? Who is partly responsible for this change?

3. After selling MITS, Ed Roberts went on to get his medical degree and became a doctor. Why did his computer quickly lose dominance in the microcomputer industry and his company eventually fold? What would you have done differently?

4. What critical agreement and what hardware decisions might have allowed Microsoft to monopolize the microcomputer world, as IBM slowly lost market share?

5. Has Microsoft been unfairly labeled a monopoly? Would the demise of Linux change your opinion?

discussion topics

1. What values are there in having embedded computers talk to one another? What dangers?

2. Imagine that Microsoft didn't get to keep the rights to its software when it moved back to Seattle. What would the software world probably look like today?

3. Programming is now carried on 24 hours a day by having development teams stationed around the globe (United States, Ireland, India, and so on). Are these developments a threat or a benefit to programmers in the United States?

4. The beginning of this chapter mentioned that almost everyone is a computer user. What do you think would classify you as a computer scientist? What would likely have classified you as a computer scientist in 1945?

5. Several schools in the United States and Western Europe have become concerned over the low numbers of women and minorities learning computer science. Recently, Carnegie Mellon focused on attracting women and minorities. How can society benefit by attracting more of these members of society to computer science? What would it mean for engineering culture, product design, management, or end users?

Internet research

1. What hardware and software system runs the New York Stock Exchange? NASDAQ?

2. In the world of the Internet, what is an RFP? Who uses them, and for how long have they been used?

3. What are the five fastest, or most powerful, computers in the world? Who created them, who operates them, and what purposes are they used for?

4. What legal arrangement protects open-source software? How has this arrangement helped or hindered development?

5. What is the *Whole Earth Catalog*, and why was it important in the development of the graphical user interface?

chapter **2**

computing security and ethics

in this chapter you will:

- Learn about the origins of computer hacking
- Learn about some of the motivations for hackers and crackers
- Learn about technologies that system intruders use
- Learn about malicious code
- Learn what social engineering is and how it works
- Learn how security experts categorize types of system attacks
- Learn about physical and technical safeguards
- Learn how to create a good password
- Learn about antivirus software
- Learn about encryption
- Learn about preventive system setup, including firewalls and routers
- Learn about laws to protect intellectual property and prosecute cracking
- Learn about ethical behavior in computing
- Learn about privacy in computing and ways to ensure it

the lighter side of the lab
by spencer

Have you ever noticed that the only "cool" computer people in movies are computer hackers? It's not often you see a scene with dramatic music playing in the background while Larry from down the hall sits in his cubicle and configures his router.

Sometimes I wish that I were a computer hacker. I don't want to break into government files or the university database. (Not even a hacker could make my grades look good.) I just want to be able to get into my computer the day after I change my password.

We've all heard that changing your password frequently is important to make your computer more secure. The only problem with this advice is that my brain seems to contain only "virtual memory" these days. As soon as I "shut down" at night, the password information disappears from my brain.

Trying to guess your password is almost like a game. "Okay, so I was thinking about my aunt when I created this password. She has a dog named Fluffy. She got Fluffy in May. My password must be fluffymay!" BUZZ! "mayfluffy?" BUZZ! "05fluffy?" BUZZ! "fluffy05?" BUZZ! "$%*&!" BUZZ! "Where's Chloe from *24* when I need her?!"

I've finally resorted to writing my usernames and passwords on yellow sticky notes that I paste all over my monitor. So now I'm completely secure—as long as someone isn't sitting at my computer. (Professional hackers would have a hard time getting into my computer from around the globe, but a kindergartner sitting at my desk shouldn't have any problem.)

Yellow sticky notes are an essential tool for any computer person. My computer often resembles a big yellow piñata. Besides holding my username and password information, the yellow sticky notes on my monitor also contain appointments, to-do lists, important phone numbers and dates, dates' phone numbers, reminders to pay bills, and the names of the Jonas Brothers (just in case).

One thing I could do to improve my personal security is to clean my desk. I'm currently on the annual cleaning schedule. At this very moment, I face the risk of paper avalanche in my office. I'm considering buying one of those cannons that ski resorts use to prevent avalanches. I'd better check to see if one's available on eBay. Now, what was my password . . .?

why you need to know about...
computing security and ethics

Clifford Stoll, a systems manager at Lawrence Berkeley National Laboratory in California, was tracking a 75-cent accounting error. His search for the source of that error led to a year of investigation and eventually to a programmer in West Germany who turned out to be part of a spy ring that sold computer secrets to the Soviet Union's KGB in return for money and drugs. Stoll's 1989 book about his experience, *The Cuckoo's Egg*, was a bestseller.

When it comes to computer security and ethics, it's tempting to think in such dramatic images: The clean-cut genius nerd catches the lone wolf, evil scientist hacker. This characterization isn't totally inaccurate, as it turns out. However, creating computer security and frustrating would-be intruders is a much broader, more complex, and more mundane undertaking than Hollywood's typical portrayal. It involves more than computer detectives and lurking intruders. Good computer security is primarily a matter of prevention—including preventing and recovering from accidental and natural events. Computer security must not exist in a vacuum but must link to good security practices and professional ethical standards for computing. Good computer security, then, is as much about locking doors, storing backups, and following protocol as it is about writing smarter software to catch the bad guys.

Computer security is important because it affects everyone and everyone can affect it. You have probably already been subjected to a virus or worm attack and perhaps played unwittingly into propagating the infection to other computers. You have probably also had the unpleasant experience of losing important files (usually right before you have to hand them in to your professor). Being aware of threats and how to prevent or counteract them, as well as being conscious of the possible effects of your actions as a computer scientist, is becoming increasingly important.

Business computers are better protected than home computers, mainly because corporations make a conscious effort to secure them; many home users just want to use their computers and not worry about other details. Some users are simply uninformed or don't care about security and think downloading a game, video, or song is more important than worrying about the file's authenticity or a possible security threat. The goal of this chapter is to help you become more aware of the risks involved with security issues so that you can become more security minded. You can minimize the level of risk by learning how to identify risks and install software to take precautions.

the intruder

The term *hacker* (or *cracker*) is often used to refer to an intruder who breaks into a computer system with malicious intent. The term originated in the 1960s, and it meant an insider who was to able to manipulate a system for the good of the system. At that time, programming was a difficult and esoteric art practiced by very few people. The best programmers were called hackers as a sign of respect, and a good program that took advantage of the system as best it could was called a "hack." Over time, however, the connotation of "hacker" in the eyes of the general public has become more negative and synonymous with "cracker," although the computer security industry still differentiates between a hacker (technically proficient person) and a cracker (unwelcome system intruder).

hacker – A technically proficient person who breaks into a computer system; originally denoted good intent, but general usage today is similar to "cracker"

cracker – An unwelcome system intruder with malicious intent

Around the same time, some people began illegally manipulating the AT&T phone system, mimicking certain tones to get free long-distance calls. A fellow who called himself Cap'n Crunch discovered that a whistle that came in boxes of this cereal could be used to subvert the phone system. The practice was called *phreaking*, and those who did it became known as phreaks.

phreaking – Subverting the phone system to get free service

Some phreaks were becoming more interested in computers as the microcomputer revolution took hold. In fact, some of these characters went legit and became beneficiaries of the revolution. Cap'n Crunch, whose real name is John Draper, helped write some of the most important applications for Microsoft. Unfortunately, a number of characters applied their technical proficiency to computers in a negative way. By breaking into mainframes and creating viruses, they changed the word "hacker" from meaning a technically savvy insider helping to make the system better to a potentially dangerous outsider. The labels "cracker" or just plain "criminal" are also used.

These hackers are now the semi-romantic figures from movies, books, and magazines who wear the "black hat" and threaten the world or the "white hat" and promise to save the world. Remember the movie *War Games*? Matthew Broderick was a computer "geek" immersed in computer games and dialed random numbers in the hope he could break into a company's system to play games. He ended up breaking into the Pentagon's defense system and almost started World War III. But who are these hackers in reality? Many intruders are fairly innocent computer users who stumble into a security hole and cause problems. Intentional intruders are generally divided into two classes: those motivated primarily by the challenge of breaking into a system, called *undirected* (or *untargeted*) *hackers*, and those motivated by greed or malicious intent, called *directed* (or *targeted*) *hackers*. In this book, "cracker," "malicious hacker," "directed hacker," and "undirected hacker" are used to indicate an unwanted system intruder.

undirected (untargeted) hacker – A cracker motivated by the challenge of breaking into a system

directed (targeted) hacker – Generally, a cracker motivated by greed and/or politics

Generally, the cracker profile is a male between 16 and 35 years old considered by many to be a loner. The person also tends to be intelligent as well as technically savvy. Novice crackers who know how to use only existing tools earn the

script kiddie – An amateur hacker who simply uses the hacking tools developed by others

moniker *script kiddie*. Crackers intent on remaining anonymous while they steal or damage (directed hackers) are usually the most proficient.

For undirected hackers, one of the biggest motivators for cracking is bragging rights. Often these undirected hackers comb the Internet looking for vulnerable systems that haven't yet been cracked. After they've cracked a system, they boast about it on Internet Relay Chat (IRC), on message boards, or in magazines such as *2600: The Hacker Quarterly*. Many crackers close the security hole that they've taken advantage of after they've gained entry so that no other cracker can follow. Their justification might be to have sole control of the system. Another justification is *hacktivism*. Many crackers believe they're doing society a favor by discovering these security holes before "real criminals" do. A document on the Internet called the *Hacker's Manifesto* justifies cracker activity for this very reason.

hacktivism – Cracking into a system as a political act; one political notion is that cracking itself is useful for society

Hacker's Manifesto – A document, written anonymously, that justifies cracking into systems as an ethical exercise

Greed tends to motivate directed hackers, who unfortunately are usually more proficient and do not advertise their exploits. This type of hacker looks for information that can be sold or used to blackmail the organization that owns it. Hackers of this type tend to target corporations that have assets of monetary value. Smart young Russian hackers, for instance, are becoming a global threat by extorting money from banks and betting firms. The Russian police have said this particular racket is just the tip of the iceberg, and no one is safe from these attacks.

Malicious hackers—interested in vandalizing or terrorism—can be both directed and undirected. Undirected hackers tend to write viruses and worms, without knowing where they will end up. They're content with the random violence of the act. These intrusions can damage systems at many levels. Some attacks are fairly benign, but others can cause billions of dollars of damage. Directed hackers usually direct their efforts at organizations or individuals where there's some perceived wrong. For example, a directed hacker might vandalize a company's Web site because he or she was fired or was dissatisfied with the company's product. Directed hackers might also be interested in making political statements. Usually, directed hackers intend to damage, not gain quiet access.

Whether directed or undirected, malicious, greedy, or benign, hired by a competing corporation or the Mob, or part of a terrorist organization, hackers are an increasingly expensive and dangerous aspect of computing. In monetary terms, illegal hacking becomes more expensive each year, and there seems to be no end in sight. So how do unwanted visitors hack into systems?

how do they get in?

The sad truth is that most intrusions could have been avoided with good system configuration, proper programming techniques, and adherence to security policies: Directed hackers can quickly take advantage of these failures to follow sound security practices. Even more quick to take advantage of systems are malicious software programs, commonly known as viruses. It takes milliseconds for a virus (or worm) to invade an unprotected system over a network. Finally, crackers take advantage of the innocent human tendency to be helpful. By starting a friendly dialogue and then asking for help, often they can get answers that help them guess passwords, for example, and use them to break into a system. This nontechnical approach—called social engineering—is often one of the most effective tools for intruders.

holes in the system

One major benefit to crackers is the open nature of the Internet. The point of the Internet when it was created was to allow sharing information and computer resources. The same could be said of the World Wide Web and networks. Unfortunately, this openness benefited malicious intent. For example, in UNIX, the Network File System (NFS) allows a user on one machine to mount (or see) a drive on another machine as though it were local (called cross-mounting). In the early days of computers, all a cracker had to do was mount someone else's drive by using the appropriate user ID number. Even more dangerous was that the root file system (where passwords and configuration files are stored) was open for reading and writing. Protecting user IDs and system files was something system administrators had to learn quickly. Users also became vulnerable to this type of intrusion when they began using remote terminal access or pcAnywhere-type programs to share Windows drives with remote users. A naive user could open his or her entire system to the world easily without knowing or intending it.

backdoors – Shortcuts into programs created by system designers to facilitate system maintenance but used and abused by crackers

Crackers have taken considerable advantage of *backdoors* left by programmers and administrators for their own convenience. The UNIX rlogin (remote login) command allows an administrator to log in to one system and then log in to other machines remotely without having a password. This command benefits system managers in maintaining machines. Unfortunately, it can also benefit a cracker because a configuration error could allow anyone to have the same kind of access. Early versions of the UNIX e-mail program Sendmail had a backdoor in which a three-letter command could gain you access to system-level control (called "root" on UNIX systems), where you could delete, modify, and replace protected operating system programs.

buffer overflow – A program tries to place more information into a memory location than that location can handle

Sloppy programming plays a major role in creating holes crackers can exploit. For example, many online shopping sites have kept information about the purchase a customer is making right in the URL string displayed in the address bar. If the site doesn't verify the item's price in the cart at purchase and a cracker modifies the price, the cracker potentially walks away with some cheap merchandise. Buffer overflows are another vulnerability of many systems. They are fairly easy to fix (but even easier to not allow in the first place) but are widespread in computer programs. A *buffer overflow* happens when a program tries to place more information into a location in memory than that location can handle. For example, if you try to put an 8-byte integer into a 1-byte character variable, it causes an overflow. A cracker aims for an overflow that overloads memory all the way to a section of memory critical to the machine's operation. The most critical memory sections in a computer are in the instruction stack. A cracker's goal is to stuff an address of a program he or she wants run onto the stack, which gives the cracker control of the machine.

viruses, worms, and other nasty things

Crackers can create *malicious code* to do their work for them. This code is designed to breach your system security and threaten your digital information. Malicious code comes in a few major forms: the virus, the worm, and the Trojan program.

A *virus* is a program that, when executed, can infect the machine directly or actively search for programs to infect and embed itself into these programs. When these programs run, they activate the virus program, which infects the machine. Sometimes the virus is silent—or at least silent for a while. Usually, the virus affects the host machine. It can do anything from playing a little tune and then eliminating itself to destroying files on the hard drive. Some other evidence that you have a virus might be the following:

- Programs don't run properly. Files don't open correctly.
- Disk space or memory becomes far less than it should be.
- Existing files or icons disappear.
- The machine runs very slowly.
- Unknown programs, files, or processes appear.

Viruses can also target particular files, such as system files, and become difficult to remove. Technically, viruses, unlike worms, require assistance in moving between machines; a common way to move is by users sharing files. The first viruses seem almost quaint now. They appeared in the early 1980s and were spread by users swapping floppy disks. Booting from an infected disk was a common means of infection. With the widespread adoption of e-mail, however, viruses can spread like wildfire. Beware of attachments: They can host a virus that runs when the attachment is opened. Figure 2-1 shows a typical virus warning from a system administrator.

A *worm* is a program that actively reproduces itself across a network. This code is a type of *bot* (short for robot) because of its capability to work on its own. Worms seek out vulnerable systems, invade them, and continue to seek more systems. They're far more active than a virus, which requires humans to move it between machines. The first catastrophic worm event was the Great Worm or Morris Worm of 1988, written by graduate student Robert T. Morris. It was a "benign" worm—he intended it to do no damage—yet it brought down more than 10% of the Internet.

malicious code – *Code designed to breach system security and threaten digital information; often called a virus, although technically a virus is only one kind of malicious code*

virus – *An uninvited guest program with the potential to damage files and the operating system; this term is sometimes used generically to denote a virus, worm, or Trojan program*

worm – *A type of bot that can roam a network looking for vulnerable systems and replicate itself on those systems; the new copies look for still more vulnerable systems*

bot – *A software program that can roam the Internet autonomously; bots can be quite benign and useful, such as those used by Google and other search engines to find Web pages to list in search results*

Figure 2-1, A typical virus e-mail warning

Trojan program – *A program that poses as an innocent program; some action or the passage of time triggers the program to do its dirty work*

A *Trojan program* disguises itself as something innocent, such as a game or, the worst possible example, an antivirus program. After it's on a host system, it can lie dormant and then do obvious damage or clandestine system analysis, potentially compromising the system by finding backdoors, and so on.

the human factor: social engineering

For crackers intent on breaking into a particular system, the best approach turns out to be not exploiting technical holes, but *social engineering*. "Social engineer" is a contemporary term for something that has been around for a long time. You might better recognize the labels "con artist," "grifter," or "flim-flam man." Social engineers use their understanding of human behavior to get important information from trusting "marks."

social engineering – *Social interaction that preys on human gullibility, sympathy, or fear to take advantage of the target, for example, to steal money, information, or other valuables—basically, a con*

The ability to lie persuasively is the most effective tool in the social engineer's arsenal. After learning an employee's name, the social engineer might pose as that employee, call the human resources department, get just a little more information, and then call computer support looking for a password, for example. Posing as an insider, the social engineer strings together bits of information, gaining more information from a variety of sources. Many support personnel just doing their jobs have unwittingly given away passwords to a caller posing as an authorized user. After all, it's the job of technical support staff to be helpful.

dumpster diving – *Picking through people's trash to find things of value; although often innocent, it has been used by thieves to glean potentially damaging information*

Social engineers can also find information just by hanging out in the right places: the smokers' circle that forms around 10 a.m. outside or a favorite coffee shop down the block. If they can't get the kind of information they want over the phone or in person, there's always *dumpster diving*—essentially sifting through trash and suffering through a few rotten banana peels to find information about companies and employees. Even things as seemingly innocent as the corporate phone book can be used by a social engineer to pick out the right people and use the right corporate lingo to dupe people into revealing more than they should. For this reason, shredders are used more often, and corporate dumpsters are locked. Home users should consider doing the same.

Generally, social engineers try to maintain a low profile and not show their faces if possible. Something as simple as browsing the company Web site— which the company wants casual users to do—is a good way to gather information. Some companies have also combined what should be an internal intranet with their public Web site. In that case, details about employees, corporate events, and other information might be available to outsiders.

A social engineer might also use traditional cracker techniques to augment the attack. Installing a fake login text box on a user's computer that captures the person's name and password is one technique. Another is sending out a spam e-mail for a chance to win money that requires a username and password. Many people use the same username and password as they do in other programs. As another example, you might be familiar with the e-mail from a wealthy foreigner who needs help moving millions of dollars from his homeland and promises a reward for your assistance, if you just supply your bank account information. Remember that if it sounds too good to be true, *run away* (said in a Monty Python King Arthur voice)!

One notorious social engineer was Kevin Mitnick. At one point in the 1990s, he was on the FBI's 10 most wanted list. He was subsequently caught, tried, and sent to jail. Since then, in an effort to turn over a new leaf, he has revealed many of his techniques for the benefit of the security community.

types of attacks

As you've seen, crackers use a variety of techniques (both directed and undirected) to gain entry to or compromise a system. There are too many attacks to list, and the number continues to grow daily. However, security managers divide these attacks into four main categories:

- Access
- Modification
- Denial of service
- Repudiation

access attacks – *Attacks on a system that can include snooping, eavesdropping, and interception; more commonly known as spying or illicitly gaining access to protected information*

sniffer – *A software program, such as Wireshark, that allows the user to listen in on network traffic*

modification attacks – *Attacks on a system that alter information illicitly*

denial-of-service (DoS) attacks – *Attacks that prevent legitimate users from using the system or accessing information*

repudiation attacks – *Attacks on a system that injure the information's reliability; for example, a repudiation attack might remove evidence that an event (such as a bank transaction) actually did occur*

risk – *The relationship between vulnerability and threat; total risk also includes the potential effect of existing countermeasures*

Access attacks include snooping, eavesdropping, and interception. Snooping can be anything from looking around a person's desk with the hope of finding something interesting to browsing through a person's files. Eavesdropping is putting a bug in an office, wiretapping, or tapping into a network to listen to communication across that medium by using a *sniffer*. Interception is a more invasive form of eavesdropping, in which the attacker determines whether the information is sent on to its intended receiver. An access attack can occur on backup tapes and CDs, hard drives, servers, and file cabinets as well as on a network. USB flash drives have become a new source of threat because they are small and easily hidden, hold a lot of information, and can be plugged into most machines easily. Usually, permissions protection can prevent casual snooping, although crackers try to get around this protection or give themselves that permission level. This kind of attack is mostly used in espionage.

Modification attacks alter information illicitly. This attack can occur on the devices where the information resides or when the information is in transit. In this attack, information is deleted, modified, or created. It turns out that electronic information is much easier to modify (especially undetected) than information stored on paper. Electronic information, however, can be replicated easily. As long as system administrators know what has been modified during an attack, they should be able to restore the information.

Denial-of-service (DoS) attacks prevent legitimate users from using resources. The attack can make information, applications, systems, and communications unavailable. This attack is usually pure vandalism. In the physical realm, a cracker could burn the records that users require or cut the communications cable that users need for communication. Computers can be destroyed or even stolen. Digitally, one way to deny communications is to overwhelm a system or network with information: inundating an address with e-mail messages, for example.

Repudiation attacks seek to create a false impression that an event didn't occur when it actually did or did occur when it really did not. Forging someone's signature on a document is an obvious physical example of repudiation. Electronically, an e-mail, for example, can be sent to someone as though it came from someone else. A repudiation attack in the electronic world is much easier than in the physical world because of the potential for eliminating or destroying evidence. Destroying a paper document with a signature requires that someone with malicious intent gain physical access to it.

managing security: the threat matrix

To manage security in a cost-effective manner, people involved in system administration and security need to manage risk. Managed risk is the basis of security. *Risk* is essentially the relationship between vulnerability and a threat. In risk

2

vulnerability – The sensitivity of information combined with the skill level the attacker needs to threaten that information

threat – The likely agent of a possible attack, the event that would occur as a result of an attack, and the target of the attack

assessment, *vulnerability* is characterized by the sensitivity of the information potentially threatened and the skill level an attacker needs to threaten that information. A *threat* is characterized by three things: *targets* that might be attacked, *agents* (attackers), and *events* (types of actions that are a threat). After identifying risks, measuring total risk includes evaluating countermeasures.

For example, information on when a bank is open is usually widely available—on the bank's Web site or posted on the door of the bank. It's important for customers to know the hours of operation, and this service to customers outweighs the possible risk of an agent (a bank robber) creating an event (a bank robbery) against the money in the bank (target). The amount of money a robber typically takes in a holdup is very small compared to the bank's assets, which lowers the vulnerability. In addition, countermeasures, such as cameras, possible witnesses, proximity of police, silent alarms, and so on, lower the total risk.

vulnerabilities

Vulnerabilities in a network or computer system might include Internet connections, hard or soft connections to partner organizations, open ports, physical access to the facilities, phone modem access, and more. Evaluating a system's vulnerabilities is essential.

threat: agents

Who is potentially attacking? You have already learned about crackers and their motivations. Other possible threat agents include employees, ex-employees, commercial rivals, terrorists, criminals, partners, customers, visitors, natural disasters, and the general public. When you examine these agents, look at their access capability (whether physical or electronic) to information, their knowledge (for example, the agent knows user ID numbers, passwords, names and addresses, file locations, security procedures, and so on), and their possible motivation (such as the challenge of the attack, greed, or some kind of malicious intent).

threat: targets and events

In systems security, targets are broken down into these four main areas:

confidentiality – Ensuring that only those authorized to access information can do so

encryption – Transforming original data (plaintext) into coded or encrypted data (ciphertext) so that only authorized parties can interpret it

- Confidentiality
- Integrity
- Availability
- Accountability

Confidentiality means that only those authorized to see or modify a certain level of information can do so. For most organizations, information is classified as public, proprietary (available internally to the company), and restricted (available to only some employees). The government has many levels of confidentiality. *Encryption* is often used for information that has a high level of confidentiality.

Designs for complex weapon systems, employee medical records, your bank account information—all are targets. An event in this target area is an access attack—in other words, viewing the confidential information.

Integrity ensures that the information is correct. Mechanisms must exist to ensure that information—whether physical files, electronic files, or electronic information—has integrity. Digital signatures on files and encryption for data transmissions are some approaches for ensuring integrity. A typical target is a transaction record for a bank account. An example of an event is removing the record by using a repudiation attack or altering the record in a modification attack.

Availability involves making systems where information is stored accessible and useful to those who should use them. Backup electronic and paper copies, the capability for failover (other systems taking over if one fails), the reconstruction of information after an intrusion, and disaster recovery plans are techniques that create availability in the face of an attack. A denial-of-service attack that prevents users from accessing their e-mail is an example of a successful attack on availability.

Accountability works with confidentiality, availability, and integrity to ensure that those who are authorized (and no others) for access to information have that access. This target area is where *identification* and *authentication* (I&A) come in. Accountability is usually not attacked solely. Usually, it's a means to attacking one of the other security targets. However, a secret attack on accountability could be used for a future attack against availability, integrity, and confidentiality. For example, a cracker might break into a system and leave a backdoor to return to later. If the cracker eliminates all traces of entering the system, accountability has been compromised.

measuring total risk

After vulnerabilities, threats, and existing countermeasures are identified and evaluated, the organization can measure risk and determine what needs adjustment. Unfortunately, risk is sometimes difficult to measure. Money is one way to measure risk. The cost of lost productivity, security consultants, and employee overtime to fix the problem, plus replacing stolen equipment—these things add up. Less easily calculated is the time the event might take to fix if a key system is down, physical resources that need to be used, the damage to the organization's reputation, or the cost of lost business during the crisis. Although risk assessors can look at other cases for a clue to these costs, many of them can't be calculated until an event actually occurs.

managing security: countermeasures

Start getting paranoid! As should be obvious by now, there are many avenues for intrusions and system break-ins: from the trash barrel to the corporate firewall to the hard drive on your laptop. The first few parts of this section—clean living,

---

integrity – Assurance that information is what you think it is and hasn't been modified

availability – Accessibility of information and services on a normal basis

accountability – Making sure a system is as secure as feasible and a record of activities exists for reconstructing a break-in

identification – A technique for knowing who someone is; for example, a Social Security number can be identification

authentication – A technique for verifying that someone is who he or she claims to be; a password is one type of authentication

passwords, antivirus software, and encryption—are useful for users as well as system administrators. The second half—system setup—concerns system administrators but might also benefit home or business users.

clean living (or only the paranoid survive)

Here are some pointers on keeping computer systems secure:

- *Have a security policy*—None of the other advice in this list will do any good if you or your employees don't follow it. Have a written policy and follow it. In addition, have regularly scheduled information and "rah-rah" sessions tying the importance of employees' work to the importance of securing information about them and their work. Some companies even hire consultants to pose as social engineers and crackers to test the policy.
- *Have physical safeguards*—Do you lock your house when you leave? Well, maybe you don't. Maybe you figure you don't have anything worth stealing, or an unlocked door will convince potential thieves that someone is actually home. You do have something worth stealing, however, even if you think you're the poorest person on the planet: your identity. Records with personal information (bank accounts, Social Security numbers, tax returns, documents related to work, and so on) should be secured or shredded. Don't throw valuable information into the trash. In addition, secure your trash. Your corporate dumpster should be in a visible, secure location and be locked. Your corporation should have a policy that doesn't allow visitors to roam at will without badges or escorts. Computers, even laptops, can be locked to desks (see Figure 2-2). Computers can have removable hard drives that can be locked in a secure location. The premises can be guarded with security guards and cameras. Employees who have quit or been terminated should be escorted off the premises, have their passwords deleted, and turn in their badges.

Figure 2-2, A computer lock as a physical safeguard

Courtesy of Kensington Technology Group

- *Use passwords to protect everything*—Use passwords to protect entry to your computer at startup, entry to your e-mail, entry to your router, entry to software with personal information, entry to your personal digital assistant (PDA), and entry to your phone. Set your password-protected screen saver to engage after a few minutes of inactivity. (See the next section on creating a strong password.)
- *Destroy old copies of sensitive material*—Use a shredder for paper and office storage media. Incinerate the material for added protection. Overwrite magnetic disks with specialized overwrite software to eliminate any electronic trace data. Another approach is to use a degausser, which creates a magnetic field so powerful that it realigns all the magnetic information on a disk. Some people argue that these techniques are still not enough and recommend completely destroying old hard drives.
- *Back up everything of value*—This measure includes copies kept off site or in a bombproof lockbox. Many people and corporations have begun to use online backup services that provide convenience and the assurance that someone else is doing it properly. A typical approach is to have full backups of all systems in at least a couple of locations and then have a number of generations (going back the last three dates modified, for example) of backups for important files. Software developers use programs such as SourceSafe and the UNIX archive program for this task.
- *Protect against system failure*—Use a power surge suppressor. A surge in electricity from a lightning strike or electrical fluctuations typical in brownouts can damage and even destroy electronic equipment. Some experts recommend replacing surge suppressors every couple of years. Systems also benefit from an uninterruptible power supply (UPS). This device is essentially what your laptop has built in—a battery backup in case the power goes out. A personal UPS gives you enough juice for your computer to work for a few hours without electricity. Servers that need to be up can benefit from an industrial power backup—perhaps a diesel generator that keeps running as long as the supply of fuel lasts. Figure 2-3 shows two physical means to secure your system: a surge suppressor and a UPS.

Figure 2-3, Two technologies that help back up your system: a surge suppressor and a UPS

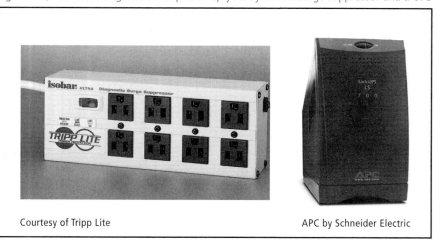

Courtesy of Tripp Lite   APC by Schneider Electric

acceptable use policy (AUP) – *An organizational policy that defines who can use company computers and networks, when, and how*

callback – *A method that allows users to connect only by having the network initiate a call to a specified number*

virtual private network (VPN) – *A private network connection that "tunnels" through a larger, public network and is restricted to authorized users*

- *Create an acceptable use policy for your company*—An *acceptable use policy (AUP)* defines who can use company computers and networks, when, and how. If your employees can't or shouldn't use company resources for personal activities or use is limited to certain times, state that in the policy. If you allow employees, vendors, or partners to connect to the network from outside, address this possible vulnerability as well. One requirement you might stipulate for off-site users is to allow connections only through *callback* numbers. This way, users can connect to a system only after it calls them back at an established number. Another approach is to have a *virtual private network (VPN)*, a sophisticated setup in which a private connection is established within a larger network, such as the Internet. The private network connection "tunnels" through the larger network, taking advantage of the larger network's reach and management facilities, but is accessible only to authorized users.

- *Protect against viruses*—Install antivirus software and configure it to scan any downloaded files and programs as well as incoming and outgoing e-mail automatically. Even so, be careful with e-mail. You should open letters, especially attachments, only from trusted sources. Mail-filtering programs, such as MailFrontier Matador and SpamKiller, can be configured to discover fraudulent e-mail messages. Have your antivirus program automatically and regularly check for and download new virus definitions. Don't start a computer with a floppy in the A drive unless it's a secure disk. Scan any disk before using it—even ones in packaged software can be infected. Have your operating system and other applications automatically and regularly check for and download security update patches. Create backups of your important files. If you don't need file sharing, make sure it's turned off in your operating system. Look into antispam, antispyware, and anticookie programs (detailed later in the "Privacy" section). Install intruder detection software that can analyze network traffic and assess vulnerabilities. It also watches for suspicious activity and any unauthorized access.

disaster recovery plan (DRP) – *A written plan for responding to natural or other disasters, intended to minimize downtime and damage to systems and data*

- *Have a disaster recovery plan (DRP)*—Whether you experience a naturally occurring or human-caused disaster, a *disaster recovery plan (DRP)* is designed to minimize any disruption a disaster might create. Depending on your situation, a disaster could be anything from the death of the CEO to a major earthquake. DRPs include documentation that creates a chain of command with a checklist of alternative recovery processes, depending on the crisis. Disaster recovery support teams should be formed and brainstorm about responding to disasters, examining who and what might be affected and how to react.

Some key resources that need to be addressed in a DRP are as follows:

- Data storage and recovery
- Centralized and distributed systems recovery
- End-user recovery
- Network backup
- Internal and external data and voice communication restoration

- Emergency management and decision making
- Customer services restoration

Recovery operations might require off-site storage or operations with or without immediate "go live" capabilities, alternative communication technologies or techniques between recovery team members, and end-user communication parameters. After a DRP has been completed, it should be tested, performing dry runs of various scenarios, and it should be retested on a regular basis.

passwords

Easily guessed passwords are a serious problem for system security. Common and simple passwords that can be guessed include a carriage return (that is, pressing Enter), a person's name, an account name, a birth date, a family member's birth date or name, or even the word "password" possibly repeated and spelled frontward or backward. Do you use anything like that? Then you are vulnerable.

Better passwords are longer and more obscure. Short passwords allow crackers to simply run through all possible combinations of letters and numbers. Take an extreme example. Using only capital letters, how many possibilities are there in a single-character password? Twenty-six. Expand that to an eight-character password, however, and there are more than 200 million possible combinations (see Table 2-1).

Table 2-1, Password protection using combinations of the letters A through Z

number of characters (A through Z)	possible combinations	human avg. time to discovery (max time/2) tries per second: 1	computer avg. time to discovery (max time/2) tries per second: 1 million
1	26	13 seconds	.000013 seconds
2	$26 \times 26 = 676$	6 minutes	.000338 seconds
8	26 raised to 8 = 208,827,064,576	6640 years	58 hours
10	26 raised to 10 = 1.4×10 raised to 14	4.5 million years	4.5 years

2

A good password should be long (at least eight characters), have no real words in it, and include as many different characters as possible. Maybe a password such as "io\pw83 mcx?$" would be a good choice. Unfortunately, passwords this complicated are often written down and taped up in plain view, which negates the purpose of having a password. One mnemonic for remembering a password is to come up with an easily remembered phrase and use its acronym as a password. Say you take the last sentence of the opening for the original *Star Trek*: "To boldly go where no man has gone before." You get "TBGW0MHGB" (replacing the "no" with a zero just to confuse things a bit). Not a bad password. Of course, if you have *Star Trek* posters on your walls, wear Spock ears, and wander around spouting off about "the prime directive" all the time, a proficient social engineer might still figure it out.

Although people can make significant changes to protect themselves and their companies, corporate cultures can include many subtle and dangerous security weaknesses. Proficient crackers become aware of corporate cultures and find these weaknesses. For example, when Clifford Stoll, mentioned in the introduction, was tracking a cracker in 1987, he became aware that many system administrators thought their VAX minicomputers were secure—and they were certainly capable of being secure. However, the machines had been shipped with an easy access service account—an account named FIELD with the password Service. The cracker had become aware of the account and password—which hadn't been kept a secret—and took advantage of system administrators neglecting to change the account password after installing the machine.

Many major institutions also confuse what's essentially public identification information (but often perceived as private because it's less readily accessible), such as a Social Security number or birth date, with a password. What identification questions were you asked the last time you called your credit card company? Name, birth date, last four digits of your Social Security number, possibly? This practice confuses identification (who the person is) with authentication (proof that the person is who he or she claims to be). Because of the problems with passwords, many secure locations are moving to a combination of three authentication techniques:

biometrics – *Biological identification, such as fingerprints, voice dynamics, or retinal scans; considered more secure than password authentication*

- Something you know—such as a password
- Something you have—such as an ID badge
- Something you are (often called *biometrics*)—such as a fingerprint, retinal scan, or DNA sample

Figure 2-4 shows these three authentication techniques. Combining them over the phone or through the Web, however, can be difficult and expensive.

Figure 2-4, Three potentially combined authentication methods, from left to right: what you know, what you have, what you are

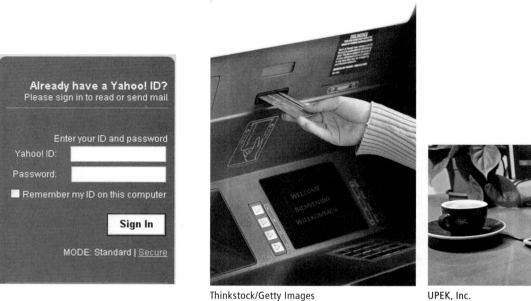

Thinkstock/Getty Images   UPEK, Inc.

antivirus software

antivirus software – A program designed to detect and block computer viruses

Installing *antivirus software* is one of the smartest things you can do to protect your machine, your software, your data, and your sanity—especially on college networks, which are notoriously open and vulnerable to attack. These networks are also where a lot of script kiddies can be found. Popular antivirus software is produced by companies such as eSafe, eTrust, F-Secure, McAfee, Norton, RAV, and AVG.

Antivirus software uses numerous techniques. One technique searches for a match with what's called a *virus signature* (or *virus definition*) of known viruses—bits of code unique to a virus. Usually, you can select where to look for the signature match—in the boot sector, all hard drives, certain folders or directories, memory, and so on. This technique is an efficient way of searching for and potentially eliminating a virus. The drawback is that the program must have the signature in its database. Antivirus vendors are continually watching their *honeypots* (programs or systems set up to deliberately lure and then track intruders) and have their ears to the ground, hoping to catch the newest viruses and put out a signature. The idea is that you need to update your signature database regularly by downloading the latest signatures before a virus infects your system. Most antivirus programs offer a service that updates virus definitions automatically on a set schedule.

Two other techniques attempt to get around the possible signature match lag by predicting how a virus will behave and then signaling possible anomalies. One

> **save your system and your sanity**
>
> · Choose a difficult password.
> · Install antivirus software.
> · Configure automatic download of antivirus software and operating system updates.

virus signature (or virus definition) – Bits of code that uniquely identify a particular virus

honeypot – A trap (program or system) laid by a system administrator to catch and track intruders

2

double safe

Even if you think your system is adequately protected from intrusion, it's essential to back up your system and data files regularly.

uses a set of *heuristics* (rules) to detect a possible virus. The other uses a *checksum* on known clean and likely target files and checks for anomalies between the files. The downsides of both techniques are that they aren't as sure as signature matching and are more likely to give false positives—labeling clean files as infected. One final approach that antivirus software can take is to alert you to activity that might be malicious. Usually, you can select the level of alarm you get: anything from probable virus events, such as writing to the boot sector in your hard drive or formatting your hard drive (alarm set to "nonchalant" level), to writing anything at all to your hard drive (alarm set to "really paranoid" level).

Antivirus software has options for scanning and dealing with viruses. For instance, the software can be operating in continuous mode, in which it's always scanning the hard drives and system. It can also work in on-demand mode, in which the user tells the software to scan. Most antivirus software can repair infected files. Some viruses are particularly nasty, however, and create files that can't be repaired. They do this by not just attaching to a file, but by essentially copying over (deleting) the good code. In this case, the antivirus software might quarantine the file—labeling it and removing it to a separate location on the hard drive. If the file is important to the operating system, quarantining could be a problem, but most antivirus software allows you to create a recovery disk that contains critical OS programs. In a worst-case scenario, you might have to reformat your hard drive. That's when a backup of the drive becomes important.

Antivirus software continues to add features. If your software supports it, activate the feature to scan macro scripts, incoming and outgoing e-mail messages, files when opened, compressed files, ActiveX controls, Java applets, and potential Trojan programs.

using encryption to secure transmissions and data

The content of information sent over the Internet could be seen by every computer through which it passes. Your e-mail is like a postcard that anyone can read. Not only that, many different machines owned by many different entities handle your postcard along its way, so sensitive e-mail and Web content need to be secured in some way. One way to ensure that your transmissions remain private is to use encryption. Encryption uses a computer code called an *encryption key* to scramble the transmission so that only a user or system with the matching decoding key can read it. Encryption can be used for securing stored information as well.

When you install a Web browser, you usually have a choice of installing a protection level of 40-bit or 128-bit encryption. The number of bits refers to the encryption key's size. The more bits, the longer the key, and the more secure the encryption. If you're going to be doing any online banking or shopping, you likely need 128-bit encryption.

note

E-mail can be encrypted with programs such as Email Protector and Pretty Good Privacy (PGP); both are shareware programs available online.

Web pages use a secure encryption system, such as Secure HTTP (S-HTTP), Secure Electronics Transactions Specification (SET), or Secure Sockets Layer (SSL). Typically, financial institutions use S-HTTP or SET because they are more secure. Their complexity makes them potentially slower, however, and because S-HTTP comes in both 40- and 128-bit flavors, it's also used in some credit card transactions. Credit card transactions don't have the same security needs as online banking because the credit card owner is not ultimately responsible for fraudulent activity on the card. Credit card companies assume this risk. In addition, unless you specify otherwise, online retailers do not store your credit card information. This information is passed on directly to credit card–verifying organizations. In many cases, organizations choose SSL because it's easy to implement and fast, two advantages that can increase customer satisfaction and, it's hoped, sales.

digital certificate – The digital equivalent of an ID card; used with encryption and issued by a third-party certification authority

S-HTTP and SSL both use a *digital certificate*, which is issued by a certification authority (CA) to both the user's browser and the vendor's server. The information in the certificate—including username and certificate number—is encrypted and verified by the CA. VeriSign is one company that manages digital certificates.

Encryption has been used to secure information for thousands of years—mostly by spies, the military, and government officials. With the need for secure financial transactions over the Internet, everyone who makes a purchase over the Web has become a user of cryptography, even if it happens in the background. Encryption uses simple to sophisticated algorithms to encode (encrypt or encipher) plaintext into ciphertext, and then the recipient uses a reverse algorithm to decode (decrypt or decipher) the message back into plaintext. Julius Caesar has been said to be the first to use a fixed-place substitution algorithm (replacing a letter with another a fixed distance away in the alphabet). For example, the letter A might become C, which is two letters later (see Table 2-2). The letter B then becomes the letter D, and so on.

Table 2-2, Simple substitution encryption algorithm for the alphabet

plaintext	ciphertext
A	C
B	D
C	E

Table 2-2, Simple substitution encryption algorithm for the alphabet (*continued*)

plaintext	ciphertext
D	F
. . .	. . .
X	Z
Y	A
Z	B

Substitution combined with algorithms for transposition, compaction, and expansion can make the original message hard to break—at least by hand. Table 2-3 shows some of these techniques.

Table 2-3, The plaintext words "JULIUS CAESAR" converted to ciphertext by substitution, transposition, and expansion

algorithm	technique	plaintext	ciphertext
substitution	Replace characters; example: replace with letter two to the right and make a space a #	JULIUS CAESAR	LWNKWU#ECGUCT
transposition	Switch order of characters; example: put in reverse	LWNKWU#ECGUCT	TCUGCE#UWKNWL
expansion	Insert characters; example: insert @ after every sixth character	TCUGCE#UWKNWL	TCUGCE@#UWKNW@L

Even with this new confusing string of characters—TCUGCE@#UWKNW@L— a cryptanalyst using cryptanalysis (breaking a cipher) can probably decipher it. One weakness in this example is that the space character never changes from the substitution phase. Given enough to work with, a cryptanalyst sees the obvious reuse of the character—or any of the characters, for that matter—and begins to deduce their significance.

Encryption and cryptanalysis have become far more sophisticated with the advent of computing and the Internet. Although there are a number of encryption standards, three have become popular in the commercial world: Data Encryption Standard (DES), RSA (named after the inventors Rivest, Shamir, and Adelman), and Advanced Encryption Standard (AES). These encryption standards are key-based standards. That is, they rely on an agreed-on starting point for encryption and decryption. In the previous example of substitution, the key might be something that indicates substitution of two letters to the right. The key might be secret (also called *symmetric encryption*) or public (*asymmetric encryption*). Secret keys work well between two people, but the system begins to break down when more than two are involved. Even with only two, distributing keys between people can be difficult because the key must remain secret. For this reason, public keys are often used. Public key systems actually use both a public key and a corresponding private key. Figure 2-5 shows asymmetric encryption. As shown, public/private key encryption can be likened to a process in which the sender sends the information locked in a box that can be opened only with the sender's public key. The box from the sender is in turn locked in a box that can be opened only by the receiver's private key. Only the receiver can open this box with the private key; even the sender can't open this outer box.

symmetric encryption –
Encryption using a private key to both encrypt and decrypt

asymmetric encryption –
Encryption using both a public key and a private key

Figure 2-5, Using a public and private key (asymmetric encryption)

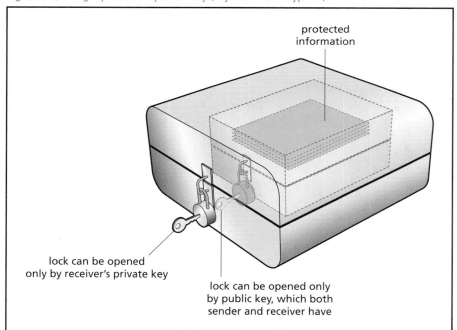

protected information

lock can be opened only by receiver's private key

lock can be opened only by public key, which both sender and receiver have

securing systems with firewalls

firewall – *Software and/or hardware that sits between an external network and an internal computer system; monitors requests for entry to the internal system and allows entry only to designated or authorized entrants*

A *firewall* is software or hardware that acts as a protective filter between an internal computer system and an external network, such as the Internet. A firewall functions to prevent all traffic into the system, except traffic that's explicitly allowed. At a minimum, it's located between an Internet service provider (ISP) and the rest of the system or between a router (which links to the ISP and is often owned by the ISP) and the rest of the system. Internal firewalls can be set up as well. The outside world shouldn't see the details of the system behind the firewall. Some companies that offer firewall software include McAfee, Symantec, and Sygate. Microsoft began including a firewall (Internet Connection Firewall) in Windows XP. A firewall can also be part of hardware; it's often offered on routers, for example (which you learn about in the next section).

proxy firewall – *A firewall that establishes a new link between each packet of information and its destination; slower but more secure than a packet-filtering firewall*

There are two main types of firewalls. One type is called a *proxy firewall*. It has different software (proxies) that must deal with each type of packet as it comes in (HTTP, FTP, and so on). For each packet that passes inspection, a new link is created between the firewall and the internal network, and the packet is sent on its way. With this type of firewall, internal IP addresses are different from IP addresses made visible outside the network. Another type is the *packet-filtering firewall* that inspects packets as they arrive and sends them directly to the required server (again, HTTP, FTP, and so on). No proxies are involved and a new link is not necessary; therefore, it's faster. However, it's probably less secure because internal and external IP addresses are the same, so they're visible to anyone outside the network.

packet-filtering firewall – *A firewall that inspects each packet and moves it along an established link to its destination; usually faster but less secure than a proxy firewall*

A firewall also allows you to configure a single entry point to your network. You can configure firewalls to allow traffic based on a number of criteria: the IP address of the destination or originator, the identification of the user making a service request, and more. What's called the firewall's "rule set" should be set to accommodate the needs of high traffic for certain requests (for example, Simple Mail Transfer Protocol for a system that has a mail server). You want the firewall to make the fastest reasonable ruling on traffic that you label as high priority, without allowing easy entry of undesirable traffic. A firewall also logs traffic so that an attack can be investigated.

protecting a system with routers

Another way to protect a network is with a router. Filtering software in a router can be a front line of defense against certain service requests. The router's job, unlike the firewall's, however, is to move packets as quickly as possible toward their intended destination. With the rise of home networks, hybrid router systems have been created especially for the home user that claim to perform both routing and firewall functions adequately.

Placing a system on the Internet, especially one with numerous services that you want to allow for internal and external users, requires some thought in terms of system architecture. For example, you might want to allow people on the inside to surf the Web, transfer files, access e-mail, and log on to external systems. Each of these services has a unique port, an opening to the Internet, through which it travels. The point is to close the ports that are not allowed, resulting in fewer points of entry to secure. Table 2-4 shows some typical ports and their associated services.

Table 2-4, Some of the many ports available on a router and what they do

service	port	description
FTP	21, 22	File transfer
HTTP	80	Access the Web
SSH	22	Create a remote session
Telnet	23	Create a remote session
POP3	110	Access remote e-mail accounts

Keeping available ports to a minimum goes for services you want to offer to others on the outside, too. High-risk services include Telnet and FTP (using SSH is more secure for both services), Microsoft NetMeeting (Internet conferencing software that opens a large number of ports at once), and Network File System (NFS) or NetBIOS (services that allow file sharing).

For more information about Telnet, FTP, and SSH, see Chapter 4, "Networks," and Chapter 5, "The Internet."

In addition to port selection, you can determine where to place servers on the network and what services are offered outside the firewall. For example, Domain Name System (DNS) is what allows you to type a URL in a browser instead of an IP address. Networks often have an internal DNS server to resolve internal names and rely on an external DNS server for external names. You want to keep internal and external DNS names separate to prevent outsiders from directly accessing machines behind the firewall. This means having a DNS server outside the firewall (owned by you or your ISP).

Services outside the firewall? Weren't you just advised to keep everything behind the firewall? Well, everything you want to protect should be behind a firewall, but there's also the demilitarized zone.

the DMZ

demilitarized zone (DMZ) –
A location outside the firewall (or between firewalls) that's more vulnerable to attack from outside

The *demilitarized zone (DMZ)* separates services you want to offer internally from those you want to offer externally. A Web service for your customers is a good example of something you want to offer externally; so is an incoming e-mail server. A database with all employees' names, addresses, and salaries, however, is not something you want to offer externally. Because systems in the

DMZ are more vulnerable to attack, they need some protection. One source of protection is filters on the router. Another is to allow each server to serve *only* the service it's intended to serve. (Say that five times fast.) In other words, you don't allow FTP, SMTP, or any other service on your Web server; you have different servers for those services. Another approach is yet another firewall on the other side of the DMZ. Figure 2-6 shows a system configuration for a network that includes a firewall, a DMZ, and a router.

Figure 2-6, System configuration of a network that includes a firewall, a DMZ, and a router

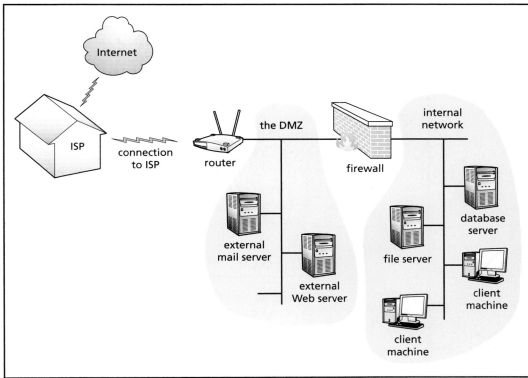

protecting systems with machine addressing

Another critical area for security administration is machine addressing. The original designers of TCP/IP defined an IP address as a 32-bit number in the format xxx.xxx.xxx.xxx. This system was called IPv4. Because of the limited number of IP addresses in the world, organizations from small to large usually had more machines than IP addresses. One way this shortcoming is being handled is by increasing the number of bits used for the IP address. (IPv6 will use 128 bits.) Change is inevitable and consistent, so IPv7 is already being discussed. Another way to handle the limited number of available IP addresses is through dynamically allocating IP addresses (with Dynamic Host Configuration Protocol [DHCP], for example). Organizations also use private class addressing. Nodes on the internal network have a different address (up to 16 bits) from what's seen outside the network. This conversion of internal to external IP addresses and vice versa is called Network Address Translation (NAT). NAT is usually provided by the firewall.

putting it all together

To ensure that your computer systems are as secure as they can be, the approaches to system security and countermeasures outlined in this chapter should be considered part of a comprehensive security plan, not implemented in a piecemeal fashion. An organization doesn't just install a firewall and figure it's immunized. Neither should you. Your approach to security is a concerted effort that includes firewalls and antivirus software. It also includes restricting physical access to buildings and hardware by using locked doors, identification, and authentication systems. It includes constant reminders of the dangers of letting your guard down, and it means training employees to remain alert to possible threats. It demands a security policy that's continually audited and updated as well as enforced. It demands that systems be updated and patched regularly to fix security holes. Files and systems must have appropriate access controls. In many ways, a successful security system can be quite boring (because "nothing ever happens"), and you as an administrator might have to deal with people (maybe even yourself) who don't want to bother with all the "bureaucracy" involved in creating and maintaining good security. In the end, however, that's what you want: a boring system where nothing ever happens.

computer crime

The preceding sections dealt with many approaches to securing the hardware, software, and data on computer systems. If these approaches aren't used or fail, and an intrusion occurs, there are some legal safeguards and avenues for prosecuting and punishing computer intruders. The next sections discuss types of computer crime and applicable legislation.

defining computer crime

In the IT world, computer crime most often relates to *intellectual property* rather than physical theft (although physical theft can also be a problem, addressed earlier in this chapter). Intellectual property can consist of a trademarked symbol, a patented design or process, a copyrighted program, digital information, or programming and hardware trade secrets. For software and hardware, protections generally fall into three categories:

- Copyright
- Patent
- Trade secrets

Copyright protects the expression of the idea, not the idea itself. In other words, you can copyright Mickey Mouse and how he's drawn, but you can't copyright all

intellectual property – An idea or product based on an idea that has commercial value, such as literary or artistic works, patents, business methods, industrial processes, and trade secrets

copyright – The legal right granted to an author, a composer, an artist, a publisher, a playwright, or a distributor to exclusive sale, publication, production, or distribution of literary, artistic, musical, or dramatic works

drawings of mice. Copyright gives the author the exclusive right to make copies of the work. Filing for a copyright is easy. Actually, if you put a copyright symbol on your work, it's essentially marked as copyrighted, although in a legal dispute you have to prove origination. A copyright lasts the life of the human originator plus another 70 years—which is a topic of debate in legal, political, and economic circles. If an unauthorized copy is made of your copyrighted material, you can sue. Your chances of successfully suing increase if an unauthorized copy is made and sold. Copyrights are often used for software. Although there's always the possibility that someone will *reverse-engineer* the program, that kind of programming takes considerable effort. The copyright at least protects against someone creating an illegal duplicate. Copyrights (or patents) have not proved very successful for protecting a user interface, however. Lotus Development, for example, tried unsuccessfully to sue Borland and Microsoft because it felt these companies copied the "look and feel" of the Lotus 1-2-3 spreadsheet in their products Quattro and Excel.

A *patent* protects inventions, the workings of a device, or a process. In the United States, you file a design at the Patent Office for a fee. The design can be a fairly rough sketch, but again, if the case ever goes to court, the design could be torn apart as insufficient for proving unique origination. Filing for a patent is a fairly expensive and complicated undertaking and requires a specialized lawyer (or someone with a lot of time). Large corporations, with embedded legal staffs, have become much better at filing for patents. The life of a U.S. patent is 19 years. If the invention is copied, you can sue. Software typically is not patented, although the U.S. Patent Office no longer discourages software patents. (Before the mid-1980s, successful bids for software patents were rare.) The problem lies in the typically fast software development and revision cycle compared with the fairly slow patent process. In addition, a patent requires that you show your design, which for software means showing the source code. Most companies don't want to reveal their source code, so they rely on copyright law and trade secrets to protect their products.

Trade secrets are another form of intellectual property. Trade secrets are methods, formulas, or devices that give their companies a competitive advantage and are kept from the public. One famous longstanding trade secret is the recipe for Coca-Cola. For a long time, only three people in the organization—and, therefore, in the world—knew the recipe. There's no time limit on trade secrets. They last as long as they can be kept secret. If trade secrets are stolen, perpetrators can be sued. Privacy laws protect the original owner in some cases.

prosecuting computer crime

The United States has a number of laws designed to protect intellectual property, personal privacy, and computer systems from fraud and abuse. Many laws that relate to securing intellectual property, for example, have a long history. The first copyright protection in the United States was created in 1787 and signed into

reverse-engineer – To figure out the design of a program or device by taking it apart and analyzing its components; for example, source code can be reverse-engineered to determine a design model

patent – A government grant that gives the sole right to make, use, and sell an invention for a specified period of time

trade secret – A method, formula, device, or piece of information that a company keeps secret and that gives the company a competitive advantage

law in 1790. It predates the ratification of the Bill of Rights—before free speech, freedom of the press, and the right to bear arms. The U.S. Patent Office was also created in 1790 to protect the exclusive rights of inventors. Privacy is not written into the Bill of Rights but has been the concern of several acts, such as the Fair Credit Reporting Act (1970) and the Video Privacy Protection Act (1988). Table 2-5 lists many of the important U.S. laws of the past 40 years that have been used to prosecute intellectual property theft, computer system intrusion, and invasion of personal privacy.

Table 2-5, Some important U.S. federal laws used to prosecute intellectual property theft, computer system intrusion, and invasion of privacy

law (U.S. code)	date	purpose/notes
Interception Act (18 U.S. Code 2511)	1968	Outlaws wiretapping; a computer network "sniffer" would fall under this statute
Fair Credit Reporting Act (15 U.S. Code 1681)	1970	Allows people to review their credit ratings and disallows companies from releasing credit information
Family Educational Rights and Privacy Act (20 U.S. Code 1232)	1974	Protects students' records from parties other than the student and parents
Privacy Act (5 U.S. Code 552)	1974	U.S. statute that stops federal agencies from using "bonus" information—information collected while an agency was investigating—for another purpose
Electronic Funds Transfer Act (15 U.S. Code 1693)	1978	Prohibits the use, sale, and supply of counterfeit (or obtained without authorization) debit/credit instruments
Computer Fraud and Abuse Act (18 U.S. Code 1030)	1984	Makes intentional access to a computer without authorization illegal
Credit Card Fraud Act (18 U.S. Code 1029)	1984	Makes unauthorized access to 15 or more credit card numbers illegal; means that accessing a system with 15 or more numbers on it, even if the person does not use the cards, is illegal

Table 2-5, Some important U.S. federal laws used to prosecute intellectual property theft, computer system intrusion, and invasion of privacy (*continued*)

law (U.S. code)	date	purpose/notes
Access to Electronic Information Act (18 U.S. Code 2701)	1986	Further defines illegal access to electronic communication; also protects access by authorized users and includes the owner of the information as an authorized user
Electronic Communications Privacy Act (18 U.S. Code 1367)	1986	Extends privacy protection beyond postal and phone communication to e-mail, cell phones, voicemail, and other electronic communications
Video Privacy Protection Act (18 U.S. Code 2710)	1988	Prohibits retailers from selling or giving away movie rental records
Telephone Consumer Protection Act (15 U.S. Code 5701)	1991	Restricts telemarketing activities to ensure privacy
Computer Abuse Amendments	1994	An extension of the 1984 Computer Fraud and Abuse Act that includes transmission of malicious code, such as viruses and worms
National Information Infrastructure Protection Act	1996	Further nationalizes the law against stealing information electronically and computer trespassing across state lines; also extends to theft of information related to national defense
Economic Espionage Act (18 U.S. Code 793)	1996	Makes any theft of information or trade secrets across international lines a crime
No Electronic Theft (NET) Act	1997	Further refines copyright law to disallow freely distributing copyrighted material without authorization
Digital Millennium Copyright Act (DMCA)	1998	Makes using anti-antipiracy technology, as well as selling anti-antipiracy technology, a crime

(continued)

Table 2-5, Some important U.S. federal laws used to prosecute intellectual property theft, computer system intrusion, and invasion of privacy (continued)

law (U.S. code)	date	purpose/notes
Provide Appropriate Tools Required to Intercept and Obstruct Terrorism (PATRIOT) Act	2001	Gives law enforcement agencies broader rights to monitor the electronic (and other) activities of individuals; in addition, the Computer Fraud and Abuse Act is further refined; causing damage (even unintentionally) to a computer system is punishable

It should be noted that these laws are always open to interpretation in the courts. (In addition, the laws are constantly changing, and keeping abreast of these changes is critical.) For example, at this writing, to prosecute computer fraud and abuse, the damage must be shown to exceed $5000. In some cases in the past, it has been proved that entering a system and viewing the information there could not be construed as damage because the plaintiff could not prove the damage exceeded the minimum amount of $5000. With credit card fraud, the attacker has to be shown to be in possession of 15 or more counterfeit or illegally acquired credit card numbers.

Many states have laws concerning computer crimes, but the laws differ widely. Some specify no minimum damage requirements, and others do. Some states, such as Minnesota, specifically target viruses. What constitutes accessing a system—actual entry or merely an attempt—also differs from state to state.

When you start looking at laws in other countries, it gets even messier. First, there's the matter of jurisdiction. For the most part, one country has to give another country permission to pursue a case. In most of the Western world, there are established agreements for reciprocity and sharing of information, and that aspect of investigation can go fairly smoothly. In many other cases, the U.S. Federal Bureau of Investigation (FBI) has had to specifically ask for help from countries that don't have any computer crime laws—even if the country is an ally. For countries openly hostile to the United States, getting this type of assistance is nearly impossible.

Prosecuting a computer crime is also a complex matter. Can you prove there was monetary damage? Can you gather enough evidence? That means you have to show traces of the intrusion on your systems. The computers in your organization become part of a criminal investigation, which means they must be replicated entirely or not used for their normal purposes during the investigation and prosecution. Of course, all this assumes you have actually discovered the perpetrator—a difficult matter in its own right. Unfortunately, although the record is improving, many people have gotten away with major intrusions and even when caught have been given no or light sentences.

I fought the law and the law won

So if computer crimes have been difficult to prosecute, you might as well commit a few, eh? Not so fast! The Western world has come a long way in prosecuting computer intrusions and other IT-related crimes since 1987 when Clifford Stoll had difficulty convincing the FBI to pursue a cracker. Increasing numbers of crackers are being caught and prosecuted. Since 1987, the laws have changed to make prosecution and conviction even more likely. In addition, authorities are far more likely to pursue electronic and computer crime than in the past.

For example, corporations are willing to pursue copyright violations more aggressively. In 2003, the Recording Industry Association of America (RIAA) began to target not just the Web sites, but also the end users who had downloaded copyrighted music from such Web sites as Napster and KaZaA. At the same time, the music and movie industries have begun to give people incentives for staying within legal boundaries. In 2003, Napster was reborn as a Web site for legally downloading songs at a reasonable cost. Apple did the same with its iTunes site. RealNetworks and the Starz Encore Group recently created a similar movie download service.

End users who engage in software piracy are also liable. They can be prosecuted and punished with up to five years in jail and fines of up to $250,000. Corporations can be liable for software piracy as well. In an effort to avoid prosecution, many organizations have been reviewing all machines periodically to check for illegal copies of software. The software industry might also try to thwart potential thieves by making the purchase of a copy of a software title a thing of the past. Currently, when you buy software, you don't actually own it. You purchase the right to use a copy with certain conditions, specified in the end-user license agreement (EULA, where you have to click "I accept" to continue). The EULA usually disallows using the software on more than one machine, loaning or renting it out, or otherwise distributing it. With another type of agreement, you purchase time on a program and connect to it through a network. Microsoft Remote Desktop Services, a program that many organizations use, is headed in this direction, in which you link to a server that's running Microsoft Office or Visual Studio, for example. This setup makes stealing software more difficult and protects organizations who want to be sure they're on the right side of the law.

n o t e

More information on software piracy can be found online at the Business Software Alliance (BSA) Web site, *www.bsa.org.*

ethics in computing

Although ethics and law are intertwined, they are separate systems for defining right and wrong behavior. Sometimes they even conflict. Nevertheless, despite differences between them and differences in the way people view them, some strong generalizations can be made about ethically and legally acceptable conduct concerning property, general welfare, health, and privacy in the world of information technology. Just because an act you engage in is difficult to prosecute or is even legal does not make it ethical.

ethics – *Principles for judging right and wrong, held by a person or group*

Ethics are the moral principles a person or group holds for judging right and wrong behavior. People often confuse ethics with religious rules because most religions attempt to instill some set of moral principles. However, ethics can be amazingly similar across religions and even for those with no particular religious affiliation. The reason is simple: Ethical systems (along with laws) help create a stable platform for living life comfortably with other people and, it's hoped, in a manner to benefit all. People generally make fairly rational decisions, and most can see beyond their own noses enough to know what's rational and right.

Organizations of computer professionals have outlined ethical standards for their members, often predating laws that now reflect these ethics. The Institute of Electrical and Electronics Engineers (IEEE), Association for Computing Machinery (ACM), Data Processing Management Association (DPMA), Computer Ethics Institute, and other IT organizations created codes of ethics that their members have sworn to uphold. Many companies create codes of ethics, too. Figure 2-7 shows an excerpt from the ACM code of ethics.

People approach ethical reasoning from different perspectives. These approaches can be generalized along two continuums: orientation toward consequences versus orientation toward rules and orientation toward the individual versus orientation toward the universal. Most people don't fit entirely within one square, or at least not for all situations they might face. Nevertheless, these approaches can help you understand a situation in terms of ethics no matter what your ethical reasoning is.

Figure 2-7, An excerpt from the ACM Code of Ethics and Professional Conduct

1.1 Contribute to society and human well-being
1.2 Avoid harm to others
1.3 Be honest and trustworthy
1.4 Be fair and take action not to discriminate
1.5 Honor property rights including copyrights and patents
1.6 Give proper credit for intellectual property
1.7 Respect the privacy of others
1.8 Honor confidentiality

2.1 Strive to achieve the highest quality, effectiveness, and dignity in both process and products of professional work
2.2 Acquire and maintain professional competence
2.3 Know and respect existing laws pertaining to professional work
2.4 Accept and provide appropriate professional review
2.5 Give comprehensive and thorough evaluations of computer systems and their impacts, including analysis of possible risks
2.6 Honor contracts, agreements, and assigned responsibilities
2.7 Improve public understanding of computing and its consequences
2.8 Access computing and communication resources only when authorized to do so

These approaches can be generally described with the following terms:

- *Egoism*—Ethical principles based on possible consequences to an individual
- *Deontology*—Ethical principles based on individual duties and rights
- *Utilitarianism*—Ethical principles based on possible consequences to many or all individuals
- *Rule-deontology*—Ethical principles based on what an individual considers to be universal rules or duties

Many of the issues facing the information technology industry and those who work in it can be analyzed in terms of the schema in Table 2-6, as shown in the next few sections.

Table 2-6, People base their ethical decisions on different principles

	oriented toward consequences	oriented toward rules
oriented toward the individual	*Egoism* The person bases his ethics on the possible good and bad consequences to himself. An	*Deontology* The person bases her ethics on a sense of duty. Consequence is not

(continued)

Table 2-6, People base their ethical decisions on different principles *(continued)*

	oriented toward consequences	oriented toward rules
	example: A student might judge the possibility of getting caught cheating on a test as high and, therefore, not cheat.	considered relevant. An example: An employee believes that telling the truth is important, no matter what the situation. When she realizes her team leader has misled her manager as to the progress of the program she's working on, she tells her manager what her true progress is, even though it puts her own abilities in a worse light.
oriented toward the universal	*Utilitarianism* The person bases her ethics on the possible good and bad consequences to all people, including herself—and to the universe in general. This can include a sense of empathy— for example, what if I were the victim of X? An example: A programmer realizes that an unintended consequence of the emissions-checking program she is writing will allow some polluting cars to pass. She determines that many people will feel the negative effects, so she takes the time to fix the code.	*Rule-deontology* The person bases his ethics on what he considers universal rights or natural or inherent rules— rules that make people responsible to one another. Consequences are not considered relevant. An example: An employee believes in the right to privacy. His boss asks for the names and addresses of people in his neighborhood as possible customers for the company's new product. He refuses.

software piracy

software piracy – Illegal copying of software; a problem in the United States and Europe, but rampant in the rest of the world

Software piracy is unethical from a number of perspectives. It's illegal and violates one or more rules in organizations' rules of conduct. For an honest, rule-based person, that's enough reason to avoid piracy. If you believe the right to private property is a natural right, then as a rule-deontologist, that should be enough for you. In addition, software piracy is detrimental to everyone in a number of ways.

virus hoax – E-mail that contains a phony virus warning; started as a prank to upset people or to get them to delete legitimate system files

As the software is spread illegally, it increases the likelihood of spreading viruses. Because it lowers the revenue of the company producing the software, it increases the cost of software for everyone. In terms of consequence, this would give any good utilitarian pause. It decreases the resources that can be put toward improving the product or toward hiring people such as you or improving your salary. Depending on the country, estimates of pirated software run from 60% to 80% of all copies. That's a lot of lost revenue for owners of stock in the software company. Even an egoist would find reasons to avoid software piracy—such as the possibility of getting a virus, losing a job, or losing share value on stock holdings.

viruses and virus hoaxes

What about passing viruses along? Writing them isn't the only unethical practice. You should also do what you can to stop their movement, such as running updated antivirus software, regularly updating your system, and not opening strange e-mail attachments. It's not against the law if you don't install antivirus software, but not doing so is imprudent and unconscionable because of the havoc viruses can wreak. A number of schools and corporations discipline anyone found passing along a virus—intentionally or not. All the codes of ethics of the IT organizations mentioned previously cover virus prevention in at least one rule. You should do what you can to eliminate viruses and inform others you communicate with if you get a virus. However, you should *not* pass along *virus hoaxes*, which add to the overwhelming amount of information people already get via junk e-mail and can cause unnecessary panic.

note You can find information on virus myths and hoaxes on several Web sites, such as *snopes.com, vmyths.com, hoaxbusters.ciac.org*, and *internet-101.com*.

weak passwords

Using weak passwords could also be considered unethical because they give online vandals access to systems. In addition to harming computers, they might take advantage of any other system weaknesses and cause further damage.

plagiarism

Many schools have an honor code that includes prosecuting not only the person who cheats, but also anyone who allows the cheating, including "innocent" bystanders. Therefore, if it's discovered you knew about other people cheating, you have also cheated. Cheating usually occurs because students feel under pressure to perform, don't understand that stealing intellectual property is a crime, or don't believe they will be caught. None of these reasons makes the behavior correct, however. Cheating also affects instructors because it forces them to spend time dealing with the issue of cheating instead of instructing.

Cheating might achieve a short-term goal of getting through a particular assignment or test. In the long run, however, the student doesn't learn the information or skills developed by doing the assignment. Even if the student avoids being caught and eventually finds a job, chances are he or she isn't going to have the skills to do the job properly and could wind up being fired. Plagiarism contradicts many ethical standards and rules of conduct, such as Rule 2.1 of the ACM code, which mentions striving to achieve the highest quality of work. The more a person engages in plagiarism, the more likely he or she will be caught. If you're going to borrow the work of others who freely share, whether it's text or a program, cite where the work came from originally.

cracking

Cracking or hacking into computers is the same as trespassing on someone's land. Would many of the crackers trespassing on computer systems be as bold in the physical world? Unlikely. The physical world contains more deterrents, including the possibility of bodily harm, but that's rarely the case in the virtual world. In dollar terms, however, the damage someone can cause by trespassing can be even more serious than in the real world. A cracker could wipe out your bank account, run up your credit cards, steal your identity, and ruin your credit rating, or a cracker could wipe out important files and kill your career. Even if a cracker didn't intend it, he or she might cause damage. Many writers of worms have been as surprised and impressed as their victims at how effectively the worms have moved across the Internet. Many program and system crackers justify their actions in terms of social Darwinism ("survival of the fittest"). They argue that stupidity should be punished and society is better off for their actions. Yet how many privately contact an organization and tell them of a flaw, giving the organization time to fix it?

Mistakes made while programming complex systems aren't necessarily a matter of stupidity. Programming is still more art than engineering. There are millions of programs running everything from the stock exchange to the charger on your electric toothbrush. The chances that some programmers are better than others are high, but many programs still need writing, and many systems still need administration. The best and brightest can't do everything. If you consider yourself one of the budding best and brightest, and you want to go counterculture, think about joining the open-source movement. The evidence from Linux and other open-source programs suggests that having many great minds around the world working on a large software program makes for better—and definitely more robust and secure—software.

health issues

Rule 1.2 of the ACM code specifies avoiding harm to others. Rule number 1 for both the IEEE and the Computer Ethics Institute concerns not using a computer to harm others. Computers have been instrumental in many injuries—large and slight—to health and the environment. A repetitive strain injury (RSI), such as carpal tunnel syndrome and tendonitis, is common for people using keyboards and mice. The U.S. Occupational Safety and Health Administration (OSHA) has issued guidelines addressing these problems. As a software or hardware designer concerned with user interfaces, you should be aware of the *ergonomics* of how an interface is used. In addition, proper disposal of computer equipment could be considered ethical. Many of the components of computers, monitors, and peripherals are made of toxic materials. For the sake of the water supply, you should think about disposing of computer equipment properly.

ergonomics – Science of the relationship between people and machines; designing work areas to facilitate both productivity and human ease and comfort

In the end, ethics are principles held by an individual. You can't be forced to write good software that won't harm others or to eliminate viruses. With this introduction to tools for evaluating complex issues in information technology, intellectual property, rules, laws, and privacy, it's hoped that you will for ethical reasons.

privacy

privacy – Freedom from unwanted access to or intrusion into a person's private life or information; the Internet and computerized databases have made invasion of privacy much easier and are an increasing cause for concern

Not all cultures have the same set of ethics or laws concerning *privacy*. In the United States, there's much discussion and legislation on privacy and a number of laws designed to safeguard personal information. However, laws also exist (as do holes in the laws) that allow information about you to be gathered and disseminated by the government and corporations without your consent. If you're concerned about your privacy, you might have to proactively defend it. In the workplace, where you are using your employer's equipment, you're likely to have fewer legal protections for your privacy. There are a number of techniques for protecting your private information at home, however. You should also be aware of the tools—such as spyware and cookies—used to gather information about you and your online activities. Finally, privacy and intellectual property are issues of information accuracy, an area not well addressed by legislation.

With so much information now available online—doctors' records, government records, credit records—that once needed to be viewed in person, the importance of information privacy has become paramount. Many people believe that information about them acts as though it were still kept in file cabinets in an office: little movement and little access. This isn't the case, however. Just going to the doctor's office for a checkup passes your information through several organizations (credit card, insurance, hospital, lab, and so on). Browsing the Web and buying things online can also leave your Web habits open for viewing. All this information is potentially helpful for companies trying to sell you something or a government agency interested in determining how suspicious your behavior might be.

In general, starting in the late 1960s, laws related to ensuring privacy have become more protective of the privacy of U.S. residents. The creation of the "do not call list" in 2003 to thwart telemarketers was the latest effort by Congress to shield Americans from intrusive marketing behavior and violations of privacy. The one legislative act that runs counter to this trend is the PA- TRIOT Act of 2002, a response to the destruction of the World Trade Center in New York City by terrorists on 9/11/2001. It specifies, in part, that law en- forcement organizations have the right to monitor individuals' Web and e-mail activity if they're suspected terrorists. At present, a debate rages about the con- stitutionality of this act, which will likely be challenged in the years to come.

As of this writing, no law currently exists to protect the privacy of employees working for a corporation. Employees' activities can be monitored through e-mail, log records, Web traffic, time spent using software, keystrokes, and other mechanisms. Companies aren't required to tell their employees about the types of monitoring and can use the information for performance review, firing, and even legal action. To the company, communicating electronically from within a company or using a company's equipment is considered no different from punching a time clock. You are in the company confines, on company property, and the company has a right to know how you're using your (its) time. The use of spyware (discussed later in this section) facilitates this monitoring.

A number of specialized technologies are used to gather information about your Web habits and sell you products and services. Most are fairly harmless, some are used by crackers, and several are considered obnoxious by many people.

spam – Unsolicited (and almost always unwanted) e-mail; usually trying to sell something

Spam is unsolicited (and usually unwanted) e-mail. Most are attempts to sell something to you. Spammers don't expect a high return ratio, but depending on the size of their distribution list, they can be successful with a small percentage of recipients "clicking through"—that is, clicking on the e-mailed advertisement. Most corporations that engage in mass e-mailing do so cautiously because they don't want to alienate their customers. The most suc- cessful mass e-mails are sent to people who have a defined relationship to a company's existing customer base. These e-mails tend to make it easy to be removed from the distribution list—a sign of goodwill toward the customer that actually reduces the chances of customers asking to be removed because they perceive it as something they can do at any time. These e-mails are sent to customer lists created mostly through product registration and support logs. In this case, you can likely reply to an e-mail with "Unsubscribe" in the subject line and be removed from the list.

The opposite of this approach is unsolicited e-mail that doesn't make it clear how your e-mail address has been obtained or how to stop receiving these e-mails. Often they come from a single person or organization using multiple return addresses to fool antispam programs used by e-mail systems such as Yahoo! and Gmail. Spammers get addresses from many sources. One technique is to use common sense with addresses. They have programs that search for combinations of common first and last names, but you can use a slightly odd e-mail name with nonalphabetic characters to help thwart this approach. Other approaches are to find public declarations of e-mail addresses (on Web pages, for example) or to buy or steal lists of names and e-mail addresses. Many people fear that their e-mail address is being sold or given to others by the latest online merchant they visited. Using a special e-mail address, such as a free Web e-mail account, just for merchant interactions is one way to find out if this is happening. However, many merchants won't sell their lists to the lowest common denominator spammers (who likely couldn't afford them anyway). These spammers probably use other tools, even spyware, to gather names. It's best to never reply to spam e-mails.

spyware – *Software that can track, collect, and transmit to a third party or Web site certain information about a user's computer habits*

Spyware is a catchall phrase for programs installed on your computer, with or without your knowledge, that observe your computer activities. Spyware can collect information about your computer use: anything from program use to Web browsing habits. More intrusive spyware can collect e-mail addresses from your address book. Spyware is often passed into your computer through a virus, worm, or Trojan program. Some legitimate software products also include a spyware program (they might call it adware) and inform you of it in the fine print. Whether spyware is used with a program you install should be specified in the license or registration agreement, and you should read it carefully to see whether information about you will be communicated to other vendors or advertisers. Spyware/adware is not necessarily illegal, but it can be, and many criticize it as an invasion of privacy, especially if the user is unaware of the program's existence.

cookie – *A program that can gather information about a user and store it on the user's machine*

Cookies are related to and sometimes used with spyware but are considered different because the user is assumed to be aware of their use. *Cookies* are files on your hard drive used to communicate with Web pages you visit. Your Web browser searches for a cookie with a unique identification when it's pointed to a Web page. If it doesn't find one, it might download one if the Web page uses them. If one does exist, it sends information to the Web page from the cookie, and the Web page might in turn update the cookie. Cookies are used by Web sites for many things and are sometimes helpful to users: keeping track of items in your shopping cart as you move from page to page on a merchant's site, your Web site preferences, or usernames and passwords so that you don't have to retype them every time you visit the site. Cookies can also be used to track visits to a site and to better target advertisements.

Spyware and cookies can be controlled. Cookies can be tracked, reduced, or eliminated. Your Web browser has settings that alert you when a cookie is sent and allow you to block some or all cookies. Occasionally clearing history files, cookies, and favorites from your browser is also a good move. A number of third-party programs (some are free) can also help manage spyware and cookies.

Antispyware programs, such as Spy Sweeper, Spyware Eliminator, and AntiSpy, work like antivirus checkers; they scan disks for intruders and warn you when spyware exists or is being installed. Cookie manager programs include Cookie Cruncher, Cookie Crusher, CookieCop, and WebWasher. Spam can also be filtered. Antispam programs include Brightmail, MailWasher, and SpamKiller. A final category of privacy tool is an anonymous Web surfer setup, such as Anonymizer.com or WebSecure. These programs prevent your Web surfing from being identified with you. To find these programs, try searching online with your favorite search engine.

Here are some other steps that can be taken to secure your privacy—some drastic and some less so:

- Avoid leaving a record of your purchases when possible. Use cash if possible, then debit cards, then credit cards, and then checks. Don't join purchasing clubs. Don't give out information to be put on a call or an e-mail list. Skip filling out warranty and registration information. You don't need them to get product support. Avoid tempting rebates.
- Guard against telephone and mail intrusion. Have an unlisted phone number. Use caller ID to block unknown numbers. Don't have your phone number and address printed on your checks.
- Review privacy rules and write to all financial institutions with which you interact. Get off their mailing lists. Inform merchants that you don't want your personal information shared.

Information accuracy is as much an issue as access to information. Questions arise as to who's ultimately responsible for the accuracy of information that's so readily available, especially online. You are responsible for ensuring that the information credit organizations have is up to date. Some argue that you should review your credit history once a year from the big three reporting agencies: Equifax, Experian, and TransUnion. You should do the same with your medical records.

note   You can find more information about your health records at the Medical Information Bureau, *www.mib.com*.

The accuracy of Web pages is another issue. With print media, incorrect or false information is often discovered and corrected in the editorial process. For many of the billions of Web pages, there's no editorial process or "quality control." The possibilities for misleading and even harmful information about almost any subject—including, possibly, information about you—have increased exponentially. This problem doesn't apply just to text. Digital pictures can be modified and used to present false or misleading information. On the extreme end, the National Photographers Association has stated that any alteration to an original photograph is dangerous. Legal precedents for determining the accuracy of photographs have yet to be set.

one last thought

This chapter has examined many vulnerabilities of computer systems, from technical to social, and has reviewed many of the laws related to system intrusion, intellectual property, and privacy. Most pragmatically, it has explored the ethical imperative of securing computer systems and a number of critical ways to make these systems less vulnerable. As a computer user, you must realize you're not just personally vulnerable; you are part of an overall vulnerability. For most users, lessening this vulnerability is fairly straightforward: Install and constantly update antivirus software, firewalls, and operating system patches. You also need to guard against communicating information and allowing access that increases vulnerability. People and organizations need to reassess the balance between ease of use, customer service, time, and cost on the one hand and system security on the other. Maintaining system security is a long-term investment for personal and organizational viability. As a computer user and potential system designer and programmer, you play an essential role in creating and supporting secure systems.

chapter summary

- Computer security is more than the hunt for intruders; it also includes creating a protective mindset and abiding by security policies.

- The terms "hacking" and "hacker" did not originally have the negative connotation they often do today.

- Intruders to systems can be classified as directed and undirected hackers, each with different motives but often having a similar effect on the systems they target.

- Crackers can find holes in systems put there intentionally or unintentionally by system administrators and programmers.

- Crackers use malicious software, such as viruses, worms, and Trojan programs, to infiltrate systems.

- One of the greatest risks to a company and its computers is social engineering—human (not technological) manipulation.

- There are four types of attacks on computer systems: access, modification, denial of service, and repudiation.

- Total risk to an organization is made up of vulnerability, threat, and existing countermeasures.

- Intruders target the confidentiality, integrity, availability, or accountability of a system's information.

- Countermeasures in managing security include common sense behavior, creating and following security procedures, using encryption, antivirus software, firewalls, and system setup and architecture.

- You need to install antivirus software, perform system updates, physically restrict access to your computers, and have a good backup system.

- Users support cracking by using weak passwords—you need to have strong passwords.

- One way to secure communication over a network is to encrypt the information by using one of a number of encryption schemes, such as using private and public keys.

- Firewalls and routers can be set up so that certain ports are unavailable and certain servers—such as the company Web site server—can sit in a DMZ, a more public and less protected part of the network.

- Prosecuting computer attackers has often been difficult because of variations in national and international laws as well as the difficulty of proving a case.

- Despite the difficulties in prosecuting computer crimes, there are laws and ethical reasoning that dictate commiting such crimes is unwise.

- Law enforcement and the courts are cracking down on computer criminals more than ever.

- A number of issues in computing can be viewed from an ethical perspective and seen as wrong; software piracy, virus propagation, plagiarism, breaking into computers, and doing harm to people through computers are some.

- Privacy is protected by law, but employees have fewer rights to privacy while on the job.

- There are many things you can do to protect your privacy; give out your personal information only when you must.

- Computer and network security are everyone's responsibility, from basic users to system designers.

key terms

acceptable use policy (AUP) (*61*)

access attacks (*56*)

accountability (*58*)

antivirus software (*64*)

asymmetric encryption (*68*)

authentication (*58*)

availability (*58*)

backdoors (*52*)

biometrics (*63*)

bot (*53*)

buffer overflow (*52*)

callback (*61*)

checksum (*65*)

confidentiality (*57*)

cookie (*85*)

copyright (*72*)

cracker (*50*)

demilitarized zone (DMZ) (*70*)

denial-of-service (DoS) attacks (*56*)

digital certificate (*66*)

directed hacker (*50*)

disaster recovery plan (DRP) (*61*)

dumpster diving (*55*)

encryption (*57*)

encryption key (*65*)

ergonomics (*83*)

ethics (*78*)

firewall (*69*)

hacker (*50*)

Hacker's Manifesto (*51*)

hacktivism (*51*)

heuristics (*65*)

honeypot (*64*)

identification (*58*)

integrity (*58*)

intellectual property (*72*)

malicious code (*53*)

modification attacks (*56*)

packet-filtering firewall (*69*)

patent (*73*)

phreaking (*50*)

privacy (*83*)

proxy firewall (*69*)

repudiation attacks (*56*)

reverse-engineer (*73*)

risk (*56*)

script kiddie (*51*)

sniffer (*56*)

social engineering (*54*)

software piracy (*80*)

spam (*84*)

spyware (*85*)

symmetric encryption (*68*)

threat (*57*)

trade secret (*73*)

Trojan program (*54*)

undirected hacker (*50*)

virtual private network (VPN) (*61*)

virus (*53*)

virus hoax (*81*)

virus signature (or virus definition) (*64*)

vulnerability (*57*)

worm (*53*)

test yourself

1. Who is Cliff Stoll?

2. What is the term for people who thwarted the AT&T phone system?

3. What did the term "hacker" originally describe?

4. What's the difference between a directed and an undirected hacker?

5. What other potential intruders do systems managers need to guard against, other than crackers?

6. What document justifies hacker activity?

7. How could most computer intrusions be avoided?

8. What login technique on a UNIX system could crackers take advantage of?

9. Explain one careless programming problem connected to URLs.

10. Explain a buffer overflow and how it can be used by a cracker.

11. What is the difference between identification and authentication?

12. What is the main difference between a virus and a worm?

13. A system attack that prevents users from accessing their accounts is called what?

14. Give an example of a repudiation attack.

15. What four types of targets are there for an information security specialist?

16. Name four ways you can "get paranoid" and safeguard your system from losing data.

17. What is the term for the most common and accurate antivirus software search technique?

18. Name three laws you could use to prosecute a cracker.

19. How expensive should the damage caused by a cracker be to be prosecuted by the U.S. Computer Fraud and Abuse Act? Explain.

20. Name four ways you could protect your privacy.

practice exercises

1. Computer security affects:

   a. Programmers and system administrators
   b. Naive users
   c. All users of computers
   d. Everyone

2. John Draper created:

   a. A whistle in Cap'n Crunch cereal
   b. Software for Microsoft
   c. Software for Apple
   d. A secure router

3. The term "hacker" originally had a negative connotation.

   a. True
   b. False

4. The term "script kiddie" refers to what?

   a. Con man
   b. Youthful hacker
   c. Unsophisticated cracker
   d. A game for hackers

5. What is the likely motivation of an undirected hacker?

   a. Technical challenge
   b. Greed
   c. Anger
   d. Politics, economics, poverty

6. What is the likely motivation of a directed hacker?

   a. Technical challenge
   b. Anger, greed, politics
   c. Fear
   d. Improving society

7. The term hacktivists refers to:

    a. Hackers motivated by greed
    b. Hackers motivated by economics
    c. Hackers who use social engineering
    d. Hackers motivated by politics

8. The Hacker's Manifesto does what?

    a. Specifies how to break into systems
    b. Justifies hacking as an end in itself
    c. Justifies prosecuting hackers and crackers for their crimes
    d. Uses Communist theory to justify hacking for its inherent justice

9. What was the backdoor on a basic e-mail program in early versions of UNIX?

    a. rlogin
    b. login
    c. ls -l
    d. blogin

10. Trojan programs are different from viruses because they need to be transported by an e-mail program and viruses do not.

    a. True
    b. False

11. One of the most notorious social engineers of the 1990s was:

    a. Clifford Stoll
    b. John Draper
    c. David L. Smith
    d. Kevin Mitnick

12. In a social engineering attack, a company phone book can be the target.

    a. True
    b. False

13. What does a modification attack do?

    a. Denies users access to the system
    b. Changes software and information
    c. Modifies evidence of system entry
    d. Allows access to a computer system

14. One way to ensure that you have a backup of information is to use a UPS.

    a. True
    b. False

15. Which of the following doesn't stop virus and worm attacks?

    a. SpamKiller
    b. Opening e-mail attachments
    c. A disaster recovery plan
    d. Updating your antivirus software

16. The best passwords are 8 to 10 letters long.

    a. True
    b. False

17. A virus-checking program that uses heuristics uses:

    a. A honeypot
    b. A virus signature
    c. A checksum on files to check their validity
    d. A set of rules to anticipate a virus's behavior

18. Encryption algorithm standards used in computers today are:

    a. Substitution, transcription, compaction, expansion
    b. S-HTTP, SEC, SSL
    c. DES, RSA, AES
    d. Proxy, packet, DMZ

19. SSN is a more secure way of transferring files than Telnet.

    a. True
    b. False

20. What kind of service is best placed in a DMZ?

    a. FTP and SMTP
    b. Internal DNS server
    c. Web server
    d. Database server

21. The legal protection usually sought for software source code is:

    a. A patent
    b. A copyright
    c. A trademark
    d. A trade secret

22. Utilitarianism is a set of ethical principles that focuses on individual consequences of an action.

    a. True
    b. False

23. The set of ethical principles that puts principles in terms of natural rights is:

    a. Rule-deontology
    b. Deontology
    c. Egoism
    d. Utilitarianism

24. According to an argument in the chapter concerning piracy, an egoist would consider piracy unethical because:

    a. It is illegal.
    b. It could affect many systems if a virus is released.
    c. It is against the ACM rules of conduct.
    d. The company that sells the software could lose share value.

25. You should always reply to spam e-mail with "Unsubscribe" in the subject line.

    a. True
    b. False

digging deeper

1. Why was a simple whistle able to subvert the phone system in the 1970s?

2. Is a firewall useful in a home computer hooked up to the Internet? When? How?

3. What is likely to happen with IP addresses, given that the world is running out of them?

4. A number of system holes that allow crackers to enter a system were introduced in this chapter. Can you find another?

5. How much does the microcomputer revolution owe to cracking and vice versa?

discussion topics

1. What value for society is there in having rogue programmers breaking into systems because they say it's valuable for society as a whole? What dangers?

2. The companies that battle viruses and market antivirus software actually share information about new viruses. Do you think this practice helps the fight against viruses, or is the power of the marketplace not given its proper due?

3. The chapter notes that it is everyone's responsibility to combat malicious hacking. Do you believe this is true? Why or why not?

4. Who holds the bulk of the blame for how easily viruses are propagated around the globe: companies or users?

5. Examine some of the reasons people don't bother to protect their systems against intrusions. Look at passwords, software, software updates, architecture, costs, and so on.

Internet research

1. List 10 companies that make antivirus software. Which one is supposedly the best? Why?

2. Find a good online source for the constantly changing vocabulary of the hacker or cracker.

3. Find a Web site that gives awards for antivirus software.

4. Who is Mikko Hyppönen?

5. Find the Hacker's Manifesto. What reasons does the author give for hacking?

3

computer architecture

the lighter side of the lab
by spencer

I recently got a call from a friend asking if I could "take a look" at his computer.

IMPORTANT NOTE TO COMPUTING MAJORS: If any friends or neighbors ask what you're studying in school, you are a history major. Trust me.

If you've ever "taken a look" at someone's computer, you know you'd better not have anything planned for the next four days. I thought about telling my friend I had a date that night, until I realized he knew me well enough that he'd never buy it. So I told him I'd be right over. It turns out he needed help setting up his brand-new computer.

IMPORTANT NOTE TO COMPUTING MAJORS: When upgrading your computer, it's important to take notes—that way, when you're tempted to think you want to upgrade your machine again, your notes will remind you that you'd rather eat fiberglass.

As we sat there during Hour 1 of 152 of the transfer process (installing programs, upgrading software, transferring his business data, and, most important, moving 300 GB of movies and music), my friend asked, "So is this a good computer?"

"A 'good' computer?" I replied.

He said, "Yeah, I've seen computers advertised for a lot cheaper, and $1500 seemed like a lot to spend." He had a good point. Just imagine what you could do with $1500! You could buy groceries for a year, pay rent for five months, or buy a textbook.

So I asked him why he chose the computer he did. I found out he had used the method most nontechie people prefer: He went to a computer store and told the salesperson he needed a computer. The salesperson pointed to a computer and said, "You want this one," so he bought it. Imagine if the same method were used in making other purchases. Car Salesperson: "No, no, Mrs. Jones. You don't want a minivan. You want a Ferrari. It's much faster!" Mrs. Jones: "Who do I make the check out to?"

In the end, we got everything but the printer working in just under four hours. That's a personal best! I guess all the practice is starting to pay off.

IMPORTANT NOTE TO COMPUTING MAJORS: I'd love to be able to help you when you're asked to "take a look" at someone's computer, but unfortunately I can't—I have a date.

why you need to know about...
computer architecture

Anyone can use a computer. Then again, more than a few people have a hard time figuring out where the power button is. Most people, however, are able to use the computer for things such as e-mail, personal finances, or browsing the Web. Nearly every adult can drive a car, but how many can build one? How many know how to fix them? Would you take your car to be repaired by a person who knew only how to drive one?

To be a computer professional, you need to understand what goes on "under the hood" of a computer. When you write a computer program, you need to understand what happens inside the computer when it executes your instructions. When it breaks (and it will), you should have some idea of what the problem might be. Knowing how a computer works is not only interesting, but also can set you above other computer professionals who don't have this depth of knowledge.

A computer is a collection of hardware designed to run programs (software) and accomplish tasks. This chapter is primarily about hardware and how that hardware is designed to work together as a computer system. In later chapters, you learn more about software.

inside the box

If someone asked to see your computer, what would you show him or her? A desktop computer normally consists of something you look at, something you type on, something you point with, and a big boxlike thing that does something, but you might not be sure exactly what.

Figure 3-1 shows a typical home computer, but what is the actual computer? Is it the thing you look at? Is it the big box thing? Or is it all the parts together? The answer is that it's all of the above, and it's also none of the above. The combination of the monitor (the thing you look at), the keyboard (the thing you type on), the mouse (the thing you point with), and the computer case (the big

Figure 3-1, Typical personal computer system

Image © 2009, Dmitry Melnikov; used under license from Shutterstock.com

*main board or mother-
board* – *The physical circuit
board in a computer that
contains the CPU and
other basic circuitry and
components*

box) can be referred to as a computer system. For example, if you asked someone to move your computer to another desk, he would probably move all four items and the printer, too. Everything together is often referred to as a computer, but the actual computer isn't the whole thing. The computer case is closer to being the actual computer, but it isn't either. The computer is actually just the central processing unit (CPU) inside the case on the *main board* (sometimes called the *motherboard*). Everything else on the board exists to support the CPU in its computing efforts. Figure 3-2 shows a main board and its primary components, and Table 3-1 describes the functions of these components.

Figure 3-2, Main board with labeled components

Courtesy of Intel Corporation

Table 3-1, Main board components

component	function
CPU	The actual "computer" in the computer; executes instructions to read from and write to memory and input/output (I/O) devices and to perform math operations
memory slots	Random access memory (RAM) dual inline memory module (DIMM) cards provide the computer's main memory (RAM); memory can be expanded by plugging additional DIMMs into the spare slots

(continued)

Table 3-1, Main board components (*continued*)

component	function
external I/O connectors	Provide connections for I/O devices, such as a mouse, printers, speakers, and other I/O devices
CMOS battery	Powers the small amount of CMOS memory that holds the system configuration while the main power is off
PCI and PCI Express bus slots	Slots to connect PCI expansion cards to the main board, used to add capabilities to the computer that aren't included on the main board; examples are sound, network, video, and modem cards
power connector	Connection to the power supply that provides electricity to all components and expansion cards on the main board
SATA connectors	Connectors for attaching hard drives and CD/DVD-ROM drives

To begin exploring computer architecture, you can start with the CPU.

the CPU

The CPU *is* the computer. It contains the digital components that do the actual processing. It's made up of millions of transistors organized into specialized digital circuits that perform operations such as adding numbers and moving data. Transistors are simply small electronic switches that can be in an on or an off state. The first Intel 8088 CPU had approximately 29,000 transistors. The Pentium IV has about 42 million. The transistors' ons and offs are treated as binary 1s and 0s and are used to accomplish everything that happens in a computer.

In Chapter 7, "Numbering Systems and Data Representations," you learn how binary 1s and 0s are used to represent data.

Inside the CPU, transistor circuits implement four basic functions:

- Adding
- Decoding
- Shifting
- Storing

Nearly everything that happens in a computer is done by using these four specialized circuits. You'll see examples of each circuit later in the chapter, but for now, here are brief descriptions:

- Adder circuits add numbers together. They are also used to perform other mathematical functions, such as subtraction, multiplication, and division.
- Decoders are used to react to specific bit patterns by setting an output of 1 when the pattern is recognized. Decoders are often used to select a memory location based on a binary address.
- Shifters are used to move the bits in a memory location to the right or left. They are often combined in a circuit with adders to provide for multiplication and division.
- Flip-flops (also called latches) are used to store memory bits. Flip-flops provide a way to maintain a bit's state without having to continue providing input.

how transistors work

semiconductor – A medium that's neither a good insulator nor a good conductor of electricity, used to construct transistors

Because everything a CPU does happens by the process of transistors turning on and off, an explanation of how a transistor works might be a good place to start your quest to learn how a computer works. Transistors are made of *semiconductor* material, such as altered silicon or germanium. A transistor consists of three parts: an emitter, a collector, and a base. A power source is placed across the collector and emitter, but the nature of the semiconductor doesn't allow electricity to flow between the two unless another voltage is placed between the base and the emitter. Therefore, the base of a transistor can be used to control the current through the transistor and the voltage on the collector and emitter. Figure 3-3 shows a diagram of a transistor and how voltages are placed on it to switch it on and off. By switching on and off, the transistor can be used to represent the 1s and 0s that are the foundation of all that goes on in the computer. In this circuit, a positive voltage considered to be a binary 1 is the output when the transistor is not conducting. When a 1 is applied to the base, the transistor is switched on (conducts), and the output goes to 0.

Figure 3-3, Transistors are used to build basic logic circuits, such as this circuit that reverses (NOTs) the input signal

power supply

when a voltage is placed on the base, the collector voltage goes toward the ground

output

collector

base

input

emitter

the transistor can conduct electricity only if a voltage is placed on the base

ground

The size of each actual transistor circuit is very small. In the Intel Core 2 Duo CPU, transistors are only 45 nanometers wide. A nanometer is one billionth of a meter. If you have a little time on your hands, you could think about dividing a meter into a billion parts.

digital logic circuits

Transistors are the smallest units in the computer; the only thing they can do is turn on and off. They have to be grouped into specialized circuits to allow actual computing to take place. The next level in the computer's design is the logic circuit. These circuits allow the computer to perform Boolean algebra. Boolean algebra is concerned with the logic of *Boolean operators*: AND, OR, and NOT.

You interact with devices using Boolean logic in much of what you do daily. Your microwave oven has circuitry that says, in effect, "When the door is closed AND the time has been set AND the start button is pushed, turn on the microwave." Or you might have a light circuit in your house that uses this logic: "If the switch by the front door is on OR the switch by the back door is on, turn the overhead light on."

Boolean operator – *A word used in Boolean algebra expressions to test two values logically; the main Boolean operators are AND, OR, and NOT*

An understanding of Boolean algebra helps you understand logic circuits. Boolean algebra is a branch of mathematics that deals with expressing logical processes involving binary values. The binary values are 0 and 1, which happen to be ideal for using transistor circuits. Boolean algebra specifies expressions, or functions, that describe the relationship of binary inputs and outputs. Perhaps the best way to visualize these Boolean expressions is by using a *truth table*. Figure 3-4 shows a truth table for the Boolean operator AND. The x, y, and z are simply variables that represent values to be inserted in the truth table. Any letters could be substituted in place of the ones used in these examples. In this case, x and y are inputs, and z is the output.

truth table – *A table representing the inputs and outputs of a logic circuit; truth tables can represent basic logic circuits as well as complex ones*

Figure 3-4 Truth table for the AND operator

inputs		output
x	y	z
0	0	0
0	1	0
1	0	0
1	1	1

Truth tables are tabular representations of Boolean expressions and always follow the same format. On the left are one or more columns representing inputs. On the right is usually one column representing the output, although sometimes multiple outputs are shown in the same truth table. A truth table should contain one row for each possible combination of the inputs. For example, a truth table with two inputs has four rows (2^2), and a three-input truth table has eight rows (2^3).

Boolean expressions are made up of Boolean variables and Boolean operators. Boolean variables are usually single letters that represent a value of 0 or 1. The variables are then connected with Boolean operators. For example, $z = (xy) + (x + y') + x'$ is a Boolean expression that can also be represented by a truth table. Boolean expressions such as this one will make more sense as you learn more about truth tables and logic circuits.

n o t e

Any Boolean expression can be represented by a truth table, and any truth table can be used to represent a Boolean expression.

the basic Boolean operators

Three basic operators are used in Boolean expressions: AND, OR, and NOT.

AND

AND – Boolean operator that returns a true value only if both operands are true

The truth table shown previously in Figure 3-4 is a tabular representation of the AND Boolean operator. The *AND* operator takes two values as input. As mentioned, there's one row in the table for every possible combination of the two inputs. Each input combination has a specified output. As you can see, the AND operator has an output of 1 (true) only if both inputs are 1. Any other combination of inputs gives an output of 0. Later in this chapter, you see when and why the AND operator is used in the computer. In Boolean algebra, the AND operator is sometimes represented by a dot or, more commonly, no symbol at all between the letters. The truth table in Figure 3-4 can be represented by the Boolean expression $xy = z$, which can be restated by saying "x AND y results in z." In other words, the truth table describes the output for any set of inputs.

OR

OR – Boolean operator that returns a true value if either operand is true

Figure 3-5 shows the truth table for the Boolean *OR* operator, which returns a 1 only when either or both of the inputs are 1. The Boolean expression $x + y = z$ is equivalent to the information represented in the truth table for the OR operator. This expression can be restated as "x OR y results in z."

Figure 3-5, Truth table for the OR operator

inputs		output
x	y	z
0	0	0
0	1	1
1	0	1
1	1	1

NOT

NOT – Boolean operator that returns a false value if the operand is true and a true value if the operand is false

The *NOT* operator works with a single input, and its purpose is to reverse the input. Figure 3-6 shows the truth table for the NOT operator. The Boolean expression for the NOT operator can be represented by $x' = z$ or $\overline{x} = z$. This expression is stated as "NOT x results in z."

Each basic Boolean operator can be combined with Boolean variables to form complex Boolean expressions. In addition, as you see later, Boolean expressions

Figure 3-6, Truth table
for the NOT operator

input	output
x	**z**
0	1
1	0

can be used to describe a circuit that gives an output for a given set of inputs. That's just about all the computer does. It has millions of circuits that respond to particular inputs. Simple circuits are grouped together to form more complex circuits. These circuits in turn are grouped together to form circuits that are even more complex and have specialized purposes, such as adding, decoding, and storing bits.

digital building blocks

gate – A transistor-based circuit in the computer that implements Boolean logic by creating a single output value for a given set of input values

Each basic Boolean operator can be implemented as a digital circuit made of one or more transistors that's designed to carry out the function of its Boolean operator. These circuits are often referred to as *gates*, and each one has a specific schematic symbol shown in the following figures. In the computer, the binary 1s and 0s are actually different electrical voltage levels. A high voltage, which is typically a positive 3 to 5 volts, is treated as the 1. A low voltage, negative 3 to 5 volts, represents the 0. These voltages ultimately come from the power supply, but they're applied to logic gates in the computer, and the output of one gate becomes one of the inputs to another gate. The combinations of gates then enable the computer to do all the things it does. Each gate in a circuit reacts in a completely predictable way. Gates can be combined to give a certain output when a specific input occurs. For example, a circuit could be designed to light up the correct elements of a seven-segment numeric display when a bit pattern representing the number is placed on the circuit inputs.

AND gate

Figure 3-7 shows the symbol and truth table for the AND gate.

Figure 3-7, Symbol and truth table for the AND gate

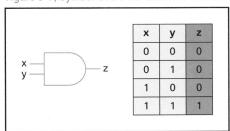

x	y	z
0	0	0
0	1	0
1	0	0
1	1	1

The AND gate allows two inputs and has one output. The truth table gives the output values for all possible inputs. Note that the truth table for the AND gate is identical to the truth table for the AND Boolean operator.

OR gate

Figure 3-8 shows the symbol and truth table for the OR gate.

Figure 3-8, Symbol and truth table for the OR gate

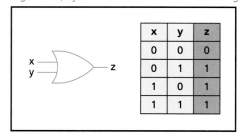

x	y	z
0	0	0
0	1	1
1	0	1
1	1	1

The OR gate also allows two inputs and one output. The truth table for the OR gate again has output values for all possible combinations of input signals. The OR gate truth table matches the truth table for the OR Boolean operator.

NOT gate

Figure 3-9 shows the symbol and truth table for the NOT gate.

Figure 3-9, Symbol and truth table for the NOT gate

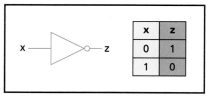

x	z
0	1
1	0

The NOT gate has only one input and one output. The truth table for the NOT gate just shows that the output is the opposite of the input. That is, the NOT gate's function is to reverse the input. Again, this truth table is the same as its Boolean operator counterpart.

The AND, OR, and NOT gates are the basic building blocks of the CPU. There are three additional gates that can be created by using the basic gates: NAND, NOR, and XOR, explained in the following sections. Sometimes they are grouped with AND, OR, and NOT as basic gates.

NAND gate

NAND – *A logical AND followed by a logical NOT that returns a false value only if both operands are true*

Figure 3-10 shows the NAND gate symbol and truth table. The **NAND** gate is a combination of an AND gate and a NOT gate. In effect, it takes the output of the AND gate and then reverses it with the NOT gate. The output in the truth table for the NAND is exactly the opposite of the AND gate's output. The symbol for the NAND gate is an AND gate symbol with a small circle added at the output to indicate the NOT.

Figure 3-10, Symbol and truth table for the NAND gate

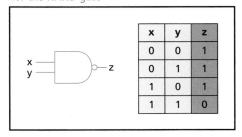

x	y	z
0	0	1
0	1	1
1	0	1
1	1	0

NOR gate

NOR – *A logical OR followed by a logical NOT that returns a true value only if both operands are false*

Figure 3-11 shows the NOR gate symbol and truth table. The **NOR** gate is a combination of an OR gate and a NOT gate. The output of the OR is fed into the input of the NOT, effectively reversing the OR's output. The NOR gate's symbol is the same as the OR with a circle added at the output, indicating the NOT.

Figure 3-11, Symbol and truth table for the NOR gate

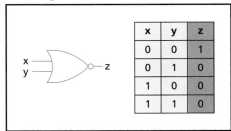

x	y	z
0	0	1
0	1	0
1	0	0
1	1	0

XOR gate

In Figure 3-12, note that the truth table for the *XOR* (exclusive OR) gate indicates that the output is 1 only when the inputs are different. If both inputs are 0 or 1, the output is 0. The symbol for an XOR gate is similar to the OR gate with a parallel curved line added at the left.

Figure 3-12, Symbol and truth table for the XOR gate

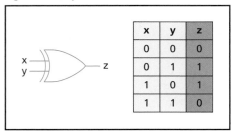

x	y	z
0	0	0
0	1	1
1	0	1
1	1	0

gate behavior

With any gate, you can predict the output for any given set of inputs. Gates are designed and built with transistors so that the output for any set of inputs follows the specifications in the truth table. Therefore, if you were told the inputs to an XOR gate are 0 and 1, you could correctly predict that the output is 1. If the inputs are both 0, the output is 0.

Note that gates can be chained together to form more complex specialized circuits. The output from one gate is connected as an input to another gate. One of the first things you might notice from this connection is the capability to connect multiple gates of the same type to form a version of the basic gates that has more than two inputs. Figure 3-13 shows how a 3-input AND gate can be constructed

Figure 3-13, Constructing a 3-input AND gate from two 2-input AND gates

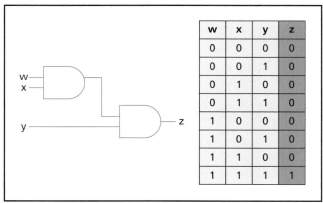

w	x	y	z
0	0	0	0
0	0	1	0
0	1	0	0
0	1	1	0
1	0	0	0
1	0	1	0
1	1	0	0
1	1	1	1

from two 2-input AND gates and the truth table resulting from this construction. The output of the first AND gate is 1 only if both *w* and *x* are 1. The output of the second gate at *z* is 1 only if the output of the first gate is 1 and *y* is also 1. Therefore, the truth table for the entire circuit shows that the output is 1 only if all three inputs are 1s.

complex circuits

Now that you understand the basic gates and how truth tables work, you're ready to start combining basic gates to form a few of the main circuits that make up the CPU. These circuits are the adder, decoder, shifter, and flip-flop.

adder

adder – The circuit in the CPU responsible for adding binary numbers

One of the main functions of the arithmetic logic unit (ALU) of the computer's CPU is to add numbers. A circuit is needed that adds two binary numbers and gives the correct result. To build an *adder* circuit from the basic logic circuits, start with the truth table showing the outcome for each set of circumstances. Figure 3-14 shows the truth table for adding 2 bits, including carry-in (ci) and carry-out (co). You might recognize that the terms carry-in and carry-out mean the same thing as borrow and carry in decimal addition and subtraction. In the adder, the bits are added according to the rules of the binary numbering system.

Chapter 7, "Numbering Systems and Data Representation," explains the rules for adding binary numbers.

Figure 3-14, Truth table for adding 2 bits with carry-in and carry-out

inputs			outputs	
x	**y**	**ci**	**s**	**co**
0	0	0	0	0
0	0	1	1	0
0	1	0	1	0
0	1	1	0	1
1	0	0	1	0
1	0	1	0	1
1	1	0	0	1
1	1	1	1	1

Note in this truth table that there are three inputs: the first bit to be added, *x*; the second bit, *y*; and the carry-in, *ci*, from a previous addition. Truth tables normally have only one output, but because both the sum, *s*, and the carry-out, *co*, work with the same set of inputs, they are shown in the same truth table in this case. The truth table indicates that for a given combination of the 2 bits you want to add, along with a carry-in from a previous addition, the sum bit has a fixed value, as does the carry-out bit.

The truth table for the adder circuit explains what needs to be done in the circuit. Figure 3-15 shows a circuit built from the basic logic gates that implement the truth table for the adder. You can experiment with the circuit by putting combinations of 1s and 0s on the three inputs, and then following the circuit through to see whether it generates the correct outputs, according to the truth table.

Figure 3-15, Adder circuit

decoder

Decoder circuits are used heavily in the computer to perform functions such as addressing memory and selecting I/O devices. The idea behind decoders is that for a given input pattern of bits, an output line can be selected. Figure 3-16 shows a 2-bit decoder along with the truth table for the circuit. Each of the output lines—*a*, *b*, *c*, and *d*—can be selected, or set to 1, by a specific bit pattern on the input lines *x* and *y*. The circuit doesn't seem too impressive with just two inputs that can control only four lines, but a circuit with only 32 inputs could control 4 billion lines!

The truth table for the circuit in Figure 3-16 is best represented by showing all possible combinations of the two inputs on the left and showing all four possible outputs on the right. Remember that a basic truth table has only one output, so this truth table is actually four truth tables in one. It shows that for any of the four possible combinations of the 2 input bits, there's only one output line set to a 1 (selected).

Figure 3-16, Decoder circuit with two input lines controlling four output lines

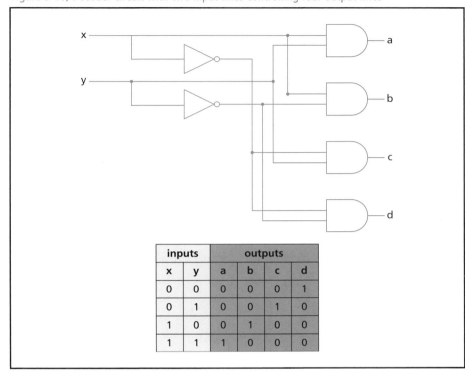

inputs		outputs			
x	y	a	b	c	d
0	0	0	0	0	1
0	1	0	0	1	0
1	0	0	1	0	0
1	1	1	0	0	0

flip-flop

flip-flop or latch – A digital circuit that can retain the binary value it was set to after the input is removed; static RAM is constructed by using flip-flop circuits

The *flip-flop* isn't just footwear for the beach—it's also a special form of a digital circuit called a "latch." The *latch* is so named because it latches onto a bit and maintains the output state until it's changed.

In the basic AND gate shown previously in Figure 3-7, the output of 1 is maintained only while both inputs are 1. In the OR gate, one or both inputs must be a 1 before the output goes to 1. If both inputs are 0, the 1 in the output also changes to 0.

The flip-flop circuit, shown in Figure 3-17, holds the value at the output even if the input changes. There are two inputs to this type of circuit: S (set) and R (reset). The output is labeled Q. The designator Q' is the inverse of the value of Q.

Figure 3-17, A basic SR (set and reset) flip-flop circuit implemented with NOR gates

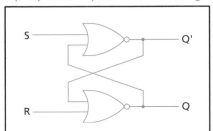

You can use the diagram in Figure 3-17 and the truth table for the NOR gate in Figure 3-11 to observe the operation of the flip-flop circuit. When the power is first turned on, all inputs and outputs start at logical 0. Because a NOR gate outputs 1 if both inputs are 0, both NOR gates begin to switch their outputs to 1. However, the first gate that switches to 1 sends that 1 to the feedback input of the other NOR gate, and it then switches its output to 0. As that 0 is fed back to the input of the first NOR, the output stays at 1. The circuit is then stable with either $Q = 1$ and $Q' = 0$ or $Q = 0$ and $Q' = 1$. The circuit stays in that state until a 1 is placed on S or R.

If a 1 is placed on the input S, the circuit flips to a state wherein the output Q goes to a 1. If the input S then returns to 0, the output Q remains 1. The circuit is now stable and remains in that state until a 1 is placed on the R input. Placing the 1 on R flips the circuit to the opposite state wherein Q is 0. Then it stays in that state until 1 is again placed on the S input.

The capability of the flip-flop circuit to maintain a set state after the input voltage that set it goes away makes it ideal for storing bits. The registers and high-speed cache memory in your computer are made of many thousands of flip-flop circuits. In fact, virtually all high-speed memory in the CPU or on video cards is made from flip-flop circuits. This type of memory is usually referred to as static RAM (*SRAM*).

shifter

Many operations in a computer benefit from using a *shifter* circuit. Shifters are used in math operations, such as multiply and divide. The shifter circuit takes a fixed number of inputs and converts them to outputs that have the bits shifted a fixed number to the left or right. Figure 3-18 shows the result of a shift right.

Figure 3-18, Inputs and outputs of a shifter circuit (1-bit right shift)

inputs	1	0	1	1	0	0	1	1
outputs	0	1	0	1	1	0	0	1

In Figure 3-18, you can see that each bit is copied to the bit to the right. A 0 is moved into the leftmost bit, and the rightmost bit is discarded. Shifter circuits can be designed that have the capability to shift any number of bits to the right or left and to carry bits in or out.

SRAM – Static RAM, a type of high-speed memory constructed with flip-flop circuits

shifter – A circuit that converts a fixed number of inputs to outputs that have bits shifted to the left or right, often used with adders to perform multiplication and division

other circuits

Other specialized circuits are used in the computer, such as the multiplexer, parity generator, and counter. Building them involves the same process described for the adder, decoder, and flip-flop circuits:

1. A truth table is constructed showing the output for each possible arrangement of inputs.

2. A Boolean algebra expression equivalent to the truth table is created. The expression might then be optimized by using a set of mathematic rules governing Boolean expressions. These rules are called *Boolean basic identities*.

3. A circuit diagram is created to implement the finished Boolean expression.

Because a Boolean expression contains only AND, OR, and NOT operators, a circuit designed from an expression might ultimately be made up of only AND, OR, and NOT gates. The benefit of this process is that designers can use Boolean expressions to accurately predict what a circuit will do before spending a penny to construct the circuit.

In the early days of computers, computer scientists and electronics engineers had to spend many hours working with Boolean expressions and truth tables to design computer circuits. Now current computers are used to design new computers. Large and complicated software programs do most of the work of designing and optimizing new logic circuits to perform tasks. Yet the basic building block of the computer has not changed: It's still the lowly transistor.

integrated circuits

The first computers were made to accomplish specific tasks in the same manner described previously, but the earliest computers used mechanical switches instead of transistors to represent 1s and 0s. Later, vacuum tubes were used for switching. Vacuum tubes work in a similar manner to transistors, but they are much larger, use much more power, and generate tremendous heat. Early computers made from vacuum tubes filled whole rooms and required extensive air-conditioning to keep them cool. When vacuum tubes were replaced with transistors, computers became much smaller, but they were still nearly room size and required air-conditioning, too. In the late 1960s, scientists learned how to put thousands of transistors and, therefore, logic circuits on a single piece of semiconductor material. They were called integrated circuits (ICs). About 10 years later, scientists again found ways to make transistors even smaller and combined them into specialized complex circuits, called *Very Large-Scale Integration (VLSI)*. The computers you use today are made up of VLSI chips containing millions of circuits. With this technology, the millions of transistors that make up all the specialized circuits in the CPU can be etched onto a single piece of silicon not much bigger than a pencil eraser.

Boolean basic identities – A set of laws that apply to Boolean expressions and define ways in which expressions can be simplified; they're similar to algebraic laws

Very Large-Scale Integration (VLSI) – The current point of evolution in the development of the integrated circuit; VLSI chips typically have more than 100,000 transistors

Von Neumann architecture

As you learned in Chapter 1, the first mechanical computers were special-purpose computers—computers designed and built to accomplish a specific task, such as tabulating census information or calculating ballistic trajectory tables. These special-purpose computers could do only what they were designed to do and nothing else. Engineers searched for a way to design a computer that could be used for multiple purposes.

The Von Neumann architecture described in Chapter 1 had digital logic circuits designed to execute different types of tasks, based on binary instructions fetched from some type of storage device. Most computers today are still based on the Von Neumann architecture and are sometimes still called Von Neumann machines.

From a technical standpoint, Von Neumann architecture is defined by the following characteristics:

- Binary instructions are processed sequentially by fetching an instruction from memory, and then executing this instruction.
- Both instructions and data are stored in the main memory system.
- Instruction execution is carried out by a central processing unit (CPU) that contains a *control unit (CU)*, an *arithmetic logic unit (ALU)*, and *registers* (small storage areas).
- The CPU has the capability to accept input from and provide output to external devices.

Figure 3-19 shows a diagram of Von Neumann architecture.

control unit (CU) – *The part of the CPU that controls the flow of data and instructions into and out of the CPU*

arithmetic logic unit (ALU) – *The portion of the CPU responsible for mathematical operations, specifically addition*

register – *A small unit of very high-speed memory located on the CPU; used to store data and instructions for the CPU*

Figure 3-19, Von Neumann architecture

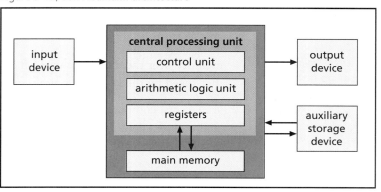

At a basic level, a Von Neumann machine operates on what's called a "fetch-execute" cycle. Simply put, the CPU fetches an instruction from memory and then executes this instruction. The actual process can be slightly more complex. For example, the following is a typical fetch-execute cycle:

1. The control unit uses the address in a special register called a program counter to fetch an instruction from main memory.

2. The instruction is decoded to determine what, if any, data it needs to com plete execution.

3. Any data that's needed is also fetched from memory and placed into other registers.

4. The ALU then executes the instruction by using the data in the registers, if necessary.

5. Input or output operations required by the instruction are performed.

system clock – *A crystal oscillator circuit on a main board that provides timing and synchronization for operating the CPU and other circuitry*

The computer has a crystal clock called the *system clock* that times, or synchronizes, each step in the fetch-execute cycle. A computer is often referred to by its clock speed. A Pentium IV 3 GHz computer has a clock frequency of 3 billion clock pulses per second, which means it can complete 3 billion fetch-execute steps each second. It makes you wonder why your computer ever seems slow!

This fetch-execute architecture on a general-purpose computer has been the mainstay of computer design for more than 60 years. By using increasingly faster clocks, computers have been able to get steadily faster. The first PC processor, using an Intel 8088, had a clock speed of 4.7 MHz. The next generation, the 80286, had a clock speed of up to 12 MHz and ran about three times faster than the 8088 machine. The 80386 could clock up to 25 MHz and ran twice as fast as the 80286. The 80486 was four times as fast, with a clock speed of 100 MHz. This steadily increasing speed, however, hit a "wall" at around 100 MHz. Increasing the clock speed much beyond 100 MHz presented a problem. The processor still had to fetch instructions and data from memory over the electronic wires and circuitry of the bus that was limited to that speed by the laws and physics of electricity.

bus – *A collection of conductors, connectors, and protocols that facilitates communication between the CPU, memory, and I/O devices*

system bus – *The main bus used by the CPU to transfer data and instructions to and from memory and I/O devices*

bus protocol – *The set of rules governing the timing and transfer of data on a computer bus*

buses

A *bus* in computer terminology is a set of wires and rules, or protocols, to facilitate data transfer. Von Neumann architecture involves using a *system bus* to get information from memory to the processor and back and to carry information to and from I/O devices. The electrical signals are the 1s and 0s used by the digital logic circuits that make up components in the computer. For this electrical signaling to be orderly, buses operate under a set of rules governing the level and timing of all signals on the bus. This set of rules is called the *bus protocol*. The bus, then, is the combination of wires and a protocol.

Bus wires are divided into three signal groups:

- Control
- Address
- Data

The control group contains a clock-timing signal for the bus as well as other wires pertaining to timing and the bus protocol. The address wires, or lines, contain 1s and 0s representing the binary address of the main memory or an I/O device. All devices connected to the bus have an address. When the CPU puts an address onto the bus, the device responds by putting data on the data lines of the bus for the CPU to read. The logic circuit used to detect and respond to a particular address is a decoder similar to the one you learned about earlier in the chapter. The data wires contain the binary data being read from or written to memory and I/O.

Early PCs used buses with names such as PC/XT, ISA, EISA, MCA, and Peripheral Component Interconnect Express (PCIe). Most PCs now use the *PCI* bus. As with all other buses, the PCI bus is a set of wires, protocols, and connectors that have been defined and standardized for use in computer systems. Everything that interacts with the CPU does so through a bus and most often via the PCI system bus.

Bus speed is determined by many factors, but one factor is the length of wires in the bus; the longer the wires, the slower the bus. When computer designers reached the limit in bus speed, their solution was splitting the bus into separate specialized buses, with each one designed for a specific data transfer situation. That way, the bus between the CPU and memory can be short and fast and doesn't have to share traffic with slower devices connected to the main system bus.

A typical computer has several buses, including a memory bus and a high-speed graphics bus. The front-side bus architecture in many computers has been used for several years but is beginning to be replaced by point-to-point buses, such as HyperTransport and Intel QuickPath Interconnect. Another common bus is the Low Pin Count (LPC) bus, a special Intel bus used to connect low-bandwidth devices to the CPU.

Buses also allow external devices to have access to the CPU. Bus connectors on the main board allow video adapter cards, network adapter cards, sound cards, and other devices to be connected to the computer system.

peripheral buses

In addition to the main system bus, there are many other secondary buses in a computer. Many of these buses are used to connect storage and other peripheral devices to the system bus. One of the most popular is the *SCSI* (Small Computer System Interface) bus, used to connect many different types of I/O devices to the

PCI – A system bus to connect a microprocessor with memory and I/O devices; PCI is widely used in personal computers

SCSI – A high-speed bus designed to allow computers to communicate with peripheral hardware, such as disk drives, CD/DVD-ROM drives, printers, and scanners

computer. Although it's known for its high performance and reliability, perhaps its most important characteristic is the capability to allow bus mastering. Bus mastering occurs when a device other than the normal controlling device (such as the CPU) has the capability and permission to take control of the bus, directing and facilitating data transfers. Bus mastering allows the CPU to perform other tasks while two devices are communicating. This capability is especially important when copying data from one device to another. Another popular and important peripheral bus used to connect storage devices is *SATA* (Serial AT Attachment). It's replaced the older Parallel ATA bus because of its smaller cable size, higher speed, and more efficient data transfer.

storage

A computer would be nearly useless if it couldn't retain programs and data when the power is turned off. In addition to needing the capability to read from and write to electronic memory, memory contents need to be stored in a more permanent manner. The term "storage" refers to the family of components used to store programs and data. Storage includes both primary storage (memory) and secondary or mass storage.

memory

As you've seen, one of the basics of Von Neumann architecture is the fetch-execute cycle. Each instruction is fetched from memory into the CPU for execution. Electronic memory is key to this architecture and to the speed of execution of computer processing.

Memory comes in two basic types: *ROM* (read-only memory) and *RAM* (random access memory). The name ROM indicates memory that's permanently etched into the chip and can't be modified; however, some special types of ROM can be rewritten under certain conditions. ROM isn't erased when the computer power goes off. It responds to a set of addresses and places requested data on the bus, but the CPU can't write to it.

ROM is used in a chip on the motherboard called the *BIOS* (basic input/output system). The BIOS contains instructions and data that provide startup programs for the computer and basic I/O routines.

Although the name ROM indicates the memory can't be written to, certain types of ROM can be modified under special conditions. These ROM types usually have additional designators, such as electrically erasable programmable read-only memory (EEPROM), and can rewrite all or portions of the memory on the chip.

RAM is called "random" because it doesn't have to be read sequentially; instead, any location in memory can be accessed by supplying an address. It's memory that

SATA (Serial AT Attachment) – A popular bus used to connect hard drives and other mass storage devices to the computer

ROM (read-only memory) – A type of memory that retains its information without power; some types of ROM can be reprogrammed

RAM (random access memory) – A generic term for volatile memory in a computer; RAM is fast and can be accessed randomly but requires power to retain its information

BIOS (basic input/output system) – A ROM (or programmable ROM) chip on the motherboard; the BIOS provides the startup (boot) program for the computer as well as basic interrupt routines for I/O processing

can be read from or written to, unlike ROM. RAM is also volatile, meaning it can be changed at will and requires constant power to maintain data stored in it.

Every program that runs on the computer is loaded into RAM, and the CPU fetches and executes the program from there. Program data is also stored in RAM. As you type your term paper into a word processor, the characters you type are written to RAM and stored there until you click Save. As mentioned, RAM is volatile, meaning that when the power goes off, RAM is cleared.

RAM is a generic term for read/write memory. Actually, there are different types of RAM. In general, *DRAM* (dynamic RAM) is typically made of circuits that use just one transistor per bit. These DRAM circuits need to be refreshed constantly to maintain the data stored in them. This refreshing process takes time, which is the main reason DRAM is so much slower than SRAM (static RAM). Remember that the CPU's fetch-execute cycle depends on the bus and on memory speed. Slower RAM could mean a slower computer.

DRAM – Dynamic RAM, a generic term for a type of RAM that requires constant refreshing to maintain its information; various types of DRAM are used for the system main memory

A few companies have created improved versions of standard DRAM. An ad for a computer might specify that it uses DDRRAM or SDRAM in main memory. These acronyms stand for special types of DRAM designed to be somewhat faster than normal RAM. DDRRAM, which allows memory access twice in each clock cycle, is used in many computers. DDR2 and DDR3 RAM speed up memory access even more by providing two and three memory accesses per clock cycle, respectively.

SRAM, made from flip-flop circuits, is the fastest type of memory. It's normally used only in the CPU's registers and in cache memory. *Cache memory* is a small amount of SRAM used to speed up the computer. When CPU clock speeds began to exceed the maximum possible bus speed, computer designers needed to find a way around the problem. They came up with a technique that makes use of high-speed, expensive SRAM as a go-between for the CPU and the main DRAM. Instructions and data are initially fetched from DRAM into SRAM at the slower bus speed, but when the CPU needs the instruction or data again, it can be fetched at the higher speed. Using high-speed memory and caching techniques allows the CPU speed to increase, even though the system bus speed has topped out at around 800 MHz.

cache memory – High-speed memory used to hold frequently accessed instructions and data in a computer to avoid having to retrieve them from slower system DRAM

Personal computers typically have two levels of cache memory, referred to as Level 1 cache and Level 2 cache. Level 1 cache is manufactured as part of the CPU. Level 2 cache is normally a separate chip connected to the CPU via a high-speed local bus.

Conventional asynchronous DRAM chips have a rated speed in nanoseconds (ns), or billionths of a second, a speed that represents the minimum access time for reading from or writing to memory. This includes the entire access cycle. Memory speeds in modern systems range from 5 to 10 ns.

mass storage

Mass storage is so named because it uses devices such as hard drives or DVDs with much more storage capacity than RAM or ROM. It's usually a much cheaper form of storage per megabyte, and its contents stick around after the power is turned off.

hard drives

The most commonly used form of mass storage is still the hard drive. It's called a hard drive because the information is stored on metal platters.

Hard drives are made up of one or more metal platters (see Figure 3-20) with a coating consisting of magnetic particles. These particles can be aligned in two different directions by an electromagnetic recording head, with the two different directions representing 1s and 0s. The particles remain aligned in the same direction until the read/write head changes their direction.

Figure 3-20, Hard drive platters and read/write heads

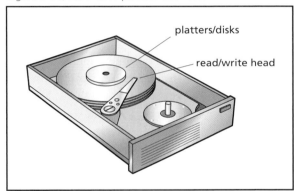

platters/disks

read/write head

The platter spins very fast, typically at speeds of 7200 or more revolutions per minute. As it spins, the read/write head moves horizontally across the disk's surface, positioning over and writing on a specific area. A disk is formatted by the read/write head recording marks on the disk's surface in concentric circles, called tracks. Each track is further divided into sectors. Organizing the surface of the disk in this way allows the hard drive to find a specified track and sector on the disk quickly for reading or writing. Hard drives can access data randomly, much like RAM. They're a standard in computers for storing large amounts of information and can store thousands of gigabytes of information inexpensively.

When deciding on the type of mass storage, one factor to consider is the cost per megabyte. For example, a 500 GB hard drive that costs $100 has a cost per megabyte of .02 cents. Compare that with a 1 GB DDRRAM memory chip that sells for $20. That has a cost per megabyte of 2 cents. You can see that hard drive storage is much cheaper than RAM.

When hard drive storage needs to be exceptionally fast and/or exceptionally reliable, multiple hard drives are connected to work together as a unit. These arrays of disks are called **RAID** (redundant array of independent disks) systems. There are seven levels of RAID, each designed to provide a different level of speed or reliability.

Hard drives can typically access information in a matter of milliseconds. That sounds quite fast, but the nanosecond speeds of the CPU and SRAM make hard drives seem like snails. Computer engineers are constantly striving to design computers and operating systems so that memory is used as much as possible.

RAID *(redundant array of independent disks) – A collection of connected hard drives arranged for increased access speed or high reliability*

n o t e

One way to speed up a computer system dramatically is to increase the amount of memory so that the hard drive is used less during operation.

optical storage

CD-ROM *– A 120-mm disc used to store data, music, and video in a computer system by using laser technology; CD-ROMs are capable of holding up to 850 MB of information*

Unlike hard disks, CDs and DVDs store data by using optical (light) technologies. **CD-ROM** (compact disc read-only memory) and **DVD** (digital video disc) have become popular forms of mass storage. Most PCs now have DVD-R/RW (read/write) drives that use a laser to burn microscopic pits in the surface of both CDs and DVDs. These pits are then interpreted as 1s and 0s when reading the disc. Like a hard disk, an optical disc spins, and the laser head moves horizontally across the surface. Unlike a magnetic hard disk, an optical disc is written to in a continuous spiral from the inside to the outside. CDs can store up to 850 MB of information. DVDs are the same physical size as CDs but can store nearly 9 GB of information and are often used to store video data.

DVD *– A technology that uses laser and layering technology to store data, music, and video on 120-mm discs; DVDs are capable of holding up to 9 GB of information*

flash drives

In the past few years, **USB** (universal serial bus) devices have replaced floppy disks as the choice for portable storage. This device, known as a *flash drive* or thumb drive, plugs into a USB port on a computer and stores thousands of megabytes of data in a package small enough to fit on a keychain. To the computer's operating system, a flash drive appears as a removable hard drive, but it really uses a special type of electronic memory, called flash memory. Flash memory is nonvolatile, meaning the data is retained when the power is turned off.

USB *(universal serial bus) – A high-speed interface between a computer and I/O devices; multiple USB devices can be plugged into a computer without having to power off the computer*

flash drive *– A small, thumb-size memory device that functions as though it were a disk drive; flash drives normally plug into a PC's USB port*

input/output systems

I/O systems are the final component in the Von Neumann architecture. The CPU fetches instructions and data from memory, and then executes the instructions. If the instruction is a math operation, shifter and adder circuitry might perform the math, placing the new values in the CPU's registers. The instruction might also transfer binary values from the registers or memory to an I/O device. I/O devices make up an essential part of Von Neumann architecture and the computer system. A computer without any I/O devices would be completely useless because I/O devices are the computer's connection to the user.

input devices

The main input device for most computer systems is the keyboard. The keyboard connects to the CPU through the keyboard controller circuit and the system bus. Your keystrokes are translated in the keyboard to binary signals of 1s and 0s that the CPU interprets as letters, numbers, and control codes. Keyboards, and most other I/O devices, connect to the main board through a *port* (see Figure 3-21). Ports are connectors on the outside of the computer that allow I/O devices to be plugged into the system bus.

port – In the context of I/O devices, the physical connection on the computer that allows an I/O device to be plugged in

Figure 3-21, The main board provides numerous ports for connecting peripheral devices

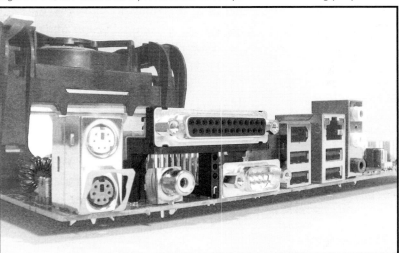

The mouse also serves as a primary input device. It works by sensing movement and translating it into binary codes. Other input devices include trackballs, styluses (pens), touch pads, touch screens, and scanners. Modems and network cards could be included in the list of input devices, although they're often categorized as networking or communication devices.

Networking and communication devices are covered in Chapter 4, "Networks."

output devices

A computer system would be of little worth if it couldn't communicate with the outside world, so a number of output devices are necessary.

monitors

The primary output device for home and business computer systems is, of course, the video display, or monitor. For years, monitors have been *CRT* (cathode ray tube) devices. In an *RGB* (red, green, blue) CRT, three electron streams (one for each color) are encoded with the color information and then aimed from the back of the monitor to the front, where they strike corresponding phosphor dots of each color. When the beam hits one of these dots, it lights it up. The beams are swept horizontally and vertically over the tube's face, varying the intensity to make up different patterns and colors. This process, called raster scanning, has been used nearly as long as computers have been in existence. The display quality is defined by the resolution and the refresh rate.

Resolution is the number of dots (pixels) on the monitor, usually measured in terms of the number of pixels or dots horizontally and vertically. A monitor advertised as 1600 × 1200 / 68 Hz is capable of displaying 1600 by 1200 (1,920,000) pixels, and its *refresh rate* (number of times an image is renewed onscreen) is 68 times per second. (The faster the refresh rate, the less the image flickers.)

LCD (liquid crystal display) monitors are much thinner and run at a much cooler temperature than CRT displays (see Figure 3-22). Originally, they were just used in notebook computers, but they have become standard on most desktop computers as their prices have decreased. Instead of an electron beam, LCD displays use small transistors that block light when a voltage is applied. As with CRT displays, LCDs are rated in terms of resolution and refresh rate.

CRT (cathode ray tube) – The technology used in a conventional computer monitor; CRTs use electron beams to light up phosphor displays on the screen

RGB (red, green, and blue) – A type of computer monitor that displays color as a function of these three colors

resolution – A measurement of the granularity of a computer monitor or printer; usually given as a pair of numbers indicating the number of dots in a horizontal and vertical direction or the number of dots per inch

refresh rate – The number of times per second an image is renewed onscreen; a higher refresh rate results in less flickering in the display

LCD (liquid crystal display) – A type of electronic device used as a computer monitor; popular in notebook computers and PDA devices and now used widely for desktop monitors

Figure 3-22, Comparison of CRT and LCD monitors

CRT: Image © 2009, androfroll; used under license from Shutterstock.com
LCD: Image © 2009, Dmitry Melnikov; used under license from Shutterstock.com

printers

The printer is another main output device. Perhaps the most popular is the inkjet printer, which creates pictures and text on pages by spraying tiny droplets of ink onto the paper as the print head moves back and forth.

Laser printers are also popular, especially in business settings. They can typically print faster than inkjet printers at a lower cost per page. Laser printers first scan the print image onto an electrostatic drum. The drum then contacts a fine, black powder called toner, and the toner sticks to the drum where the image has been drawn. The drum is then placed in contact with the paper, and the toner is transferred to it. The last step is a heat-fusing process that melts the toner onto the paper's surface. Color laser printers work similarly, except they have cyan (blue), magenta (red), and yellow inks in addition to black.

The quality of printer output is measured in resolution (dots per inch, or dpi) in both horizontal and vertical directions. Resolution ranges from 300 dpi to 2400 dpi for both inkjet and laser printers. Printers are also rated by the number of pages per minute (ppm) the printer is capable of printing. Laser printer ratings typically range from 6 to 15 ppm, inkjets are rated at 4 ppm and higher for black text, and photo-quality inkjets range from 0.3 to 12 ppm, depending on the type and quality of printing.

sound cards

Another common output device is the sound card. Although many main boards have sound capability as part of the chipset, sound cards are typically used as well. The sound card fits into the PCI bus expansion slot on the main board. At the back of the sound card are connectors for audio input and output. Analog sounds can be converted to digital codes and stored in memory or storage devices on the computer. The sound card is used to digitize sounds for storage or to read binary sound files and convert them back into analog sounds.

interrupts and polling

As you have learned in this chapter, the CPU fetches and executes at a rate equal to the processor's clock speed. Each clock pulse causes the CPU to fetch, decode, or execute a binary machine code instruction. As the CPU goes through this process continuously, how does it know when a keyboard key has been pressed?

polling – A technique in which the CPU periodically interrogates I/O devices to see whether they require attention; polling requires many more CPU resources than interrupt handling

For the keyboard and other I/O devices, there are two techniques designed to process input and output information: polling and interrupts. In *polling*, at regular intervals the processor asks each I/O device whether it has any requests for service pending. It's a bit like driving with small children who repeatedly ask "Are we there yet?" "Are we there yet?" "Are we there yet?"

interrupt handling – A computer process in which a signal is placed on the bus to interrupt normal processing of instructions and transfer control to a special program designed to deal with events such as I/O requests

Polling works, but it's inefficient because much of the CPU's time is spent asking the question (interrogating). *Interrupt handling* is a more efficient method. The CPU has a companion chip with connections, known as interrupt lines, to wires in the control section of the system bus. When an I/O device places a voltage signal on one of these lines, the interrupt chip checks the interrupt's priority and passes it on to the CPU. The CPU then stops executing its current program and jumps to a special program designed to handle that specific interrupt.

choosing the best computer hardware

As you learn more about how the computer works, you're better prepared to answer the question "Which system or device is better?" Many times in your computer science career, you'll need to make decisions on hardware and software purchases. For example, "Which is better, an Intel Core 2 processor or an Intel Core 2 Quad mobile processor?" Your answer to this and any other "Which is better?" question should be "It depends!" The question can't be answered unless you know the task the computer or device is going to be used for. You have to know what outcome you need before you can say which computer or I/O device can best solve the problem.

For example, by now you should know that a computer's speed depends on more than just the CPU clock speed. Factors such as the memory type, bus speed, and even hard drive speed can affect overall speed far more than the CPU clock. Many people have purchased a new computer only to find that it didn't solve the problem they were trying to solve.

one last thought

This book is just the beginning of your study of computer hardware and software. You should stay current on new technologies and see where they fit into your existing understanding of computers. Remember that having a better understanding of how a computer works and how the parts of a computer system interact can improve your skills in whatever computer specialty you choose.

chapter summary

- Understanding the inner workings of a computer is important if you're planning a career in computers.
- The CPU is the "real" computer in a computer system.
- Transistors are the smallest hardware unit in a computer and are used to represent the 1s and 0s in a computer.
- Transistors are arranged into circuits that provide basic Boolean logic.
- The basic Boolean operators are AND, OR, and NOT.
- The basic Boolean operators can be implemented as digital circuits or gates; simple gates can be combined to form complex circuits that perform specific functions.
- The main circuits that make up the CPU are adders, decoders, shifters, and flip-flops.
- Von Neumann architecture, characterized by a fetch-execute cycle and the three components of CPU, memory, and I/O devices, is the current standard for computers and has been for more than 60 years.
- Buses transfer information between parts of the Von Neumann architecture.
- Memory consists of different varieties of ROM and RAM.
- Mass storage is nonvolatile and used to store large amounts of data semipermanently.
- I/O systems consist of input devices, such as keyboards and mice, and output devices, such as monitors and printers.
- The CPU interfaces with I/O devices via techniques such as polling and interrupt handling.

key terms

adder (*112*)

AND (*106*)

arithmetic logic unit (ALU) (*116*)

BIOS (basic input/output system) (*119*)

Boolean basic identities (*115*)

Boolean operator (*104*)

bus (*117*)

bus protocol (*117*)

cache memory (*120*)

CD-ROM (compact disc read-only memory) (*122*)

control unit (CU) (*116*)

CRT (cathode ray tube) (*124*)

decoder (*112*)

DRAM (dynamic RAM) (*120*)

DVD (digital video disc) (*122*)

flash drive (*122*)

flip-flop or latch (*113*)

test yourself

1. What is the purpose of a main board?
2. What does CPU stand for?
3. What are the four basic functions implemented in the CPU?
4. What is the purpose of a decoder circuit?
5. What are the three parts of a transistor?
6. What are the main Boolean operators?
7. What type of table is used to represent the inputs and outputs of a logic circuit?
8. Which complex circuit is used to address memory?
9. What is the output of an XOR gate if both inputs are 0?
10. Which gate is combined with an AND to form the NAND gate?
11. What symbol is used for the OR Boolean operator in a Boolean expression?
12. Which of the complex digital circuits is used to construct SRAM?

13. Which memory type is faster: SRAM or DRAM?

14. What are the characteristics of Von Neumann architecture?

15. In computer terminology, what is a bus?

16. What are the three signal groups of a bus?

17. What is the purpose of cache memory?

18. What is polling?

19. Which is more efficient: polling or interrupt handling?

20. How is resolution measured?

practice exercises

1. Which of the following circuit types is used to create SRAM?

    a. Decoder
    b. Flip-flop
    c. LCD
    d. ROM

2. Which of the following is not one of the basic Boolean operators?

    a. AND
    b. OR
    c. NOT
    d. XOR

3. Transistors are made of _____ material.

    a. Semiconductor
    b. Boolean
    c. VLSI
    d. Gate

4. Which of the following is not one of the bus signal groups?

    a. Control
    b. Address
    c. Data
    d. Fetch

5. Which type of memory can't be written to easily?

    a. RAM
    b. SRAM
    c. ROM
    d. Flip-flop

6. Which of the following memory types is the fastest?

   a. DRAM
   b. ROM
   c. XOR
   d. SRAM

7. In a truth table, inputs are represented on which side?

   a. Top
   b. Bottom
   c. Left
   d. Right

8. Any Boolean expression can represented by a truth table.

   a. True
   b. False

9. Inputs of 1 and 0 to an XOR gate produce what output?

   a. 0
   b. 1

10. In a computer, what function does a decoder usually perform?

    a. Adding
    b. Shifting
    c. Addressing memory
    d. Multiplying

11. Boolean expressions are simplified through the use of:

    a. Basic identities
    b. Gate logic
    c. Algebraic expressions
    d. Specialized circuits

12. Which type of I/O processing is most efficient?

    a. Boolean
    b. Polling
    c. Logic
    d. Interrupt

13. Which of the following defines the display quality of a monitor?

    a. Resolution
    b. Flip rate
    c. Beam strength
    d. Inversion

14. Most computers today are based on:

    a. Von Neumann architecture
    b. Upscale integration
    c. Tabulation basics
    d. Small-Scale Integration

15. Which part of the CPU is responsible for mathematical operations?

    a. CU
    b. ALU
    c. RLU
    d. VLSI

16. A _____ in computer terminology is a set of wires and protocols designed to facilitate data transfer.

    a. Gate
    b. Bus
    c. Boolean circuit
    d. CPU

17. Most computers these days use the _____ bus.

    a. VLSI
    b. ACM
    c. ASI
    d. PCI

18. The _____ contains instructions and data that provide the startup program for a computer.

    a. RAM
    b. DRAM
    c. BIOS
    d. CPU

19. High-speed _____ is used to speed processing in a computer system.

    a. Mass storage
    b. Cache memory
    c. ROM
    d. CD-ROM

20. The quality of printer output is measured in _____.

    a. ppm
    b. cu
    c. dpi
    d. rom

digging deeper

1. What are the Boolean basic identities, and how are they used in reducing Boolean expressions?

2. How does the quality of laser printer output compare with an inkjet? Which has a lower cost per page?

3. What are the newest types of memory, and how are they faster than older memory technologies?

4. Compare the different storage media currently on the market. Which is fastest? Most cost effective? Most portable? Most durable?

5. What do you think standard monitor resolution should be and why?

discussion topics

1. If you could afford any computer, what would you have? Why? List the different hardware components you would include.

2. What new computer hardware technology do you think will have the largest effect on the computer industry in the next decade?

3. Why learn Boolean expressions and gate logic?

4. What could be some possible alternatives to Von Neumann architecture?

5. What are some of the ways logic gates are used in your everyday life?

Internet research

1. What is the fastest clock speed currently used in desktop and notebook computers?

2. Who are the main vendors of CPUs? Which one appears to be the leading vendor and why?

3. Compare three desktop computers from different vendors. Describe the advantages and disadvantages of each.

4. What Web sites display speed rankings for hardware components?

5. List three manufacturers of main boards and describe their products.

chapter

4

networks

in this chapter you will:

- Learn how computers are connected
- Become familiar with different types of transmission media
- Learn the differences between guided and unguided media
- Learn how protocols enable networking
- Learn about the ISO OSI reference model
- Understand the differences between network types
- Learn about local area networks (LANs)
- Learn about wide area networks (WANs)
- Learn about wireless local area networks (WLANs)
- Learn about network communication devices
- Learn how WANs use switched networks to communicate
- Learn how devices can share a communication medium
- Learn about DSL, cable modems, and satellite communications

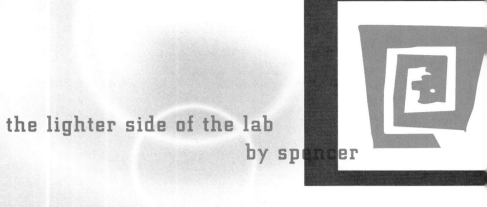

the lighter side of the lab
by spencer

I love technology. To give you a glimpse into my mind, when someone comments (as they often do) that I might as well glue my cell phone to my ear, I think, "Hey, that's actually not a bad idea. It would free up both hands to play Call of Duty." (*You* try sniping one-handed!)

Luckily, I can save the money I would have spent on glue because I recently got a Bluetooth headset for my birthday. Instead of facing the embarrassment of having a cell phone glued to my ear, now I can talk on my phone all the time, and to people around me, I just seem to be talking to myself. Phew!

Whether it's a cell phone, an MP3 player, a digital camera, or all of the above combined in one device, I love it. I've often wondered what I would have done had I been born 500 years ago. I probably would have been the first one on the block with an Abacus Core Duo.

I'm well aware of where this love for technology comes from: my dad. As far back as I can remember, we were always the most technologically advanced family on the block. In fact, my dad has exclusive ownership of a top-secret, cutting-edge piece of technology.

A few years back, I was lying on the couch watching TV and noticed construction sounds coming from the basement (hammering, sawing, drilling, and so on). My dad and our neighbor kept walking upstairs and past the couch out to the backyard and then back into the house and downstairs again.

After ~~Battlestar Galactica~~ the football game was over, my curiosity got the best of me, and I went downstairs to see what in the world was going on. I noticed they were building a tray to rest on the arms of a treadmill. On the tray was a mouse and keyboard, and on the wall above it was another tray holding a computer and monitor. I looked at my dad, who said matter-of-factly, "It's a Walk-n-Work."

My family is the only one with a Walk-n-Work, but technological miracles are all around us. I think we can all agree, however, that greater than any technological miracle is the miracle that I was ever born.

why you need to know about...
networks

Imagine life without e-mail, Web browsers, and search engines. Picture a bored teenager with no instant messaging, having to resort to using the telephone or (heaven forbid) snail mail to communicate with friends. Networking is the glue that connects computers together. Without networking, computer users couldn't share printers. Online shopping, banking, and research would be impossible. Soon after the computer was invented, computer scientists realized that computers needed to be connected to other computers and peripheral devices and began working on technologies and standards that would make networking possible.

Networking has now moved from government research centers, universities, and large corporations to home computing. As people began to have more than one computer at home, they needed to share resources, such as printers and Internet connections. Networking has indeed become central to computing. The network has effectively become an extension of the computer's system bus.

Now that networking has become an integral part of computing for homes and enterprises, designing, implementing, and maintaining networks have become increasingly important. Many types of security management and performance tuning can be done only by trained professionals. In your computing education, you'll learn more about networks and networking. You probably already use networks in nearly all that you do. Networks are beginning to extend to almost all aspects of daily life, from mobile devices to game consoles and even to household appliances. Networks, including the Internet, are becoming an integral part of personal computers, and as a computing professional, you'll have to incorporate network technologies into nearly everything you develop for computers. This chapter gives you a basic understanding of how networks operate and introduces you to the communication protocol at the heart of the Internet.

connecting computers

As you learned in Chapter 3, computers are binary devices. Instructions, numbers, pictures, and sounds are all stored and transferred by using 1s and 0s, which are actually electrical voltage signals. Computers could be connected to each other to share information by just extending the bus signals—if the computers were right next to each other. Buses consist of many wires. The PCI bus has 98, for example. A cable to extend the PCI bus to another computer would have to be very thick and wouldn't be practical at all. Because of the difficulties of extending the system bus to connect computers, new technologies had to be developed. Although computers next to each other are sometimes connected, connecting computers that are physically farther apart is often necessary. In all situations, connecting computers requires a medium, such as wire, to carry electrical signals and a communication protocol to control and manage the process.

transmission media

Sending 1s and 0s from one computer to another requires a *transmission medium*. A transmission medium is some type of material that conducts electrical and/or electromagnetic signals. One popular medium is copper wire, which is a good conductor of electricity and is less expensive than other media. It's also quite flexible and easy to work with.

note

More than one transmission medium is referred to in the plural form as "transmission media."

Transmission media are rated in four different ways:

- *Bandwidth*—The speed the medium is able to handle, measured in bits per second. Bandwidth is a function of how much the medium is affected by outside electrical influences, referred to as noise.
- *Signal-to-noise ratio*—The proportion of signal compared to noise, which is calculated by the formula $stnR = 10 \log_{10}$ (signal/noise). High ratios are better than low ratios because a high ratio indicates that the signal is stronger than the noise.
- *Bit error rate*—The ratio of the number of incorrectly received bits to the total number of bits in a specified time period. A medium's capability to transmit binary information usually drops off (the error rate increases) as the transfer rate increases.
- *Attenuation*—The tendency of a signal to become weaker over distance. Because of resistance to electrical flow, an electrical signal gets weaker as it travels, especially on copper wire. This attenuation means that all transmission media have limitations on the distance the signal can travel.

transmission medium – A material with the capability to conduct electrical and/or electromagnetic signals

bandwidth – A measurement of how much information can be carried in a given time period over a wired or wireless communication medium, usually measured in bits per second (bps)

signal-to-noise ratio – A measure of the quality of a communication channel

bit error rate – The percentage of bits that have errors in relation to the total number of bits received in a transmission; a measure of the quality of a communication line

attenuation – A reduction in the strength of an electrical signal as it travels along a medium

Transmission media are classified as two general types: guided and unguided. *Guided media* are physical media, such as copper wire or fiber-optic cable. The term *unguided media* describes the air and space that carry radio frequency (RF) or infrared (IR) light signals.

guided media

The most common guided medium is copper wire in the form of twisted pair or coaxial cable. Another type of guided medium is fiber-optic cable, which uses glass and light to transmit data. Figure 4-1 shows these common types of cables.

guided media – Physical transmission media, such as wire or cable

unguided media – Transmission media you can't see, such as air or space, that carry radio or light signals

Figure 4-1, Coaxial, twisted pair, and fiber-optic cable are guided media

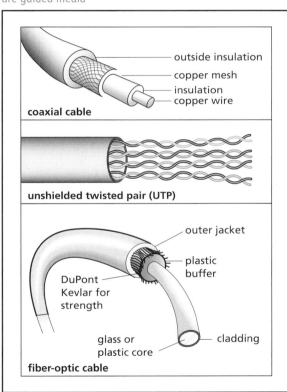

copper wire: coaxial and twisted pair

Copper wire has been the network conductor of choice for many years. It's also used to carry satellite or cable TV signals inside your house. Copper wire is manufactured in two basic formats: *coaxial* (sometimes called "coax") and *twisted pair*.

Transmitting data requires two wires: one to carry the signal and one for the ground, or return line. Two copper wires could be used to connect computers together. Just using two wires has problems, however. Electronic noise is

coaxial – Communication cable that consists of a center wire surrounded by insulation and then a grounded foil shield wrapped in steel or copper braid

twisted pair – A pair (sometimes pairs) of insulated wires twisted together and used as a transmission medium in networking

all around. It's emitted by all electronic wiring and equipment and even by the sun. Because copper is affected by this noise, one way to increase the bandwidth of copper wire is to protect it from noise by surrounding it with a metal shield. Cable manufactured in this way is called coaxial cable. It has a high signal-to-noise ratio and can support bandwidths up to 600 MHz. Different types of coaxial cable have been used over the years to network computers. The cable types usually have names such as *10BaseT*. Coaxial cable has been a popular medium in the past, but it's being replaced in most instances by twisted pair cables that are less expensive to produce and have even higher bandwidths. Coax is still used when computers connect to the Internet through a cable TV service via a cable modem.

The main copper transmission medium currently in use is called twisted pair because it consists of pairs of copper wires that are twisted. The reason the wires are twisted has to do with the electrical property of *inductance*. When metal wires run parallel to each other in close proximity, electrical current in one wire induces an electrical signal in the wire or wires next to it. In motors and generators, this property is good, but in computers and networking, inductance is a big problem. Because the electrical signals on the wires are treated as 1s and 0s, and because 1s and 0s make up the data being transmitted, it would be bad if a 0 were changed to a 1 or vice versa by some type of interference on the line. It would especially be a problem if the bit error involved a substantial increase in your credit card balance. Twisting the wires nearly eliminates inductance, enabling higher bandwidth and longer wires. All copper wires are also subject to *impedance*, which makes electrical signals weaken as they travel along the wire. The reduction in signal is called attenuation, as mentioned earlier.

Twisted pair cable comes in two configurations: shielded and unshielded. Like coaxial, the twisted pair can be wrapped in an aluminum foil–like shield to protect the wires from outside interference. Shielded twisted pair is designed to be faster and more reliable than unshielded cable, but it's more expensive and less flexible. The less expensive unshielded twisted pair (UTP) cable continues to be the more popular of the two.

Twisted pair cables have been rated by the Electronic Industry Alliance/ Telecommunications Industry Association (EIA/TIA) according to the maximum frequency the cable can reliably support. Table 4-1 lists the category ratings of twisted pair cable. Categories above 2 normally have four pairs of twisted wire.

10BaseT – *A twisted pair Ethernet networking cable capable of transmitting at rates up to 10 Mbps (megabits per second)*

inductance – *The magnetic field around a conductor that opposes changes in current flow*

impedance – *The opposition a transmission medium has toward the flow of alternating electrical currents*

Table 4-1, EIA/TIA twisted pair cable categories

category	maximum frequency
1	4–9 KHz
2	1 Mbps or less
3	10 MHz
4	20 MHz
5	100 MHz
5e	100 MHz
6	250 MHz
6a	500 MHz
7	600 MHz

Cat 5 – *A popular Ethernet twisted pair communication cable capable of carrying data at rates up to 100 Mbps*

100BaseT – *A fast Ethernet networking cable made up of four twisted pairs of wire and capable of transmitting at 100 Mbps*

10GBaseT – *The fastest Ethernet networking cable, capable of transmitting at 10 Gbps (gigabits per second) over twisted pairs of wires*

fiber optic – *Guided network cable consisting of bundles of thin glass strands surrounded by a protective plastic sheath*

You might have heard the term Cat 5 used to refer to networking cable. *Cat 5* (Category 5) is the most common twisted pair cable in use for homes and businesses. The maximum frequency of 100 MHz for Cat 5 cable is fast enough for most home and business networks. Twisted pair cables are also known by names such as *100BaseT* and *10GBaseT*.

Copper has been used for many years in coaxial and twisted pair configurations, but as the need for faster data transmission has increased, the computer industry has turned to optical media.

fiber-optic cable

Copper wire "guides" electrical signals along the wire. *Fiber optic* uses glass fibers to guide light pulses along a cable in a similar manner. Fiber-optic cables are made of a thin strand of nearly pure glass surrounded by a reflective material and a tough outer coating. These cables can transmit binary information in the form of light pulses. Transmission speeds are much higher than with copper because fiber-optic cables are much less susceptible to attenuation and inductance. In fact, inductance doesn't apply to fiber-optic cables at all. Light, unlike electricity, is immune to inductance and electronic noise on the cable. Because inductance isn't a problem at high frequencies, as in copper cable, fiber-optic cables have bandwidths hundreds of times faster than copper.

If fiber optic is faster, why hasn't the world switched to it? In the past, the problem has been the cost. Fiber-optic cable is complicated to manufacture, and the glass used in the cable has to be very pure. In the early days of fiber-optic development, the cables were expensive. As more businesses have chosen the speed and reliability of fiber-optic cable, however, economies of scale have brought the price down. In some cases, fiber-optic cable is becoming even cheaper than copper. As the price of fiber optic continues to drop and the quality increases, you can expect fiber optic to become the most widely used guided medium. Although fiber optic will continue in popularity, many factors are contributing to an increased use of the unguided media of wireless technologies.

unguided media: wireless technologies

Wouldn't it be nice if you could skip wires and use radio waves to connect your computers? Well, you can. The convenience and low price of wireless networking have allowed the computing industry to make inroads into many businesses and nearly all home networks. The main benefit of wireless technologies is that there's no need to run cables between computers. Cabling is expensive in both materials and labor. Another benefit is that computers can be mobile, instead of having to be attached to the network at a single location. Table 4-2 lists some wireless technologies, many of which are illustrated in Figure 4-2.

Table 4-2, Wireless technologies

wireless technology	transmission distance	speed
Bluetooth	33 feet (10 meters)	1 Mbps
WLAN 802.11b	112 feet (34 meters)	11 Mbps
WLAN 802.11a	65 feet (20 meters)	54 Mbps
WLAN 802.11g	112 feet (34 meters)	54 Mbps
WLAN 802.11n	200 feet (68 meters)	600 Mbps
satellite	worldwide	1 Mbps
fixed broadband	35 miles (56 kilometers)	1 Gbps
WAP (cell phones)	nationwide	384 Kbps

To understand wireless technologies, you need to understand how radio transmissions work. You use the technology behind wireless networking all the time—cell phones, walkie-talkies, garage door openers, microwave ovens, and, of course, radio. In all these products, an electronic signal is amplified and then

Figure 4-2, Wireless technologies

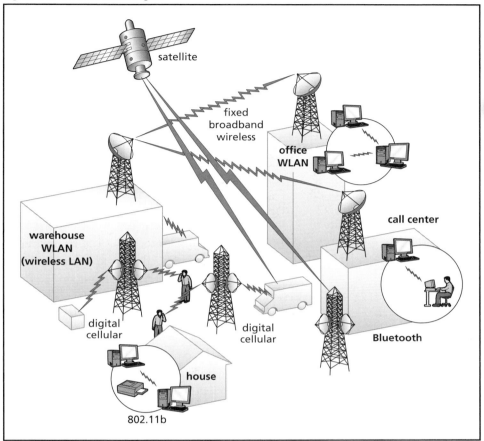

radiated from an antenna as electromagnetic waves. These waves travel through the air and sometimes through outer space and are picked up by another antenna and converted back to an electronic signal. Electromagnetic waves can be transmitted at many different frequencies. The difference between a low-pitched sound and a high-pitched sound is the frequency of the sound waves, or vibrations. The frequency of radio waves works in much the same way, except that radio waves deal with electromagnetic waves instead of vibrations. Each time you tune to a new radio station, you're actually changing frequencies.

Wireless networking uses the same technology as the radio in your car and the cell phone in your pocket. The complete possible range, or spectrum, of radio frequencies has been divided by international governing bodies into bands of frequencies. Each band is allocated for a specific industry or purpose. The frequency band at the 2.4 GHz range has been allocated for unlicensed amateur use, making it a perfect fit for wireless networking for home and businesses.

hotspots

802.11 wireless connections have been installed in airports, bookstores, coffee shops, and other commercial locations to enable people to access the Internet with their wireless-enabled notebook computers or PDAs. These locations are known as "hotspots."

IEEE (Institute of Electrical and Electronics Engineers) – *An organization involved in formulating networking standards*

802.11 – *A family of specifications for WLANs developed by IEEE; currently includes 802.11, 802.11a, 802.11b, 802.11g, and 802.11n*

Bluetooth – *A specification for short-range RF links between mobile computers, mobile phones, digital cameras, and other portable devices*

The Institute of Electrical and Electronics Engineers (*IEEE*) formulated a standard for wireless networking using the 2.4 GHz range and numbered it *802.11*. Later variations have included 802.11b, 802.11g, and 802.11n, which have been used heavily in wireless networking. If you have a wireless home networking system, it's probably using one of the 802.11 wireless standards.

These wireless standards allow wireless networks to transmit data between computers and wireless devices in much the same manner as guided media, such as copper and fiber optics. The goal in both is to transmit binary information between computer systems. Selecting the right medium, however, is only part of the problem. There's a lot more to networking computers than choosing a transmission medium.

Bluetooth is another wireless protocol that's becoming popular for connecting keyboards, mice, printers, and other I/O devices to the computer. Bluetooth isn't really a networking protocol but can be used to interface to a LAN. The Bluetooth specification allows the maximum distance between devices to range from 3 inches to 328 feet, depending on the transmitter's power. The most common distance for Bluetooth is 30 feet.

light transmission

For short distances, infrared light is also used to send and receive information through the transmission medium of the air. For infrared to work, there must be a clear line of sight between the sending device and the receiving device. Portable devices, such as PDAs, cell phones, and notebook computers, often have this capability. Many types of wireless keyboards and mice also use infrared technology. Pulses of infrared light are used to represent the 1s and 0s of binary transmission. Infrared transmissions are capable of transmission rates up to 4 Mbps.

n o t e

Remote controls for home entertainment devices also use infrared transmission.

protocols

protocol – *A set of rules designed to facilitate communication; protocols are heavily used in networking*

A *protocol* is a set of rules designed to facilitate communication. In both human and computer interactions, protocols are essential.

You deal with protocols in your life every day. For example, you deal with classroom protocol each day you attend class. (For some of you, that's less often than it should be!) When you're in a classroom with the professor talking and you have a question, the normal protocol is for you to raise your hand and keep it up until the professor acknowledges you. At some point, the professor indicates that you can ask your question. When you have finished your question, the professor answers it and then asks if the question was resolved. If so, the professor resumes the lecture.

n o t e   Networking would be impossible without the use of protocols.

The classroom protocol used in this example is designed to facilitate communication and understanding in the classroom by providing for an orderly flow of information transfer. This description is simple, but the classroom protocol is actually quite a bit more complex. Protocols are often represented with a timing diagram, which shows the protocol interactions between two entities. Table 4-3 is an example of timing for the classroom protocol.

Table 4-3, Protocol timing diagram

time period	professor	student
1	Lecturing	
2		Raises hand to show the need to ask a question
3	Notices student's hand and finishes thought	
4	Tells student to proceed	
5		Lowers hand to acknowledge professor's recognition
6		Asks question
7		Stops talking to indicate question is complete
8	Answers question	
9	Continues lecturing	

A similar process occurs throughout computer communications, especially in networking. If you design a circuit to put a binary signal on a transmission medium, you have to take into consideration the protocol for communicating data from one machine to another. It isn't enough to just put voltages on the line. You must also provide for an orderly flow of information from one machine to the other. This flow happens through a transmission protocol. In fact, many protocols are used in your computer. One example is with Web pages, covered in Chapter 5. You have probably typed "HTTP" in your browser's address bar. The "P" in "HTTP" stands for protocol, as it does in TCP/IP and FTP. Without protocols, there would be no Internet. Actually, without protocols, computers would not function.

You learn a lot more about protocols, such as HTTP, FTP, and TCP/IP, in Chapter 5, "The Internet."

Communication protocols, such as Transmission Control Protocol (TCP), allow two computers to establish a communication connection, transfer data, and terminate the connection. A timing diagram for a protocol such as TCP (see Table 4-4) might look similar to the one for the classroom protocol. Instead of words, however, computers use special codes to facilitate the communication process.

Table 4-4, Timing diagram for a communication protocol

time period	computer 1	computer 2
1	Listening	Listening
2	Are you ready?	
3		Yes, I am
4	Here comes part 1	
5		I received part 1
6	Here comes part 2	
7		I received part 2
8	I'm finished	
9		Terminate

TCP is actually a little more complicated, but the process is similar. Computers use communication protocols to ensure that the information gets from the sender to the receiver exactly as it's sent. This means the protocol must have provisions to check for errors and retransmit parts of the information, if necessary. This process happens whenever you're browsing the Internet, playing streaming files, or chatting over an instant messenger. You haven't had to worry about the process because in 1984, two standards groups, the International Organization for Standardization (*ISO*) and the Comité Consultatif International Téléphonique et Télégraphique (International

ISO (International Organization for Standardization) – *An organization that coordinates worldwide standards development*

Telegraph and Telephone Consultative Committee, *CCITT*), formulated the ISO Open Systems Interconnect reference model (*ISO OSI reference model*), usually called just the OSI model.

ISO OSI reference model

The OSI model was designed to formulate a standard for allowing different types and brands of computers to communicate with one another. It's a conceptual model for the communication process that has seven discrete layers, each with a specific responsibility or function:

1. *Physical*—The Physical layer defines the electrical, mechanical, procedural, and functional specifications for activating and maintaining the physical link (such as the cable) between end systems.

2. *Data Link*—The Data Link layer provides reliable transit of data across the physical link and is responsible for physical addressing, data error notification, ordered delivery of frames, and flow control.

3. *Network*—The Network layer provides connectivity and path selection between two end systems. This layer uses routing protocols to select optimal paths to a series of interconnected subnetworks and is responsible for assigning addresses to messages.

4. *Transport*—The Transport layer is responsible for guaranteed delivery of data. It uses data units called *datagrams*. The Transport layer is also responsible for fault detection, error recovery, and flow control. This layer manages virtual circuits by setting them up, maintaining them, and shutting them down.

5. *Session*—The Session layer is responsible for establishing, maintaining, and terminating the communication session between applications.

6. *Presentation*—The Presentation layer is responsible for formatting data so that it's ready for presentation to an application. This layer is also responsible for character format translation, such as from ASCII to Unicode, and for syntax selection.

7. *Application*—The Application layer is responsible for giving applications access to the network.

note

Networking protocols and topologies don't always use all seven layers of the OSI model.

Each layer is defined in terms of a header and a protocol data unit (*PDU*). The headers for each layer contain fields of information related to the layer's function and the message data being sent. The sending side of the communication creates the header, and then the corresponding layer on the receiving side uses this header. The PDU is used to communicate information about the message to the next layer on the same side. Figure 4-3 shows the communication process of the OSI layers.

Figure 4-3, How the OSI model processes data

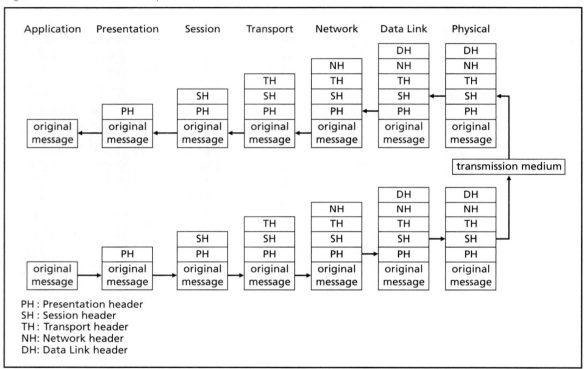

PH : Presentation header
SH : Session header
TH : Transport header
NH: Network header
DH: Data Link header

Note in Figure 4-3 how the layers function when a message is transmitted. The message originates at an application, such as your Web browser. The message is then passed down to the Presentation layer. The Presentation layer adds a header pertaining to the message and the layer's responsibilities. It's then passed to the Session layer and another header, specific to the Session layer, is added to the message and the presentation header. This same process continues down to the Physical layer. The Physical layer places the new message, consisting of the original message along with all headers from previous layers, on the transmission medium. When the receiving side gets the message, each layer examines its header and acts on the information it contains. Normally, each layer passes the message, minus the layer's header, up to the next layer. If a layer detects a problem, it can request retransmission of the message.

You can see that layers in the OSI model are defined and designed to provide services for the process of communicating between computers. The description here is brief but gives you enough information about each layer's responsibilities. The actual ISO OSI definition consists of many pages of specific information about the responsibilities of each layer. The effect of breaking down a communication process into layers is that each layer can be programmed and designed independently of the others. During the design phase, after a layer has been tested and is working correctly, it can be plugged into the other layers. Different types of networks can use the same programming code for all the layers, except the layer specifically responsible for that type of network. For example, if all the layers have been programmed to handle Internet communication over copper wire, a change to a wireless technology requires modifications to the Physical layer only. The rest of the layers could remain as they are for the network on copper wire.

You might have noticed that learning about networks requires learning a whole new vocabulary—and you've barely started. Learning these new terms, however, can help you when interviewing for jobs and communicating with other computer professionals.

network types

LAN (local area network) – A network of computers in a single building or in close proximity

WAN (wide area network) – A network in which computer devices are physically distant from each other, typically spanning cities, states, or even continents

WLAN (wireless LAN) – A local network that uses wireless transmission instead of wires; the IEEE 802.11 protocol family is often used in WLANs

One way of classifying networks is in terms of their proximity and size. A *LAN* (local area network) is a small number of computers connected in close proximity, usually in a building or complex, and over copper wire. A *WAN* (wide area network) consists of many computers spread over a large geographical area, such as a state or a continent. Sometimes you hear the term MAN (metropolitan area network) to describe a network that spans a city or metropolitan area. Deciding whether to use the term LAN or WAN to describe a network isn't always easy. There's no standardized definition, although if the network is confined to a single building, it's usually called a LAN. If multiple physical locations are connected through a combination of copper wire and/or telephone or other communication services, the network is normally referred to as a WAN. The Internet is the largest example of a WAN. Figure 4-4 shows an example of a WAN composed of a combination of LANs and WLANs.

Because of the increasing popularity of wireless networking, especially in home and small businesses, a new term has entered into the vocabulary. *WLAN* (wireless LAN) describes a LAN that uses a wireless transmission medium, instead of copper wire or fiber optics.

Figure 4-4, Example of a WAN configuration

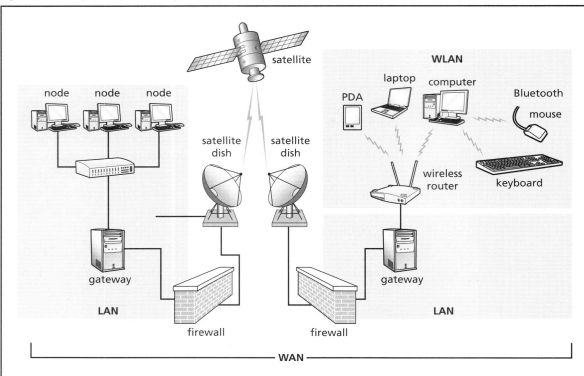

LAN topologies

After the transmission medium and protocols are in place, the computers can be connected in different configurations. These network configurations are often referred to as *network topologies*. The computers attached to a network are often referred to as *nodes*.

There are three basic topologies, or ways of connecting computers, in a LAN:

- *Ring topology*—This method connects all the computers in a ring, or loop, with a cable going from one computer to another until it connects back to the first computer. When a computer wants to send a message or data to another computer on a ring network, it sends the message to the next computer in the ring. Each computer on the ring network has a unique address. If the message isn't addressed to the computer receiving it, the computer forwards the message to the next computer. This process repeats until the message reaches the correct computer.
- *Star topology*—In a star topology, a computer or a network device, such as a switch, serves as a central point, or hub, for all messages. When a computer in this configuration wants to send a message to another computer, it sends the message to the

network topology – A schematic description of the arrangement of a network, including its nodes and connecting lines

node – Any addressable device attached to a network that can recognize, process, or forward data transmissions

central node, which forwards the message to the computer it's addressed to. Again, all computers on the network must have a unique address.

- *Bus topology*—A network in a bus topology is configured much like a system bus on a computer. Each computer, or node, on the network is connected to a main communication line, or bus. Any computer attached to this bus can place a message on the bus that's addressed to any other computer on the bus. All the computers "listen" to the bus, but only the one with the correct address responds. The bus line requires a special terminator at its end to absorb signals so that they don't reflect back down the line.

The bus topology has historically been one of the most popular methods of connecting computers in a LAN, but the advent of the Internet and home networking has increased the star topology's popularity. Figure 4-5 shows these three network topologies.

Figure 4-5, LAN topologies

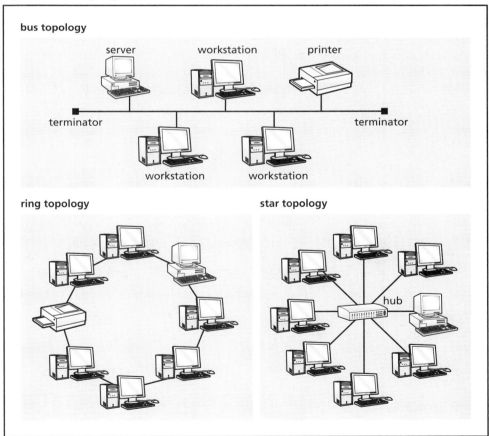

Ethernet – A common method of networking computers in a LAN, using copper cabling at speeds up to 100 Mbps

token ring – A LAN technology that has stations wired in a ring, in which each station constantly passes a special message token on to the next; whichever station has the token can send a message

FDDI (Fibre Distributed Data Interface) – A token-passing, fiber-optic cable protocol with support for data rates up to 100 Mbps; FDDI networks are typically used as the main lines for WANs

LAN communication technologies

LANs can also be classified according to the technology used to connect nodes to the network. A widely used technology that has become the industry standard for LANs is *Ethernet*. Ethernet is based on a bus topology, but it can be wired in a star pattern, sometimes called a star/bus topology. Today, Ethernet is the most popular LAN technology because it's inexpensive and easy to install and maintain. The original Ethernet standard transferred data at 10 Mbps, and a more recent standard, Fast Ethernet, transfers data at 100 Mbps. Many PCs come with built-in Ethernet 10/100 ports to accommodate both speeds. Gigabit Ethernet provides even faster transfer rates of up to 1 Gbps (1 billion bits per second), and recently 10 Gigabit Ethernet appeared on the scene.

The second most popular LAN technology is *token ring*, which uses a ring topology and controls access to the network by passing around a special signal called a token. Standard token ring networks support data transfer of 4 or 16 Mbps. Other LAN technologies that are generally faster and more expensive are *FDDI* and *ATM*. Table 4-5 summarizes the bandwidths of LAN technologies.

Table 4-5, Bandwidths of LAN technologies

LAN technology	bandwidth
Ethernet	10 Mbps (megabits per second)
Fast Ethernet	100 Mbps
Gigabit Ethernet	1 Gbps (gigabits per second)
10 Gigabit Ethernet	10 Gbps
token ring	4 or 16 Mbps
fast token ring	100 or 128 Mbps
FDDI	100 Mbps
ATM	Up to 2.488 Gbps

ATM (Asynchronous Transfer Mode) – A network technology based on transferring data in cells or packets of a fixed size at speeds up to 2.488 Gbps

network communication devices

LANs, WANs, and WLANs can be connected to form larger, more complex WANs. These larger WANs might consist of LANs of different types, located physically far apart. To connect them, various communication devices are used. To connect to a network, a computer or network device needs a network interface card. Networks also use repeaters, hubs, switches, bridges, gateways, routers, and firewalls to solve networking issues.

NIC

Each physical device connected to a network must have a *network interface card (NIC)*. This card is usually in an expansion slot on the motherboard or in a card slot on a notebook computer and includes an external port for attaching a network cable or an antenna for wireless connection. Each NIC has a unique, 48-bit address—the Media Access Control (MAC) address or a physical address assigned by the NIC manufacturer—used to identify it on the network (by the OSI Physical layer). The NIC becomes the interface between the physical network and your computer, so it normally connects to the main system bus.

repeater

As mentioned, signals decrease (attenuate) as they travel through a transmission medium. Attenuation limits the distance between computers in a network. *Repeaters* alleviate this problem by amplifying the signal along the cable between nodes. Repeaters don't alter the content of data in any way. They just boost the signal.

hub

A *hub* is a special type of repeater with multiple inputs and outputs, unlike the standard repeater that has just one input and one output. All the inputs and outputs are connected. The hub allows multiple nodes to share the same repeater.

switch

A *switch* is similar to a hub, in that it's a repeater with many input and output ports. A switch differs from a hub because not all the inputs and outputs are connected. Instead, the switch examines the input's packet header and switches a point-to-point connection to the output addressed by the packet. Because it's not just a passive device, as a hub is, a switch has the OSI Layer 2 (Data Link) responsibilities of examining headers for addresses.

bridge

A *bridge* is similar to a switch, in that it amplifies signals that it receives and can connect inputs with outputs, but it can allow dividing a network into segments to reduce overall traffic. Recall that in a bus network, all messages are presented to all computers on the network. That places a heavy load on each computer, as every message must be examined to see whether the computer needs to respond. In a large network, this traffic can slow the network quite a bit. A bridge can prevent this slowdown because it can read the address of each message it receives and then forward it to just the network segment containing the addressed computer.

gateway

A *gateway* is similar to a bridge but has the additional capability to interpret and translate different network protocols. Gateways can be used to connect networks of different types or to connect mainframe computers to PCs. Your PC no doubt connects to the Internet through a gateway. Most gateways are simply a computer with software that provides gateway functionality.

router

Routers are small, special-purpose devices or computers used to connect two or more networks. Routers are similar to bridges and gateways, but they function at a higher OSI layer. Because they can "route" network traffic based on the logical (IP) addresses assigned at Layer 3 (the Network layer), they aren't dependent on the physical (Layer 1) MAC address of the computer's NIC. Routers can also understand the protocol information placed in messages by the Network layer and make decisions based on it. Routers are at the heart of the Internet. You learn more about the Internet and IP addresses in Chapter 5, but routers are essential for getting your Web page request to its intended destination.

firewall

A *firewall* is a device designed to protect an internal network or node from intentional or unintentional damage from an external network. Firewalls limit access to networks. Many firewalls are router based, meaning that firewall functionality is added to the router. A firewall can examine inbound and outbound network traffic and restrict traffic based on programmed parameters and lists. A well-designed firewall can do much to protect an internal network from unwanted or malicious traffic. Although most firewalls are separate hardware devices, many operating systems, such as Windows XP and Vista, have built-in software firewalls.

The use of firewalls and other network security techniques is discussed in more detail in Chapter 2, "Computing Security and Ethics."

note

A network firewall is named after the physical firewall in buildings designed to slow the spread of a fire from room to room.

switched networks

So far, you have read about computers being connected in LAN and WAN configurations. You might have pictured these computers being connected via copper cable, such as coaxial and twisted pair, or via wireless networks. If you have two computers you want to connect, you can run a Cat 5 wire between them—if they're close to each other. What if one computer is in San Francisco and the other is in New York? You could get a huge spool of wire and start walking, or you could try to find someone who already has a wire running from San Francisco to New York and share that wire.

Well, someone already does have a wire going from nearly any location in the world to any other location: the telephone company. By the time computers were invented and, more important, by the time people wanted to network them, telephone companies already had cables all over the place. It was natural to want to use this existing network of wires to connect computers. The problem, however, was that the phone system was designed to carry analog voices, not digital data. The first hurdle of using the phone system to transmit data was finding a way to convert bits into sounds. Engineers came up with a device called a *modem* (modulator/demodulator). Modems convert binary digits into sounds by modulating, or modifying, a tone so that one tone can indicate a 0 bit and another tone can indicate a 1 bit. If you have connected to the Internet with a modem, you have heard the different tones as the sending and receiving modems begin communicating with each other.

Voices require only a small frequency range to be understood. For this reason, telephone companies were able to split the bandwidth of a copper conductor into multiple ranges or bands and let homes and businesses share the total bandwidth. Doing so made running the wires more cost effective. The small bandwidth required for voice presented a new problem for engineers, however. The standard voice-grade telephone line is designed to carry frequencies in the range of 300 to 3300 Hz. This means the highest data range is 3300 bits per second. So how does a 56K (56,000 bps) modem go faster than that? Modem manufacturers achieved higher speeds by coming up with some tricks.

First, they realized they could modulate not only the frequency of a sound (how fast it vibrates) with a technique called frequency modulation (*FM*), but also the volume (amplitude) of sound waves with amplitude modulation (*AM*). The combination of the two allows fitting more bits into the same frequency range. Additionally, it's possible to shift the starting point, or phase, of an audio waveform and measure the shift on the other end. This technique is called phase modulation (*PM*). Figure 4-6 shows FM, AM, and PM. Using a combination of all three allows transmission speeds of approximately 30,000 bps. To get the additional speed and approach 56,000 bps, the data has to be modified so that it doesn't take up as much bandwidth, and different rates are used for sending and receiving.

modem – A device that converts binary signals into audio signals for transmission over standard voice-grade telephone lines and converts the audio signals back into binary

FM (frequency modulation) – A technique of placing data on an alternating carrier wave by varying the signal's frequency; this technique is often used in modems

AM (amplitude modulation) – A technique of placing data on an alternating carrier wave by varying the signal's amplitude; this technique is often used in modems

PM (phase modulation) – A technique of placing data on an alternating carrier wave by varying the signal's phase; the most common modulation type in modems

Figure 4-6, Frequency modulation, amplitude modulation, and phase modulation

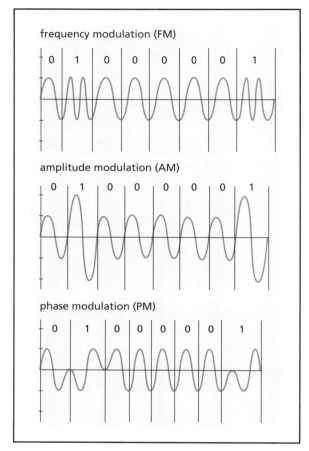

The main method for modifying data to take up less bandwidth is compressing it. A number of techniques have been developed for compressing data so that more information can be sent in a given bandwidth. You'll likely learn more about them in future computing courses. One technique is replacing repeating patterns with a code. For example, as you've been reading this chapter, you might have noticed that words such as "protocol," "bandwidth," "frequency," and "network" have been repeated often. This repetition might be a bit annoying to read, but it's great for transmitting over a modem. A modem's compression capabilities can take repeating patterns of letters and numbers and replace them with a much shorter code. The word "bandwidth" has nine letters, for example. If it's replaced with a 2-byte code, that saves 7 bytes for every occurrence of the word and allows sending more data within the limits of the telephone frequency range.

Finally, frequency is a function of the number of transitions from a sound wave's high point to its low point in a second. If the bits in a message could be rearranged so that the 1s and 0s were grouped better, the number of transitions would be reduced, and more bits could be sent in the same amount of time.

The combination of these three techniques has pushed modems to their 56K limit, which probably isn't fast enough for most people these days. Although voice-grade modems aren't used much now, many of these same techniques are used in cable and DSL modems.

high-speed WANs

Because most WANs use the telephone company's existing wires, they have to operate within the constraints established by telephone companies. With standard voice-grade lines, the maximum data rate for modem dial-up is 56K, as stated previously. For most network applications, this rate is painfully slow. Because networking is becoming an extension of the system bus, it stands to reason that there's a need for high-speed network connections. The normal copper wire used in your home or business is actually capable of speeds faster than 1.5 Mbps. The telephone company limits the bandwidth, however, so that more subscribers can share the wiring's cost. One way of getting a faster connection is by leasing all the bandwidth on the wire. Normal copper wire is capable of carrying 24 voice channels, so you could lease all 24 channels on the wire. This dedicated line is called a *T1 line*. As you might imagine, leasing a T1 line can be quite expensive.

T1 line – A digital transmission link with a capacity of 1.544 Mbps; T1 uses two pairs of normal twisted wires, the same twisted wire used in most homes

If you need a faster connection, you can lease one of the higher-speed lines the telephone company offers. The T3 line consists of 28 T1 lines. For even faster speeds, fiber-optic lines with optical carrier (OC) designations are used. Table 4-6 lists the high-speed WAN options available from telephone companies.

Table 4-6, High-speed WAN connections

connection	speed	equivalent
T1	1.544 Mbps	24 voice lines
T3	43.232 Mbps	28 T1 lines
OC3	155 Mbps	84 T1 lines
OC12	622 Mbps	4 OC3 lines
OC48	2.5 Gbps	4 OC12 lines
OC192	9.6 Gbps	4 OC48 lines

multiple access

FDM (frequency-division multiplexing) – *A technique for combining many signals on a single circuit by dividing available transmission bandwidth by frequency into narrower bands, each used for a separate communication channel*

Most WAN connections use one of two techniques to divide a connection's bandwidth among multiple users. Normal telephone voice-grade lines use frequency-division multiplexing (*FDM*) to divide the bandwidth among subscribers so that each has a certain frequency or channel for the duration of the communication session. For example, with a T1 line, the total bandwidth or frequency range of the copper wire is divided among the 24 possible users as voice-grade lines.

FDM is inefficient because in most cases, many of the subscribers sharing a line aren't using it. Think right now of what your home phone line is doing. Of course, you're not talking while you're reading, but how about while you're working or at school? At any given instant, much of the bandwidth isn't being used. Even in a normal telephone conversation or Internet session, the bandwidth is effectively wasted when you're not talking or sending data.

TDM (time-division multiplexing) – *A technique for combining many signals on a single circuit by allocating each signal a fixed amount of time but allowing each signal the full bandwidth during an allotted time*

A better way of dividing bandwidth might be based on time instead of frequency. You could allow each user the entire bandwidth but just for small amounts of time. By managing this process, each user could have an effective speed that exceeds the speed achieved with FDM. This technique is called time-division multiplexing (*TDM*). Figure 4-7 compares how bandwidth is shared by FDM and TDM.

Figure 4-7, FDM and TDM

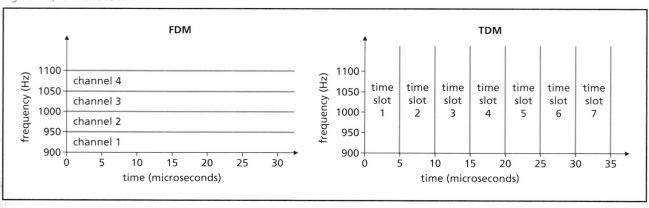

DSL

DSL (digital subscriber line) – *A method of sending and receiving data over regular phone lines, using a combination of FDM and TDM*

Many homes and businesses use a high-speed Internet connection called digital subscriber line (*DSL*). DSL is a combination of FDM and TDM, incorporating the best features of both. In DSL, the total bandwidth of the copper phone wire is divided into 247 different frequency bands. Your voice travels over the lower 4 KHz band, and the remaining bands are used in various combinations for uploading and downloading data. DSL uses a special "modem" to place voice communication into the frequency band reserved for it and data in the area above the voice band. This composite signal is then digitized and combined with signals from other customers using TDM, placed on a high-speed medium, and sent to the central office (telephone switching station) to be redirected to its final destination. These techniques allow DSL speeds to range from 256 Kbps to 1.5 Mbps, and upload speeds and download speeds can differ. Because of attenuation, a DSL subscriber is required to be no more than 18,000 feet away from the nearest telephone switching station. Much effort, however, is being put into developing new DSL techniques that can overcome this distance barrier.

cable modems

Another popular method of implementing a WAN, especially for home Internet connections, is through a *cable modem*. The coax cable that comes into a home for cable television (CATV) can carry hundreds of channels. Each channel is allocated a 6 MHz bandwidth. One or more of the channels is reserved for data transmission, although these channels might not be used if you use only cable TV. When you subscribe to a cable Internet service, the cable company connects your computer's Ethernet connector to a cable modem, which is connected to the CATV cable. Downstream from each home is a device that takes the signals from all nearby homes and uses TDM to combine them into one signal for transmission to the Internet provider. Cable modems are capable of speeds up to 42 Mbps, but normally, the provider limits speeds to less than 1 Mbps. This limitation allows more customers to share a single cable line. Cable modems also allow different upload and download speeds.

wireless technologies

Most cell phone providers now offer wireless broadband capabilities with smartphones and other portable devices. Technologies such as EDGE, EVDO, and 3G allow people to have high-speed Internet access wherever there's cell phone coverage. As these technologies mature, they might become the standard method of wireless networking.

satellite technologies

Wireless WAN technologies are becoming more widely used as the technology improves and the price comes down. Some homes and businesses are restricted to dial-up connections because they're located out of range of DSL, cable, and other wired or short-range wireless technologies. One of the few alternatives is a satellite connection. The same satellite dish used for TV broadcasts or one

---

cable modem – *A type of digital modem that connects to a local cable TV line to provide a continuous connection to the Internet*

much like it is placed outside to receive and send signals to an orbiting satellite. As unguided media improve, they might surpass guided media, especially copper cable, as the most widely used transmission media.

one last thought

As networks become more tightly integrated with computers and computing, computer scientists will have a greater need to program for and interact with networks and to understand networking topologies and protocols. The list of key terms in this chapter is long, but it barely scratches the surface. There are many textbooks much thicker than this one that examine just a single networking topic. The IEEE specifications for the 802.11a wireless protocol alone consist of 91 pages! There's a lot to learn, but this chapter should serve as a good foundation for your future networking and computing studies.

chapter summary

- Networking is essential to modern computing.

- Networking requires a transmission medium to carry information from one computer device to another.

- Transmission media are rated in terms of their bandwidth, signal-to-noise ratio, bit error rate, and attenuation.

- Copper wire has been the most widely used network conductor, primarily in the form of coaxial and twisted pair cable.

- Fiber-optic cable has a much higher bandwidth than copper conductors.

- Cat 5 is a twisted pair copper cable used most commonly in Ethernet networks; it has a transmission speed of up to 100 Mbps.

- Wireless technologies allow networking to be conducted by using electromagnetic waves or light.

- The IEEE 802.11 family of standards applies to wireless networking.

- A protocol is a set of rules designed to facilitate communication and is essential to networking.

- The OSI model defines a set of protocols necessary for data communication; the seven protocol layers are (1) Physical, (2) Data Link, (3) Network, (4) Transport, (5) Session, (6) Presentation, and (7) Application.

- The main network types are WAN, LAN, and WLAN.

- LAN topologies are ring, star, and bus.

- The most popular LAN technology is Ethernet, and token ring is another LAN technology.

- Various hardware devices are used in networking, such as NICs, repeaters, hubs, switches, bridges, gateways, routers, and firewalls.

- Voice telephone service is widely used to extend networks, and modems handle the conversion from digital binary to analog audio to make using voice networks possible.

- Transmission media are shared among users by using FDM and TDM techniques.

- DSL, cable modems, and satellite are popular broadband WAN solutions.

key terms

10BaseT (*140*)

100BaseT (*141*)

10GBaseT (*141*)

802.11 (*144*)

AM (amplitude modulation) (*155*)

ATM (Asynchronous Transfer Mode) (*152*)

attenuation (*138*)

bandwidth (*138*)

bit error rate (*138*)

Bluetooth (*144*)

bridge (*153*)

cable modem (*159*)

Cat 5 (*141*)

CCITT (Comité Consultatif International Téléphonique et Télégraphique) (*147*)

coaxial (*139*)

datagram (*147*)

DSL (digital subscriber line) (*158*)

Ethernet (*152*)

FDDI (Fibre Distributed Data Interface) (*152*)

FDM (frequency-division multiplexing) (*158*)

fiber optic (*141*)

firewall (*154*)

FM (frequency modulation) (*155*)

gateway (*154*)

guided media (*139*)

hub (*153*)

IEEE (Institute of Electrical and Electronics Engineers) (*142*)

impedance (*140*)

inductance (*140*)

ISO (International Organization for Standardization) (*146*)

ISO OSI reference model (*147*)

LAN (*149*)

modem (*155*)

network interface card (NIC) (*153*)

network topology (*150*)

node (*150*)

PDU (protocol data unit) (*148*)

PM (phase modulation) (*155*)

protocol (*144*)

repeater (*153*)

router (*154*)

signal-to-noise ratio (*138*)

switch (*153*)

T1 line (*157*)

TDM (time-division multiplexing) (*158*)

token ring (*152*)

transmission medium (*138*)

twisted pair (*139*)

unguided media (*139*)

WAN (wide area network) (*149*)

WLAN (wireless LAN) (*149*)

test yourself

1. What are the two general types of transmission media?
2. What are the four ways to rate transmission media?
3. What are the two basic copper wire formats?
4. What is the maximum frequency of Cat 5 cable?
5. What are examples of networking protocols?
6. How many layers are in the OSI model?
7. What is a WAN?
8. What are the three LAN topologies?
9. Which of the three LAN topologies has emerged as the most popular?
10. What is a NIC?
11. Which network device can interpret and translate different network protocols?
12. What is the difference between a hub and a switch?
13. Which network device is designed to prevent damage to an inside network from an outside source?
14. What frequency range are voice-grade telephone lines designed to carry?
15. What is the speed range of DSL?
16. What is bandwidth?
17. How does a WLAN differ from a LAN?
18. What is the difference between AM and FM?
19. How many standard voice lines are equivalent to a T1 line?
20. Which type of multiplexing combines signals on a circuit by dividing available transmission bandwidth into narrower bands?

practice exercises

1. Which is a better signal-to-noise ratio?

    a. High
    b. Low
    c. Guided
    d. Unguided

2. Fiber-optic cable is made of:

   a. Glass
   b. Nylon
   c. Braided copper
   d. Copper

3. Which is a faster networking cable?

   a. 10BaseT
   b. 100BaseT

4. Which of the following standards is used in wireless networking?

   a. Cat 5
   b. ISO OSI
   c. 802.11
   d. TCP

5. Which of the following is not one of the OSI model layers?

   a. Physical
   b. Wireless
   c. Transport
   d. Application

6. Which of the OSI layers is responsible for guaranteed delivery of data?

   a. Transport
   b. Network
   c. Data Link
   d. Presentation

7. Which of the OSI layers is involved with a network's electrical specifications?

   a. Physical
   b. Network
   c. Session
   d. Transport

8. Which of the following is a LAN topology?

   a. Cat 5
   b. Coaxial
   c. Star
   d. Repeater

9. A hub has a single input and a single output.

   a. True
   b. False

10. Normal speeds of a cable modem are approximately:

    a. 56 KHz
    b. 1 Mbps
    c. 10 Mbps
    d. 100 Mbps

11. DSL speeds range from:

    a. 256 Kbps to 1.5 Mbps
    b. 256 Mbps to 15 Mbps
    c. 56 Kbps to 256 Kbps
    d. 100 Kbps to 156 Kbps

12. Standard voice-grade lines are designed to carry frequencies in the range of:

    a. 1.5 MHz to 15 MHz
    b. 500 MHz to 1 MHz
    c. 56 KHz to 100 KHz
    d. 300 Hz to 3300 Hz

13. Modems convert binary digits into sounds by modulating tones.

    a. True
    b. False

14. Which of the following is not a network device?

    a. Router
    b. Gateway
    c. Ramp
    d. Hub

15. Which of the following is used to connect a computer to a network?

    a. Gateway
    b. NIC
    c. Ramp
    d. Router

16. What factor reduces the strength of an electrical signal as it travels along a transmission medium?

    a. Bandwidth
    b. Signal-to-noise ratio
    c. Bit error rate
    d. Attenuation

17. Which of the following is the most commonly used twisted pair cable category?

    a. Cat 1
    b. Cat 5
    c. 10Base2
    d. 10Base5

18. Which type of guided medium is the least susceptible to attenuation and inductance?

    a. Coaxial cable
    b. Twisted pair cable
    c. Fiber-optic cable
    d. They are all the same

19. Which topology has become more popular with the advent of the Internet and home networking?

    a. Token ring
    b. Star
    c. Bus
    d. Loop

20. DSL is a combination of what two types of multiplexing?

    a. FDM and TDM
    b. FDM and FM
    c. AM and TDM
    d. AM and FM

digging deeper

1. What is a TCP packet? How is it used? What does it look like?

2. How many of the seven OSI layers are used in the TCP/IP protocol suite?

3. What is a connection-oriented protocol?

4. How can a bus topology handle more than one computer transmitting at the same time?

5. What are the characteristics of each IEEE 802.11 wireless standard?

discussion topics

1. What are the advantages of wireless networking? What are the disadvantages?

2. What are examples of protocols in your everyday life?

3. Why is it necessary for a computer scientist to have a knowledge of networking?

4. What are the advantages of using twisted pair cable for networking? What are the disadvantages?

5. How do you think the OSI model helped further networking progress?

Internet research

1. What other standards have the ISO, IEEE, and CCITT groups formulated?

2. Where is the ISO standards group located, and who are the members of the group?

3. What are the costs of setting up a wireless home network compared with a wired home network?

4. What types of jobs are available in the field of networking?

5. Explain the history and evolution of the ring, star, and bus network topologies.

5

the Internet

in this chapter you will:

- Learn what the Internet really is
- Become familiar with the architecture of the Internet
- Become familiar with Internet-related protocols
- Understand how TCP/IP protocols relate to the Internet
- Learn how IP addresses identify devices connected to the Internet
- Learn how DHCP can be used to assign IP addresses
- Learn how routers are used throughout the Internet
- Learn how a DNS server translates a URL into an IP address
- Learn how port numbers are used with IP addresses to expand Internet capabilities
- Learn how NAT is used in networking
- Learn how to determine your own TCP/IP configuration
- Learn how HTML and XML are used with the World Wide Web
- Learn how to develop a simple Web page by using HTML
- Learn how search engines make the World Wide Web more usable

the lighter side of the lab
by spencer

The power went out not too long ago. Because my family lives on such a reliable (and by "reliable," I mean completely unreliable) power grid, we're experts at dealing with power outages. We simply lit the 450 scented candles located throughout the house, compliments of my mom. Soon the house was well lit and smelling very good.

The real crisis came when my parents, who were fixing dinner when the power went out, tried to finish cooking. Fortunately, we have a gas range that isn't dependent on electricity. However, nobody could remember how they heated a can of refried beans before microwaves were invented.

I can remember buying our first microwave oven. It was the size of a small Buick and a little bit heavier. Little did I know that 20 years later as a college student, I would depend on the microwave to do what little cooking Taco Bell and McDonald's didn't do for me.

Luckily, we got dinner figured out eventually, but I realized how many things I depend on every day that have been invented during my lifetime. I can remember my family getting our first VCR, camcorder, video game (Pong), and cell phone, to name a few.

I can also remember logging on to the Internet for the first time. Talk about a life-changing event! Little did I know then that if somebody told me I had to choose between losing the Internet or one of my kidneys, I would have to say, "Let me think about it."

A good chunk of my online time is spent shopping on eBay, which is way more fun than normal shopping. It's like shopping mixed with cage fighting. Right after I signed up, I bid on a set of golf clubs. I had responsibly set a personal bidding limit of $200.

With only a minute to go and winning the bid, I noticed someone had outbid me. Now I was really mad. "I'll show you!" I threatened. I bid and was almost immediately outbid. I bid again, and the bids flew back and forth until the time expired.

I stared at the screen as it refreshed for the last time, holding my breath in anticipation. Suddenly the words I had been waiting for appeared on the screen: "You have won the item!" "Yes!" I yelled. "Take that, suckers!" I was extremely excited—until I realized I'd gone $25 over my responsibly set limit.

In summary, I don't know how I'm going to survive if the power goes out and I can't use the Internet. I guess it's time to buy a generator. Maybe I can find one on eBay.

why you need to know about...
the Internet

You might have heard of the Industrial Revolution in your history classes. The world was forever altered by the invention of powered machinery and mass production. The computer revolution has also changed the world. Nearly everything you use is in some way related to computers. Either it has a computer embedded in it, like your car, or its design was made possible by computers.

You're now living through one of the world's greatest technological revolutions, one that's changing the way we think and act. Computers and the Internet are changing the face of nearly every industry. In the past, all workers had to be located at their place of business. Now workers in many fields can perform their jobs from home just as easily as at the office or plant. Education is certainly benefiting from this revolution. It might be that you're reading this textbook as part of an online course, where all your interaction with the instructor and other students is via the Internet.

Perhaps the biggest change is in the areas of knowledge and learning. People with access to a computer have nearly all the world's knowledge at their disposal, and in much of the world that's nearly everyone because Internet-connected computers are available in homes, workplaces, libraries, and public Internet centers. Cell phones also provide access to the Internet. You can be almost anywhere and check the news and weather, compare prices, and shop online. You can do your banking, renew your car registration, and apply for a student loan. You probably registered for your college courses online.

In your studies, you're required to do a lot of research on various topics. Although you probably spend time in the library, much of your research takes place online (or online at the library). This chapter shows you how the Internet can help you to do research.

The field of computing is heavily involved in all aspects of the Internet revolution. Nearly all networks, protocols, and server and client programs have been programmed and are maintained by computer professionals. That's why the focus of this chapter is on helping you gain a basic understanding of not only how the Internet works, but also of the technologies involved in its everyday use. You, as a computing specialist, are on the leading edge of the knowledge and information revolution. You might be involved with formulating new uses for the Internet and perhaps with regulating and providing ways to limit misuse.

what is the Internet?

In Chapter 4, you learned about LANs and WANs. The Internet is actually just a collection of LANs and WANs connected to form a giant WAN. When you connect your computer to your Internet service provider (*ISP*), you become part of this WAN. You have already learned much of the history of the Internet. From small beginnings, the Internet has evolved into a massive network that involves nearly every computer in the world.

You might be surprised to learn that the Internet is not just one thing; rather, it's a collection of many things. You might also be surprised to know that nobody owns the Internet. A few groups propose rules for the Internet and other organizations manage the way it works, but no one owns the whole Internet. Everyone who is connected to, or provides communication to, other computers on the Internet owns a part of it. What's interesting about the Internet is that everyone who gets involved in it is doing so for his or her own purposes but still benefits many others. For example, companies providing communication lines or companies providing content on the Internet do it for profit, but they still benefit everyone by playing a role in disseminating information.

n o t e   It's estimated that there are more than a billion Internet users in the world.

Understanding the Internet requires understanding many of the technologies that make up the whole. These technologies build on one another in such a way that they're best discussed in sequential fashion, starting with the general structure or architecture of the Internet.

the architecture of the Internet

Your computer might be part of an existing LAN, or it might be a stand-alone computer. Either way, it's likely connected to the Internet. Your LAN is connected to the Internet through communication lines, normally leased from the phone company to an ISP. You might also be connected to a LAN via a wireless access point, a wireless router connected via wire to a LAN. If you connect with a cable modem, you're connecting to your ISP through the cable TV system. Your Internet provider maintains a switching center called a point of presence (*POP*). This POP might be connected to a larger ISP with a larger POP and connections to communication lines with much higher speeds. This larger ISP is probably connected to national or international ISPs that are often called national backbone providers (*NBP*s), as shown in Figure 5-1. All these ISPs,

ISP (Internet service provider) – A company that provides access to the Internet and other related services, such as Web site building and virtual hosting

POP (point of presence) – An access point to the Internet

NBP (national backbone provider) – A provider of high-speed network communication lines for use by ISPs

Figure 5-1, Internet data can pass through several levels of ISPs

from large to small, have network-switching circuitry, such as routers and gateways, and are eventually connected to optical cables capable of transmitting many billions of bits per second.

After reading Chapter 4, you have an understanding of LANs and WANs and the specialized equipment, such as NICs, routers, gateways, and firewalls, used to control the flow of information between computers on a network. The components you have already read about are what make up the hardware of the Internet. To understand how the Internet works at a hardware level, you need to learn a little more about these pieces of equipment. However, before you can understand these specialized network devices, you need to know about protocols and addressing.

protocols

Hardware is only part of what makes the Internet work. As you have learned, a protocol is a set of rules established to facilitate communication. In the context of the Internet, the importance of protocols can't be overstated. There are many protocols involved with the Internet. You have probably typed HTTP at the beginning of a Web address many times. *HTTP* stands for Hypertext Transfer Protocol. You've certainly used e-mail, which uses *SMTP* (Simple Mail Transfer Protocol). You might also have sent or received a file via *FTP* (File Transfer Protocol). Computing in general, and networking in particular, is made possible by protocols.

A more thorough explanation of protocols is in Chapter 4, "Networks."

HTTP (Hypertext Transfer Protocol) – *A protocol designed for transferring files (primarily content files) on the World Wide Web*

SMTP (Simple Mail Transfer Protocol) – *A TCP/IP-related, high-level protocol used in sending e-mail*

FTP (File Transfer Protocol) – *A protocol designed to exchange text and binary files via the Internet*

TCP and IP

TCP/IP (Transmission Control Protocol/Internet Protocol) – The suite of communication protocols used to connect hosts on the Internet

TCP (Transmission Control Protocol) – An OSI Transport layer, connection-oriented protocol designed to exchange messages between network devices

The basic networking protocols for the Internet are a pair of protocols that work together to deliver binary information from one computer to another. This protocol pair is called *TCP/IP*. The first protocol, *TCP* (Transmission Control Protocol), is responsible for the reliable delivery of data from one computer to another. It accomplishes this task by separating data into manageable, fixed-size packets, and then establishing a virtual circuit with the destination computer to transmit them. TCP also manages the sequencing of each packet and handles retransmitting packets received in error. Each data segment is appended to a header containing information about the total packet, including the sequence number and a checksum for detecting errors in the packet's transmission. Table 5-1 lists the sections of a TCP header, which is at the beginning of every TCP data packet. Although it's not necessary for you to know all the details of a TCP header, a few of these fields are used in the explanations that follow.

Table 5-1, TCP header fields

header field	size in bits
source port	16
destination port	16
sequence number	32
acknowledgment (ACK) number	32
data offset	4
reserved	6
flags	6
window	16
checksum	16
urgent pointer	16
options	32

IP (Internet Protocol) – The protocol that provides for addressing and routing Internet packets from one computer to another

TCP ensures reliable delivery of packets, but it has no provision for addressing packets to ensure that they get to the correct place. This is the job of Internet Protocol (*IP*). TCP packets are sent to the IP software, where another header is added containing addressing information. Table 5-2 shows the fields in an IP header. As with the TCP header, you don't need to be concerned with all the details of the header.

Table 5-2, IPv4 header fields

header field	size in bits
version	4
header length	4
type of service	8
total length of data packet	16
packet identification	16
flags	4
fragment offset	12
time to live (TTL)	8
protocol number	8
header checksum	16
source IP address	32
destination IP address	32
IP options	32

IP addresses

IP address – A unique 32-bit number assigned to network devices that use Internet Protocol

IPv4 – Version 4 of Internet Protocol, the most widely used version of IP

IPv6 – Version 6 of Internet Protocol has more capabilities than IPv4, including providing for far more IP addresses

Central to the operation of Internet Protocol is the *IP address* of both the source and destination. During the design of Internet Protocol, it was established that every computer (or device) attached to the Internet would have a unique identifying number. This number, or address, is a 32-bit binary value. Having a 32-bit address allows 4,294,967,296 (2^{32}) different addresses. You'd think this number would be plenty, but the addresses are in danger of running out. The most widespread version of IP, *IPv4*, uses 32-bit addresses. A new version of IP (*IPv6*) has been designed and has 128-bit addresses, allowing 2^{128} possible addresses. Considering that the world has around 6.7 billion people, there should be plenty of addresses to spare with IPv6. Converting every device to support this new version will take some time, but eventually all devices connected to the Internet will support it.

It's difficult for humans to deal with the 32-bit binary numbers that computer equipment uses, so an IP address is normally represented as a set of four decimal numbers, separated by periods. A typical IP address looks like this: 192.168.0.12. Each decimal number in an IP address represents 8 bits (an octet) of the overall 32-bit address, so each decimal value can range from 0 to 255.

For example, 192.168.0.12 is actually 11000000101010000000000000001100 in binary. See how much easier it is to remember a decimal address than a long binary number?

The total pool of IPv4 addresses is separated into groups called classes, designated by the letters A, B, C, D, and E (see Figure 5-2). The idea behind classes is that some entities, such as large corporations and universities, need to have and manage more IP addresses than small companies do. The first group of bits of the IP address identifies the network class, the next group of bits identifies the host on the network, and the final group of bits identifies the node connected to the host.

Figure 5-2, IP address classes

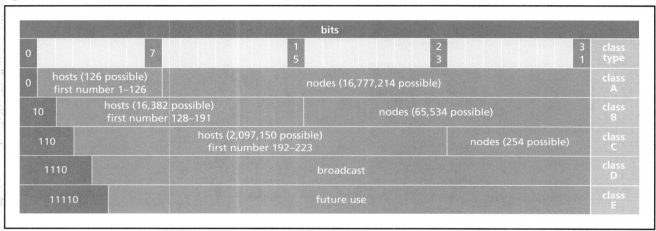

There are some special reserved addresses:

- Address 0.0.0.0 is reserved for the default network.
- Address 127.0.0.1 is used for testing as a loopback address (the local computer).
- Address 255.255.255.255 is reserved for network broadcasts (sending the same data to every computer on the network).
- Address range 10.0.0.0 to 10.255.255.255 is reserved for private networks.
- Address range 172.16.0.0 to 172.31.255.255 is reserved for private networks.
- Address range 192.168.0.0 to 192.168.255.255 is reserved for private networks.

Looking at the IP address classes shown in Figure 5-2, you can see how the range of IP addresses has been divided. A host corresponds to a corporation, university, or some other entity that needs IP addresses. Nodes are the number of devices with unique IP addresses that each host can have. Notice that Class A addresses are designed for large entities that need up to 16 million nodes,

5

but only 126 entities in the entire world can have a Class A network. An entity with a Class B license can have up to 65,534 IP addresses for its nodes, and there's room for only 16,382 Class B hosts in the world. More than two million Class C hosts are possible, but each can have only up to 254 nodes.

You can tell from the first number of your IP address what class of license your institution has. At home, you get the node part of your IP address from your ISP, which in turn might get it from a larger ISP or NBP.

IANA (Internet Assigned Numbers Authority) – The organization under contract with the U.S. government to oversee allocating IP addresses to ISPs

So who is in charge of allocating these addresses? The *IANA* (Internet Assigned Numbers Authority) maintains a high-level registry of IP addresses for the entire world, but IP addresses are actually assigned by regional agencies. *ARIN* (American Registry for Internet Numbers) is a nonprofit agency that allocates IP addresses in the United States, among other areas.

ARIN (American Registry of Internet Numbers) – The U.S. organization that assigns IP address numbers for the country and its territories

IP addresses are the key part of Internet Protocol. If a computer "knows" the IP address of another computer, components of the network, from computer to router to router to computer, can respond to the address and direct the packet to the correct communication line.

subnet – A portion of a network that shares part of an address with other portions of the network and is distinguished by a subnet number

IP addressing also supports the concept of a *subnet*, which consists of a block of IP addresses that form a separate network from a routing standpoint. Subnets are defined with a subnet mask that looks much like an IP address. For example, the subnet mask 255.255.255.0 defines a subnet in which all devices have the same first three parts of the IP address. The zero in the last position of the subnet mask indicates that each device has a different last number in the range 0 to 255.

DHCP

DHCP (Dynamic Host Configuration Protocol) – A communication protocol that automates assigning IP addresses in an organization's network

Another protocol that's a key part of the Internet is *DHCP* (Dynamic Host Configuration Protocol), which is used between a computer and a router. Usually, institutions are given a block of IP addresses they can use for their own networking purposes. They could configure each computer and set an IP address manually for each computer. DHCP, however, allows assigning each computer an IP address automatically every time it's started. This dynamic allocation of IP addresses saves network administrators time. Each computer configured for DHCP uses this protocol to communicate with the router and get an IP address. That way, the network administrator has to set up only the DHCP server to allocate a block of addresses. After the server is configured, nodes can be moved around and new computers can be added without having to determine what IP addresses are available.

router – *A device or software in a computer that determines the next network point to which a packet should be forwarded*

routers

The network hardware component that makes the Internet work is the *router*. The key to the Internet is that IP packets can be routed to the correct destination via a number of different routes. The Internet was originally designed to be immune to problems on a particular network. With routers, a packet can be sent on another line if the original line is damaged or busy (see Figure 5-3).

Figure 5-3, Routers provide many alternative routes for packets

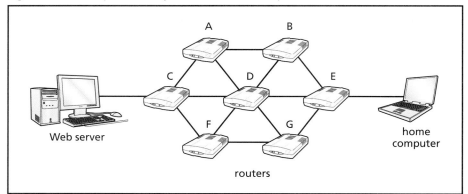

A router is actually a specialized computer connected to many different communication lines and is programmed to examine the packets it receives on one line and route them to the communication line that can get each packet closer to its final destination. Routers are used to join networks. The Internet, as mentioned, is a collection of many different networks. Routers, therefore, make the Internet possible by connecting all these networks and forwarding IP packets to other routers or to their final destination.

n o t e   The Internet would not exist without the capability of routers.

Routers work in a manner similar to the way mail is delivered. Consider a package with the address:

Cengage Learning
20 Channel Center Street
Boston, MA 02210

The postal service examines the zip code and puts the package on a truck that takes it to another truck or the airport. The postal workers, or machines in some cases, do what's necessary to get the package closer to its ultimate destination. Along the trip to Boston, various workers examine the zip code and place the package on some type of transportation that gets it closer to its destination. When the package arrives at the post office in Boston, another worker places the package on a truck that's driven to the street address for final delivery.

Now consider the IP address 69.32.142.109, which is the IP address for the Cengage Learning Web site. If you're sending some data to this IP address from your home computer, the first packet that leaves your computer is sent to a router at your ISP. The router examines the destination address in the packet header to see whether the address is within your ISP's LAN. If so, it forwards your data packet on a communication line that takes it to the computer within the ISP. Because your computer is probably on a different LAN from Cengage Learning, the router checks its internal tables (called a "table lookup") and places the packet on a communication line that takes it to another router that's closer to the ultimate destination.

When the next router gets the packet, it follows the same process. First, it examines the address to see whether it's part of the LAN to which the router is connected. If not, a table lookup is done again, and the packet is placed on another communication line that takes it to another router that's even closer to the specified address.

Finally, the packet is forwarded to a router on the Cengage Learning LAN. This router notes that the destination address is within the LAN and places the packet on the communication line connected to the specified computer.

Each packet that makes up your message is sent in this same manner, and not all packets take the same path. Routers can communicate with each other by using another special protocol. They share information about the amount of traffic on the lines to which they're connected. If the communication line the router normally uses is down or heavily congested, the router sends the packet out on another line, usually one that's still close to the destination specified by the IP address.

So that packets don't keep bouncing from router to router forever, the *time to live (TTL)* field in the IP packet header is initialized to a value (normally 40 to 60). Each time a packet passes through a router, the field is decremented by one. When the count reaches zero, the packet is discarded.

If packets can be discarded and some might never reach the specified destination, how can you be certain the data you sent is received just as you sent it? Also, because of the way routers work, the packets that make up your complete message might take many different routes to the final destination. How can you guarantee that your packets are received in the correct order? As mentioned, TCP ensures reliable delivery of data from one computer to another and checks that the data received in the packet is identical to the data that was sent.

how much is that router?

Prices of routers vary widely. Large commercial routers can cost more than $100,000; small routers for home use can sell for less than $50.

time to live (TTL) – A field in the IP header that enables routers to discard packets that have been traversing the network for too long

TCP also includes information about the order in which packets were originally sent and uses these sequence numbers to order packets after it has received all of them. If any packet is missing, the receiving TCP software sends a message back to the sending TCP software, requesting a retransmission of the missing packet. Any packets containing data errors are also requested for retransmission. Errors are detected when the receiving side detects that the checksum doesn't match the sent packet.

The combination of TCP and IP ensures that data sent from one computer to another gets there in a fast, orderly, and reliable manner. Without TCP/IP and routers, there would be no Internet.

high-level protocols

In Chapter 4, you learned about the OSI networking model and its seven layers of protocols. The suite of protocols that work with TCP/IP can be compared with the OSI layers (see Figure 5-4). TCP and IP span the Session,

> ### UDP
>
> UDP (User Datagram Protocol) is another protocol that works with IP to broadcast data. UDP differs from TCP in that it doesn't have the capability to guarantee delivery or recover from errors in transmission. UDP is often used for streaming audio or video.

Figure 5-4, TCP/IP protocols compared with the OSI model

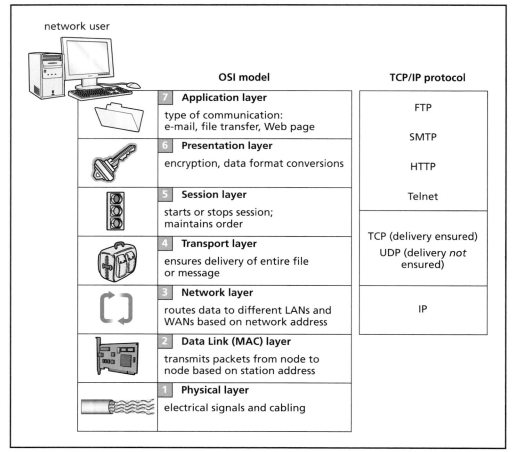

network user	OSI model	TCP/IP protocol
	7 Application layer — type of communication: e-mail, file transfer, Web page	FTP
	6 Presentation layer — encryption, data format conversions	SMTP
		HTTP
	5 Session layer — starts or stops session; maintains order	Telnet
	4 Transport layer — ensures delivery of entire file or message	TCP (delivery ensured) UDP (delivery *not* ensured)
	3 Network layer — routes data to different LANs and WANs based on network address	IP
	2 Data Link (MAC) layer — transmits packets from node to node based on station address	
	1 Physical layer — electrical signals and cabling	

Transport, and Network layers. SMTP, HTTP, FTP, and Telnet are called "high-level protocols" because they're "above" TCP and IP in the networking model. Remember that these high-level protocols use TCP/IP over the Internet to accomplish their tasks. Messages are passed from a high-level protocol to the TCP layer, which splits them into packets (if necessary), adds TCP headers, and forwards them down to the IP layer for addressing. From there, packets are sent down to the Data Link and Physical layers for transmission across the communication medium. These high-level protocols can also be used in environments other than the Internet. In that case, messages from these protocols are passed down to a lower protocol for transmission and error detection and correction.

SMTP

Simple Mail Transfer Protocol is used to send e-mail messages over the Internet. This protocol establishes a link from an e-mail client, such as Microsoft Outlook, to a mail server, such as Microsoft Exchange, and then transfers a message according to the protocol's rules. This protocol, like all others, exchanges a series of messages, called handshaking, to establish the parameters of the intended communication of data. Receipt of e-mail is handled by another protocol, *POP3* (Post Office Protocol version 3) or *IMAP* (Internet Message Access Protocol).

POP3 (Post Office Protocol version 3) – The most recent version of a standard protocol for receiving e-mail from a mail server

IMAP (Internet Message Access Protocol) – A standard protocol for accessing e-mail from a mail server

FTP

File Transfer Protocol is used for reliable and efficient transmission of data files, especially large files. FTP has been in use for many years. As with SMTP, it requires both a client program and a server program to transfer files. Most operating systems include a default command-line FTP client. In Windows, you can get to the command-line client by opening a command prompt window and typing FTP at the prompt. You can also use a Web browser to connect to an FTP server by entering the server's address in the address bar. For example, you could enter *ftp://ftp.aol.com* to connect to the AOL FTP site, as shown in Figure 5-5.

FTP clients are an important tool for computing specialists, as described in the online chapter "Software Tools for Techies."

Figure 5-5, Command-line FTP session

SSH

SSH (Secure Shell) – A network protocol for secure data exchange between two networked devices, usually in a Linux environment.

Secure Shell (*SSH*) is another network protocol used primarily with Linux and UNIX operating systems. It was designed as a secure replacement for Telnet, an early data exchange protocol. SSH enables users to connect to a remote host computer to issue commands and transfer data. Numerous SSH clients are available for download or purchase.

HTTP

Secure HTTP (S-HTTP)

A Web address that begins with *https* instead of *http* indicates a secure Web site capable of sending Web pages back in an encrypted format. Internet Explorer and Firefox show a small closed padlock icon in the status bar to indicate that a page is secure. If the padlock is open, the page is not secure.

Although all the protocols discussed so far are widely used with the Internet, Hypertext Transfer Protocol is the protocol that makes the Web possible. In the early days of the Internet, files were transferred between computers by using FTP and other older protocols. Researchers and scientists wanted a better way to transmit data, so in 1990, Tim Berners-Lee came up with the idea of the World Wide Web and built the first rudimentary browser program. Central to the idea of the World Wide Web was a Web server, a Web browser, and a protocol that allowed the two to communicate. HTTP is the protocol that allows Web browsers and Web servers to "talk" to each other. When you type in a Web address, such as *http://www.cengage.com*, the *http* tells the browser you're using Hypertext Transfer Protocol to get the Web page you're looking for.

URLs and DNS

Trying to remember the IP address of every Web site you would like to visit is difficult. When there were only a few computers on the Internet, Web pages were accessed by IP addresses. As the Internet grew, the problem of having to remember IP addresses was solved by allowing Web servers to have *domain names* and by developing Domain Name System (*DNS*). To locate a Web page or send an e-mail message, you use a Uniform Resource Locator (*URL*), which consists of the domain name followed by specific folder names and filenames, as shown in Figure 5-6. Domain names are mapped to IP addresses by a special computer called a DNS server. This computer's job is to translate domain names from URLs into IP addresses.

domain name – A name used to locate the IP address of an organization or other entity on the Internet, such as www.cengage.com

DNS (Domain Name System) – A method of translating Internet domain names into IP addresses; DNS servers are servers used in this process

URL (Uniform Resource Locator) – The English-like address of a file accessible on the Internet

Figure 5-6, Structure of a URL

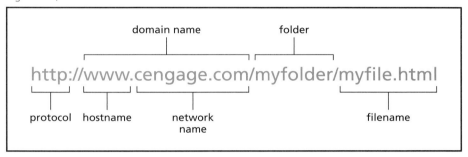

If there were only one DNS server for the entire Internet, it would get overwhelmed quickly. Instead, there are many thousands of DNS servers distributed throughout the Internet. Your ISP maintains a DNS server, but it doesn't have to contain every domain in the world. Instead, each DNS server is responsible for just a portion of the world's domains.

A domain has levels (listed in Table 5-3). You're probably familiar with the original top-level domains (TLDs) of .com, .edu, .gov, .net, .org, and .mil. You might have also heard of some newer ones, such as .biz and .info. There are also top-level, two-character domains for every country and a top-level DNS server for each top-level domain. Each of these servers has information about all the DNS servers in that domain.

Table 5-3, Top-level domains on the Internet

TLD	meaning
.aero	air-transport industry
.arpa	Address and Routing Parameter Area
.biz	business
.com	commercial
.coop	cooperative
.edu	U.S. educational
.gov	U.S. government
.info	information
.int	international organization
.mil	U.S. military
.museum	museum
.name	individuals, by name
.net	network
.org	organization
.pro	profession
.ca, .mx	Canada, Mexico, and other countries are represented by two-letter codes

For example, there's a top-level .edu server. This server has information on the IP addresses of all the lower-level servers managing domains within .edu. An educational institution, such as Weber State University, has a domain server containing information on all domains under *weber.edu*. There might be additional servers under this domain, such as *faculty.weber.edu*. The server at each level has knowledge of a lower-level server that might have better knowledge of the IP address you're looking for.

When you type a URL in a browser's address bar, you send a DNS lookup request to the DNS server at your ISP. If the URL is outside your ISP's domain, the DNS server contacts a top-level DNS server. This server might then give the address of another DNS server, and that server might give another address, until your ISP's DNS server has contacted the DNS server that knows the correct IP address and can return it to your browser. After the DNS server at your ISP has located an IP address for a URL, it saves, or caches, the address in case there's another request for the same URL.

DNS servers are smart, in that they can communicate (using a protocol, of course) with other DNS servers and stay updated with the correct IP address for any URL. Each DNS server is maintained by the network administrators of that domain. This is another example of how people acting for their own purposes on the Internet actually benefit all.

n o t e

PING is a commonly used command-line utility for resolving IP addresses from domain names and testing communication between two IP devices.

port numbers

Another problem in the early days of the Internet was that one computer with one IP address needed to be able to use multiple protocols at the same time. In addition, people wanted to be able to have multiple browsers open simultaneously, much like having multiple chat windows open so that you can chat with a dozen of your closest friends at once.

port number – An addressing mechanism used in TCP/IP as a way for a client program to specify a particular server program on a network computer and to facilitate Network Address Translation

To solve this problem, the concept of a *port number* was established. With TCP, you can go beyond specifying an IP address by specifying a unique port number (sometimes just called a port) for each application and for the sending and receiving computers in the TCP header. The combination of IP address and port number is much like a street address and apartment number. The street address gets you to the building, and the apartment number takes you to the correct apartment. Similarly, the IP address gets you to the computer, and the port number gets you to the specific program or window.

Most protocols have a standard port number. The standard port number for HTTP is 80, and for FTP, it's 21. There are 65,636 possible port numbers that can be used with each IP address. You can specify a port by appending a colon and port number following the domain or IP address. For example, *http://192.168.2.33:8080* specifies the IP address 192.168.2.33 and the port number 8080. Only the specific program set to "listen" on port 8080 can respond to the IP packets coming in to this address. Table 5-4 lists some commonly used port numbers.

Table 5-4, Commonly used TCP/IP port number assignments

port number	protocol
21	FTP (File Transfer Protocol)
22	SSH (Secure Shell)
25	SMTP (Simple Mail Transfer Protocol)
53	DNS (Domain Name System)
68	DHCP (Dynamic Host Configuration Protocol)
80	HTTP (Hypertext Transfer Protocol)
110	POP3 (Post Office Protocol version 3)
139	NetBIOS

NAT

NAT (Network Address Translation) – Used to translate an inside IP address to an outside IP address; NAT is often used to allow multiple computers to share one Internet connection

Now that you have an understanding of how TCP/IP, routers, and port numbers work, you're ready to learn a new term: *NAT* (Network Address Translation). If you set up a home network, you might use a wireless router with NAT. Your school labs probably use routers and NAT, too. With NAT, multiple computers can share one Internet connection.

NAT depends on DHCP and port numbers. A range of IP addresses reserved for internal LAN use is 192.168.0.0 to 192.168.255.255 (subnet mask 255.255.0.0). This IP address range is often used for internal LANs connected to a DHCP router. On the Internet side of a router, one IP address is presented to the Internet. That way, many computers can share one IP address. Because the 192.168 subnet is never presented to the outside Internet, all LANs can use the same addresses if they are behind a DHCP NAT router.

All computers using DHCP-assigned IP addresses can share the same Internet connection through one IP address because of ports. Each internal IP address is assigned a port number to be used with the main IP address. When HTTP or other messages come to the router from the Internet, TCP routes them to the computer with the corresponding port number.

checking your configuration

IPCONFIG – *A Windows command-line utility that can be used to display currently assigned network settings*

You can check your computer's network configuration in Windows by using the *IPCONFIG* command-line utility. To do this, click Start, Programs, Accessories, Command Prompt. At the command prompt, type IPCONFIG and press Enter. Your current IP address, subnet mask, and address of your gateway to the Internet are then displayed onscreen. The IP address is the one assigned to your computer by your network administrator or ISP. The subnet mask is a set of numbers used to identify the subnet to which you're connected. The gateway address is the IP address of a computer or router that serves as your gateway to the next level in the Internet. Figure 5-7 shows the result of typing the IPCONFIG command. You can get even more information about your network connections by typing IPCONFIG /ALL at the command prompt.

Figure 5-7, Results of using the IPCONFIG command

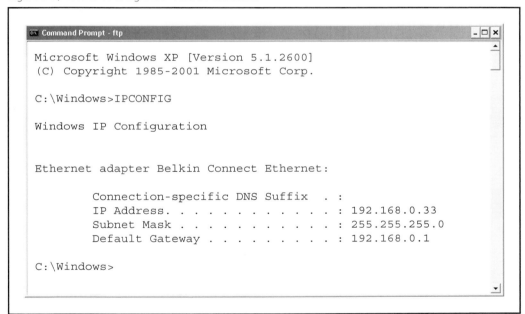

n o t e   You can get help on all available IPCONFIG options by entering IPCONFIG /H at the command prompt.

www

The www (for World Wide Web) in front of many domain names is part of the URL. The URLs *www.foxnews.com* and *foxnews.com* are not necessarily the same. Web site URLs aren't required to start with "www."

Web server – *A program running on a computer that responds to HTTP requests for Web pages and returns the pages to the requesting client*

HTML (Hypertext Markup Language) – *Markup symbols or codes inserted in a file that specify how the material is displayed on a Web page*

n o t e

HTML

You have discovered the network aspects of what goes on when you type a URL in a browser's address bar, but you might still have the question "What exactly is a Web page?"

When you type *http://www.cengage.com* in your browser's address bar, what happens? As described previously, first the URL is sent to your ISP's DNS server, and you receive the actual IP address corresponding to the domain you entered. Your browser then sends an HTTP request to this IP address. When the HTTP request gets through all the routers to the Web server you addressed, the *Web server*, which is just a computer programmed to respond to HTTP requests, sends back the requested Web page. In this case, only a domain was specified, so the server sends back a default page. Default pages typically have names such as index.htm or default.htm. The person responsible for the Web server, sometimes referred to as the Webmaster, can specify the default Web page.

What is a Web page? There are a few possible answers to this question, but most Web pages are simply text files containing the page's text information and *HTML* (Hypertext Markup Language) tags. HTML tags are formatting commands that enable the browser to display the page content in a graphical, easy-to-read format. Table 5-5 lists some commonly used HTML tags.

HTML tags are enclosed in less-than signs (<) and greater-than signs (>), and most tags come in pairs, with an opening and closing tag.

Table 5-5, Common HTML tags

tag	purpose
<HTML> </HTML>	Used to provide a boundary for the HTML document; everything between <HTML> and </HTML> is considered part of the Web page.
<HEAD> </HEAD>	The <HEAD> tags are placed inside the <HTML> tags; they provide a boundary for items that aren't part of the document but are used to direct the browser to do certain things, such as displaying a page title in the title bar.

Table 5-5, Common HTML tags (*continued*)

tag	purpose
<TITLE> </TITLE>	The <TITLE> tags surround the Web document's title, which appears in the browser's title bar when the page is displayed. The <TITLE> tags go inside the <HEAD> tags.
<BODY> </BODY>	The <BODY> tags enclose the part of the Web page document that's displayed in the browser; they're placed inside the <HTML> tags but not inside the <HEAD> tags.
 	 forces the browser display area to go to a new line. Note that there's no closing tag.
<P> </P>	The <P> tags define a paragraph in the Web document and cause a paragraph break.
<SPAN></SPAN>	The <SPAN> tags replaced a number of formatting tags. They define an area of the document and specify the way this area should be formatted.
<A> </A>	The <A> tags specify a link to another Web page or a specific location on the current page; the opening <A> tag has arguments that reference the linked page or position.
<IMG />	The <IMG> tag is used to insert an image in the document; it has arguments for specifying the location and size of the image.
<FORM> </FORM>	The <FORM> tags provide the boundaries for an input form on the Web page; other tags are placed inside the <FORM> tags to create items such as input boxes and buttons on the Web page.
<INPUT />	The <INPUT> tag specifies data input objects inside the <FORM> tags; this tag allows users to enter data on a Web page.
<TABLE> </TABLE>	The <TABLE> tags define an area on the Web page that displays data in rows and columns.
<TR> </TR>	The <TR> tags are placed inside the <TABLE> tags to signify the start of a table row.
<TD> </TD>	The <TD> tags are placed inside the <TR> tags to define a column in a table row.

Many more HTML tags are available. If you're going to design Web pages, you need to know how to use HTML, even if you use a Web page design tool, such as Adobe Dreamweaver or Mozilla SeaMonkey.

creating a simple Web page

You can create a simple Web page on your own computer and test it with your browser. Others won't be able to get to your Web page because your computer is probably not set up to be a Web server, but you can test Web pages you create without having a Web server. Simply start Notepad and type the HTML document shown in Figure 5-8. After you have entered the HTML tags exactly as shown, save the file to your hard drive or other storage media. HTML files should normally have the file extension .htm or .html. Then use Windows Explorer to find the document where you saved it. Double-click the file to open your browser and display the document with the formatting your HTML code specified (see Figure 5-9).

Figure 5-8, HTML tags for a simple Web page

```
<html>
<head>
<title>My First Web Page</title>
</head>
<body>
<p>My First Web Text<br>
 <span style="font-weight:bold; font-size:16px; font-family:Arial, Helvetica, sans-serif">
My First Table
</span>
</p>
<table width="30%" border="1">
  <tr>
    <td><b>Protocol</b></td><td><b>Purpose</b></td>
  </tr>
  <tr>
    <td>TCP</td><td>Reliable Delivery</td>
  </tr>
  <tr>
    <td>IP</td><td>Addressing</td>
  </tr>
  <tr>
    <td>HTTP</td><td>Web Pages</td>
  </tr>
</table>
</body>
</html>
```

Figure 5-9, Simple Web page displayed in a browser

HTML is not case sensitive. Even though Table 5-5 shows tags in uppercase, the browser accepts them as uppercase or lowercase. Note that HTML ignores white space, too, such as excess spaces, tabs, or lines. The HTML tags in Figure 5-8 could all be on the same line, and the browser would still display the page correctly. However, formatting HTML tags as shown in the example makes it easier for you, as an HTML developer, to create and maintain the page.

Creating Web pages in HTML is tedious, so most Web designers don't create Web pages by using straight HTML. They create pages visually with a Web design tool. You need to know HTML, however, because many times design tools don't do exactly what you want, and you have to go into the HTML code to fix it.

hyperlinks

hyperlink – A link that allows users to select a connection from one word, picture, or information object to another

One of the most powerful aspects of the Web and HTML is the ability to provide links to other pages. The HTML <A></A> tags are used for this purpose. The format of the *hyperlink* tag pair is shown in Figure 5-10, and its result in a browser window is shown in Figure 5-11. The user can click the underlined hyperlinks to be taken to the specified URL.

Figure 5-10, Using the <A> tag to create hyperlinks in a Web document

```
<html>
<head>
<title>My Second Web Page</title>
</head>
<body>
<p><span style="font-weight:bold">My Set of Hyperlinks to News Sources</span><br/>
  <a href="http://cnn.com">CNN</a><br/>
  <a href="http://foxnews.com">FOX NEWS</a><br/>
  <a href="http://www.nbc.com/nbc/NBC_News/">NBC</a><br/>
  <a href="http://abcnews.go.com/">ABC</a><br/>
  <a href="http://www.cbsnews.com/sections/home/main100.shtml">CBS</a></p>
</body>
</html>
```

Figure 5-11, Browser view of the sample hyperlink Web page

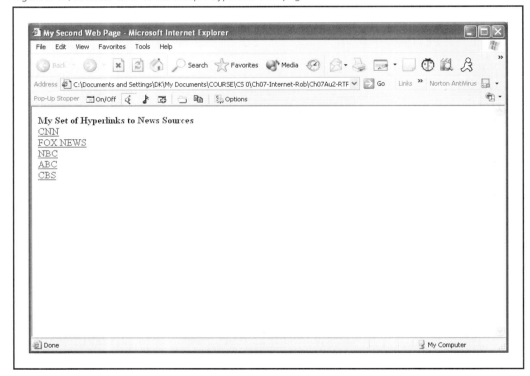

5

DHTML (Dynamic HTML) –
*An extension to HTML tags
and options for producing
Web pages that are responsive to user interaction*

JavaScript – *An interpreted
programming or script language from Netscape;
somewhat similar in capa-
bility to Microsoft VBScript*

VBScript – *An interpreted
script language from
Microsoft that's a subset of
the Visual Basic program-
ming language; often used
by Web browsers and
Active Server Pages (ASP)
servers*

**CGI (Common Gateway
Interface)** – *An older Web
server technology used for
dynamic Web page creation*

Perl – *A script programming
language similar in syntax
to the C language; often
used to develop CGI
dynamic Web pages*

ASP (Active Server Pages) –
*A Web server technology
that combines features of
HTML and JavaScript or
VBScript programming code;
used on a Web server to create Web pages dynamically*

JSP (Java Server Pages) –
*Comparable with Microsoft's
ASP technology, except it runs
only programs written in Java*

PHP – *In Web programming, a free script
language and interpreter
used primarily on Linux
Web servers*

Python – *An interpreted,
object-oriented program-
ming language similar to
Perl that has gained popularity in recent years*

Web server programs

HTML is the language Web browsers use to display Web pages. Normally, HTML pages are static; they never change from one request to another. To make information on a Web page dynamic—that is, have it be different each time it's accessed—you need a technology with more programming capabilities than the simple formatting available in standard HTML.

Web browsers allow dynamic Web pages in the form of *DHTML* (Dynamic HTML), which provides Web page animation and more responsive user interactions. Therefore, both HTML and DHTML allow including scripting code, such as *JavaScript* or *VBScript*. With these scripting languages, Web page developers can include dynamic properties, such as changes to an area of the Web page based on keystrokes, mouse movement or clicks, and timers. The Web page is still static, in that the page stored on the Web server doesn't change between accesses, but when it's displayed in the browser, items can be altered dynamically in response to various events.

For a Web page to be *completely* dynamic—to be different each time it's accessed—it has to be created at the time it's accessed. There are Web server technologies that allow this capability. *CGI* is an older technology that allows using older programming languages, such as *Perl*, to create Web pages dynamically as they're requested. CGI/Perl is being replaced by newer technologies, such as *ASP*, *JSP*, *PHP*, and *Python*. These new technologies perform the same function: They are used to create programs stored on a Web server, and when they're accessed via HTTP and a browser, they create an HTML or DHTML Web page dynamically and return it to the browser as though it were a static page.

Server-side Web technologies are used heavily on the Internet now for everything from Internet banking and shopping to television program guides. If you choose a career in computer programming, you'll probably be doing server-side dynamic Web page programming.

Web services

An outgrowth of dynamic server-side Web page programming is a fairly new technology called Web services. A *Web service* is a server-based Web program containing data to be used by other programs or Web pages, instead of being viewed. Web services are becoming popular in business to provide information, such as stock quotes, to other programs. For example, Amazon.com provides Web services that allow other Web sites to include information from Amazon.com. Web services have expanded to include "cloud computing," which is used to provide entire applications as a service on the Web.

XML

The original specification for HTML was derived from a document specification for *SGML* (Standard Generalized Markup Language). SGML is not a markup language like HTML; rather, it's a specification for what a markup language should consist of. HTML has been enormously popular because it enables people to format Web pages in appealing ways. However, HTML deals only with the *form* of a Web page, not its content.

Another implementation of SGML that has become popular is *XML* (Extensible Markup Language). XML is similar to HTML in structure, but it serves a different purpose. HTML is used only to format content for display in a browser. XML goes beyond that and provides data and information *about* that data; this information is called *metadata*. XML can be used to display Web pages, but its capability to transfer data is more useful. XML has become the standard for transferring data via the Internet. Figure 5-12 shows an example of an XML data document. You can see its similarities to HTML. The main difference is that HTML is used to format the output of a text document, whereas XML is used to transfer data via the Web. XHTML is HTML that conforms to XML syntax restrictions.

Web service – *Programming and data on a Web server designed to make data available to other Web programs*

SGML (Standard Generalized Markup Language) – *A standard for how to specify a document markup language or tag set*

XML (Extensible Markup Language) – *A markup language designed to create common information formats and share the format and data on the World Wide Web*

metadata – *In XML and in database systems, information about characteristics of the data in a file; sometimes called "data about data"*

Figure 5-12, An example of an XML data document

```xml
<?xml version="1.0" encoding="ISO-8859-1"?>
<?xml-stylesheet type="text/xsl" href="sample.xsl"?>
<dvd_library>
   <dvd>
      <id>D0146</id>
      <title>The Lord of the Rings: The Return of the King</title>
      <rating>PG-13</rating>
      <price>24.95</price>
      <review>****</review>
   </dvd>
   <dvd>
      <id>D3218</id>
      <title>Dumb and Dumber</title>
      <rating>PG-13</rating>
      <price>14.95</price>
      <review>****</review>
   </dvd>
   <dvd>
      <id>D4482</id>
      <title>Mom and Dad Save The World</title>
      <rating>PG</rating>
      <price>8.95</price>
      <review>*****</review>
   </dvd>
</dvd_library>
```

using the Internet

While you're in school, you often need to research assigned topics. The Internet has become a tremendous resource for this task. Spending time developing skills in searching the Internet can aid you in all your educational pursuits. In the early days of the Internet, newsgroups were the primary method of research.

The widespread use of the Internet has opened up many new security concerns and ethical issues, covered in Chapter 2, "Computing Security and Ethics."

search engines

The World Wide Web has hundreds of millions of Web pages. Many are useless for research, but many others are relevant and accurate. As the number of pages on the Internet has grown, it has become obvious that there's a need to search the Web for information. Many indexing methods have been tried, but the *search engine* has emerged as the preferred method for finding information on the Web. Figure 5-13 shows an example of the Bing search engine in Internet Explorer.

search engine – A program, usually accessed on the Web, that gathers and reports information available on the Internet

Figure 5-13, A search engine provides capabilities for Web searching

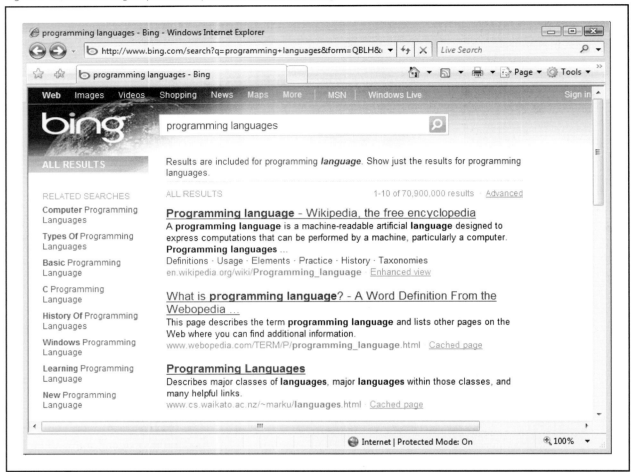

bot – *A small program, also called a spider or crawler, that accesses Web sites to gather their content for search engine indexes*

spider – *Also called a bot or crawler, a program that visits Web sites and reads their pages and other information to create entries for a search engine index*

Search engines use many different methods to build a database of Web sites that people can search, but probably the most widely used method is "crawling." Crawling makes use of a special program called a *bot* (for robot) or a *spider*. A bot starts with a few Web pages that have been submitted for indexing, and then scans these pages for links to other Web pages. The program then follows the links to these Web pages and repeats the process for every page it finds.

As the program identifies each page, it retrieves relevant words on the page and uses them to create an index to each page, based on words on the page and a special section of the HTML header called the <META> tag. This tag contains keywords that describe the Web page's content.

Most search engines make use of crawlers; others consist of human-created directories. Some search engines, such as Dogpile.com, aren't actually search engines but compilations of results from other search engines in a relevant format. Table 5-6 lists some popular search engines.

Table 5-6, Some popular Web search engines

search engine	URL
Google	*www.google.com*
AlltheWeb	*www.alltheweb.com*
Yahoo!	*www.yahoo.com*
Bing	*www.bing.com*
Ask	*www.ask.com*

As you might imagine, search engines get millions of hits per day. Therefore, search sites have to be well designed from the standpoint of both hardware and software to maintain quick response with such a high hit rate. All aspects of designing and maintaining a search site require high technical skills of the type learned in a computer science program.

As a computing student and as a professional, you'll have many opportunities to benefit from the power of search engines. You would do well to spend some time learning how to enter keywords for searches so that you can maximize your productivity when using search engines.

one last thought

From a humble start, the Internet has grown into perhaps the most widely used medium for information gathering. From research to entertainment, the Internet has become part of nearly everyone's life. Even third-world countries are beginning to use and benefit from the Internet and its resources. Many good things have come about as a result of the Internet's growth and acceptance; however, there are also problems with the Internet.

Perhaps the biggest problem with the Internet is its anonymity. When you go to a Web page, you don't know where it is. When you type your user ID, account number, or password in an input field on a Web form, you can't be completely sure where you're sending it. It's difficult to tell whether the information on a page is reliable. Identity theft and virus replication are just two of the many ethical and societal problems related to Internet use.

New technologies related to the Internet are described in the online chapter "Emerging Technologies."

One thing is certain—the Internet is here to stay. As time goes on, the Internet will become more a part of everyday life. As the Internet grows in use, computing professionals will be required to develop and use new Internet-related technologies continually.

chapter summary

- The Internet has revolutionized the world.
- The Internet is just a giant collection of LANs and WANs.
- The Internet is not owned by any single person or entity.
- You connect to the Internet through ISPs and NBPs.
- Protocols are vital to the operation of the Internet.
- TCP/IP is the protocol set that makes the Internet possible.
- TCP is used for accurate delivery of data packets.
- Every device connected to the Internet has a unique IP address.
- IP is used for addressing and routing data packets.
- IP addresses are organized into classes for block allocation.
- DHCP is a protocol for assigning IP addresses to devices automatically.
- Internet networks are organized into subnets.
- Routers are key to the operation of the Internet.
- SMTP, POP3, and IMAP are protocols for sending and receiving e-mail.
- FTP is widely used to send and receive files of various types.
- HTTP is the protocol for sending and receiving data on the Web.
- A URL is translated into an IP address by DNS.
- Port numbers are used to extend the capability of IP addressing.
- NAT is often used to allow multiple computers to share an Internet connection.
- You can check your computer configuration with the IPCONFIG command.
- HTML is the language of the World Wide Web.
- XML is a markup language used to create common information formats.
- Web pages consist of information surrounded by HTML formatting tags.
- Scripting languages can be used on Web pages to make them dynamic.
- Hyperlinks are used on Web pages to connect to other pages.
- Web services make data available to other programs.
- Search engines are used to find Web pages on the Internet.

key terms

ARIN (*177*)	NAT (*186*)
ASP (*193*)	NBP (*172*)
bot (*196*)	Perl (*193*)
CGI (*193*)	PHP (*193*)
DHCP (*177*)	POP (*172*)
DHTML (*193*)	POP3 (*181*)
DNS (*183*)	port number (*185*)
domain name (*183*)	Python (*193*)
FTP (*173*)	router (*178*)
HTML (*188*)	search engine (*195*)
HTTP (*173*)	SGML (*194*)
hyperlink (*191*)	SMTP (*173*)
IANA (*177*)	spider (*196*)
IMAP (*181*)	SSH (*182*)
IP (*174*)	subnet (*177*)
IP address (*175*)	TCP (*174*)
IPCONFIG (*187*)	TCP/IP (*174*)
IPv4 (*175*)	time to live (TTL) (*179*)
IPv6 (*175*)	URL (*183*)
ISP (*172*)	VBScript (*193*)
JavaScript (*193*)	Web server (*188*)
JSP (*193*)	Web service (*194*)
metadata (*194*)	XML (*194*)

test yourself

1. The Internet is a collection of _____ and _____.
2. What does the acronym ISP stand for?

3. What is an NBP?

4. What is the protocol SMTP used for?

5. Which Internet protocol is responsible for reliable delivery of data from one computer to another?

6. Which Internet protocol manages sequencing data packets?

7. Which Internet protocol maintains port information?

8. What is the size, in bits, of an IPv4 address?

9. Which IPv4 class allows the greatest number of hosts?

10. What is the IP address 255.255.255.255 reserved for?

11. What is the regional agency that assigns IP addresses for the United States and its territories?

12. What is the function of DHCP in networking?

13. What is a router?

14. What prevents TCP/IP packets from bouncing from router to router forever?

15. What is the purpose of FTP?

16. Which network device is used to resolve domain names into IP addresses?

17. What is the Windows command-line utility to check your computer's network configuration?

18. What is the language of the World Wide Web?

19. What programs are used to "crawl" the Web?

practice exercises

1. The Internet is owned by:

   a. ARIN
   b. The FCC
   c. The United Nations
   d. None of the above

2. Internet providers maintain a switching center called a:

   a. Point of presence
   b. Backbone
   c. Router
   d. None of the above

3. The purpose of HTTP is to:

   a. Format Web pages
   b. Transfer Web pages
   c. Route addresses
   d. None of the above

4. Which of the following is not an Internet-related protocol?

   a. HTTP
   b. HTML
   c. TCP
   d. FTP

5. How many possible ports are allowed in TCP?

   a. 8
   b. 16
   c. 65,536
   d. 16,137,285

6. Which portion of the TCP/IP protocol suite provides error detection and correction?

   a. TCP
   b. IP
   c. Both
   d. Neither

7. How many different hosts can be granted a Class A IP address allocation?

   a. 16,137,285
   b. 65,536
   c. 16,382
   d. 126

8. Which Internet protocol is used to assign IP addresses dynamically?

   a. TCP
   b. DHCP
   c. HTTP
   d. DNS

9. Routers are critical to the operation of the Internet.

   a. True
   b. False

10. Which Internet component is responsible for decrementing the TTL field?

   a. Router
   b. Switch
   c. DNS
   d. Packet

11. Which of the following is an example of a high-level protocol?

   a. TCP
   b. IP
   c. DHCP
   d. SMTP

12. Which of the following protocols makes the Web possible?

   a. FTP
   b. Telnet
   c. HTTP
   d. None of the above

13. Which of the following is an example of a URL?

   a. www.cengage.com
   b. 192.168.0.22
   c. 1110111010111010110101
   d. HTTP

14. How many DNS servers does the Internet have?

   a. 1
   b. 2
   c. Thousands
   d. Millions

15. What is the standard port number for HTTP?

   a. 1
   b. 21
   c. 50
   d. 80

16. How many IP addresses are presented to the Internet when NAT is used?

   a. 1
   b. 21
   c. Thousands
   d. Unlimited

17. Which of the following is an example of an HTML tag?

   a. <HTTP>
   b. <HTML>
   c. <TCP>
   d. <DHCP>

18. Which HTML tag is used to provide links to other pages?

   a. <HTTP>
   b. <LINK>
   c. <A>
   d. <P>

19. XML is just another name for HTML.

    a. True
    b. False

20. Bots are used by _____ to crawl the World Wide Web.

    a. Routers
    b. Search engines
    c. XML
    d. TCP/IP

digging deeper

1. What is the purpose of each field in a TCP packet header?

2. What is the purpose of each field in an IP packet header?

3. How are routers programmed?

4. What is the difference between a router, a gateway, and a switch, as applied to the Internet?

5. What is the process for obtaining a block of IP addresses for your business?

discussion topics

1. In what ways has the Internet affected society?

2. What is meant by the term "digital divide"?

3. What are the security issues related to the Internet, and how are they being addressed?

4. What are the steps involved in an HTTP request?

5. How does your school's computer lab connect to the Internet?

Internet research

1. What are the major search engines, and what are the strengths of each?

2. Find a map of Internet backbone communication lines. Where are the main lines located?

3. What are the major Web browsers? What are their strengths and weaknesses?

4. What is the membership makeup of ARIN?

5. Research some domain names of your choosing to see whether they're available.

chapter

6

database fundamentals

- Consider the widespread use of databases
- Take a brief tour of database development history
- Learn basic database concepts
- Be introduced to popular database management software
- See how normalization makes your data more organized
- Explore the database design process
- Understand data relationships
- Gain an understanding of Structured Query Language (SQL)
- Learn some common SQL commands

the lighter side of the lab
by spencer

I don't know any two words that make me cringe more than the words "corrupted data." I've spent the past four years working in technical support for a local software company. If you haven't had the opportunity to work in technical support, here's a sample of a typical call:

ME: Hi, you've reached technical support. This is Spencer. CUSTOMER: Hi. I got an error message yesterday when I did something in the program. What do I do to fix it?

ME: All right. Do you remember what the message said? CUSTOMER: No.

ME: Do you remember what you were doing when you got the error message? CUSTOMER: Who am I, Einstein?

ME: Okay, try opening the program. CUSTOMER: Oh, here we go! It says the data is corrupted. What do I click?

ME (cringing): We'll need to restore from one of your backups. CUSTOMER: Okay. Is that something I need to order?

(Brief pause) ME: Backups. You know—the thing you're supposed to do every time you leave the program. CUSTOMER: Oh, yeah! That message is so annoying. It comes up every time I close. I always just click No. Is there any way to turn that message off?

(Brief pause) ME: All right, let's search your computer to see whether we can find a recent backup. Click Start. CUSTOMER: Is that a right-click or left-click? ME: Left-click. Now click Search. CUSTOMER: Is that a right-click or a left-click? ME: Left-click. It will always be a left-click unless I say it's a right-click. CUSTOMER: Got it.

ME: Now click All Files and Folders. CUSTOMER: That's a left-click, right? ME: Yes! Now, do you see where it says "All or part of file name"? CUSTOMER: My computer doesn't have that. ME: Okay, it should be the first thing on the Search screen. CUSTOMER: No, it's not here.

(Brief pause) ME: Okay, it has to be there somewhere. CUSTOMER: Nope . . . nope . . . oh, wait! You mean right here in the middle of the screen? ME: (Sigh)

And so it goes for the next hour. The good news is that I've discovered my head actually supports bus mastering. My mouth handles the technical support with absolutely no communication to or from my brain! I sometimes catch myself 20 minutes into a call not remembering a word anybody has said. This is good because it frees up brain cycles to think about more important things—like the day I won't have to take another support call.

why you need to know about...
databases

Can you imagine a world where no data was organized? How could a baseball announcer know that the batter hits .357 every other Thursday against this right-handed pitcher when the temperature is below 60 degrees, the moon is full, and the umpire ate tacos for dinner? Who would ever think to relate this information to listeners? Baseball announcers have a multitude of facts at their fingertips because someone has entered information into a database, allowing announcers to extract it based on any criteria they want.

Without databases, how could a shopper find that rare DVD of *Godzilla Versus the Centrino Processor* with so many other DVDs to choose from? It would be like finding a needle in a haystack! Instead of searching through all DVD titles by name, you would have to start at the first DVD offered for sale and scan through each item one at a time, hoping you find the DVD you want.

To be an effective computer professional, you must know the correct way to design databases. Designing a database begins with analyzing the information that needs to be stored. At the end of the design phase is a process called normalization, which ensures that the database is accurate and reliable. You should also know the basics of how information is retrieved from relational databases with statements called Structured Query Language (SQL, pronounced "sequel" or sometimes S-Q-L) and be familiar with the major players in the database management software arena.

database applications

database – *Data that has been logically related and organized into a file or set of files to allow access and use*

Data that has been organized and logically related to allow access, retrieval, and use of that data is called a *database*. A database is a storage mechanism that enables you to relate data logically so that you can extract it later with little effort and even "query" the data to create new information.

Many software applications use some type of database as the data repository. Think of what would happen if applications had no way to track information. How could a bank keep track of your account? How could a healthcare provider keep track of your medical history? How could the government keep track of criminals? Without a database, most applications would be useless and send the technical world spiraling back decades into the past. The paper trails would be endless, and trees all over the world would have shivers of fright running up their bark. It's amazing to think of all the places databases are being used and how they make your life simpler.

What type of database applications have you seen today? If you can't think of any, reflect on the last time you went to the grocery store. Information about all the food items is stored in a database. How else would the store know how much to charge for an item? At the same time you're purchasing the item, a "Quantity" column in the food item database is probably being updated automatically in a database file. As another common example, where did that telemarketer get your phone number? It was probably purchased from a vendor who supplied a database including your name, phone number, address, and other pertinent information. Here are other examples of activities that use database applications:

- Student grading
- Library inventory
- Genealogy studies
- Social Security payments
- Real estate sales
- Video store rentals
- Retail sales
- Space shuttle missions

Database applications are everywhere, so database development is an essential part of your daily life. As a computer professional, working with databases will likely be an important part of your career. Before diving into the fundamentals of databases and the systems developed to manage them, take a short historical tour.

brief history of database management systems

Back in the mid-1970s, kids were frantically searching neighborhoods for empty pop bottles. Each unbroken bottle meant a nice return of at least five cents that could be applied toward a pack of baseball cards. Although the hard stick of bubble gum that came with the card lost its flavor within minutes, kids spent hours reading the information on the cards and sorting them in different orders. Some liked their cards sorted by team name, and others sorted the cards by position. Some cards were even sorted by team, position, and name or by card number. In other words, the information could be sorted in many different ways, with each owner determining the sort order.

A more recent craze is sharing music files over the Internet. People organize their music files by artist, song title, music category, or other attributes. Like baseball card collectors, music lovers spend hours organizing their music files. Whether it's baseball cards or music files, things are collected and organized according to personal preferences.

So what do these crazes have to do with databases? In the early 1970s, while many thoughts turned to impeachment of Richard Nixon, the end of the Cold War, and the movie *The Exorcist*, E. F. Codd and C. J. Date were hard at work for IBM creating a theoretical model for designing data structures. This model became the foundation on which database applications have been designed for almost the past three decades. Believe it or not, kids collecting and sorting baseball cards and people collecting and sorting music files were putting into practice some of the database theories Codd and Date conceived.

The development of software for organizing and sorting large amounts of data began with two mainframe products: System R by IBM and Ingres, created at the University of California, Berkeley. Both systems used *Structured Query Language (SQL)* to query or extract information from databases. This language became a standard database feature. As PCs became more popular in businesses, users clamored for the type of software packages they were accustomed to using on large mainframes. Therefore, the road was paved for other software vendors to create *database management system (DBMS)* packages.

Structured Query Language (SQL) – A special language used to maintain database structure and modify, query, and extract information

database management system (DBMS) – A program for managing storage, access, and modifications to a database

In 1978, while working for Martin Marietta and managing the database for the Viking spacecraft ground support system, C. Wayne Ratliff developed a database program called Vulcan. In 1980, the program was renamed dBASE II and was marketed for PCs by Ashton-Tate. (There never was a dBASE I, but the name dBASE II was chosen to give consumers more confidence in a product that seemed to have been tested already.) dBASE II was such a success that soon Ashton-Tate dominated the PC DBMS market. The popularity of dBASE opened the door for other companies to market PC database products, such as Paradox, Microsoft Access, and FoxPro, trying to include features dBASE II lacked or improve on weaknesses in dBASE II.

note

In 1991, Borland Software Corporation acquired Ashton-Tate and its dBASE products. Today, dBASE is not a serious contender in the PC database market.

distributed data

Databases were originally created to act as a central data repository, but today, a database might be stored on several computers that can be in different physical locations. This arrangement is called a distributed database. The main advantages of a distributed database are flexibility, reliability, expandability, and efficiency. Disadvantages are cost and complexity.

As mainframe database systems, such as System R and Ingres, and PC systems, such as dBASE, became widespread, it became evident just how powerful databases were in providing essential information for corporate decision making and enhancing almost all business systems, from inventory management to customer support. Since then, databases have become an essential and critical part of business and, therefore, of software development.

In today's computer industry, every company that wants to use a database must decide which DBMS package to use. There's a wide variety of databases on the market (see a sample in Table 6-1), each with its own strengths and weaknesses.

Table 6-1, Popular database management systems

DMBS name	vendor	computer type
Access	Microsoft	PC, server, PDA
DB2	IBM	PC, mid-range server, mainframe
InterBase	Embarcadero Technologies	PC, server
MySQL	MySQL AB (public domain)	PC, mid-range server
Oracle	Oracle	PC, mid-range server, mainframe, PDA
Paradox	Corel	PC, server
SQL Server	Microsoft	server
Sybase	Sybase	PC, mid-range server, PDA

note

Microsoft Access was developed in the early 1990s and is included in the Microsoft Office Professional suite.

n o t e

MySQL is one of the most popular open-source databases, often used on Web sites.

database management system fundamentals

take a test drive

As a computer professional, you might have to recommend a specific DBMS to use as the company standard. What will you recommend? If you look at advertisements and product literature, all DBMSs look good. One thing you can do now to prepare is to start learning popular DBMS packages. Take them for a test spin and formulate your own opinions as to what you like and dislike about the products. Many database vendors have trial versions you can download and test to see whether you like what the package has to offer.

A DBMS helps manage data and extract information from a database by using a query language. It also manages the database structure and controls access to data stored in the database, thus guaranteeing data integrity and data consistency.

The main functions of a DBMS are the following:

- Manage database security.
- Manage multiple users' access to the database.
- Manage database backup and recovery.
- Ensure data integrity.
- Provide an end-user interface to the database.
- Provide a query language that allows users to modify and view database information easily.

n o t e

The person who maintains the database in a company is called the database administrator (DBA).

database concepts

table or entity – *Data arranged in rows and columns, much like a spreadsheet*

column, field, or attribute – *A specific piece of information in a table row*

row, record, or tuple – *A collection of columns*

To understand the functionality of a DBMS, you must first understand the basic elements of a database. A database can contain one or more tables. Each *table* or *entity* is divided into rows and columns, much like a spreadsheet. Figure 6-1 shows a database table with information about a music collection. Each *column* (also called a *field* or an *attribute*) represents a specific piece of information (Song_Name, Track_Num, Album_Num, Album_Name, and so on), and a *row* (*record* or *tuple*) represents a collection of columns. Each song is considered a record or row in the database and contains information that can be arranged in columns describing the row.

Figure 6-1, A database table consists of rows and columns

domain – Set of possible values for a column

The set of possible values for each column is called the *domain*. For instance, the domain for the column labeled Genre_Code in Figure 6-1 is as follows:

- ALT—Alternative
- BLU—Blues
- CLA—Classic Rock
- CW—Country Western
- EL—Easy Listening
- GOS—Gospel
- HR—Hard Rock
- JAZ—Jazz
- NW—New Wave
- POP—Pop
- RAP—Rap
- RB—R & B

n o t e

Sometimes a program developer designs software so that a drop-down list box displays all the domain values users can select. This feature helps keep data consistent and prevent user entry errors.

As mentioned, a collection of columns referring to one item is called a row or tuple. A collection of rows forms the table's contents, and a collection of one or more tables makes up a database. A database can contain one or more tables that are related through columns designated as key columns. This organized structure gives software developers and end users easy access. The information in each table can be accessed more quickly by using indexes, discussed next.

indexes

An *index* is a special file that occupies its own space and specifies one or more columns that determine how information stored in a table can be accessed more efficiently. For example, a table consisting of rows and columns can represent music in your music database. The rows represent songs, and the columns contain more detailed information, such as Song_Name, Track_Num, and Album_Num. Many different types of information you encounter every day are accessed with an index. Can you imagine a phone book with the information ordered sequentially? In other words, new phone numbers are placed at the end of the phone book. You would have to search for hours to find the phone number you want. Instead, information in a table (or phone book) is organized into an index or order by choosing specific columns. For instance, the Last Name and First Name columns organize the phone book so that you can retrieve phone numbers simply by knowing the alphabet.

tables versus databases

How do tables and databases relate to each other? In most database packages, the terms database and table are *not* synonymous. *Database* refers to the file that stores information about the tables; *table* is the data file with rows and columns of information.

Think of all of the MP3 files stored on your favorite music Web site. What if the songs were stored in a random order? Would you want to spend all night searching row by row, trying to find a song? Definitely not! You have better things to do, such as reading this textbook and excelling in your computer courses.

note

The primary advantage of using an index is being able to find data in a table without scanning the entire table.

more's company

A company can (and usually does) have many databases, with each database acting as a virtual filing cabinet for related information.

By using an index, you can access all songs in columns that have been indexed more quickly. For instance, you can sort songs by artist in ascending order, with As at the top, or you can sort songs alphabetically in descending order, with Zs at the top. You could even sort songs by using a combination of two columns, such as artist and song title. Using indexes with these sorts can speed up access time dramatically. The disadvantage of using indexes is that they require more storage space in the database, and operations for updating data take a little longer because the indexes must also be updated.

Every table in a database should have some type of index defined to make searching quicker and data retrieval more organized.

an example of indexing

Imagine you're walking down the aisle in a grocery store, pushing the cart with wobbly wheels. The cart acts like a database because it holds the food items you want to purchase and store at your home. As you pass the frozen foods section, you open one of the freezer doors and grab the cheap one-item frozen pizza with simulated cheese (an essential substance for serious database developers). You take note of the UPC, brand name, amount, description, and price and throw it in your cart. You push your wobbly cart over to the drinks aisle and pick up a six-pack of your favorite beverage loaded with caffeine so that you can finish your projects on time. Again, you notice the UPC, brand name, amount, description, and price and add it to your cart. The process of gathering food items continues until your cart is full or you have bought all the food items on your list. You might not have realized it, but you have created your own database by placing food items in your shopping cart. Your database of food items is compared against the store's database when you go through the checkout stand. Each item can be related to a row in the database. Figure 6-2 shows how some items purchased at the grocery might appear in a database.

Figure 6-2, You use database concepts in your everyday life

	UPC	Brand_Name	Amount	Description	Price
▶	020188081029	Beefies	1	Frozen Pizza	$3.25
	993059377373	Pure Juice	6	Electrify Soda	$2.29
	768498522313	Popper	6	Microwave Popcorn	$2.59
	869488263567	SugarD	12	Sweet Cakes	$3.79
	896746255671	Beefies	2	Chimichanga	$0.79
	233254518898	CoolQ	1	Root Beer Ice Cream	$4.25
	574827764671	CheesePleeze	6	Macaroni and Cheese	$0.49
	985183848511	CoolQ	1	Cookie Dough Ice Cream	$4.25
	372883718232	Popper	3	Grandma Goose Popcorn	$1.79
✱			0		$0.00

Record: |◀ ◀ | 1 | ▶ ▶| ▶✱ | of 9

Each row in the database has similar attributes that might have different information describing the product. Notice that each food item purchased has information that's shared by other food items, such as brand name, amount, description, and price.

As stated earlier, columns can be specified as an index for quicker access when rows are sorted. When columns are used to determine the sort order of information, they are called *sort keys*. There can be one key or a combination of keys determining the sort order.

The information stored in a database is kept in natural or sequential order, so the first record you see in the database is the first record you created and stored in the database file. Using keys to sort database information allows you to view

sort key – *In a database table, one or more columns used to determine the data's sort order*

the data in any order you want. To see how keys are used to determine sort order, refer to the shopping cart data in Figure 6-2. The order in which records are displayed is the order in which they were entered. For example, if the UPC column is the sort key, records in the database are sorted in ascending order, using the value stored in the UPC column. The view of the database is then the same as in Figure 6-3.

Figure 6-3, Database records sorted by using the UPC column as a key

UPC	Brand_Name	Amount	Description	Price
020188081029	Beefies	1	Frozen Pizza	$3.25
233254518898	CoolQ	1	Root Beer Ice Cream	$4.25
372883718232	Popper	3	Grandma Goose Popcorn	$1.79
574827764671	CheesePleeze	6	Macaroni and Cheese	$0.49
768498522313	Popper	6	Microwave Popcorn	$2.59
869488263567	SugarD	12	Sweet Cakes	$3.79
896746255671	Beefies	2	Chimichanga	$0.79
985183848511	CoolQ	1	Cookie Dough Ice Cream	$4.25
993059377373	Pure Juice	6	Electrify Soda	$2.29
*		0		$0.00

Food_by_UPC : Table — Record: 1 of 9

You can also combine sort keys to further organize the data. For example, Figure 6-4 shows data ordered by Brand_Name and Description. That is, first it's sorted by Brand_Name, and then it's sorted by Description, in ascending alphabetical order.

Figure 6-4, Database records sorted by Brand_Name and Description

UPC	Brand_Name	Amount	Description	Price
896746255671	Beefies	2	Chimichanga	$0.79
020188081029	Beefies	1	Frozen Pizza	$3.25
574827764671	CheesePleeze	6	Macaroni and Cheese	$0.49
985183848511	CoolQ	1	Cookie Dough Ice Cream	$4.25
233254518898	CoolQ	1	Root Beer Ice Cream	$4.25
372883718232	Popper	3	Grandma Goose Popcorn	$1.79
768498522313	Popper	6	Microwave Popcorn	$2.59
993059377373	Pure Juice	6	Electrify Soda	$2.29
869488263567	SugarD	12	Sweet Cakes	$3.79
*		0		$0.00

Food_by_Brand_Desc : Table — Record: 1 of 9

All the information for the database is kept in the database file. This file acts as a repository of information and can be viewed or manipulated with a wide variety of media, such as reports, forms, labels, low-level file I/O, and source code, to name a few.

normalization

With all the information being stored around the world, a set of database standards has evolved to ensure that information is retrieved and stored correctly. The set of rules that dictates how databases are designed is called *normalization*. Normalization is the process of structuring tables to eliminate duplication and inconsistencies in the data structure. In plain language, normalization tells you how to organize data stored in the database so that the application functions correctly, and the amount of duplicate and unwanted information stored is minimized. The process of normalization works in stages called normal forms, such as first normal form, second normal form, and third normal form. From a database design point of view, second normal form is better than first normal form, and third normal form is better than second normal form. There are five normal forms (or six, if you count a refinement called Boyce-Codd normal form, BCNF), but for most database applications, third normal form is as high as you need to go.

note

The rules of normalization have been standardized and accepted by the computer industry. By following existing standards, the database work that computer professionals perform is consistent, no matter what the company or project is.

Normalization solves three problems that often occur when designing databases. First, if a database isn't normalized correctly, it can't represent certain real-world information items. Second, a database can contain redundancies (repetitions) in data, which wastes time and storage space. Third, important information might have been excluded during the design of data structures. By following the rules of normalization, you can make sure your tables are defined accurately to ensure the integrity and stability of your database application.

preparing for normalization: gathering columns

Before you begin creating a database and following the normalization process, you need to make a list of all pertinent fields (columns or attributes) you think are needed in the database application. Often you can create this list by looking at reports end users have given you, such as the Song inventory report shown in Figure 6-5.

Figure 6-5, End-user report with table columns highlighted

Songs

Artist_Name	*Song_Name*	*Track_Num*	*Album_Name*	*Media_Type*	*Genre_Code*
B.B. King	The Thrill is Gone	8	The Best of B.B. King	MP3	BLU
Nirvana	Come As You Are	3	Nevermind	MP3	NW
Nirvana	Lithium	5	Nevermind	MP3	NW
Oingo Boingo	Only a Lad	16	Best O Boingo	CD	NW
Peter Gabriel	Big Time	14	Shaking the Tree	CD	POP
Peter Gabriel	Sledgehammer	3	Shaking the Tree	CD	POP
The Beach Boys	Sloop John B	7	Pet Sounds	Vinyl	CLA
Toby Keith	American Soldier	3	Shock'n Y'all	MP3	CW
Toby Keith	Beer For My Horses	5	Unleashed	MP3	CW
U2	One Tree Hill	9	The Joshua Tree	CD	NW
U2	With or Without You	3	The Joshua Tree	CD	NW

Often each field in a report is a field or column in a table or consists of one or more combined table fields. Write these fields in your column list and continue this process for each report supplied by end users.

The next step is to review the input forms users have specified. Each field in an input form used in an application (see Figure 6-6) should be a column in a table. Add these columns to your master column list and continue the process for each form in the program you're creating.

Figure 6-6, Additional table columns can be gleaned from input forms

Songs	_ □ ×
Song_Name	Sledgehammer
Track_Num	3
Album_Num	10
Album_Name	Shaking the Tree
Media_Type	CD
Artist_Code	PG
Artist_Name	Peter Gabriel
Genre_Code	POP

Record: ◄◄ ◄ [1] ► ►► ►* of 11

The next step is to review all documentation for any fields that aren't in the end-user reports or forms. After gathering and documenting all the columns on your master column list, you're ready to move to the next step: creating tables of columns by combining associated fields. For this task, you logically group information that depends on other information, such as information pertaining to an artist and all his or her song files. To create the music database, you need to gather all the data for the rows and columns that relate to each other, such as the ones in Figure 6-7.

Figure 6-7, Columns relating to song files are placed in one table

Song_Name	Track_Num	Album_Num	Album_Name	Media_Type	Artist_Code	Artist_Name	Genre_Code
Sledgehammer	3	10	Shaking the Tree	CD	PG	Peter Gabriel	POP
Big Time	14			CD	PG	Peter Gabriel	POP
Lithium	5	24	Nevermind	MP3	NIRV	Nirvana	NW
Come As You Are	3			MP3	NIRV	Nirvana	NW
Sloop John B	7	45	Pet Sounds	Vinyl	BB	The Beach Boys	CLA
Only a Lad	16	78	Best O Boingo	CD	OB	Oingo Boingo	NW
The Thrill is Gone	8	98	The Best of B.B. King	MP3	BBK	B.B. King	BLU
With or Without You	3	146	The Joshua Tree	CD	U2	U2	NW
One Tree Hill	9			CD	U2	U2	NW
Beer For My Horses	5	826	Unleashed	MP3	TK	Toby Keith	CW
American Soldier	3	911	Shock'n Y'all	MP3	TK	Toby Keith	CW

getting ready for normalization

1. Create a list of all columns or fields you need in the database application by reviewing the specifications and forms supplied by end users.

2. Create tables of columns by grouping associated fields logically.

3. Continue grouping fields until all the columns have been assigned to one big table.

first normal form (1NF) – Eliminating repeating fields or groups of fields from the table and confirming that every column has only one value by creating a new record in the table

All these fields relate to each other and describe song files. Continue this process until all the columns/fields have been assigned to one table. With all the fields defined and placed in one table, you're ready to begin the normalization process of refining your database design.

first normal form

After you have data in column and row format, you have what's known as an unnormalized table. At this point, you could define a database table based on this design, but redundancies and dependencies can cause problems when the table is in use. The table needs to be normalized to a stable state to prevent these problems.

The first step in the normalization process is to modify tables' rows and columns to ensure that each row-column intersection has only one value. As each new row is created to accommodate repeating groups, cell data from the original row needs to be copied into each column.

In the unnormalized table of Figure 6-8, the Song_Name column has two values in the first row. Note that some columns of the first row have one value and some have two values. To put the table into *first normal form (1NF)*, any columns containing two values need to be separated into two rows. The columns that didn't originally have two values are duplicated in the new row.

Figure 6-8, Columns with duplicate data need to be simplified

Unnormalized Data

Artist_Code	Song_Name	Artist_Name	Album_Num	Album_Name	Track_Num	Media_Type	Genre_Code
TK	American Soldier	Toby Keith	911	Shock'n Y'all	3	MP3	CW
	Beer For My Horses		826	Unleashed	5		
P G	Big Time	Peter Gabriel	10	Shaking the Tree	14	CD	POP
	Sledgehammer				3		
NIRV	Come As You Are	Nirvana	24	Nevermind	3	MP3	NW
	Lithium				5		
U2	One Tree Hill	U2	146	The Joshua Tree	9	CD	NW
	With or Without You				3		
OB	Only a Lad	Oingo Boingo	78	Best O Boingo	16	CD	NW
BB	Sloop John B	The Beach Boys	45	Pet Sounds	7	Vinyl	CLA
BBK	The Thrill is Gone	B.B. King	98	The Best of B.B. King	8	MP3	BLU

first normal form

Eliminate repeated column values by making a new row in the table and copying the common data to the column values.

You can see that the Songs table in Figure 6-8 is not in first normal form because the Album_Num, Album_Name, Artist_Code, Artist_Name, Media_Type, and Genre_Code columns contain multiple values in a row-column intersection. First normal form requires that columns contain only single values, as shown in Figure 6-9. To solve this problem, create a new record for the duplicated column values and then fill in the blanks so that every column in the record has a value.

Figure 6-9, Songs table in 1NF

First Normal Form Data

Artist_Code	Song_Name	Artist_Name	Album_Num	Album_Name	Track_Num	Media_Type	Genre_Code
TK	American Soldier	Toby Keith	911	Shock'n Y'all	3	MP3	CW
TK	Beer For My Horses	Toby Keith	826	Unleashed	5	MP3	CW
P G	Big Time	Peter Gabriel	10	Shaking the Tree	14	CD	POP
P G	Sledgehammer	Peter Gabriel	10	Shaking the Tree	3	CD	POP
NIRV	Come As You Are	Nirvana	24	Nevermind	3	MP3	NW
NIRV	Lithium	Nirvana	24	Nevermind	5	MP3	NW
U2	One Tree Hill	U2	146	The Joshua Tree	9	CD	NW
U2	With or Without You	U2	146	The Joshua Tree	3	CD	NW
OB	Only a Lad	Oingo Boingo	78	Best O Boingo	16	CD	NW
BB	Sloop John B	The Beach Boys	45	Pet Sounds	7	Vinyl	CLA
BBK	The Thrill is Gone	B.B. King	98	The Best of B.B. King	8	MP3	BLU

Notice that there's still redundant (repeated) data in some columns. This problem is addressed during a later stage of normalization.

second normal form

primary key (PK) – A column or combination of columns that uniquely identifies a row in a table

The next step is assigning a primary key to the table and identifying the functional dependencies in the table. A *primary key (PK)* is simply a column or combination of columns that uniquely identifies a row in a table. For instance, for all the students in your computer science course, the primary key could be the Student ID because there are no repeating IDs in the school. Every student has a unique number that identifies him or her. Other examples of primary keys that make a record unique are the following:

- Car VIN (vehicle identification number)
- SSN (Social Security number)
- Driver's license number
- Purchase order number
- Tax ID
- Bank account number

Before you learn the second step to normalization, you need to understand the concept of a *determinant*. A determinant in a database is any column you can use to determine the value assigned to another column in the same row. In simpler terms, the Artist_Code column is a determinant for the Artist_Name column. The value PG determines that the Artist_Name is Peter Gabriel.

determinant – *In a database, any column you can use to determine the value assigned to another column in the same row*

note

By default, a primary key is a determinant.

---

second normal form

Apply 2NF to tables with multiple keys to eliminate redundant data.

A functional dependency is the combination of a determinant and the columns it determines. For example, the Artist_Name column is functionally dependent on the Artist_Code column. The artist name "Peter Gabriel" is dependent on the code PG.

Still confused? Here's another example. You probably have a student ID number. In a database, your ID number can be used to determine your name, address, and other information. Your name, however, couldn't be used to determine your student ID because other students might have the same name.

second normal form (2NF) – *First normal form has already been applied to the table, and every column that isn't part of the primary key is fully dependent on the primary key*

functional dependency – *A column's value is dependent on another column's value*

composite key – *A primary key made up of more than one column*

A table is in *second normal form (2NF)* if it's already in first normal form and every column that isn't part of the primary key is fully dependent on the primary key. This concept is called *functional dependency*. A column is functionally dependent on another column if for each value of the first column, there's only one value for the second column.

Note that the primary key for the Songs table in Figure 6-9 is a composite key of Artist_Code, Song_Name, and Album_Num. These three fields combined account for unique song records because the song title could be duplicated by multiple artists, but adding Album_Num makes each record unique. This type of combined key is called a *composite key* because more than one column makes up the primary key. To put a table in second normal form, you must determine which columns in the table aren't dependent on the entire primary key.

6

n o t e   If a 1NF table does not have a composite key, by default, it's in second normal form.

For example, the Track_Num column is dependent on the Song_Name, Artist_Code, and Album_Num columns because there's only one track number for a specific combination of song, artist, and album. On the other hand, the Album_Name column is not dependent on the composite primary key, so these types of values should be removed to a separate table. Figure 6-10 shows how the Songs table is split into three tables: a Songs table with Album_Num dependent on the Song_Name and Artist_Code PKs; an Album table with Album_Name dependent on the primary key Album_Num; and an Artist table, where Artist_Name is not dependent on the entire primary key. Artist_Name was also removed from the Songs table and put into its own table, using Artist_Code as the primary key and Artist_Name as a dependent column.

Figure 6-10, 2NF: Remove any columns that aren't dependent on the composite primary key and create a new table

Second Normal Form Data

Songs Table

Artist_Code	Song_Name	Album_Num	Track_Num	Media_Type	Genre_Code
BB	Sloop John B	45	7	Vinyl	CLA
BBK	The Thrill is Gone	98	8	MP3	BLU
NIRV	Come As You Are	24	3	MP3	NW
NIRV	Lithium	24	5	MP3	NW
OB	Only a Lad	78	16	CD	NW
PG	Big Time	10	14	CD	POP
PG	Sledgehammer	10	3	CD	POP
TK	American Soldier	911	3	MP3	CW
TK	Beer For My Horses	826	5	MP3	CW
U2	One Tree Hill	146	9	CD	NW
U2	With or Without You	146	3	CD	NW

Artists Table

Artist_Code	Artist_Name
BB	The Beach Boys
BBK	B.B. King
NIRV	Nirvana
OB	Oingo Boingo
PG	Peter Gabriel
TK	Toby Keith
U2	U2

Album Table

Album_Num	Album_Name
10	Shaking the Tree
24	Nevermind
45	Pet Sounds
78	Best O Boingo
98	The Best of B.B. King
146	The Joshua Tree
826	Unleashed
911	Shock'n Y'all

There are many advantages in placing a table into second normal form. The main advantage is that it eliminates repetition of data, which can result in a lot of wasted disk space.

third normal form

*third normal form (3NF) –
Eliminate columns that are
not dependent on only the
primary key*

*transitive dependency –
One column is dependent
on another column that
isn't a primary key*

Third normal form (3NF) eliminates columns that aren't dependent on only the primary key. In database parlance, putting a database in 3NF eliminates transitive dependencies. A *transitive dependency* exists when one column is dependent on another column that isn't the primary key.

To show transitive dependency, a new column called Genre_Desc has been added to the Songs table, as shown in Figure 6-11. This column describes the Genre_Code column.

Figure 6-11, Songs table with the Genre_Desc column added

Songs Table

Artist_Code	Song_Name	Album_Num	Track_Num	Media_Type	Genre_Code	Genre_Desc
BB	Sloop John B	45	7	Vinyl	CLA	Classic Rock
BBK	The Thrill is Gone	98	8	MP3	BLU	Blues
NIRV	Come As You Are	24	3	MP3	NW	NewWave
NIRV	Lithium	24	5	MP3	NW	NewWave
OB	Only a Lad	78	16	CD	NW	NewWave
PG	Big Time	10	14	CD	POP	Popular
PG	Sledgehammer	10	3	CD	POP	Popular
TK	American Soldier	911	3	MP3	CW	Country Western
TK	Beer For My Horses	826	5	MP3	CW	Country Western
U2	One Tree Hill	146	9	CD	NW	NewWave
U2	With or Without You	146	3	CD	NW	NewWave

third normal form

Eliminate columns that aren't dependent on only the primary key. 3NF is the same concept as 2NF, but it applies only to tables having single primary keys.

Each column that isn't part of the primary key should be a fact about the primary key. For example, the Genre_Desc column is dependent on the Genre_Code column, which is not part of the primary key for the Songs table. In this case, Genre_Desc isn't dependent on the Songs table's primary key. Instead, it depends on the Genre_Code column.

To put the Songs table into third normal form, you create a Genre table containing the Genre_Code and Genre_Desc columns, with Genre_Code as the primary key, as shown in Figure 6-12.

Figure 6-12, Songs and Genre tables in 3NF

Third Normal Form Data

Songs Table

Artist_Code	Song_Name	Album_Num	Track_Num	Media_Type	Genre_Code
BB	Sloop John B	45	7	Vinyl	CLA
BBK	The Thrill is Gone	98	8	MP3	BLU
NIRV	Come As You Are	24	3	MP3	NW
NIRV	Lithium	24	5	MP3	NW
OB	Only a Lad	78	16	CD	NW
P G	Big Time	10	14	CD	POP
P G	Sledgehammer	10	3	CD	POP
TK	American Soldier	911	3	MP3	CW
TK	Beer For My Horses	826	5	MP3	CW
U2	One Tree Hill	146	9	CD	NW
U2	With or Without You	146	3	CD	NW

Genre Table

Genre_Code	Genre_Desc
BLU	Blues
CLA	Classic Rock
CW	Country Western
NW	New Wave
P OP	Popular

As shown in Figure 6-13, putting the database in 3NF eliminates the repetition of the Genre_Desc, Artist_Name, and Album_Name columns in the Songs table, which saves disk space.

n o t e   The fourth and fifth normalization forms break data down into smaller pieces to eliminate redundancy. These forms apply only in rare situations and are not used often.

Figure 6-13, Eliminating repetition saves storage space

Third Normal Form Data

Songs Table

Artist_Code	Song_Name	Album_Num	Track_Num	Media_Type	Genre_Code
BB	Sloop John B	45	7	Vinyl	CLA
BBK	The Thrill is Gone	98	8	MP3	BLU
NIRV	Come As You Are	24	3	MP3	NW
NIRV	Lithium	24	5	MP3	NW
OB	Only a Lad	78	16	CD	NW
PG	Big Time	10	14	CD	POP
PG	Sledgehammer	10	3	CD	POP
TK	American Soldier	911	3	MP3	CW
TK	Beer For My Horses	826	5	MP3	CW
U2	One Tree Hill	146	9	CD	NW
U2	With or Without You	146	3	CD	NW

Genre Table

Genre_Code	Genre_Desc
BLU	Blues
CLA	Classic Rock
CW	Country Western
NW	New Wave
POP	Popular

Artists Table

Artist_Code	Artist_Name
BB	The Beach Boys
BBK	B.B. King
NIRV	Nirvana
OB	Oingo Boingo
PG	Peter Gabriel
TK	Toby Keith
U2	U2

Album Table

Album_Num	Album_Name
10	Shaking the Tree
24	Nevermind
45	Pet Sounds
78	Best O Boingo
98	The Best of B.B. King
146	The Joshua Tree
826	Unleashed
911	Shock'n Y'all

the database design process

Trying to understand the normal forms and then normalizing the tables you have designed can be quite cumbersome. However, your goal in normalization should be moderation: to reach a balance between redundant data and redundant keys. There are six steps you can follow to make designing data structures easier while adhering to the basic normalization forms. The following sections use an example of the database design and normalization process based on creating a student-grading system.

step 1: investigate and define

The first step in the database design process is to investigate and research the information you plan to model. Define the purpose of the database and how it will be used. Use any documents end users use to perform their jobs. These documents can be a basis for defining the database and tables needed to create forms and reports. The more you involve end users, the better your chances of designing the database accurately. The student-grading system is based on a course syllabus that defines all items for which students can receive grades.

step 2: make a master column list

Create a list of all fields where you need to store information along with their properties. The properties might include such items as the following:

- Field name
- Data type (char, varchar, number, date, and so on)
- Length
- Number of decimal places (if any)

Again, review the users' documents. Forms and reports are good indicators of fields you need so that you can manipulate and manage data. For this example, you might have fields such as Student ID, First Name, Last Name, E-Mail, Grade Level, Grade Level Description, Homework Average, Quiz Average, Test Average, Final Exam, Final Grade, Letter Grade, Course ID, and Course Description.

step 3: create the tables

After all the fields or columns have been defined, it's time to group them into tables logically. This step is the heart of the design process and relies heavily on normalization rules. The main rules in database design are the first through third normal forms. After a table is in 3NF, for the most part, it has been accurately defined.

The task of normalizing databases can be compared with cleaning up a toy closet. At first, the job looks monumental, but if you take one shelf at a time, the project's mammoth scope dwindles. Organize the toy shelves by first cleaning out the closet into one big pile of toys. Then decide which types of toys go on which shelves. Now you're ready to begin placing one toy at a time on the right shelf.

This process applies to database design. Logically organize the columns into the right "shelves." As you're organizing columns, look for any duplicates or ways you can save "shelf" space. Why keep two games that are the same when both have all their pieces? You can only play one game at a time, so get rid of one and keep the other on the toy shelf. Similarly, why keep two copies of the same column when both represent the same data? Get rid of one and keep the other in the table. Figure 6-14 shows the tables created for the student-grading system.

Figure 6-14, Tables created for the student-grading system

Student : Table

Student_ID	First_Name	Last_Name	E_Mail	Grade_Level
111111111	SpongeBob	SquarePants	SpongeBob@wsu.edu	Fr
223212578	Squidward	Tentacles	Squidward@wsu.edu	So
543768893	Yosemite	Sam	Yosemite@wsu.edu	Ju
984367183	Bugs	Bunny	Bugs@wsu.edu	Sr

Record: 1 of 4

Grades : Table

Course_ID	Student_ID	Homework_Ave	Quiz_Ave	Test_Ave	Final_Exam	Final_Grade	Letter_Grade
1829388133	111111111	70	65	60	72	67	D+
1829388133	223212578	80	85	90	86	85	B
1829388133	984367183	96	92	94	98	95	A
2731288812	543768893	84	82	86	78	83	B-
3712883828	223212578	100	90	88	92	93	A-
3712883828	984367183	100	98	98	96	98	A
4311223112	111111111	60	70	82	80	73	C-
4311223112	223212578	82	84	78	90	84	B
		0	0	0	0	0	

Record: 1 of 8

Grade_Level : Table

Grade_Level	Grade_Desc
Fr	Freshman
Ju	Junior
So	Sophomore
Sr	Senior

Record: 1 of 4

Courses : Table

Course_ID	Course_Desc
1829388133	Underwater Programming
2731288812	Intro to Computer Science
3712883828	Software Engineering for Cartoons
4311223112	Database Design in a Toon Environment

Record: 4 of 4

step 4: work on relationships

After the database is normalized, it's time to finalize the relationships you have observed during the design and normalization process. As in your everyday life, a relationship defines how one entity works with or relates to another. If you don't work on your personal relationships, your life will likely be a mess. Likewise, if you don't spend time working on table relationships, your database design will be a mess.

In database design, a *relationship* defines how one table works with another. Two types of relationships are discussed in this chapter:

- One-to-many (1:M)
- One-to-one (1:1)

Each relationship determines what type of data is stored in each table. Relationships need to have primary and foreign keys defined in each table. The primary key was discussed earlier in this chapter. A *foreign key (FK)* is a column in one table that relates to the primary key in another table.

relationship – How one entity or table works with another

foreign key (FK) – A column in one table that relates to a primary key in another table

For instance, the Genre_Code column in the Genre table (refer back to Figure 6-12) is the primary key in the Genre table, so it's considered a foreign key in the Songs table. The same applies to Artist_Code and Album_Num. Both are considered foreign keys in the Songs table because they relate to primary keys in other tables.

The following sections show how primary keys and foreign keys function in table relationships.

one-to-many relationship

one-to-many (1:M)
relationship – One instance
of an entity (parent table)
is associated with zero to
many instances of another
table (child table)

A *one-to-many (1:M) relationship* is the most common relationship and states that each record in Table A (the Student table in Figure 6-15) relates to zero to many records in Table B (the Course Grade table). In other words, for each student (the 1 part of 1:M), there can be zero to many grades (the M part of 1:M).

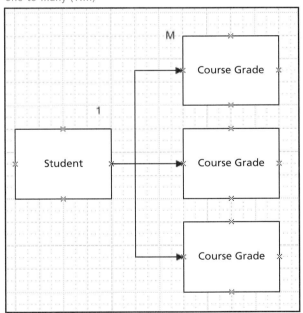

Figure 6-15, The relationship of Student to Course Grade is one-to-many (1:M)

A one-to-many relationship requires that foreign key columns in the "many" table have a value that refers to the primary key column in the "one" table. Referring back to Figure 6-14, you can see that the Student_ID column is a foreign key in the Grades table and a primary key in the Student table.

one-to-one (1:1) relationship – One instance of an entity (parent table) is associated with only one instance of another entity (child table)

M:M

Although some consider it poor data design, another relationship is a **many-to-many (M:M) relationship**, in which Table A can have more than one matching record in Table B, and Table B can have more than one matching record in Table A. Many-to-many relationships can often be broken down into several one-to-many relationships.

many-to-many (M:M) relationship – Many instances of one entity or table (parent table) are associated with many instances of another entity (child table)

entity relationship (ER) model – A data model that represents how all tables interact and relate to each other in the database

cardinality – Shows the numeric occurrences between entities in an ER model

one-to-one relationship

A *one-to-one (1:1) relationship* dictates that for every record in Table A, there can be only one matching record in Table B (see Figure 6-16). This type of relationship is quite unusual and often indicates that the two records actually belong in the same table.

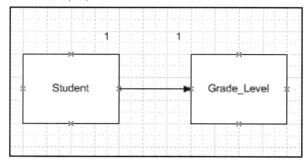

Figure 6-16, The relationship of Student to Grade Level is one-to-one (1:1)

The first thing you should consider if you find a 1:1 relationship is whether you can combine these tables into one table. Although a 1:1 relationship should exist in some situations, normally the two tables can be combined into one table.

step 5: analyze the design

With all the data pieces in place, it's time to analyze the work you've completed. Search for design errors and refine the tables as needed. Follow the normalization forms (ideally to third normal form) and correct any violations that might hamper the database's performance.

ER modeling

At this point, creating a data model is helpful to give a visual representation of how all the tables or entities interact and relate to each other in the database. This model is called an *entity relationship (ER) model*.

An ER model is composed of entities (tables) and relationships. Entities represent the database tables, and relationships show how each table relates to another table. The model can also include cardinality to show the type of relationship between tables. *Cardinality* shows the numeric occurrences between entities in an ER model. The different types of cardinality, along with their standard notations, include the following:

- 0..1, 0:1 (zero to one)
- 0..M, 0:N, 0..*, 0..n (zero to many)
- 1..1, 1:1 (one to one)

- 1..M, 1:M, 1:N, 1..*, 1..n (one to many)
- M..1, M:1, N:1, *..1, n..1 (many to one)
- M..M, M:M, N:N, *..*, n..n (many to many)

For example, an ER model for the student-grading system shows the four tables (Student, Grades, Grade_Level, and Courses) and how they relate to each other (see Figure 6-17).

Figure 6-17, The student-grading system ER model in Visio

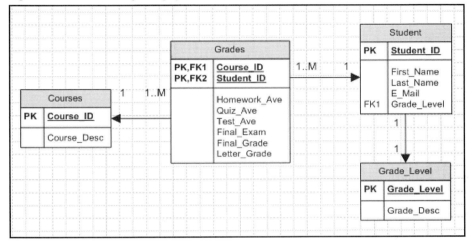

The PK and FK labels in Figure 6-17 represent the defined primary and foreign keys in each table. The numbers next to the foreign key are created by Microsoft Visio and simply indicate that one foreign key is different from another in that table.

step 6: reevaluate

Reevaluate database performance and ensure that it meets all your reporting and form needs. Include end users and explain each table and field being used. Make sure fields have been defined to address end users' requirements. You've probably played the gossip game, in which one person starts a rumor and whispers it to the next person. If so, you know that by the time the rumor reaches the last person, it isn't even close to the original. Similarly, end users' requirements might get altered during the design process, so reevaluating and checking with end users is always a good idea to make sure the database design meets their goals.

If you find your database "toy closet" can't hold all the toys, you have to leave some toys out of the closet or stuff in as many toys as possible, which results in a mess. In other words, spend the time and effort to get the database design right the first time so that you don't have to backtrack to get your design process on the right road.

After designing a database, you need to modify the data structure. You do this by using SQL commands.

Structured Query Language (SQL)

As mentioned, Structured Query Language (SQL) is a powerful database language for defining, querying, modifying, and controlling data in a database. With SQL, you have a way to do the following:

- Manipulate data
- Define data
- Administer data

Manipulating data involves retrieving and modifying data. For this task, you use SQL statements that become part of a query, with the intent to search a database and retrieve information.

Many different "dialects" of SQL are available, but after you learn the basic statements in one version, you can usually transfer this knowledge to other SQL versions.

n o t e

Only the basics of SQL are discussed in this chapter. For more information on SQL, you can review the many available book options from Course Technology at *http://cengage.com/coursetechnology/*.

SQL offers the following advantages:

- *Reduces training time*—Because SQL is English based, it's easy to understand and learn.
- *Makes applications portable*—SQL is standardized and works similarly on many different databases. So after you learn SQL and move to a different database, you should still be able to use your SQL knowledge.
- *Reduces the amount of data being transferred*—Instead of transferring all data stored in the table, SQL deals with only the data you want to see, thus reducing how much data is sent to users.
- *Increases application speed*—SQL sends you only the data you want to see instead of sending the entire set of data, which results in faster transfer of information.

SQL isn't a hard language to learn because it uses simple descriptive statements, such as CREATE TABLE, INSERT INTO, and SELECT. For example, Figure 6-18 shows a SQL statement that produces a list of all songs in your music database that are in the NW (New Wave) category.

Figure 6-18, A sample SQL statement and results

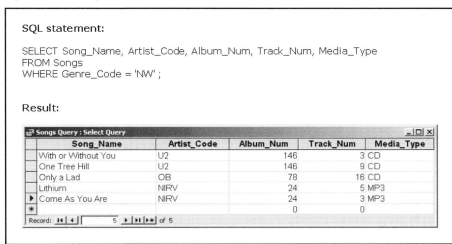

The following sections show the basic SQL commands for creating tables, adding (inserting) rows of data, and querying the table to select certain information.

CREATE TABLE statement

An advantage of SQL is that the statements are fairly easy to figure out. For instance, the CREATE TABLE statement is used to—you guessed it—create a table! This statement uses the following syntax:

```
CREATE TABLE table_name
( column_name datatype [NULL | NOT NULL]
[, column_name datatype [NULL | NOT NULL] . . . );
```

The CREATE TABLE statement is straightforward. Its job is to create a new table in a database. The *table_name* is the name of the table you want to create. Make sure this name describes the data being stored. For example, you could name a table of information about songs in your music database "Songs."

The next line, beginning with a parenthesis, is the clause for defining the table's columns/fields. Again, make sure you use descriptive names that represent the data. Type the name of the first column in the table (for example, Song_Name), followed by a space and the data type: int (integer), char (character), currency, date, and so on. Some data types, such as char, need a length specified inside parentheses, such as char(10). Table 6-2 describes some data types you can use in a CREATE TABLE statement.

Table 6-2, Common SQL data types

type	description
char	fixed number of characters
int	whole numbers
varchar	variable number of characters
date	calendar dates
number	numbers that include decimals; must specify the field's total length and the number of decimal positions

Anything declared with square brackets is considered optional. The square brackets are *not* part of the statement you enter. For example, the keywords NULL and NOT NULL in the CREATE TABLE syntax are optional and indicate whether data is required for the specified column. The vertical bar separating them means you can use one or the other.

The third line of the statement is also optional, meaning that you can have a table with only one column. If there are more columns, continue adding their names, separating each column with a comma. The last thing to do when writing a SQL statement is make sure you end it with a semicolon (;) to tell the database system the statement is complete.

The following SQL statement creates a table called Songs with six columns: Song_Name, Album_Num, Artist_Code, Track_Num, Media_Type, and Genre_Code. Some columns require data (NOT NULL), and others do not (NULL). Note that SQL commands can be uppercase or lowercase, but the convention is to use uppercase for SQL keywords.

```
CREATE TABLE Songs
(Song_Name char(50) NOT NULL,
Album_Num number NOT NULL,
Track_Num number NULL,
Media_Type char(5) NULL,
Artist_Code char(5) NOT NULL,
Genre_Code char(5) NOT NULL
);
```

n o t e

Some database developers like to place a table specifier before each column name. For example, in the preceding statement, you could include an "s" to represent the Songs table, as in `s_Song_Name char(50)` `NOT NULL`. When you're creating several tables, this method makes it easier to see which table a column is in.

INSERT INTO statement

The INSERT INTO statement is used to add new rows of data to the table and follows this syntax:

```
INSERT INTO table_name [(column1, column2, . . . )]
VALUES (constant1, constant2, . . . )
```

The syntax for the INSERT INTO statement requires a table name so that the system knows into which table to insert data. If you aren't entering data for every column in the table, you need to specify which columns are receiving data. The square brackets indicate that the column listings (*column1*, *column2*, and so on) are optional.

The only fields required to have data in the Songs table are Song_Name, Album_Num, Artist_Code, and Genre_Code because they were declared as NOT NULL in the CREATE TABLE statement. The rest of the fields aren't required to have data when you add a new record to the table. To add information about the song "Where the Streets Have No Name" by U2, you use the statement shown in Figure 6-19.

Figure 6-19, SQL INSERT INTO statement to add a record to the Songs table and its result

SQL statement:

```
INSERT INTO Songs (song_name, album_num, artist_code, genre_code)
VALUES ( 'Where the Streets Have No Name', 146, 'U2', 'POP' );
```

Result:

	Song_Name	Album_Num	Track_Num	Media_Type	Artist_Code	Genre_Code
	American Soldier	911	3	MP3	TK	CW
	Beer For My Horses	826	5	MP3	TK	CW
	Big Time	10	14	CD	PG	POP
	Come As You Are	24	3	MP3	NIRV	NW
	Lithium	24	5	MP3	NIRV	NW
	One Tree Hill	146	9	CD	U2	NW
	Only a Lad	78	16	CD	OB	NW
	Sledgehammer	10	3	CD	PG	POP
	Sloop John B	45	7	Vinyl	BB	CLA
	The Thrill is Gone	98	8	MP3	BBK	BLU
▶	Where the Streets Have No Name	146	0		U2	POP
	With or Without You	146	3	CD	U2	NW
*		0	0			

Songs : Table

Record: |◄| |◄| | 11 |►| |►I| |►*| of 12

You don't have to put each column and column value on a separate line, but many developers do so to make statements more readable and easier to maintain. Also, note that not every column needs to be "initialized" with data (which means including it in the INSERT INTO statement). Columns defined as NULL, such as Track_Num, could be omitted in both the column list and value list.

If you don't supply column names, SQL assumes you're inserting a row into the table, using the order of the columns as defined in the table structure, as shown in this example:

```
INSERT INTO Songs
VALUES (
'Where the Streets Have No Name',
146,
NULL,
NULL,
'U2',
'POP');
```

If you don't specify the column list, you *must* enter data for columns defined as NULL to gain access to the NOT NULL columns that follow the NULL column. The preceding SQL statement implies there are two fields in front of the field receiving the U2 Artist_Code data. The previous SQL statement that listed columns didn't need to specify NULL values because it listed each column receiving data.

note

Make sure you know the table's format, which means you need to know the order of columns.

SELECT statement

The SELECT statement is the most commonly used SQL statement and is responsible for retrieving data from tables in a database. The syntax for this statement is as follows:

```
SELECT [DISTINCT] column_list
FROM table_name
[WHERE search_condition]
[ORDER BY order_list]
```

For example, Figure 6-20 shows the statement to select the Song_Name, Media_Type, and Track_Num fields from the Songs table and the results in Microsoft Access.

Figure 6-20, SQL SELECT statement to return the name, media type, and track number for songs

Looking at Figure 6-20, notice that the columns being selected are separated with commas, and the statement ends with a semicolon. The order of fields doesn't have to match the order in the defined table structure. The order you specify in the SELECT statement determines the order in which data is retrieved and displayed.

WHERE clause

The WHERE clause in a SQL SELECT statement specifies additional criteria for retrieving data from a table. Think of it as being the search criteria, in that you can exclude or include specific rows depending on their column values. Figure 6-21 shows a SQL SELECT statement with a WHERE clause that searches for and retrieves Song_Name and Track_Num for songs with the Media_Type CD.

Figure 6-21, SQL SELECT statement with a WHERE clause and the results

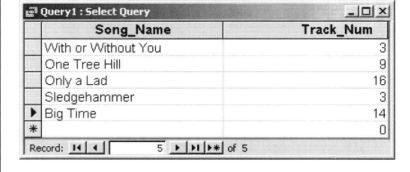

SQL statement:

SELECT Song_Name, Track_Num
FROM Songs
WHERE Media_Type= 'CD' ;

Result:

Song_Name	Track_Num
With or Without You	3
One Tree Hill	9
Only a Lad	16
Sledgehammer	3
Big Time	14
	0

Record: 5 of 5

Notice that the Media_Type column doesn't have to be specified as part of the SELECT column list. When you're using a field in a WHERE clause, however, including it in the SELECT statement's column list is best to make sure the data retrieved is accurate. Figure 6-22 shows a more descriptive version of the SELECT statement in Figure 6-21.

Figure 6-22, More descriptive SQL SELECT statement with a WHERE clause

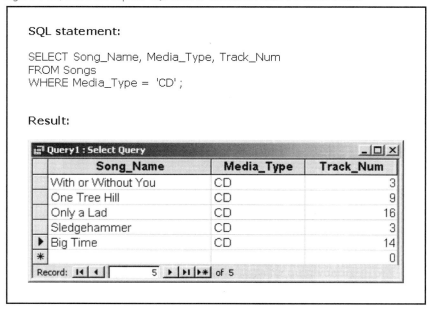

SQL statement:

SELECT Song_Name, Media_Type, Track_Num
FROM Songs
WHERE Media_Type = 'CD' ;

Result:

Song_Name	Media_Type	Track_Num
With or Without You	CD	3
One Tree Hill	CD	9
Only a Lad	CD	16
Sledgehammer	CD	3
Big Time	CD	14
		0

Record: 5 of 5

You can also specify more than one search criterion by using the AND and OR keywords. AND indicates that all criteria *must* be met; OR is more flexible, indicating only one criterion needs to be met. Try this next query. What do you think the results will be?

```
SELECT Song_Name, Media_Type, Track_Num
FROM Songs
WHERE Media_Type = 'CD' AND
Track_Num > 6 ;
```

If you guessed that the results would be the rows "Only a Lad," "Big Time," and "One Tree Hill," you were right: The Media_Type for all these songs is CD AND the Track_Num is greater than 6. Now what do you think the results of the following SELECT statement will be?

```
SELECT Song_Name, Media_Type, Track_Num
FROM Songs
WHERE(Media_Type = 'CD' OR Media_Type = 'MP3')
AND
Track_Num > 6 ;
```

Figure 6-23 shows the results of these two SELECT statements, one using AND and one using OR. As you can see, the OR result contains more entries because it selects songs that are CD *or* MP3 *and* have a track number greater than 6.

Figure 6-23, SQL SELECT statement with a WHERE clause and AND versus OR

SQL statement:

```
SELECT Song_Name, Media_Type, Track_Num
FROM Songs
WHERE(Media_Type = 'CD' OR Media_Type = 'MP3')
AND
Track_Num > 6 ;
```

Result:

Song_Name	Media_Type	Track_Num
One Tree Hill	CD	9
Only a Lad	CD	16
Big Time	CD	14
The Thrill is Gone	MP3	8
*		0

Record: 1 of 4

ORDER BY clause

Now that you have seen how to specify search criteria, you're ready to specify the order in which the rows of data are returned.

The ORDER BY clause enables you to change how data is returned from the SELECT statement. By default, data is returned in sequential order, meaning rows are kept in the order in which they're entered. Therefore, the first row of data returned is the first record that matches the search criteria and the first record entered in the table.

If you want to arrange the data more meaningfully, you can specify the ORDER BY column names. For example, Figure 6-24 shows the SQL statement to select songs with a track number greater than 6, arranged in order by Song_Name and then by Track_Num, and the results.

Figure 6-24, SQL SELECT statement with an ORDER BY clause and the results

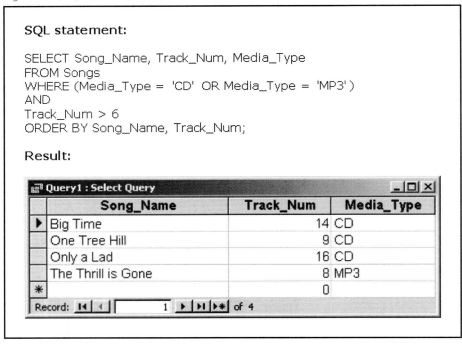

The first time these commands were run without the ORDER BY clause (refer back to Figure 6-23), the results were a little different. The same number of records was returned, but they were in a different order. The first record was "One Tree Hill," which means that of the four records returned, it was the first record entered in the table that satisfied the search criteria. Adding the ORDER BY clause allows the data to be rearranged and displayed in a more meaningful order. Now the first record you see is "Big Time" because the results are in alphabetical order by song title.

n o t e   Notice that when you have multiple fields in the ORDER BY clause, they are separated by commas.

The ORDER BY clause also allows the SQL statement to return data in ascending (default) or descending order. Figure 6-25 shows a SQL SELECT statement that displays Song_Name and Track_Num for all Media_Type columns that are CD *or* MP3 *and* have Track_Num column values greater than 6. The information is in ascending order by Track_Num and Song_Name, with the smallest Track_Num value at the top of the list and the largest value at the bottom of the list. Because ascending is the default order, you don't have to use a special keyword to specify this order.

Figure 6-25, SQL SELECT statement, using an ORDER BY clause with the default ascending option

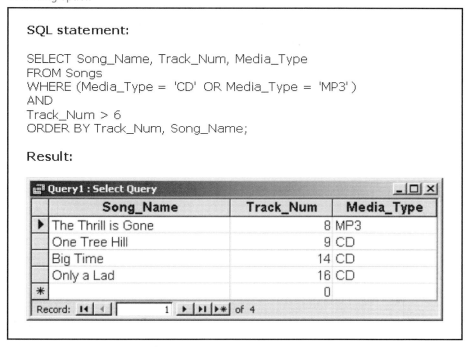

SQL statement:

```
SELECT Song_Name, Track_Num, Media_Type
FROM Songs
WHERE (Media_Type = 'CD' OR Media_Type = 'MP3')
AND
Track_Num > 6
ORDER BY Track_Num, Song_Name;
```

Result:

Song_Name	Track_Num	Media_Type
The Thrill is Gone	8	MP3
One Tree Hill	9	CD
Big Time	14	CD
Only a Lad	16	CD
	0	

Record: 1 of 4

If you want data returned in descending order, you simply place the keyword DESC next to the column in the ORDER BY clause. Figure 6-26 shows the SQL statement to order songs by Track_Num and Song_Name, using Track_Num in descending order, and the results.

Figure 6-26 SQL SELECT statement, using an ORDER BY clause with the DESC option

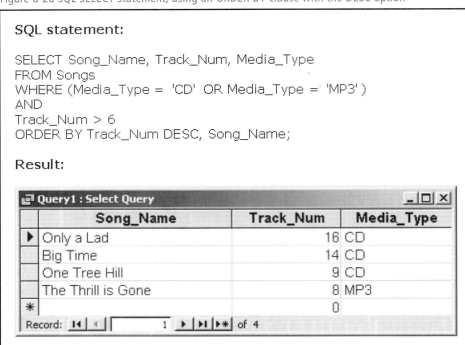

SQL statement:

SELECT Song_Name, Track_Num, Media_Type
FROM Songs
WHERE (Media_Type = 'CD' OR Media_Type = 'MP3')
AND
Track_Num > 6
ORDER BY Track_Num DESC, Song_Name;

Result:

Song_Name	Track_Num	Media_Type
Only a Lad	16	CD
Big Time	14	CD
One Tree Hill	9	CD
The Thrill is Gone	8	MP3
	0	

You have barely scratched the surface of SQL's power. Many more options for the SELECT statement are available for using more specific search criteria or being more specific about the format of the returned results. Also, there are many SQL commands for maintaining, defining, and administering the data in a database.

one last thought

A database that isn't organized well can be more of a hindrance than a benefit. You have to carefully plan how data will be structured and stored, apply normalization rules, and use the right SQL statements to extract the kind of information you want. With these structures, a database becomes a powerful tool used in many areas, including business and computing.

6

chapter summary

- A database is a collection of logically related information used in an application to create meaningful output for end users.
- Normalization is the process of structuring tables to eliminate unwanted redundancies and dependencies.
- Database information is kept in sequential order, but you can view the order of records in different formats by creating indexes and assigning sort keys.
- Primary keys are used to uniquely identify table entries; foreign keys are columns in one table that reference a primary key in another table.
- The manner in which one table relates to another table is called a relationship.
- The three types of relationships discussed are one-to-one (1:1), one-to-many (1:M), and many-to-many (M:M).
- First normal form eliminates repeated fields.
- Second normal form dictates that every column that isn't part of the primary key is fully dependent on the primary key.
- Third normal form states that no column can depend on any other column than the primary key.
- Fourth and fifth normal forms are rarely used but further break down tables into nondependent, nonredundant forms.
- The six steps for designing a database are investigate, create a master column list, create the tables, assess the relationships, analyze the design, and reevaluate.
- Structured Query Language (SQL) is a powerful database language for defining, maintaining, querying, and administering data.

key terms

cardinality (*228*)

column (field or attribute) (*211*)

composite key (*220*)

database (*207*)

database management system (DBMS) (*209*)

determinant (*220*)

domain (*212*)

entity relationship (ER) model (*228*)

first normal form (1NF) (*218*)

foreign key (FK) (*226*)

functional dependency (*220*)

index (*213*)

many-to-many (M:M) relationship (*228*)

normalization (*216*)

one-to-many (1:M) relationship (*227*)

one-to-one (1:1) relationship (*228*)

primary key (PK) (*219*)

relationship (*226*)   *Structured Query Language (SQL)* (*209*)

row (record or tuple) (*211*)   *table (or entity)* (*211*)

second normal form (2NF) (*220*)   *third normal form (3NF)* (*222*)

sort key (*214*)   *transitive dependency* (*222*)

test yourself

1. What is a database? Give an example of a database in current use that affects you.

Use the following table for Questions 2–7:

record #	team	wins	losses
1	Anteaters	10	2
2	Byrds	8	0
3	Monkeys	6	6
4	Admirals	10	2
5	Sapsuckers	5	7

2. The table is listed in what order (primary key)?

3. Write a SQL SELECT statement to list the table's contents in order of wins.

4. Write a SQL SELECT statement to list the table's contents in order of wins and team.

5. Write a SQL INSERT INTO statement to add the team Bears. The Bears have 3 wins and 9 losses.

6. Write a SQL INSERT INTO statement to add the team Lions. The Lions have 9 wins and 3 losses.

7. Write a SQL SELECT statement to list all the table's contents.

8. What is normalization, and what problems does it solve?

9. Explain the first three normalization forms.

10. List and explain the six steps for designing a database.

11. Create a normalized database to support a space shuttle launching application. The government wants to keep track of astronauts, space shuttles, and launch history. Define the tables, primary and foreign keys, and indexes. Make sure the tables are finalized in the third normalized state.

12. Draw an ER model to represent the space shuttle launching application designed in Question 11. Make sure you show the relationships, label the cardinality, and show primary and foreign keys.

Use the following table for Questions 13–20:

field name	field size	field type	sample data
Error_Log_Date		Date	12/15/2010
Error_Log_Time		Time	2:24:32 PM
User_Code	8	Text	KATIE
User_First	15	Text	KAYTLEN
User_Last	25	Text	ANDERSON
Error_Code	4	Text	LOG
Error_Code_Desc	40	Text	INCORRECT LOGIN
User_Password	10	Text	MONK
Error_Log_Desc	80	Text	USER INPUT WAS BAD
Error_Status_Code	1 if Text	Yes/No or Text	C—Completed, U—Unresolved, I—In process of being fixed
Error_Priority_Code		Number	Can contain a number from 1 to 5: 1—Very high 2—High 3—Medium 4—Low 5—Very low

13. Using the fields listed, normalize the data by organizing the fields into tables. *Hint*: You should end up with at least three tables.

14. Write a SQL CREATE statement to create each table. Make sure you identify which fields you think should or should not allow NULL values.

15. Write a SQL INSERT INTO statement to add at least three records to each table you created.

16. Using the normalized tables, write a SQL SELECT statement to show all users (User_Code, User_First, and User_Last). Sort the information by the User_Last and User_First columns.

17. Using the normalized tables, write a SQL SELECT statement to show all errors (Error_Log_Date, Error_Log_Time, Error_Code, Error_Status_Code, Error_Priority_Code, Error_Code_Desc, and Error_Log_Desc). Sort the information by the Error_Log_Date and Error_Log_Time columns.

18. Using the normalized tables, write a SQL SELECT statement to show all information on each error along with the first and last name of the user who created the error.

19. Review the Error_Status_Code column in the normalized tables. The user wants to see the description displayed for the Error_Status_Code column. This description will also be used in a drop-down list box when the user is entering information for the error. What can you, as the database designer, do to enhance the tables' current design and make the database structure more flexible so that more Error_Status_Codes can be added to the system?

20. Review the Error_Priority_Code column in the normalized tables. The user wants to see the description displayed for the Error_Priority_Code column. This description will also be used in a drop-down list box when the user is entering information for the error. What can you, as the database designer, do to enhance the tables' current design and make the database structure more flexible so that more Error_Priority_Codes can be added to the system?

practice exercises

1. Which of the following is *not* a valid DBMS?
   a. SQL Server
   b. C++
   c. Oracle
   d. DB2

2. A table is divided into databases.
   a. True
   b. False

3. A column is divided into tables.
   a. True
   b. False

4. What is the set of possible values for a column?

   a. Domain
   b. Table
   c. SQL
   d. Index

5. What specifies how the information in an entity is organized?

   a. Domain
   b. Table
   c. SQL
   d. Sort key

6. First normal form says:

   a. No nonkey columns depend on another nonkey column.
   b. Every column that's not part of the primary key is fully dependent on the primary key.
   c. Eliminate repeated fields.
   d. None of the above

7. Second normal form says:

   a. No nonkey columns depend on another nonkey column.
   b. Every column that's not part of the primary key is fully dependent on the primary key.
   c. Eliminate repeated fields.
   d. None of the above

8. Third normal form says:

   a. No nonkey columns depend on another nonkey column.
   b. Every column that's not part of the primary key is fully dependent on the primary key.
   c. Eliminate repeated fields.
   d. None of the above

9. What uniquely identifies a row in a table?

   a. Index
   b. Column
   c. Primary key
   d. Tuple

10. A composite key is a column containing unique information.

    a. True
    b. False

11. Which is *not* a step of the database design process?

    a. Create the tables
    b. Create the relationships
    c. Investigate
    d. Add the data

12. When creating a table in SQL, you *must* specify whether the column is NULL or NOT NULL.

    a. True
    b. False

13. The SQL INSERT INTO statement allows adding multiple records in one statement.

    a. True
    b. False

14. By default, data returned by the SQL SELECT statement is in descending order.

    a. True
    b. False

15. Which of the following SQL SELECT options is used to organize the data being returned?

    a. ORDER BY
    b. SORT BY
    c. WHERE
    d. None of the above

digging deeper

1. Talk to at least three different companies that use databases and find out which DBMS packages they use. Ask them why they selected those particular DBMSs and report your findings.

2. List at least five SQL statements that haven't been discussed in this chapter. Describe what they do and give an example of each.

3. Research the fourth and fifth normal forms. Describe them and demonstrate in examples how they're applied to a database.

4. Are there any other database relationships besides 1:M and 1:1? If so, describe the relationship and use tables you have defined to show how it's implemented.

5. What are the advantages and disadvantages of using Oracle versus SQL Server?

discussion topics

1. When have you encountered databases being used?

2. If you could create a database to make some aspect of your life easier, what type of information would it contain?

3. If you were creating a registration database system for your university, what tables would it contain? What columns would be in the tables?

4. If you were creating a database system to hold all your music files, what tables would it contain? What columns would be in the tables?

5. What are some possible negative effects on privacy and citizens' rights that the use of databases might involve?

Internet research

1. List and describe at least five Web sites that give SQL tutorials. Share this information with your class.

2. Choose a particular database format (such as Oracle, SQL Server, or another product) and research the following information: current version, current price, training options, available certifications, company information, and company stock price. Create a spreadsheet or table to display your results.

3. What types of computer jobs require knowledge of a DBMS package? Search the Internet, using sites such as Dice, Monster, CareerBuilder, and so on, and write down the jobs, types of DBMS packages, and required tasks or skills.

4. List at least five Web sites that use databases to store information. Describe the information they are storing, and try to identify some tables they might have created to use on their Web sites.

5. Identify the advantages and disadvantages of the DBMS packages listed in this chapter. Use the Internet to search for opinions, reviews, and other articles.

6. List and describe three tools (other than Microsoft Visio) for creating ER models.

7

numbering systems and data representations

in this chapter you will:

- Learn why numbering systems are important to understand
- Refresh your knowledge of powers of numbers
- Learn how numbering systems are used to count
- Understand the significance of positional value in a numbering system
- Learn the differences and similarities between numbering system bases
- Learn how to convert numbers between bases
- Learn how to do binary and hexadecimal math
- Learn how data is represented as binary in a computer
- Learn how images and sounds are stored in a computer

the lighter side of the lab
by spencer

The term "numbering systems" is an excellent example of why computer geeks have a hard time getting dates (until they graduate and become gazillionaires). I guess a more boring term could be used in place of "numbering systems," such as "quantitative analysis protocols" or maybe "algorithmic processes for deriving alternative radix notation." (If your eyes are lighting up and you're saying, "Yeah, they *should* use these terms instead!" please seek professional help.)

Why not just say "different ways of counting things"? Or better yet, "different ways to count doughnuts"? Imagine you had opened this book to Chapter 7 to see the title "Different Ways to Count Doughnuts." Now that's a chapter you're going to read!

Sesame Street understands this principle. You never heard a conversation like this between Maria and Big Bird:

Big Bird: "Hi, Maria. What are you doing?"

Maria: "Hi, Big Bird. I'm just executing conversions between numbering systems."

Big Bird: "Huh?"

Maria: "I'm converting this series of digits from the binary base 2 numbering system to the decimal base 10 numbering system by multiplying each digit's value in base 2 by its positional value in base 10 and calculating the total sum of all values."

Big Bird (running away): "Snuffyyyyyyy!"

No, *Sesame Street* uses fun terms to teach. Everyone remembers the Count. ("One! One ball! Ah, ah, ah!") Give the Count 5 minutes and a dozen doughnuts, and he'd have the entire class counting in hexadecimal: "C! C doughnuts! Ah, ah, ah!"

In conclusion, don't be intimidated by terms such as "numbering systems" and "positional value." They're just really, really boring terms for stuff that's actually interesting. If computer geeks who make up terms such as "numbering systems" took a lesson from the Count, they might be saying "One! One Friday night spent with someone whose name isn't Pentium! Ah, ah, ah!"

I'm just giving you a hard time, computer geeks. Remember that if Bill Gates had a dollar for every time someone made a joke about him . . . Oh, wait—he does. Ah, ah, ah!

why you need to know about...
numbering systems

Every computer game, program, picture, or sound is stored in the computer as a series of binary digits. Because humans don't normally talk binary, if you want to be better at telling a computer what to do, you must learn to understand binary and hexadecimal.

Terms such as "data representation," "numbering systems," and "hexadecimal" might seem intimidating; however, as with anything new you learn, you just have to become familiar with these terms to understand them. Most people are born with 10 fingers and 10 toes, so it's no accident that people are most familiar with the base 10 numbering system. You probably learned it from watching *Sesame Street* and then again in elementary school. You might have counted on your fingers and even your toes. (Then again, you might still be counting on your fingers and toes.) If people were born with only two fingers and two toes, maybe this computer binary thing would be easier to understand. In any case, understanding numbering systems is quite simple if you just take a deep breath, relax, and go through it one step at a time.

Understanding numbering systems and data representations will help you be more comfortable as you interact with computers in later computing courses and throughout your career. Many times, you'll need to be able to read displays containing the contents of a computer's memory or hard disk, often referred to as hexadecimal memory dumps. You have probably seen the dreaded "blue screen" fatal error message, which looks something like this:

```
an exception OE has occurred 0028:CICA38F1 in VXD MXECPV (02) +00000251.
This was called from 0028:C02A50EE in VXD VWIN32(05) +00001F16.
```

The hexadecimal numbers in this error message probably don't mean anything to you now, but as you continue your studies in computer science, you'll learn what these numbers mean and how they can be used to explain computer errors.

powers of numbers: a refresher

Before you get into numbering systems and data representations, think back to a concept you learned in elementary school: powers of numbers.

You might remember that 2 squared equals 4 and is displayed with the power as a superscript, as 2^2. Remember that raising a number to a positive power simply means multiplying that number by itself the number of times specified by the power indicator (often called an exponent). The number 2^3, for example, is just $2 * 2 * 2$. The number 2 is multiplied by itself 3 times, giving a value of 8. In working with computers, multiplication is represented with an asterisk (*).

That's all there is to positive powers, with the exception of two special cases: the exponents (powers) 0 and 1. First, raising a number to the 0 power always results in 1, no matter what the original number was. The number 10^0 is 1. The number 2^0 is also 1. Second, raising a number to the 1 power always results in the number itself. So 2^1 is always 2, and 16^1 is always 16.

note

An important mathematical concept is that any nonzero number raised to the 0 power gives a value of 1.

Try practicing with base 10 numbers by raising 10 to the fourth power. The number 10^4 is just $10 * 10 * 10 * 10$, or 10,000. The number 10^2 is $10 * 10$, which equals 100.

Numbers can also be raised to negative powers, which are used to represent fractional portions of numbers. Raising a number to a negative power is similar to raising it to a positive power, with one final step. After you multiply the number as many times as specified by the exponent, you divide that result into 1. The number 2^{-3} is 1 divided by 2 cubed ($2 * 2 * 2$) and is equivalent to .125. For 10^{-4}, the calculation is $1 / (10 * 10 * 10 * 10)$, or .00001. In other words, you multiply 10 by itself 4 times, which gives you 10,000. Then divide that value into 1.

Understanding powers of numbers is handy when you start to learn more about numbering systems.

counting things

In essence, numbers are used to count things. Whether you're dealing with money or miles, numbers are used to count how many things are represented. Whether numbers are negative, positive, whole numbers, or fractions, they're used to count. If your tuition is $2395, it means that attending school costs you two thousand, three hundred, and ninety-five dollar units. You should be accustomed to this unit of measurement by now. What does it mean, however? In elementary school, you learned that $2395 is 2 thousands plus 3 hundreds plus 9 tens and 5 ones, but what does it *really* mean? The number 2395 really means $(2 * 10^3) + (3 * 10^2) + (9 * 10^1) + (5 * 10^0)$.

You're accustomed to counting in the decimal, or base 10, numbering system. You can also count in other numbering systems or bases. Computers use a numbering base of 2, which is called *binary*. So unlike base 10, which has 10 unique digits—0, 1, 2, 3, 4, 5, 6, 7, 8, and 9—base 2 has only 2 unique digits, 0 and 1. Hexadecimal has 16 digits: 0, 1, 2, 3, 4, 5, 6, 7, 8, 9, A, B, C, D, E, and F. A base is identified by the number of digits a numbering system has, including the digit 0.

binary – *Numbering system with two digits, 0 and 1; also known as base 2 and is the basis for modern computer systems*

When you count in base 10, you start with 0 and count up to 9. Because there aren't any more digits after 9, you have to put a 1 in the tens column and then go back to 0 in the ones column, as shown in the following example:

```
0, 1, 2, 3, 4, 5, 6, 7, 8, 9, 10, 11, 12, 13, 14, 15,
16, 17, 18, 19, 20, . . . , 99, 100
```

The process of counting in this manner is the same for any base. In base 2, you start counting at 0 and then go to 1. When you get to 1, you have run out of digits, as you did at 9 in base 10. So you put a 1 in the twos column and go back to 0 in the ones column. When you get to 11, you have to go to 100, as you do with 99 in decimal:

```
0, 1, 10, 11, 100, 101, 110, 111, 1000
```

> **who's on base?**
>
> The base of a numbering system is the number of digits in that system.
>
> Base 10 (decimal) has 10 digits, 0–9.
>
> Base 2 (binary) has 2 digits, 0 and 1.
>
> Base 16 (hexadecimal) has 16 digits, 0–F.

hexadecimal (hex) – *Numbering system with 16 digits, 0–9 and A–F; also known as base 16 and often used as shorthand for binary (one hex digit = four binary digits)*

Base 16 (*hexadecimal*) has more digits than base 2 or base 10. Counting still starts at 0 and continues in the same column until you reach the highest possible value, F. Then you put a 1 in the sixteens column and set the ones column back to 0:

```
0, 1, 2, 3, 4, 5, 6, 7, 8, 9, A, B, C, D, E, F, 10, 11,
12, . . . , FF, 100
```

What's important is not stressing over counting in other base numbering systems. Because you already know how to count in base 10, you actually know how to count in the others.

n o t e

To help you become familiar with different names for numbering systems, the following terms are used interchangeably in this chapter: base 10 or decimal, base 2 or binary, and base 16 or hexadecimal.

positional value – The numerical value each position in a number has; calculated by raising the base of the number to the power of the position

radix point – The point that divides the fractional portion from the whole portion of a number; in the decimal numbering system, it's referred to as a decimal point

positional value

A key principle of numbering systems is *positional value*. In any numbering system, each position or digit in a number has a positional value. You're familiar with the base 10 positional values of ones, tens, hundreds, thousands, ten thousands, and so on. This concept exists in all numbering bases. The value of each position in a number (positional value) is found by raising the base of the number to the power indicated by the position. The positions of a number start with a power of 0 in the rightmost place, and then increase by 1 for each position going left. Negative powers begin with -1 at the right of the *radix point*. The term "radix point" is used instead of decimal point because the number might not be in decimal. "Radix" is synonymous with "base."

For the number 436.95, the 4 is in position two, the 3 is in position one, and the 6 is in position zero. To the right of the radix point, the 9 is in position -1, and the 5 is in position -2.

The positional value of each digit in a number specifies what multiplier the position gives to the overall number. For example, in the decimal (base 10) number, 4321, the digit 3 is multiplied by the positional value of the position it's in, which is 100 (10^2). The rest of the digits in the number are multiplied by their positional values: The 4 is in the thousands position, the 2 is in the tens position, and the 1 is in the ones position. The digit in each position is multiplied by the value of the position. Then the results of these multiplications are added, giving you the total number of things being counted. Figure 7-1 shows how positional values work in base 10 numbers.

Figure 7-1, Positional values for a base 10 number

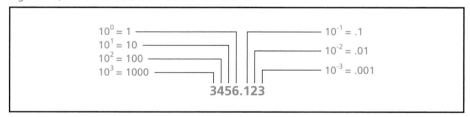

Figure 7-1 shows the positional values for the number 3456.123 as a power of 10, which is the base, and as a number. You can see that 3 thousands, 4 hundreds, 5 tens, and 6 ones precede the radix point. Following the point is 1 tenth, 2 hundredths, and 3 thousandths.

Now consider a base 2 (binary) number, such as 1011_2. (The subscript 2 in the number 1011_2 indicates that the number is in base 2.) With binary numbers, each position also has a place value, as in base 10 numbers. Following the rule established previously, the rightmost position has a positional value of the base (2) raised to the 0 power. Again, any number raised to the 0 power has a value of 1. So the positional value of the rightmost digit is 1. The next position has a value of 2 raised to the power of 1. The next position is 2 squared, and the next is 2 to the third. Figure 7-2 shows the positional values for a base 2 number.

Figure 7-2, Positional values for a base 2 number

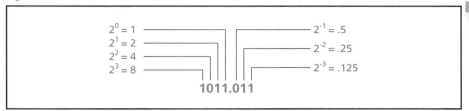

As shown, the positional value of a number is significant because it gives the weight each digit contributes to the number's overall value. You have probably never given this concept much thought, as you have dealt with decimal numbers all your life. As you begin using numbers from other bases, however, you have to pay attention to and deal with positional values.

how many things does a number represent?

Positional values are used to calculate how many of something a number represents. The process is to multiply each digit of the number by its positional value and then add all those values together. So the number 1001_2 is equivalent to nine things. The number 9 is calculated like this: $(1 * 2^0) + (0 * 2^1) + (0 * 2^2) + (1 * 2^3)$.

With a little practice, you should become comfortable evaluating numbers in any base by using the following steps:

1. Calculate the value for each position of the number by raising the base value to the power of the position.

2. Multiply the positional value by the digit in that position.

3. Add all the calculated values together.

Now try applying these steps to a decimal, binary, and hexadecimal number. Start with the number 2345_{10}. Using this process with a base 10 number might seem a little redundant, but the practice will help when you're calculating in other bases.

1. Calculate the value for each position of the number by raising the base value to the power of the position:

$$10^0 = 1 \quad \text{(Any number to the 0 power is 1.)}$$
$$10^1 = 10 \quad \text{(Any number to the 1 power is the number itself.)}$$
$$10^2 = 100$$
$$10^3 = 1000$$

2. Multiply the positional value by the digit in that position:

$$1 * 5 = 5$$
$$10 * 4 = 40$$
$$100 * 3 = 300$$
$$1000 * 2 = 2000$$

3. Add the calculated values together:

$$5 + 40 + 300 + 2000 = 2345$$

Calculating the number of things represented by a base 2 number, such as 10100110_2, is a bit more difficult, but the steps are the same as for a base 10 number.

1. Calculate the value for each position of the number by raising the base value to the power of the position:

$$2^0 = 1$$
$$2^1 = 2$$
$$2^2 = 4$$
$$2^3 = 8$$
$$2^4 = 16$$
$$2^5 = 32$$
$$2^6 = 64$$
$$2^7 = 128$$

2. Next, multiply the positional value by the digit in that position:

$$1 * 0 = 0$$
$$2 * 1 = 2$$
$$4 * 1 = 4$$
$$8 * 0 = 0$$
$$16 * 0 = 0$$
$$32 * 1 = 32$$
$$64 * 0 = 0$$
$$128 * 1 = 128$$

3. Finally, add the calculated values together:

$$0 + 2 + 4 + 0 + 0 + 32 + 0 + 128 = 166$$

Performing the same process in base 16 (hexadecimal) is more difficult because the numbers are larger, but it works exactly the same as the others. For the hex number 5678_{16}, the process goes like this:

1. Calculate the value for each position of the number by raising the base value to the power of the position:

$$16^0 = 1$$
$$16^1 = 16$$
$$16^2 = 256$$
$$16^3 = 4096$$

2. Next, multiply the positional value by the digit in that position:

$1 * 8 = 8$
$16 * 7 = 112$
$256 * 6 = 1536$
$4096 * 5 = 20{,}480$

3. Finally, add the calculated values together:

$8 + 112 + 1536 + 20{,}480 = 22{,}136$

Remember that in base 16 (hexadecimal), digits larger than 9 are A–F. These digits have (decimal) values of 10–15. Otherwise, the process is exactly the same. For the hex number $ABCD_{16}$, the process goes like this:

1. Calculate the value for each position of the number by raising the base value to the power of the position:

$16^0 = 1$
$16^1 = 16$
$16^2 = 256$
$16^3 = 4096$

2. Next, multiply the positional value by the digit in that position:

$1 * D\ (13) = 13$
$16 * C\ (12) = 192$
$256 * B\ (11) = 2816$
$4096 * A\ (10) = 40{,}960$

3. Finally, add the calculated values together:

$13 + 192 + 2816 + 40{,}960 = 43{,}981$

converting numbers between bases

Because all numbering system bases are just a way of counting things, it stands to reason that for any quantity, there's a number in any base to represent it. Table 7-1 shows how quantities from 0 to 20 are represented in bases 2, 10, and 16. Note that as you're counting, when you reach the highest digit for a base, you must add 1 to the next higher position to the left and return to 0 in the position you're working with. For example, base 2 counting starts with 0, and then goes to 1. Because there are no more digits to work with in base 2, you add a 1 to the column to the left and return to 0. There wasn't a value in the column to the left, so in effect, you added 1 to 0 to get the next value, 10. Base 10 runs out of digits at 9 and doesn't need to go to 10 until then. Base 16 doesn't run out of digits until F. When F is reached, the next value is 10.

Table 7-1, Counting in different bases

base 10	base 2	base 16
0	0	0
1	1	1
2	10	2
3	11	3
4	100	4
5	101	5
6	110	6
7	111	7
8	1000	8
9	1001	9
10	1010	A
11	1011	B
12	1100	C
13	1101	D
14	1110	E
15	1111	F
16	10000	10
17	10001	11
18	10010	12
19	10011	13
20	10100	14

If you created a giant counting table going from 0 to a huge number, you could convert numbers from one base to another by looking up the number for one base and finding its counterpart in another column. No one wants to carry around a book containing a table this big, however. Fortunately, there's an easier way. You can use some simple mathematics to convert from one base to another.

converting to base 10

Converting to base 10 from any other base makes use of what you have learned about the positional value of numbers.

You can experiment with a simple conversion from base 2 to base 10. Using Table 7-1, look down the base 2 column to the value 10011. Remember that each position in a number has a positional value, which is calculated by raising the base to the power indicated by the position. The first position on the right has a positional value of 1 (2^0). Because a 1 is in that position, the positional value is multiplied by 1, resulting in 1. The next position has a value of 2 (2^1) and is multiplied by the digit 1 in that position. The next two digits are 0s. These positions could be calculated by using their positional values, but 0s don't contribute to the value of a number, so they can be skipped. The final digit 1 is in position 4. The base of 2 raised to the power of 4 is 16. Because a 1 is in that position, 16 needs to be added to the total. To finish the calculation, add $16 + 2 + 1$, which equals 19. This conversion process calculates the binary value 10011 to be equivalent to the decimal value 19. Table 7-1 confirms that this calculation is correct.

Converting base 16 (hexadecimal) to base 10 (decimal) follows the same process. (Remember that hexadecimal has 16 possible digits, 0–F.) The letters A–F are used in hexadecimal to represent numeric values above 9.

To convert the hexadecimal value 13_{16} to its decimal counterpart, multiply the digit in each position by its positional value, and add the results. The first digit on the right is a 3 and is in position 0. Because position 0 always has a value of 1 in any base (16^0), the 3 in that position is multiplied by 1, resulting in 3. The next digit to the left, 1, is in position 1. Raising the base 16 to the power of 1 gives 16. Multiply the positional value of 16 by the digit in that position ($16 * 1 = 16$). Adding the calculated values for each position ($16 + 3$) results in 19. Refer to Table 7-1 to verify your answer.

Although larger numbers result in larger total values, the process is the same. Converting from any base to decimal always follow these steps.

converting from base 10

Converting from base 10 to any other base (the target base) is the reverse of converting to base 10. To use this positional value method, follow these general steps:

1. Examine the decimal number to determine which positional value in the target base is the nearest to or equal in value to the decimal number, without going over. If the number is less than or equal to the highest value in the base, it's the last (rightmost) digit of your converted number. Otherwise, you go on to Step 2. Example: For the decimal number 2604, the nearest hexadecimal positional value that isn't greater than 2064 is 256. The next hexadecimal positional value, 4096, is greater than 2604.

2. Determine how many times that positional value can be divided into the decimal number, and write down that value. Example: 256 goes into 2604 10 times, so write down a hexadecimal A, which is the hex equivalent for a decimal 10.

3. Multiply the number from Step 2 by the associated positional value, and then subtract the product from the number you chose in Step 1. The result is the remainder. Example: Subtracting 2560 (10 * 256) from 2604 gives a remainder of 44.

4. Use the remainder from Step 3 as a new starting value, and repeat Steps 1 through 3 until the Step 1 value is less than or equal to the maximum value in the target base. Example: Use decimal 44 as the starting point in repeating Steps 1 to 3.

5. The converted number is the digits you've written down, in order from left to right.

This method might seem confusing, but an example makes it clearer. Try a small number first, such as converting the decimal number 815 to its hexadecimal counterpart:

1. Hexadecimal numbers have positional values that are powers of 16:

$$16^0 = 1$$
$$16^1 = 16$$
$$16^2 = 256$$
$$16^3 = 4096$$

The highest positional value (without going over) nearest to 815 is the 256 position, so choose this value.

2. The positional value 256 goes into 815 three times, so write down a 3.

3. Next, multiply the hexadecimal 3 by the positional value 256, which gives you 768. Subtract this value from 815, resulting in 47, which is the remainder.

4. The remainder from Step 3 becomes the new starting point for repeating Steps 1 through 3, as shown in the next steps.

5. The highest positional value (without going over) nearest to 47 is the 16 position, so choose this value.

6. The positional value 16 goes into 47 two times, so write down the value 2.

7. Next, multiply the 2 by the positional value 16, which gives you 32. Subtract this value from 47, resulting in 15 (hex F). The value F is equal to the highest hexadecimal value (F), so you're finished with the conversion process.

8. Finally, write down 32F as the hexadecimal equivalent of the decimal number 815.

Working through a few more of these conversions helps you get comfortable with them. Of course, you can always use a calculator that converts from one base to another, but knowing how the conversion process works is important.

n o t e

The Windows calculator (Start, [All] Programs, Accessories) can convert between hex, binary, and decimal. Try a few examples manually, and then use the Windows calculator to check your work. Make sure the calculator is in the Scientific view.

binary and hexadecimal math

You have been adding and subtracting decimal numbers for most of your life but probably haven't given much thought to exactly what you're doing. Try adding the decimal numbers 685 and 925. Did you get 1610? What process did you go through to get this result? The process is important because you use the same process for any base.

You started by adding the rightmost digits of the numbers (5 + 5 = 10). Because 10 is larger than 9, you put a 0 in that position and carried the 10 as a 1 to the next position. Then you added the carried 1 to the 8 and 2 in the next numbers you were adding. Adding 8 + 2 + 1 results in 11, so again a 10 was carried as a 1 to the next position to the left. Finally, 6 and 9 were added to the carried 1, resulting in 16. The 6 was placed in that position, and the 10 was carried as 1 to the next position. The result was the number 1610.

Adding numbers in other bases follows nearly the same steps as in decimal numbers. The only difference is the carry process. In decimal, you carry 10 to the next column. What you're actually doing is carrying the base to the next column. So when you add numbers in other bases, you still carry the base to the next column.

Figure 7-3 is an example of adding two binary numbers by using the process described previously. Note that in binary, 1 + 1 doesn't equal 2. In binary, there isn't a digit 2, so 1 + 1 equals 10.

Figure 7-3, Adding numbers in binary

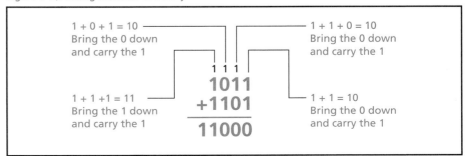

Subtraction in other bases follows the same process used in subtracting base 10 numbers. When the top number is smaller than the bottom, you borrow an amount equal to the base from the column to the left. In decimal, you borrow 10s. In binary, you borrow 2s. Borrowing from the column to the left reduces it by 1. Figure 7-4 shows an example of subtraction with base 2 numbers.

Figure 7-4, Subtraction with base 2 numbers

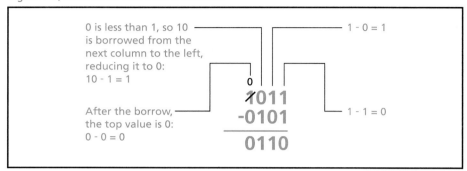

You can also multiply and divide in any base, much as you do with decimal numbers, but these topics are beyond the scope of this book.

data representation in binary

Remember, computers are capable of storing only binary information. The transistors that make up a computer can exist in only one of two states: on or off. So everything that takes place in the computer and is stored in the computer must be stored as base 2 values. Therefore, you need to understand binary to examine and analyze the contents of memory, hard disk data, and Internet packets.

Each 1 and 0 (on and off) in a computer is referred to as a *bit* (*b*inary dig*it*). A *byte* is a group of 8 bits. Computer systems also have larger groups of bits referred to as *words*. In addition, half a byte is 4 bits, sometimes referred to as a *nibble* (a term no doubt coined by a computer scientist with a sense of humor).

Humans have a difficult time dealing with the large binary numbers that computers use. To make it easier, computer scientists sometimes use hexadecimal as a shorthand method for representing binary values. Each hexadecimal digit corresponds to a 4-bit binary pattern. Therefore, a long binary value can be represented in hexadecimal by using one-fourth as many digits. For example, the binary number 1111101011001110 is equivalent to the hexadecimal number FACE. Test it for yourself by taking the binary number and grouping the bits into sets of four, beginning on the right. The groups are 1111, 1010, 1100, and 1110. Then check Table 7-1 to get the hexadecimal counterpart of each 4-bit binary number. When separating these binary digits into groups of

bit – The abbreviation for "binary digit"; a bit is a 1 or a 0 and is the smallest unit of representation in a computer system

byte – A group of 8 bits considered as one unit and used as the basic unit of measurement in a computer system; memory is measured in number of bytes, for example

word – A group of bits in a computer system; the number of bits in a word depends on the machine, but common word sizes are 16, 32, and 64 bits; a typical computer system manipulates bits in word increments

nibble – A term sometimes used to refer to 4 bits (half a byte)

four, you must begin grouping on the right. Grouping from the left gives you an erroneous value if the number of binary digits isn't an even multiple of four.

n o t e

Each hexadecimal digit corresponds to a 4-bit binary pattern. Table 7-1 shows the relationship between hex and binary.

You can also create a binary equivalent for a hexadecimal value by replacing each hexadecimal digit with its 4-bit counterpart. The hex value C2D4, for example, is equivalent to the binary value 1100001011010100. Again, you can use Table 7-1 to do this conversion.

With this information, you can understand some of what's displayed in "blue screen" errors and other messages. The error message shown at the beginning of this chapter contains hexadecimal values representing the actual binary information stored in the computer at the time the error occurred. Computer programmers can use this information to pinpoint the exact location of the error.

Everything that's stored in or displayed on a computer is in binary. The next time you play a game on your computer, you might ponder the fact that everything you're seeing—and everything the computer is doing that you don't see—is the result of little transistors turning on and off to form binary bit patterns. Or you might concentrate on the game so that you can win!

representing whole numbers

whole (integer) number – A number (positive, zero, or negative) that has no fractional portion

Whole numbers, or *integer numbers*, can be represented internally in a computer as simple binary integers, similar to the ones you worked with earlier in the chapter. These whole numbers are always stored in a fixed number of bits. For example, the year 2010 is stored as the 16-bit integer value 0000011111011010. This binary value is displayed as the equivalent hex value 07DA.

Negative numbers need to be represented in a computer, too. The binary numbering system contains only the value of the number, or its magnitude. It doesn't contain the number's sign, so techniques need to be devised to allow storing both the sign and magnitude of a number. Various ways of storing signed numbers in binary have been devised, but the most commonly used is the twos complement method. In this method, the leftmost bit of the binary number is reserved as a sign bit: A 0 is used to indicate positive numbers, and a 1 indicates negative numbers. The remaining bits are used to store the number's absolute value, or magnitude. The *twos complement* method involves performing a conversion on binary digits if the number is negative. If the number is positive, it's left as is.

twos complement – A method of representing negative numbers in a computer system; a binary number is converted to twos complement format by flipping, or reversing, the state of each bit and then adding 1 to the entire word

To perform a twos complement operation on a number to store it as a negative value, the number is first converted from decimal to binary, as described earlier. Then each bit of the number is reversed, or flipped, to the opposite state. Finally, a binary 1 is added to the complete binary number (the word).

Say your checkbook has a negative balance of $124. In a 16-bit signed integer field, this value is represented as 1111111110000100_2 ($FF84_{16}$) by using the following process:

1. Convert the decimal value 124 to binary:

   $124_{10} = 1111100$

2. Place the binary value into a fixed-length field of 16 bits, extending leading 0s to the left:

   0000000001111100

3. Then reverse or flip the bits:

   1111111110000011

4. Finally, add a 1 to the entire number, using binary addition:

   1111111110000100

The final result containing the twos complement negative binary number can also be represented in hex as FF84. Figure 7-5 shows the process of converting both positive and negative numbers to the twos complement format.

Figure 7-5, Storing numbers in a twos complement 8-bit field

	+52	**-52**	
52 decimal is equivalent to binary 110100			52 decimal is equivalent to binary 110100
00110100			**11001100**
In twos complement, positive numbers are simply stored as binary values, with leading 0s to fit the field size			Start with 00110100 Flip the bits to get 11001011 Add 1 to get 11001100

Computers distinguish between signed binary numbers and unsigned binary numbers by examining a number's first bit. If the first bit is a 1, the number is treated as a twos complement negative number. If the first bit is 0, the number is positive and left as it is.

To ensure that the number's sign is always in the first bit, both signed and unsigned numbers in a computer are designed to always take up the same number of bits. Having a 32-bit, signed integer field indicates that a positive or negative number stored in this field always has 31 bits, with the sign being in the remaining bit. Positive numbers have leading 0s to fill the 31 bits. Negative numbers have leading 0s before the twos complement process.

Note that having a fixed number of bits reserved to hold a number also limits the maximum value the number can represent. A number placed in a 32-bit field can't exceed the binary value that the 31 available bits can represent.

representing fractional numbers

In the real world, numbers other than whole integer numbers need to be represented. For example, if the ATM shows your balance as $1.53, the computer needs to store the 53 cents somehow. You've learned how the computer stores integers, both positive and negative. How does it store fractional portions of numbers or numbers to the right of the decimal point? In addition to storing a fractional number, computers must also be able to store whether the number is positive or negative.

Computer designers faced the question of how to store fractional numbers years ago and came up with a technique that the Institute of Electrical and Electronics Engineers (IEEE) adopted. You might be familiar with this *floating-point* or *scientific notation* of numbers. Perhaps you've seen a number such as 1.345E+5 on a calculator display. This method of displaying numbers uses a *mantissa* and an *exponent*. The mantissa (1.345) contains the number's significant digits (that is, excluding zeros), and the exponent (+5) indicates where to place the decimal point. The E in base 10 notation means "10 to the power of." The number 1.345E+5 means the actual number is 134,500.

The *IEEE-754* specification, which dictates how floating-point numbers are stored in most Intel-based computers, uses binary mantissas and exponents. The details of the IEEE-754 specification and other floating-point storage techniques will come later in your studies. For now, you just need to understand that they exist, and you might have to interpret them at some point in your career.

representing characters

In addition to numbers, computers need to be able to store characters. Characters have no mathematical relationship between them, however, so the method of storing them is different from storing numbers.

Early in the history of computers, the *American National Standards Institute (ANSI)* met to standardize the way characters are represented in computers. This

---

floating-point or scientific notation – A method of representing numbers containing fractional values consistently; uses a mantissa and an exponent, such as 3.144543E+8

mantissa – In scientific notation, it contains the number's significant digits and is placed before the exponent

exponent – In scientific notation, it's the power of the base and is multiplied by the mantissa to give the actual number

IEEE-754 – A standard for the binary representation of floating-point numbers; it's the 754th standard proposed by the IEEE

American National Standards Institute (ANSI) – An organization that works with industry groups to formulate and publish standards

group formulated a character set coding scheme of 7-bit patterns as a standard way of representing characters with specific bit patterns. This scheme is called *American Standard Code for Information Interchange (ASCII)*.

Table 7-2 shows a partial listing of the ASCII character set. (For a more complete chart, see Appendix B.) The ASCII character set provides for uppercase and lower-case English characters, numerals, punctuation, and additional special characters. It also has bit patterns set aside to represent control characters for video displays and printers. In total, ASCII provides for 128 (2^7) different characters.

Table 7-2, Sample standard ASCII characters

symbol	decimal representation	hex representation	binary representation
space	32	20	00100000
$	36	24	00100100
1	49	31	00110001
9	57	39	00111001
A	65	41	01000001
Z	90	5A	01011010
a	97	61	01100001
z	122	7A	01111010
}	125	7D	01111101

As computers became used more globally, additional characters needed to be supported. The original ASCII specification was limited to 128 characters, so a new character set was defined with 8 bits instead of 7. This new code, *Extended ASCII*, allowed for 128 additional characters, bringing the total to 256.

Still, for script languages, such as Arabic and Asian languages, Extended ASCII didn't provide for enough characters. Another group met and proposed a new standard called *Unicode*. Unicode provides for 34,168 unique characters and is compatible with ASCII. It's becoming the standard method of character representation.

When you're typing characters into your computer, they're being stored as binary patterns in ASCII, Extended ASCII, or Unicode format. All character data, such as data in databases, is stored on the hard disk in this format, too.

American Standard Code for Information Interchange (ASCII) – *A standard for storing text characters in computers; the ASCII standard allows representing 128 possible characters with 7 bits*

Extended ASCII – *A method for storing characters with an 8-bit code; adds 128 more characters to the original 7-bit ASCII code*

Unicode – *A 16-bit standard for storing text or script information; defines 34,168 unique characters and control codes*

representing images

You've learned now that everything going on in a computer is done in binary. Video displays and printers are no exception.

If you look closely at your computer monitor, you can see that what's displayed on the screen is not a solid image. It's made up of small dots of colored light. Each dot is referred to as a *pixel (picture element)*, which is the smallest unit that can be displayed on a computer monitor. Pixels are arranged in rows and columns. The number of pixels in each row and column defines the display device's resolution. A common resolution on a PC monitor is 1024 × 768, which means the monitor is displaying 768 rows with 1024 dots, or pixels, in each row. As the resolution numbers get larger, the size of each pixel gets smaller.

pixel (picture element) – The basic unit of programmable color on a computer display or in a computer image; its physical size depends on the display device's resolution

As you might have guessed, each pixel is stored in the computer as a binary pattern containing information about its color and brightness. This binary pattern can be 8 bits and allow up to 256 different levels of color and brightness, or, it might be 24 bits per pixel, allowing more than 16 million different colors. One common way of encoding pixel information is assigning a value to each of the colors red, green, and blue, with each color using 8 of the 24 bits. This method is referred to as *RGB encoding*. If all 24 bits are 1s, the pixel is displayed as bright white. If all the bits are 0s, the pixel is displayed as black. Values other than all 0s or all 1s are perceived as colors made up of the amount of red, green, and blue specified in each 8-bit section.

RGB encoding – A method of defining a pixel's color and brightness in terms of intensity of the colors red, green, and blue

Images, such as photos, can also be stored in the same manner. When a pattern of bits is stored for each pixel, these bitmap (BMP) files can be very large. A photo with 1024 × 768 resolution consists of 786,432 pixels. If each pixel uses 24 bits to store color information, the file size is more than 2 million bytes (2 MB). Large image files can be slow to send over the Internet, so compression techniques have been devised to allow storing the same image information in a smaller file. JPG and GIF are examples of compressed image formats. The compression techniques used in these formats take advantage of repeating patterns and colors to replace the pixels they consist of with special codes.

Moving images are stored in a similar manner. Movies on DVDs, for example, are just series of still images displayed one after another at a rate of nearly 30 images per second. Compression is essential to store and display images at this rate. Examples of video compression formats are MPEG (MPG), QuickTime (MOV), and Windows Media Video (WMV).

representing sounds

Sounds are stored in the computer in a manner similar to images. A sound consists of a waveform with amplitude (volume) and frequency (pitch). The computer samples sounds at fixed intervals, and each sample is assigned a binary value, according to its amplitude (see Figure 7-6). The number of bits used for each sample determines how many unique amplitude levels can be represented. You might have noticed that an audio file's properties contain information about the file's sampling rate and size. To achieve CD-quality audio, the sound must be sampled more than 44,000 times a second, and each sample must be 16 bits, allowing more than 65,000 different amplitudes.

Figure 7-6, Digital sampling of a sound wave

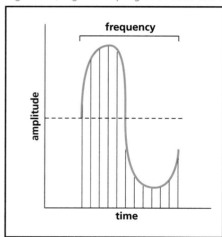

WAV – An audio file format that has become a standard for everything from PC system and game sounds to CD-quality audio

MP3 (MPEG-1 Audio Layer-3) – A standard technology and format for compressing a sound sequence into a small file, compared with an uncompressed sound file, such as a WAV file

Raw audio samples are often stored in uncompressed file formats, such as *WAV* files. Sound files can also be quite large, so compression techniques, such as *MP3*, are useful.

Representing sounds and images is an evolving science. Computer scientists are constantly striving to make sound and image files smaller. Perhaps you'll come up with a new method of compression that will revolutionize the multimedia industry. If you're interested, you can find more detailed information about image and sound formats on the Internet.

one last thought

Understanding number conversions and data representations is vital to excelling in the computer field. Because everything that's stored in or takes place on a computer is ultimately done in binary, being able to "talk" binary is necessary to create new ways of executing instructions and storing data.

Although learning to program or to manage a database without understanding binary and hexadecimal is possible, having this understanding gives you a better foundation than others who don't have it. Computer professionals who have a strong understanding of the concepts in this chapter are better at whatever they specialize in. For this reason, they're usually more essential in their organizations. Typically, they're the last ones to go when there are layoffs, and they're more likely to find new employment soon. Wouldn't you want to be this type of person?

chapter summary

- The powers of a number can be calculated by multiplying the base, or radix, by the exponent.
- Numbering systems are used to count things.
- The positional value of each digit in a number can be calculated by raising the base of the number to the power indicated by the position.
- Numbers in one numbering system can be converted to any other numbering system.
- Converting to and from base 10 and any other base follows a set procedure.
- The hexadecimal numbering system is used as a shorthand for binary values.
- Whole numbers can be represented in binary by using signed or unsigned techniques.
- Fractional numbers can also be represented in binary.
- Binary values are also used to represent characters, images, and sounds.

key terms

American National Standards Institute (ANSI) (*265*)

American Standard Code for Information Interchange (ASCII) (*266*)

binary (*253*)

bit (*262*)

byte (*262*)

exponent (*265*)

Extended ASCII (*266*)

floating-point or scientific notation (*265*)

hexadecimal (hex) (*253*)

IEEE-754 (*265*)

integer number (*263*)

mantissa (*265*)

MP3 (*268*)

nibble (*262*)

pixel (*267*)

positional value (*254*)

radix point (*254*)

RGB encoding (*267*)

twos complement (*263*)

Unicode (*266*)

WAV (*268*)

whole number (*263*)

word (*262*)

test yourself

1. What does the subscript 10 indicate in the number 3456_{10}?

2. What does the superscript 10 indicate in the number 2^{10}?

3. What is the value of 2^8?

4. What is the positional value of the first digit on the left of the binary number 10110?

5. What is the largest number of items that can be represented with 4 binary bits?

6. What is the positional value of the A in the hexadecimal number CAFE?

7. What numeric value in base 10 does the binary number 10101010 represent?

8. What is the binary equivalent of the decimal number 345?

9. What base 10 value is equivalent to $1C4B_{16}$?

10. What base 16 value is equivalent to 2576_{10}?

11. What numeric value in hexadecimal is equivalent to the binary number 1011111010101101?

12. What binary value is equivalent to the hexadecimal number C43A?

13. What is the binary result of adding the binary numbers 1001 + 1111?

14. What is the twos complement value of the binary number 01110110?

15. How many unique characters does Extended ASCII allow?

16. How many pixels is a computer monitor with a resolution of 1024 × 768 capable of displaying?

17. What is the ASCII code (in hex) for the uppercase letter A?

18. How many different colors can be represented with a 24-bit pixel?

19. Which of these image formats—BMP, JPG, GIF—is not compressed?

20. Any number raised to the 0 power returns a value of what?

practice exercises

1. What does the subscript 16 indicate in the number C4A6$_{16}$?

    a. An exponent of 16
    b. A positional value of 16
    c. A base 16 number
    d. None of the above

2. What does the superscript 3 indicate in the number 16^3?

    a. An exponent of 3
    b. A positional value of 3
    c. A base 3 number
    d. None of the above

3. What is the value of 16^3?

    a. 163
    b. 48
    c. 4096
    d. 256

4. What is the positional value of the 1 in the binary number 100000?

    a. 64
    b. 32
    c. 16
    d. 8

5. What is the largest number of items that can be represented with four hexadecimal digits?

    a. 4096
    b. 40,960
    c. 65,536
    d. None of the above

6. What is the positional value of the A in the hexadecimal number BEAD?

    a. 2
    b. 10
    c. 16
    d. 32

7. What numeric value in base 10 does the binary number 10000001 represent?

    a. 129
    b. 10,000,001
    c. 65
    d. None of the above

8. What is the binary equivalent of the decimal number 543?

   a. 11111011110111
   b. 101100111
   c. 1011010011
   d. 1000011111

9. What base 10 value is equivalent to $3C0D_{16}$?

   a. 15,373
   b. 32,767
   c. 68,536
   d. 10,125

10. What base 16 value is equivalent to 1234_{10}?

    a. ABC
    b. 4D2
    c. C34
    d. A65

11. What numeric value in hexadecimal is equivalent to the binary number 1101111010101101?

    a. BCAF
    b. BE6C
    c. 6FAD
    d. DEAD

12. What binary value is equivalent to the hex number C43A?

    a. 1100100100010110
    b. 1100110101111010
    c. 1100010000111010
    d. 1100001101011101

13. What is the binary result of adding the binary numbers 0110 + 1101?

    a. 10011
    b. 1111
    c. 01101101
    d. 101001

14. What is the twos complement value of the binary number 010100110?

    a. 101011001
    b. 101011010
    c. 010100111
    d. None of the above

15. How many unique characters does ASCII allow?

    a. 16
    b. 32
    c. 128
    d. 255

16. How many total bits are required to store 24-bit color information for a 1024 × 768 display?

   a. 18,874,368
   b. 786,432
   c. 1024
   d. 24

17. What is the ASCII code (in hex) for the lowercase letter z?

   a. 7A
   b. 80
   c. 32
   d. AB

18. What is the minimum number of bits required to represent 256 colors?

   a. 4
   b. 8
   c. 16
   d. 32

19. What color is represented if all the pixel bits are 1s?

   a. Red
   b. Black
   c. Cyan
   d. White

20. Any number except 0 raised to the power of 1 is what?

   a. 1
   b. The positional value times the digit
   c. The number itself
   d. None of the above

digging deeper

1. Can all numbering system bases be used as shorthand for binary? If not all bases, which bases can?

2. What other image formats are there, besides JPG, BMP, and GIF? What are the strengths and weaknesses of each?

3. How would you calculate the value of a number with a fractional power?

4. What are some alternative methods of converting from base 10 to other numbering system bases?

5. What is the purpose of the ASCII codes 0_{10} to 26_{10}?

discussion topics

1. What are possible implications for computing if a transistor-type device could be created with 10 stable states?

2. In working with computers, what types of situations require knowledge of numbering systems?

3. What types of compression techniques can be used to make image and sound files smaller?

4. What are the word sizes in the most widely used computer systems? What's the significance of a word size?

5. How can a hex editor be used to examine the contents of memory and disks?

Internet research

1. Where are standards, such as IEEE-754, available on the Internet?

2. What is the history of numbering systems?

3. What are some examples of Web pages and downloadable programs that can convert between different forms of data representations and numbering systems?

4. What are the advantages and disadvantages of each image and sound format discussed in the chapter?

5. What do the hexadecimal values in a typical "blue screen" fatal error message represent?

chapter

8

data structures

in this chapter you will:

- Learn what a data structure is and how it's used
- Learn about single-dimensional and multidimensional arrays and how they work
- Learn what a pointer is and how it's used in data structures
- Learn that a linked list allows you to work with dynamic information
- Understand that a stack is a linked list and how it's used
- Learn that a queue is another form of a linked list and how it's used
- Learn that a binary tree is a data structure that stores information in a hierarchical order
- See an overview of several sorting routines

the lighter side of the lab
by sp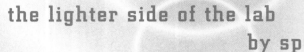er

As soon as you flip the page, you're going to be bombarded with a list of words you're probably not familiar with, such as "pointers," "arrays," "stacks," and "queues." Don't stress out! Calmly pick up your book, slowly walk to the nearest open window, gently hurl the book through the open window, and change your major to art. I'm kidding, of course. Change it to sociology.

Actually, these concepts aren't as complicated as they seem at first. There are examples all around you. You see an example of a pointer when you attend a commencement and somebody in the audience uses a laser pen to point out to the rest of the audience where the speaker's forehead is.

Arrays can be extremely useful for keeping track of large quantities of information when all the entries are of the same type. This technology has given NASA scientists the ability to keep track of Brangelina's kids.

Stacks are found everywhere, too. In fact, I was near the bottom of a stack the other day. This stack consisted of my two cousins, my three brothers, and myself and was created when my brother initialized the stack with the command "Doggypile!" NOTE: FIFO doesn't work with doggypile stacks, as demonstrated by my cracked ribs. (Feel free to return and laugh at this statement after you've read the chapter.)

Most of us stand in at least one queue (or "line," as it's called in the United States) on a daily basis, whether it's in the supermarket, at a restaurant, or for the shower in the morning when all your roommates and you try to get ready for school at the same time. In fact, I almost had a little "buffer overflow" as I stood in the extremely long queue for the restroom at a football game recently.

You see, data structures aren't that difficult. When these technical terms are applied to aspects of everyday life, learning these principles becomes easy enough that anybody can do it—even an art major.

why you need to know about...
data structures

A doctor, an engineer, and a computer scientist were discussing which of their professions had been around the longest. The doctor said, "In the beginning, there was Adam and Eve. Someone had to know medicine to create Adam and Eve." The engineer turned to the doctor and said, "Before Adam and Eve could live on the earth, it had to be created. Someone had to know engineering to create the earth." The computer scientist just laughed and said, "You're both wrong! In the beginning, there was chaos. Who do you think created all that chaos?"

For a computer to be effective, there must be some type of organization. Without it, chaos would run rampant. The computer couldn't access and retrieve memory effectively, and system response time would be unbearably slow. In fact, computers would perform so horribly that they would be worthless. Data structures organize data in a computer and make it possible to access and process data in an efficient and meaningful way.

All programs use some form of data, and to be able to write effective computer programs, you must understand the basics of a data structure and how it's used. As you learn more about programming and begin writing computer programs, you'll find many occasions for using the kinds of data structures introduced in this chapter.

data structures

Why worry about organizing data on your computer? Think of your bedroom. How hard is it to find something you're looking for? If your room is organized and clean, finding an item is a lot easier and quicker. If it's messy and disorganized, you have to look through everything to try to find an item, which takes time and energy.

data structure – A way of organizing data in memory, such as arrays, lists, stacks, queues, and trees

A *data structure* can be defined as a way of organizing data. There are different types of data structures in memory, such as arrays, lists, stacks, queues, and trees. There are also ways of organizing data on storage media, such as file structures.

Chapter 10 focuses on file structures, and this chapter focuses on memory structures.

A computer's memory is organized into cells. Each memory cell has a memory address through which the cell's contents can be accessed. As shown in Figure 8-1, memory addresses are organized consecutively: If the first memory cell has an address of 0, the next memory cell has an address of 1.

Figure 8-1, Consecutive memory locations

position	value
0	Mercury
1	Venus
2	Earth
3	Mars
4	Jupiter

Luckily for you, data structures make it possible to use a computer without having to worry about the details of how information is stored in consecutive memory locations. The most common data structures are arrays and lists.

arrays

array – A set of contiguous memory cells used for storing the same type of data

An *array* is the simplest memory data structure and consists of a set of contiguous memory cells that must store the same type of data. So if the first memory cell contains a number, all memory cells associated with the array must also contain numbers.

Arrays are used for storing similar kinds of information in memory. This information can then be sorted or left in the order it was entered in the array. Arrays can be used to store student grades, book titles, names of college courses, a space shuttle launch checklist, and so on. As long as the information is of the same type and you want to store it in memory, an array is the data structure to use.

For example, if you want to write a computer program that asks users to enter five different numbers, prints them onscreen in reverse order, and then calculates the sum of the numbers, you can create an array of five positions to hold the number values temporarily. The number values can be accessed by using the array. As shown in Figure 8-2, if you didn't use an array, you would have to create five different holding areas or variable names, with each area having its own name. Using an array makes program logic easier to understand and use. Instead of having to worry about five different memory variables or names, using an array requires you to remember only the array name.

Figure 8-2, Arrays make program logic easier to understand and use

array name:	aNumbers				
position	value				value
0	95		0	Variable1	95
1	88		1	Variable2	88
2	92		2	Variable3	92
3	78		3	Variable4	78
4	85		4	Variable5	85

how an array works

When an array is first defined, you must tell the computer what type of data to store and how many memory cells to use. For example, in the Java programming language, you create a new array and specify its type and size by using the "new" keyword. You also specify a name for the array, which is used to access the contents of the array's cells. Take a look at this statement, and then read the following explanation:

```
int[ ] aGrades = new int[5];
```

- The int[ ] part of the statement tells the computer that the array will hold integer (numeric) values. If you want the array to hold character values, char[ ] is used.
- The word "aGrades" is the array's name, the name by which memory contents are accessed.
- The "new" keyword tells the computer that a new array is being created.
- The int[5] part of the statement, for specifying array type and size, tells the computer to reserve five memory locations to store numeric (int) values for the array.

element – *A memory cell in an array*

- The = sign (equal sign, called an assignment operator) takes the newly created array of five memory cells and assigns aGrades as the "manager" of these memory cells.
- The ; (semicolon) tells the computer that the end of the statement has been reached.

Note that the array name includes a lowercase "a" in front of "Grades." This convention is called Hungarian notation, a variable-naming standard devised to make a program's statements more readable.

The five contiguous memory cells are reserved in memory and can be referenced by using the word that has been set up as the manager—in this case, aGrades. The aGrades array is considered a single-dimensional array because it contains only one row or column of elements (see Figure 8-3). (An *element* is another name for a memory cell in an array.) An array's dimension is how many levels are created to hold the array elements.

Figure 8-3, Five contiguous memory cells managed by aGrades in a single-dimensional array

array name:	aGrades	
position	value	one row of memory locations
0	95	
1	88	
2	92	
3	78	
4	85	

Think of a single-dimensional array as a row of mailboxes on a street (see Figure 8-4). Each mailbox has an address associated with it. For this example, the street name is aGrades. There are five property locations on the street, each with its own unique mailing address. All the mailboxes are lined up in a row on the street so that the postal carrier can organize and deliver the mail easily. Also,

Figure 8-4, A row of mailboxes is similar to a row of contiguous memory cells (an array)

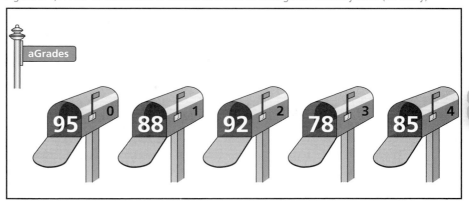

there are strict rules for the postal carrier. The only type of items that can be delivered to mailboxes must be defined when the mailboxes are first built. In this example, the mailboxes allow receipt of only letters containing numbers. As the postal carrier drives up to the mailboxes, the address on each letter determines which mailbox receives the information being mailed.

So how is the process of putting values into an array's cells accomplished in a computer? The first address or position in the array starts with 0. Arrays start at element 0 because they're implemented by using memory addresses. When you create a new array and assign it a name, the computer reserves some memory locations to accommodate the array's size. The name is actually assigned the memory location where the array begins in memory. This memory location is used just as a postal carrier uses an address to find a specific mailbox. After the memory location (or mailbox) is found, the computer knows that the next element in the array is one position, or *offset*, over from the starting address. The offset specifies the distance between memory locations. The computer has been told that to locate the next element in the array, it must use the array's starting memory location, stored in the first position of the array, and then move over the number of offsets representing different positions in the array.

offset – *Used to specify the distance between memory locations*

For example, the array's first position, referenced as position 0, can be found by using the starting memory location of the array plus zero offsets. In other words, it's equal to the array's starting position. The next position of the array, referenced as position 1, is found by using the starting memory location plus one offset. The third position of the array, referenced as position 2, is found by using the starting memory location plus two offsets (see Figure 8-5).

Figure 8-5, Arrays start at position 0 and use an offset to know where the next element is located in memory

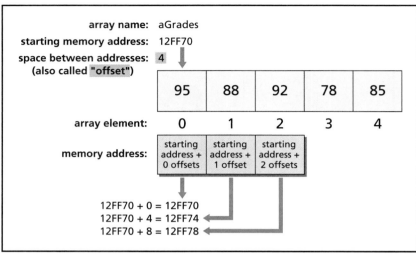

index (subscript) – *How an array accesses each element stored in its data structure*

To make using an array easier, an *index* or a *subscript* is used. It tells the computer which memory cell to access in the array by looking at the element's position. The index is placed between square brackets ([ ]) after the array name. To store a value of 50 in the first element, you use this statement:

```
aGrades[0] = 50;
```

When the array was created, it was specified with five contiguous memory locations. The preceding statement places the value 50 in the first position. Remember that position 0 is the first position, so when an array has positions 0 to 4, there are actually five memory cells, or addresses. If you want to store a value in the fifth element, you need to access position 4, as shown:

```
aGrades[4] = 100;
```

If you store a value in every element of the array, as shown in the following code lines, it might look like Figure 8-6:

```
aGrades[0] = 50;
aGrades[1] = 30;
aGrades[2] = 25;
aGrades[3] = 85;
aGrades[4] = 100;
```

upper bound – *The highest position in an array*

lower bound – *The lowest position in an array*

The *upper bound* of the array is the element with the highest position (4), and the *lower bound* is the lowest position used (0). These bounds can be used with the array's length to process through the array element by element, until all elements have been processed.

Figure 8-6, The array with all elements stored

position	value
0	50
1	30
2	25
3	85
4	100

multidimensional arrays

multidimensional array –
An array consisting of two
or more single-dimensional
arrays

Besides single-dimensional arrays, there are *multidimensional arrays*, which consist of two or more single-dimensional arrays. In the mailboxes example, there's just one row of mailboxes in a single-dimensional array. In a multidimensional array, there are multiple rows of mailboxes stacked on top of each other, as shown in Figure 8-7. In this example, the apartment building has a mailbox for

Figure 8-7, A multidimensional array is like apartment mailboxes stacked on top of each other

apartment #:	0	1	2	3	4
floor 0	floor 0 apartment 0	floor 0 apartment 1	floor 0 apartment 2		
1	floor 1 apartment 0	floor 1 apartment 1			
2	floor 2 apartment 0				

each tenant. The building's floor numbering starts on 0 because it's ground level. Each floor is offset by the number of flights of stairs above ground level, so the second floor is floor 1, or one flight of stairs above ground level (floor 0). The address of each mailbox is the combination of the floor number plus the apartment number. For example, the first mailbox has the address of floor 0, apartment number 0. The last mailbox (not numbered in the figure) has the address of floor 2, apartment number 4. Each floor has five apartments numbered 0 through 4. The only way the postal carrier knows which apartment receives the letter is by also knowing the floor.

Are you officially confused? You can make it easier by starting with the simplest multidimensional array. Almost everyone has played tic-tac-toe. A tic-tac-toe board (see Figure 8-8) is actually a two-dimensional array—that is, an array within an array.

Figure 8-8, Tic-tac-toe board

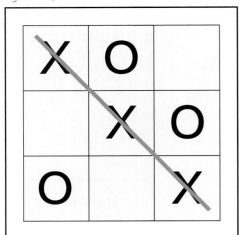

The tic-tac-toe board array consists of three positions in the first row, three in the second, and three in the third. The first row contains an array of three positions, as shown in Figure 8-9. The rows are numbered from 0 to 2, and the columns are numbered from 0 to 2. All the array elements in the first row have a row value of 0 with a column value of 0, 1, or 2.

The second and third rows are also arrays (see Figure 8-10). All the array elements in the second row have a row value of 1 with a column value of 0, 1, or 2, and all the array elements in the third row have a row value of 2 with a column value of 0, 1, or 2.

Figure 8-9, First row of the tic-tac-toe board

column:	0	1	2
row:			
0	row 0 column 0	row 0 column 1	row 0 column 2
1			
2			

Figure 8-10, Second and third rows of the tic-tac-toe board

column:	0	1	2
row:			
0	row 0 column 0	row 0 column 1	row 0 column 2
1	row 1 column 0	row 1 column 1	row 1 column 2
2	row 2 column 0	row 2 column 1	row 2 column 2

Creating the tic-tac-toe board as a multidimensional array in memory is easy. Using the array syntax defined earlier in the chapter, the statement looks like this:

```
char[ ][ ] aTicTacToe = new char[3][3];
```

Don't get confused into thinking you would declare a three-by-three array as [2][2] because array indexes are zero-based. In declaring an array size, you don't need to worry about the fact that arrays start at 0. You just need to remember

multidimensional arrays

In C++, you create a multidimensional array and store a value in one of the array elements by using these statements:

char aTicTacToe[3][3];

aTicTacToe[1][1] = 'X';

In Delphi (Pascal), you create a multidimensional array and store a value in one of the array elements by using these statements:

var aTicTacToe : array[0..2,0..2] of char;

aTicTacToe[1,1] := 'X';

that array indexes are zero-based when you begin accessing the elements. When you're declaring the array's size, you need to think only of how many elements are needed.

The preceding statement creates three arrays, each having three storage locations. It's a lot easier to think of it as having three rows and three columns (much like a spreadsheet).

If you're playing a game of tic-tac-toe, you might want to start by putting an X in the center position (see Figure 8-11). To place the character X in the second row of the second column, you use the following statement:

```
aTicTacToe[1][1] = 'X';
```

Why isn't the location shown as [2][2]? That's right—because array indexes are always zero-based, so the first row is index row 0, and the second row is index row 1, and so on.

Figure 8-11, Storing a value in an array location

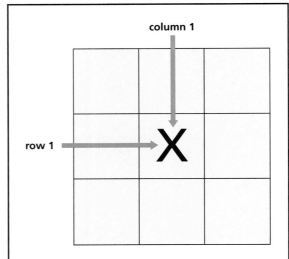

Take a look at Figure 8-12, an example of a three-dimensional array. It can be explained as having three arrays or levels. On each level (array) is a two-dimensional array containing rows and columns.

Are you ready to try a four-dimensional array? Actually, many programmers suggest that you go no further than three levels deep on an array because the more levels you have, the more complicated the array becomes. Remember that simplicity makes writing and maintaining data structures a lot easier.

Figure 8-12, Three-dimensional array

uses of arrays

Arrays are an excellent data structure for storing information in memory because they can be accessed sequentially without any knowledge of the memory cell contents. As long as you know the array name and the data type for elements, you can retrieve and store data with an array. Arrays are also easy to create and are useful for people who write computer programs. For example, you have a program that stores 20 student names. Instead of creating 20 separate storage locations, each with its own name, you have to create only one array containing 20 storage locations, accessed by a single name plus an index. That's a lot easier to remember and use.

You have learned that an array is a collection of homogeneous data items. Chapter 14, "Programming I," introduces a data structure called a class, which is a collection of heterogeneous data items.

A disadvantage of using arrays is that a lot of overhead (computer power) can be expended in trying to insert new elements into a defined array structure. The array is a contiguous list data structure, which means memory cells are located one after the other in memory. What if you define an array to hold 20 student names, but then one more student registers for the course? Now you have run out of room in the array and have to redefine the array's size and make sure all the information in the first array is copied to the second array correctly. This method is quite inefficient and cumbersome.

Another disadvantage of arrays is that data in memory cells can be accessed only sequentially—that is, one at a time, in order. So if you want to find a specific value stored in an array, you have to start at the first position in the array and look at every single position until you find the value you're looking for. You can't randomly search the data stored in elements based on search criteria. If you're using arrays for random searching of data, the computer is performing work that can be done more efficiently by using a different data structure.

The real benefits of arrays become more apparent when you learn how to program loops, discussed in Chapter 15, "Programming II."

lists

As you've learned, the process of changing array size dynamically is quite inefficient and daunting. Another data structure, the list, was developed to overcome some disadvantages of arrays. This data structure holds dynamic lists of data, meaning the lists vary in size. Examples of lists that grow or shrink include class enrollment, cars brought in for repairs, and e-mail inboxes. In fact, whenever the amount of data is unknown or could change, you have a good candidate for a list data structure. The amount of storage needed for the list is unknown and needs to be flexible so that the list can accept new items or have existing items removed.

The forms of lists that can be implemented to work efficiently with dynamic data are as follows:

- Linked lists
- Queues
- Stacks

The following sections describe these data structures.

linked lists

linked list – A data structure that uses noncontiguous memory locations to store data; each element in the linked list points to the next element in line and doesn't have to be contiguous with the previous element

A *linked list* is used when the exact number of items is unknown or the length of the structure might change. For example, a linked list could be used to store the names of students who visit a professor's office in a day, points you have scored against an opponent in your favorite video game, or companies that have sent you spam e-mail. You use the logic behind a linked list every day.

A linked list differs in use from an array in that it stores data noncontiguously (not in order). Instead of allocating a block of memory with array cells following each other contiguously, a linked list maintains the data and the address of where to go next. Remember that each cell of an array uses an address as a reference for accessing the data. A linked list also uses addresses but implements them as "The memory locations I'm using can be stored anywhere in memory, so what memory location is next in line for me to jump to?"

Linked lists are the basic constructs for more advanced data structures, such as queues and stacks. All these structures use pointers. Learning how pointers work is not rocket science, but it tends to be a topic that can confuse beginning computing students. In fact, you have already used pointers but probably didn't realize it. All you have to know is that a *pointer* is a memory variable containing the address of a memory cell as its data. Just think "address," and it's easier to grasp. You have already worked with addresses while learning about arrays. An address is simply a location in memory.

pointer – A memory variable containing the address of a memory cell as its data

For example, say you're playing a game in which students sit in a circle. Each student has a piece of paper with a box in the upper-left corner indicating a student number and another box in the center divided into two more boxes (see Figure 8-13). The students are told to write their favorite color in the center box on the left and leave the box on the right alone, as it already has a number printed in it.

Figure 8-13, The piece of paper used in the linked list game

The professor also has a piece of paper, but it contains only a student number. The professor starts the game by reading this number aloud and pointing to the student whose piece of paper contains that number. This student reads aloud the color written in the left box, and then reads the student number printed in the right box on his piece of paper. The student with this number then states her color and calls out the student number written on her paper. This process continues until all the students have had a turn to read aloud the color they wrote and call out the number in the right box. How does this game end? The last student's paper doesn't have a student number printed in the right box. Instead, the last student's "go next?" box contains a null (also called a *null value*).

This game demonstrates how a linked list is used in memory and how a pointer is used to tell the computer which memory location is the next one in the list. Each piece of paper represents the structure of a linked list: As Figure 8-14 shows, it contains both data (the color) and a pointer to where to go next (the student number). The professor's piece of paper represents the *head pointer*, the beginning of the linked list that indicates where to get the first piece of information.

null value – *The absence of a value, meaning there's no value stored; null is not the same as blank or zero*

head pointer – *A pointer indicating the beginning of the first element in a data structure*

Figure 8-14, Structure of a linked list

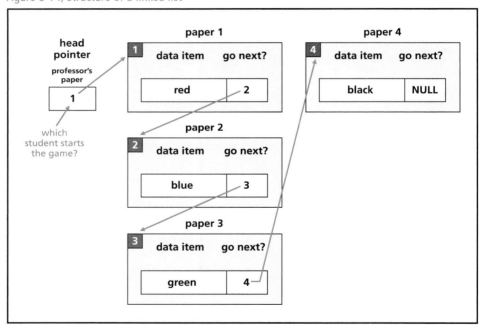

What happens if you want to insert a new element into the list? If it's an array, you have to resize it, which causes the computer to allocate a new block of memory big enough for the entire array, and then the old array's contents must be copied to the new array's memory cells. This method isn't an efficient way of storing data in memory if you're adding and deleting elements.

A linked list, on the other hand, simply creates a new "piece of paper" with one location for the data and another for the "where to go" pointer address. Then the pointer before the location where the new paper is to be inserted is changed to point to the new paper. The pointer on the new paper is made to point to the next paper in the sequence. For example, a new student joins the class. The professor hands a piece of paper with the number 5 on it to the new student and tells the student to sit at the end of the line and write a favorite color in the box on the left. The professor then tells the student to follow student 3 in telling the class the color, and then the new student should point to student 4 (see Figure 8-15).

Figure 8-15, Inserting an element into a linked list

A linked list doesn't have to work with contiguous memory, which makes it more efficient for dynamic structures. The professor could even put the new student at the beginning of the line without affecting how the information is processed. Why? Because the professor would still tell student 1 to start. Student 1 would read the color "red" and then call on student 2, who would read the color "blue." This process would continue until after student 3 reads the color "green" and calls on the new student, who is number 5. Student 5 would read "purple" and then call on student 4, who would read "black" and then stop.

The same concept applies when you want to delete an element from a linked list. The element that points to the item being deleted must have its pointer modified to point to the item that the deleted item used to point to (see Figure 8-16).

Figure 8-16, Deleting an element from a linked list

Without having to move any students in the class, a student can be deleted from the game. All that has to happen is that whichever student was pointing to the deleted student needs to change his or her "go next?" value to point to the student who follows the deleted student. In other words, before an item is deleted from a linked list, the "go next?" value is saved so that the previous item can be updated to skip the deleted item.

stacks

stack – A list in which the next item to be removed is the item most recently stored

A *stack* is a special form of a list that allows you to "push" new items onto the list and "pop" existing items off the list. It's similar to how some all-you-can-eat buffet restaurants provide plates for customers (see Figure 8-17). The plate holder is spring-loaded, and as a customer removes a plate from the stack, every plate moves up one position. As clean plates are added to the stacks, the current plates move down, away from the top of the stack. The kitchen employee pushes plates onto the stack, and customers pop plates up from the stack. Looking at the top plate to inspect it without removing it from the stack is called *peeking*.

peeking – *Looking at the top item in the stack without removing it from the stack*

Figure 8-17, The stack concept

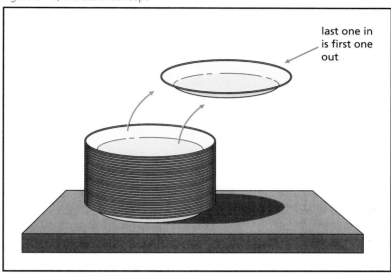

last one in is first one out

last in, first out (LIFO) – *The last item placed on the stack is the first item removed from the stack*

push – *Place an item on the stack*

pop – *Remove an item from the stack*

A stack is considered a *last in, first out (LIFO)* data structure. The last or most recent item *pushed* (put) onto the stack is the first item *popped* (removed) from the stack. Another example of a LIFO data structure is a text editor. As you type characters, the character insertion pointer is placed at the end of the last character typed. If you press the backspace key, the last character typed is removed. Or think of a can of Pringles potato chips. The factory pushes chips into the cylinder so that the first chip pushed in sits at the very bottom and is the last one to come out.

Notice that in a stack, items are added to or taken away from the top of the stack. In other words, the first value popped from the stack is the value that has remained on the stack for the shortest amount of time. The very last item popped from the stack has remained on the stack for the longest time.

uses of a stack

How a stack is used can best be explained by understanding how a computer processes the lines of source code in a program. As the computer executes a program, it understands the tasks it's supposed to accomplish by using source code. A line of source code is simply a command to do some work. This work might include storing a value in memory, performing a mathematical calculation, displaying a value onscreen, sending information to the printer, or a plethora of other tasks.

procedure – A group of one or more related commands that perform a task

The source code is logically organized into *procedures*, groups of related commands that perform a task. Another line of source code might call the procedure and tell it to execute its lines of source code. The called procedure might in turn call another procedure and so on, until there's a long list of procedures that have called each other.

The computer must keep track of the calling procedure so that when the called procedure's source code is completed, it can return to where it left off in the program. Think of it as the computer creating a "lifeline" so that it always knows how to get back to where it came from. This backtracking is accomplished by using a stack. The computer pushes the address of a procedure call onto the stack. As the called procedure finishes executing its source code, the address of the procedure is popped off the stack, and the computer proceeds to the next statement in the program.

back to pointers

stack pointer – A pointer that keeps track of where to remove or add an item in a data structure

In most stack implementations, a pointer called the *stack pointer* keeps track of the top of the stack. The computer knows where to push new items and remove current items from the data structure by using the memory location pointed to by the stack pointer. Remember that stacks, like linked lists and arrays, are just memory locations that have been organized into structures to facilitate reading from them and writing to them. Figure 8-18 shows how the stack pointer is adjusted when an item is popped off the stack.

Figure 8-18, Stack pointer is decremented when the item is popped off

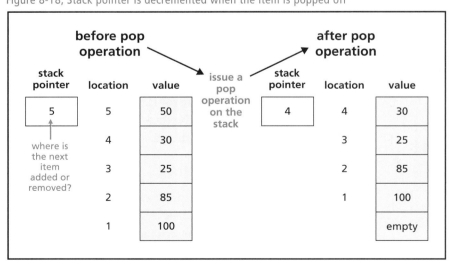

Before an item is popped from the stack, the status of the stack must be checked to make sure there's an item to pop. Before an item is pushed onto the stack, the computer must check to make sure there's room for the new item. Otherwise, pushing or popping could cause an error.

queues

queue – *A list in which the next item to be removed is the item that has been in the list the longest*

first in, first out (FIFO) – *The last item placed on the stack is the last item removed from the stack, and the first item removed from the stack is the first item placed onto the stack*

A *queue* is another type of linked list that uses a *first in, first out (FIFO)* structure. Insertions are made at the end of the stack, and deletions are made at the beginning. The implementation of this data structure is much like waiting in line. For example, the first customer in line is the first one to leave the line. The last customer in the line is in line the longest. You have encountered FIFO structures when you have gone to a bank, bought food at the supermarket, driven your car on and off a ferry, or lined up at the school bookstore to buy this book.

uses of a queue

A queue is used in many situations in a computer system, and you hear it referenced by people who work with computer task management. For example, as you print documents, they're placed in a print queue. The first item to be printed is the document that has been in the queue the longest. As the item is printed, it's deleted from the queue, and the next item is printed. If you request to print another document, it's placed at the end of the queue. This process continues until the queue is emptied. The queue is a "worker bee" that simply accepts what it's given and pushes it out if it can. It keeps pushing out the oldest items and putting the newer items at the end of the list.

In a queue, all insertions of new data occur at the rear of the queue, and removal of data occurs at the front of the queue.

pointers again

tail pointer – *Keeps track of the end or rear position of the data structure*

dequeue – *To remove an item from a queue*

A queue uses a head pointer and a tail pointer. The head pointer keeps track of the beginning of the queue. As you might have guessed, the *tail pointer* keeps track of the end of the queue (see Figure 8-19). If the queue contains no items, both the head and tail pointer point to the same location.

When an item is removed from the queue (to *dequeue* an item), the head pointer is changed to point to the next item in the list following the item recently removed. Look at the queue shown in Figure 8-20. If you dequeue an item from this queue, the oldest entry (stored in location 1) is removed. The head pointer is then updated to point to location 2, signifying that it's currently the oldest entry in the queue.

Figure 8-19, A queue uses a FIFO structure

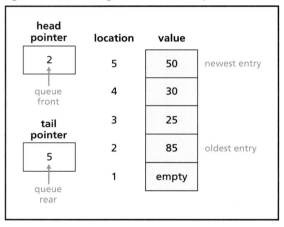

head pointer	location	value	
1	5	50	newest entry
queue front	4	30	
tail pointer	3	25	
5	2	85	
queue rear	1	100	oldest entry

Figure 8-20, Removing an item from the queue

head pointer	location	value	
2	5	50	newest entry
queue front	4	30	
tail pointer	3	25	
5	2	85	oldest entry
queue rear	1	empty	

enqueue – *To insert an item into a queue*

When an item is inserted into the queue (to *enqueue* an item), it's placed at the end of the list, and the tail pointer is updated. As shown in Figure 8-21, a new entry containing the value 18 is enqueued, thus adding a new item to the list and updating the tail pointer to point to the newest item added to the queue.

note

There are many different ways to implement data structures in programming, depending on how the programmer wants to do it.

As you can see, both stacks and queues use pointers to keep track of items in their data structures.

Figure 8-21, Inserting an item into the queue

head pointer	location	value	
2	6	18	newest entry
↑ queue front	5	50	
tail pointer	4	30	
6	3	25	
↑ queue rear	2	85	oldest entry
	1	empty	

trees

Another data structure that uses pointers to manipulate storage of information, but is not a list, is a binary tree. A *tree* represents a hierarchical structure, similar to that of organizational or genealogical charts, and is useful for keeping the list of data in a hierarchy and for speeding up searches (see Figure 8-22).

tree – A data structure that represents a hierarchical structure, similar to that of organizational or genealogical charts

Figure 8-22, Tree data structure

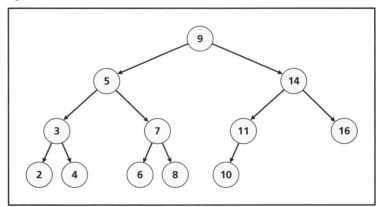

node or vertex – A position in a tree data structure

left child – The child node to the left of the parent node

right child – The child node to the right of the parent node

Each position in the tree is called a *node* or *vertex*. The tree is binary because each node has at most two child nodes. A node can have zero, one, or two child nodes. The child node to the left of the parent node is called the *left child*. The child node to the right of the parent node is called the *right child*.

root – *The node that begins the tree*

leaf node – *A node that has no child nodes*

The node that begins the tree is called the *root* and is not a child of any node. A node that has no children is called a *leaf node* (see Figure 8-23).

Figure 8-23, Tree nodes

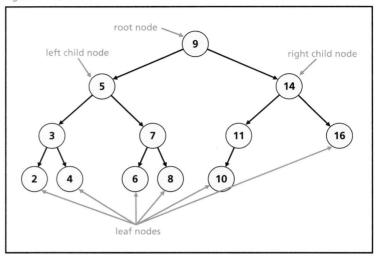

depth or level – *The distance from the node to the root node; the root's depth or level is 0*

height – *The longest path length in the tree*

The *depth* or *level* of the binary tree refers to the distance from the root node. The maximum number of levels is called the *height* of the tree (see Figure 8-24).

Figure 8-24, The level and height of a binary tree

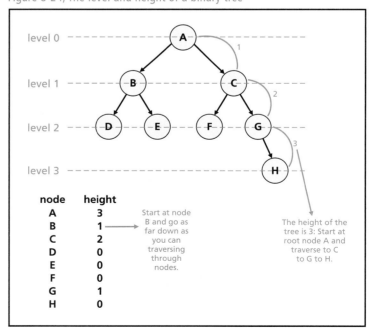

uses of binary trees

Binary trees can also be called *binary search trees (BSTs)*, as long as the tree follows two rules:

- The data value of the left child is less than the value of the parent node.
- The data value of the right child is greater than the value of the parent node.

Binary search trees, when arranged correctly, are a useful data structure for searching through stored data. One use is storing information in a hierarchical representation, such as the file system shown in Figure 8-25.

You learn more about file systems in Chapter 10.

Huffman coding

David A. Huffman, a student at MIT in 1952, constructed an encoding method that uses binary search trees in file compression algorithms. The method is called the Huffman Coding Tree.

Figure 8-25, A file system structure can be stored as a binary search tree

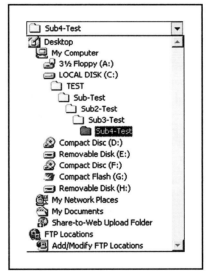

searching a binary tree

A node in a binary search tree contains three components, shown in Figure 8-26:

- Left pointer
- Right pointer
- Data

In the binary tree is a root pointer containing the root node's address and providing initial access to the tree. If the left or right child pointers contain a null (empty) value, the node is not a parent to other nodes down that specific path. If both left and right pointers contain null values, the node is not a parent down either path.

Figure 8-26, A node in a binary search tree

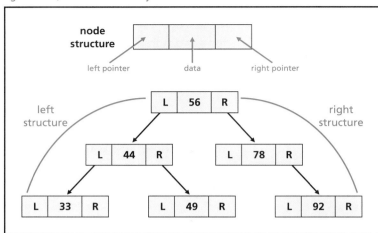

A binary tree must be defined properly to be searchable. In a binary tree, the left child node always has a value less than the right child node's. Searching for a particular value in a binary tree requires starting at the root position and determining whether the path will move to the left child or the right child. If the left pointer is NULL, there's no node to traverse down the left side. If the left pointer does have a value, the path continues down that side. If you have found the value you're looking for, you stop at that node.

Searching for the value 8 in Figure 8-27 requires the following steps:

1. Start at the root node.

2. Does the value 8 = the root value (9)? No. Then is the value 8 > the root value (9)? No. Move to the left child (5).

3. Does the value 8 = 5? No. Then is the value 8 > 5? Yes. Move to the right child (7).

4. Does the value 8 = 7? No. Then is the value 8 > 7? Yes. Move to the right child (8).

5. Does the value 8 = 8? Yes. Stop traversing the tree.

Figure 8-27, Searching a binary tree for the value 8

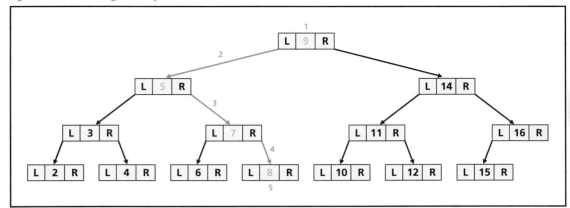

To see an example of what happens with a null value, try searching for the value 1 in Figure 8-28:

1. Start at the root node.

2. Does the value 1 = the root value (9)? No. Then is the value 1 > the root value (9)? No. Move to the left child (5).

3. Does the value 1 = 5? No. Then is the value 1 > 5? No. Move to the left child (3).

4. Does the value 1 = 3? No. Then is the value 1 > 3? No. Move to the left child (2).

5. Does the value 1 = 2? No. Then is the value 1 > 2? No. Attempt to move to the left child, but stop traversing the tree because the left pointer (2) is NULL.

Figure 8-28, Searching a binary tree for the value 1

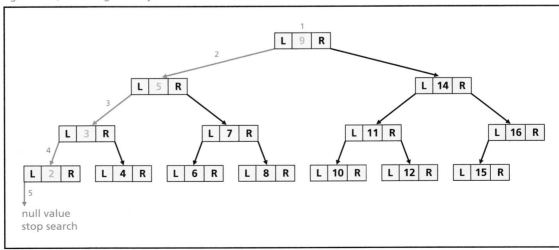

You can perform these same searches for any number, with the result being that the value is found or not found.

sorting algorithms

In addition to the array, list, and tree data structures, there's another essential way to organize data: sorting. In many cases, even if data is in a list or other structure, if you can't sort the data, it's useless. Can you imagine a phone book that simply entered data sequentially in order of new phone numbers assigned to customers? The last person in the phone book would be the last person to sign up for a phone number from the telephone company. Finding anyone's phone number would take forever (or longer)!

Almost any type of computer output is in some type of sort order so that the reader can interpret it easily. Here are some other examples of data being sorted:

- Words in a dictionary
- Files in a directory
- Index of a book
- Course offerings at a university

Think back to Chapter 6 on databases. The Songs table contained a list of all songs stored in the music inventory. Sorting the songs by title made finding a song easier. If the data wasn't sorted, you would have to look through each song record until you found the one you're looking for. If you have five songs, the search takes no time at all. If you have more than 2000 songs, you might as well start canceling all your extracurricular activities so that you can search through music records.

Remember that an algorithm is a procedure or formula for solving a problem. To sort data, you first need to create an algorithm that defines the process for sorting. There are many algorithms for sorting data; each one has advantages and disadvantages. In fact, the list of sorting algorithms continues to grow as more computer scientists try to improve established sort routines. Two sorting routines covered in this chapter are the selection and bubble sorts.

selection sort

selection sort – A sorting routine that selects the smallest unsorted item remaining in the list, and then swaps it with the item in the next position to be filled

The *selection sort* is a simple sorting routine that mimics closely how you might sort a list of values. To sort from lowest to highest, for example, it starts at the first value in the list, and then processes each element, looking for the smallest value. After the smallest value is found, the selection sort places it in the list's first position and simultaneously moves the value that was in the first position to the location that originally contained the smallest value. Then the sort moves on to the next position, looking for the next smallest value. It continues to "swap places" between the current position and the position where it finds the smallest value. For example, you have an array containing the following numbers: 14, 8, 2, 4, and 10. Follow the example of the selection sort shown in Figure 8-29.

Figure 8-29, A selection sort

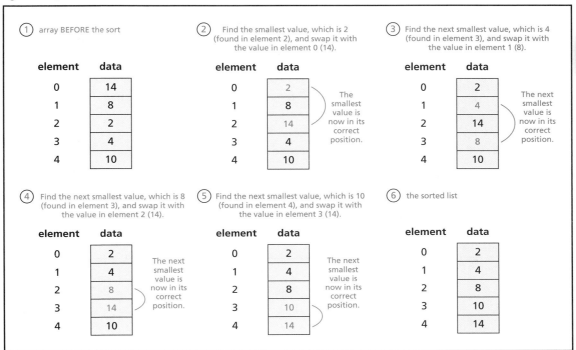

In a selection sort for lowest to highest values, the computer starts processing through the list until it finds the smallest value. In this example, the number 2 in element 2 is the smallest value, so the value 2 is moved into element 0 (the first location), and the value 14 is moved to element 2 (Step 2 in Figure 8-29).

The computer accepts that the value in element 0 is the smallest and ignores that position for the rest of the sort. Instead of looking at element 0, it moves on to the next element (1) and begins searching for the next smallest value. It finds the number 4 in element 3. It moves the value 4 up to element 1 and moves the value 8 to element 3 (Step 3).

Again, the computer knows that memory location 1 now has the next smallest value stored and moves on to element 2. This process of searching for the smallest value and swapping it with the current location continues. It finds the number 8 in element 3. It moves the value 8 up to element 2 and moves the value 14 to element 3 (Step 4).

This process of searching for the smallest value and swapping it with the current location continues. It finds the number 10 in element 4. It moves the value 10 up to element 3 and moves the value 14 to element 4 (Step 5). This list is finally sorted (Step 6).

The selection sort is simple to use but isn't very efficient for sorting large lists. For this task, you need a different sorting routine, explained in the next section.

bubble sort

bubble sort – A sorting routine that compares each item in the list with the item next to it; if the first item is greater than the second, it swaps them, and then repeats this process until it makes a pass all the way through the list without swapping any items

The *bubble sort* is an older and slower sort method. It works by starting with the last element in the list and comparing its value with that of the item just above it in the list order. If it's smaller, it changes positions and continues up the list, comparing itself with the other items until an item doesn't pass the "I am smaller, so I move up" test. If it isn't smaller, the next item is compared with the item above it and swapped if it's smaller. The system continues checking values until the smallest value "bubbles" up to the top. Then the entire process starts over but stops at the second item because it already knows that the first item contains the smallest value.

Now try an array containing the following numbers: 14, 8, 2, 4, and 10. Follow the example of the bubble sort shown in Figure 8-30.

Figure 8-30, A bubble sort

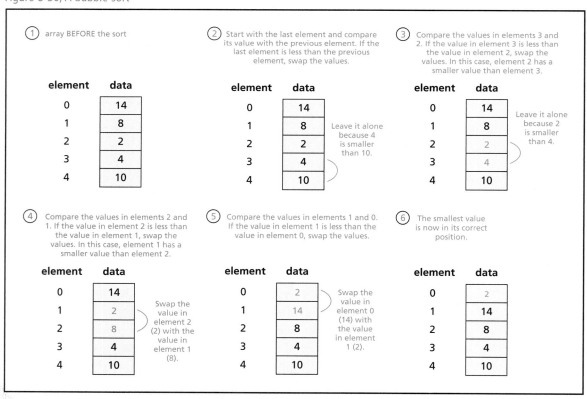

The computer starts the processing with element 4. It compares the value 10 with the value 4 in element 3. Because the value in element 3 (4) is smaller than the value in element 4 (10), it leaves the 10 alone and uses the value in element 3 (4) for the next comparison (Step 2 in Figure 8-30). Next, the value 4 in element 3 is compared with the value 2 in element 2. Because the value 2 is smaller than 4 and is already higher up in the list, it leaves them alone (Step 3).

Next, the value in element 2 (2) is compared with the value in element 1 (8). Because 2 is less than 8, the values are swapped so that the value 2 is now in element 1, and the value 8 is in element 2 (Step 4).

Now compare the value in element 1 (2) with the value in element 0 (14). Because 2 is less than 14, the values are swapped so that the value 2 is now in element 0, and the value 14 is in element 1 (Step 5).

After all that work, the smallest value has "bubbled" up to the top of the sorted list (Step 6). Now you have to continue this process with the remaining four elements in the array! The only nice thing about the bubble sort, besides being easy to implement, is that you don't have to worry about the value in element 0 anymore because you already know it's the smallest.

Figure 8-31 shows the entire process starting over with the bottom position and its value. The only difference is that you don't have to worry about the element in position 0.

Figure 8-31, The bubble sort continues

Element 4 has the value 10 and is compared with the value in element 3 (4) (Step 2). No change occurs, so the computer moves on to comparing elements 3 and 2. The value in element 3 (4) is smaller than that in element 2 (8), so it's swapped (Step 3).

On you go, comparing the value in element 2 (now 4) with the value stored in element 1 (14). Because the value in element 2 is smaller, it's swapped (Step 4). The second smallest value has now bubbled its way to the second position in the list (Step 5).

The process continues as shown in Step 1 in Figure 8-32, with the first two elements now locked into place. Element 4 still has the value 10 and is compared with the value in element 3 (now 8). Because element 3 has a value smaller than element 4, no change occurs (Step 2). Element 3 (8) is compared with element 2 (14). Because element 3 (8) has a value smaller than element 2 (14), the values are swapped (Step 3). The third smallest value has now bubbled its way to the third position in the list (Step 4).

Figure 8-32, The bubble sort still swapping along

Hang in there because you're almost done! The process continues as shown in Step 1 of Figure 8-33, with the first three elements now locked into place. Element 4 still has the value 10 and is compared with the value in element 3 (now 14). Because element 4 (10) has a value smaller than element 3 (14), the values are swapped (Step 2). The fourth smallest value has now bubbled its way to the fourth position in the list (Step 3). Because there's only one element left and nothing to compare it against, element 4 *must* have the largest value in the entire list of values.

Figure 8-33, The bubble sort's last comparison

As you can see, a bubble sort involves a lot of comparisons—and this list has only five values. The bubble sort is simple to use but requires many comparisons, so it's quite inefficient in terms of processing speed.

other types of sorts

Selection sorts and bubble sorts are easy to use but run too slowly because they make too many comparisons for large lists of information. For this reason, other sort routines have been created with the specific purpose of sorting data in a shorter time with fewer comparisons. Some of these other routines are as follows:

- *Quicksort*—This routine incorporates the logic that sorting two small lists is easier and faster than sorting one large list (divide and conquer). It's very fast and useful when a large amount of information needs to be sorted. The routine

recursion – *The process of a routine calling itself*

keeps breaking the data down into smaller lists until they're quite manageable to sort. The routine does this by calling itself over and over until each list is sorted. The process of calling itself is called *recursion*. After the lists are sorted, the sorted sets are simply combined into one big sorted set. Believe it or not, you have already encountered the basics of a quicksort in the discussion of a binary search tree. The quicksort is fast but difficult to comprehend.

n o t e

Do you suppose if you looked up recursion in a dictionary, it would say, "See recursion"?

- *Merge sort*—Similar to the quicksort, the merge sort splits data into sets. Instead of splitting data over and over into small sets, however, the merge sort splits data into two equal halves. Each half is sorted, and then both halves are merged back together into one list. This sort also uses recursion by calling itself over and over until the data is sorted. It's fast but not as efficient as the quicksort because it uses twice the memory to perform its sorting algorithm.
- *Insertion sort*—This sort requires two list structures into which sorted items are inserted. The first list is the data structure containing the information, and the second list is the sorted data structure. This routine simulates sorting a deck of cards. As you select a card, it's put in its correct place in the sorted list. You continue this process of moving cards around until all cards are in their correctly sorted locations. This sort isn't complex and has the advantage of being efficient with lists of fewer than 1000 elements.
- *Shell sort*—This efficient routine makes multiple passes through the list, grabbing a set of values to sort. It then uses the insertion sort routine to sort the data. For each pass, the system grabs a larger set of data. As the size of the set increases, the number of sets that need to be sorted decreases until the entire list is sorted.

Other sort routines are available, with each having its own advantages and disadvantages. One consideration might be the complexity of programming code needed to implement the sort. Another might be the amount of memory the routine needs to complete the sort.

one last thought

Algorithms are used everywhere in the computer industry. They're used for creating and working with data structures, searching for information, and sorting data. As you progress through your computing education, you might even be the person who develops the fastest sorting algorithm ever known in the computer industry!

Knowing how to work with data structures and sorting algorithms is necessary when you begin writing computer programs. Many algorithms have already been written and are available for your use. Also, knowing what tools are available and which sort routine will perform best for a situation can save you a lot of time because you won't have to reinvent the sort routine.

8

chapter summary

- Data structures are used to organize data.
- Arrays are stored in contiguous memory cells (one right after the other).
- To define an array, you must specify the array name, type, and size.
- A single-dimensional array is a structure consisting of one level of array elements.
- A multidimensional array is a structure consisting of more than one level, and each level consists of an array.
- The array's size is stored internally by using an upper and lower bound.
- A pointer is a memory variable that points to a memory cell location.
- A linked list is a data structure that can be used when the size of the information to be stored is unknown or will change. Stacks and queues are forms of linked lists.
- A stack uses a last in, first out (LIFO) structure.
- A queue uses a first in, first out (FIFO) structure.
- A tree data structure represents a hierarchical storage method.
- Each position in a tree is called a node.
- Binary search trees are efficient for searching for information.
- There's a wide variety of sorting algorithms, including selection, bubble, quicksort, merge, insertion, and shell sorts.

key terms

array (*280*)

binary search tree (BST) (*301*)

bubble sort (*306*)

data structure (*279*)

depth or level (*300*)

dequeue (*297*)

element (*282*)

enqueue (*298*)

first in, first out (FIFO) (*297*)

head pointer (*292*)

height (*300*)

index (subscript) (*284*)

last in, first out (LIFO) (*295*)

leaf node (*300*)

left child (*299*)

linked list (*290*)

lower bound (*284*)

multidimensional array (*285*)

node (vertex) (*299*)

null value (*292*)

offset (*283*)

peeking (*295*)

pointer (*291*)

pop (*295*)

test yourself

1. Describe the uses of an array.

2. How would you define an array to keep track of five students' ID numbers (integer value) and their final averages, rounded to the nearest whole number (integer value)?

3. Using the array defined in question #2, write the statements to store information for the five students' ID numbers and final averages in each array element.

4. Describe in your own words how a stack works.

5. Describe in your own words how a queue works.

6. Describe in your own words how a binary tree works.

For questions 7 and 8, use Figure 8-34.

Figure 8-34, Sample data for questions 7 and 8

element	data
0	32
1	4
2	7
3	2
4	25
5	10

7. Show each step to sort the data by using a bubble sort.

8. Show each step to sort the data by using a selection sort.

For questions 9 and 10, use Figure 8-35.

Figure 8-35, Sample data for questions 9 and 10

element	data
0	5
1	32
2	30
3	1
4	2
5	20

9. Show each step to sort the data by using a bubble sort.

10. Show each step to sort the data by using a selection sort.

For questions 11–15, use Figure 8-36.

Figure 8-36, Sample data for questions 11–15

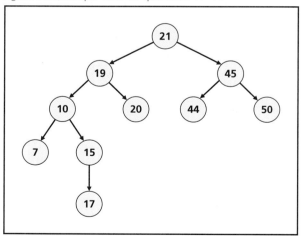

11. Label the root and leaf nodes.

12. What is the maximum height of the tree?

13. On what level is the node with the value 15?

14. Show the steps to find the value 7.

15. Show the steps to find the value 17.

practice exercises

1. A(n) _____ is a data structure consisting of contiguous memory locations.

   a. Array
   b. Stack
   c. Queue
   d. Tree

2. A(n) _____ is used in an array to access each element.

   a. Index
   b. Subscript
   c. Both a and b
   d. None of the above

3. A single array can contain information of different data types (integers, characters, decimals, and so on).

   a. True
   b. False

4. The statement char[] aAnswers = new char[5] declares an array that has memory locations of 1 through 5.

   a. True
   b. False

5. The offset is used to specify the distance between memory locations.

   a. True
   b. False

6. Arrays are a good data structure to use with dynamic data.

   a. True
   b. False

7. A stack uses a LIFO structure.

   a. True
   b. False

8. A queue uses a FIFO structure.

   a. True
   b. False

9. LIFO is an acronym for:

   a. List in, first order
   b. Last in, first out
   c. Last in, first order
   d. List in, first out

10. FIFO is an acronym for:

   a. First in, first out
   b. First in, first order
   c. First in, final out
   d. First in, final order

Use Figure 8-37 to answer questions 11–15.

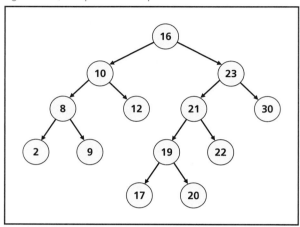

Figure 8-37, Sample data for questions 11–15

11. How many comparisons does it take to find the following numbers?

   a. 8
   b. 2
   c. 23
   d. 30
   e. 17

12. What is the number of nodes on level 3?

13. What is the number of nodes on level 4?

14. What is the maximum height of the tree?

15. How many right and left child nodes are there?

Given the following numbers—1, 2, 3, 4, 5, 6, 7, 8, 9, 10, 11, and 12—answer questions 16 through 20.

16. Draw a binary search tree for these numbers. Make sure binary search tree rules are applied.

17. How many comparisons does it take to find the number 4?

18. How many comparisons does it take to find the number 11?

19. What is the maximum height of the tree?

20. On what level is the number 6?

digging deeper

1. Write a sorting routine different from those discussed in the chapter to organize information, and explain how it's implemented.

2. Using six different numbers in any order, draw a diagram that shows how the merge sort works.

3. Draw a diagram that shows how the insertion sort works, using six different numbers in any order.

4. Draw a diagram that shows how the quicksort works, using six different numbers in any order.

5. Draw a diagram that shows how the shell sort works, using six different numbers in any order.

discussion topics

1. Which sorting routine do you think is best to use when sorting the information in a phone book for a large city? Why?

2. List five scenarios for using an array.

3. List five scenarios for using a stack.

4. List five scenarios for using a queue.

5. Write the statements to define an array for a three-dimensional tic-tac-toe board, and then play the game with other class members by specifying the array location where you want to place an X or an O.

Internet research

1. What are some sorting routines currently being used that haven't been mentioned in this book? What are the advantages and disadvantages of using them?

2. Find a Web site that demonstrates different sorting algorithms, and share it with the class.

3. Find at least three Web sites that demonstrate how a stack and queue work, and share them with the class.

4. Find at least three Web sites that explain binary trees, and share them with the class.

5. Describe how a binary search works, using the pre-order, post-order, and in-order traversal methods.

chapter

9

operating systems

in this chapter you will:

- Learn what an operating system is

- Become familiar with different types of operating systems

- Identify the major functions of an operating system

- Understand how operating systems manage processes

- Understand how operating systems manage resources

- Understand how operating systems provide security

- Learn how to perform basic operating system file management functions in Windows and Linux

the lighter side of the lab
by spencer

I recently took a trip to Texas to visit family. (For those who are wondering: Yes, the stars at night *are* big and bright.) We went to a fun little place called Sundance Square in Fort Worth to have some dinner. I had been tasked with finding a restaurant for the group, usually a simple 2-minute job for normal people. "This place looks good. Done." For me, it involved four hours scouring the Internet and one spreadsheet.

I have this problem wherever I travel. I realize that I won't be returning to the city often, so I want to find the best place to eat at the best price. So even before I arrived in Fort Worth, I got on the Internet and started searching. I read review after review and list after list. I made note of the ones that looked good and their prices, and then I started trying to rank them. (I was still working on this list as we were being seated at the restaurant the group finally chose because I couldn't decide.)

This problem carries over to watching TV, too. Every time I'm channel surfing and see a VH1 *Top 100* show, I can't resist, no matter how stupid the topic. Even with *Top 100 Music Videos Featuring Kitties*, I have to know what #1 is!

This is why I don't like other operating systems gaining ground against Windows. Linux has been getting more popular for a while, and Apple has made a huge comeback with its Pentium-based computers and Leopard operating system. I want a clear winner! Bring on the monopoly! Then I won't have to choose.

Windows is obviously the big hitter in the group, but more people are making the switch to other operating systems because of cost, security, and cool features, among other reasons. Linux is usually free, so how can you beat that value? Worse yet, for me, there are a bunch of different GUIs to choose from, so picking the one I like best is impossible. Even Bill Gates has to admit that the new Apple computers are pretty dang sweet.

In the computer world, the Linux vs. Windows debate rivals that of Ford vs. Chevy or Coke vs. Pepsi. (In fact, the only debate that gets more heated in these circles is the Kirk vs. Picard debate. If you bring this one up, look out!) So which operating system is the best? We might never know.

If you traveled to Fort Worth, where would you eat? Maybe a place with some famous Texas barbecue or authentic Mexican food? There are lots of tasty choices. After all my work, however, where did we end up eating in Fort Worth? A Chicago-style pizzeria.

why you need to know about...

why you need to know about...
operating systems

If you try to run a program on a computer without an operating system—save a file, print a file, or any other task you can think of—as they say in the movies, "It just ain't gonna happen!"

Operating systems are essential to the functioning of computers. Everything that takes place on a computer goes through, uses, or gets permission from the operating system. Inside the computer, the operating system is the boss. Outside the computer, you can be the boss—if you know how to control the operating system. This chapter helps you understand what an operating system is, what it does, and how it works. It also explains how to perform some basic folder and file functions in Windows and Linux, the operating systems you'll most likely use in your study of computers. Armed with a better understanding of what the operating system is doing and how it works, you and your computer can be more efficient. If you learn how to use operating systems now, everything else becomes easier because you can concentrate on new material in future courses and not have to spend time trying to find your files. As you've probably guessed, your professors have heard the "I lost my file" story too many times.

what is an operating system?

operating system (OS) –
The program responsible for managing the user interface, system resources, and processes

An *operating system (OS)* is the software "control center" of modern computer systems. It's the first program loaded into memory when the computer starts (boots). The OS then remains resident in memory to load and supervise all other programs that run on the computer. Both people and application software interface with the CPU and I/O devices through the OS (see Figure 9-1).

how does a computer boot?

The process of starting a computer is often referred to as **booting**. The term "boot" comes from the idea of using bootstraps to pull on boots. Computers are hard-wired with a small program called a bootstrap loader that checks the status of all hardware devices before going to a storage device and loading the OS into memory so that it can be executed. The process of checking hardware is called **POST**, which stands for power-on self test. You have probably seen the flashing lights and onscreen messages as the POST is performed.

Figure 9-1, An OS provides an interface between the user, applications, and hardware

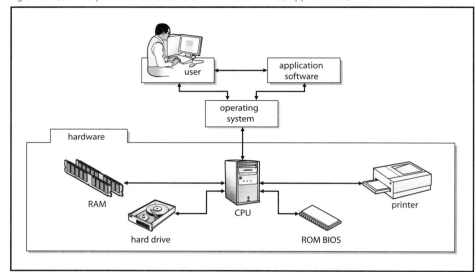

note

In computing, there's a strong distinction between system software and application software. Operating systems, drivers, and other utilities are considered system software. Word-processing and accounting programs, for example, are considered application software, or just "applications."

booting – The process of starting a computer system

POST (power-on self test) – A procedure performed by the computer boot routine to check hardware devices

driver – A special program that provides an interface to a specific I/O device

The OS provides a way for application software, such as a word-processing program or Web browser, to interact with computer hardware. It also contains special interfaces that allow the computer to interact with peripheral devices. These interface programs are called *drivers*, short for device drivers. For example, when you click the Print icon in your word-processing program, a signal is sent to the OS that a document should be sent to the printer. The OS then communicates the document data to the driver for the printer, and the driver controls the printer as it prints your document.

note

Many problems on a computer are caused by outdated drivers, especially video drivers. Check the Web site of your device's manufacturer for updated drivers, which are widely available and can be downloaded and installed.

Operating systems have the capability to connect with standard devices, such as the keyboard and monitor. For most other I/O devices, such as printers, scanners, and cameras, drivers must be installed. These drivers, often written by the device manufacturers, usually ship with the I/O device, but checking the manufacturer's Web site for an updated driver is always a good idea. You can avoid many problems by making sure you have the most current driver for a device.

An OS is just a computer program, although it's an essential one. Like other programs, OSs are written in programming languages, such as C and C++. They generally consist of two parts: the core program (called the *kernel*) and other system components that support and extend the kernel (see Figure 9-2). The kernel, the core of the OS, is a small program that's loaded first and remains in memory the entire time the computer is on. The program responsible for loading the kernel is in the BIOS chip on the main board. When power is turned on, the CPU begins executing the instructions stored in the BIOS chip. These instructions perform the POST and then load the OS kernel from the boot device specified in the CMOS RAM. After the kernel is loaded into memory, the BIOS program transfers control to it.

The BIOS and CMOS are also described in Chapter 3, "Computer Architecture."

before the OS

Early computers didn't have operating systems. A program had to be entered bit by bit, using switches on a front panel. This program was the only thing running on the computer and remained in memory only as long as the computer had power.

kernel – *The core of an operating system; controls processor, disk, memory, and other central functions*

Figure 9-2, Users and computer components interact with the OS kernel

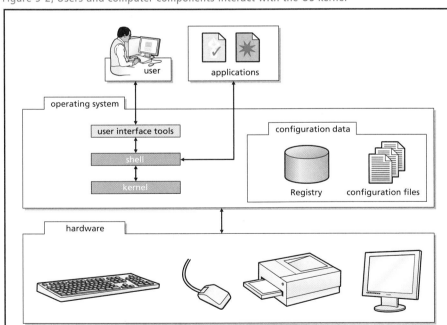

Windows – *A popular Microsoft GUI operating system for Intel-based systems*

DOS (Disk Operating System) – *A single-user, single-tasking, command-line operating system; the Microsoft predecessor to Windows*

Linux – *A multitasking, multiuser, open-source variation of the UNIX operating system*

UNIX – *A multitasking, multiuser, command-line operating system known for its stability and reliability*

The other part of the OS is made up of system components, or modules. The main module is the program responsible for the user interface. In Windows, this module provides the graphical desktop you use to perform computer functions. In Linux, it might be the Gnome, KDE, or Xfce graphical interface. Drivers are other modules that interface with I/O devices, such as printers, monitors, and network cards. All these modules work together to give the user and applications access to the CPU and other connected devices.

Most OSs are loaded on the computer's hard disk, although on smaller handheld computers and personal digital assistants (PDAs), the OS can reside on a ROM chip. Currently, Microsoft *Windows* is the most widely used OS. Years ago, you might have used *DOS (Disk Operating System)*. The "Disk" part of the name indicates that this OS has support for disk drives, a novel feature at the time. Many companies now are using the *Linux* or *UNIX* operating system on their servers. You might have also used the Macintosh operating system (Mac OS) at school. Operating systems vary in style and special features, but they all perform similar functions. Table 9-1 shows how the main operating systems fit into the overall scheme of OS development.

n o t e

Linux is an open-source variation of the UNIX operating system. Many of the Linux commands and features described in this chapter also apply to UNIX.

Table 9-1, OS development summary

OS	approx. date	description
UNIX	1968	First widely used multiuser, multitasking OS; initially for mid-range computers.
CP/M	1975	First OS that allowed business work on PCs, with its VisiCalc spreadsheet software.
MS-DOS	1980	First OS for the IBM PC.
PC DOS	1981	IBM version of Microsoft MS-DOS.
Mac OS	1984	First widely distributed OS to use a graphical user interface (GUI) and a mouse, for Apple PCs; Mac OS X is closely related to UNIX but runs only on Apple computers.

Table 9-1, OS development summary (*continued*)

OS	approx. date	description
Windows 3.x	1990	Early Microsoft Windows versions, including Windows 3.1 and Windows 3.11 (collectively referred to as Windows 3.x), provided a graphical interface to what was essentially still DOS "under the hood."
Linux	1990	*Open source*, meaning it was developed, tested, and enhanced by many people as a collaborative effort. Based on UNIX, Linux was created by Finnish computer science student Linus Torvalds in 1990 and has expanded to include a GUI and many other modules. Those participating in development make the OS available free to everyone, although some companies charge to package or support Linux. Because of its low cost, availability for many types of computers, and stability, Linux has become popular in the past few years.
Windows NT	1993	Included more advanced security features, network support, and user administration features than Windows 3.x. It came in two versions: Windows NT Workstation for end-user computers and Windows NT Server for managing and maintaining a network. Designed mainly for businesses and technical users rather than home users.
Windows 9x	1995	These OSs—Windows 95, Windows 98, and Windows Me (Millennium Edition)—relied on a DOS core but had a more user-friendly interface and advanced features, such as automatic recognition and configuration of I/O devices (Plug and Play), more integrated Internet capabilities, and support for hardware devices, such as CD/DVD-ROM drives.
Windows 2000	2000	An upgrade of Windows NT with additional features, including improved network support and increased speed and stability. There are several versions: Windows 2000 Professional is popular for business desktops, and Windows 2000 Server, Windows 2000 Advanced Server, and Windows 2000 Datacenter Server are network OSs.

open source – *Computer programs, including operating systems, developed as a public collaboration and made available free for use or modification*

(continued)

Table 9-1, OS development summary (*continued*)

OS	approx. date	description
Windows XP	2001	Combined the user-friendly features of Windows 98 and Windows Me with the strengths of Windows 2000. Included an upgraded user interface, support for multiple users, better performance, and more support for multimedia, such as audio and video. Available in three versions: Home Edition, Professional, and Tablet PC Edition.
Windows Server 2003	2003	A network OS with additional features for managing and maintaining a network; provides increased security, enhanced file and print server support, support for remote access, and more. Available in several versions, including Standard Edition, Enterprise Edition, Datacenter Edition, Web Edition, and Small Business Server 2003.
Windows Vista	2006	Designed to improve security in Windows to address criticisms of security vulnerabilities in previous versions. Its release was delayed because of the extra work required for improving security aspects of the OS. Includes improvements in networking and multimedia. A new server OS, Windows Server 2008, was also released at this time.
Windows 7	2009	The most recent Windows version has improvements over Windows Vista yet maintains compatibility with existing Vista drivers. It has new features for voice and handwriting recognition as well as a complete reworking of the taskbar.

n o t e

Versions of Microsoft Windows are installed on nearly 90% of desktop computers worldwide.

platform – *The OS running on a computer*

The OS running on a computer is often called its *platform* and is typically tied to a particular CPU. Applications that run on one platform won't run on another platform without modification. For example, the Microsoft Word application that runs on the Windows XP platform can't run on an iMac computer running Mac OS. Applications that have been converted to run on multiple platforms are called "cross-platform" applications and should run nearly identically in different OSs.

types of operating systems

Operating systems can be classified by their features or intended uses. For example, older OSs, such as DOS and Windows 3.x, were designed to be *single-tasking* operating systems, meaning only one program or task could be running at a time. Current versions of Windows, Linux, and Mac OS X are examples of *multitasking* OSs, meaning they can service many different program tasks at a time. Most of today's OSs are multitasking. Some, such as NetWare, UNIX, Linux, and Windows Server 2008, are designed as *network operating systems*, with capabilities to configure and manage networks of computers.

Each OS has been designed to be strong in a particular area. For example, recent versions of Microsoft Windows and Mac OS have been designed to have an easy-to-use interface and multimedia capabilities to appeal to home and small-business users. UNIX and Linux are designed to be very strong in multi-tasking, security, and *multiprocessing* (using more than one CPU). UNIX and Linux are also known for their stability. Windows is installed on the over-whelming majority of desktops, but UNIX and Linux are often the OSs of choice in the server environment. Servers—database servers and Web servers, for example—are computers used to service many different users.

Many other OSs run on equipment such as PDAs and cell phones. In some cases, the OS is just a scaled-down version of a larger OS, as with the Android OS, based on the Linux kernel, used in the T-Mobile G2. It's important to remember that every multipurpose device with a CPU must also have an OS.

functions of an operating system

Although they have different features and strengths, all OSs perform the same basic functions. For example, they provide a user interface, schedule and manage program execution, manage memory, configure devices, provide file management and security, provide basic networking capability, and monitor performance. The basic functions that all OSs perform can be classified into four main categories:

- Providing a user interface
- Managing processes
- Managing resources (including memory)
- Providing security

single-tasking – *An OS that allows running only one process (task) at a time*

multitasking – *An OS's capability to effectively support more than one process running at a time*

network operating system – *An OS designed to provide strong network services*

multiprocessing – *Coordinated execution of a process, using two or more CPUs at the same time*

running backward?

In the world of computers, ensuring that older hardware and software are compatible with newer computers is referred to as "backward compatibility" and is crucial to the success of a new OS or CPU. Many past failures in PCs can be traced to their lack of backward compatibility.

providing a user interface

As a computer user, you're no doubt familiar with the function of providing a user interface. The user interface is a program that enables you to communicate with the computer. Operating systems provide for input from devices such as the keyboard, mouse, and touch screen as well as audio commands.

There are two basic types of user interfaces: the *command-line interface* and the *graphical user interface (GUI)*, shown in Figure 9-3. DOS and Linux use a command-line interface and are sometimes called console operating systems.

command-line interface – A method of communicating with the OS by typing commands and receiving responses in text format

graphical user interface (GUI) – A method of interacting with the OS, in which information is displayed in a graphical format, and the user can select items by using a pointing device, such as a mouse

Figure 9-3, The Windows command prompt emulates a DOS environment (top); the default GUI interface of Windows Vista (middle); and the GUI interface of Linux (bottom)

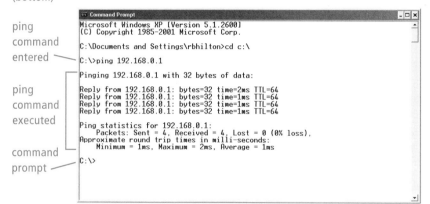

Figure 9-3, (*continued*)

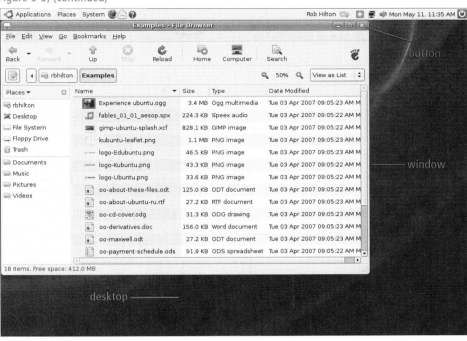

command prompt –
*Words and symbols
displayed onscreen that
indicate the OS is waiting
for user input*

Users interact with the OS by typing commands at a ***command prompt***, with the output displayed as characters and numbers. Windows, Mac, and some Linux versions use a GUI, which allows users to interact with the OS by using the keyboard and mouse or other pointing device to click icons and buttons, open graphical windows, and make menu selections instead of typing text commands.

Although Windows is primarily a graphical OS, you can also access a command prompt, usually via the All Programs, Accessories menu. The command prompt emulates a DOS environment. DOS, the first Microsoft operating system, is a command-line OS with no graphical interface. GUIs can be added to Linux, but standard Linux uses a command-line interface. To provide backward compatibility, Windows has always included the capability to interface with the OS via the command prompt. Many computing courses require you to have some knowledge of the command prompt interface in Windows so that you can run Linux or DOS programs and back up your files in a console environment.

the first GUI

The GUI was invented by scientists at Xerox Corporation in 1970. It was adopted later by Apple Computer and used extensively in Macintosh computers before being adopted by Microsoft for its Windows product. Now virtually all home and business OSs have a GUI.

managing processes

process – A small program running on a computer; can be part of a larger program

Operating systems are responsible for loading, starting, running, and stopping processes—or programs—on the computer. Each program you run is a *process*. Processes might then start (sometimes called "spawn") other processes to support them. In Windows, for example, you can view running processes by pressing Ctrl+Alt+Delete to open Task Manager and then clicking the Processes tab to display information on all running processes (see Figure 9-4).

Figure 9-4, Windows Task Manager

Image Name	User Name	CPU	Memory (...	Description
csrss.exe		00	808 K	
dwm.exe	rbhilton	00	436 K	Desktop ...
explorer.exe	rbhilton	00	17,244 K	Windows ...
MSASCui.exe	rbhilton	00	1,080 K	Windows ...
sidebar.exe	rbhilton	00	3,700 K	Windows ...
taskeng.exe	rbhilton	00	2,080 K	Task Sche...
taskmgr.exe	rbhilton	03	1,476 K	Windows ...
VMwareTray....	rbhilton	00	496 K	VMwareTray
VMwareUser....	rbhilton	00	544 K	VMwareUser
wermgr.exe	rbhilton	00	2,488 K	Windows ...
winlogon.exe		00	876 K	
wmdSync.exe	rbhilton	00	780 K	User sessi...
wuaudt.exe	rbhilton	00	184 K	Windows ...

Show processes from all users   End Process

Processes: 43   CPU Usage: 2%   Physical Memory: 51%

Linux has a similar function for displaying information on active processes. At the console prompt, you can type the ps command to get a list of all running processes. Figure 9-5 shows an example of the output of this command. There's no DOS command to list currently running processes because only one process can be running at a time. DOS was designed to be used by a single user, completing one task at a time. Linux, on the other hand, was designed to accommodate multiple users and multiple tasks.

Figure 9-5, Viewing processes in Linux with the ps command

```
                    rbhilton@rbhilton-ubuntu: ~
File  Edit  View  Terminal  Tabs  Help
rbhilton@rbhilton-ubuntu:~$ ps
  PID TTY          TIME CMD
 6226 pts/0    00:00:00 bash
 6270 pts/0    00:00:00 ps
rbhilton@rbhilton-ubuntu:~$
```

In reality, only one process can run at a time on all single CPU systems. For example, in Windows you might be listening to an MP3 while you're downloading a file and, at the same time, using a word-processing program to write your term paper. If you opened Task Manager and looked at active processes, you would probably see even more processes running. It would seem you're running many processes at once; however, the computer is likely carrying out only one process at a time. Von Neumann architecture supports only serial execution of instructions; during any given clock cycle, only one instruction from a single program can be executed. If the computer has multiple processors, some parts of some processes might be executing in parallel.

The parts of a computer system, such as the CPU, memory, keyboard, monitor, and network adapter, function at different speeds. The CPU is the fastest and can execute billions of instructions per second. Main memory is slower and can be accessed only millions of times per second. Because memory and other devices are slower than the CPU, the CPU has time to spare. It uses this spare time to execute a few instructions at a time for each running process. Of course, the CPU is also much faster than users. Say the average user types 60 words per minute. In the time between each keystroke, the CPU can execute billions of instructions.

time slicing

Computers can run many programs with only one processor by using effective time management. College students also have to be good at time management—at least, those who want good grades *and* a social life do. You have probably observed students talking on cell phones while eating breakfast while studying for a history assignment and maybe even putting on makeup. (Actually, maybe that was you.)

time slicing – A method of allocating fixed time units to running processes so that it appears to users that all processes are running simultaneously

The method that allows multiple processes to share the CPU is called *time slicing*, and it's an important responsibility of the OS. It works by allocating small segments of CPU time to each running process, one after another. To users, it seems that multiple processes are running at the same time, but in reality, the processor is just using its time efficiently. Time slicing works because often the CPU is waiting for I/O devices to return information.

Time slicing, managed by the OS, allows computers to accomplish much more work than they would otherwise, but this process is complicated. The OS must be able to decide which process is ready for execution and which process is waiting for some I/O to take place. Sometimes processes need to have CPU time immediately—for example, to act on special keystrokes, such as Ctrl+Alt+Delete, which can be used in Windows to view and terminate processes. Because the OS might be allocating time to other processes when keystrokes are entered, the OS must also allow processes to interrupt the CPU and jump to the head of the line of processes requesting CPU time. This procedure takes place with *interrupt handling*.

Interrupts can be initiated by programs or devices. When an interrupt occurs, the CPU stops what it's doing and goes to a program in memory called an interrupt handler. Multiple interrupt handlers reside in memory waiting for their number to be called. The main interrupt handler is part of the OS and is executed when the time-slicing timer ticks. This interrupt routine is coded to decide which processes are ready for more execution time and which process is next in the execution schedule.

managing resources

Devices such as the main memory, hard disk, and CD/DVD-ROM drive are the computer's *resources*. The CPU uses them to accomplish program tasks. Each process running on the computer might need to access and use these resources. Therefore, another responsibility of the OS is to manage the computer's resources.

I/O devices have to be configured to work correctly in the environment in which they're installed. In the past, configuration was performed by users setting physical switches or jumpers or running special software utilities. In 1995, a new technology was introduced with Windows 95. This technology, called *Plug and Play (PnP)*, was intended to create a computer with hardware and software that worked together to configure devices and assign resources automatically, making hardware changes and additions easier. Plug and Play has been a feature of all subsequent versions of Windows and has been used in other operating systems as well.

Theoretically, it's possible for each program or process running on a computer to access I/O devices directly. For example, sometimes DOS-based games access the video card directly to try to improve performance. Having programs access I/O devices directly isn't a good idea, however. Each program accessing I/O devices directly would need drivers for the specific I/O devices attached to the computer. It makes more sense to have the OS be responsible for all interfacing with I/O devices. That way, any program can simply request that the OS perform the I/O operation, and only the OS has to be set up to recognize and interface with I/O devices.

interrupt handling – A method of allowing processes and hardware I/O devices to interrupt the processor's normal executing so that it can handle specific tasks

resources – Devices connected to the CPU, such as the main memory, hard disk, and CD/DVD-ROM drive; all running processes have to share these devices

Plug and Play (PnP) – A technology that allows the OS and hardware to work together to detect and configure I/O devices automatically

Managing a computer's resources is tricky, in that the OS must assign and keep track of priorities for each device and each running process. It's even more difficult when a process is waiting for a resource allocated to another process, and the second process is waiting for a resource allocated to the first. This rare situation is called *deadlock*. Unless the OS can break the deadlock by recognizing it and releasing one of the resources, processing ceases and the system freezes up. Although deadlock occurs only rarely, if the OS didn't provide a remedy for it, the system couldn't continue processing without a reboot.

<aside>

deadlock *– A rare situation in which I/O devices and/or processes are waiting for each other for use of resources; this situation would continue indefinitely without intervention by the OS*

</aside>

managing memory

Another important resource that an OS manages is memory. All programs and processes running on a computer are stored in main memory, or RAM. Program data is also stored there. When a user issues a command to run a program, the OS determines the location of free space in memory and loads the program from the disk to this memory location. As processes and programs come and go, the OS must constantly manage memory and communicate with the CPU about where to begin executing a program.

providing security

Some processes running on a computer are programs the user has initiated, and others are initiated by programs running on the system. Still others are part of the OS itself. All these processes theoretically could have access to all memory and all system resources. However, one process writing into the memory area of another process can cause problems. Operating systems are responsible for protecting memory and other resources and serve as the "resource police," ensuring that resources are distributed evenly among competing processes.

Allowing unauthorized users to access programs or devices is also dangerous. Most computer systems contain sensitive data, and access to this data needs to be controlled. The OS provides a means for allowing only authorized users to access programs or devices as another measure for keeping the computer and its resources secure. One way OSs provide security is by allowing system administrators to set up password-protected user accounts. Many OSs also allow administrators to set up group policies that govern which resources a class or group of users is allowed to access. When a new user is created and assigned to a group, he or she gains the group's rights and permissions automatically. The system administrator saves time by not having to list every permission a new user should have.

<aside>

recovery partition to the rescue

Most major OSs allow you to create a recovery partition on the main hard drive that can be used in case you can't boot your system.

</aside>

using an operating system

As you continue your education in computing and embark on a career, you'll have to use and interact with many different operating systems. Although understanding how an OS works is helpful, knowing how to perform basic tasks is just as important. Much of your interaction with an OS is simply starting and running programs. At other times, you need to know how to use the OS to manage your computer's resources. In the following sections, you learn how to perform some basic file management tasks with two of the most widely used operating systems.

managing disk files

From the user's point of view, one of the main functions of an OS is to organize files on the computer's drives. For this task, the OS needs a formal filing structure. Nearly all operating systems allow users to give names to files as they're stored. For better organization, OSs allow you to organize files into structures called *folders* or *directories*. Folders are organized into a treelike structure with a single *root level* and one or more branches. The files can then be viewed as leaves (nodes) on the tree structure. Figure 9-6 shows an example of this tree structure in Windows.

folder – *Structure on a formatted disk that enables storing and organizing files; also known as a directory or subdirectory*

directory – *Same as folder; "folder" is often used in Windows, and "directory/subdirectory" is more often used in DOS and Linux*

root level – *The main folder/directory level on a drive*

Figure 9-6, The Windows interface for working with files and folders

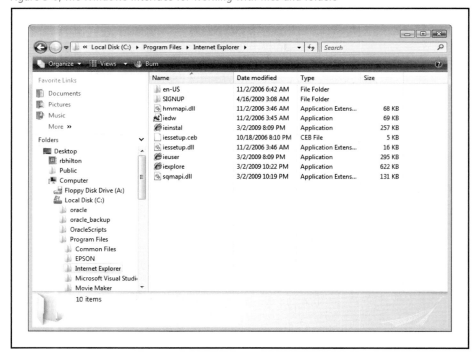

In command-line operating systems, such as Linux and DOS, a similar structure is used, but you can't view it as a tree structure. You need to enter commands at the prompt to display files and folders, as shown in Figure 9-7.

how are files organized on CDs?

CDs have their own filing system, but each OS translates the CD filing system into a format common to the OS so that users can treat it the same as any other drive on the system.

Figure 9-7, Linux command-line interface for displaying files and folders

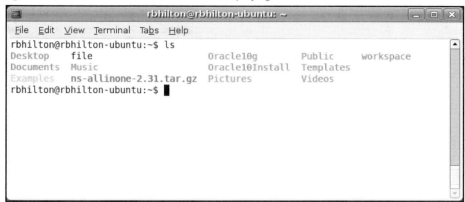

DOS in Windows

You can practice DOS commands by opening a command prompt window in Windows.

The graphical interface of Windows makes it easy for users to view and work with the folder structure. Windows Explorer is one way of viewing and managing files in Windows. In Figure 9-6, shown previously, the system's drives and folders are shown in the left pane, and subfolders and files are shown in the right pane. You can set the right pane to display folders and files in different ways. For example, Figure 9-6 shows the Details view, which displays information on file size, type, and date modified. Graphical interfaces can improve user productivity substantially because working with files and folders is fast and easy.

The next sections show you how to perform some basic file management functions in Windows and Linux. If you can become familiar with these tasks, you'll be more effective in everything else you do in the computing field.

Normally, Linux uses a command-line interface, so the following sections list commands you enter at the command prompt. Many GUIs are available for Linux, but because they're similar to the Windows GUI, only the command-line interface is described in these examples.

Linux commands have what are called command-line switches (sometimes called parameters or flags), used in this format:

```
ls -lrt
```

just in case

Linux commands are case sensitive. For example, LS or Ls won't work for the ls command.

The ls command lists files in the specified directory or subdirectory. The switches shown with this command, listed after the hyphen, list all files located in the current directory. Switches modify the way a command works. The "l" switch indicates that the output should be in long format. The "r" specifies reverse order for the output sorted by file modification time, which is indicated by the "t" switch.

Although the syntax for commands is shown in the following sections, you need to consult each operating system's Help feature to find detailed information on switches. In Linux, entering man *command* gives you the manual pages with information on the command you specify. Note that nearly all switches are optional, and you don't need to worry about them most of the time. To exit manual pages, simply type "q."

The basic operations for creating and managing folders and files, explained in the following sections for Windows and Linux, are as follows:

- Partitioning disks
- Formatting disks
- Creating folders (subdirectories)
- Listing folders and files
- Renaming folders and files
- Deleting folders and files
- Copying folders and files
- Moving folders and files

partitioning disks

partition – *An area of a hard disk reserved to hold files of a particular OS type*

format – *Organizing the disk's surface in a way that allows writing folders and files to it*

Before a disk can be used, it must be divided into *partitions* and *formatted*. Both tasks are accomplished by running a program that's part of the OS. Partitioning a disk prepares it to be formatted by dividing it into areas called partitions. The partitions are simply broad divisions of the disk's total capacity into specific OS areas. Partitions aren't prepared to receive folders and files until they have been formatted.

Both Windows and Linux use the fdisk command to partition hard disks. As mentioned, Linux is case sensitive, so the fdisk command must be lowercase. Windows isn't case sensitive, so FDISK works, too. Partitioning commands should be used only when necessary, however, because they're somewhat complicated and can erase your entire hard drive easily. If you're fond of the files on your hard drive, you'll pay close attention to the following note.

n o t e

CAUTION: The FDISK command completely and irreversibly erases disk drives. Never run FDISK unless you are sure of what you're doing.

formatting disks

command syntax

In the command syntax shown in this chapter's tables, words in bold are required, and italic words are replaced with the specified information. Items in square brackets are optional and can be omitted.

After a disk has been partitioned, it can be formatted by the OS. The process of formatting arranges the disk surface into addressable areas and sets up the basic directory tree structure on the disk. Formatting can also be used to place a copy of the OS on the disk so that it can be used as a boot disk for starting the computer. Table 9-2 shows the commands for formatting in Windows and Linux.

n o t e

CAUTION: Formatting a disk erases its contents completely. Never format a disk unless you are certain you don't need any files on it.

Table 9-2, Formatting disks

OS	commands/procedures to format disks
Windows	Nearly all types of disks can be formatted in Windows Explorer. Some specialized removable drives have their own format program, but most can be formatted with the OS program.
	In Windows Explorer, right-click the drive to be formatted and click Format. The Format dialog box that opens has options you can set. Most are defaults and shouldn't be changed. You can do a full format or a quick format. A full format marks tracks and sectors on the disk and puts the basic tree structure on the disk. The quick format just puts an empty tree structure on the disk. You can also select an option to place system startup files on the disk.
	After you select options and click the Start button, the disk is formatted. The OS informs you when the formatting is finished and the disk is ready to use.
Linux	Use the fdformat command to format a disk. The command takes this form:

```
fdformat [-dDeEfHlLmMUqvx]
[-b label] [-B filename]
[-t dostype] [devname]
```

The items in brackets are optional switches that modify the command.

The fdformat command performs a low-level formatting on the disk. To complete the formatting process, you also need to use the mkfs command to create the file system on the disk. You can get more detail on the fdformat command by entering `man fdformat` at the command prompt.

Linux also has the format command to format hard disks. Enter `man format` at the command prompt for more help on formatting hard disks.

n o t e

CDs and DVDs are usually formatted only when they're written to. Exceptions are rewriteable CDs and DVDs.

creating folders (subdirectories)

After a disk has been partitioned and formatted, files can be stored on it. As mentioned, OSs allow you to divide the disk further into folders or directories that can also contain subfolders or subdirectories. At the root level, you can create folders, and every folder you create there is considered to be "under" the root folder. You can also create child folders inside these folders, and they're called subfolders or subdirectories. Folders containing "children" are called parent folders or parent directories. A folder that's a child to one folder can also be a parent to another folder. Any folder on a disk can contain files and/or additional child folders.

Note that there's always a current subdirectory (folder) in use. Typically, it's shown as part of the prompt in command-line interfaces and on the status bar in Windows. Commands for subdirectories act on the current subdirectory unless you specify otherwise.

The parent-child structure has nearly unlimited depth, but as a practical matter, you should avoid creating more than 10 levels in the structure. Nesting more than 10 folders results in lengthy file pathnames and makes the files in those folders difficult to find.

For users to be able to create this structure, the OS needs to provide a method of creating folders. Folders are given names, and each OS has specific rules for naming them. In general, folder names must start with a letter and can include additional numbers or letters and some special characters, up to a maximum length of 255 characters. Linux is case sensitive, meaning that it treats uppercase and lowercase letters as different letters. DOS and Windows aren't case sensitive.

n o t e

Windows uses the term "folder," but Linux more often uses the terms "directory" and "subdirectory." In most of this chapter's discussion, the terms are used interchangeably.

Table 9-3 shows commands and procedures for creating folders in Windows and Linux.

Table 9-3, Creating folders

OS	commands/procedures to create folders
Windows	Folders can be created in Windows in two ways: • In Windows Explorer, select a drive or folder, and then right-click the blank area in the right pane, point to New, and click Folder. A folder called New Folder is appended to the list of files and folders in the right pane. You can then click this folder and rename it with whatever name you like. • Select the folder you want to be the parent to the new folder, and then click File, New, Folder from the Windows Explorer menu. (In Windows Vista and later, you select the folder you want to be the parent in the navigation pane on the left, and then click Organize, New Folder on the command bar.)
Linux	Use the mkdir command to create subdirectories (folders). To change your current (default) subdirectory, use the cd command. The following command creates a subdirectory named homework as a child under the current directory: `mkdir homework`

listing the contents of drives and folders

Table 9-4 shows the procedures and commands to list the contents of drives and folders in Windows and Linux.

Table 9-4, Listing the contents of drives and folders

OS	commands/procedures to list contents of folders or drives
Windows	The main program for viewing drives, folders, and files is Windows Explorer. To open it, click Start, All Programs, Accessories, Windows Explorer, or double-click the desktop icon (if you have one). You can also hold down the Windows (flag) key and press E. In Windows Explorer, you can browse the tree structures of your drives. Clicking the plus symbol next to a folder opens the folder's contents. (In Windows Vista and later, right arrows and down arrows are used instead of plus and minus symbols.) In general, folders are on the left and files on the right, although subfolders are sometimes displayed on the right. If you right-click a file or folder and click Properties, you can view details about it.

(continued)

Table 9-4, Listing the contents of drives and folders (*continued*)

OS	commands/procedures to list contents of folders or drives
Linux	To list files and folders, use the ls command (for "list") with the following syntax: **ls** [-a] [-A] [-b] [-c] [-C] [-d] [-f] [-F] [-g] [-i] [-l] [-L] [-m] [-o] [-p] [-q] [-r] [-R] [-s] [-t] [-u] [-x] [*pathnames*] The ls command has many switches for modifying how files are displayed. You can find information on them by entering man ls at the command prompt.

renaming folders and files

After you have created folders, the OS provides a method for renaming them, as shown in Table 9-5.

Table 9-5, Renaming folders and files

OS	commands/procedures to rename folders or files
Windows	In Windows Explorer, right-click the folder or file and click Rename. The cursor moves to the name of the highlighted folder or file, and you can type the new name. You can also select a file or folder, press F2, and enter the new name.
Linux	The Linux syntax for renaming a file or directory is as follows: **mv** *directory newname* In this command, *directory* is the full pathname to the subdirectory or file, and *newname* is the new name for the subdirectory or file.

deleting folders and files

An OS must also provide a method for deleting folders. Note that deleting folders requires care because it can also delete all files and subfolders contained in the deleted folder. Command-line OSs such as Linux don't allow recovering folders and files after they have been deleted. In Windows, deleted files and folders reside in the Recycle Bin folder until it's emptied.

9

wildcard – A symbol that stands for one or more characters, used in selecting files or directories

Both these OSs allow the use of wildcards. *Wildcards* are characters that are used to match any character, much as the joker can match any card in many card games. In Windows and Linux, wildcard characters are the asterisk (*) and the question mark (?). The asterisk matches any group of characters, and the question mark matches a single character. For example, the following path includes all files in the c:\windows\system32\drivers folder tree with .inf as a file extension:

```
c:\windows\system32\drivers\*.inf
```

Here are some more examples of wildcards:

*.exe	All .exe files	?xyz	Files such as 1xyz, 2xyz, and so on
a*.bat	All .bat files beginning with "a"	??xyz	Files such as 10xyz, abxyz, and so on

Wildcards can be used with many Linux and Windows commands to include groups of files and folders in file manipulation commands. As with other commands, wildcard specifications are case sensitive in Linux.

Table 9-6 shows the commands and procedures for deleting folders and files in Windows and Linux.

Table 9-6, Deleting folders and files

OS	commands/procedures to delete folders and files
Windows	There are two ways to delete a folder: • Right-click the folder you want to delete and click Delete. • Click the folder you want to delete and press Delete. With both methods, you see a message asking whether you're sure you want to delete; click Yes or press Enter to confirm. Note that deleting a folder also deletes all the files and folders it contains.
Linux	The rm command is used to delete folders (subdirectories) or files. For subdirectories, the -r switch must be used to indicate that a subdirectory, rather than a file, is being deleted. In the following command, rm deletes the file or files specified by *filename*. The optional switch -i prompts you before each file is deleted. You can use Linux wildcards to specify groups of files to be deleted. **rm** *filename* [-i] For more information on the rm command, enter `man rm` at the command prompt.

copying files and folders

After the basic folder and file structures have been set up, files can be copied into folders or stored at the root level. One of the most essential functions of an OS is to allow saving files to disk drives. Partitioning, formatting, and creating folders are done to prepare the drive to receive files. As a user, manipulating files and folders is one of the most important skills you can learn. Few things are more frustrating than losing a file on the hard drive or losing all your unsaved work when the power goes out. Knowing how to copy files and folders and organize drives into folders makes you more effective in your work and helps you perform proper backups. Table 9-7 shows you how to copy files in Windows and Linux.

Table 9-7, Copying files and folders

OS	commands/procedures to copy folders and files
Windows	The easiest, safest, and most consistent method in Windows Explorer is using the copy and paste functions. Simply right-click a file and click Copy. Next, right-click the folder or drive you're copying the file to and click Paste. A copy of the file is placed in this location.
	You can also hold down the Ctrl key, click the file, and drag it to the folder or drive. This process is risky, however, because if you accidentally let go of the key or button before the file gets to its destination, it might wind up in the wrong location, and you might also delete the file from its original location.
	Folders can be copied in the same manner as files. Any files or subfolders in the copied folder are also copied.
	To select multiple files or folders for copying, click one in the group and press Shift or Ctrl. Shift selects contiguous folders or files; click the first item to copy, hold down Shift, and click the last item in the group to select the entire group. For files or folders that aren't contiguous, click the first item to copy, hold down Ctrl, and click each additional item to add it to the selection.
Linux	The cp command is used to copy files and has this syntax:

```
cp filefrom fileto
```

The *filefrom* and *fileto* are full pathnames to the "from file" location and the "to file" location. Linux has more wildcards but still uses the asterisk and question mark. Using the asterisk after *filefrom* or *fileto* instructs the cp command to include all files and subdirectories in the main subdirectory specification.

moving files and folders

Moving files is similar to copying, but the file is deleted from its original location after it's moved. The command to move a file is actually a copy command followed by a delete command. Table 9-8 shows procedures and commands to move files and folders in Windows and Linux.

Table 9-8, Moving files and folders

OS	commands/procedures to move folders and files
Windows	The safest method is right-clicking the folder or file you want to move and clicking Cut. Next, right-click the location where you want to move the folder or file and click Paste.
	You can also click the folder or file, drag it to its new location, and release the mouse button. This method is called "drag and drop" and isn't as reliable as cutting and pasting.
Linux	The mv command is used to move subdirectories as well as files and follows this syntax:
	`mv oldname newname -r`
	The -r switch is used to include all child subdirectories and files in the move process. Note that the mv command is also used to rename files and folders, as you learned earlier.

one last thought

Because operating systems are a central part of computing, learning the basic OS concepts and how to use them is essential. In later computing courses, you'll expand your knowledge of the theory of OSs. In almost all your later courses, you'll have to interact with OSs to complete your studies and assignments. The coverage in this chapter isn't exhaustive by any means, but it gives you some common OS tools for managing files and folders.

chapter summary

- Operating systems are essential to the operation of computers.
- Operating systems are special programs designed to manage overall computer operation.
- An OS is the software control center of a computer system.
- Applications interface with a computer's hardware through the OS.
- Operating systems consist of a core program called a kernel and other system components that support and extend the kernel.
- Operating systems provide a user interface. The two main OS interface types are graphical (GUI) and command line (console).
- The OS is loaded as a result of the loader program in the system BIOS.
- The OS normally resides on the system's hard drive and is loaded into memory.
- The OS running on a computer is often referred to as the system's platform.
- Operating systems can be single-tasking or multitasking.
- Operating systems provide a user interface, manage processes, manage resources, and provide security for the system.
- Operating systems are responsible for loading, starting, running, and stopping processes.
- Operating systems allow multiple processes to share the CPU through a procedure called time slicing.
- Some operating systems use Plug and Play (PnP) technology to detect and configure I/O devices automatically.
- The most popular operating systems are Windows and Linux.
- Operating systems also provide for managing and organizing disk folders and files.
- Commands can be modified by using switches or parameters.
- Disks can be organized into folders (directories) and files.
- Learning to use OS file management functions can help you work more efficiently.

key terms

booting (*322*)

command-line interface (*328*)

command prompt (*329*)

deadlock (*333*)

directory (*334*)

DOS (Disk Operating System) (*324*)

driver (*322*)

folder (*334*)

format (*336*)

graphical user interface (GUI) (*328*)

interrupt handling (*332*)

kernel (*323*)

Linux (*324*)

multiprocessing (*327*)

multitasking (*327*)

network operating system (*327*)

open source (*325*)

operating system (OS) (*321*)

partition (*336*)

platform (*326*)

Plug and Play (PnP) (*332*)

POST (*322*)

process (*330*)

resources (*332*)

root level (*334*)

single-tasking (*327*)

time slicing (*331*)

UNIX (*324*)

wildcard (*341*)

Windows (*324*)

test yourself

1. What is the first program loaded into memory when a computer is started?

2. Special programs designed to allow the computer to communicate with peripheral devices are called what?

3. What is the core program of an OS called?

4. What is multitasking?

5. What is multiprocessing?

6. What are the four main categories of OS functions?

7. What are the two basic types of user interfaces in an OS?

8. What is a process in an OS?

9. What method allows multiple processes to share the CPU?

10. What is the purpose of an interrupt handler?

11. Folders and files in an OS are organized into what type of structure?

12. In Linux, how do you access information on OS commands?

13. What is the purpose of formatting a disk?

14. Give an example of a case-sensitive OS.

15. What command is used in Linux to create a folder?

16. What command is used in Linux to list folders and files on a drive?

17. In an operating system, what's a wildcard?

18. In Windows, what key is used to rename a file?

19. For what task is Plug and Play used in an OS?

20. Do PDA devices require an OS?

practice exercises

1. DOS stands for:

   a. Demand Open Sources
   b. Disk Operating System
   c. Device Outer Shell
   d. Direct Operating System

2. Multitasking operating systems can service many different _____ at once.

   a. Users
   b. Program tasks
   c. User interfaces
   d. Operating systems

3. The _____ portion of an OS remains in memory the entire time the computer is on.

   a. CPU
   b. Overlay
   c. Interrupt
   d. Kernel

4. Which of the following is not a multitasking OS?

   a. Linux
   b. UNIX
   c. Windows
   d. DOS

5. An OS method of allowing multiple processes to share the CPU is:

   a. Time slicing
   b. Multiuser
   c. I/O
   d. Command line

6. Deadlocks are resolved by:

   a. Interrupts
   b. Time slicing
   c. Memory segments
   d. The OS

7. Graphical interfaces can be added to the Linux OS.

   a. True
   b. False

8. Command-line switches are used to:

   a. Modify the command's operation
   b. Disable the OS
   c. Enable the graphical interface
   d. Remove folders

9. Before a disk can be used, it must be:

   a. Erased and locked
   b. Partitioned and formatted
   c. Filled with folders and files
   d. Time sliced

10. The process of _____ arranges the disk's surface into addressable areas and sets up the disk's basic directory tree structure.

    a. Partitioning
    b. Time slicing
    c. Booting
    d. Formatting

11. The main level of a disk is called the:

    a. Root
    b. Platform
    c. Head
    d. Subdirectory

12. Windows is case sensitive.

    a. True
    b. False

13. In Windows, the md command must be used to create a folder.

    a. True
    b. False

14. What is the Linux command to list files and folders on a disk?

    a. ls
    b. lsdir
    c. chdir
    d. list

15. Which of the following is the Linux command to rename files?

    a. rename
    b. F11
    c. mv
    d. ls

16. The Linux command for deleting a folder is:

    a. del
    b. rd
    c. rmdir
    d. rm

17. In Windows Explorer, you can select multiple folders and files by using the left mouse button combined with which of the following?

    a. Right mouse button
    b. Shift key
    c. Alt key
    d. Spacebar

18. The Linux wildcard _____ can be used to match multiple characters.

    a. ? (question mark)
    b. - (hyphen)
    c. / (forward slash)
    d. * (asterisk)

19. The Linux command to delete a file is:

    a. del
    b. delfile
    c. rm
    d. filedel

20. Windows Explorer can be used to drag and drop both files and folders.

    a. True
    b. False

digging deeper

1. What functions are performed by the OS kernel?

2. What is a thread, and how does it relate to a process?

3. Who is responsible for developing device drivers for an OS?

4. What is spooling, and what function does it perform in an OS?

5. What shells are used with Linux to provide a GUI? What is the strength of each?

discussion topics

1. Could there be a computer system that doesn't have an OS?

2. What other functions could an OS perform?

3. What techniques other than time slicing could be used for process management?

4. Which is better: a graphical user interface or a command-line interface?

5. What makes an OS stable?

Internet research

1. What is the most popular graphical interface available for Linux, and how does it compare with Windows?

2. What is the next version of Windows called, and what new features will it have?

3. Who created Linux, and for what purpose was it created?

4. What is the process for locating and downloading device drivers for major operating systems?

5. What is the difference between Linux and UNIX?

chapter

10

file structures

the lighter side of the lab
by spencer

Recently, I was hired to work in the technology section of the university newspaper and was excited until it came time to get paid. No, that's not just a lame reporter joke. I would have to actually get paid to be able to joke about it.

Shortly after I got the job, I received an e-mail instructing me to stop by the payroll office to fill out some forms for tax purposes. Sounds easy enough, right?

The forms were simple by IRS standards, so I had to ask "What does this line mean?" only 37 times. In just six or seven hours, I was done with the two forms and walked up to the counter to hand them in. The nice person behind the desk said, "Okay, I'll just need to see your Social Security card."

I was pretty sure I'd had a Social Security card at some point. I could picture what it looked like. It had popped up now and then, but now it had completely disappeared from existence (much like my dating life).

I explained that I didn't have my Social Security card, nor did I know where it was. She explained that they would hold my checks until I found it. (Judging by how well I kept track of the Social Security card, the checks were probably safer in their hands anyway.)

I began my search in my bedroom. Unfortunately, my room needs a little "defragmentation," if you know what I mean. I checked the stack o' junk in my closet, facing severe risk of avalanche. I checked the pile o' clothes on the bed and didn't find anything other than a pair of pants I'd forgotten I owned. (They passed the smell test, so I wore them when I went out that night.)

At this point, I was out of ideas, so I pulled out the big guns—I asked my mom. (This is a luxury that all you smarty-pants who moved out of your parents' house before you were 27 don't have. Who's laughing now?) Unfortunately, she couldn't find it either.

I've worked for the university newspaper for nine weeks without receiving a check. I can't help but think that none of this would have happened if I had used file structures. I could have created a linked list with yellow sticky notes, beginning at my baby book and leading from place to place until it pointed to my Social Security card. Defragging would be fun—almost like a scavenger hunt. It would be impossible to lose anything!

If you happen to find my Social Security card lying around, let me know. I'll send you reward money—after I get paid.

why you need to know about...
file structures

Have you ever thought what it would be like if you were listening to your favorite song, and a third of the way through it, the system prompted you to go find a file containing the next part because not all the song was in one location? Or what if you were reading a book and had to check out five different books because each one contained a couple of chapters? In either situation, you would be frustrated. Instead of being able to complete the task without interruption, you would be distracted by having to spend time locating the resources you need. Listening to an entire song or reading a book from start to finish is certainly more productive and enjoyable.

Files containing information (such as songs or books) are commonly used in everyday computer tasks. The operating system is responsible for managing files and making sure tasks are uninterrupted. These tasks involve using a file manager and file management system. By understanding how an operating system stores and maintains data in a computer, you can better comprehend how a computer handles files, learn how to manipulate files, and keep your computer running as efficiently as possible.

what does a file system do?

file system – The part of the OS responsible for creating, manipulating, renaming, copying, and moving files to and from a storage device

One function of an operating system (OS) is organizing and maintaining files on secondary storage media, such as hard drives, CDs, and removable media. A *file system* is the part of the OS responsible for creating, manipulating, renaming, copying, and moving files to and from these storage devices. A hard drive is the most common place to store files. Besides being a place to store all your documents, music files, and movies, it's the central location for storing the OS, applications, and user files.

In this book, you have learned about many operating systems and been introduced to many different applications and tools for making your life as a computing student easier. Each of these operating systems and applications uses files to perform its tasks.

User files are files you create for your own use, such as the following:

- Word-processing documents
- Source code for programs you have written
- Music files
- Movie files
- Spreadsheets
- Photos

The list could go on and on because so many different applications and tools are available. Each file takes up storage space on a hard disk or other storage medium, and the file system must keep track of these files. One way the file system does this is to organize files into directories, which are common storage areas. In fact, the file system acts much like a filing cabinet, with each piece of paper representing a file, and each file folder representing a directory or subdirectory (see Figure 10-1). Windows, Mac OS X, and many Linux versions use a file folder icon to represent a directory and call directories

Figure 10-1, Files and directories in a file system are similar to documents and folders in a filing cabinet

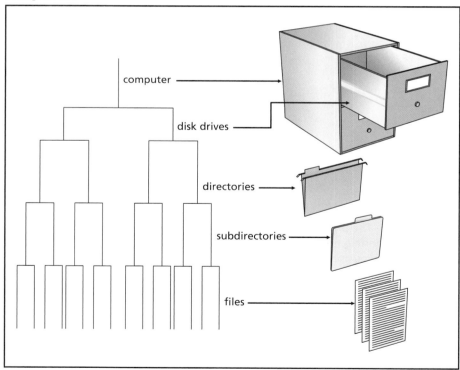

"folders." As you saw in Chapter 9, the OS uses a similar treelike hierarchical structure to organize files into directories and subdirectories (folders), as shown in Figure 10-2.

Figure 10-2, Folders and files in Windows

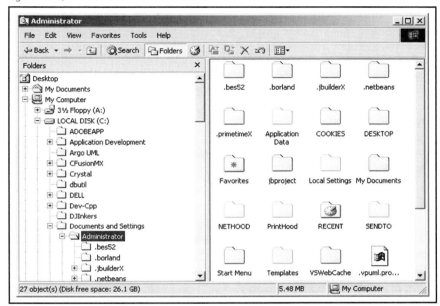

The file system's job is to keep track of where files and directories are located and assist users by relating their locations to the storage medium's physical structure. Hard disks, for example, are physically organized into tracks and sectors, and read/write heads move over specific areas of the hard disk to store (write) or retrieve (read) data.

random access – Reading data from or writing data to anywhere on a disk

sequential access – Reading and writing data in order from the beginning

A hard disk is a *random access* device, meaning you can read data from or write data to anywhere on the disk. (Another type of access is *sequential access*, in which you must start at the beginning of data and read until you get to the data you want. You learn more about access methods later in this chapter.) Random access is a faster way to access data, but users want to store and organize information in a more orderly (less random) fashion. That's where the file system comes in. Various file systems have been developed to allow users to organize their files as they want and still take advantage of the speed of random access (also called relative access).

file systems and operating systems

The type of file management system used depends on the OS. The first Microsoft file system was File Allocation Table (*FAT*). Different versions of FAT were used from MS-DOS in the 1980s through Windows 95, 98, and Me. Beginning with Windows NT, the default Windows file system changed to New Technology File System (*NTFS*), although FAT was still supported. Current Windows OSs use NTFS by default. UNIX and Linux support several different file systems, including XFS, JFS, ReiserFS, ext3, and others. The original Macintosh Filing System (MFS) evolved into the Hierarchical Filing System (HFS) and then the Hierarchical Filing System Extended Format (HFS+), the current Mac OS X file system.

Each of these file management systems was suitable at the time it was developed to handle storing and maintaining the OS's file structure, but unlike fine wine, filing systems become outdated, and new ideas and methods are discovered. NTFS has many advantages over the older FAT file management system, but before you can appreciate them, you need to understand how FAT came to be and what it accomplished.

FAT

Many people worry about being overweight, but computers are weight conscious, too: They incorporate FAT into their system and try their best to manage it!

FAT was introduced with the first PC operating system, MS-DOS. In those days, you could store the entire OS on a single floppy disk. As you learned earlier, a hard drive stores information in sectors. In many file management systems, including FAT, sectors are grouped to form *clusters* (also called allocation units), as shown in Figure 10-3.

Figure 10-3, Sectors are grouped into clusters on a hard disk

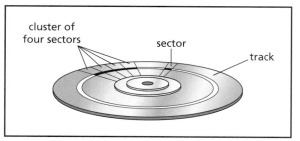

FAT (File Allocation Table) – File management system used to locate files on a storage medium

NTFS (New Technology File System) – File management system introduced in Windows NT and incorporated into all desktop and server Windows OSs since then; used to locate files on a storage medium

what's your file system?

To see which file system your Windows computer uses, open the My Computer window, right-click the hard drive, and click Properties. The file system is listed near the top of the General tab.

cluster – Area of the hard drive containing a group of the smallest units that can be accessed on a disk (sectors)

Data is stored in 512-byte sectors on the hard drive, and depending on the file size, data might occupy one or more sectors. For performance reasons, sectors are organized into contiguous (one after the other) clusters on the disk. So in reality, a file might occupy one or more clusters that consist of one or more sectors. FAT simply keeps track of which files are using which clusters and where files are located by using entries in the FAT table.

FAT organizes the hard drive into several areas, as shown in Figure 10-4:

- Partition boot sector
- Main FAT
- Backup FAT
- Root directory area
- Data area (measured in clusters)

Figure 10-4, Typical FAT file system

Partition boot record (1 sector)
Main FAT (size depends on total number of disk clusters)
Backup FAT (same size as main FAT)
Root directory area
Data area (size varies, depending on total number of disk clusters; stores all other files and directories)

The partition boot sector contains information the file system needs to know how to access volumes. (A volume is a drive or a drive partition formatted with a file system. A hard disk can have more than one volume, or one volume can span several disks.) Two FAT tables are stored in fixed locations: main FAT and backup FAT. If an error occurs in reading main FAT, the backup FAT can be copied over the main FAT to ensure system stability. The root directory area keeps an entry for every file and folder stored in the root directory. Each entry contains information on the file or folder, including name, size, and number of the cluster holding the beginning of the file.

The FAT format progressed from FAT12 through FAT16 to FAT32. The numbers refer to the number of bits in each FAT entry. As the number of bits for FAT entries increased, so did the size of partitions and files that could be used with FAT.

Every file and folder on a drive is stored in units called clusters, which consist of smaller units called sectors. The computer needs to know which clusters are used for each file. The FAT table contains this information and maintains the relationship between files and clusters used for files. Each cluster has two entries in the FAT table: The first shows the current cluster information, and the second contains a link to the next cluster to use.

n o t e

Flash memory devices, such as SmartMedia, Compact Flash, and memory sticks, emulate popular file management schemes, such as FAT.

VFAT

Microsoft created Virtual FAT (VFAT) in the mid-1990s as an extension of FAT so that the OS could handle filenames longer than eight characters.

defragging

To access Disk Defragmenter in Windows XP and Vista, click Start, All Programs, Accessories, System Tools, Disk Defragmenter. To defragment the drive properly, you might need to turn off virus checkers, screen savers, and other running programs.

disk fragmentation – Occurs when files' clusters are scattered in different locations on the storage medium instead of being in contiguous locations

Because clusters are linked this way in the FAT table, FAT is a form of a linked list. The process of linking a file's clusters continues until the end of the file is placed in the final cluster. It's marked with a special code so that when the file system is looking for all the file's pieces, it knows when it has reached the last cluster and doesn't need to look for more of the file.

FAT keeps track of which clusters it can use for writing information and which are already in use storing file data. It also marks which clusters are bad and no longer usable so that the file system doesn't attempt to use them.

When you first format a hard drive, many clusters are available for use, although some might have been marked as bad already. If you store a file on a newly formatted hard drive, the file system usually stores the information in a contiguous block of clusters. As time goes by and you store, delete, and move files, the contiguous blocks might not be contiguous any more. The file system then puts data into clusters wherever it fits best, often in noncontiguous blocks. Having data scattered all over the disk in this fashion can create some problems, discussed next.

disk fragmentation

As more files are stored on the hard drive and clusters become less contiguous, the file system begins to slow down because it's moving the hard drive's read/write heads all around trying to locate the clusters for a particular file. Every time a new file is stored, the system tries to recover open space. Eventually, a file can have its clusters stored in every corner of the hard drive. This state of affairs is called *disk fragmentation* (see Figure 10-5).

Figure 10-5, Files become fragmented as they're stored in noncontiguous clusters; a defragmenting utility moves files to contiguous clusters and improves disk performance

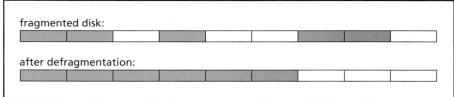

Fragmentation can occur in NTFS as well, but it's a bigger problem with FAT. To compensate for this unorganized storage method, Windows provides the Disk Defragmenter utility to reorganize clusters on the hard drive so that they're contiguous again. This utility acts like the computer system's mom: It comes into the hard drive, takes a look at how messy it is, and cleans everything up. It's a helpful tool that should be used regularly to make sure your system runs at peak performance. Disk Defragmenter improves performance by minimizing how much read/write heads have to move to access data.

advantages of FAT

The main advantage of FAT is its efficient use of disk space. Because large files aren't required to have contiguous clusters, FAT can place the parts of the file wherever they fit.

Another advantage is that filenames can now have up to 255 characters. Under FAT16, filenames were limited to eight characters for the name and three characters for the file extension. FAT32 supports 255-character filenames.

One more advantage of using FAT is how easy it is to recover files that have been deleted. When a file is deleted, the file system doesn't actually remove it from the hard drive; instead, it places the hex value E5h in the first position of the filename. The actual file and its contents remain on the drive and can be recovered easily by using special software, such as a hex editor, to replace the E5h with the original first letter of the filename. In fact, unless you fill up the hard drive with files or do a low-level format, in which the file system formats the drive by removing all the stored data, you can usually recover deleted files.

disadvantages of FAT

Compared with NTFS, using FAT has many disadvantages. One is that overall performance slows down as more files are stored on the drive. Another problem, as mentioned, is that the drive can become fragmented quite easily.

In addition, FAT lacks many of the security features in NTFS, such as being able to assign access rights to files and directories. It can also have file integrity problems, such as lost clusters, invalid files and directories, and allocation errors. All these problems have been addressed in NTFS.

NTFS

NTFS was developed with the goal of overcoming FAT's limitations. Introduced with Windows NT, it's the default file system in all current Windows operating systems. NTFS is often referred to as a "journaling" file system because it keeps track of transactions performed when working with files and directories. If any errors are encountered, the file system "rolls back" transactions until it's stable again. This feature is a benefit of using NTFS because the file system is less likely to become corrupt, but if it does, it's usually smart enough to fix itself.

Master File Table (MFT) – A table used in NTFS to store data about every file and directory on the volume

NTFS uses the *Master File Table (MFT)* to store data about every file and directory on the volume, and the OS uses data in this table to retrieve files. Data stored in the MFT includes a file's size, name, and permissions, among other information.

The MFT is similar to a database table containing attributes about files and can be thought of as a table of contents for files and folders in a volume. When a file or folder is created on the volume, a record is also created in the MFT. If the file is smaller than 700 bytes, it's also stored in the MFT entry. Like FAT, NTFS uses clusters (allocation units) for storing data. It reserves blocks of space so that the MFT can grow.

n o t e

Not all hard drives in a computer must use the same file management system. One can use FAT, and another can use NTFS, for example.

from FAT to NTFS

If you're converting a FAT drive to an NTFS drive, the reserved blocks of space are usually located somewhere in the middle of the partition, resulting in slower performance. For this reason, doing a clean install on a new drive when converting to NTFS is always recommended.

advantages of NTFS

The structure of NTFS makes file access fast and reliable. When you want to view a file in FAT, first the file system has to read the FAT entry and make sure it's valid. Then it accesses the file by searching for clusters assigned to the file. In NTFS, the file system simply goes right to the file as soon as you request it.

In addition, with the MFT, the file system can recover from problems without losing a lot of data. The journaling feature also makes restoring to a stable system state easy. There's also a backup (mirrored) copy of the MFT in case of damage to the main MFT, which is useful for system restoration.

Security has been improved compared with FAT, too. Under NTFS, an administrator can specify which users or groups of users can perform certain operations on files and directories (also called file and directory permissions). These permissions include both reading and writing data. FAT was designed during the single-user era, but NTFS is geared more toward a networked environment, so security measures have been increased.

Encrypting File System (EFS) – An encryption technology that converts data in a file to unreadable information by using an encryption algorithm and key value; to make the information readable again, you must decrypt it with another key value

NTFS also supports file encryption with *Encrypting File System (EFS)* and file attributes, so you can encrypt files to protect them from unauthorized access. If other users are able to access a file owned by a different user, they can see information about the file but not the actual data in the file.

Finally, NTFS includes a file attribute that controls file compression. A user can set a file to be compressed and save disk space. *File compression* is the process of reducing a file or folder's size. The entire process is transparent to the user, meaning the file doesn't have to be uncompressed before the user can read it. The system handles compressing and uncompressing for you. You simply sit back and reap the benefits of saving disk space.

n o t e

> There are many different types of file compression, but hard drives have become so inexpensive that many users don't want to sacrifice performance to save disk space.

file compression – The process of reducing file size and, therefore, taking up less disk space

why not compress?

There are two disadvantages of using file compression:

- It slows performance.
- You can't encrypt a compressed file.

disadvantages of NTFS

There are also disadvantages of using NTFS on a volume. Because NTFS has a larger system overhead than FAT, it's not recommended as a file management system on volumes smaller than 4 GB. For example, on a 100 MB drive, NTFS needs about 4 MB of disk space. This also means you can't format a floppy disk with NTFS because the file system wouldn't fit on the disk.

Another disadvantage is that you can't access NTFS volumes from MS-DOS, Windows 95, or Windows 98. Also, many Linux distributions can't write to NTFS drives.

comparing file systems

Table 10-1 compares the features of FAT16, FAT32, and NTFS. Which file system you use depends on the OS you're using and the features you need. For example, if you're using Windows 9x as an OS, you use FAT; if you're using Windows XP or Vista, you use NTFS. Choosing the correct file system rarely depends on hardware; it depends more on the OS.

Table 10-1, Fat16, FAT32, and NTFS compared

feature	FAT16	FAT32	NTFS
total volume size	4 GB	2 GB to 2 TB	2 TB
maximum file size	2 GB	4 GB	Size of drive (theoretical limit of 2^{64} bytes)
OS support	DOS, Windows 3.x, 9x, NT, 2000, XP, Vista, and Server 2003/2008	Windows 95 (OSR2), 98, NT, 2000, XP, Vista, and Server 2003/2008	Windows NT (service pack 4), 2000, XP, Vista, and Server 2003/2008
compatible with floppy disks	yes	yes	no
security	limited security	limited security	extensive security features
file compression	supported with extra utilities	supported with extra utilities	included as part of NTFS
journaling (tracking file transactions)	none	none	yes
large database support	limited	yes	yes
multiple disk drives in one volume	no	no	yes

All PCs with Windows operating systems are now formatted with NTFS. FAT is used only with older small hard drives and small removable devices, such as flash drives, which are usually formatted with FAT32. NTFS can support drive sizes up to 16 TB (1600 GB), so it should remain a viable file system for the foreseeable future.

In the UNIX/Linux environment, you also have a variety of file system choices; some are listed in Table 10-2. As with Windows file systems, some Linux file systems support journaling, some support long filenames, and all have specified maximum file sizes.

Table 10-2, Some UNIX/Linux file systems

file system	description
Extended File System (ext) and the newer versions, ext2 and ext3	The default Linux file system; the current version, ext3, supports journaling
Unix File System (UFS)	Original file system for UNIX; compatible with virtually all UNIX systems and most Linux systems
MS-DOS	Compatible with FAT12 and FAT16 (doesn't support long filenames); typically installed to enable UNIX to read floppy disks created in MS-DOS or Windows
Network File System (NFS)	Developed by Sun Microsystems for UNIX systems to support network access and file sharing (such as uploading and downloading files); supported in almost all UNIX/Linux versions and many other operating systems

The best way to determine which file system to use, barring any specific hardware requirements, is by checking your current OS and determining what type of file system environment you want to work in. Then evaluate the advantages and disadvantages of each file system.

file organization

Now that you have an idea of what a file system does and the different types of file systems that are available, take a closer look at file characteristics and how files are stored on disks and other media.

binary or text

A file is a storage location containing data that's treated as binary or text. All files are stored as binary files, and as you learned in previous chapters, all data on the disk is actually stored as 1s and 0s. The difference between text files and binary files is that text files consist of ASCII or Unicode characters. Each time you type a character in a file (including letters, punctuation, and spaces), the file system stores a byte in the file. Text files are typically read with word-processing programs or text editors, such as Notepad in Windows or gedit in UNIX/Linux, and are easy to view and modify.

Binary files can't be read with these programs, and the term "binary" is often used to refer to any file that isn't a text file. Binary files can be read by computers but not humans and contain coded and numeric information. They're also more compact than text files. Some examples of binary files are executable programs, applications, and sound and image files.

sequential or random access

Data is usually stored sequentially or randomly (see Figure 10-6). Sequential storage means data is accessed one chunk after the other in order, and random storage means data can be accessed in any order. Random access is also called direct or relative access.

Figure 10-6, Sequential versus random access

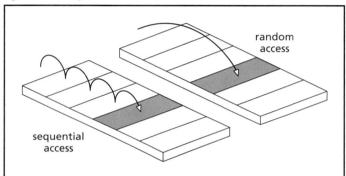

sequential access

A sequential file is accessed starting at the beginning of the file and is processed to the end of the file. The data stored in the file can be thought of as one long row of information. An example of a sequential file is an audio file or a video file. When you add new data, it's written at the end of the file. Because data is appended to the end of the file, the writing process is fast. On the other hand, retrieving data can be extremely slow, depending on the data's location.

Sequential file access allows storing information in the file row by row, much like a database table record. Each line of the sequential file can be organized or logically grouped as though you're describing a record. For example, a line in a sequential file might consist of a student ID, first name, last name, and letter grade. As shown in Figure 10-7, a comma (or another character, such as a tab) can be used as a field delimiter to separate each field in the line.

Figure 10-7, A comma can be used as a field delimiter

```
1234,Joseph,Blow,C
2452,Mary,Lamb,A-
5839,Alexander,Roma,B
8983,Marissa,Anderson,A
7738,Miles,Gregory,A
8442,John,Jones,C+
```

Instead of using a character as a delimiter, you can use a fixed length for each field. Data that isn't long enough to fill the entire field can be padded with spaces. Figure 10-8 shows the layout of student records in fixed-length format:

- Student ID: 4 characters
- First name: 10 characters
- Last name: 15 characters
- Grade: 2 characters

Figure 10-8, Data can also be in fixed-length format

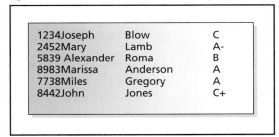

```
1234Joseph      Blow           C
2452Mary        Lamb           A-
5839 Alexander  Roma           B
8983Marissa     Anderson       A
7738Miles       Gregory        A
8442John        Jones          C+
```

By the time you're finished creating a sequential file, you have stored one or many rows of data in order.

A major drawback of sequential access is that when you insert, delete, or modify existing records, you must process the entire file by writing all the information with changes to a new file. In addition, although sequential access is often used in computer systems, it has a serious drawback: The only way to get to a specific record in a file is by starting at the beginning of the sequential file and reading through it until you get to the record you want. If the file has only a few records, this method isn't a problem. When files contain many records, or the records are very large, sequential access can be a real problem. It takes time to read each record, especially when the disk's read/write head has to be moved. Therefore, to deal with large amounts of data, another method is needed: random access, discussed next.

random access

Accessing a particular record in a file is faster if you can position the read/write head directly on the record without having to read all the records in front of it. If all records are the same size, you can mathematically calculate the record's position on the disk surface and go right to it. This is the principle behind random access. Random access requires fixed-length records; Figure 10-9 shows the difference between variable-length and fixed-length records.

Figure 10-9, Record organization and file access

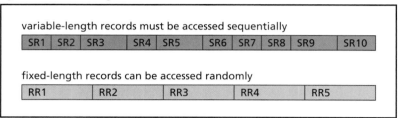

For example, you have a file of 1000 records, and each record is 100 bytes. If you want to access record 538, you multiply the record number by the record size (538 * 100) and calculate that the record you're looking for is 53,800 bytes into the file. Depending on how many bytes per sector and per track are on the disk, you can position the read/write head at that exact point.

An added benefit of random file access is that records can be updated in place. If you want to make a change in a record, you calculate the record's position and then write directly to the record. You can't do this with sequential access because variable-length records can be different sizes. Updating a sequential file requires copying the entire file to a new file and modifying the record as it's written to the new file.

The advantages of random file access are getting to a particular record faster and being able to update the record in place. The disadvantage is that disk space can be wasted if data doesn't fill the entire record or if some record numbers don't have data. Random file access works well when a sequential record number can identify records easily.

hashing

hashing – A common method for accessing data in a file or database table with a unique value called the hash key

hash key – A unique value used in hashing algorithms and identifying records

When records can't be identified by a sequential numeric value, or the numeric identifying value isn't in sequential order beginning with 1, another technique has been developed that allows using nonnumeric record keys to access relative records. This technique, called *hashing*, is widely used in database management systems. Hashing uses a hashing algorithm to generate a unique value called a *hash key* for each record. The hash key is then used as a key value in a list of rows or records of information. Combining hash keys establishes an index similar to what you learned about in Chapter 6.

why hash?

The goal of hashing is to create an algorithm that allows converting a key field, such as a phone number, that isn't suited for relative (random) file access into a relative record number that can be used. Even ASCII character fields can be converted by using a hashing technique.

For example, if you're storing customer information, you can use a phone number as the identifying key in a relative access file, but the file would have large blocks of unused spaces reserved for unused phone numbers. With a customer living in area code 702, you would have to waste the space for relative records 0 through 7019999999, which isn't acceptable.

To solve this problem, you use a simple hashing technique. You subtract 7019999999 from the customer's phone number and use the result as the relative key. Doing so solves the problem of wasting space on relative record numbers for phone numbers less than 702-000-0000. This hashing technique still isn't the most efficient, however, because you still waste many blocks of space lying between the ranges of your customers' phone numbers, as it's unlikely their phone numbers are in order beginning with 701-000-0001. You need to come up with a better hashing technique. Although devising an efficient *hashing algorithm* might be difficult, there are a few basic techniques you can use to formulate one.

hashing algorithm – A routine of logic used for determining how hash values are created

A moderately simple technique for hashing a number such as a phone number is to first determine the maximum number of records you might have. The records in the relative file should have a key value from 0 to the highest number possible, minus 1. This range is then used to allocate space for the file to store all the records it might end up using. After you know how many records you need to store, you can create an algorithm that converts the customer's phone number into a number in the specified relative record range.

An easy way to accomplish this is to divide the highest possible phone number by the expected number of customers, with the result being an algorithm key. After you have this key, you can use it on customer phone numbers to calculate their relative record numbers.

For example, a phone number in the United States is made up of 10 numeric digits (999-999-9999, not including parentheses or dashes). You make a rough estimate and decide that you could have approximately 2000 customers. So you divide 9999999999 by 2000 to come up with the algorithm key, which, rounded, is 5,000,000. If your first customer has a phone number of 702-555-1234, the relative record is calculated as 7025551234 / 5000000, or 1045. The record for this customer is then stored in relative record 1045.

This hashing technique might be useful if the 2000 customer phone numbers were evenly spread throughout the range of 0000000000 to 9999999999. In a normal situation, however, phone numbers are more likely grouped in a single area code and in just a few three-digit prefixes. In this case, the algorithm generates a lot of collisions.

dealing with collisions

collision – In hashing, what happens when the hashing algorithm generates the same relative key for more than one original key value

Collisions happen when the hashing algorithm generates the same relative key for more than one original key value. In the previous example, the same relative key is generated for the phone numbers 522-500-5000 through 522-999-9500. This isn't acceptable, so a better algorithm needs to be developed.

A simple remedy for the collision problem might be expanding the algorithm. For example, the previous algorithm could be expanded to include the sum of the phone number's digits, with the hope of lessening the chances of a collision. Again, using the phone number 702-555-1234 gives you the relative key 1045. Add to it the sum of the phone number's digits: 34 (7 + 0 + 2 + 5 + 5 + 5 + 1 + 2 + 3 + 4), giving 1045 + 34, or 1079. Another phone number, such as 702-555-5678, would have a relative record number of 1045 + 50, or 1095, and a collision is avoided. Using this technique doesn't completely prevent collisions, but it does lessen them. Note that if one customer has the phone number 702-555-1234 and another has the phone number 702-555-4321, a collision occurs.

With a little skill and mathematical ability, you can develop an efficient algorithm for the range of customer phone numbers and nearly eliminate collisions. Even the best hashing algorithm occasionally has collisions, however, so you must make some provisions for dealing with them. One common method is creating an *overflow area* in the relative file that holds records with duplicate relative record numbers.

overflow area – Area in a file that's used in case a collision occurs during the hashing algorithm

The overflow area works in this manner (shown in Figure 10-10): The first record with a relative key calculated by the hashing algorithm is placed in the

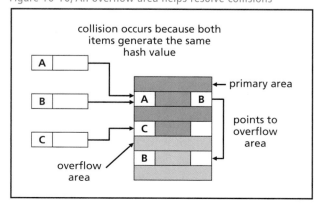

Figure 10-10, An overflow area helps resolve collisions

specified place on the disk. When the hashing algorithm generates the same key for a different phone number, the system goes to the specified relative location on the disk and checks to see whether the phone number of the record there matches the customer's phone number. If not, the second record is written to the overflow area at the end of the file.

When a record is retrieved, the process is similar. The hash key is calculated from the phone number, and the record at the calculated position is retrieved. If the record at that location isn't the correct one, the overflow area is searched sequentially until the matching record is found.

hashing and computing

In the past, creating hashing algorithms has been the focus of computer-related education programs. The most efficient hashing algorithm for a certain key was awarded a prize—maybe something like a deluxe pocket protector.

Hashing benefits companies that produce database management systems. Each company wants the most efficient storage and lookup routines so that their systems outperform the competition.

Many different hashing algorithms are used in computing. Some are based on encryption and decryption, and others focus on indexing. Many programming languages have specialized built-in libraries of hashing routines, but don't be surprised if one day you need to create your own hashing routine.

one last thought

A computer system's worth is often measured in terms of what's stored on its hard drives. Power supplies, main boards, CPUs, and monitors can be replaced easily. Data, on the other hand, can be difficult, if not impossible, to replace. All aspects of data storage depend on the file system that's used. Computing professionals who have a strong understanding of file systems can make data available more readily and know how to protect it. Who knows? Your career path might lead to participating in the design of the next-generation filing system for a new form of mass storage device.

chapter summary

- A hard drive is an example of a random access device that stores information in tracks and sectors and accesses data through read/write heads.
- A file system is responsible for creating, manipulating, renaming, copying, and moving files on a storage device.
- Windows uses FAT or NTFS as the file system.
- The File Allocation Table (FAT) file system keeps track of which clusters files are using.
- FAT is prone to disk fragmentation.
- New Technology Filing System (NTFS) is the default file system on current Windows operating systems and uses a Master File Table (MFT) to keep track of files and directories on a volume.
- NTFS has many advantages over FAT, such as better reliability and security, journaling, file encryption, and file compression.
- Linux can be used with many file systems, such as XFS, JFS, ReiserFS, and ext3, but ext3 is used most commonly.
- A file contains binary or text data.
- Data is usually stored and accessed sequentially or randomly (relative access).
- Hashing is a common method for accessing a relative file and uses a hashing algorithm to generate a hash key value for identifying a record location.
- Collisions occur when the hash key is duplicated for more than one relative record location.
- The goal of hashing is to create an algorithm that allows converting a key field into a relative record number with few collisions.

key terms

cluster (*356*)

collision (*368*)

disk fragmentation (*358*)

Encrypting File System (EFS) (*361*)

FAT (File Allocation Table) (*356*)

file compression (*361*)

file system (*353*)

hash key (*366*)

hashing (*366*)

hashing algorithm (*367*)

Master File Table (MFT) (*360*)

NTFS (New Technology File System) (*356*)

overflow area (*368*)

random access (*355*)

sequential access (*355*)

test yourself

1. Describe what a file system does.

2. Describe the key characteristics of FAT.

3. Describe how a drive becomes fragmented.

4. Explain how defragmentation works and how it can improve system performance.

5. How does FAT differ from NTFS, and when is each used?

6. What are the advantages and disadvantages of FAT?

7. Describe the key characteristics of NTFS.

8. What are the advantages and disadvantages of NTFS?

9. Describe the Master File Table (MFT) and how it works.

10. What are the advantages and disadvantages of file compression?

11. What's the difference between a text file and a binary file?

12. How does sequential file access differ from random file access?

13. What are the strengths and weaknesses of sequential file access and random file access?

14. Explain how hashing works.

15. You're trying to create a hashing algorithm to work with information stored for a student registration system. Each student is identified by a student ID, which is seven characters. The numbers for student IDs range from 1000000 to 9999999. Write a hashing algorithm that minimizes collisions.

practice exercises

1. Which of the following is *not* a responsibility of the file system?

   a. Creating files
   b. Manipulating files
   c. Renaming files
   d. Copying files
   e. None of the above

2. Sectors are made up of clusters.

   a. True
   b. False

3. In FAT, files don't need to be stored in a contiguous block of memory.

   a. True
   b. False

4. Which of the following FAT formats allows the largest volume size?

   a. FAT12
   b. FAT16
   c. FAT32
   d. All FAT formats have the same maximum volume size.

5. Which tool is used to reorganize clusters so as to minimize drive head movement?

   a. Disk Defragmenter utility
   b. Sequential Access utility
   c. FAT
   d. NTFS

6. FAT32 provides the capability to assign access rights to a file and directory.

   a. True
   b. False

7. Which is *not* an advantage of using NTFS?

   a. Journaling
   b. File encryption
   c. Efficient disk use on small volumes
   d. Security

8. Which is *not* a file system used in Linux?

   a. HFS+
   b. XFS
   c. JFS
   d. ext3

9. You're tracking information on rocket launches. Each launch is assigned a number from 1000 to 100000. There will probably be around 5000 launches, and you're using a hashing algorithm that divides the highest possible number of launches by the expected number of launches. What is the hashing algorithm key in this situation?

   a. 200
   b. 20
   c. 500000
   d. 5000000

10. Using the information from problem 9, if you have a rocket launch number of 80000, what is the relative record?

   a. 4000
   b. 400
   c. 50
   d. 5000

digging deeper

1. What is a journaling file system?

2. Are there any other types of file systems besides journaling, FAT, and NTFS? If so, describe them.

3. Does disk defragmenting really make a difference in your system's overall performance? Why or why not?

4. What is a hash table, and how is it used?

5. Create a hashing algorithm for uniquely identifying records. Make sure you describe how it works.

discussion topics

1. Using question 15 from the Test Yourself section, determine which hashing algorithm is best suited for reducing the number of collisions.

2. What situations are best for using sequential file access?

3. What situations are best for using random file access?

4. What are the maximum file and volume sizes for the NTFS and ext3 file systems? What happens when storage devices exceed these sizes?

5. Which of the common file systems is the least prone to fragmentation? Why?

Internet research

1. What are the most current file systems used in Windows? Describe their differences.

2. What are the most current file systems used in Linux? Describe their differences.

3. Find five Web sites that explain hashing and demonstrate a hashing algorithm. Share your findings with the class.

4. How do you convert a FAT drive to an NTFS drive?

5. How does ext3 organize a hard drive?

6. How does NTFS organize a hard drive?

11

the human-computer interface

in this chapter you will:

- Learn the origins of human-computer interface development
- Learn about human interaction technologies
- Learn the foundations of human interface design
- Understand how to build an effective user interface
- Discover how contemporary design experts create cutting-edge technologies
- Find out what human emotion has to do with good design

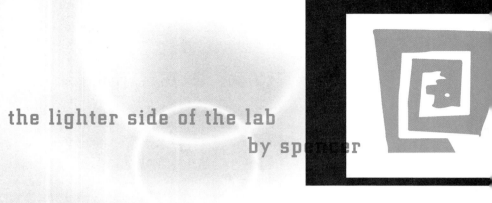

the lighter side of the lab
by spencer

Recently, I got my first Bluetooth headset. I had resisted buying one for a long time because in the past, I'd been startled by strangers suddenly talking to me out of the blue in a store, saying something like, "Yeah, I laughed so hard it frightened my Chihuahua." After a second or two, I'd respond with something vague, such as "Oh . . . that's good to hear." These strangers would then look at me blankly as they turned their heads, and I'd finally notice the tiny Bluetooth headset.

My dad just gave me one for my birthday, so now *I'm* the stranger who startles people in the store as I walk up and down the aisles chatting seemingly to myself. I don't know what I ever did without it. It's nice to not have a numb arm from holding the phone up to my ear for long periods or a kinked neck from the old-fashioned version of "hands free."

That has me thinking about what else could be hands free. The other day when I was driving, I thought about how cool it would be if I could hook up a voice-activated Web browser in my car, with a small display in the windshield, so that I could browse the Internet while on the road. (My next thought was that I really need to seek professional help.)

Some of you might remember the 1989 movie *The Wizard*, starring cute and lovable Fred Savage. It introduced the newest and coolest technology around at the time: the "Power Glove" Nintendo controller. Like every other kid, my brothers and I were blown away as we watched the screen follow the movements of the Power-Gloved hand.

Today's technology makes the Power Glove seem silly. We've moved beyond the keyboard and mouse to voice recognition, touch screens, and bowling games where you actually bowl. The only way to make bowling more real would be to add the scent of used bowling shoes.

Sophisticated technology makes programming more difficult because, let's face it, users can be idiots. For example, I always wondered why Wii remotes need straps, until my neighbor mentioned that his cute and lovable daughter was playing Wii tennis and, on a big serve, threw the remote through the screen of his big-screen TV.

Of course, I'd never do anything like that. I am a trained professional. Whoa! What just happened? Why is my computer typing every word I say? How did my speech-recognition software get turned on? Why won't this window close? CLOSE!

why you need to know about...
the human-computer interface

Software developers often put off designing a program's user interface until the end. Even with the advent of GUI rapid prototyping tools and extreme programming techniques, system and engineering needs often drive development, not the needs of the people who will be using the program. Also, it's all too easy to blame the user when there are problems. Software developers even have a quick response to users having trouble with software: RTFM, or Read the Fabulous Manual (although other words starting with "F" are also used). However, although people are ultimately responsible for their actions in using technology (they are, after all, using it), expecting excellent results from poorly designed technology is like expecting someone to be able to open the door shown in Figure 11-1 without a struggle.

Figure 11-1, A poorly designed door

the evolving interface

There are many examples of how technology often doesn't do what's intended and is even dangerous to use. Look at the glass exit doors with a push bar in your bank. Is it obvious which side the door hinges are on? People have broken their wrists on them. Look at your stove, too: The burners are in a square pattern, and the dials to control them are in a line across the front of the stove. Even though you've used the stove for years, you probably still have to stop and think about which burner you're turning on—the front one or the back one?

A project's design and its usability often get second-level status, despite the importance users give to usability. Studies have shown that users rate a computer's ease of use as up to 45% of their overall satisfaction. Operation, noise, repair service, system capacity, and other considerations rated much lower. Users often get second-level status, too, despite the importance of their satisfaction in selling them a product or service.

Companies give many reasons for not focusing on users—in other words, for using a system-first rather than a user-first development approach. For example, a company might have small development teams without the necessary skills in user interface design. Other reasons companies cite for using a system-first approach include having established development processes, developers protecting their turf, and the belief that extra steps in development, such as gathering requirements, result in increased costs. Some have even argued that the computer industry is economically geared toward creating more features in faster releases instead of focusing on creating a quality user-centered experience. An argument has also been made that PCs are the problem because they're more of a multipurpose device than any other consumer item.

note

In 1990, Bill Gates said, "We need to do a better job of thinking about technology from the point of view of all individuals—how they work, how they think, what they need to work and think more effectively."

Although Microsoft, like any company, hasn't always created the most usable products, many of its efforts have been successful, and it has spent a lot of money trying to make its products usable. Despite having software on many of the world's desktop computers, Microsoft must still compete for users, as must any company in the computer industry. Competing for users should be enough of an incentive to strive for well-designed software and hardware: That's the financial bottom line.

by any other name...

The focus on addressing users'
needs can go by many names,
such as "user-centric design,"
"consumer-driven design," and
"user-first design." Although the
meaning of these terms can differ slightly, they all mean
addressing users' needs as the
starting point in design.

*user interface – The
component that handles
interaction between a
technology and the user;
consists of what the user's
senses can perceive and
what the user can manipu-
late to operate the
technology*

The software industry, like no other, has involved consumers in the development process by releasing software in beta format and updating it based on user
feedback. This process is a form of rapid prototyping (discussed later in "The
User-Centric Design Process"). However, engaging in this process doesn't necessarily mean that a company has done a good job of addressing users' needs.

Understanding a particular user base and its needs—whether spoken or
unspoken—and developing and evaluating technological responses to these
needs require many skills. Naturally, unspoken needs are the most difficult to
determine. For this reason, companies such as Microsoft, Yahoo!, IBM, IDEO,
Google, and others employ people with skills that are useful in determining
users' needs. A design team might include someone with good visual design
skills, someone who understands behavior, someone who's good at creating
prototypes, and someone who knows how to test and observe behavior. Finding
one person with all these skills is rare, so usually, a team is necessary. The team
can also include people from marketing, engineering, and manufacturing to get
different perspectives.

Although this chapter doesn't delve into details on anthropological methods of
observation, psychologists' understanding of human responses, and principles
of visual design, it does give you an appreciation of how these skills are used in
developing *user interfaces*. The goal of this chapter is to broaden your outlook
as a potential programmer. Remember that at the other end of the program
you're writing are people trying to use it. You want them smiling serenely, not
cursing loudly.

This chapter starts with an overview of some interface technologies for interacting with computerized technologies. You then continue with the foundations of
user interface design, including understanding the psychology of how people use
technology, analyzing technology use in different settings, fitting user interface
design into the software engineering cycle, and evaluating interface designs. You
also look at some cutting-edge interactive design methods, with special attention
on Web development as well as the newest research in emotion and design.

user interface technologies

Human-computer interface technologies are more than just a mouse, keyboard,
screen, and GUI. With ubiquitous and embedded computing technologies, the
interface to a computer could be a teddy bear, the human body, your car's dash-
board, or a number of other objects. A computer might receive input through
voice, leg movements, biochemical changes, pulse and respiration rates, or
where the user's eyes are looking. It might give feedback in the form of a visual
display but also as sound, movement, heat, or some other response. In this
section, you look at some technologies that allow for "multimodal" interfaces—
many modes of interaction.

gaze system – *A system that uses users' eye movements as input*

With *gaze systems*, users can type letters, play chess, and perform other tasks in a number of ways. Many gaze systems use an infrared sensor to gauge where the user's eyes are looking on a screen and respond by measuring the length of time the eyes stay in one location or by using some other trigger that acts as the "mouse click." Measuring eye movements is useful in other ways. For example, Web page developers can use an eye movement analysis tool to track the amount of time a user spends on parts of an interface to determine whether the design makes sense. On the left, Figure 11-2 shows a gaze system with an infrared camera to track eye movements. On the right is an example of a program that captures and displays the user's eye movements.

Figure 11-2, Gaze systems in action

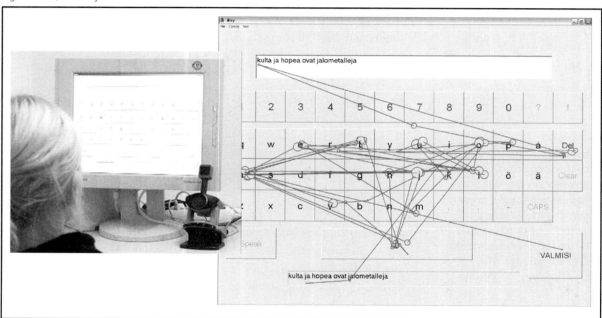

Courtesy of Päivi Majaranta and Harri Rantala from the Tampere Unit for Computer-Human Interaction at the University of Tampere, Finland

voice-recognition technology – *A technology that can recognize human speech and process instructions*

Computer *voice-recognition technology* has improved considerably since the mid-1990s, and you're probably familiar with the increasing use of voice-activated help systems or answering systems that companies use. Recognition systems trained for individual users, such as Dragon NaturallySpeaking (*www.nuance.com/naturallyspeaking/*), are quite good at processing both voice commands and text input, and they continue learning and improving as they interact with users.

11

natural-language processing – *A system that recognizes the natural way in which humans communicate verbally (by speech or text) and can discern meaning from this communication*

haptics technologies – *Technologies that allow users to feel a response from a system, not just see or hear a response; optimally, can replicate the sensation of feeling an object in real life to create a virtual tactile experience*

Systems designed to interact with many users, such as the ones at utility companies, obviously need to accommodate many different voices. To achieve voice recognition, they limit the number of phrases understood—collectively called the system's "grammar"—during a conversation. In other words, the system can understand when you speak a number but won't understand you talking about your grandmother. Being able to recognize "normal" conversation is called *natural-language processing*. Although it often isn't a major component of speech recognition because of limitations with voice recognizers, it's a critical component of search engine parsing and is growing in sophistication.

Haptics technologies allow users to feel—not just see or hear—some kind of response, called "feedback," from the system. If you've played with a Wii, you have already experienced this feedback with the hand unit's vibrations. Haptics have a long history in aviation; they originated with flight simulation projects the United States developed during World War II that used a type of analog computing.

note

One common haptics system is the fly-by-wire controls on airplanes. Pilots don't control the plane's components directly with cables and pulleys; instead, a computer sends signals to servos that move the control surfaces. Airplane manufacturers added a "feel" to controls so that the pilot feels the drag and shudder that emulate actual physical control.

Figure 11-3 shows a girl using a pen-like device attached to an arm that gives feedback depending on what the girl sees and "touches" while looking at the monitor. On the right is an example of what the user might see in the monitor. Notice the black pointer touching the toothpaste tube. When the user touches the toothpaste tube, she can "feel" its texture. When she touches the rubber bulb of the horn to the left of the toothpaste tube, she can feel it and press hard enough to get the horn to honk. Outlines of images are delineated by feel.

Figure 11-3, An example of haptics technology

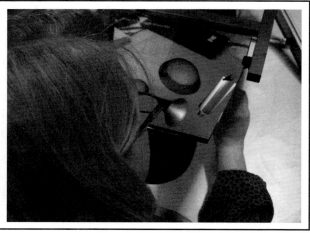

Courtesy of Arto Hippula (left) from the Tampere Unit for Computer-Human Interaction at the University of Tampere, Finland, and author David Ferro (right)

Along with tactile systems that sense pressure the user exerts and advanced human-machine interface technologies that allow a direct neural connection to the body, haptics are also used in many advanced prosthetic limbs and remote operations (called "haptic teleoperation"), such as flying remote drones, operating on a patient in another location, and controlling an underwater robot. Haptics can also be used with virtual reality technologies to train people for working in real situations. Given their capabilities to measure force, they allow practical training that previously was possible only with on-the-job training.

User interfaces to computers started with entering data by flipping switches, but since then, attention has been paid to many other methods of sensing input. Tracking eye, head, and body movements, sensing neural output, measuring brain activity, hearing and understanding speech, sensing the motion of a pen or mouse, and many other ways of entering data are possible now. Computer output has become just as sophisticated, with the use of heat, movement, vibration, and speech, among others. The opportunities to work on how humans and computers interact are many, varied, and increasing.

foundations of user interface design

People's capabilities, experiences, opinions, needs, expectations, and worldviews are included in the way they expect certain technologies to interact with them. Designers have to take these personal factors into account when developing technology, despite the tendency to design solely for physical capabilities. Designers also bring their own personal factors into their work, which explains why a perfect user interface will never exist. It's still a goal worth striving for, however.

For any technology, people have a model, or idea, of how the technology works. Models, metaphors, and analogies can be distinguished from one another, but generally, they all describe the mental view people have of a technology. Models allow users to predict what will happen given certain input, to find causes for the system's behavior, and to determine what actions cause the changes they want. A model can also serve as a device for recalling relationships between actions and events. Users can map a model to another similar device and get similar results. For example, your understanding of how a car wheel changes the car's direction gives you a clue for how to steer a powerboat. If you had to steer a boat controlled by a tiller, however, you might find mapping a car's steering mechanism to the boat more difficult.

Everyone involved in the development process has his or her own model. In software design, designers should take the users' and programmers' models into account and build on these models to create common metaphors. The result of not bringing these mental models into some accord or not incorporating everyone's expectations is what creates *superstitious behavior*. User interface specialist Paul Heckel stated, "Most software is run by confused users acting on incorrect and incomplete information, doing things the designer never expected."

superstitious behavior – Users with incomplete information on how to use a technology create an incorrect model of the way a technology works

Superstitious behavior is why consistency in the user interface is important. For example, look at the user interface of the world and gravity. If your shoes seemed to start floating to the ceiling after you took them off at night, you might start building a model in your head of gravity's effects that includes all sorts of unlikely behavior, such as believing you need to pat your head three times before untying your shoelaces to counteract your shoes floating away. You might see superstitious behavior in users restarting their systems every time they install software because they had to do it before with other software and now believe it must be done no matter what.

human psychology in human-computer interaction

To design an interface, you need to understand a few things about how humans think and work—an important factor in human-computer interface design. Many studies examine physiological capabilities to, say, move a mouse or a person's eyes across the screen by measuring the chemical reactions in saliva, electrical impulses in the brain, and other physiological reactions to stimuli.

sensory storage – Where sensory information is first processed by the human brain before passing it to short-term memory; can handle a lot of information simultaneously but can't store it for long

Humans have sensory storage, short-term memory, and long-term memory. *Sensory storage* works as a buffer to store all the sensory information coming in. Unfortunately, although sensory storage can absorb massive amounts of information, it can't hold on to it for very long because more information is always coming in. However, if you pay any attention to the information, it's moved into the higher memory functions. This is how you process movies, for example.

Sensory storage takes in each frame of film as it comes in at a high speed, and higher-level functions smooth out the images to make them continuous.

Another example is how your sensory system works at a party. It's always on, keeping an eye, ear, and so forth on your surroundings for anything that might be important. So even if you're involved in chatting with someone at a party, if you hear your name spoken from across the room or spot a cute guy or gal by the punch bowl, you're able to pick up on this sensory information. This phenomenon is why bells, whistles, blinking red lights, and other sounds and visuals are used in interfaces to grab your attention.

note

Interestingly, repeated actions can cause the sensory system to ignore a stimulus. This reaction, called "habituation," is why bells, whistles, blinking red lights, and the like should be used sparingly.

short-term memory – *Where information is sent after the sensory system receives it; limited to storing five to nine items temporarily*

Short-term memory, the next stage, is where you do information processing, such as mathematics. It's limited to holding between five and nine items. New information bumps out the old, unless it's moved to long-term memory. Also, information is held in short-term memory only temporarily, up to 30 seconds. Because of short-term memory's limitations, people use tactics such as repetition and chunking to retain information. Chunking groups bits of information, essentially tricking short-term memory into remembering fewer items. Phone numbers are a good example. Instead of remembering nine digits, you can remember a phone number as three chunks: area code, prefix, and suffix.

Designers need to be aware of the limits of short-term memory. Moving users to another page when they need information from the previous page can be a problem, for example. Pop-up windows placed over the information users need to do their work cause trouble, particularly when they obscure information a user is trying to get help on. In addition, systems that "forget" information from one page to another force users to remember and reenter information, further taxing their short-term memory and patience.

long-term memory – *Where information is stored on a semipermanent basis; can store a potentially limitless amount, but retrieving information can be more difficult*

Long-term memory is the next stage. The amount of information that can be stored there is potentially limitless, but unfortunately, the information isn't as easy to access. You've probably experienced the "tip-of-the-tongue" phenomenon when you're trying to remember something. People often use mnemonics as memory hooks to recall information, and chunking can work, too. Storytellers often remember key events in a story and what comes next. This way, they don't have to remember the entire story at once; instead, they retrieve it as needed. An example of a user interface moving away from having users rely on long-term memory is the way a word-processing program prompts you with a list of documents you have opened recently. Your long-term memory still needs to come

11

into play, however. Word-processing programs haven't gotten so sophisticated that they can remind you what you wanted to say in the document!

ignoring human psychology?

So should you be designing only for accessing long-term memory through recognition? Taking a look at the advantages and disadvantages of GUI menu systems can shed some light on this question. GUIs are not the answer for all applications. More important, they're not the answer for all users. After users become familiar with an application, they often use keyboard shortcuts or sometimes command-line input so that they don't have to drag and click a cursor all over the screen. Take a simple task such as moving just executable files from one folder to another. By the time you open a view, sort and select information, open another view, and drag or copy and paste the files, someone with expertise working at the command line could have typed "copy c:*.exe d:" and moved on to other things.

Menu interfaces have advantages and disadvantages as well. With menus, users don't have to memorize commands, functions are easy to recognize and access, keyboard entry errors are reduced, nonexperts can learn the application quickly, and menu selections are flexible with the use of shortcut keys. A menu doesn't necessarily make an interface easier to use or learn, however; that requires good design. Menu interfaces can include the following drawbacks:

- Users might get lost in a broad or deep menu structure.
- Menu terms might not be recognizable or meaningful for users.
- Menu graphics require a lot of computing power to work quickly.
- Menus use more screen space.
- Combining commands with a menu isn't as easy as with a command-line interface.

The importance of each of these concerns depends on your target users and their needs as well as the application platform. Designing applications takes more into account than human memory storage.

design criteria for a quality user interface

The following *design criteria* are useful in creating a quality user interface:

- *Quality of the experience*—How does the design give people a satisfying experience? What need does the product satisfy?
- *An understanding of users*—How well did the design team understand the needs, tasks, and environments of users? How well was this understanding reflected in the product?
- *An effective design process*—Is the product a result of a well-thought-out and well-executed design process? What design issues came up during the process, and what method was used to address them? How were budgeting, scheduling, and other practical issues managed to support the goals of the design process?

---

recognition versus recall

Designers must accommodate long-term memory capabilities and limitations. One strategy is using the long-term memory access approach of recognition versus recall. You can see this approach by comparing a GUI with menus, which shows available commands, and a command-line interface that requires users to remember (recall) available commands. Recall-activated functions have their place, however. In fact, they're a recommended alternative for experienced users who want shortcuts.

---

design criteria *– Factors to consider in creating a good design, including users' needs and experiences and what's appropriate given the design's constraints*

- *Learnability*—Is the product easy to learn and easy to remember how to use? Are the product's features obvious to users? How well does the product support the different ways people will approach and use it, considering their varying levels of experience, skills, mental models, and strategies for problem solving?
- *An aesthetic experience*—Is using the product aesthetically pleasing or satisfying? Does it show consistency of style and operation? Does the design perform well within technological constraints?
- *Changeability*—Have the designers considered whether the product's changeability is appropriate? How well can the product be adapted to suit users' needs and preferences? Does the design allow the product to evolve for new, perhaps unforeseen, uses?
- *Manageability*—Does the product account for and help users manage needs such as installation, training, and maintenance?

Well-designed software should act like a good teacher, creating a working relationship with ease of entry for the student (user). In addition, users can be stretched incrementally to achieve more sophisticated results. To optimize the user experience, you should put users in control of the interface, reduce users' memory load, and make the user interface consistent. The following sections discuss these principles in more detail.

guidelines for user control

There's a classic story in user interface design. A campus planner had to determine where to lay sidewalks for a new quad between buildings. First, he decided to see where people walked on the grass. Wherever heavy traffic had pressed down the grass, that's where he decided to put a sidewalk. The point of this story is letting users have control or, at the very least, creating the perception of them having control, even when control of the task is mostly out of their hands. Here are some guidelines for user control:

- Use modes judiciously, and strive to make the application as modeless as possible. For example, in older text editors, keystrokes are used to move between text entry mode and text modification mode. Knowing which mode you're in is often confusing. However, both modes are important and need to be accommodated.
- Give users flexibility in using different interfaces (keyboard, mouse, voice, and so forth) for input.
- Allow users to change focus so that they can interrupt what they're doing without being trapped in a long, and possibly unwanted, sequence. A tutorial should allow them to save their place and return when they're ready, for example.
- Display descriptive messages that are helpful and not distracting. When users are engaged in a critical task, they don't want to see tips on unrelated features, for example.

- Provide immediate feedback and reversible actions. People want to know what's happening, so the system should be informative about where the user is in correcting an unwanted action, for example. Sometimes this feature is called the "illusion of progress," which has the added benefit of giving users a better impression of software. Allowing users to engage in another activity at the same time can also create the illusion of progress. If you have a slow-loading Web page in your browser, for example, you can still edit your Facebook page in another browser window and listen to the Benedictine monks of St. Michael's in your media player.
- Provide meaningful, helpful navigation paths and exits. The system should be easy to navigate.
- Accommodate users with different capabilities. The system should be accessible to users with varying skill levels and physical capabilities.
- Make the user interface "transparent" (not literally, of course!), meaning it's so easy to use and understand that users don't have to focus on learning it. The tasks they need to perform should be the focus.
- Allow users to customize the interface. They should be able to set preferences for how they use the software.
- Allow users to manipulate interface objects directly, as in moving files on the desktop. This guideline has its downside, however. For example, selecting an object accidentally and losing it by dropping it in the wrong folder can happen. Does the desktop metaphor give users a cue for undoing this action?
- Encourage exploration. Why not include the fun of discovery in an interface? Designers can look for ways to encourage users to find faster ways to do tasks or do more complex tasks. It's a delicate balance, however. Word used to have an animated paper clip icon called "Clippy" that suggested new ways of doing things, but many users found this feature annoying. Similarly, many users disable the helpful hint boxes that open in many programs when they're started. Games are much better at encouraging exploration.

guidelines for users' memory load

Interface designers need to consider how humans process information, and reducing users' memory and processing loads is a critical component. The following guidelines have some similarities with the guidelines for user control:

- Reduce the need to rely on short-term memory by making sure the information needed to operate the program is readily available.
- Rely on recognition more than recall by including cues (visual, audio, and so forth) for what actions are available. Menus work well for this purpose.
- Provide visual cues, such as a blinking cursor to indicate where a user is in a document or a status bar that shows what font size you're using.
- Provide defaults and undo and redo actions. The undo and redo buttons in a word-processing program are a good example. The program's defaults, such as what mode it's in or what task it's ready to perform, should be obvious. For

example, when using a word-processing program, it should be obvious that you're in the mode for entering text, not the mode for looking up a word in the thesaurus.

- Provide interface shortcuts. Using shortcut letters to represent menu items is one method, such as F for File, E for Edit, and S for Save. Alt, Ctrl, Esc, and function (F1, F2, and so on) keys tend to work more on recall than recognition, but they can work for this purpose, too.

- Promote an object-action syntax. A good example is using a word in a document as an object and an action menu (in Windows, a right-click menu) that allows performing actions on that object. For example, if you right-click a word in Microsoft Word, you get options such as Cut, Paste, Font, and so on. Actions that can't be performed are disabled ("grayed out") or aren't displayed. In iTunes, for instance, you can't choose options on the Edit menu for cutting or pasting a song until you've selected a song.

- Use real-world metaphors. If you understand 95% of a subject, grasping the remaining 5% is easier than if you start from 0%. Real-world metaphors help get users farther along the path they want to follow. Look at the editing toolbar in Word, for example. Do the icons make sense? Some have argued that the scissors icon for the Cut option is a good clue to its function, but the clipboard icon for the Paste option isn't. Not all metaphors work well or are obvious to all users.

- Reveal information progressively, especially for new or infrequent users. Information should be given to users on a need-to-know basis—in other words, when it makes sense for what they're doing and when they're doing it. Wizard interfaces often use this step-by-step approach.

- Promote visual clarity. This guideline is where graphics artists and designers are essential. Take a look at Google's interface, for example, which is very streamlined and straightforward. Visual clarity is discussed in more detail later in "Designing for the Web."

guidelines for consistency of the interface

Consistency helps users recognize what's available in the interface. You've probably noticed that many programs have similar icons: a picture of a chain for a link to another document or a floppy disk icon for saving a file (although maybe it's time to update this icon). The following guidelines help in creating consistency:

- Sustain the context of users' tasks. For example, if users start a task by using voice recognition for input, they should be able to complete the task by using the same input method. The information for them to finish the task should be readily available without having to change modes, windows, and so forth.

- Maintain consistency within and across products. Why have an icon that means "save file" in one program but has a different meaning in another program? Why have "save file" mean "save the existing file" in one part of the program but mean "save another version" in a different part of the program? Why have the shortcut key S mean "save" at 3 minutes into using the program but mean "slow down, big fella" at 6 minutes? Okay, the last question is a bit exaggerated, but you get the point: Inconsistency confuses people.

- Keep interaction results the same to avoid creating superstitious behavior in users.
- Strive for aesthetic appeal. Does the interface make people feel good (see "Human Emotion and Human-Computer Interfaces" later in this chapter)? In addition, designers have to make sure that images used in the interface correspond with the company's brand image. For example, a company that markets itself as cutting edge doesn't want icons in its software that look old-fashioned. Companies often have user interface guidelines that dictate the look of products, Web pages, marketing brochures, and the like.

designing for the Web

The explosion of Web pages since the mid-1990s, both external Web pages for users and intranet Web pages for internal company information, and the use of Web pages as a design model for many types of applications make designing for the Web a special category of user interface design.

what do designers know about their users?

Servers handle retrieving the Web pages you want, but they're displayed on your screen by Web browsers. Because users have a fair amount of control over how their browsers render pages, such as text and window size, and run their browsers on different hardware, programmers must accommodate these variations. Designers don't know what browser, platform, preference settings, window size, monitor size or screen resolution, connection speed, color settings, or font users have chosen. This problem is even more obvious with handheld devices, such as the iPhone and BlackBerry, used to browse the Web.

So what choices do you have as a designer or developer? Generally, you can try to force the display to your way of thinking as much as possible by using graphics and Flash programs instead of text, for example, but this approach has problems. Search engines can't search for information in graphics, and graphics take longer to load. Non-GUI users (visually impaired people, for example) can't "see" the content, although the ALT attribute in HTML can help remedy this problem.

However, instead of forcing a particular view, you can design your pages to reflect users' needs and wants. Some users' impairments might mean that larger text, for example, makes the difference between maneuvering around a Web page slowly or not at all. To help address these needs, you can code to the lowest common denominator in terms of browser, platform, and screen size. It's more likely, however, that modern Web servers query the client and then serve pages appropriate for that client and its settings, which means more server-side coding (invisible to users) than in the past.

note
Server-side coding also means more customized pages, but that never hurts customer relations.

There are still programming elements you should be aware of. Any font you use that doesn't exist on users' machines is displayed in their default font. However, you can specify a backup font by using style sheets. A collection of fonts called TrueType is built into both Apple and Microsoft operating systems, including Comic Sans, Courier New, Times New Roman, Verdana, and many others. With style sheets, you can specify one of these TrueType fonts as a backup in case users don't have the font you've used. Now you know why so many sites use the same font.

In addition, images are rendered differently on different platforms because of variations in gamma settings. A PC has a higher gamma setting (meaning it's darker) than a Mac, for example. Images created on a Mac might look darker on a PC, and images created on a PC might look washed out on a Mac. Users with 24-bit monitor settings see 16 million color combinations—all the colors you can use digitally. Using a lower bit setting or resizing the image forces the color to the next available color, which often causes "dithering" (a mottled appearance in solid colors). With Web-authoring tools, such as Photoshop, you can use the 8-bit Web-safe palette, if you want to be on the safe side. This palette has only 216 colors; the other 40 colors needed for the typical 256-color palette are used to smooth out colors that are difficult to display.

Web developers need to be aware of usable screen space, too, so monitor resolution is important. Because browser windows can be resized to any dimension, on any size monitor, designing for unknown screen "real estate" is a challenge. For example, you might need to design for monitors set at a range from 800 × 600 pixels to 1600 × 1200 pixels. If you design in pixels, your design takes up less real estate at the 1600 × 1200 end of the range, but everything you've designed should be in proportion. New wide-screen monitors have less vertical space, however. Don't forget that the OS and program also take up screen space. For example, in Windows the taskbar might take 28 pixels, and the browser window might take up to 160 pixels for just the status, menu, title, navigation, and location bars.

note
Web pages and services that keep track of client preferences are available, such as InternetNews.com (*www.internetnews.com*). Web developers can use them to see what their clients' platforms, browsers, monitor sizes, and so forth are.

deconstructing Web pages

There are many guidelines for addressing the basic need of serving the customer in Web page design. The following list summarizes a few of them:

- *Communicating the site's purpose*—The company name and logo should be easily visible and summarize what the site or company does, and they should be placed on what's clearly the site's home page. You don't have to actually welcome people to the site, however, and you don't need to use "home page," ".com," ".org," or so forth in the page title unless it's part of the organization's name. In addition, the highest priority tasks should be emphasized and clear. For example, if the most important feature of a bank's Web site is allowing users to access their accounts, you might put the logon feature in the middle of the page or another likely place that users' eyes will travel to.

note

Registering other domain names for your site, such as names with alternative spellings, abbreviations, or common misspellings, is a good idea. For example, *nytimes.com* and *newyorktimes.com* both lead to the *New York Times* Web site.

- *Communicating the organization's information*—The Web page is part of a company's corporate presence and should be in sync with its brand image. Having "Contact Us" and "About Us" sections builds trust in the site and the company. In addition, include a privacy policy if you collect information from users. For security reasons, don't include internal company information, such as employees' phone numbers, on the public site.
- *Writing good content*—The language should be focused on customers, not on the corporate hierarchy or other internal interests. Avoid redundant content and labeling and "clever" phrases that might be hard to understand. Use a consistent style throughout the site, and follow guidelines for clear writing, such as spelling out abbreviations and writing in the present tense.
- *Revealing content through examples*—If the content is self-explanatory, it doesn't need a label. Examples (with links to more detail and "more of this type of content") can explain content better than descriptions can. Indicate clearly which links drill down to more detail and which go to more general information.
- *Making links obvious*—Differentiate links from other content. They should follow the universal convention of blue underlined words and indicate which parts of the site the user has already visited (typically with a color change to the link text). Avoid generic instructions such as "Click here." The link should make it clear what type of content is being linked to, such as an audio file, a PDF, a video file, and so forth.

- *Using clear navigation*—Place navigation features in the noticeable area below a banner. Similar navigation items should be grouped, not repeated on the page. The home page shouldn't link to itself. Make it clear where navigation titles and icons lead users. Avoid unfamiliar and confusing words and images in navigation features.
- *Making search capabilities obvious*—Give users a clearly labeled search text box on the home page that can accommodate the length of typical search keywords. A Search button to the right of the text box is usually the clearest label. You don't need to offer a "search the Web" feature on your site.
- *Using graphics, animation, and widgets wisely*—Graphics should show real content, not just add decoration. If an image's meaning isn't clear, add a label. Avoid semitransparent backgrounds because they add visual clutter. Photos and diagrams should be sized to fit the intended display device. Use animation sparingly, and don't use it on important elements, such as headers and navigation areas, because it detracts from useful content. Drop-down or roll-over menus can help reduce visual clutter but are limited to users who have the technology for viewing them (typically Flash or JavaScript, which are add-ons that many people don't install). Also, these menus don't allow a quick visual scan of the site hierarchy, so use them judiciously. Using too many text boxes on the home page is confusing, so reserve their use for the page where they're specifically needed.
- *Following good graphics design principles*—The main principle is don't overdesign. Therefore, keep the number of font styles and other text formatting to a minimum, and avoid horizontal scrolling. (If possible, avoid vertical scrolling, too.) Strive for a high contrast between text and background to make type legible. Keep all critical page elements above the bottom of the display window.
- *Following other guidelines for content*—Make new content, such as recent news stories or new product offerings, easy to access. If you have news items, link headlines to full stories. Time-critical content, such as stock quotes, should display an update time, although it depends on how often users expect the information to be updated. News less than a day old probably doesn't need a date stamp, for example, but a timestamp might be helpful. Avoid pop-up windows because most users see them as annoying advertisements, especially if they multiply. You should have one main page, not many, although you might need to bend this rule and route people to main pages in different languages. Ads from companies other than your own should be on the edge of pages, not in the middle or along the top, where they could be confused with your site's content. When possible, only new content should be refreshed, not the whole page.

note

The bottom line is to stay focused on the reason users come to your Web site. Anything else is a distraction.

To see examples of these Web design principles, take a look at Figure 11-4, the home page of the Visual Arts Department at Weber State University (*www.weber.edu/dova*).

Figure 11-4, The home page of the Visual Arts Department at Weber State University

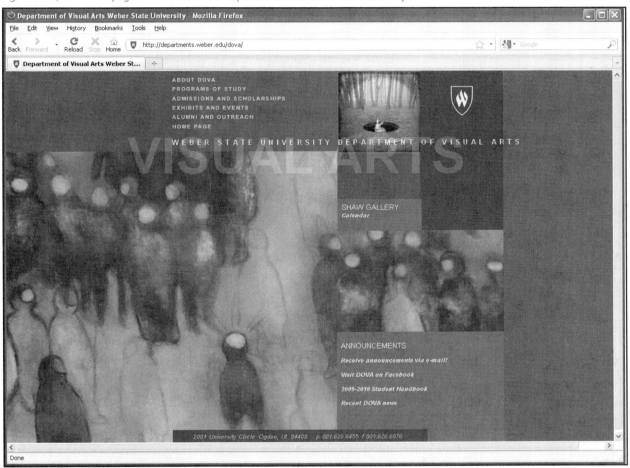

According to the designers, the site's intent is to provide information for prospective and current students as well as the general public. Another goal is to make it appealing to users so that they appreciate it as an example of visual design. Because of this goal, the page doesn't follow all the functional guidelines discussed previously:

- It's difficult to tell what on the page is a link. For example, the items at the top are menu items with a Flash rollover feature, so users without Flash won't be able to use the menu. Other links on the page aren't in the blue underlined text typically used for links.
- The HOME PAGE link at the top is active, which isn't usually recommended.

- The SHAW GALLERY title with the Calendar link could be missed easily in the middle of the complex image.
- Under the ANNOUNCEMENTS title are four links, and only the second—Visit DOVA on Facebook—indicates clearly what the link takes you to. The first link doesn't indicate whether it takes you to a form or opens a message window in your e-mail program, for example. The third is a slow-loading PDF, and the fourth is another HTML Web page.
- The image at the upper right is actually a link, as is the "W" to the right of it. However, they don't give you a hint that they're links or indicate what the link might take you to.

On the plus side, the design is eye catching and encourages visitors to explore and see what the site has to offer. In addition, the design indicates the site's purpose clearly, and the menu at the top persists in many (although not all) pages, so navigation is consistent.

the user-centric design process

*user-centric design –
Designing by focusing
on users' needs before
considering other
constraints of the system*

The main phases of *user-centric design* are as follows:

- Gather and analyze user information.
- Design the user interface.
- Construct the user interface.
- Test the user interface.

Frank Lloyd Wright said, "You can use an eraser on the drafting table or a sledgehammer on the construction site." In other words, design is essential before building anything, and spending some time on the design process can save time in the construction process. However, as you'll see in Chapter 13, design processes have become more iterative, and prototyping tools have become more powerful and widely used. So although designing user interfaces still follows the four main phases of development, designers often repeat phases or delve into subphases. Interface design phases can also reflect the software development life cycle and use many of the tools used in this approach, such as use case diagrams, flowcharts, and the like.

See Chapter 13, "Software Engineering," for more information on the software development life cycle.

Because the process is often iterative, the design team might continue to gather data while designing a pilot (prototype) of the interface. This prototype is then tested with real or hypothetical users while the team works on a more complex prototype, which then evolves based on additional information from data gatherers and is tested with users, and so on. While all this is happening, an actual product might be created and go through field tests, maintenance, and upgrades based on feedback from the continuing prototyping process.

phase 1: gathering and analyzing user information

Phase 1 involves steps such as developing user profiles, analyzing users' tasks, gathering user requirements, and analyzing the user environment. In developing *user profiles*, you ask "Who are the users?" and look at demographic information, skills, knowledge, background, and more. Techniques such as conducting interviews, taking surveys, and examining historical data are helpful.

Analyzing *user tasks* involves examining what users do and how they do it. You can discover this information with interviews, but observation is more helpful. Design team members ask questions about what tasks users perform, what tasks are most critical, what steps are involved in their tasks, what their goals are, what information they need, how they do their work, how often tasks are performed, and how they interact with others in business processes.

Gathering *user requirements*, usually with focus groups, interviews, and surveys, focuses on what users expect the product to do for them. Typical questions users ask are who installs and supports the product and how much it will cost.

User environment analysis examines where users perform their tasks and is usually best done through observation and reviewing existing data. Environmental factors include lighting, noise, temperature, and ergonomics (how people's bodies interact with technology). Designers must also consider the interfaces typically used for input (voice, keyboard, handheld devices, and the like), users with special needs, and any cultural needs, such as requiring keyboards for different character sets.

Comparing user requirements with user tasks is a reality check to verify that your understanding of users and their needs is accurate. However, understanding human activities is so complex that simply listing requirements, putting them into a system, and popping out the perfect technology for users' needs isn't possible. Finding the "perfect" technology takes continuous evaluation.

phase 2: designing the user interface

In this phase, a product's usability goals and objectives are defined, *user scenarios* are developed, and interface objects and actions are defined.

user profiles – *Written descriptions of who the users are, including backgrounds, skills, and so forth*

user tasks – *What users do and how they do it*

user requirements – *What users want and need to do*

user environment – *Where users perform their tasks*

putting yourself in the user's fins

The head of the design firm IDEO, Bill Moggridge, says some of the best-designed products have been designed by the people who use them, such as code for the Linux operating system and outdoor equipment from Black Diamond. When the designer of a technology isn't the user of the technology, developing a sense of empathy with the user is critical. For example, a team designing an underwater camera (a device without much peripheral vision) tried to look at the design from a diver's point of view by attempting to find a coffee cup on a desk while looking through paper towel tubes.

user scenarios – *Examples of user activities, written to show the steps users go through in using a technology*

usefulness – *A measure of how many of the intended tasks users can perform with the technology*

effectiveness – *A measure of how well the technology helps users perform their tasks; often expressed as how quickly, how easily, how safely, and so forth*

learnability – *A measure of how quickly users can learn to use the technology to perform their tasks*

attitude – *A measure of how much users enjoy their experience with the technology*

---

brainstorming with the client

One of the world's most famous design firms, IDEO (*www.ideo. com*), uses a number of methods for discovering what clients need and for brainstorming solutions to meet these needs. The methods fit into four categories:

- *Learn*—For example, doing historical analysis to spot patterns in customers' past browsing habits on a Web site
- *Look*—Observing current behaviors, such as following users around for a day to see how they interact with the technologies they use
- *Ask*—Having users fill out questionnaires or asking them to create a collage as a way of discovering the importance they place on aspects of the potential system
- *Try*—Finding ways to create empathy with users, such as simulating their work environments

---

Usability goals and objectives are defined in terms of *usefulness*, *effectiveness*, *learnability*, and *attitude*. For usefulness, the goal might be ensuring that users can use the program to perform their tasks, and an objective might be that 90% of users can perform a simple task on the first attempt. Effectiveness might refer to how fast users can perform their tasks, learnability might refer to how quickly they can learn to operate at 100% effectiveness, and attitude might refer to how high users rate their satisfaction with the product.

User scenarios can be documented in numerous ways, some of which are discussed in Chapter 13. Developing as many scenarios as possible is often useful for designing the final user interface. Interface objects and actions are defined from the user scenarios and tasks, and they should be reviewed with end users or their representatives. To identify objects and actions, typically you start by identifying nouns and verbs from the user scenarios; interface objects are derived from nouns, and interface actions are derived from verbs.

phase 3: constructing the user interface

You should prototype early and often, have plenty of alternatives, and be prepared to throw many away. The risk of prototyping is that many people consider a prototype the final product that needs just a little refinement. The more sophisticated the prototype and the more work that has gone into developing it, the more people make this assumption. Prototyping has become a specialized skill, and it takes a person who's willing to chuck the work and start over. A prototype is developed to gain support for the approach. It helps managers and eventual users realize the possibilities and limitations of a technological solution. It isn't supposed to be the final product that needs just a few modifications and add-ons. Prototypes can often be quite rickety—barely held together with tape and chewing gum. In addition, they don't need to be constructed of the materials the final product is made of. A software program, for example, might be prototyped with paper and pencil.

phase 4: validating the user interface

This phase is where the usability goals and objectives of usefulness, effectiveness, learnability, and attitude defined in Phase 2 come into play. To assess how effectively you met the objectives, you can create a variety of tables and measures. To do so, you use the traditional social science methods of observing, surveying, and interviewing users or trial users. Many companies, for example, pay people to try out their products and give feedback on them. Figure 11-5 shows a typical user interface testing lab. The user on the left is working with the interface being tested, and the researcher on the right is observing him. The user's actions are also captured by the camera and microphone on the left, and his keyboard and mouse actions are recorded by a logging program. In addition, researchers behind the mirror are observing him. The researchers can examine all impressions, from facial expressions to pauses in mouse clicks, to determine where the user interface succeeds and fails.

Figure 11-5, An example of a user interface testing lab

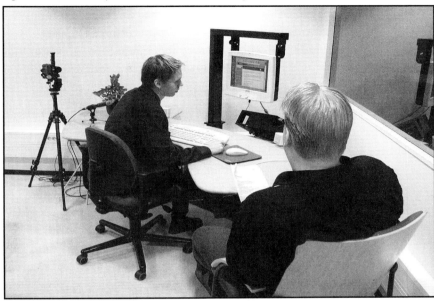

Courtesy of Päivi Majaranta from the Tampere Unit for Computer-Human Interaction at the University of Tampere, Finland

human emotion and human-computer interfaces

As it turns out, aesthetically pleasing user interfaces work better. This might seem obvious, or maybe it seems to you that aesthetics shouldn't have a major effect on function. For example, you wouldn't expect color to influence function, but if you think about your relationships with various technologies, you might see the link.

An aesthetically pleasing interface can make users feel good, and if they feel good, they'll be more patient in working with the interface and finding creative solutions to difficulties in doing their work—in short, they'll be more forgiving of any functional problems. When users are willing to find solutions, they become more adept at using the interface. The emotional commitment to an interface can even influence users' opinions of how practical the interface is to use. This emotional effect has contributed to Apple's success with its product line, which is generally considered aesthetically pleasing. Think of things in your life that give you such emotional joy that you put up with their many flaws (not your significant other—well, maybe).

affect system – How emotions and potentially aesthetics play a role in decision making

The study of emotions in decisions about using technology, part of what's called the *affect system* of decision making, has its origins in an early 1990s study by two Japanese researchers, Masaaki Kurosu and Kaori Kashimura. They examined ATM control layouts and found that users were more adept at using attractive interfaces. An Israeli scientist, Noam Tractinsky, was skeptical of whether the study's results were universal. Aesthetic differences are generally considered part of cultural differences. However, he found the same effect: Attractive interfaces were easier to use.

Since Tractinsky's study, many other studies have shown the relationship between attractiveness and ease of use. For example, uniform proportionality—in anything from facial features to buttons on a phone—has universal appeal and can be applied to user interface design, among other things. Figure 11-6 shows a system that measures emotional responses. The headset the researcher is wearing measures activity in certain parts of the brain, and this information is displayed on the monitor. This system can be used to observe users' responses while working with programs.

Figure 11-6, Measuring users' emotional responses

Courtesy of Toni Vanhala from the Tampere Unit for Computer-Human Interaction at the University of Tampere, Finland

There are three levels of design: visceral, behavioral, and reflective. The design of most objects is perceived on all three levels, so good design should address all three.

Visceral thinking is snap judgment about an object. Is it dangerous? Is it good? It's an instinctive, nearly universal attitude about what feels, looks, tastes, sounds, and smells good. The response to sweetness is visceral, for example, whereas a love of salty licorice or limburger cheese is learned and controlled at a higher level. The visceral level can be controlled by the behavioral and reflective levels, especially as you get older. In designing a user interface, you might appeal to the visceral level by choosing appealing colors, for example. The weight and feel of an object in your hand, such as a smartphone, also appeal to the visceral level. Visceral design is all about immediate emotional impact. It has to feel good and look good.

visceral thinking – *Immediate, instinctive thinking; an object's look and feel play a role in how it's perceived*

behavioral thinking – *Thinking about how something works*

reflective thinking – *Thinking about how something reflects on the user and his or her relationship to others*

Behavioral thinking drives most human behavior. You might also think of it as the functional level. The main driver is how useful the object is. Appearance doesn't matter; only performance does. Most user interface designers focus on appealing to behavioral thinking by answering the questions "How well does it work? How easy is it to understand?"

The highest level, *reflective thinking*, isn't directly affected by sensory input or the control of behavior. Reflective thinking is more sophisticated but can be susceptible to changes in fashion and culture because it appeals to more learned behaviors. To appeal to reflective thinking in design, you have to focus on the cultural meaning of a product or its use. This level also involves a user's self-image and what message his or her ownership of a product sends to others, as with people who believe that driving the "right" car or living in the "right" house is important. Reflective thinking is where a sense of belonging to a community or status level plays a role. For example, what does a product say about how the user wants to be perceived by others? Many successful products can demonstrate the three levels of thinking at work in a product's appeal. Take the Toyota Prius. To many, it's attractive (visceral), works well (behavioral), and creates pride in ownership and a sense of community among its users (reflective). Reflective thinking can be powerful. Those uninterested in being in the Prius community, for example, might not find the product particularly attractive or might focus on ways it doesn't work.

personalization and customization

Products such as the iPhone offer another feature for increasing all three levels of appeal to users: personalization. You can choose from many different cases, screen savers, and other gadgets for the iPhone, which appeals to the visceral level, and you can download a wide variety of applications, which appeals to the behavioral level. Appealing to the reflective level, you can gain easy entrance into the community of iPhone application developers.

Personalization can work with mass-produced commodities quite well, which is easily seen in cars. Many people add details and engine enhancements to their Honda Civics, for example. However, there are a limited number of choices for personalization. You can make a product yourself, but that's time consuming, and few people have the skills for making something as complex as a car or a computer system. You can have objects made to order, but this approach is usually expensive. You can also buy add-ons or choose specific options, as with iPhones and modified Hondas.

True total customization is difficult; turning a car into a helicopter, for instance, isn't likely. The flexibility of software can allow personalization, if users have access to the software and tools to manipulate it. However, even with software, customization does have its costs. Creating a system that's easy to use and understand but also allows making unlimited customizations is difficult. You often end up with a complex system that's difficult to understand, thus making it hard to customize. That's why many technologies offer limited customization. Whatever approach to personalization you allow in a product, however, users' personalization of it creates an emotional involvement with the product and, therefore, taps into the affect system to create a sense of goodwill toward the product.

one last thought

The user interface development process depends on the resources an organization is willing to spend on it, how much an organization values satisfying end users, and organizational politics involved in defending the needs of production, marketing, engineering, system, and accounting departments. It takes a strong leader with vision to focus an organization on end users, but one advantage of a technocratic society is that everyone can be a leader in technology in one way or another. User interface specialist Donald Norman ends one of his books with the following call (from *The Design of Everyday Things*, p. 216):

"Now you are on your own. If you are the designer, help fight the battle for usability. If you are a user, then join your voice with those who cry for usable products. Write to manufacturers. Boycott unusable designs. Support good designs by purchasing them, even if it means going out of your way, even if it means spending a bit more. . . . And enjoy yourself. Walk around the world examining the details of design. . . . Realize that even details matter, that the designers may have had to fight to include something helpful."

So fight the good fight in interface design. Your organization will benefit from customers' loyalty and goodwill as a result of your efforts.

selected references

Carroll, John M. *Human-Computer Interaction in the New Millennium.* Addison-Wesley, 2002 (ISBN 0-201-70447-1).

Mandel, Theo. *The Elements of User Interface Design.* John Wiley & Sons, Inc., 1997 (ISBN 0-471-16267-1).

Moggridge, Bill. *Designing Interactions.* MIT Press, 2007 (ISBN 0-262-13474-8).

Nielsen, Jakob and Marie Tahir. *Homepage Usability.* New Riders, 2002 (ISBN 0-7357-1102-X).

Norman, Donald A. *The Design of Everyday Things.* Doubleday, 1988 (ISBN 0-385-26774-6).

Shneiderman, Ben. *Designing the User Interface: Strategies for Effective Human-Computer Interaction.* Addison-Wesley, 1998 (ISBN 0-201-69497-2).

chapter summary

- Design is often a secondary concern, but it should be the first.
- Poorly designed technology is often the cause of poor sales, poor usability, and user confusion.
- Many technologies for interacting with computers are available, including a mouse, a pen or stylus, gaze systems, voice recognition, haptics, and other input and output devices.
- People bring a variety of personal factors to the technologies they use.
- Designers should strive to create systems that discourage users from engaging in superstitious behavior.
- Humans have three levels of memory storage that designers should take into account: sensory storage, short-term memory, and long-term memory.
- Although understanding psychology is important, it's not the only matter to take into account when designing interfaces.
- The design criteria for user interfaces are the quality of the experience, an understanding of users, an effective design process, learnability, an aesthetic experience, changeability, and manageability.
- Three main goals of a user interface are giving users control of the interface, reducing users' memory load, and aiming for consistency in the interface.
- Programming for the Web is complicated because of the many different Web technologies end users use.
- Remember the basic rules for building effective Web pages, such as communicating a site's purpose and organization, making links obvious, and creating helpful navigation.
- The user-centric design process starts with the end user, not system needs. Its main phases are gathering and analyzing user information, designing the interface, constructing the interface, and testing the interface.
- User interface design can be iterative rather than sequential, meaning steps can be revisited many times in the process. Prototyping is a key component of iterative design.
- Human emotional response is a new but growing area for designers to take into account when building technology.
- Personalization can help get positive emotional responses from users.

key terms

affect system (*397*)

attitude (*396*)

behavioral thinking (*399*)

design criteria (*385*)

effectiveness (*396*)

gaze systems (*380*)

haptics technologies (*381*)

learnability (*396*)

long-term memory (*384*)

natural-language processing (*381*)

reflective thinking (*399*)

sensory storage (*383*)

short-term memory (*384*)

superstitious behavior (*383*)

usefulness (*396*)

user-centric design (*394*)

user environment (*395*)

user interface (*379*)

user profiles (*395*)

user requirements (*395*)

user scenarios (*395*)

user tasks (*395*)

visceral thinking (*398*)

voice-recognition technology (*380*)

test yourself

1. What does the poorly designed door symbolize?

2. List three obstacles to user-centric design.

3. List three career paths that could be useful in creating a good design.

4. What technology do many gaze systems use to track eye movement?

5. Technology with inconsistent responses to user input often creates what kind of human behavior?

6. What are the three levels of memory storage?

7. What two techniques help improve short-term memory?

8. When might users prefer to use recall instead of recognition in using a technology's interface?

9. Describe five design criteria discussed in this chapter.

10. What is one major reason that designing for the Web is different from designing for other user interfaces?

practice exercises

1. What technologies in your daily life could be designed better to meet your needs?

2. What technologies in your daily life could be designed better to meet the needs of someone with impaired vision?

3. What technologies in your daily life could be designed better to meet the needs of someone with limitations in mobility?

4. What technologies in your daily life could be designed better to meet children's needs?

5. In what ways do the technologies you use every day require recall and recognition?

6. In what ways could the technologies you use every day be safer?

7. After reading Chapters 14 and 15, pick a programming exercise from each chapter, and attempt to design the program with the user-first approach.

8. Create a paper-and-pencil prototype of a better smartphone, and explain how user interface technologies, such as gaze systems and haptics, come into play. *Optional*: Simulate using the phone with a partner. What works and what doesn't work?

9. Create a verbal simulation of a conversation with a "professor program" that reports your grades. Imagine that the computer can recognize only four phrases per exchange. Have someone test it as a user. How complex is it? What needs does it have? How well did the first conversation go? Where did it fail?

10. Interview classmates about their expectations for technologies they use frequently. How well do the technologies meet their expectations?

11. Observe your professor's behavior. How would you improve his or her interaction with technology in the classroom? What could be solved with new technology, and what might require only a change in how it's used?

12. Test a partner in short-term memory ability. How easy is it to remember the sequence 1 7 7 6 1 9 4 5 2 0 0 1 1 4 9 2? What tactics can your partner use to remember all the numbers? Come up with similar examples of short-term memory tactics.

13. Find a partner with similar interests, and test each other on long-term memory questions. For example, if you both like movies, start naming actors in movies you both know. Describe how you recall these names.

14. Make a spreadsheet with the design criteria discussed in the chapter and a ranking system of 1 (poor) to 10 (excellent). Interview and observe other students in your class using a technology of their choice, and see how well the technology corresponds to the criteria.

15. After creating a paper-and-pencil prototype of a smartphone (exercise 8), conduct a usability study with other students in your class. Give them a short description, and then observe them as they pretend to use it. Ask them questions about their use of the prototype.

digging deeper

1. Have a class discussion about the value of command-line interfaces and menu-based interfaces. If some people have strong preferences for one or the other, ask them for specific examples.

2. Have a class discussion comparing the user interfaces of some technologies (for example, Mac OS, Windows, and Linux operating systems or standard versus automatic transmission in cars). Ask those who have strong preferences for one to give specific reasons. How much do emotions seem to come into the interaction between students and technologies?

3. Create a class project to design a toy, using teams with members representing different aspects of the design process (gathering and analyzing user information, designing the prototype, constructing the prototype, and testing the prototype) and members representing users of the system. Assign an observer to take notes during the exercise and report on how well the teams followed the phases of user-centric design.

4. You can find many pragmatic exercises for understanding users' needs. One example is a team-building exercise in which a blindfolded person is led by the guide's voice through an obstacle course, with ambient noise, such as other people talking, to confuse the blindfolded person. Use this exercise to think of ways to improve the process of understanding users' needs.

discussion topics

1. Should users of technology be called "users"? What if they were just called "people"?

2. This chapter discussed considering users' needs as the first step in the design process. Would it make more sense to consider the technology first? What about considering all constraints simultaneously?

3. Some design experts have called computer interfaces the "weak link" in computing. How would you approach designing computers to have multiple capabilities but still make them as easy to understand as, say, a hammer?

4. What do you think business practices, law, and economics have to do with how technology is designed? Give specific examples.

5. If users matter so much, why don't designers do a better job of designing for their needs? Give specific examples.

6. Some have speculated that the perfect personal computer should be as simple to use and as unobtrusive as a common kitchen appliance, such as a toaster. What would it take for computers to progress to the ease of use of a toaster?

Internet research

1. Go to your favorite Web page. Does it meet the guidelines in the "Deconstructing Web Pages" section? Explain why or why not.

2. Find a Web resource with statistics on users' platforms, browsers, and screen resolutions. How would this information change the way you design a Web page?

3. Numerous Web resources on designing good user interfaces are available. Find three, and compare their design criteria with the criteria covered in this chapter.

4. Numerous Web resources on designing good user interfaces are available. Find three, and compare their approaches to addressing human memory capabilities with the approaches discussed in this chapter.

5. Numerous Web resources on designing good user interfaces are available. Find three, and compare their approaches to addressing human emotion with the approaches discussed in this chapter.

6. Find two Web sites that have similar purposes, such as two online bookstores, weather sites, news outlets, search engines, and so forth, and select one with a good interface and one with a poor one. Compare how these two sites achieve the design goals discussed in this chapter. In what ways is the good site's interface effective, and in what ways does the other site fall short?

chapter

12

problem solving and debugging

the lighter side of the lab
by spencer

Not long ago, I opened a cupboard to find what looked like little chocolate sprinkles (which I'm glad I didn't eat) scattered around the garbage can with some chewed-up wrappers. Yes, I had a mouse living in my cupboard.

I went to work to solve the problem. First, I went to the store to buy a trap. What I didn't realize is that there's a wide variety of mousetraps. (*Note*: See Chapter 9's Lighter Side on decision making.) The standard mousetraps were two for $1, and some poison cost $3 (which I thought might be good, until I realized the mouse would eat the poison and then go hide behind my dishwasher). The "humane" traps for $5 would trap the mouse inside them. Um, and then what? For $20, there was a reusable mini–electrocution chamber, which I'm guessing was manufactured in Texas.

Three hours and one spreadsheet later, I bought two standard mousetraps and set them with peanut butter as bait. I checked the traps the next day and found they were still set, but all the peanut butter was licked away. Next day, same result. I realized this was no ordinary mouse.

My dad suggested I try sticky pads, where the mouse simply gets stuck if it steps on one (and again, then what?). I laid some down, and moments later, I heard a miniature ruckus coming from the kitchen. I ran in to find that the sticky pad, containing no mouse, had been dragged to the mouse hole.

The next day I put the traps *and* the sticky pads like a minefield all under the sink. I went to check the traps later and heard a little rustling from the garbage can. I picked it up, and a GIGANTIC mouse bailed out of the can and onto the floor near my feet. I did what any man would do in this situation: I screamed like a girl, jumped, and ran out of the room.

To make a long story short, this scene was repeated a number of times over the next few weeks, as I tried to trap the mouse inside the garbage can, always followed by a bail, a scream, and a scramble. I considered the electrocution chamber, but instead bought some industrial-strength steel traps. That did it. I came home a couple of days later to find that not one, but two mice had met their fate! They were followed by their brothers: Three, Four, Five, Six, and Seven.

In conclusion, if you run into a problem, don't give up. Perseverance leads to victory. Also, don't eat the chocolate sprinkles.

why you need to know about...
problem solving and debugging

Do you like reading or watching mysteries? Playing video games? Fixing cars? Solving puzzles? Whether your mystery-solving hero is Sherlock Holmes, Adrian Monk, or your local mechanic, the joy of solving mysteries will serve you well in the world of computing. Although this chapter is short, the importance of its topic can't be overstated. Computer science is essentially the art and science of developing solutions to problems—in other words, problem solving. For example, software engineering and user interface design are essentially processes for developing solutions to meet users' needs. What you've learned so far is how to prevent problems through good design, not how to fix something that doesn't work. There are all sorts of ways to prevent problems: software standards, code reviews, risk management, quality assurance processes, test automation, and the like. Unfortunately, in computer development, inevitably a program you write won't do what you think it should because it has a "bug" (although some programmers prefer to call it a "feature"). Whatever the problem is called, you must fix it. In programming, this process of finding and fixing a problem is called "debugging." This chapter focuses on that process by giving you some rules to follow and examples of how they're used.

the mental game of problem solving

Obviously, people have been solving problems for a long time, so you're in good company. However, the scientific study of how people solve problems is more recent. Psychologists have been studying it only since the early 20th century. They originally focused on people in a laboratory setting solving stripped-down math or logic problems, such as the Tower of Hanoi (see Figure 12-1). The assumption was that problem-solving processes discovered in the lab would be the ones used in real-life situations. Since the 1970s, however, research has moved to specific problem domains—medical, automotive, scientific, engineering, and other fields—and has become less focused on finding general processes for problem solving. In addition, researchers have found that more complex problems elicit more complex approaches to solutions.

In addition, a key discovery that emerged is the role that less quantified approaches, such as intuition and emotion, play in problem solving. A fun book on the power of intuition is Malcolm Gladwell's *Blink: The Power of Thinking*

Figure 12-1, The Tower of Hanoi puzzle

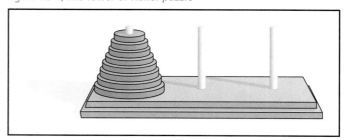

Figure 12-1, The Tower of Hanoi puzzle

Without Thinking. One of his points is that although rigorous process and formalized understanding play a role in problem solving, experience can create intuitive understanding. In other words, having the experience of seeing many similar problems is valuable in problem solving, but having a few rules and tools is always useful.

n o t e

Reliance on intuition is often why programmers say that debugging is an art.

Tower of Hanoi

The Tower of Hanoi is a puzzle consisting of three rods with several disks of gradated sizes stacked on the leftmost rod, from the largest on the bottom to the smallest on the top. To solve the puzzle, you must move the stack to another rod while following these rules:

• Move only one disk at a time.

• Taking a disk from one rod and sliding it on another rod constitutes a move.

• You can't place a disk on top of a smaller disk.

In addition to being used in psychological research, the Tower of Hanoi is a widely used method of explaining recursive algorithms to programming students.

As for the key discovery about the role of emotion, researchers realized that lab settings don't incorporate the emotional aspect of real-life situations. Emotion can be a powerful incentive or a dismaying distraction, which leads to the first concrete piece of advice: Take a deep breath, remain calm, and devise a strategy.

Want to see some amazing cases of solving problems while staying calm? Watch the 1995 movie *Apollo 13*, read about Shackleton's expedition to Antarctica, or listen to the radio program *Car Talk with Tom and Ray Maggliozzi*. They're all excellent examples for future software engineers. One of the most critical tools in an engineer's arsenal is an unwavering belief that problems can be solved. If a problem has been created by people, in all likelihood it can be solved by people. You don't want to succumb to mental inertia because a problem seems overwhelming.

Here are a few techniques to keep your chin up while debugging:

• Boast aloud and visualize or write down positive results. This technique creates a positive self-image and a positive image with peers, subordinates, and supervisors. Telling others, such as peers, managers, and teachers, that you expect to solve the problem puts a little pressure on you to solve it successfully.

• Think positively about the process, not negatively. Smile as you hunt for an elusive bug, and think about how lucky you are to solve problems for a living.

• Be patient. Debugging takes time. The amount of time it takes to understand what you don't yet know is unpredictable, although the more familiar a bug looks, the more control you'll probably have over finding it. Experience counts for a lot, and you can only get it with practice.

why are software problems so hard to solve?

Actually, software problems might be quite easy to solve, depending on their underlying cause. The following five categories describe bugs of varying complexity and are listed in order of ease of finding and fixing bugs:

- *Coding bugs*—Usually the easiest to find and fix, these bugs are the most likely to occur and are usually caused by not understanding the programming language thoroughly. Beginners are the most apt to cause these bugs and often blame anyone or anything (compiler, browser, instructor, and so forth) but themselves for the problem.

- *Logic bugs*—These bugs are more difficult to fix. An index counter counting past the end of the array and accessing an out-of-bounds memory location is a typical example. In this case, a program crash with the message "segmentation fault" means a pointer in your program is accessing a memory location outside its permitted boundaries. The C programming language is particularly susceptible to these bugs because of the lack of memory bounds checking.

- *Bad data bugs*—This bug can be considered an offshoot of the logic bug. Despite its name, the data might not actually be bad. Often it means the program isn't robust enough to handle anything other than the expected input. Expecting data input to be perfect all the time is illogical.

- *Compatibility bugs*—These problems are even more difficult to debug. Coding for the Web, for example, requires understanding that different platforms—browsers, servers, operating systems, and so forth—vary in standards. Compatibility bugs are closely aligned with coding bugs because they're usually caused by not understanding platforms thoroughly. Standards for platforms are published and available, but often you need to know more than just a single language to program for the Web, which adds to the complexity.

- *Architecture bugs*—These problems are the most difficult to debug and might require rewriting the code completely. Flaws in the underlying operating system, browser, server, database, compiler, and even debugger are certainly possible, but typically, they're the least common places for bugs to occur.

Even the easiest category, coding bugs, can be difficult to debug, however. Software is difficult to debug for these main reasons:

- *The fog of war*—Seeing what's happening in the program can be difficult, both in its source code and while it's running.

- *Multiple goals*—The program might have multiple goals that affect or even contradict each other and that aren't expressed or understood well.

- *Complexity*—The program has many interrelated items, such as processes, goals, variables, layers of connectivity, and visibility (scope), and these items contain a lot of variation.
- *Constant change*—The characteristics of program items, such as variables, change frequently, and the results can be unpredictable.

problem-solving approaches

There have been many approaches to creating group and individual problem-solving paths and getting to the root of a problem. The following are only a few examples, but they can be applied to any type of problem:

- *Straw man argument*—With this method, you build up a theory of the problem (the straw man) with the idea that it will likely be knocked down. It helps you communicate issues, find weak points, and throw away what doesn't work. The straw man can be followed by men made of a little stronger stuff (wood, steel, and so on), depending on what you discover. It's a useful tool when you don't know everything. For example, you could start with the argument "The print statement doesn't work because the program never reaches that point."
- *Rules of thumb (heuristics)*—Heuristics, used in many fields, consist of "good enough" approximations. Your experience might tell you that 60% of the time the problem of print statements not working is caused by the print statement not being formatted correctly. Other people's experiences might lead them to make other estimations. You can follow this reason with the second most likely reason, third most likely reason, and so on. These reasons become straw men that you knock down or justify.
- *Follow a procedure*—If the problem is big and complicated enough, it might need a procedure, a detailed checklist of what steps need to be followed. For example, you could create a checklist of what to do if you get a print statement that doesn't work. The checklist might have Step 1 as "Sleep on it" and Step 2 as "Make sure it's not a formatting problem because my rule of thumb is that 60% of print problems are formatting problems," and so on.

the scientific method

You can look at many other techniques, but essentially, they boil down to *inductive reasoning*, also known as the *scientific method*. It usually consists of these four steps:

1. Observe what's happening.
2. Propose a theory for why it's happening.
3. Test the theory.
4. Repeat Steps 1 to 3 until the theory is strong enough to stand on its own. In programming, you usually achieve this step by seeing the program work the way you designed it. (Realize, of course, that an even better theory might come around one day.)

inductive reasoning or scientific method – *A basic approach to problem solving, consisting of four steps: observe, theorize, test, and repeat*

Figure 12-2, The bug found by Grace Hopper

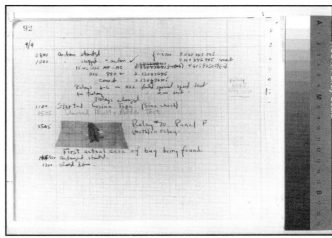

You can see that the approaches discussed previously are just mental tools for reminding you to follow the scientific method steps. For example, the straw man argument is simply creating and testing theories. Using heuristics is just applying your past experience with similar problems to create a theory. Following a procedure is a way to formalize how you plan to propose and test your theories. Steps 3 and 4 are the most important in programming: You need to get into the code, test it, and modify it. As a computing student, you might be afraid of changing anything after it's written, but of fear you must let go, young Padawan.

debugging

debugging – The process of finding and fixing problems in program code

So how do you go about solving software bugs? The following "Thirteen I's" give you a general approach for *debugging*:

1. I will own the problem.
2. I will remain calm and remember the mental game of debugging.
3. I will use the scientific method and problem-solving approaches.
4. I will read the manual.
5. I will make it fail.
6. I will look before I assume.
7. I will divide and conquer the problem.
8. I will isolate changes.
9. I will write down what I do. (Keep a debugging log.)
10. I will check the fuel level.
11. I will get another perspective.
12. I will check that the problem is fixed.
13. I will ask three questions.

debug one problem and (maybe) debug all problems

When you're debugging software, if you fix the problem, you usually fix it for every copy of the software. Unfortunately, this isn't true for solving problems such as fixing a car. Pushing a solution for an automotive design flaw to all owners of the car is difficult. For this reason, some programmers distinguish between "debugging" and "troubleshooting," with troubleshooting referring to fixing a particular instance of a program. The distinction isn't critical, however, because you're always working on a particular instance of software, no matter how much you modify the original design or how much you apply the solution to other instances.

sleeping on the job

Did you know that Thomas Edison, shown in Figure 12-3, used this approach? He was convinced that the unconscious mind had answers the conscious mind couldn't think of. So he took naps while holding a metal ball bearing in his hand. He fell asleep thinking of the problem, and when his hand relaxed, the ball dropping to the floor startled him into waking up, and then he often had the answer he was looking for. This method was so successful that he talked about it frequently, inspiring many others to try it.

At this point, you might be wondering whether these rules are so obvious that you don't need to review them. Far too many times, however, programmers forget the basics, such as Rule 8, isolating changes. As a matter of fact, forgetting these rules is so common that you should copy them and tape them above your monitor.

rule 1: I will own the problem

The name "Thirteen I's" is used for these guidelines to reinforce that you're responsible for solving problems in code you write. Don't waste time and energy looking for scapegoats. Of course, it's possible you'll discover another source for the bug, such as an underlying problem with the operating system, but you still have to find a workaround for it. Remember from the previous discussion of bug categories that coding bugs are the most common. Most likely, the bug you find is your own doing, so *you* have to fix it.

rule 2: I will remain calm and remember the mental game of debugging

Remind yourself of the tips for keeping a positive mindset and being patient. First, take a deep breath, and then recite a positive mantra. Staying calm, attack the problem patiently, and use the problem-solving approaches. (Screaming at the screen does *not* work.) Keep in mind that if you can't find the problem, you can

Figure 12-3, Thomas Edison in his lab

find someone else who might, or you can take a different path around the problem. Don't give up easily. Knowing when to say "Enough is enough" is good, but you don't want to end up with three half-finished programs. Remember that leaving things to the last minute isn't the best way to stay calm. In addition, software is complex to debug, but this complexity also means there are many ways to solve a problem. Complexity has its virtues, so focus and breathe. Sleeping on the problem might help, too, but remember that it's focus and *breathe*, not focus and *snore*!

rule 3: I will use the scientific method and problem-solving approaches

Remember the approaches you've learned for uncovering the origins of an error: straw man arguments, rules of thumb (heuristics), and following a procedure. Review the steps of the scientific method, too:

1. Observe.
2. Create a theory.
3. Test the theory.
4. Repeat Steps 1 to 3.

rule 4: I will read the manual

After writing code, one thing most programmers don't want to do is read a manual. Reading it is important, however. You want to avoid problems that happen when you don't understand what you're working with. Read whatever the pertinent manual is, whether it's help pages for the programming language you're using, HTML definitions at the World Wide Web Consortium (W3C) Web site, documentation for borrowed code, or online discussion boards, blogs, and wiki posts. Of course, manuals, no matter what form they take, are created by people and likely have their own errors. Having said that, there's a good chance you'll find information in the manual that you need. Read the manual so that you know how the system or programming language is supposed to work and how the tools you're using to fix the problem work.

rule 5: I will make it fail

If something fails once, it will probably fail again. However, you might have trouble re-creating a bug so that you can figure out how to fix it. Intermittent bugs are especially difficult to trace. In this case, you have to force the program to fail so that you can examine how it fails, determine why it fails, and look for ways to fix it. Just keep running the program repeatedly and making changes one at a time (see Rule 7) until it "breaks."

Other methods include starting over and re-creating the program, which might involve restarting the computer and running other programs (if other programs were running when the problem occurred). Another method that's helpful is having a way to automate the process of running the program repeatedly with slight variations in input each time, usually with a script. For a program that asks users to enter an address, for instance, you can create a script that enters this data automatically each time the program runs instead of having to type an address manually. This method requires recording what's happening (see Rule 9). You have to look for all external effects on the program, including user input. When you've collected and recorded enough information, you should be able to see what's going on when bugs occur and, just as important, when they don't occur. After you've built and used a debugging tool, such as a script, don't throw it away. It could be useful in the future.

rule 6: I will look before I assume

In a company with programmers and testers, the blame for errors often falls on testers, but chances are, the problem isn't caused by testers (see Rule 1). Just as you shouldn't make assumptions about the source of a bug, you shouldn't assume you know what caused the failure and fix something that isn't even broken. Double-check that what you're seeing is actually happening.

This rule doesn't mean that a good guess isn't useful. It is. However, you need to focus your debugging efforts by examining what's working and not working in the code. The best way to see what's going on is to use available debugging tools, such as including a simple print statement that shows the value of an array's index as the program runs through a loop. You can even build print statements into a program and turn them on and off as needed. If you're concerned about ruining your program during testing, make one or more copies for experimentation. Using descriptive naming conventions for these copies is useful for version control purposes. You might name one myProg_trial1_readLoopError, for example.

note   A word of caution: The Heisenberg uncertainty principle might come into play. In other words, measurement of the system actually affects the system.

rule 7: I will divide and conquer the problem

There are a number of ways to divide and conquer problems, such as starting with the low-hanging fruit, narrowing the search, and creating easy-to-spot patterns. These methods are explained in the following sections.

start with the low-hanging fruit

Often you have many bugs and even bugs hiding behind other bugs. For example, you might have a major one that crashes the program and another minor one that formats output oddly sometimes. You might assume that these bugs can't possibly be related and decide you'll correct the minor bug later because it's an easy fix, but there's a good chance the bugs *are* related. Clean up the low-hanging fruit—that is, the obvious, easily fixed problems—and you have a good chance of correcting more serious bugs. As you gain experience, you'll learn to recognize bugs that are likely to cause other bugs and will know to correct them first. Memory allocation problems can cause havoc in several places in a program, for example.

narrow the search with continual approximation

The Occam's razor principle states that the simplest explanation for a phenomenon is most likely the correct explanation. Engineers often follow the similar "Keep it simple, stupid" (KISS) rule because complexity inevitably leads to making the process of finding a problem and its solution more difficult. Complexity is already a characteristic of most programs, so you have to follow the KISS rule as best you can and realize that Occam's razor can be used proactively—that is, breaking a problem down into parts to find a simple phenomenon (bug).

To do this, you zero in on the problem by narrowing the search and using approximation continually. You use this technique naturally. If someone asks you to guess a number from 1 to 10 and tells you whether you're too high or low, you should be able to guess the number with only a few tries: "5?" "Too low." "7?" "Too high." "6?" "Yup." Of course, first you need to determine the range of possible causes. Is the bug occurring in the hardware, platform, browser, or program logic, or is it a syntax error? (Remember the categories of bugs.) Is the problem the called function or the calling function? If you assume everything in the program is involved, you have a big range of possible causes to work with. However, with approximation, you can narrow the range down quickly.

breakpoint – A stop command inserted to prevent the program from executing past that point

Breakpoints can help with this approach. Say you've determined that the program crashes. You can insert a piece of code called a breakpoint at a location in the program, and then run the program again. Does it crash before the breakpoint? If so, put in a new breakpoint about halfway to the original point. Does the program crash before this new breakpoint? If not, put in a new breakpoint about halfway between this one and the first one, and continue dividing and approximating until there's nowhere left for the bug to hide.

create easy-to-spot patterns

Another technique is using data in tests that gives you easy-to-spot patterns. If the real database content is too complex, for example, create a test database with similar but fewer records, or create an input file with the same line of text used everywhere—maybe "All work and no play make Jack a dull boy." This approach can make problems jump out more obviously. When you run the program and it loops through a print statement, displaying this line of text constantly, if you suddenly see the statement "ou,mnzxcvoiiaefeopu," you've seen the program fail and can pinpoint the problem.

rule 8: I will isolate changes

Confronted with a persistent bug, inexperienced programmers often panic and start throwing everything but the kitchen sink at the problem. In the process, the code that started out well structured and documented winds up being a mess, and they no longer remember what changes they made and when.

If you make a change to try to fix the problem and it doesn't work, don't leave the change in the program. Take it out, go back to the original program, and try the next fix. In other words, change one thing at a time. Even though this guideline is a basic of the scientific method, it's amazing how often it's ignored. If you're getting bad output from a stream of data in a database, test with only one changed field in the database, and keep the other fields the same. Change the fewest lines of code possible, and back out if this change does nothing.

note

Changing everything at once only confuses the issue and makes returning to the program's original conditions difficult.

As mentioned, you can have more than one version of a program for debugging purposes. Running both simultaneously and comparing the differences can be helpful, but make sure the two versions are mostly the same, with only one small difference. Comparing the versions by examining output files or run logs can get tedious, however. To make it easier, you can send output from the two versions to different files and then run a program that compares them, such as the UNIX diff command.

You can write an entire program and then debug it, but generally, an iterative approach is better. In other words, write a program component and debug it, write another component and debug it, and so forth. With this approach, you need to work out a framework for your program that indicates where you'll place components after you've written them. This method can save you a lot of debugging time.

Iterative program development has another benefit: giving you a baseline for debugging. You can ask, "What have I changed since the last time the program worked?" Then you can go back to that version and start over. Having a debugging log (see Rule 9) is critical for this task. Keep in mind that the version immediately preceding the problem version might still have problems, so you might have to use the technique of forcing it to fail. Isolating changes with iterative development and testing is a good way to apply the scientific method, however.

rule 9: I will write down what I do

As mentioned in the previous guidelines, keeping a record of the changes you have made (a debugging log) and keeping versions of the program you have created are critical. Version control software, such as Microsoft Visual SourceSafe, helps with keeping a debugging log, although you can do it manually with a simple text file or spreadsheet. Keeping a log electronically is best so that it can be shared with others in a programming department or team. (Remember to use descriptive filenames to help you keep track of program versions.) Generally, you should write down the changes you make, in the order in which you've made them, and the results of these changes. Getting into this habit is good practice for the real world because most managers require programmers to keep this type of log.

Sometimes it's the most minor change that ends up causing a problem, so the more details you include in your log, the better. Table 12-1 shows an example of an entry in a debugging log. Notice that it includes the program version and the result.

Table 12-1, FtoC_versionX.src debug log, 5-17-10

what did I do?	program version	what happened?
Wrote program.	Version 0	Syntax error at line 15.
Examined line 15; added semicolon at end of line.	Version 1	Program crashed.
Added breakpoint at line 30.	Version 3	Program crashed.
Added breakpoint at line 15.	Version 3b	Program ran to breakpoint.

(continued)

Table 12-1, FtoC_versionX.src debug log, 5-17-10 (*continued*)

what did I do?	program version	what happened?
Looked at lines 15 to 30 and noticed memory allocation line was overwriting program memory. Changed the value of the `last_mem_location` parameter from 3200 to 3400 and removed breakpoint.	Version 4	Program didn't crash but address output was displayed with tabs between characters.
Hard-coded value of the memory address as one character: A.	Version 5	Printed A as the output.
Hard-coded value of the memory address as two characters: AA.	Version 5b	Printed A, a tab, and another A as the output.
Noticed a tab character in the print statement and removed it.	Version 5c	Printed AA as the output correctly.
Removed the hard-coded value AA.	Version 6	Working!

After you write down events and results, you can begin to see correlations. For example, the problem discovered in Table 12-1 is a tab character in the print statement. The programmer narrowed down the problem by hard-coding a recognizable small data value (AA, in this example). When the same failure happened, the programmer realized the problem was the print statement, not the data. Other programmers can use this log as a model for repair or an insight into the program. Remember the problem-solving approach of following a procedure? Creating a procedure usually starts with writing down the problem and its solution.

Novice programmers often wonder why they should write anything down, but there are good reasons for doing so. First, in the real world, chances are you don't get to work on only your own programs. Wouldn't it be nice if other programmers had documented their code? Second, the programs you write run on a variety of operating systems and interact with other software and hardware you didn't design for. Wouldn't it be nice if the programmers of this other software had documented their code? Third, you might not have documented the program well, and now that a few weeks have gone by (or maybe one tough night at the Hard Rock Cafe), you no longer understand the reasoning behind some of your code. Wouldn't it be nice if you had documented your code?

rule 10: I will check the fuel level

If you call a help desk about problems with your printer, the first questions you're asked are typically "Is the printer on?" and "Is it connected to the computer?" You might think these questions aren't necessary, but in problem solving, starting with the simplest and most likely problems is best. If your car stops running, you don't check the axles first; you check the fuel level. Similarly, when debugging software, start with the most likely problems and move up from there: coding (syntax errors), logic problems, compatibility issues, and architecture problems.

At each step, you should make sure your assumptions are correct—that you're starting with the conditions you think you are. For example, when debugging software, first you should verify that you're running the program you think you are. Next, you should make sure you're starting the program with the correct initial conditions. With programs running on browsers, for example, often you need to reset the system or the browser. You might need to log off and then log back on or refresh the browser.

Stepping back and checking the fuel level includes checking that your debugging tools are working correctly. If you're using a device to check the electrical current, for instance, first test it on a circuit you know is working and powered on. Similarly, check print statements outside the problem area to make sure they work.

rule 11: I will get another perspective

Learning how to solve problems yourself is always good, of course, but sometimes getting input from other people can save you a lot of time and frustration. Just the process of explaining your problem out loud to someone else can give you a flash of insight. Maybe students in computing courses should try talking to themselves out loud when solving problems, although this method might make lab periods a little noisy!

The point is that getting another perspective, even just as a sounding board, is helpful. Taking advantage of others' experience is useful, too. Even if the people you're consulting don't know the specific technology or programming language you're using, they might have run across similar problems or have a fresh approach. When you ask for another perspective, keep in mind that you should report exactly what's happening, not your theory about why it's happening. You might think that eliminating what you've already tested is helpful, but it lessens your chances of getting an unbiased opinion. Stick to the facts.

note

When you ask someone else to look at your problem, provide as many details as possible. Vague statements, such as "It doesn't work," don't motivate people to help you.

rule 12: I will check that the problem is fixed

Needless to say, you have to check that your fix worked. You can't just assume that inserting a semicolon was the solution. You have to test to verify that the missing semicolon was indeed the problem. One advantage of software is that you can test both working and nonworking versions easily to verify the solution. For example, you add a new array endpoint, and the program works. You take it out, maintaining the same conditions elsewhere in the code, but the program doesn't work. You put it in again, and the program works. After this testing, you can be confident that you've solved the problem. In other words, make the program fail (see Rule 5), and then make it fail *again*.

Unfortunately, bugs don't go away by themselves. If they do seem to solve themselves, that usually means the program conditions aren't the same, and you'll probably see the bugs again. Occasionally, someone else makes a change that fixes the bug, such as updates to a programming language. This doesn't get you off the hook, however. You have to know how the bug was fixed to be confident it won't return. If the language changes again in the future, the bug might return, but your code should be robust enough to handle it. Additionally, if you can't fix a bug, at least put in some method for tracking it in case the problem happens when the program runs. Known bugs can at least be managed sometimes. It's the unknown ones, the surprises, that really cause problems. Also, be honest. Nothing bugs a professor or client more than the programmer trying to hide something.

rule 13: I will ask three questions

You should ask three questions every time you fix a bug to make sure you're not just treating the symptoms. You want to fix the underlying cause. These three questions can help you pinpoint underlying problems to prevent other bugs from occurring in the future:

- Is this mistake occurring anywhere else? For example, if you discover you didn't create an array index systematically, maybe you've made similar errors in other array indexes, even though they didn't result in a noticeable bug.
- What next bug is hidden behind this one? This question reminds you of the low-hanging fruit problem: Bugs can act like red herrings and distract you from other bugs. So if you've been careless with how array indexes read from and

12

write to the array, maybe you've been careless in writing the print statement that references arrays. In addition, how many little changes have you made to make things come out right? Maybe it's time to think of rewriting the code a bit and eliminating all the bandages you've added to get the program to run. Maybe you haven't tested some parts of the code because you assumed they would work the same way they did before you started adding fixes. Go back and look at these parts of the code.

• What should I do to prevent similar bugs? Answering the first two questions can help you answer this one, but you should go further. At what stage of program design and implementation was the bug introduced? Ask more "Why?" questions. Perhaps the language you're using is prone to allowing certain types of bugs. Verification tools, such as the W3C validator, that check syntax were created to help with investigating the cause of bugs. You might also want to look into creating new testing processes, such as devising a test specifically for array indexes.

the rules in action

Seeing some of these rules in action is helpful. This section uses some typical stories as examples and then discusses which rules are applicable. In addition, in all these stories, aspects of the scientific method of proposing a theory and testing it have been followed. The stories you see here are real, but the names have been changed to protect the guilty and innocent alike.

> **Story 1:** A student asked me why his picture wasn't showing up on his Web page. He had tried the Web page on his PC, and it worked, so he loaded the page on the server we're using. I asked, "Where's the picture file?" Frustrated, he responded, "Right here, on my computer!" I told him the picture file needs to be on the server. He uploaded it, but he still couldn't display the picture. The problem was he had changed the filename to include spaces, and the server was running Linux. I'd told my students that in Linux, spaces in filenames aren't typical and could cause problems. Of course, if you're used to Windows, you use spaces in filenames all the time. The student changed the spaces to underscores, but he also changed uppercase letters in the filename to lowercase letters, and Linux is case sensitive.

This problem starts with Rule 10: The student didn't step back, ask what he was actually testing, and look for the simplest solution to the problem. (Following Rule 2, staying calm, might have helped, too.) The problem was caused by a platform bug: differences in how Linux and Windows handle filenames. Following Rule 4, reading the manual, would also have helped this student.

Story 2: I was working on a program and wondered why a variable wasn't changing. I'm new to programming in PHP, so I assumed that variable scope (where in the program a variable is visible) was the same as in other languages I've used. I kept banging away at it, changing different parts of the program one at a time and seeing it break repeatedly. Finally, I asked a coworker for help, who suggested I look up variable scope in PHP. Sure enough, my assumptions were wrong. It took about 5 minutes of looking up information to solve the problem versus the 45 minutes I had spent changing the code every which way.

In this example, the programmer did some good debugging work. By testing it repeatedly and not assuming the variable had changed, he followed Rule 6, looking before assuming. By trying to make it fail and changing things one at a time, he followed Rule 5, making it fail, and Rule 8, isolating the changes. Finally, he even followed Rule 11, getting another perspective. However, Rule 4, reading the manual, ended up being the key. If he had understood the language better, he wouldn't have assumed that variable scope worked the same as in other languages.

Story 3: I decided to write a little client/server game as a way to learn about sockets. Based on what I'd read, I assumed the process should go like this: I send a message to the server. It responds "I'm here." Then I send the message "Here's the work to do." The server responds with "Working" or "Here's the answer." However, it didn't work that way. The server responded with one message: "I'm here and here's the answer." Now it appeared to be working the way I'd assumed it should, but the response didn't match what I'd read in the manual, so I had to experiment.

Sometimes the manual isn't complete, or worse, it's wrong. In this case, you have to go beyond the manual and find other expertise as well as digging into the problem yourself. The programmer followed Rule 4, but when confronted with evidence contradictory to what he had read, he started dividing and conquering the problem (Rule 7).

Story 4: I had to write an ASCII program for converting file types. It worked flawlessly, so I took it to my boss, and he gave me a 2.5 GB file. Well, the program wouldn't work. It took me a while to realize that the file was too big. I had to rewrite the program completely because no one told me the program had to handle such a large input. Of course, we were both at fault. I should have asked, but my boss should have told me.

This programmer is correct: Getting accurate requirement specifications is crucial. She was able to solve the problem, but following Rule 4 (in this case, understanding the requirements) would have helped her remember to ask about limits on input file size. This situation involves Rule 1, too. She should have owned the problem and asked the right questions. Clients (and bosses) are notoriously bad at giving you complete information.

> **Story 5:** My mom called me and complained that she couldn't enter her password for her e-mail account. My first question was "Can you enter text anywhere else?" Turns out she couldn't. My next thought was that the keyboard wasn't hooked up. I knew she had a wireless keyboard, so I told her to try resetting it, and if that didn't work, try replacing the batteries. It worked!

This story is a great example of Rule 10, checking the fuel level. Instead of worrying about the program his mom was trying to use, the son went back to the basics: Can anything be typed? When he realized his mom couldn't use the keyboard at all, he followed Rule 4, reading the manual. In other words, he knew his mom had a wireless keyboard. By following Rule 10 again (literally—because the keyboard had run out of battery "fuel"), he was able to solve the problem.

one last thought

Print the rules, and post them near your computer. Even experts can use reminding once in a while. This chapter is one you can return to after reading other chapters. For example, when you read Chapters 14 and 15, if you get frustrated about a program that just won't run right, come back here and reread some tips. In the world of debugging, remember that it's mind over (virtual) matter. Breathe deeply, and stay positive.

references

Agans, David J. *Debugging*. Amacom, 2006 (ISBN 0814474578).

Bezroukov, Nikolai. "A Second Look at the Cathedral and the Bazaar" (*www.softpanorama.org/Lang/debug.shtml*).

Burns, David. "The Mental Game of Debugging" (*www.softpanorama.org/Lang/debug.shtml*).

Frensch, Peter A. and Joachim Funke (eds.). *Complex Problem Solving: The European Perspective*. Lawrence Erlbaum Associates, 1995 (ISBN 0805813365).

Gladwell, Malcolm. *Blink: The Power of Thinking Without Thinking*. Back Bay Books, 2007 (ISBN 0316010669).

Krantz, Steven G. *Techniques of Problem Solving*. American Mathematical Society, 1997 (ISBN 082180619X).

Rice, David. *Geekonomics: The Real Cost of Insecure Software*. Addison-Wesley, 2007 (ISBN 0321477898).

Van Vleck, Tom. "Three Questions About Each Bug You Find" (*www.multicians.org/thvv/threeq.html*).

chapter summary

- Problem solving is inevitable, and learning how to do it well is a skill you can use in every area of your life.

- Remember that debugging can be fun, especially for people who enjoy mysteries and puzzles. Think of it as a mental game. Develop a positive mindset and stay calm.

- Categorizing bugs in a hierarchy from easiest to most complex to solve helps you determine what kind of bug you've found and how difficult it will be to correct.

- Software problems can be difficult to solve for a number of reasons, but these reasons aren't excuses for poor programming practices. Careless programming can have a bigger impact than just causing an error when a program runs.

- Some general problem-solving approaches that can be applied to almost any problem are setting up straw man arguments, using rules of thumb (heuristics), and following a procedure.

- Computing professionals use the scientific method to solve problems: observing the problem, proposing a theory, testing the theory, and repeating these steps.

- The Thirteen I's are useful guidelines for what you should remember when debugging.

key terms

breakpoint (*417*)

debugging (*413*)

inductive reasoning or
scientific method (*412*)

12

test yourself

1. What are some less quantified problem-solving approaches that have been discovered in studies since the 1970s?

2. Describe three techniques for developing the right mindset for solving problems.

3. Which type of bug is the most difficult to find and fix?

4. Which type of bug is the easiest to find and fix?

5. Explain how logic bugs and bad data bugs are related.

6. Explain how compatibility, architecture, and coding bugs are related.

7. Describe some problem-solving approaches you can use for any problem.

8. What are the steps in the scientific method?

9. Explain what "I Will Own the Problem" means.

10. Describe the approach of iterative program development, and explain its benefits.

11. What's one reason for having more than one version of a program?

12. What code technique is useful with continual approximation?

13. List three different forms in which you can find a manual for help in debugging.

14. What information should you include in a debugging log?

15. What's the main reason for asking three questions after you've found the cause of a bug and fixed it?

practice exercises

1. After doing the practice exercises on software engineering in Chapter 13, find five exercises where you could apply the Thirteen I's. For each one, state the rule, and give examples of how you could have followed it.

2. A programmer reports this problem with an HTML program: "In the line break section, I tried using the file from the <pre> section as a base and

just modifying the text with <p> and <br/> tags. Well, that didn't work because it messed up the structure of the <pre> block, and all I wanted it to do was insert line breaks. I ended up reworking the entire program and removing the <pre> block." What kind of error is it? What rules were applied, and which should have been applied earlier?

3. A student reports this problem when using HTML and JavaScript: "On the assignment with preloaded images, I had to rewrite the example from the book. I had a problem with the syntax for linking the source file to the <form> element. I solved the problem by using this syntax: document.images.img3.src = (source of file)." What kind of error is it? What rules were applied, and which should have been applied earlier?

4. A programmer reports this problem when using PHP: "It didn't take me long to find out that if you use flat files to read and write, you should change their settings. They're set to read, not write, so just click Properties to change their settings. To save time, if I saw an error I didn't understand, I Googled it." What kind of error is it? What rules were applied, and which should have been applied earlier?

digging deeper

1. A student reports this problem when using HTML and JavaScript: "I had some issues with the date display exercise. I finally realized I'd forgotten to increase the image array's size after I added the dots and slashes!" What kind of error is it? What rules were applied, and which should have been applied earlier?

2. A programmer reports this problem when using PHP: "In NetBeans and (I'm assuming) most other development environments, the project folder and the server source folders *must* have the same name, or the program won't work. I discovered this by accident when I was trying to create my project for the umpteenth time." What kind of error is it? What rules were applied, and which should have been applied earlier?

3. A student reports this problem when using HTML and JavaScript: "This assignment has been nothing but trouble. I had some problems getting things to display correctly in both IE and Firefox and having things disappear when I clicked an option button. The Web site resource has helped a little but has mostly been a headache." What kind of error is it? What rules were applied, and which should have been applied earlier?

4. A student reports this problem when using HTML: "When building my home page, I couldn't get the background color to change until I put a # in front of the value. Now it works." What kind of error is it? What rules were applied, and which should have been applied earlier?

5. A programmer reports this problem when using XML: "I forgot to put the end tag on one of my XML tags, and everything quit working. Took me forever to figure it out, and I had to use IE as a debugger." What kind of error is it? What rules were applied, and which should have been applied earlier?

discussion topics

1. With good software design, do you think bugs can be eliminated? Why or why not?

2. Can skills in problem solving be learned, or is problem solving an inherent talent?

3. Do any of the Thirteen I's seem contradictory? If so, why?

4. Could you argue that because programmers use the scientific method constantly, they're as well trained as scientists?

Internet research

1. Try opening your favorite Web page in two different browsers and on two different operating systems. Do you find any problems in how the Web page opens and performs? Do you notice any differences when opening it on different browsers and operating systems?

2. Find Web sites with statistics on error rates for different platforms, browsers, programs, and languages. Does open-source software live up to its hype of making the task of finding and fixing bugs easier?

3. Many examples of solved problems in programming are on the Internet. Find discussions of some of these problems, and then categorize the problems based on what you've learned in this chapter. What rules were applied in fixing these problems?

4. Numerous Web resources on problem solving are available. Find three, and compare their approaches to solving problems. Summarize which approach you find most useful and why.

software engineering

in this chapter you will:

- Learn how software engineering is used to create applications
- Learn some software engineering process models
- Understand how a design document is used during software development
- Review the steps for formulating a design document
- Learn how Unified Modeling Language (UML) diagrams can be used as a blueprint for creating an application
- See some pitfalls in developing software, and learn how to avoid them
- Understand how teams are used in application development

the lighter side of the lab
by spencer

I've got a little problem with procrastination that I've been meaning to take care of for a while. I'm not sure how I've made it through school so far. I can't tell you how many times I've stayed up all night working on a term project or research paper that was due the following day.

Unfortunately, I've found that the last-minute routine doesn't work in the computer world. Software isn't created overnight (although sometimes it functions as though it is). An intricate process goes into designing and creating a program.

First, it's important for the team to get together and argue for hours about which is better: Windows or Linux. This step serves no purpose, but it's a lot of fun. (*Hint*: Linux vs. Windows debate != interesting date conversation.)

Next, coming up with a programming strategy is important. How will the project be divided up among teams? Will UML (Unified Modeling Language) be used? Does the customer need a prototype? Will the programming teams be the same as those for Call of Duty?

After all these decisions are made, it's time to get to work. It's exciting when the pieces come together and the program works, although sometimes it's more exciting when the pieces come together and the program doesn't work. (The Computer Throw and Monitor Kick could be Olympic events.)

Finally, one day the program is finished, or so you think. It's then sent to a small group of customers for what's known as a "beta test." No matter how well you think you've programmed, the beta testers will find errors. Eventually, you find all the bugs, and the software is sent out to customers. They have a special ability to find errors that a normal person would never dream of.

Support Technician: What seems to be the problem?

Customer: Um, yeah. When I enter the Pledge of Allegiance backward into the Date box, I get an error.

The process is a lot of work, but it's also a lot of fun. There's nothing as satisfying as seeing someone use the program you wrote with your own two hands—other than finally going to sleep after staying up all night working on a research paper, of course.

why you need to know about...
software engineering

Every day you're faced with the task of defining a project. Whether it's mowing the lawn, buying groceries, or writing a program, you need to define the project's scope before you begin the work.

For example, a neighbor hires you to mow his lawn. You show up bright and early, and after three hours of grueling work, you finish the job. You ring the doorbell, expecting praise for your good work and a fistful of hard-earned cash. The neighbor opens the door, looks at the lawn with a sour expression, and says, "That's not how I wanted it done!" So off you go, sweating, pushing, and pulling the lawn mower, which feels heavier with each passing moment. Again, you trudge to the door and ring the doorbell. The neighbor comes to the door and again you hear "That's not what I wanted!" Finally, you scream, "How *do* you want your lawn mowed?" The neighbor explains that the correct way to mow the lawn is by pushing the mower diagonally rather than horizontally across the yard. He releases you from your duty without pay and swears to never hire you to mow the lawn again. Dejected, you leave the lawn-mowing business and join a traveling circus.

The moral of this story is, of course, that you must find out exactly what's required *before* you start the job—a principle you might have already discovered applies to programming, too. Just because you have problems making your program meet all the requirements you have been given, you shouldn't give up and change your major to basket weaving. All you need to do is design the project properly before you start writing any source code.

It's not enough to know a programming language and be able to write code. Software engineering enables you to design your programs and communicate with clients and other team members—essential elements of writing applications.

what is software engineering?

Yogi Berra said, "You've got to be very careful if you don't know where you're going because you might get there." For any application to be successful, you must have a map outlining what should be accomplished. Designing a project requires incorporating software engineering skills to meet the end user's requirements. *Software engineering* is the process of producing software applications. It involves not just the program's source code but also associated documentation, including UML diagrams, screen prototypes, reports, software requirements, future development issues, and data needed to make programs operate correctly.

An *end user* is the driving force behind software development. You might have heard that programmers are often frustrated by end users and consider them demanding or stupid, but end users serve an important purpose. End users are the ones who need the program to perform a function or meet a need, and they determine the program's required functionality. They're the ones who know what they need but don't have the resources or knowledge to create a product that helps them achieve their goals. However, keep in mind that an end user (also called "client" or just "user") doesn't always have to be a person. An end user could be a piece of machinery or even a task to be accomplished.

A major part of software engineering is the process of designing, writing, and producing software applications that are based on the needs of end users. As time goes by, end users' needs might change. In fact, their need for the application might even disappear, making the application obsolete. Therefore, there's a constant need to communicate with end users to make software applicable to their needs.

software engineering – The process of producing software applications, involving not just the program's source code but also associated documentation, including UML diagrams, screen prototypes, reports, software requirements, future development issues, and data needed to make programs operate correctly

end user – Someone or something that needs the program to perform a function or meet a need and determines the program's required functionality

note   The terms "software," "program," and "application" are often used interchangeably.

software development life cycle

During the life of a program, you continue to maintain, fix, and improve it. The *software development life cycle (SDLC)* includes several elements:

software development life cycle (SDLC) – A model that describes the life of the application, including all stages involved in developing, testing, installing, and maintaining a program

- *Project feasibility*—Determining whether the project is worth doing and specifying its advantages and disadvantages
- *Software specifications*—Determining specific functions of the software and any constraints or requirements
- *Software design and implementation*—Designing and writing the application to meet the software specifications

- *Software validation*—Testing the application to ensure that it meets the software specifications
- *Software evolution*—Modifying or changing the application to meet changing customer needs

Different models of the software development process can be used to represent software functionality, such as the following:

- *Waterfall*—The fundamental processes in creating the program are represented as phases. The output from each phase is used as the input for the next phase.
- *Build and fix (or evolutionary)*—The developer writes a program and continues to modify it until it's functional.
- *Rapid prototyping*—This process uses tools that allow end users to work with *prototypes* of program screens and other interfaces. These prototypes can then be used to build the final product.
- *Incremental*—The application is developed and released in a series of software releases.
- *Spiral*—This model starts with an initial pass, using the waterfall method. After an evaluation period, the cycle starts again, adding new functionality until the next prototype is released. The process resembles a spiral, with the prototype becoming larger and larger until all functionality has been completed and delivered to the end user.
- *Agile*—This method is used for time-critical applications. It's less formal, has a reduced scope, and encourages frequent inspection and adaptation. Tasks are carried out in small increments with minimal planning. Two well-known agile methods are scrum and extreme programming (XP). Scrum includes a "sprint," in which a team creates an increment of usable software. This method allows end users to change their minds about the application's requirements. XP includes four basic activities: coding, testing, listening, and designing. This method incorporates user stories (written by end users to describe what the application needs to do) and spike solutions (answers to tough technical or design problems).

prototype – *A standard or typical example that gives end users a good idea of what they will see when their application is completed*

Each model varies in the steps needed to complete the development tasks. This chapter focuses on the *waterfall model* (shown in Figure 13-1), a widely used model that has been around since 1970. The waterfall model resembles the process of building a house. You start by excavating the area where the foundation will be placed. You can't pour the foundation until the excavation process has been completed. After the foundation is laid, you can then proceed to the next process, framing the house. The process of finishing one step before moving on to the next one continues until the house is finally completed.

waterfall model – *An SDLC approach involving sequential application development with processes organized into phases; after a phase is completed, a new one starts, and you can't return to the previous phase*

Figure 13-1, The waterfall model of software development

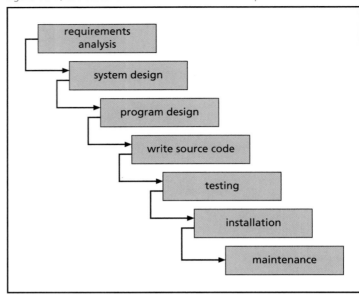

The waterfall model follows a similar approach. The first step is gathering all the requirements for the project. The second step is designing the system and software. After all the requirements have been defined and the project has been designed, it's time to build and implement the application. After the application is finished, it must be tested and then finally put into operation and maintained to meet users' needs.

Software need not become obsolete. Instead, it can be modified to meet end users' changing needs. Over time, the needs that used to be important might no longer be part of the picture. A program's requirements and functionality can change, and the software can be changed to fit.

Luckily, software engineers are prepared to deal with change because they have a set of "blueprints" for their software products, called a design document.

creating the design document

design document – A document that details all the design issues for an application

A *design document* is sometimes compared to a thesis in size. It can be quite large because it details all the application's design issues, including screen layouts, colors, reports, security, paths for files, online help, user documentation, future plans, and more. Every aspect of the application should be documented and maintained in a file or folder.

An advantage of using a software development environment as your application development tool is that you can prototype screens and reports without writing a single line of source code. In other words, you can sit down with end users and interactively design all the screens and reports to their specifications, including text, color, and field location. For instance, you have been asked to write an application to help technicians keep track of laboratory test results. You can sit down with the end users and have them help you design the input screen's appearance by specifying fonts, colors, and locations for input areas. The end users can also use a word-processing program to design sample reports as prototypes for the reports you create in the application. All this information gives you a head start in creating the application and making sure it looks pleasing to the end users.

Another important reason for using a design document is that it serves as a blueprint. If everyone agrees on the design document as the correct way of doing the work, there should be no surprises in the final product. If one party says something was done incorrectly, both parties can return to the design document to resolve the dispute.

The process of creating a design document is based on good communication with end users in determining the application's needs and requirements (see Figure 13-2).

Figure 13-2, The process of creating a design document

- learn the current system and needs
- create UML diagrams
- create a data dictionary
- design reports
- structure the application's logical flow
- start building the prototype
- put all the pieces together

To help you better understand the process, the following case study walks you through the seven steps of creating a design document.

step 1: learn the current system and needs

You're the president and programmer at Over Byte, Inc. The owner of the music store Toe-Tappin' Tunes, Mr. B. Bop, comes to you with a proposal for an application to manage the store's media inventory. Learning the end user's or client's current system and needs is your first task.

n o t e   RULE: Learn the end user's current system and needs.

First, you have to spend some time with Mr. Bop and find out how he currently handles his inventory. What are his needs? What is his goal for using a computer-based inventory system? You can even assign him the task of writing a list of reports he wants the application to generate. Then have him send you a copy of the reports so that you can review them before your next meeting.

Your job is to document the meeting's main points and come up with solutions or suggestions to address the issues of security, colors, printing, and other standard application factors. You don't have to write down every word of the meeting, but do take notes that can be used as a reference later when you begin creating the design document.

n o t e   RULE: Document the information the client gives you.

Essentially, you become a detective in trying to determine what the user really wants. If a system is already in place, you can spend time learning how it's used and discovering its good points and bad points. You should also talk to the people who will actually be using the product to make sure the application you're developing meets their needs. In other words, you have to keep digging for information.

After you have a good handle on what the user really wants, you should write the project's objectives (or an introduction), specifications, and requirements (see Figure 13-3). This part of the design document is an overall guide for the major tasks that need to be accomplished.

n o t e   RULE: Write objectives, specifications, and requirements.

step 2: create UML diagrams

After the objectives and requirements have been defined, it's time to start creating diagrams to illustrate what the program is supposed to do. *Unified Modeling Language (UML)* enables software developers to create diagrams included in the blueprint that show the program's overall functionality and provide a way for the client and developer to communicate. UML is a visual modeling approach to specifying the system functionality that's needed to create a product that meets the project requirements. The diagrams are created before any source code is written and help the software developer see what needs to be accomplished.

Unified Modeling Language (UML) – *A software modeling process for creating a blueprint that shows the progam's overall functionality and provides a way for the client and developer to communicate*

Figure 13-3, A design document includes objectives, specifications, and requirements

1. **Introduction**

    1.1. <u>**Purpose**</u>

        1.1.1.   This document lists all software requirements for the creation and implementation of a Fantasy Basketball Web site. It defines the feasibility study, operational requirements, algorithms, databases, user interfaces, error systems, help systems, cost analysis, and supporting diagrams.

                The intended audience for this document is the end user or client, development team, project manager, and any other stakeholders in the system.

    1.2. <u>**Terms**</u>

- *League Owner:* The creator of the league
- *Commissioner:* The person responsible for overseeing league actions
- *Team Owner:* Any person who owns a team in the specified league
- *Team:* Consists of 12 players, each playing in the position of guard, forward, or center
- *User:* Any person who registers to play in a league of Fantasy Basketball

    1.3. <u>**Scope**</u>

        1.3.1   The users of this product are the participants in the Fantasy Basketball game. Users can create their own league or participate in an established league.

    1.4. <u>**Overview**</u>

        1.4.1.   This product enables people to create leagues and organize teams by letting them manage and follow their teams through a basketball season. This product is Web based and requires a server, an Internet connection, and a Web browser. Every night, basketball statistics are downloaded to the server. These statistics are then updated throughout the league teams to determine a team's final score for a specific game.

2. **Specifications**

    2.1.   ...

3. **System Requirements**

    3.1.   ...

note

There's a common perception among end users that software is cheap to produce and easy to modify. After you have gained more experience with software engineering, you'll find that this perception is false. Software can be complex and take many hours to produce. Time is translated into money spent by the company or lost by the developer in creating a program.

UML provides many types of diagrams for explaining the different parts of a system. Microsoft Visio is one tool for creating UML diagrams and other types of diagrams that are useful to programmers (see Figure 13-4).

The following are some types of UML diagrams and their uses:

- *Class*—Shows how different object classes relate to each other
- *Object*—Gives details of an object created from a class
- *Use case*—Describes a system's behavior from a user's standpoint
- *State*—Shows an object's particular state at any given time
- *Sequence*—Shows how one class communicates with another by sending messages back and forth
- *Activity*—Shows activities that occur in a use case or in an object's behavior
- *Component*—Shows how system components relate to each other
- *Deployment*—Shows the physical architecture of a computer-based system

Figure 13-4, Creating UML diagrams in Microsoft Visio

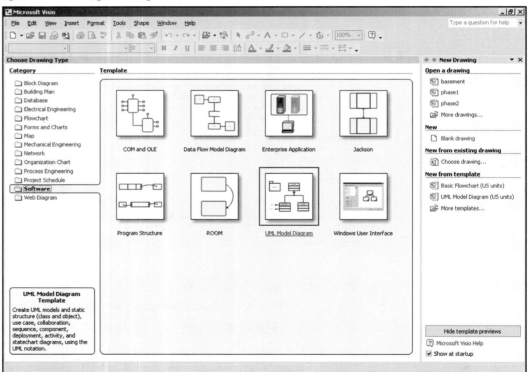

Each type of UML diagram serves a specific purpose in defining a system's functionality from the client's viewpoint. For example, you're asked to create an application to help the Toe-Tappin' Tunes music store. The use case diagram (see Figure 13-5) shows the inventory application's overall functionality and lists the main tasks the application needs to perform and the system needs to support.

Figure 13-5, Use case diagram for the music inventory application

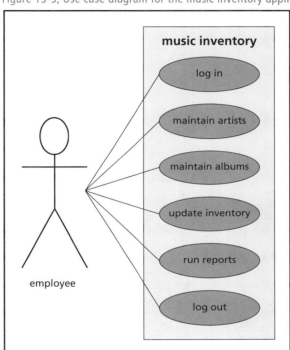

The class diagram shows what object-oriented classes need to be included when creating the application (see Figure 13-6). It also shows how the classes relate to one another. In essence, it can be used as an object-oriented programming (OOP) blueprint for creating source code built on the class relationships.

Figure 13-6, Class diagram for the music inventory application

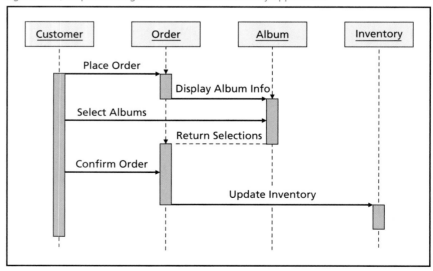

The UML sequence diagram (see Figure 13-7) shows what types of messages are passed back and forth between the classes specified in the class diagram.

Figure 13-7, Sequence diagram for the music inventory application

Each type of UML diagram describes different object-oriented functionality in a system. Developers can use these visual models as a blueprint when writing the actual source code. UML tools enable you to create a UML diagram in much the same way that you might create a drawing with a program such as Paint. Each type of diagram has defined images that you can drop onto the workspace to represent different functionality.

step 3: create the data dictionary

You know the program incorporates a database if the user wants to store information. Unless a database is already in place, it's your job to help define the structure of the database by creating a *data dictionary*. This task might be a secondary role for you. The primary person in charge of the database might be the database administrator (DBA). If the database is already in place, you should review it for accuracy by comparing it with your meeting notes and the project's objectives, specifications, and requirements.

data dictionary – *A document describing the type of data being used in the program, showing table definitions, indexes, and other data relationships*

n o t e

RULE: Determine whether a database is needed; if so, create a data dictionary.

If a database isn't in place and you're responsible for creating the database structure, you can review any reports the end user has provided to devise a list of data tables to use in the application.

The process of creating a data dictionary (also referred to as "preparing for normalization") is explained in more detail in Chapter 6, "Database Fundamentals."

n o t e

RULE: Use information from the end user to summarize the current system and organize a brief plan for the new application.

Before you meet with the end user again, review the reports so that you know what type of information needs to be stored and can design the necessary tables to be used in the application. This information is what drives the application. After all, what good is an application if it can't retrieve the information end users need?

n o t e

RULE: Review end users' reports to find possible tables and elements for a data dictionary.

Create a data dictionary of the tables by listing the table name, the order (or indexes) in which data is sorted, a description of the table's use, and a comment for each field in the table (see Figure 13-8).

Figure 13-8, Creating a data dictionary

Music Inventory Data Dictionary

Database is MIToeTappin written in Oracle 11g

Table: Artist

Indexes: ByCode   Artist_CD
               ByName   Artist_NM

Use: This table contains all the music artists.

Field	Description
ARTIST_CD	Unique code identifying the record
ARTIST_NM	Artist name

Table: Inventory

Indexes: ByCode   Media_CD
               ByType   Media_Type

Use: This table contains all the music items in the store's inventory.

Field	Description
MEDIA_CD	Unique code identifying record
MEDIA_TYPE	Media type (CD, tape, album, and so on)
ON_HAND	Quantity on hand
MRP	Minimum reorder point
COST	Store's cost
PRICE	Retail price

The data dictionary becomes a schematic describing the type of data used in the program. Both software engineers and end users can use this document to clarify the data available for use in reports, screens, file transfers, and other data operations.

step 4: design reports

It's time to meet with Mr. Bop and review your ideas for helping the store better maintain the media inventory. Bring along a notebook or desktop computer loaded with your development software. Sitting down with end users at the computer might seem like a major task, but it helps you create a program that specifically meets their needs.

Start by reviewing the data dictionary and explaining what data will be stored. Ask the user whether any other data needs to be kept. If you haven't planned the database tables before you start the project, you're asking for trouble and are likely to miss a deadline.

One way you can include the end user in the design process is with an integrated development environment (IDE), which contains design tools and wizards that make application development easier.

n o t e

RULE: Let the user help you design the reports.

For example, you can use a report wizard or a report generator, such as the one shown in Figure 13-9, to generate prototypes of the reports Mr. Bop needs to have in the application.

Figure 13-9, Example of a report created with a report generator

Music CD Catalog
ToeTappin' Tunes
Sorted by Artist and Song Title

Print Date 1/16/2010

Artist Name	Song Title	CD Title
COUNTING CROWS		
	ANGELS OF THE SILENCES	RECOVERING THE SATELLITES
	MR. JONES	AUGUST AND EVERYTHING AFTER
	RECOVERING THE SATELLITES	RECOVERING THE SATELLITES
	TIME AND TIME AGAIN	AUGUST AND EVERYTHING AFTER
ERIC CLAPTON		
	BLUES BEFORE SUNRISE	ERIC CLAPTON UNPLUGGED
	HEY HEY	ERIC CLAPTON UNPLUGGED
	HOOCHIE COOCHIE MAN	ERIC CLAPTON UNPLUGGED
	LAYLA	ERIC CLAPTON UNPLUGGED
	TEARS IN HEAVEN	ERIC CLAPTON UNPLUGGED
HOWARD JONES		
	CONDITIONING	HUMAN'S LIB
	LOOK MAMA	BEST OF HOWARD JONES
	NEW SONG	BEST OF HOWARD JONES
	PEARL IN THE SHELL	BEST OF HOWARD JONES
	WHAT IS LOVE?	BEST OF HOWARD JONES
MANHATTAN TRANSFER		
	BIRDLAND	THE MANHATTAN TRANSFER ANTHOLOGY
	BOY FROM NEW YORK CITY	THE MANHATTAN TRANSFER ANTHOLOGY
	JAVA JIVE	THE MANHATTAN TRANSFER ANTHOLOGY

When you examine a report, you see a snapshot of data that should exist in your application. Each column in the report might represent a field or column in a table. Each row of data in the report represents a record found in the table. You can sit down with the end user and design the reports interactively by using these reporting tools.

step 5: structuring the application's logical flow

Now that the data structure is in place and the reports have been designed, it's time to move on to the application's logical flow.

note

RULE: Create a logical flow before you begin writing source code.

flowchart – *A combination of symbols and text that provides a visual description of a process*

The application's logical flow details the main functionality of the system and the relationship of the tasks to be completed. You can use a *flowchart* for this task. Although some developers skip this step, it's always a good idea to sketch out or write down how the system should work before you start typing lines of source code.

Some developers like to use formal flowchart diagrams. The example in Figure 13-10 shows how a student might drive to school.

Figure 13-10, Flowchart example

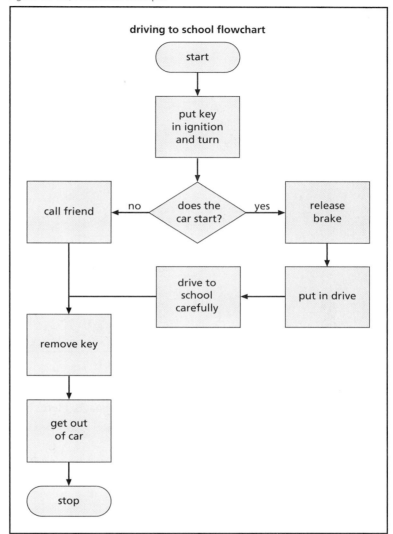

The symbols in the flowchart represent different functions in a program.
Figure 13-11 shows some symbols you might encounter in a flowchart.

Figure 13-11, Flowchart symbols

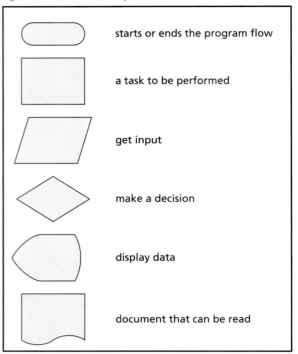

	starts or ends the program flow
	a task to be performed
	get input
	make a decision
	display data
	document that can be read

Some developers use pseudocode, which is a description of the program logic written in human language. Here's some sample pseudocode for the process of starting your car:

```
Start
Put the key in the ignition and turn
If the car does not start, call a friend to take you to
school
Else if the car does start
Release the brake
Put the car in drive
Drive to school carefully
End if
Remove key
Get out of car
Stop
```

You learn more about pseudocode in Chapter 14, "Programming I."

However you do it, you should create some kind of formal definition of how the system is supposed to work before you start typing the source code. Time spent thinking and designing before using the keyboard saves a lot of time later when you have to debug and maintain the program.

step 6: start building the prototype

Because the opening screen is the first thing the end user sees, and it forms the user's first impression of your program, it must reflect the user's goals and the program's main function. Opening screens can be clever, cute, serious, or whatever the end user wants to make the application appealing. A good way to make sure you create appealing screens is to include the end user in the design process. For example, Mr. Bop's music store focuses on disco music, so his opening screen should be representative of his store and the program's major task.

After designing the opening screen, you should take it to the end user for approval. Then it's time to move on to the data input screens. In this case, Mr. Bop wants to be able to update the inventory status, track purchase information, maintain employee information, and set up some form of program security. You also know that he needs a set of routines to manage data in tables.

Asking the end user more questions can reveal possibilities for information you never thought you had to worry about. For example, by continuing to have an open dialogue with the client, you might discover new items that need to be incorporated in your application, such as artists, media produced by each artist, types of media, and so on.

note

RULE: Ask the end user as many questions as possible until you're confident that you have a good understanding of the program's main functionality.

One way to increase your productivity and include the end user in the application's design is to use some sort of form generator to create prototypes of each screen you and the end user have decided to include in the application. Remember: Not one line of code should be written until the user has agreed to the specifications and approved the screen prototypes.

note

RULE: *Don't write any source code until the project specifications are approved!*

As mentioned, a prototype gives end users a good idea of what they'll see when the application is completed. It's *not* the final product, ready to go. It's more of an overview of what screens and reports will look like and what the general flow of the application will be.

Let end users help determine the colors, text, position of fields, and other factors so that they play an important role in determining the application's look and behavior when it's finished. By including end users, you're building their sense of ownership of the product.

n o t e   RULE: Let the user help you design the screens.

The more work end users do, the better the application will be when it's finished. In addition, users will like the application more because they had a major part in developing it.

step 7: putting all the pieces together

Almost all the pieces of the application design have been put together, and it's time to thank end users for their time and head back to your office. Take all the information you have gathered and create the design document. Much of this process is simply putting together the pieces you already have, along with dates, timelines, and price estimates.

n o t e   RULE: Be realistic in defining project completion dates.

Be careful when giving dates and price estimates to make sure they're realistic and feasible. Remember that end users will hold you to dates and figures you give, so you have to take the time to be accurate in your estimating process. End users want that application, and they want it now. If they add more details to the application, simple logic says the date of completion should be extended. End users don't always think that way, however. Although they might say, "Yeah, yeah, we know you'll need more time to complete the project if you add these other details," they often remember only the date on your first estimate.

The design document should contain the following items:

- Header page describing the contents
- Project objective
- Defined terms related to the project
- Feasibility study
- Project specifications and requirements
- Project cost analysis

13

- Data dictionary
- Copies of screens (or prototypes)
- Copies of reports
- Diagrams (UML diagrams and flowcharts of all business processes)
- Plans to test the software after it's written
- Plans to gather user feedback about the application's functionality
- Notes from meetings

You can also include information such as employee bios and company profiles or other material you think is appropriate for readers to understand the key players involved in the application and how the project's objectives will be accomplished.

Don't forget this important part of the design document: a place for end users to sign, indicating they have read the document and accept it as the basis for creating the program. If you have a signature in the design document, you can use it as a contract for work.

Almost always, something changes after the design document is signed. Whether it's a new item the end user wants to include or an item the application designer forgot, the document probably needs to be amended. In this case, you don't need to start over, designing all the screens and placing copies of reports, screens, menus, and tables in a document. Simply create an addendum detailing the new items. The end user should be required to sign an agreement to modify the deadline and your fee, if necessary, because the project scope has changed.

note

RULE: Have end users sign the design document to indicate they agree to the deadline defined by the project scope.

If the application isn't finished by the deadline because the end user has made frequent changes in the project scope, documenting these changes at least protects your reputation (and perhaps your job) in your own company.

avoiding the pitfalls

After looking at the process of software engineering and all the rules involved in creating a design document, you might feel a little hesitant. What if the project fails miserably? What might go wrong, and what can you do to help your projects succeed? The next sections warn you about some common problems and pitfalls and tell you how to avoid them.

userphobia

What if the end user messes up the whole process? One of the biggest mistakes you can make when designing an application is to be "userphobic." Userphobia is the fear that if you include end users in the design process, the application will be a failure.

Some programmers have the attitude that end users have no idea what's needed in creating an application to meet their requirements. Remember that end users are sitting in the driver's seat, however. It's their application. If they don't like yellow text on a blue background, you should change to whatever colors they want. Just make sure you document everything.

Sometimes the user's ideas aren't workable, however. If end users want something in the application that simply can't be done, tell them honestly it isn't possible. Don't get in the habit of saying, "Sure. No problem. I can do anything. I am Zeus, master of the keyboard!" Treat end users as you would any customer. Whether they're outside contacts or in-house employees, they are still considered customers and have all the rights and privileges customers should have.

Remember to keep the lines of communication open with end users. Let them know what's happening. A weekly update informing them of your progress on the application is often a good idea. An informed end user is a happy end user.

note

RULE: Keep the lines of communication open with end users.

too much work

Another problem you might run into is the "heap on the work" syndrome. For example, a manager gives a programmer a project deadline but later gives the programmer more work that has a higher priority than the first project. Of course, the manager specifies that the first deadline can't change. In this situation, the manager is setting the programmer up for failure on both projects. You, as the programmer, need to be assertive and explain to your manager what will happen to the first project's deadline if the second project takes priority. By doing so, you can save yourself a lot of frustration. Again, protect yourself by documenting everything.

scope creep – Occurs when new changes are added to a project constantly, thus changing the proposed deadline so that the project is never completed; instead, it's in a constant improvement mode

scope creep

Another pitfall that can affect whether you meet your deadline is called *scope creep*. It occurs when the end user keeps adding functionality to the application after you have already agreed on the project specifications and requirements, thus changing the deadline. This process of making changes and extending the deadline continues until finally a manager steps in and asks, "Will this project ever be completed?"

To avoid scope creep, one common tactic is using a phased approach. Any changes the user wants that have a major impact on the project's deadline can be put into a second phase. The first phase can continue as planned. After it's finished, tested, and delivered to the end user, you can begin phase two. As the program is being used, the end user might find other problems or issues that need to be addressed. They can also be placed in phase two or, if needed, pushed into phase three.

The main point is that you need to deliver something to the end user on schedule! Let end users start working with the product while you continue to make other changes. In addition, sometimes software engineers add their own unnecessary features to the design, even though the end user hasn't approved the addition. This problem is called *gold plating*.

gold plating – *Adding unnecessary features to the project design*

the project development team

An application can be developed by one developer or a team of developers. Many software development departments support team development because it allows team members to run the IDE on their workstations while storing the necessary tables on a network.

To help you understand how a successful team is built, the next sections outline the players who can be included in the team, their roles, and how they interact with other members of the team and with clients.

project manager

project manager – *Leader of the software development team; responsible for choosing the right players for the right positions and making sure the project is on schedule*

The *project manager* is the team leader and is responsible for choosing the right players for the right positions. The project manager is also responsible for determining the project's risks, costs, and schedule of tasks. In addition, the project manager pulls together all the project pieces and incorporates them into the design document.

Determining risks and costs usually requires experience. Scheduling tasks and keeping up with team member responsibilities are generally done by using project management software, such as Microsoft Project (see Figure 13-12). With this type of tool, managers can track the different tasks that need to be completed, who's assigned to each task, the status of tasks, and the costs associated with each task.

Figure 13-12, Project management software helps a manager keep track of the project's status

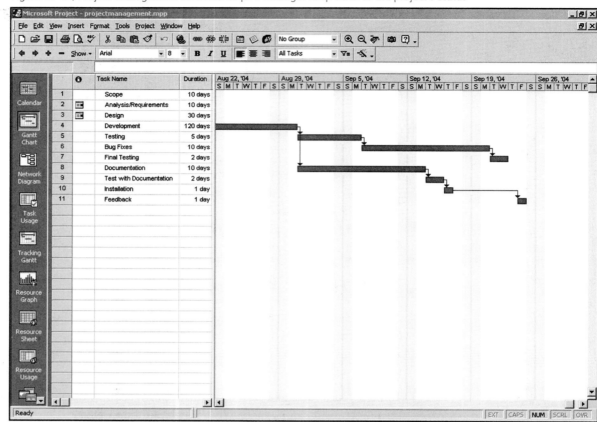

database administrator

The person assigned the role of creating the database is often referred to as the *database administrator (DBA)*. Creating the database involves taking the information from design meetings with end users and creating a data dictionary. As you've learned, a data dictionary serves as a map for the structure of tables. It's created by reviewing the screens and reports the end user wants to include in the application and determining which fields are essential to the application.

***database administrator (DBA)** – Person assigned the role of creating and maintaining the database structure*

note

Have only one person in charge of creating and maintaining databases to reduce confusion and errors.

The DBA's job is not only to create any databases needed by the project, but also to maintain them and manage changes and updates to data stored in the files. If all programmers on the team were allowed to change the database structure, the application would be heading down the path to failure. Too many DBAs in the programming kitchen spoil the application.

software developers (programmers)

Teams include one or more *software developers* (also called *programmers*) who are responsible for writing the source code. Many times, developers are also involved in creating UML diagrams. The developer turns the design document into a tangible product.

Developers use software development tools and logical skills to create programs that meet the project requirements and objectives. The source code they write also incorporates class, use case, and sequence UML diagrams.

client (end user)

The client or end user is the driving force behind the project, the one who has a need that can be met by the project development team. The client can be internal (works for the same company as the software developers) or external (doesn't work for the company creating the program).

Clients usually know what they want but often don't know how to explain it to developers. Similarly, developers usually know how to meet the client's needs but often don't know how to communicate the process to the client.

n o t e

> Clients know what they want. Your job as the software developer is to help them communicate their needs and translate those needs into a software development project.

tester

Every program has to be tested. An untested program is a program that's doomed to fail. Many companies have a quality assurance (QA) department responsible for turning out good products. The development team is responsible for testing its program before it's turned over to the QA team. The QA team then puts the program through a series of tests and reports the results to the software developers, who fix the problems, test the program again, and deliver it to the QA team for another round of testing.

The role of *tester* is one of the most critical roles in application development. Not only should developers test the application as it's being written, but at least one or two people, including the end user, should be designated as testers. Too often a product is written and presented to end users without being tested thoroughly. This oversight results in wasted time and lowers users' confidence

no bugs?

No application is bug free. You should tell this to end users when the application is being created, delivered, and tested. Be happy when end users find bugs. Thank them for letting you know, fix the problem fast, and hope that the bug is the last one you encounter!

in the application (and its developers). If an application has too many bugs, end users will stop using it and seek a different means of accomplishing the job. This could mean reverting to the previous way of handling day-to-day operations or finding another developer for the application. Either way, insufficient testing can blemish your reputation for reliability and jeopardize your career.

Here are a few pointers on testing:

- Make sure you run the application through a series of tests that mimic the end user's environment, including monitors, CPUs, printers, and other hardware.
- Make sure programmers have developed the application to handle any situation that might come up. Some developers insist that end users would never try to do something a certain way because it just isn't logical. If anyone can break the application, end users can, so put yourself in their place and try to test situations that aren't always logical.
- Keep a log of errors encountered during testing and after the application's release. Record the date the error occurred, a description of the error, the procedure you think created the bug, what was done or needs to be done to fix the problem, and who is responsible for handling the error.

Some day, you might end up in the following situation. An end user calls the developer and in a panicked voice says, "I just had a problem while I was using the application!" The developer chokes down the question "Why me?" and asks the end user to explain the process that resulted in the error and describe the error information that appeared on the screen. It's now the end user who chokes down the question "Why me?" and informs the developer that the information wasn't kept. A wave of relief passes over the developer as the popular technical support response "Call me if it happens again" echoes through the phone receiver. The developer hangs up the phone, exclaiming "Whew! Dodged that bullet!" This situation occurs every day. As a developer, you shouldn't be afraid of errors. Instead, be thankful the end user has found them and is willing to help you solve the problem.

customer relations representative

customer relations repre-sentative (or support technician) – Person responsible for interacting with testers, developers, and end users during the product's creation and early release and on an ongoing basis with end users as long as the product is being used

The *customer relations representative* (or *support technician*) is the interface between testers, developers, and end users during the product's creation and early release. After the early release stage, you might want to create a help desk to handle calls about using the application or errors users have encountered.

generator of installation media

After the application is completed, tested, and debugged, it's time to create the media (usually CDs or DVDs) to install on the end user's machine. This task is not a full-time job, so the customer relations person might be able to handle it. This role requires interacting with developers to make sure all necessary files are included. Many IDEs include a utility for creating installation media, which makes the task easier.

n o t e   Make sure to scan for viruses before copying files to any installation media!

installer of the application

It's show time! After the installation media have been created, it's time to install the program on the end user's machine. Customer relations representatives should also take on the role of installer because they already have a good relationship with end users. After the installation process, the installer should stay with end users while they test-drive the application. Take them on a guided tour of the application, showing all the bells and whistles the application has to offer.

n o t e   Train end users well so that they can train other end users.

If end users don't feel comfortable using the application, you might need to schedule additional training sessions. After one user in a department is trained, that user can train other users in his or her own department.

one last thought

Good design results in good programs. If you skip some steps in creating an application or cut corners, you'll probably see the results in poor performance, unmet client needs, or a project that runs over budget and over schedule. The project manager's main responsibilities are to build a team that can work well together and to keep the project on schedule and within budget. By making sure the project follows all the steps outlined in the design document and goes through a thorough testing cycle, the team can ensure that the program meets the client's needs.

chapter summary

- Software engineering involves many different steps to create an application that meets an end user's needs.

- The process of building an application is accomplished by following a software development life cycle (SDLC) model.

- Each SDLC model provides a different way of outlining the steps for creating a software product.

- A design document is created as a blueprint for software development and outlines an application's functionality.

- Several steps should be followed when creating a design document: researching end users' needs; communication; logical design of screens, reports, and data structures; and all other steps that must take place before any source code is written.

- Unified Modeling Language (UML) is a tool that enables developers and end users to illustrate an application's functionality.

- There are several types of UML diagrams, each serving a particular purpose or describing a part of the project being developed.

- Using reports and a data dictionary can help a developer find any oversights in the project's design.

- Software development is often a team effort; building a team involves knowing the specific roles of each member.

- Team members often include a project manager, database administrator, developers/programmers, clients/end users, testers, and customer relations representatives.

- After the application has been developed, installation media must be generated.

- After the application is installed on the client's system, spend some time training end users, who can in turn train other end users.

key terms

customer relations representative (or support technician) (*456*)

data dictionary (*443*)

database administrator (DBA) (*454*)

design document (*436*)

end user (*434*)

flowchart (*446*)

gold plating (*453*)

project manager (*453*)

13

test yourself

1. Describe what the process of software engineering includes.

2. What is a design document, and how does it affect software engineering?

3. Write the pseudocode steps for a program that processes a savings deposit in an ATM.

4. Write the pseudocode steps for a program that processes a savings withdrawal from an ATM.

5. How can UML help a developer create a program that meets an end user's needs?

6. How is a data dictionary used in software development?

7. What is a prototype, and how is it used in software engineering?

8. What are some mistakes you can make in designing and developing a software program?

9. Describe the steps in the waterfall SDLC model.

10. List each software development team role and describe the job function.

11. Draw a flowchart for using a microwave to heat a TV dinner for 2 minutes.

12. Write the pseudocode for using a microwave to heat a TV dinner for 2 minutes.

13. Draw a flowchart for making a purchase on the Internet.

14. Write the pseudocode for making a purchase on the Internet.

15. Draw a flowchart and write the pseudocode for an application that allows a professor to keep track of the following information for each student: 10 homework assignments, 4 quiz scores, and 2 test scores. The application should calculate the average grade for each type of information (homework, quizzes, and tests), and then calculate a final grade by averaging all three average scores.

practice exercises

1. End users need to be told what they want and how the program should work.

   a. True
   b. False

2. Which is *not* included as a task of software engineering?

   a. Communicating with clients in meetings
   b. Designing screens
   c. Writing the application
   d. Creating a design document
   e. None of the above

3. A design document is used as:

   a. A way to bill the client more
   b. A blueprint that shows an application's functionality
   c. A replacement for pseudocode when writing a program
   d. None of the above

4. Which is *not* part of the SDLC?

   a. Project feasibility
   b. Software design
   c. Software implementation
   d. Software proposal to client
   e. All of the above

5. Which is *not* a valid software development model?

   a. Waterfall
   b. Degradation
   c. Evolution
   d. Spiral
   e. Incremental

6. UML was designed to:

   a. Assist developers in creating visual models of the application's functionality
   b. Assist developers in designing screens and reports
   c. Incorporate object-oriented design into application development
   d. Replace the outdated notion of pseudocode

7. The best way to write a good program is to have an initial meeting with the end user to find out the requirements for the project, go back to your office and write the program, and then deliver the finished product for installation.

   a. True
   b. False

8. The document responsible for describing the type of data stored in the database is called the:

   a. Design document
   b. Data dictionary
   c. UML diagram
   d. SDLC
   e. None of the above

9. Including end users during the entire design process is recommended. In fact, you can even let them help design screens and reports.

   a. True
   b. False

10. A _____ is used as a visual model for describing a program's logical steps.

    a. Flowchart
    b. Class diagram
    c. Use case diagram
    d. Design document
    e. None of the above

11. A _____ is a standard or typical example of how something might work, but without all the built-in functionality.

    a. Flowchart
    b. Prototype
    c. Design document
    d. Data dictionary
    e. None of the above

12. Which should *not* be included in the design document?

    a. Project objectives and requirements
    b. Cost analysis
    c. Feasibility study
    d. Copies of screens and reports
    e. None of the above

13. Scope creep is good for a project because it's one of the software development life cycles.

    a. True
    b. False

14. If end users or testers find a bug in the application, you should find out why they insist on breaking the program and get them some training so that they will stop making it crash.

    a. True
    b. False

15. The tester's role is not as critical as other team roles and should be the first role eliminated if the project is behind the scheduled completion date.

    a. True
    b. False

discussion topics

1. Which member of the project development team has the most important role and why?

2. Which software engineering step do you consider the most important and why?

3. Do you think UML is a viable way of doing software engineering, and will more software development departments adopt it? Why or why not?

4. What do you think the biggest challenge is in software engineering?

5. The biggest problem with creating a design document is the time spent in determining the client's needs, researching, and organizing. How can you convince your employer or client to pay for the time spent in creating a good design document, even if it means delaying the project's completion date?

digging deeper

1. Research and describe the SDLC processes covered in this chapter.

2. What are some project management software packages on the market? Give a brief description of each product along with the vendor and cost.

3. What are some software packages on the market for generating reports? Give a brief description of each product along with the vendor and cost.

4. What are some software packages on the market for flowcharting? Give a brief description of each product along with the vendor and cost.

5. Why do you think it's so important to get the end user to sign the design document agreeing that the design meets the project's requirements? What would you do if the requirements changed after the document had been signed?

Internet research

1. What are the number of available jobs and the average salary in your state or province for software engineers?

2. What are the number of available jobs and the average salary in your state or province for developers with UML skills?

3. Find three free UML software packages and list links to their Web sites.

4. Find three Web sites with material on teaching software engineering skills, and summarize the material on these sites.

5. What are some newer software development models currently being discussed?

programming I

- Learn what a program is and how it's developed
- Understand the difference between a low-level and high-level language
- Be introduced to low-level languages, using assembly language as an example
- Learn about program structure, including algorithms and pseudocode
- Learn about variables and how they're used
- Explore the control structures used in programming
- Understand the terms used in object-oriented programming

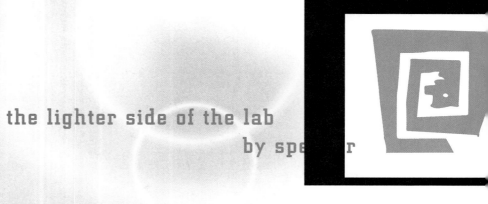

the lighter side of the lab
by spencer

I wrote my first program when I was 12 years old. My dad showed me how to fire up Basic in DOS, and I followed along with an example in a book. After just three or four hours, I had a program that asked "What is your name?" The user could then enter a name such as "Spencer," and the program displayed "Hi, Spencer!" Needless to say, I gave up programming for a number of years.

Then one day, my dad offered to pay me actual money to program some reports for him. If I hadn't had the brain of a teenager at the time, I might have been smart enough to realize there must be a reason my dad didn't want to program the reports himself. Having the brain of a teenager, however, I probably thought he wanted me to do it because he couldn't figure it out himself.

I spent the next few weeks converting between inches and twips to program the correct x and y coordinates where the report text should print. I suppose there are more tedious jobs in the world, such as searching for a grain of salt in a bag of sugar. After this experience, I might have hung up my programming hat completely if it weren't for the encouraging words from a caring father—and the massive paycheck.

I started reading how-to books on programming and taking lessons from my dad. Soon I was promoted from programming reports to working on a program's actual functionality. I've been programming ever since. Those who have never programmed can't comprehend the feelings that accompany compiling a program you wrote with your own two hands for the first time—and getting 162 compile error messages. It brings tears to my eyes just thinking about it.

Then you start the debugging process. You and your coworkers laugh at the level of stupidity that must have gone into the errors you made. One by one, you fix each error. And then one day, it happens: You compile the program, and no error messages appear. You recompile it because you think the computer must have made a mistake. When you still get no error messages, you jump up and down like a 5-year-old on Christmas morning. (This process is usually followed by your hard drive crashing and the realization that you forgot to make a backup.)

In spite of it all, programming is actually a great job. There's nothing like the sense of satisfaction in seeing someone using a program and realizing "Hey, I wrote that!" In fact, if you're interested in some programming work, give me a call—I've got some reports that need to be programmed.

why you need to know about...
programming

You've probably heard the story about the foolish man and the wise man who wanted to build houses. The wise man built his house on rock, and the foolish man built his house on sand. When the rain came, the house built on sand washed away, but the house built on rock was intact because it was built on a firm foundation.

The moral of this story applies to programming, too. Programs are used constantly, even in places you might not have thought of, such as cars, space shuttles, ATMs, and even microwaves. If these programs weren't built on a firm foundation of structured logic, your microwave would burn your food, the space shuttle wouldn't launch, the ATM would give your money away to other people, and your car would sit in the driveway gathering dust. Being a programmer involves responsibility: You're responsible for developing a quality product that might possibly mean the difference between saving or destroying lives. Would you want to fly in a plane if the navigation system's programmer hadn't structured the program on a firm foundation of quality principles?

Learning solid programming practices is essential to your future computing career and to the people who will benefit from the programs you produce. Building a strong foundation requires learning the basic language constructs and knowing how to use them when writing a program. If you can learn how to write structured, logical programs that other software developers can read and understand, you can become an asset to any organization. Good programming skills are acquired through diligent practice as well as a lot of trial and error. You can think of it as learning a foreign language: You can learn all the basics of a language, but if you don't practice using it, you'll never speak it fluently. Learning a programming language means practice, practice, and even more practice!

what is a program?

program – *A collection of statements or steps that solves a problem and needs to be converted into a language the computer understands to perform tasks*

algorithm – *A logically ordered set of statements used to solve a problem*

So many programs are used every day that trying to list them all would be mind-boggling. Focusing on what a program is and what it can do is much easier. A *program* is simply a collection of statements or steps that solves a problem and needs to be converted into a language the computer understands to perform tasks. These statements are usually written in a language that's understood by humans but not computers. They're entered as a logical ordered set (also called an *algorithm*). For the computer to execute the algorithm, the statements must be converted into a language the computer understands by using an interpreter or a compiler.

n o t e

The only language the computer understands is binary, consisting of 1s and 0s.

interpreter – *An application that converts each program statement into a language the computer understands*

compiler – *An application that reads all the program's statements, converts them into computer language, and produces an executable file that doesn't need an interpreter*

An *interpreter* is a separate application needed for a program to run. Its purpose is to translate the program's statements, one by one, into a language the computer can understand. A *compiler*, on the other hand, reads all the program's statements and converts them into computer language. The result is an executable file that doesn't need an interpreter.

Programs are developed to help people perform tasks, so programmers should communicate with users of a program to make sure the program meets their needs. A program might perform calculations, gather information, or process information and display the results. Programs are used to make vehicles run efficiently, operate an appliance, or even map out directions for your next family vacation. They're used everywhere, and people rely on them functioning correctly.

When a program doesn't perform accurately, there can be two possible causes: A piece of logical functionality was left out of the program, or the program has one or more statements containing logical errors. A program that doesn't have full functionality or doesn't have the functionality users need can be corrected by following software-engineering practices, such as getting input from users who requested the program. Think of writing a program as putting together all the pieces of a puzzle. To put all the pieces in the right spots, you need to know what pieces are available and understand how they fit with other pieces.

Putting programs together was discussed in Chapter 13, "Software Engineering."

eastern roots

The word "algorithm" came from Mohammed ibn-Musa al-Khwarizmi (c. AD 780 to 850), a mathematician and a member of the Baghdad royal court. His book later introduced algebra to the West.

I speak computer

The first step in programming is to determine what language you want to use to communicate with the computer. As stated, computers speak only one language—binary. All programming languages end up in binary, so you can focus on choosing a programming language that suits your preferences and the task the program should accomplish.

Choosing a programming language can be like trying to choose an ice cream flavor. There are so many to choose from, and all of them can satisfy your need for ice cream. Here are a few of the programming flavors you can choose:

- Ada
- Assembly
- C, C++, and C#
- COBOL
- FORTRAN
- Delphi (Pascal)
- Java and JavaScript
- Lisp
- Perl
- Smalltalk
- Visual Basic

No single language is considered the best. Each has its own strengths and weaknesses. For example, when you're trying to determine which language is best for the task, you might consider the following:

- Assembly language works well when you want to control hardware.
- COBOL was first used in business applications and continues to be popular in business.
- FORTRAN is geared toward engineering and scientific projects.
- Java and JavaScript are well suited for Internet applications.
- Lisp is well known for working with artificial intelligence.
- Pascal was created to teach people how to write programs.
- Smalltalk was created to assist developers in creating programs that mimic human thinking.
- Visual Basic was developed to provide a simple yet powerful GUI programming environment.

Lady Ada

The Ada programming language was named after Ada Byron (1815–1852), daughter of the poet Lord Byron. She was a mathematician and is considered the first programmer. She wrote to Charles Babbage about his Analytical Engine and suggested ideas for an engine that could calculate Bernoulli numbers.

The following are examples from a simple program that displays "Computer Scientists Are Wired!" in a variety of languages.

Ada:

```
with TEXT_IO; use TEXT_IO;
procedure Wired is
    pragma MAIN;
begin
    PUT ("Computer Scientists Are Wired!");
end Wired;
```

Assembly language:

```
mov ah,13h
mov dx,0C00H
mov cx,30
mov al,00
mov bh,00
mov bl,1fH
mov ah,13H
lea bp,[Msg]
int 10H
int 20H
Msg: db 'Computer Scientists Are Wired!'
EXE_End
```

C:

```
#include <stdio.h>
main()
{
    printf("Computer Scientists Are Wired!\n");
}
```

note

Dennis Ritchie developed C in the early 1970s for UNIX while working at AT&T Bell Labs. Its predecessor, B, was based on the BCPL language.

C++:

```
#include <iostream>
int main(int argc, char *argv[])
{
    cout << "Computer Scientists Are Wired!\n";
}
```

n o t e   C++ was written by Bjarne Stroustrup at Bell Labs in 1983 and is an extension of C.

COBOL:

```
000100 IDENTIFICATION DIVISION.
000200 PROGRAM-ID. WIRED.
000300* DATE-WRITTEN. 12/15/10 16:09.
000400* AUTHOR GREG ANDERSON
000500 ENVIRONMENT DIVISION.
000600 CONFIGURATION SECTION.
000700 SOURCE-COMPUTER. RM-COBOL.
000800 OBJECT-COMPUTER. RM-COBOL.
000900
001000 DATA DIVISION.
001100 FILE SECTION.
001200
100000 PROCEDURE DIVISION.
100100
100200 MAIN-LOGIC SECTION.
100300 BEGIN.
100400 DISPLAY "Computer Scientists Are Wired!" LINE 12
       POSITION 25.
100500 STOP RUN.
100600 MAIN-LOGIC-EXIT.
100700 EXIT.
```

n o t e   COBOL, an acronym for Common Business-Oriented Language, was developed in 1959 by a group called the Conference on Data Systems Languages (CODASYL).

Delphi (Pascal):

```
Program Hello (Input, Output);
Begin
    Writeln ('Computer Scientists Are Wired!');
End.
```

n o t e   Delphi is object-oriented Turbo Pascal and was released by Borland Software, Inc., in 1995. Pascal was developed in the early 1970s by Niklaus Wirth to provide more structure in programming and as a method for learning the concepts of programming.

FORTRAN:

```
PROGRAM WIRED
PRINT *,'Computer Scientists Are Wired!'
STOP
END
```

n o t e   A team of programmers at IBM, led by John Backus, developed FORTRAN (an acronym for FORmula TRANslation) in 1957.

Java:

```
class Wired {
    public static void main (String args[]) {
      System.out.print("Computer Scientists Are Wired!");
    }
}
```

n o t e   Java evolved from the Oak language, developed in 1995 at Sun Microsystems. It was created as a platform-independent language.

Lisp:

```
;;; Common LISP
(defun wired ()
    (print "Computer Scientists Are Wired!")
)
```

n o t e   List Processing Language (Lisp) was based on John McCarthy's work at IBM. It was created to support artificial intelligence and released in the mid-1960s.

Smalltalk:

```
Transcript show:'Computer Scientists Are Wired!';cr
```

n o t e

Smalltalk, an object-oriented programming language, was developed at Xerox PARC by Alan Kay, Dan Ingalls, Ted Kaehler, Adele Goldberg, and others during the 1970s.

Before you decide which programming language you prefer, you need to research them a little more. First, you should decide whether a low-level or high-level programming language is right for you. A *low-level language* gives instructions to a CPU or piece of hardware in binary code understood by computers, but not by humans. The lowest-level language is *machine language*, in which instructions are encoded as binary bit patterns. In fact, the only instructions a computer ever carries out are in machine language.

An *assembly language* program is one step up from machine language, in that it assigns letter codes to each machine-language instruction. A program called an *assembler* reads assembly-language code and translates it into machine language. A *high-level language* is more user friendly because it uses a more natural language that humans can understand. High-level languages, such as C++ or Java, require a compiler or an interpreter to translate the code into machine language. High-level languages can also be used on many different types of computers, making them more platform independent. Figure 14-1 shows how these different types of programming languages are grouped.

Figure 14-1, Different types of programming languages

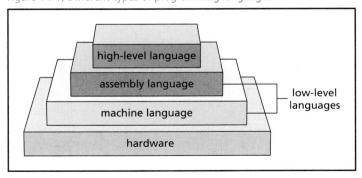

low-level language – A programming language that uses binary code for instructions

machine language – The lowest-level programming language, which consists of binary bit patterns

assembly language – A programming language that's one step up from machine language; it assigns letter codes to each machine-language instruction

assembler – A program that reads assembly-language code and converts it into machine language

high-level language – A programming language written in a more natural language that humans can read and understand

The following sections give you a taste of how a low-level language works, using assembly language as an example, and then you're introduced to how high-level languages work. In Chapter 15, you delve into high-level languages more by looking at Java and C++ examples. An introduction to every programming language would take an entire library full of books! As a computing

go for a drive

Many of these languages offer free or trial versions you can take for a test drive. Make sure you do before you make a commitment.

professional, you'll likely work with many different languages and discover for yourself what "flavor" you prefer.

low-level languages

Machine language uses only binary numbers, so few people code in this language. However, speaking in binary on a date might help you find your true love! This chapter doesn't go into detail on how machine language works, but you learn about assembly language, which simulates machine language but is written with more English-like statements. As with machine language, each assembly-language statement corresponds to one machine instruction. Assembly language produces programs that are usually smaller and run faster than programs in higher-level languages. It's a powerful language, and almost anything you can do on a computer can be written in this language, which isn't always the case with other languages. Assembly language is closely tied to the CPU type, and assemblers have been written for every type of CPU.

n o t e

The 808x architecture of early Intel processors is used to illustrate assemblers in this chapter because it's fairly simple.

assembly-language statements

In Chapter 3, you learned about the registers in a CPU, which are special memory locations for storing information programs can use. The registers AX, BX, CX, and DX are called general-purpose registers (GPRs) and are used mainly for arithmetic operations or accessing an element in an array. The 808x architecture also has special-purpose registers: pointer registers, segment registers, and a flags register.

Assembly language consists of text instructions that are converted one by one into machine (binary) instructions. Take a look at the following example. As you read the assembly code, you might think it seems cryptic. A disadvantage of assembly language is that it can be hard to read and understand.

```
;NASM-IDE ASM Assistant Assembler Project File
[BITS 16]  ;Set code generation to 16-bit mode
%include 'exebin.mac'
EXE_Begin
[ORG 100H]  ;Set addressing to begin at 100H
cls:  mov ah,06
      mov cx,0000
      mov dx,184fH
      mov al,00
```

```
            mov bh,1fH
            int 10H
            mov dx,0C22H
            lea bp,[Hi]
            mov cx,12
    wst:    mov al,00
            mov bh,00
            mov bl,1fH
            mov ah,13H
            int 10H
            cmp dh,0Ch
            jnz stop
            inc dh
            lea bp,[Bye]
            mov cx,8
            jmp wst
    stop:   int 20H
    Data:
    Hi:  db 'How Are You?'
    Bye:  db 'Goodbye!'
    EXE_End
```

syntax – Rules for how a programming language's statements must be constructed

Clear as mud? After you understand the *syntax* of a language, however, it doesn't seem as cryptic. By learning assembly language, you reap the rewards of fast executing code and the power to do anything you want in a computer system. Another problem with using assembly language is that it takes a lot of programming to accomplish very little. Also, the assembler for a particular CPU can be used only on that CPU, and assemblers for different CPUs have very different syntax.

In assembly language, each programming statement, or instruction, performs a task. The following sections explain some of these instructions.

mov

The mov instruction moves values around. For example, the following statement tells the assembler to move the value of 8 into the CX register:

```
mov cx, 8
```

get on your case

Some assemblers are case sensitive, meaning that a lowercase "a" is different from an uppercase "A." For example, the word "wst" isn't recognized as being the same as "WST." You need to know whether your assembler is case sensitive.

n o t e   Assembly statements are read from right to left.

You can move a value from memory to a register, from a register to memory, or from register to register. For example, the following statement tells the assembler to move the value stored in the CX register to the DX register:

```
mov dx, cx
```

This statement doesn't delete the value stored in CX. The CX register still has the value 8, but now the DX register has the value 8, too. So the mov statement actually copies values instead of moving them.

add

The add instruction takes a value on the right and adds it to the value on the left. In the following example, the first statement moves the value 3 into the CX register. The second statement moves the value 8 into the DX register. The last statement adds the value in the CX register (3) to the value in the DX register (8), resulting in the value 11 being stored in the DX register.

```
mov cx, 3
mov dx, 8
add dx, cx
```

inc

The inc instruction adds 1 to the register being used. The following statement takes the value in the DX register, which is currently 11 after the previous add instruction, and increases (increments) it by 1:

```
inc dx
```

The DX register then contains the value 12.

sub

The sub instruction tells the assembler to subtract one number from another number. In the following example, the first statement moves the value 4 into the CX register, and the second statement moves the value 7 into the DX register. The last statement subtracts the value in the CX register (4) from the value in the DX register (7) and places the result (3) in the DX register.

```
mov cx, 4
mov dx, 7
sub dx, cx
```

After these three statements execute, the CX register still contains the value 4, but the DX register contains the value 3 (in other words, DX = DX - CX).

cmp

The cmp instruction tells the assembler to compare two values. It works like a sub instruction but doesn't store the result in a register. Instead, the result is used to set flag bits in the flags (FL) register. If the result of the compare equals 0, the zero (ZR) flag is set to a binary 1, and the sign (SF) flag is set to 0 (meaning a positive number). If the result of the compare is a negative number, the ZR flag bit is set to a binary 0, and the SF flag is set to 1 (meaning a negative number).

In the following example, the first statement moves the value 4 into the CX register. The second statement moves the value 7 into the DX register. The last statement compares the value of the DX register with the value of the CX register.

```
mov cx, 4
mov dx, 7
cmp dx, cx
```

If DX - CX = 0, the ZR flag is set to 1. You can then use this comparison to determine whether to jump to a different location in the program with a conditional instruction, such as jnz.

jnz

The jnz instruction tests the value of the ZR flag maintained by the system. If it's set to 1, it tells the system to jump somewhere else in the program, much like a "go to" statement in other programming languages. If it isn't set, the assembler continues to process the code on the next line. The following example shows the jnz instruction added to the previous example:

```
mov cx, 4
mov dx, 7
cmp dx, cx
jnz stop
```

The jnz instruction checks the ZR flag that might have been set during the cmp instruction. If the flag is set to 1, it tells the system that the cmp instruction evaluated to 0 and it should jump or pass control to a section in the program labeled "stop." If the ZR flag is set to 0, it means the cmp instruction didn't evaluate to 0 when the two registers were compared.

Are you a master assembly programmer yet? Don't worry. Learning a new language takes practice, and low-level languages are harder to understand and learn because they're oriented more toward hardware than human speech. Now that you have seen how a low-level language works, it's time to get an overview of high-level languages.

high-level languages

With high-level programming languages, you can write programs that aren't as dependent on the type of computer or CPU, and the statements are easier to write, read, and maintain than with low-level languages. Also, you can accomplish much more with a single statement in high-level languages than in low-level languages. Unlike assembly languages, there's not a one-to-one relationship between a statement and a binary instruction. However, high-level language programs generally run slower because they must be compiled or interpreted. Some popular high-level languages were included in the list earlier in this chapter, such as Java, C++, Delphi, and C#.

Over the years, these languages have developed and become more powerful yet maintained the capability to promote productivity and flexibility. Many of these languages (as well as some assemblers) incorporate some form of *integrated development environment (IDE)*. An IDE provides several tools that programmers can use to write program code more easily. Figure 14-2 shows an example of Visual Studio .NET, a Microsoft IDE.

integrated development environment (IDE) – An interface provided with software development languages that incorporates all the tools needed to write, compile, and distribute programs; these tools often include an editor, a compiler, a graphical designer, and more

Figure 14-2, An IDE makes software development easier

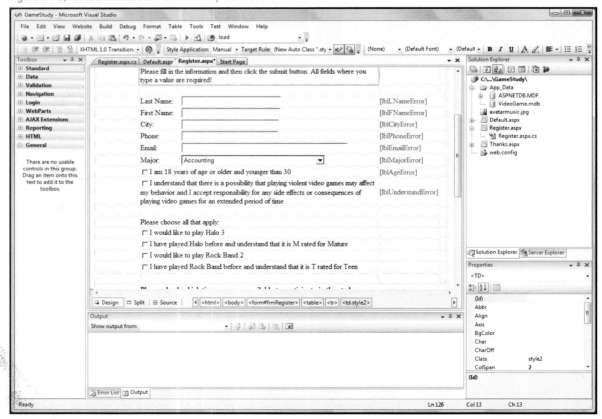

structure of a program

Before you begin to write a program in any programming language, you need to know how the program should work and how the language syntax should be incorporated. As you learned earlier, the syntax is a formal definition of how statements must be constructed in the programming language. As with any language, you have to learn not only the vocabulary, but also the rules for using the vocabulary.

When you learn a foreign language, you must start at the beginning—the alphabet, numbers, simple phrases—and then move on to grammatical rules and conjugating verbs. You can apply this same process to learning a programming language. Before you use a programming language's syntax, however, you need to understand how a program is structured. As discussed in the following sections, a program's structure is based on algorithms, and it's often represented with pseudocode.

algorithms

With any kind of problem, you have to figure out what method you're going to use to solve it. For example, if you're trying to get an A in an introductory computer science course, you need to follow a plan that might include attending lectures, taking notes, reading the chapters, doing the assignments, and studying for quizzes and exams.

You can break down each task in your plan into smaller subtasks. For example, for the task of taking notes, a subtask might be making sure you have paper and pencils. Another subtask might be learning some abbreviations for the topics in the course so that you can take notes faster and more efficiently.

For many tasks, you can plan a series of logical steps to accomplish them. Algorithms boil down to thinking logically about the solution to a problem. In programming, an algorithm consists of steps you need to follow to solve the problem. To convert an algorithm into programming statements, you need to represent the steps in some format. Programmers often use pseudocode, discussed next, for this purpose.

pseudocode

Pseudocode is a detailed yet readable description in human language that describes an algorithm so that it can be converted into programming statements. The description is in a human-understandable format but follows the steps of a program. Pseudocode can be considered a template for what needs to be converted into programming language syntax.

---

that (inter)face is familiar

Companies that develop programming language packages are working to create standard interfaces to their languages. For example, Microsoft Visual Studio .NET incorporates an IDE that allows software engineers to write statements in C++, Visual Basic (VB), or C# in the .NET environment, using the same IDE interface for all three languages. This feature saves time and money because developers have to learn only one software development tool.

pseudocode – A readable description of an algorithm written in human language

14

For example, the following pseudocode describes the algorithm for entering a student's grades and calculating the final average:

```
FIND/ADD STUDENT:
Search for a student
If the student is not found, add student
Display the student information
INPUT GRADES:
Prompt the user to select which grade to enter
(assignment, quiz, or test)
Accept the input and store it in the database
Prompt the user to see whether more grades need to be
entered
If so, return to the first prompt asking for a grade
Continue this process until there are no more grades to
be entered for the student
CALCULATE FINAL GRADE:
Calculate the final grade
     First calculate the assignment average
     Apply the appropriate weighting
     Calculate the quiz average
     Apply the appropriate weighting
     Calculate the test average
     Apply the appropriate weighting
     Add up all the weighted averages
     Compare the result with the grading scale
     Print the student's final average
     Store the average and letter grade in the database
```

This example shows how breaking the task into smaller subtasks makes it easier to define the steps needed for solving the problem. There are no formal rules for writing pseudocode, but you need to consider whether the information you're providing is enough to explain the process to someone who has no experience with solving this type of problem.

How do you learn how to write pseudocode and think logically? Again, the answer is practice. Many professors require students to write pseudocode before they start entering programming statements, but it's not because they love to assign busywork (even though you might suspect they do). It's because they know students need practice in thinking logically and putting problem-solving steps in writing before they start programming.

Here's another example of how to start defining an algorithm with pseudocode. Suppose you want to write a program to convert the temperature in degrees Celsius to degrees Fahrenheit or vice versa. (Figure 14-3 is a chart you can use as a reference for checking that the program calculates conversions accurately.)

In this case, as with many programming problems, you need to determine what formulas to use in your algorithms.

Figure 14-3, A temperature conversion chart

Celsius	Fahrenheit
0 C	32.0 F
1 C	33.8 F
2 C	35.6 F
3 C	37.4 F
4 C	39.2 F
5 C	41.0 F
6 C	42.8 F
7 C	44.6 F
8 C	46.4 F
9 C	48.2 F
10 C	50.0 F
11 C	51.8 F
12 C	53.6 F
13 C	55.4 F
14 C	57.2 F
15 C	59.0 F
16 C	60.8 F
17 C	62.6 F
18 C	64.4 F
19 C	66.2 F
20 C	68.0 F
21 C	69.8 F
22 C	71.6 F
23 C	73.4 F
24 C	75.2 F
25 C	77.0 F
26 C	78.8 F
27 C	80.6 F
28 C	82.4 F
29 C	84.2 F
30 C	86.0 F

note

Make sure any formulas you use in an algorithm are accurate! Any mistakes could make the program useless and possibly even disastrous.

Start with the formulas needed in the algorithm:

- Fahrenheit to Celsius: Celsius temp = (5/9) * (Fahrenheit temp - 32)
- Celsius to Fahrenheit: Fahrenheit temp = ((9/5) * Celsius temp) + 32

After the formulas have been proved correct, you can begin outlining the steps to write a program that gets input from the user, calculates the conversions, and then displays the results to the user. Here's the pseudocode you can use to solve this problem:

```
Menu:
     Do you want to perform a conversion?
     If Yes then
     Which conversion do you want to perform?
            If Celsius to Fahrenheit then
            Go to the Fahrenheit section
            If Fahrenheit to Celsius then
            Go to the Celsius section
     Else If No then
     Exit the program
Celsius:
     Ask the user for a temperature in Fahrenheit
     Apply the formula Celsius temp = (5/9) * (Fahrenheit
temp - 32) to the entered temperature
     Display the result, saying Fahrenheit temp ##
converted to Celsius is XX
     Return to the Menu section
Fahrenheit:
     Ask the user for a temperature in Celsius
     Apply the formula Fahrenheit temp = ((9/5) * Celsius
temp) + 32 to the entered temperature
     Display the result, saying Celsius temp ## converted
to Fahrenheit is XX
     Return to the Menu section
```

By the time you have completed the pseudocode, the program is basically written in a human-understandable language.

choosing the algorithm

You can often perform a task in many different ways, but one way is usually more effective than others. Your job as the programmer is to determine which algorithm is best for the project. For example, you want to go to Disney World during spring break and are trying to determine the best way to get there. What are some algorithms you could use for solving this problem? You can always fly, with the advantage of arriving in a short time but the disadvantage of a high cost. You can drive, with the advantage of a lower cost but the disadvantages of more time and wear and tear on your car. You can hitchhike, with the advantage of an even lower cost but the disadvantages of more time and safety risks. You can walk, with the advantage of a low cost but the disadvantage of a very long time (and sore feet).

Each algorithm for getting to Disney World solves the problem, and each has advantages and disadvantages. The critical issue is selecting the algorithm that works best for your purposes.

n o t e   The selection of an algorithm can be based on a multitude of deciding factors. Spending time investigating all the options before you begin creating the algorithm is wise.

testing the algorithm

Before you get too excited and start typing your program code (called "source code"), you should test the algorithm and pseudocode you have written. For this task, pretending you're an end user who isn't knowledgeable about the program helps you write a program that's easier to use. For the previous program, the user might not know anything about temperature conversions, for example. Putting yourself in the user's shoes also helps you predict possible mistakes users might make.

n o t e   Make sure you write your pseudocode and test the algorithm before you begin writing the source code.

Look at the part of the algorithm that takes the temperature value the user enters. It makes a big assumption—that the user enters a numeric value. What if the user enters a letter instead? There could be trouble right here in pseudocode city! Maybe the pseudocode needs to be altered as follows to confirm that the user has entered a valid numerical value:

```
Celsius:
    Ask the user for a temperature in Fahrenheit
    If the value entered is numerical
    Apply the formula Celsius temp = (5/9) * (Fahrenheit
temp - 32) to the entered temperature
    Display the result, saying Fahrenheit temp ##
converted to Celsius is XX
    Else
    Display a message stating that the value entered is
NOT allowed
    Return to the Menu section
```

```
Fahrenheit:
     Ask the user for a temperature in Celsius
     If the value entered is numerical
     Apply the formula Fahrenheit temp = ((9/5) * Celsius
temp) + 32 to the entered temperature
     Display the result, saying Celsius temp ## converted
to Fahrenheit is XX
     Else
     Display a message stating that the value entered is
NOT allowed
     Return to the Menu section
```

You can take this pseudocode one step further. Instead of having the Celsius and Fahrenheit routines display an error message, you can add a new section that handles any errors that occur. If an error occurs, you send control of the program to this new section. After the error message has been displayed and the program has handled the error, program control returns to where it left off, as shown in the following example:

```
Celsius:
     Ask the user for a temperature in Fahrenheit
     If the value entered is numerical
     Apply the formula Celsius temp = (5/9) * (Fahrenheit
temp - 32) to the entered temperature
     Display the result, saying Fahrenheit temp ##
converted to Celsius is XX
     Else
     Go to Error
     Return to the Menu section
Fahrenheit:
     Ask the user for a temperature in Celsius
     If the value entered is numerical
     Apply the formula Fahrenheit temp = ((9/5) * Celsius
temp) + 32 to the entered temperature
     Display the result, saying Celsius temp ## converted
to Fahrenheit is XX
     Else
     Go to Error
     Return to the Menu section
Error:
     Display a message stating that the value entered is
NOT allowed
     Return to the Celsius or Fahrenheit section,
depending on which section was in use
```

Testing the algorithm and expecting the worst to happen can help ensure that you create well-formed pseudocode from correct logic.

syntax of a programming language

After defining an algorithm and testing the logic thoroughly, you can begin translating the algorithm into statements in a specific programming language. Writing a program can be compared with following a recipe (the algorithm and pseudocode) to combine all the ingredients in the correct order so that you produce a culinary masterpiece (a program). A programming language consists of many different ingredients that can be used to create your application, and as the "chef," you need to know what ingredients are available and how they should be combined. Some of the ingredients you can use are the following:

- Variables
- Operators
- Control structures
- Objects

Using these ingredients allows you to build a program, but you need to know why and when to use them. Otherwise, it's like throwing a random bunch of ingredients from your refrigerator into a pot and hoping you cook something edible.

variables

Remember the old saying "Different strokes for different folks"? It's true for programming, too, as there's no one way to write a program. Even though programmers differ in style or preference, however, they all use variables.

A *variable* is a name used to identify a certain location in the computer's memory. Some programmers use variables to hold running totals; others might use variables to keep track of a company name. The type of program determines what types of variables need to be created, modified, and maintained. It's possible to write a program that doesn't use variables, but you'll probably use variables in all your programs.

When the variable is defined, the type of data that can be stored in that memory location is specified. By using the variable name, you can access the memory location's contents and use its value in your program. A variable name is simply an easy way to access computer memory without having to know the actual hardware address.

For example, you're trying to change the oil in your car. You need to find the oil plug, so you pull out your handy-dandy engine diagram. It doesn't have descriptive labels for each item, however; instead, it shows part numbers. You see two items that might be plugs, so you guess which one is the oil plug and

variable – *A name used to identify a certain location and value in the computer's memory*

14

dive under the engine. As you remove the plug and the fluid begins draining, you notice that instead of the usual dirty black color your oil is, it's purple. What started off being an oil change has unexpectedly turned into a transmission fluid replacement because the plugs in the diagram had numbers instead of names. If you think of the plugs as variables, you can see why using a variable's name (instead of its hardware address) prevents the problem of accessing the wrong memory location and using a value that doesn't apply to the programming situation. For this reason, in a high-level language, the variable name is also called an *identifier*.

identifier – Name of a variable

identifiers and naming conventions

The identifier is used to access the memory contents associated with a variable. When deciding on an identifier, be sure to use a name that describes the data being stored. For instance, if you're storing a person's salary, a variable labeled "x" isn't descriptive. It does nothing to help others understand or maintain the program. Some companies don't have variable-naming standards, so their programmers have free rein in choosing whatever variable names they want. One company's data-processing staff thought using variable names such as Fred, Wilma, and Barney was funny, but it caused some problems when they had to debug and maintain the programs.

n o t e

When choosing a name, you should also make sure it's not being used by an instruction in the programming language, which causes an error when you try to run the program.

You can use more than one word for a variable's identifier, if you like. One standard (created by Sun Microsystems, the inventor of Java) suggests making the first character of the first word lowercase and the first character of subsequent words uppercase, as in `numCookiesBought`.

If you follow the Sun standard, it's better not to use an underscore for the first character, although doing so isn't illegal. One-character names, such as "k," shouldn't be used except for variables in which you simply discard the value. Overall, giving your variables meaningful names is best.

n o t e

For ease of reading, many programmers separate words with an underscore (_), as in `num_Cookies_Bought`.

operators

In many high-level languages, *operators* are used to manipulate the data stored in variables. Operators are classified by data type. One operator might work with numbers, and another operator might be designed to work with characters.

math operators

The mathematical operators are addition (+), subtraction (-), multiplication (*), division (/), and modulus (%). The % (modulus) operator returns the remainder when performing division. There are also shortcuts you can use for math operators, listed in Table 14-1.

Table 14-1, Standard mathematical operators

operator	description
+	addition
−	subtraction
/	division
%	modulus or remainder
*	multiplication
+=	addition and then assignment
−=	subtraction and then assignment
*=	multiplication and then assignment
/=	division and then assignment
%=	modulus and then assignment

increment and decrement operators

Two of the most common programming instructions you use are incrementing and decrementing values in variables. Many languages have increment and decrement operators that perform this task so that you don't have to write the entire statement. For example, the ++ operator adds 1 to the value of a variable (called "incrementing"). The -- operator, or decrement, subtracts 1 from the value of a variable.

In the following example, the increment operator takes the value stored in the iCount variable (5), adds 1 to it, and stores the value 6 in the iResult variable:

```
iCount = 5
iResult = ++iCount
```

The decrement operator takes the value stored in the `iCount` variable (5), subtracts 1 from it, and stores the value 4 in the `iResult` variable:

```
iCount = 5
iResult = --iCount
```

There are two types of increment and decrement operators: pre and post. The pre operator places the `++` or `--` symbol before the variable name. Having the operator in front of the variable name informs the system that the increment or decrement should be the first thing to happen in that line of source code:

- Preincrement: `++variable`
- Predecrement: `--variable`

The post operator places the `++` or `--` symbol after the variable name. Having the operator after the variable name informs the system that the increment or decrement should be the last thing to happen in that line of source code:

- Postincrement: `variable++`
- Postdecrement: `variable--`

To see how these operators work, take a look at this preincrement example:

```
iCount = 5
iResult = 0
iResult = ++iCount
```

In this example, the variables are initialized (meaning values are assigned to them), and then the variable `iCount` is incremented to the value 6, which is assigned to the variable `iResult`. Here's another example of the pre operator:

```
iCount = 5
iResult = 0
iResult = ++iCount + 10
```

In this example, after the variables are initialized, the variable `iCount` is preincremented to 6 (because the pre operator is used), which is then added to 10 and stored in `iResult` (16).

Now look at this postincrement example:

```
iCount = 5
iResult = 0
iResult = iCount++ + 10
```

Because the post operator is used, first the addition between the variable `iCount` with the value 5 and the number 10 takes place. This sum of 15 is then stored in the variable `iResult`. After everything else on the line is completed, the postincrement of the variable `iCount` occurs, changing it to the value 6.

"pre" is rude

Remember that "pre" contains the letter "r," which stands for "rude"—meaning it always goes first. No matter where the pre operator is located in the code line, it's processed first, ahead of anything else in the line.

"post" is polite

Remember that "post" contains the letters "po," which stand for "polite"—meaning it always lets everything else in the code line go first. No matter where the post operator is located in the code line, it's processed last.

relational operators

The main purpose of relational operators is to compare values. The standard relational operators are listed in Table 14-2.

Table 14-2, Standard relational operators

operator	meaning
!=	not equal to
<	less than
>	greater than
<=	less than or equal to
>=	greater than or equal to
==	equals

To understand these operators, look at this example of variable declarations and initializations:

```
iFirstNum = 15
iSecondNum = 10
```

iFirstNum > iSecondNum results in a true.

iFirstNum < iSecondNum results in a false.

iFirstNum != iSecondNum results in a true.

After making these comparisons, or relations, you can use the result to determine what other action you want to take in the program.

logical operators

The main function of logical operators is to build a truth table when comparing expressions. An *expression* is simply a programming statement that returns a value when it's executed. Expressions usually use relational operators to compare variable contents or values. Table 14-3 shows the standard logical operators.

You learned about truth tables in Chapter 3, "Computer Architecture."

no strings attached

The == operator is a comparison operator, but it should never be used to compare one string (a group of characters) with another. If you use the == operator on strings, it compares whether one string points to the same memory location as another string. Instead, use the equals() method with any variable you have declared as a string, as in this example:

```
String sFirst = "Math";

String sSecond =
         "Physics";

Results:

sFirst.equals(sSecond)
         results in a false.
```

expression – A statement containing a combination of values that's interpreted and computed to produce another value

Table 14-3, Standard logical operators

operator	meaning
!	not
&&	and
||	or

Table 14-4 shows how logical operators might be used in a program, given the following variables:

```
iFirstNum = 15
iSecondNum = 10
iThirdNum = 20
iFourthNum = 15
```

Note that these expressions use Boolean variables, which means the expression can be evaluated to a true or false value. Boolean values are used with logical operators to determine what action to carry out. For example, if there's a potato chip in the bag (true), you'll eat the chip; if there's no potato chip in the bag (false), you won't eat anything.

Table 14-4, Boolean expressions

expression	value	explanation
(iFirstNum >= iSecondNum) && (iThirdNum >= iFourthNum)	T and T equals T	(15 >= 10) and (20 >= 15)
(iFirstNum <= iSecondNum) && (iThirdNum >= iFourthNum)	F and T equals F	(15 <= 10) and (20 >= 15)
(iFirstNum == iSecondNum) && (iThirdNum == iFourthNum)	F and F equals F	(15 == 10) and (20 == 15)
(iFirstNum != iSecondNum) && (iThirdNum != iFourthNum)	T and T equals T	(15 != 10) and (20 != 15)
(iFirstNum >= iSecondNum) || (iThirdNum >= iFourthNum)	T or T equals T	(15 >= 10) or (20 >= 15)
(iFirstNum <= iSecondNum) || (iThirdNum >= iFourthNum)	F or T equals T	(15 <= 10) or (20 >= 15)

Table 14-4, Boolean expressions *(continued)*

expression	value	explanation
`(iFirstNum == iSecondNum) ||` `(iThirdNum == iFourthNum)`	F or F equals F	(15 == 10) or (20 == 15)
`(iFirstNum != iSecondNum) ||` `(iThirdNum != iFourthNum)`	T or T equals T	(15 != 10) or (20 != 15)

precedence and operators

The order in which operators appear can determine the output. For instance, the following line outputs 14, not 20:

```
2 + 3 * 4
```

Even though it seems that 2 + 3 (equals 5) times 4 results in 20, the answer is really 3 * 4 (equals 12) + 2, which is 14. Why? Because operators have a *precedence*, or level of hierarchy. In other words, certain operations are performed before other operations. In this case, multiplication takes precedence and is performed before addition. Figure 14-4 shows the order of precedence of operators, with the highest (first performed) at the top of the pyramid.

precedence – *The order in which something is executed; symbols with a higher precedence are executed before those with a lower precedence*

Figure 14-4, Order of relational and mathematical precedence

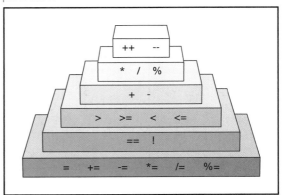

n o t e   Remember that parentheses have the highest precedence, so anything inside them is evaluated before any other operator.

Using the order of precedence, see whether you understand the output in the following examples:

(2 + 3) * 4 outputs 20

2 - 5 * 2 outputs -8

control structures and program flow

All high-level languages use a variety of control structures. A *control structure* is an element that dictates a program's flow and enforces modular structured programming.

If you don't follow structured programming practices, your programs can end up looking like "spaghetti code," that is, source code that breaks the program's modular structure and flow (see Figure 14-5). The name "spaghetti code" is used because finding the beginning and ending of a spaghetti noodle in a bowl is almost impossible. Instead of following a controlled flow of execution, "spaghetti" program flow leaps from one area to another and is extremely hard to follow. In fact, trying to maintain spaghetti code is like trying to empty a bathtub full of water with a sieve.

one bite at a time

Modular structured programming divides a programming project into smaller, more manageable pieces so that the program is easier to design, maintain, and debug. Remember the old saying: "How do you eat an elephant? One bite at a time." If you try to digest the whole thing in one sitting, you'll be unsuccessful.

Figure 14-5, Spaghetti code makes your program harder to maintain and debug

In high-level programming languages, four types of control structures are used:

- Invocation
- Top down
- Selection
- Repetition

Each control structure performs a specific task in a program, and control structures work together and can be nested within other control structures. If used correctly, these control structures provide the tools for creating a program with a logical flow of execution. Even with all the tools available, programmers can still ignore control flow and write a flawed program.

You learn more about these control structures in Chapter 15, "Programming II."

invocation

Invocation is the act of calling something. For example, you might decide that certain tasks in your program could be reused in another program. Obviously, you'd rather not rewrite this code from scratch in other programs. In this case, you can copy the code for a specific task (called "functionality") to a file and name it descriptively. When you write a new program, you can "call" (invoke) this piece of code without having to rewrite it, which saves time and money in program development. After this piece of code has been used, control can be passed back to the original program location to continue.

top down (also called sequence)

The top-down control structure is used when program statements are executed in a series, from the top line to the bottom line one at a time. So the first statement to be executed is the first line in the program. Each statement is executed in sequential order, starting with the first line and continuing until the last line is processed. This control structure is the most common, found in every programming language.

The top-down control structure is implemented by entering statements that don't call other pieces of code, as with invocation. Instead, they simply execute the current line and proceed to the next line. The other control structures do something to change the flow of this basic top-down structure, such as directing program flow to another block of code or location in the program, and generally provide a way to return control back to the top-down structure.

selection

Up to now, you have learned that statements can be executed in sequential order, and you can execute statements kept in other locations in the application by using invocation. Sometimes, however, you need the program to make a choice (selection) depending on a value or situation.

Making and evaluating selections in a program is a standard part of most programs you'll write. In the following example, if an employee's job level is equal to "Manager," the salary increase is equal to the salary times .08. If the job level isn't equal to "Manager," use a .03 salary factor. The program has to determine what the job level is and then carry out code based on that job level.

```
Salary Increase:
If Job Level = "Manager" then
     salary = salary * 1.08
else
     salary = salary * 1.03
```

Remember the algorithm for converting Fahrenheit and Celsius temperatures? This algorithm also involves selection: If the user selects Celsius, one thing happens; if the user selects Fahrenheit, something else happens:

```
Convert to Celsius:
     Ask the user for a temperature in Fahrenheit
     If the value entered is numerical
     Apply the formula Celsius temp = (5/9) * (Fahrenheit
temp - 32) to the entered temperature
     Display the result, saying Fahrenheit temp ##
converted to Celsius is XX
Convert to Fahrenheit:
     Ask the user for a temperature in Celsius
     If the value entered is numerical
     Apply the formula Fahrenheit temp = ((9/5) * Celsius
temp) + 32 to the entered temperature
     Display the result, saying Celsius temp ## converted
to Fahrenheit is XX
```

repetition (looping)

The last control structure, repetition, is used when source code is to be repeated. It's often referred to as "looping" and is commonly used with databases or when you want an action to be performed one or many times. The standard repetition constructs are the `for`, `while`, and `do-while` statements.

When you want to repeat a series of statements a known number of times, you use the `for` statement. The `while` statement can also be used to process a series of statements a certain number of times. The `do-while` statement is used mainly when processing a table or if you want the loop to execute at least one time. The `for` and `while` loops might not even execute, depending on the condition expression in the loop.

ready, set, go!

Now that you've learned some building blocks—variables, operators, and control structures—you're probably wondering what the next steps are to start programming. In this section, Java is used to show examples of programming code because it's a widely used language and is fairly easy to learn. First, you need the Java software package. There are many different vendors of Java, but Sun Microsystems offers a free version, and you can download Java and the Java

Developer's Toolkit at *www.sun.com*. This toolkit gives you all the tools you need to compile and run Java programs.

After you have downloaded and installed Java, the next step is choosing an editor, the interface used for entering code. Some Java packages include an IDE containing a program editor, compiler, debugger, and many more tools. You don't need all these tools to learn how to write Java programs, although they do make application development easier and faster.

Java programs can be written in any text editor, including Windows Notepad. Just make sure you save your program with the .java file extension. After entering the program in a text file, you can compile it from the command prompt with the `javac` command, like this:

```
javac MyProg1.java
```

This command compiles the MyProg1.java program and determines whether there are any syntax errors. If there are errors, open your text file, fix the problems, save the changes, and recompile.

After the compile works, you're ready to try out your program. To run a Java program, you use the `java` command:

```
java MyProg1
```

Before you start writing and compiling code, however, continue reading to learn more about the fundamentals of how Java and other object-oriented languages work.

object-oriented programming

object-oriented programming (OOP) – *A style of programming that involves representing items, things, and people as objects instead of basing program logic on actions*

Now that you have the skills for writing simple pseudocode for programs, you can learn about the concepts behind *object-oriented programming (OOP)*. In object-oriented programming, an object isn't simply a noun (person, place, or thing); it includes the qualities of an object, what it does, and how it responds or interacts with other objects. Objects in OOP can have three distinct features: characteristics, work, and responses. As an example, say you have an alarm clock, called the Alarm object. The Alarm object, as with any object in OOP, has the following features (see Figure 14-6):

- *Characteristics*—The Alarm object has different characteristics or attributes, such as color, wake time, current time, selected radio station, and so on.
- *Work*—The Alarm object performs some work, such as displaying the current time and ringing annoyingly when you'd rather sleep.
- *Responses*—The Alarm object responds to certain events. When your wake-up time is reached, the alarm goes off, or when you hit the snooze button, the alarm "sleeps" for another five minutes.

Figure 14-6, An object has characteristics, work, and responses

Object: Alarm

Characteristics:
- Color
- Current time
- Wake time
- Station tuned to
- ...etc

Work:
- Display current time
- Play radio station
- ...etc

Responses:
- When alarm time reached, play alarm
- When Snooze button pressed, delay alarm for 5 minutes
- ...etc

learning about objects

The best way to learn what objects are available is to read the online help included with many software packages or search the Internet for tutorials.

Most high-level languages, including Java, support object-oriented programming. Each object in Java incorporates the three features described earlier. For example, the string data type you learned about is actually an object, one of many in Java.

OOP can be defined as being able to represent part of the program as a self-contained object. The hardest parts of learning OOP are taking the time to create objects and use them in your application and trying to determine what needs to be an object and what can remain as simple source code.

The main advantages of using an OOP language are reusability and maintainability. If a certain item can be used in many programs, writing the supporting code again for every new program wastes time. For example, you wrote the source code to represent a person as an object, and it worked well when you included it in a program. Later, you had to write another program, but you had to be more specific and represent a student instead of a generalized person. Because you know the source code for a person works, and a person's characteristics are very similar to those of a student, you just need to add items that are specific to a student, such as GPA, grade level, and schedule. Because the person object was reused, you were able to decrease the amount of time writing source code.

Maintaining source code is also easier with OOP because programs can be divided into smaller, more manageable pieces. Say you want to modify how a student logs in to a system. Without OOP, you would have to track down every location in the source code where a student could log in and change the code in each location. By representing items as objects, you have to change the source code in only one location. The object handles the rest because the code is contained in the object.

how OOP works

To understand the principles of object-oriented programming, imagine you work for a toy company, and your division is responsible for creating action figures. This week, you're supposed to create a kung-fu action figure. The company could give you and every employee in the division a piece of plastic and tell everyone to carve the figure, but management would have to price the figure absurdly high to ensure that it still makes a profit, after paying all the employees. What if you make a mistake and have to get another piece of plastic? What a waste of time and money! The company won't stay in business very long with this approach. For the company to be profitable, it needs to create a mold (called a class or template in object-oriented terminology) so that the figure can be mass-produced economically and efficiently.

making the mold

The mold for action figures is probably just a skeleton or the basic outline of a finished product. It won't have all the characteristics (attributes) of a kung-fu fighter, for example. The mold just describes the basic type of figure you're going to create: two arms, a head, two legs, a certain height, and so on. In other words, the mold defines the figure's attributes.

creating the figure

To create the action figure, you must pour plastic into the mold. You might use different colors of plastic in different parts of the mold to create attributes such as hair color and eye color. The plastic is then formed to the shape of the mold. It might not be completely functional, but it has the general appearance of the figure you're creating. In other words, the mold defines what the plastic will be.

putting the figure to work

In addition to having attributes, the figure can perform some work or action. For instance, it can stand, the arms and legs can move, the head can turn, and so on. The figure's work and how it responds to certain actions are defined by the type of mold you used. For instance, because you used the kung-fu mold to create the figure, when you pull the arm back and release it, the arm shoots forward with a powerful karate chop. In other words, the figure responds to the event of pulling the arm back with a specific action.

class – A template for defining new object types and their properties (characteristics or attributes) and behaviors

object – A self-contained entity consisting of both data and procedures

instantiation – The process of creating an object based on a class and assigning memory to it

constructor – A special method for instantiating an object

property or attribute – Characteristic of an object

method – The work performed by an object; a function defined in a class

event – An action or occurrence recognized by a class

event handler – How a class responds to an event

Now that you have seen how the process of creating an action figure can be compared with creating an object, you can carry the analogy a little further to learn more about OOP terminology (see Figure 14-7):

- The mold or template for creating the figure is called a *class*. It defines the figure's characteristics, work, and responses.
- The figure is called an *object*. It's created based on the mold, or class.
- The creation process is called *instantiation*. Instantiation is simply creating an object and assigning it memory resources. The method used to instantiate an object in a class is called a *constructor*.
- A characteristic of the figure is called a *property* or an *attribute*. It defines what the object looks like.
- The work performed by an object is called a *method*. It performs a task and is linked to a class.
- An object's response to some action taken by the end user or system is called an *event* or *event handler*.

Figure 14-7, Making a plastic figure shows OOP concepts in action

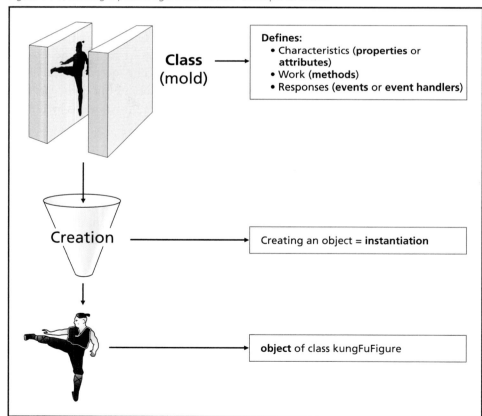

All these items describe the basic functioning of OOP. Your job, as the programmer, is deciding what items in the program need to be represented by an object and what can be represented by standard source code. The items you want to represent by an object are those the system might require and those you know will be reused in other programs.

After an object is created by using a class, it has access to all the properties, methods, and events defined for the object type. To access information for an object, use the object name, followed by a period and the qualifier. For example, the following Java code can be used to access an object containing a character string and the equals() method:

```java
String sFirstName = "Joe";
String sLastName = "Blow";
if (sFirstName.equals(sLastName))
    System.out.println("The last name equals the first
    name. Strange!");
```

The call to equals() represents calling a method in the String class.

As another example, here's the parseDouble() method (part of the Double class) that was used in the temperature conversion program:

```java
String sInput = "98.6";
double dFahrenheit = 0.0;
dFahrenheit = Double.parseDouble(sInput);
```

inheritance

Take a moment to think about who you look like. If you look like your father or mother, it's because you inherited traits from your parents. Similarly, in programming, "child" objects can inherit properties, methods, and events from "parent" objects. This process is called *inheritance*.

inheritance – The process of creating more specific classes based on generic classes

In programming, inheritance is the creation of an object from a parent class. A newly created object receives everything (properties, methods, and events) from the parent class that isn't declared as private, and it can add other capabilities the parent doesn't have. As shown in Figure 14-8, inheritance promotes code reusability. If the base class (the Person class, in the figure) has already been created and tested, whenever you need a new class with similar characteristics, work, and responses as in the Person class, you have a head start in creating your new class.

Figure 14-8, Inheritance promotes code reusability

Figure 14-8, Inheritance promotes code reusability

base (or parent) class – A general class from which other classes can be created via inheritance

subclass – A more specific class based on a parent class and created via inheritance

The general class is called the *base class* or *parent class*. The more specific classes created through inheritance are called *subclasses* and inherit everything the parent class has.

Some inherited classes that can be based on a `Person` class might include `Student`, `Employee`, `Manager`, `Salesperson`, and `Customer`. The real power of inheritance comes from creating a general class and then making it more specific to meet your needs. In this way, most of the work is already done, and you're simply reusing source code with slight modifications.

Calling a method is a chain reaction. Suppose your neighbor asks you to mow his lawn, but you don't know how to mow a lawn. If the lawn isn't mowed, your neighbor is going to be disappointed. What are you going to do? You might go to your parents and explain the situation. If your parents know how to mow a lawn, they explain it, and the lawn gets mowed. If your parents don't know how to mow a lawn, they go to their parents (and so on).

This example describes the process of calling methods. If a method is called from within a subclass and the subclass doesn't contain it, it's passed up the chain to the parent and continues until the method is located and executed or an error is generated.

What's nice about object-oriented languages is that you don't have to be concerned with what's been inherited from which class because the help documentation makes it seem as though all the information found in a class was written for that class, even though much of the information was received through inheritance. Do you care that a class has inherited a property instead of the property being written from scratch? Suppose you inherited a million dollars and want to put it in the bank. Is the bank manager going to say "Wait a minute! Is this inherited money? Get out of here! We don't take inherited money!" In reality, the bank manager will probably say "Welcome! What can I get you? Would you like a toaster to take home?"

One of the biggest questions is "Why do you want to subclass?" You subclass an object when it doesn't do everything you want it to do, but you know you'll reuse it in other situations. Think of it this way: You've been asked to clean your room, but you don't want to spend a lot of time cleaning. As a matter of fact, you'd rather have somebody else do the work. You call your mom for help, but she makes the bed differently than you do: She pulls the sheets and bedspread over the pillow and then tucks them under. So what do you do? You let Mom make the bed her way, and then you come in and pull the sheets and bedspread off the pillow. In other words, you're able to use most of the "parent class" of cleaning your room, with one modification to how the bed is made—the "subclass." In a programming example, you might subclass a Close button from the parent class, `Button`. This way, you just have to make minor changes in the button's attributes or behavior instead of re-creating all the code for the `Button` class from scratch.

encapsulation

encapsulation – The process of hiding an object's operations from other objects

Another advantage of OOP is that you don't need to know how everything works to use it because of *encapsulation*, which is the process of one object hiding its operations from other objects. For example, your monitor hides its operations from the CPU. If something happens to the monitor, you fix it or replace it. You don't have to do anything to the CPU. Similarly, when you want to print a document, do you really think about packets of data being sent to the printer, or do you just want the document to print? Encapsulation hides the details and does the work. Encapsulation also helps cut down on the chance of errors occurring because programmers can't make changes to the parts of an object's source code that are hidden.

polymorphism

polymorphism – An object's capability to use the same expression to denote different operations

To promote reusability and flexibility, OOP supports using the same expression to denote different operations, a capability called *polymorphism*. For example, a program has objects representing a word-processed document, a report, and an e-mail. Each object can be printed. If you click the Print menu item, the object's contents should be sent to the printer and printed. Polymorphism states that even though the objects are different, all can use the print operation. Each object has the capability to make a call to an operation, and the system determines at runtime how the operation is performed. Another example of polymorphism relates to geometric shapes. If you have objects representing squares, triangles, and circles and want to send them to the output device and display them, you should be able to call a draw operation for any of these objects.

You can use many different classes, methods, and events in Java programming, and you'll become more familiar with them if you take the time to practice a lot.

Java and OOP

Java follows the OOP model closely. Everything in Java revolves around classes, properties, and methods. The sooner you start using OOP in Java, the sooner you know the available classes and can reduce the number of code lines you have to write because you'll be able to reuse objects.

choosing a programming language

Now you can revisit the earlier question about which programming language to use. Java has been used in many of this chapter's examples, but as you've learned, each language has advantages and disadvantages. Take the time to choose carefully. Before you dive headfirst into the high-level programming language waters, check for rocks! Try demo versions of different languages and see whether you like what they have to offer. Talk to others who have experience with a certain language and ask about its pros and cons. You should also consider these other factors:

- *Functionality*—Does the language allow you to do everything you want to do (such as creating database and Web applications)?
- *Vendor stability*—Is the company backing the language financially stable? Will the language be around for the long haul?
- *Popularity*—How many books on the language do you see at the bookstore? Having many books available usually means the language is popular and has a lot of support.
- *Job market*—How many and what types of jobs are related to the language you want to use?
- *Price*—How much does the language's software package cost?
- *Ease of learning*—How long does it take to learn the language before you're a productive developer?
- *Performance*—Will programs created with the language have suitable response times and processing times?

Never choose a language simply because someone else says it's good. Choosing a language is like choosing a car: You have to test-drive a lot of them before you know which one you like. Compare a language with your criteria to make sure it fits your needs. Keep in mind, too, that you shouldn't get complacent after you choose a language and think you'll never have to learn another one. The world of programming changes constantly, and unless you continue increasing your skills and learning new technology, your skills will become outdated quickly.

one last thought

A program does whatever you tell it to do. You can write a program that plays your favorite music or calculates how much money you need to pay your bills, for example. In most cases, if the program doesn't work correctly, it's the fault of the programmer, not the computer. In programming, the key word is responsibility. As a programmer, you can create new programs to help society, but you can also write a program with serious negative ramifications, such as allowing a breach in security. This chapter is just a stepping stone to learning how to program. The ball's in your court now. If you want to become a good programmer, have patience and practice, practice, and practice!

chapter summary

- A program is only as good as the programmer who wrote it.
- Programs are used everywhere and in almost everything you do.
- A program can be interpreted or compiled.
- Low-level languages are more closely related to the machine language a computer understands. Assembly language is a low-level programming language.
- High-level languages are more closely related to human language.
- Algorithms are created to solve problems with a logical method.
- Programmers use pseudocode to map out how a program is supposed to work.
- Creating an algorithm is one of the most important steps in writing a program.
- Variables are temporary storage locations and are used in programs for performing calculations and storing information.
- Programming languages use mathematical, relational, and logical operators.
- Four types of control structures are used in a program: top down, invocation, selection, and repetition.
- Object-oriented programming (OOP) allows programmers to reuse code and makes programs easier to maintain.
- OOP creates classes, which are like templates or molds for creating objects.
- Objects can have properties, methods, and event handlers.
- Java follows the OOP model closely.
- To become a good programmer, you must practice, practice, and practice some more.

key terms

algorithm (*468*)

assembler (*473*)

assembly language (*473*)

base (or parent) class (*500*)

class (*498*)

compiler (*468*)

constructor (*498*)

control structure (*492*)

encapsulation (*501*)

event (*498*)

event handler (*498*)

expression (*489*)

high-level language (*473*)

identifier (*486*)

inheritance (*499*)

instantiation (*498*)

test yourself

1. What is an algorithm?
2. Write an algorithm for calculating your checkbook balance.
3. Write the pseudocode for a program that can calculate your checkbook balance.
4. Write an algorithm for operating a gas pump when filling up a car.
5. Write the pseudocode for a program that maintains a gas pump's operation.
6. Write an algorithm for calculating your final grade, based on information in your course syllabus.
7. Write the pseudocode for a program that calculates your final grade, based on your course syllabus.
8. Write the pseudocode describing how to play tic-tac-toe.
9. Write the pseudocode describing how you get to school.
10. Write the pseudocode describing how you complete a 3 × 3 sudoku puzzle.

practice exercises

14

1. Which is *not* an example of a high-level programming language?

   a. Ada
   b. Boolean
   c. C++
   d. Java

2. Which of the following converts source code into a computer language and results in an executable file?

   a. Compiler
   b. Interpreter
   c. IDE
   d. Algorithm

3. Which of the following translates a program's statements, one by one, into a language the computer can understand?

   a. Compiler
   b. Interpreter
   c. IDE
   d. Algorithm

4. Pseudocode should be written after the source code to ensure that the program was written correctly.

   a. True
   b. False

5. Which is *not* a type of programming language?

   a. Low-level
   b. Assembly
   c. High-level
   d. Machine
   e. None of the above

6. The only language computers can understand consists of 1s and 0s.

   a. True
   b. False

7. All languages include an integrated development environment (IDE).

   a. True
   b. False

8. What is a name used to identify a specific location and value in memory?

   a. Variable
   b. Operator
   c. Control structure
   d. Object

9. What is the final result of the expression 5 + 2 * 4 - 2?

   a. 26
   b. 11
   c. 9
   d. 0
   e. Can't be determined

10. What is the final result of the expression 5 % 4 + 3 - 2?

    a. 2
    b. 6
    c. 1
    d. 0
    e. Can't be determined

11. The postincrement operator increments the variable and then processes the remainder of the statement.

    a. True
    b. False

12. The preincrement operator increments the variable and then processes the remainder of the statement.

    a. True
    b. False

13. Which is *not* a type of control structure?

    a. Invocation
    b. Top down
    c. Algorithm
    d. Selection
    e. Repetition

digging deeper

1. What language is considered the most complex to learn? Why?

2. What integrated development environments can be used for Java?

3. What integrated development environments can be used for C++?

4. What is the specialty of each high-level language listed in this chapter?

5. What is a disadvantage of each high-level language listed in this chapter?

discussion topics

1. What are the advantages and disadvantages of OOP languages?

2. Find a business in your area, or a department at your school, that hasn't switched to using an object-oriented language, and ask about the reasons for not making this change.

3. How could a programming language be made easier to use? What would the language look like? Why hasn't someone already developed a language like it?

4. What is the future of COBOL? Is there a need for programmers to learn this language? Why or why not?

5. What are some common tasks that require thinking in terms of an algorithm?

Internet research

1. What are some famous banking errors caused by bugs in programs?

2. Search the Internet or ask software developers to find out whether learning object-oriented programming is worth the effort. Why or why not?

3. Does a programming language ever really "die"? If so, which languages are no longer used? What process do software developments follow when the languages they're using become obsolete?

4. What are some suggested standards for pseudocode? If you could create your own standard, what would it be?

5. Research the term "embedded software." Describe what this term means, and explain what programming languages are used for it.

15

programming II

- Gain an understanding of the basics of high-level programming languages, using Java and C++ as examples
- Learn about variable types in Java and C++ and how they're used
- Explore the different control structures in Java and C++

the lighter side of the lab
by spencer

Many years ago, my dad shared some words of wisdom with me: "Son, a good computer programmer is lazy." (Coincidentally, it was the same day I decided I wanted to make a living as a computer programmer.) He makes a good point. Here's an example to describe what I'm talking about:

Recently, I came home to discover that my dad had spent many hours on his latest "home improvement" project. He had screwed a hook into the frame of the back patio door, and then screwed in two or three hooks along the top of the door. He tied some fishing line to the hook in the frame, ran the line through the hooks on the door, and then tied some weights on the other end. Like you, I wondered what this contraption did—until I noticed our dog approaching the door, which had been left ajar, from the backyard. He pushed the door open with his nose, and I watched as the weights pulled the line to shut the door neatly behind him. I realized we would no longer have to get up from the couch and trek the 10 feet to shut the door after the dog came in. (Needless to say, my dad is an excellent programmer!)

My dad's point was that good computer programmers are willing to spend massive amounts of time and effort to automate a process so that they won't ever have to do that task again. Obviously, he was being a little facetious; programming is actually hard work.

For example, I once spent two weeks debugging one simple error. I was creating an install disk, and every time I got to a certain point in the installation process during testing, I got an error. I tried everything I could think of to fix it. I burned about 100 test install CDs. I went through the installation code line by line, retraced my steps, and modified every setting I could find. I paced the room and beat my head on the keyboard out of frustration.

After literally 80 hours of debugging, about the time I was considering changing my major to psychology, it occurred to me that the error might not be in the installation wizard but in my code. (Hard to believe, I know.) After about 30 seconds of looking at my code, I found the error. To "save time," I had copied and pasted a section of code from one part of my program to another. Unfortunately, the variable I was using was named "gsDPath" in one part and "DPath" in the other, and the install program didn't recognize it. (Laziness did *not* work out so well in this case.)

Now that you have a little programming under your belt, you'll understand these next statements:

```
if (two_Letter_Error == two_Weeks_Worth_of_Work)
{
    pink_slip;
}
else
{
    you_did_not_let_your_boss_know_about_the_error;
    //This is the option I took.
}
```

Well, I'd better get back to work on my latest project. I call it the Automatic Lighter Side Writer.

why you need to know about...
programming languages

During the Depression, a family struggling to survive wanted to provide opportunities for their children to develop their talents. The father often skipped meals and took on extra jobs to pay for his daughter's piano lessons. Despite these sacrifices, he wanted to give his daughter the opportunity because he knew how much music meant to her.

Time went by, and the daughter married and had a family of her own. Her father was visiting one day and noticed a piano in her house. He had fond memories of her practicing daily, so he asked her to play him a song. Embarrassed, she said she hadn't played for a long time, but he persuaded her to play. As she stumbled through the song, she noticed her father becoming more emotional. She was touched, thinking that she and her father were sharing a special moment. By the time she finished the song, her father was sobbing. She turned to him and said, "I hope you liked that, Dad." He replied, through tears, "I can't believe it. All that money down the drain!"

Students invest a lot of time, money, and effort learning computer programming languages. However, the only real way to learn is through practice, practice, and more practice. If you want to learn Java or C++, you can't stop your learning after you finish reading this chapter. You must sit down at the computer and practice the concepts frequently.

Java and C++ programming languages

As you learned in Chapter 14, you can choose from a wide variety of programming languages to develop software. Your choice of language should be based on what tasks the program needs to perform, your programming skills, the program's lifetime (how long it will be used), and the complexity of the software you're designing.

C++ and Java are widely accepted in industry and academia. Both languages support an object-oriented environment and can be used on different operating systems. Either language gives you a strong foundation for learning how to program and can be a springboard to other languages.

learning to cook with Java and C++

As discussed in Chapter 14, you can use the following ingredients to write programs:

- Variables
- Operators
- Control structures
- Objects

Java and C++ are high-level programming languages, meaning you can interact with a computer without having to speak in binary 1s and 0s. Java, designed for Internet use, was introduced by Sun Microsystems in 1995. It was intended for small tasks or small applications (called "applets"), without the need to write an entire program. However, Java has become a full-blown programming language and the language of choice to develop applications for communication devices and media, such as PDAs, cell phones, the Internet, and networks.

The main advantages of Java are the following:

- *It uses familiar syntax*—Its syntax is similar to the popular C++ language but easier to use.
- *It's very portable*—You can run a Java program written for one operating system on other operating systems without recompiling it. This advantage is the most important one for software developers.
- *It's powerful*—It has an extensive library of classes and routines to do most of the necessary programming tasks.
- *It's popular*—Java is widely used in many different computing environments and is currently one of the most popular languages.

C++, created in 1983 by Bjarne Stroustrup at Bell Labs, was based on C, which was used to develop UNIX. Stroustrup added features to the C language and called it "C with Classes," which later became known as C++. C++ is an object-oriented programming language that provides reusable and extendable source code, so modifying software is easier. It maintains the basics of the C language but offers simplified memory management and access to low-level memory.

Because Java and C++ are such popular and widespread languages, often used in schools to teach programming skills, both languages are used in this chapter to illustrate programming concepts. The building blocks you learn with these languages can be used in almost every other high-level language. Also, people with knowledge of both languages are in high demand because so many companies are using these languages.

variables

Just as ingredients can affect how a dish you're preparing turns out, variables have specific effects on a program's outcome. Before you can use a variable in your program, it must have an identifier, or name. Associating an identifier with a variable is called declaring a variable, so a *declaration* is a statement that associates an identifier with a variable (or an action or another programming element that can be given a name).

> *declaration* – A statement that associates an identifier with a variable (or an action or another programming element)

When you declare a variable, you specify its attributes, which define how the variable is processed. Some attributes are as follows:

- Identifier (name)
- Type (character, numeric, Boolean, and so forth)
- Content

For example, the following statement can be used to declare a variable for storing the integer number of tickets bought:

```
int numTicketsBought;
```

note

Java and C++ are case-sensitive languages, so make sure you're consistent with naming conventions. For example, "Amount" isn't the same as "amount." The same letter case must be used every time you use a variable.

variable naming conventions

The rules for declaring a variable in Java or C++ are as follows:

- Use only letters, underscores, and numbers.
- Begin the name with a letter.
- Avoid Java and C++ *reserved words* that have specific programming meanings.

> *reserved word* – A keyword with a specific instructional meaning; the name can't be used for a variable because the programming language is already using it as an instruction

variable types

All variables in Java and C++ are strongly typed, meaning you must declare the type of data a variable can hold. Many data types are used in Java and C++, and not all are discussed in this introductory chapter. However, you learn about the major data types. In Java, six data types are number related, one is character related, and one is for true and false (Boolean). C++ uses many of the same data types as Java but adds a data type for signed or unsigned numbers. A signed variable includes positive and negative values, and an unsigned variable includes only positive values. This is the syntax for declaring a variable:

```
type variableName;
```

integer data types

Integer data types are used for positive and negative whole numbers. Table 15-1 shows the Java integer data types, and Table 15-2 shows some C++ integer data types for working with positive and negative whole numbers.

Table 15-1, Java integer data types

data type	storage requirement	values
int	4 bytes	-2,147,483,648 to 2,147,483,647
short	2 bytes	-32,768 to 32,767
long	8 bytes	-9,223,372,036,854,775,808L to 9,223,372,036,854,775,807L (Long integers have the suffix L.)
byte	1 byte	-128 to 127

Here are some examples in Java:

```
int studentTickets;
short studentFees;
long studentTuition;
byte studentGrade;
```

Table 15-2, C++ integer data types

data type	storage requirement	values
short int	2 bytes	-32,768 to 32,767
unsigned short int	2 bytes	0 to 65,535
int	4 bytes	-2,147,483,648 to 2,147,483,647
unsigned int	4 bytes	0 to 4,294,967,295

The following are some examples in C++:

```
int studentTickets;
short int studentFees;
unsigned int totalPoints;
```

floating-point data types

Floating-point data types are used for positive and negative numbers that can also have decimals. Tables 15-3 and 15-4 list some examples of floating-point data types in Java and C++.

Table 15-3, Java floating-point data types

data type	storage requirement	values
float	4 bytes	3.4E +/- 38F (approx. 6 to 7 significant digits)
double	8 bytes	1.7E +/- 308 (approx. 15 significant digits)

Table 15-4, C++ floating-point data types

data type	storage requirement	values
float	4 bytes	3.4E +/- 38F (approx. 7 significant digits)
double	8 bytes	1.7E +/- 308 (approx. 15 significant digits)
long double	16 bytes	1.2E +/- 4932 (approx. 19 significant digits)

Here are some examples of declaring variables in both languages:

```
float salary;
double billGatesSalary;
```

character data type

The character (char) data type is used in Java and C++ for variables that hold only one character (see Tables 15-5 and 15-6).

Unicode

Unicode was discussed in Chapter 7. It's a 16-bit character set that defines 34,168 unique characters and control codes.

Table 15-5, Java character data type

data type	storage requirement	values
char	2 bytes	Character is enclosed in single quotes and stored as Unicode.

Table 15-6, C++ character data types

data type	storage requirement	values
char	2 bytes	-128 to 127
unsigned char	2 bytes	0 to 255

Here's an example of declaring the char type:

```
char studentMiddleInit;
```

Boolean data type

The Boolean data type is used for only one of two values: true or false. In Java and C++, you can't associate a number with a Boolean value. In other languages, such as Visual Basic, you use the numeric value 1 to mean true and the value 0 to mean false. Java and C++ simply rely on a "true" or "false" value (see Tables 15-7 and 15-8).

Table 15-7, Java Boolean data type

data type	storage requirement	values
boolean	1 byte	true or false

Table 15-8, C++ Boolean data type

data type	storage requirement	values
bool	1 byte	true or false

In Java, a Boolean variable declaration looks like this:

```
boolean deserveRaise;
```

In C++, it looks like this:

```
bool deserveRaise;
```

string data type

The char data type is used to recognize one character, which is enclosed in single quotation marks. If you want more than one character, such as a student's name, you need to use the string data type. A string variable can be used to store a piece of information that isn't a number and contains more than one character.

Strings are declared by using double quotes. Even if only one character is enclosed in double quotes, it's still considered a string. String variables use the String or string keyword. Notice in the following examples that the keyword is capitalized in Java but not in C++:

```
String sName; //Java String
string sName; //C++ string
```

> **n o t e**   In Java, the String keyword is the only one that's capitalized for data types.

The preceding statements declare a string variable called sName that contains no characters, so it's considered an empty string. In the following statements, the characters enclosed in double quotes are the contents of the string variable sName:

```
String sName = "Joe Blow"; //Java
string sName = "Joe Blow"; //C++
```

The plus (+) operator works a little differently with strings than with numeric values. It's a *concatenation* operator, meaning it combines one string with another. The following statement (in Java and C++) takes the value stored in sFirstName (Joe), adds the string ", ", and then adds the value stored in sLastName (Blow), resulting in the variable sFullName containing "Blow, Joe":

```
//Java example
String sFirstName = "Joe";
String sLastname = "Blow";
String sFullName;
sFullName = sLastName + "," + sFirstName;
```

---

when is a quote not a quote?

In both Java and C++, 'a' is *not* the same as "a" because the value enclosed in single quotes is a character, and the value enclosed in double quotes is a string.

---

concatenation – The process of combining or joining strings into one value

```
//C++ example
string sFirstName = "Joe";
string sLastname = "Blow";
string sFullName;
sFullName = sLastName + "," + sFirstName;
```

n o t e   Integer and character data types are also referred to as "scalar," meaning they reference a specific value. Strings are a combination of values, so they can't be represented by scalar values.

Hungarian notation

Hungarian notation –
A variable-naming method that adds a letter at the beginning of a variable name to indicate its data type

Another standard for variable identifiers is called *Hungarian notation*. Charles Simonyi, a Microsoft programmer, decided that adding a letter at the beginning of an identifier to indicate its data type would be helpful. For instance, a variable named `bBirth` indicates a Boolean value. Table 15-9 shows Hungarian notation for other data types.

Table 15-9, Hungarian notation examples

notation	data type	example
c	char	cMiddleInit
f	float	fSalary
i	int	iStudentCount
li	long integer	liSecondsLived
si	short integer	siStudentsPaid

Just because a variable uses Hungarian notation doesn't mean it must contain the specified data type. It's used only for the sake of readability. Java and C++ compilers ignore the name when determining whether programming statements are valid. They're concerned only with naming rules, such as whether reserved words are used in a variable name and whether the variable is used correctly.

variable content

variable initialization –
Supplying a value when a variable is first declared

When a variable is declared, you can assign it a value immediately by using the equal sign (=). Assigning a value to a variable is called *variable initialization*, or "initializing a variable." You don't always have to initialize a variable, but sometimes if you don't, the programming language assigns it a default value.

For example, the following statements use Hungarian notation to declare a variable called `iStudentCount` and assign it a value of 456:

```
int iStudentCount;
iStudentCount = 456;
```

You can also initialize a variable on one line:

```
int iStudentCount = 456;
```

When you assign a value to a character variable, it should be enclosed in single quotes:

```
char cMiddleInit;
cMiddleInit = 'S';
```

If you prefer, you can combine these statements on one line:

```
char cMiddleInit = 'S';
```

When you assign a value to a string variable, it should be enclosed in double quotes:

```
//Java
String sMiddleName;
sMiddleName = "S";

//C++
string sMiddleName;
sMiddleName = "S";
```

Again, you can combine the statements on one line:

```
String sMiddleName = "S"; //Java
string sMiddleName = "S"; //C++
```

better safe...

No matter which programming language you use, initializing variables to some starting value is wiser than wondering whether the system is going to initialize them. In programming, follow the principle "Better safe than sorry."

n o t e

Make sure you use blank lines and spaces to help make your source code more readable.

Java and C++ control structures and program flow

As you learned in Chapter 14, the four types of control structures are invocation, top down, selection, and repetition. Using these control structures correctly helps make a program readable and easier to maintain.

n o t e   Java examples in this chapter were compiled with JGrasp, and C++ examples were compiled with Dev-C++.

n o t e   As mentioned in Chapter 14, you can download a free version of Java and the Java Developer's Toolkit at *www.sun.com*. Many different versions of C++ are available; you can download a free version at *www.bloodshed.net/ devcpp.html*.

invocation

function *– A block of code that performs a task and can return a value*

Every Java or C++ program has a block of code called the `main()` function that tells the operating system it's the starting point. A *function* performs a task and can, if needed, return a value. For example, take a look at this source code in the Save_Ferris.java file:

```java
public class Save_Ferris
{
  public static void main(String[] args)
    {
        System.out.println("I could have been the Walrus!");
    }
}
```

The first two lines are a statement to the compiler declaring that the following source code is part of the Save_Ferris program:

```java
public class Save_Ferris
{
```

You can put the opening brace ({) at the end of the first line, but putting it on a separate line improves readability. The opening brace indicates that there's a block of code associated with the Save_Ferris Java program. Any opening brace must have a closing brace paired with it. The `public` keyword tells the Java

the `main()` **function**

The Java `main()` function doesn't return a value, so it must be declared to return void. Other languages, such as C and C++, allow `main()` to return a value to the operating system.

scope – *Where source code can be seen and whether other programs can see and use it*

compiler that this source code can be seen by any other program that wants to use it and is included with the Save_Ferris program. The `class` keyword identifies what type of source code is being used.

The next line of code promotes modular programming by breaking down parts of the program into blocks:

```
public static void main(String[] args)
  {
```

This block of code is called `main` and, as mentioned, it's the starting point for any Java program. Again, the `public` keyword indicates the *scope* of the source code, meaning where code can be seen. Public scope means the source code is visible for any other program to use.

The `static` keyword indicates that the function belongs to a class. In this example, the `main()` function belongs to the Save_Ferris class. The `void` keyword indicates that the `main()` source code isn't going to return anything to the operating system when it has finished running. It still displays output onscreen, but it doesn't return anything for the operating system to use.

n o t e

In Java, make sure you use the standard naming convention of capitalizing the first letter of each word in a function name (except in the `main()` function).

parameter – *A received value assigned to a variable; used by a block of source code*

The words inside parentheses—`String[] args`—are used as data receivers when the program runs. When a Java program runs, it can receive *parameters* (values). To pass parameters as values, simply enter them on the same line after the Java program name. For example, if you want to pass the number 10 to a Java program called "hello" containing this line, enter the following:

```
C:\>hello 10
```

This line runs the Java program and passes the value 10 to the variable called `args` of type `String`.

C++ also has a `main()` function in every program. However, software engineers often have to include other files of source code to perform common tasks, such as displaying information onscreen. Notice the `#include` statements in this example:

```
#include <cstdlib>
#include <iostream>
using namespace std;
int main()
```

```
    {
        cout << "I could have been the Walrus!\n";
        system("PAUSE");
        return 0;
    }
```

n o t e

In C++, many of the statements you use are contained in "include" files. The standard include files you should use in programs are `cstdlib` and `iostream`. They give you access to statements such as `cout` and `cin`.

Like Java, C++ can also have words inside parentheses, such as `int argc`, `char *argv[]`, to indicate parameters that receive data when the program runs. These parameters allow users to pass data to `main()` and then use the data in the program:

```
//C++ main receiving parameters
int main(int argc, char *argv[])
```

top down (or sequence)

The top-down control structure is used when program statements are executed in sequential order, starting at the top and working down to the bottom. In other words, statements are carried out one after another. The following source code in the Add_It_Up.java and Add_It_Up.cpp files shows examples of the top-down control structure:

```
//Java example
public class Add_It_Up
{
    public static void main(String[] args)
    {
        int iFirstNum = 15;
        int iSecondNum = 10;
        int iThirdNum = 20;
        int iFourthNum = 15;
        int iResult = 0;
        iResult = iFirstNum + iSecondNum;
        System.out.print("15 + 10 = ");
        System.out.println(iResult);
        iResult = iThirdNum - iFourthNum;
        System.out.print("20 - 15 = ");
```

```
        System.out.println(iResult);
        System.out.println("Have a nice day!");
    }
}

//C++ example
#include <cstdlib>
#include <iostream>

using namespace std;

int main()
{
        int iFirstNum = 15;
        int iSecondNum = 10;
        int iThirdNum = 20;
        int iFourthNum = 15;
        int iResult = 0;

        iResult = iFirstNum + iSecondNum;
        cout << "15 + 10 = " << iResult << endl;
        iResult = iThirdNum - iFourthNum;
        cout<< "20 - 15 = " << iResult << endl;
        cout<< "Have a nice day!\n";

        system("PAUSE");
        return 0;
}
```

Here's the output generated by the preceding code:

```
15 + 10 = 25
20 - 15 = 5
Have a nice day!
```

n o t e   Don't forget to end a block of code with a closing brace (}). Every opening brace must be paired with a closing brace.

In a top-down control structure, the first statement to be executed is the first line in the program. In the example, `int iFirstNum = 15;` is the first statement executed. Next, control is passed to the next line, which declares and initializes the variable `iSecondNum`. This process continues until all the variables are declared and initialized. Then the mathematical operations begin. First, the contents of `iFirstNum` are added to `iSecondNum` and stored in `iResult` with the line `iResult = iFirstNum + iSecondNum;`. Second, the system displays a string of characters onscreen with the Java line `System.out.print("15 + 10 = ");` or the C++ line `cout << "15 + 10 = " << iResult << endl;`. The program flow continues until no more lines are left to process.

Each statement is executed in sequential order, starting with the first line and continuing until the last line is processed. This control structure is the most common, found in every programming language. The top-down control structure is implemented by entering statements that don't call other pieces of code, as with invocation. Instead, they simply execute the current line and proceed to the next line.

Before continuing with the other control structures, you need to know how to use indenting and line breaks to make code more readable, discussed in the following section.

blocks of code

A sequence of several statements can be enclosed with opening and closing braces to indicate that they're related to each other in functionality and constitute a block of code. This format helps make your program more readable and accurate. (Leaving out braces can actually cause your program to function incorrectly, as you see in later code examples.) Here's an example of using braces to create a block of code:

```
{
    statement 1;
    statement 2;
}
```

Braces are used most often when you're working with invocation, selection, and repetition control structures. The following sections show some examples in Java and C++ output and input statements.

Java output data

You can send data to the output device (usually the monitor) with the Java `System.out` statement. `System.out` has two methods to output (sometimes called "print") data to the output device:

```
System.out.print(expression);
System.out.println(expression);
```

insertion point – *Where the cursor is placed*

The `print()` method prints the expression or string but leaves the *insertion point* at the end of the data being output. In other words, it's like writing words on a piece of paper but keeping the pencil ready to write more on the same line if needed.

The `println()` method prints the expression or string, and when it's finished, it moves the insertion point to the next line. This method is like writing a line and then picking up the pencil and moving it to the beginning of the next line on the paper.

You can output all types of data. Table 15-10 lists some examples of Java output statements.

Table 15-10, Java output statements

statement	output
`System.out.println(15 + 10);`	25
`System.out.println(15 + iFirstNum);`	30
`System.out.println("Hello, Kitty!");`	Hello, Kitty!
`System.out.println("Computer scientists \nhave better memory!");`	Computer scientists have better memory!
`System.out.println("iFirstNum + 15 = " + (15 + iFirstNum));`	iFirstNum + 15 = 30

Notice a couple of things in Table 15-10. First is the \n, called the newline escape sequence in Java and C++. It moves the insertion point to the beginning of the next line, as though someone pressed the Enter key. Whatever follows it continues printing at this new location.

Second, you can concatenate (join) values. The last statement in the table joins a string with an expression in ("iFirstNum + 15 = " + (15 + iFirstNum)). System.out is flexible in displaying data and is definitely a useful tool for Java programming.

C++ output data

In C++, you can send data to the output device with the cout statement. This statement uses the redirection symbols (<<) to direct output, as shown in this example:

```
cout << "15 + 10 = " << iResult <<endl;
```

The cout statement instructs the compiler to direct anything following the << symbols to the defined output device (typically, the monitor). First, the string "15 + 10 =" is displayed. Second, the content of the iResult variable is displayed on the same line, and third, the endl statement, which is much like using a newline escape sequence (\n), is sent to the output device so that the insertion point moves to the beginning of the next line.

note

The endl statement shown in Table 15-11 flushes the buffer and inserts a new line. The \n just inserts a new line.

Table 15-11, Sample C++ output statements

statement	output
cout << 15+10 << endl;	25
cout << 15 + iFirstNum << endl;	30
cout << "Hello, Kitty!\n";	Hello, Kitty!
cout << "Computer scientists \nhave better memory!\n";	Computer scientists have better memory!
cout << "iFirstNum + 15 = " << 15 + iFirstNum << endl;	iFirstNum + 15 = 30

typical typos

A common mistake programmers make is typos—switching the order of letters, misspelling words, or using the wrong letter case, for example. When a program doesn't compile successfully, start by checking that words are spelled correctly, and the correct letter case has been used.

input data

Displaying data is great, but you need a way to get data from users, too. Java and C++ provide input statements to read data from the input device (usually the keyboard).

System.out provides methods to display data in Java, so it makes sense that there's a System.in to provide methods for retrieving data from the input device. To get input from System.in, you must create a new variable from the Scanner class. This variable is responsible for reading characters from the input stream (keyboard) and then putting them, one by one, into another variable that acts as a memory buffer for storing the entered string. The input can be assigned to a string variable you have declared by making a call to the next() method.

In C++, the cin statement is used to retrieve data from the input device. Take a look at the following examples in Java and C++, paying particular attention to the bolded lines:

```java
//Java example of input using strings
//Author: Alfalfa Sprouts
//Description: Get a user's name and print it by using a string

import java.io.*;
import java.util.*;

public class MyProg1
{
    public static void main(String[] args)
    {
      //Create a variable of type Scanner to get input
      Scanner console = new Scanner(System.in);

      String sFirst_Name; //Declares a string variable
      String sLast_Name;  //Declares a string variable
      System.out.println("Enter your first name:");
      sFirst_Name = console.next(); //Gets input from the
      keyboard

      System.out.println("Enter your last name:");
      sLast_Name = console.next(); //Gets input from the keyboard

      System.out.println("Hello " + sFirst_Name + " " +
      sLast_Name);
    }

}
```

```
//C++ example of input using strings
//Author: Alfalfa Sprouts
//Description: Get a user's name and print it by using a string

#include <cstdlib>
#include <iostream>

using namespace std;

int main()
{
    string sFirst_Name; //Declares a string variable
    string sLast_Name;  //Declares a string variable

    cout << "Enter your first name: ";
    cin >> sFirst_Name; //Gets input from the keyboard
    cout << "Enter your last name: ";
    cin >> sLast_Name;  //Gets input from the keyboard

    cout << "Hello " << sFirst_Name + " " + sLast_Name << endl;
    system("PAUSE");
    return 0;
}
```

Both examples read two string values from the keyboard and assign them to two different variables. Then the program combines (concatenates) these variables with a space between them (indicated as " ") and prints all variables to the output device.

note

The Java and C++ programs shown in this chapter contain many new elements you haven't seen yet. For those of you chomping at the bit to become Java and C++ experts, you can find a plethora of Web sites with free tutorials that open the doors to the vast world of programming. Just go to your favorite search engine and enter "Java tutorial" or "C++ tutorial."

back to control structures

The other control structures do something to change the flow of the basic top-down structure, such as directing program flow to another block of code or location in the program, and generally provide a way to return control to the top-down structure.

Java and C++ implement invocation with calling functions and methods. A function, as you've learned, performs a task and can return a value. A method is simply a function that belongs to a class. The invocation control structure executes the statements in a function or method. In other words, when the system encounters a function name, it passes control to the first line of code in this function. The function finishes carrying out its statements and then returns control to the original calling point.

For example, the Java `equals()` method associated with string variables returns a Boolean value determining whether two strings are equal. When this method is used, the system passes control (although you don't see it happen) to the source code associated with `equals()`, carries out the statements, makes the comparison, and then returns a Boolean value.

The following Java example combines the top-down and invocation control structures. The variable declaration and initialization statements are carried out in sequential order, and the statement `bCompare = sName.equals(sNewName);` is an example of invocation because it calls the `equals()` method:

```java
//Java example
public class Combining_Strings
{
public static void main(String[] args)
    {
        String sName;
        String sNewName;
        boolean bCompare;

        sName = "Mary Lamb";
        sNewName = "Joe Blow";

        bCompare = sName.equals(sNewName);
```

```
System.out.println(sName);
System.out.println(sNewName);
System.out.println(bCompare);
        }
    }
```

After all statements in the equals() method have been carried out, control is returned to the assignment statement, and the value returned from the method is placed in the bCompare variable. Control is then passed to the next statement, continuing the top-down control structure.

C++ also uses method and function calls for invocation. As the following example shows, the _strdate statement calls ("invokes") the source code that copies the current date into the sDate variable:

```
//C++ example
#include <cstdlib>
#include <iostream>
#include <time.h>

using namespace std;

int main()
{
    char sdate[9];
    _strdate(sdate); //needs a group of characters as a parameter
                     //instead of a string variable

    cout << "Date: " << sdate << endl;

    system("PAUSE");
    return 0;
}
```

The invocation control structure is used when the same code module is executed more than once in an application. Code that's repeated should be placed in a function or method and then called when it's needed. The reasons are to cut down on the amount of code you have to write, which saves time and money, and make the program more modular and structured. Learning more about functions and methods is an important part of learning Java and C++ and continuing your computing education.

selection

You use the selection control structure every day, although you might not have realized it. For example, "If I want an A in this course, I study.

Otherwise, I won't study." is an example of using a selection control structure to make a choice. To make sure the program meets the requirements of the language you're using, writing an algorithm with pseudocode first is recommended. An algorithm can be used as a guide or template for writing source code. Using the algorithm and pseudocode from Chapter 14 to convert Celsius to Fahrenheit temperatures and vice versa results in the following Java source code:

```java
//Java example
//Lines starting with // are comment lines and are ignored by
//the Java compiler. Information about the program, including your
//name and a description, is usually placed in the comment section
//at the beginning.
//Java has many class libraries for performing common tasks.
//java.io is the library for input and output, so for keyboard I/O,
//this library must be imported. java.util is needed for the Scanner class.
import java.io.*;
import java.util.*;

public class test
{
//This statement is required exactly as written
public static void main(String[] args)
    {
    //Declare strings to hold input from the keyboard and
    //floating-point (double) variables to hold temperatures
    String sInput = "";
    double dCelsius = 0.0;
    double dFahrenheit = 0.0;
    String sChoice = "";

    Scanner sConsole = new Scanner(System.in);

    //This statement prompts the user to choose which conversion to perform
    System.out.print("Enter F for Fahrenheit to Celsius OR ");
    System.out.print("Enter C for Celsius to Fahrenheit: ");
    sChoice = sConsole.next();

    if (sChoice.equals("F"))
      {
      //This statement prompts the user to enter a Fahrenheit temperature
      //Input from the keyboard comes in as a text string
```

```
          System.out.print("Enter the Fahrenheit temperature: ");
          sInput = sConsole.next();
          //and must be converted into a floating-point number
          //so that it can be used in a calculation
          dFahrenheit = Double.parseDouble(sInput);
          //This statement calculates the Celsius temperature
          dCelsius = (5.0/9.0) * (dFahrenheit - 32.0);
          System.out.println(sInput + " converted from F to C is " + dCelsius);
          }
      else
        {
        //This statement prompts the user to enter a Celsius temperature
        //Input from the keyboard comes in as a text string
        System.out.print("Enter the Celsius temperature: ");
        sInput = sConsole.next();
        //and must be converted into a floating-point number
        //so that it can be used in a calculation
        dCelsius = Double.parseDouble(sInput);
        //This statement calculates the Fahrenheit temperature
        dFahrenheit = ((9.0/5.0) * dCelsius) + 32.0;
        System.out.println(sInput + "converted from C to F is " + dFahrenheit);
        }
      }
  }
```

n o t e

In Java, the variable `dTemp` is the double data type. If you need to convert a string to a double, use the `Double.parseDouble()` method, which accepts a string value and returns a double value.

The C++ source code looks like this:

```
//C++ example
//Lines starting with // are comment lines in C++, too.
#include <cstdlib>
#include <iostream>
#include <string>

using namespace std;

int main()
{
    //Declare strings to hold input from the keyboard and
    //floating-point (double) variables to hold the temperatures
```

```
double dCelsius = 0.0;
double dFahrenheit = 0.0;
string sChoice;

//This statement prompts the user to choose which conversion to perform
cout << "Enter F for Fahrenheit to Celsius OR \n";
cout << "Enter C for Celsius to Fahrenheit: \n";
cin >> sChoice;

  if (sChoice == "F")
    {
    //This statement prompts the user to enter a Fahrenheit temperature
    //Input from the keyboard comes in as a text string
    cout << "Enter the Fahrenheit temperature: ";
    cin >> dFahrenheit;
    //This statement calculates the Celsius temperature
    dCelsius = (5.0/9.0) * (dFahrenheit - 32.0);
    cout << dFahrenheit << " converted from F to C is " << dCelsius << endl;
    }

  else
    {
    //This statement prompts the user to enter a Celsius temperature
    //Input from the keyboard comes in as a text string
    cout << "Enter the Celsius temperature: ";
    cin >> dCelsius;
    //This statement calculates the Fahrenheit temperature
    dFahrenheit = ((9.0/5.0) * dCelsius) + 32.0;
    cout << dCelsius << " converted from C to F is " << dFahrenheit << endl;
    }
  system("PAUSE");
  return 0;
}
```

The if statement in the preceding examples—if (sChoice == "F")—is interpreted as "If the user enters an F, the program should convert from Fahrenheit to Celsius. Otherwise, convert from Celsius to Fahrenheit." Java and C++ implement the selection control structure with if, if-else, if-else-if, and switch statements.

if and if-else statements

You use if and if-else statements every time you need to weigh the results of making a decision. If you choose what's behind door number one, you win a new car. If you choose what's behind door number two, you win a donkey. For every choice, there's a result. The syntax for the `if` statement is as follows:

```
if (condition)
    {
    one or more statements;
    }
```

The `condition` in the syntax is an expression that returns a true or false value. If needed, you can add an `else` part to the control structure to perform some other function if the `if` control structure evaluates to a false value, as shown in this example:

```
if (condition)
    {
    one or more statements;
    }
else
    {
    one or more statements;
    }
```

ABCs of blocks

New programmers often make the mistake of having more than one statement associated with an `if` control structure but forgetting to group the statements in a block. The result is that only the first statement depends on the `if` control structure, and the remaining statements are always carried out, no matter what (which might not be what you intended).

If the expression evaluates to true, the system executes the nested commands below the `if` statement up to the `else` keyword. If the expression evaluates to false, the system executes the nested commands below the `else` statement up to the closing brace.

In the temperature conversion program, the system checks to see what type of value the user entered that's stored in the sChoice variable. The variable's contents are compared with the string `"F"`. If the user enters an F, the system asks the user to enter the temperature in Fahrenheit; if the user doesn't enter an F, the system prompts the user for a Celsius temperature. The following example shows the `if-else` structure used in the previous Java and C++ programs:

```
//Java example
    if (sChoice.equals("F"))
      {
      //This statement prompts the user to enter a Fahrenheit temperature
      //Input from the keyboard comes in as a text string
      System.out.print("Enter the Fahrenheit temperature: ");
```

```
      sInput = sConsole.next();
      //and must be converted into a floating-point number
      //so that it can be used in a calculation
      dFahrenheit = Double.parseDouble(sInput);
      //This statement calculates the Celsius temperature
      dCelsius = (5.0/9.0) * (dFahrenheit - 32.0);
      System.out.println(sInput + " converted from F to C is " + dCelsius);
      }
  else
      {
      //This statement prompts the user to enter a Celsius temperature
      //Input from the keyboard comes in as a text string
      System.out.print("Enter the Celsius temperature: ");
      sInput = sConsole.next();
      //and must be converted into a floating-point number
      //so that it can be used in a calculation
      dCelsius = Double.parseDouble(sInput);
      //This statement calculates the Fahrenheit temperature
      dFahrenheit = ((9.0/5.0) * dCelsius) + 32.0;
      System.out.println(sInput + " converted from C to F is " + dFahrenheit);
      }

//C++ example
      if (sChoice == "F")
      {
      //This statement prompts the user to enter a Fahrenheit temperature
      //Input from the keyboard comes in as a text string
      cout << "Enter the Fahrenheit temperature: ";
      cin >> dFahrenheit;
      //This statement calculates the Celsius temperature
      dCelsius = (5.0/9.0) * (dFahrenheit - 32.0);
      cout << dFahrenheit << " converted from F to C is " << dCelsius << endl;
      }
  else
      {
      //This statement prompts the user to enter a Celsius temperature
      //Input from the keyboard comes in as a text string
      cout << "Enter the Celsius temperature: ";
      cin >> dCelsius;
      //This statement calculates the Fahrenheit temperature
      dFahrenheit = ((9.0/5.0) * dCelsius) + 32.0;
      cout << dCelsius << " converted from C to F is " << dFahrenheit << endl;
      }
```

The if or if-else statement is used any time you need a series of statements to be executed depending on a certain expression.

if-else-if statement

There's a problem with the if statement used in the previous example. What if the user enters G? The system assumes the user wants to convert from Celsius to Fahrenheit, but that might not be what the user intends. Remember that when you write a program, you should imagine end users as computer novices and plan for the worst. In this situation, the program should perform the calculations only if the user enters the correct choice: F or C. The way to solve this problem is by adding an else-if to the if control structure. In fact, it also gives you a way to inform the user that the valid choices are F and C. Here's an example of adding an else-if statement to the if statement in Java and C++:

```java
//Java example
    if (sChoice.equals("F"))
    {
    //This statement prompts the user to enter a Fahrenheit temperature
    //Input from the keyboard comes in as a text string
    System.out.print("Enter the Fahrenheit temperature: ");
    sInput = sConsole.next();
    //and must be converted into a floating-point number
    //so that it can be used in a calculation
    dFahrenheit = Double.parseDouble(sInput);
    //This statement calculates the Celsius temperature
    dCelsius = (5.0/9.0) * (dFahrenheit - 32.0);
    System.out.println(sInput + " converted from F to C is " + dCelsius);
    }
    else if (sChoice.equals("C"))
    {
    //This statement prompts the user to enter a Celsius temperature
    //Input from the keyboard comes in as a text string
    System.out.print("Enter the Celsius temperature:");
    sInput = sConsole.next();
    //and must be converted into a floating-point number
    //so that it can be used in a calculation
    dCelsius = Double.parseDouble(sInput);
    //This statement calculates the Fahrenheit temperature
    dFahrenheit = ((9.0/5.0) * dCelsius) + 32.0;
    System.out.println(sInput + " converted from C to F is " + dFahrenheit);
    }
    else
    {
      System.out.println("Your valid choices are F or C");
    }
```

```
//C++ example
    if (sChoice == "F")
      {
      //This statement prompts the user to enter a Fahrenheit temperature
      //Input from the keyboard comes in as a text string
      cout << "Enter the Fahrenheit temperature: ";
      cin >> dFahrenheit;
      //This statement calculates the Celsius temperature
      dCelsius = (5.0/9.0) * (dFahrenheit - 32.0);
      cout << dFahrenheit << " converted from F to C is " << dCelsius << endl;
      }
    else if (sChoice == "C")
      {
      //This statement prompts the user to enter a Celsius temperature
      //Input from the keyboard comes in as a text string
      cout << "Enter the Celsius temperature: ";
      cin >> dCelsius;
      //This statement calculates the Fahrenheit temperature
      dFahrenheit = ((9.0/5.0) * dCelsius) + 32.0;
      cout << dCelsius << " converted from C to F is " << dFahrenheit << endl;
      }
    else
      {
      cout << "Your valid choices are F or C";
      }
```

The if-else-if structure provides a way to perform certain blocks of code depending on the variable's state in the program while it's running. It's easy to use and makes your program more flexible in handling data and processing information.

switch statement

As you can see in the previous examples, putting one if control structure inside another—called *nesting*—can decrease the code's readability.

nesting – Putting one control structure inside another

Sometimes you need a statement that allows testing many options but still groups blocks of code to be executed depending on the results. In Java and C++, this statement is the switch statement, which uses this syntax:

```
switch (expression)
    {
    case value_1 :
      statement_1;
      break;
```

```
case value_2 :
  statement_2;
  break;
case value_3 :
  statement_3;
  break;
default :
  statement_4;
  break;
}
```

A `switch` statement allows you to test an expression's value and, depending on the value, jump to some location in the `switch` statement. The expression must be a scalar data type, such as an integer or a character. When the expression is evaluated, the system begins searching through the `case` statement values, trying to find a match. If it finds a match, all the `case` statements are executed. That's why you need to put a `break` statement at the end of each `case`: to tell the system to quit processing `case` statements and send control to the end of the `switch` statement. With the `break` statement, you can make sure the system performs only the `case` statement that has a matching value. If no match is found, the statements for the `default` section are executed. The `default` section is optional, but displaying a message stating that no match was found is helpful for users.

n o t e

You can't use the `switch` statement to compare string variables. It works only with scalar variables, such as integer and character variables.

The following example shows the `switch` statement in Java:

```
//Java example
import java.io.*;
import java.util.*;

public class Switch_Time
{

public static void main(String[] args)
    {
    Scanner console = new Scanner(System.in);
    //String variable to hold the input
    String sInput = "";

    System.out.print("Enter the letter grade: ");
    sInput = console.next();
```

```
            //Process the first character of the entered string
            switch (sInput.charAt(0))
              {
              case 'A' :
                System.out.println("You get an A");
                System.out.println("Great job!");
                break;
              case 'B' :
                System.out.println("You get a B");
                System.out.println("Nice job!");
                break;
              case 'C' :
                System.out.println("You get a C");
                System.out.println("Good enough!");
                break;
              default :
                System.out.println("You get a D");
                System.out.println("See you next semester!");
              }
          }
      }
```

In C++, the switch statement looks like this:

```
//C++ example
#include <cstdlib>
#include <iostream>

using namespace std;

int main(int argc, char *argv[])
{
    char cInput;

    cout << "Enter the letter grade: ";
    cin >> cInput;

    //Process the first character of the entered string
    switch (cInput)
      {
      case 'A' :
        cout << "You get an A\n";
        cout << "Great job!\n";
        break;
```

```
            case 'B' :
              cout << "You get a B\n";
              cout << "Nice job!\n";
              break;
            case 'C' :
              cout << "You get a C\n";
              cout << "Good enough!\n";
              break;
            default :
              cout << "You get a D\n";
              cout << "See you next semester!\n";
            }

        system("PAUSE");
        return EXIT_SUCCESS;
    }
```

n o t e

The switch statement in C++ requires comparing the expression against integer scalar values or one unit of data. If you're evaluating multiple characters, you use nested if statements.

If more than two values execute the same block of code, you can simply place them one on top of the other in a top-down structure. For example, if you want the same code carried out whether the value is A, B, or C, you can do the following:

```
//Java example
switch (cInput)
    {
    case 'A' :
    case 'B' :
    case 'C' :
        System.out.println("You get a(n) " + cInput);
        System.out.println("You passed!");
        break;
    default :
        System.out.println("You get a " + cInput);
        System.out.println("Do NOT pass go and go directly to jail!");
    }
```

Because a string can't be used in a C++ or Java switch statement, you have to rethink your program logic. The following example prompts the user to enter a score and then uses the switch statement to display the grade:

```cpp
//C++ example
#include <cstdlib>
#include <iostream>

using namespace std;

int main()
{
    //string variable to hold the input
    int iInput;

    cout << "Enter the test score: ";
    cin >> iInput;

    //Process the first character of the entered string
    switch (iInput)
      {
      case 100 :
      case 99 :
      case 98 :
      case 97 :
      case 96 :
      case 95 :
      case 94 :
      case 93 :
      case 92 :
      case 91 :
      case 90 :
         cout << "You get an A\n";
         cout << "Great job!\n";
         break;
      case 89 :
      case 88 :
      case 87 :
      case 86 :
      case 85 :
      case 84 :
      case 83 :
      case 82 :
      case 81 :
      case 80 :
```

```
                           cout << "You get a B\n";
                           cout << "Nice job!\n";
                           break;
                      case 79 :
                      case 78 :
                      case 77 :
                      case 76 :
                      case 75 :
                      case 74 :
                      case 73 :
                      case 72 :
                      case 71 :
                      case 70 :
                         cout << "You get a C\n";
                         cout << "Good enough!\n";
                         break;
                      default :
                         cout << "You get a D\n";
                         cout << "See you next semester!\n";
                   }

          system("PAUSE");
          return 0;
     }
```

The `switch` statement makes your source code easier to read and maintain than an `if-else-if` statement, as you can see in this example:

```
//Java example
if (cInput == 'A')
    {
    System.out.println("You get an A");
    System.out.println("Great job!");
    }
else if (cInput == 'B')
    {
    System.out.println("You get a B");
    System.out.println("Nice job!");
    }
else if (cInput == 'C')
    {
    System.out.println("You get a C");
    System.out.println("Good enough!");
    }
```

```
else
    {
    System.out.println("You get a D");
    System.out.println("See you next semester!");
    }

//C++ example
if (cInput == 'A')
    {
    cout << "You get an A\n";
    cout << "Great job!\n";
    }
else if (cInput == 'B')
    {
    cout << "You get a B\n";
    cout << "Nice job!\n";
    }
else if (cInput == 'C')
    {
    cout << "You get a C\n";
    cout << "Good enough!\n";
    }
else
    {
    cout << "You get a D\n";
    cout << "See you next semester!\n";
    }
```

note

Because if statements are used in the preceding examples, break statements aren't needed to stop the condition testing.

Like the if statement, the switch statement is used any time you need a series of statements to be executed depending on a certain expression. The difference between if and switch is that the switch statement is used when there are many different expressions to evaluate, and the if statement is used more often to evaluate one expression.

repetition (looping)

Although typing duplicate statements in your code when you want something to happen multiple times might not seem like much trouble, it makes code harder to read and maintain. The repetition control structure (called "looping") allows repeating statements multiple times without having to retype statements.

The following sections explain the statements used for looping: for, while, and do-while.

for statement

When you want to repeat a group of statements a known number of times, you use the for statement, which has this syntax in Java and C++:

```
for (variable declaration; expression; increment/decrement)
{
    statement(s);
}
```

The *variable declaration* is where you declare and initialize a variable. A common oversight in working with the for loop is forgetting to declare the counter variable. All that's needed is a statement similar to int iCount.

note

You can also declare a variable in the for statement. It's then visible only in the for statement. After the for statement is over, the variable is gone. Every variable has scope (where it can be seen) and duration (how long it occupies memory).

The starting value is the number used to initialize the counter variable (in the *variable declaration* part) and inform the system of the beginning value in the loop. The *expression* part checks whether the statements inside the for loop should be executed and acts as an ending boundary for processing the loop. The *increment/decrement* part is where you increment or decrement the counter variable. The *variable declaration* part contains the value used in the *expression* part to determine whether to continue processing the for loop. The following examples show how to use the for loop:

```
//Java example
public class For_Loop
{
    public static void main(String[] args)
    {
      int iCount;

      for (iCount = 1; iCount <= 5; iCount++)
      {
        System.out.println("I am on number " + iCount);
      }
    }
}
```

```cpp
//C++ example
#include <cstdlib>
#include <iostream>

using namespace std;

int main()
{
    int iCount;

    for (iCount = 1; iCount <= 5; iCount++)
    {
      cout << "I am on number " << iCount << endl;
    }

    system("PAUSE");
    return 0;
}
```

Output:

```
I am on number 1
I am on number 2
I am on number 3
I am on number 4
I am on number 5
```

The for loop assigns the value 1 to the iCount variable by using the iCount = 1 statement and makes sure it's less than or equal to the ending value 5 by using the iCount <= 5 statement. The iCount variable is incremented by 1 with the iCount++ statement, so the numbers displayed onscreen are 1 through 5. In simpler terms, the variable declaration starts the loop counter at 1, and then checks to see whether the variable's value is <=5. If so, the for loop is processed, and after the loop executes all statements inside the braces, it returns to the for loop to increment the counter variable with iCount++.

The next for loop program repeats the same process as the first loop, but instead of using the increment value 1, the increment statement tells the system to use the increment value 2 by using the iCount+=2 statement. Therefore, the numbers displayed are 1, 3, and 5.

```java
//Java example
public class For_Loop2
{
    public static void main(String[] args)
```

```
      {
        int iCount;

        for (iCount = 1; iCount <= 5; iCount+=2)
        {
          System.out.println("I am on number " + iCount);
        }
      }
    }

//C++ example
#include <cstdlib>
#include <iostream>

using namespace std;

int main()
{
    int iCount;

    for (iCount = 1; iCount <= 5; iCount+=2)
    {
        cout << "I am on number " << iCount << endl;
    }

    system("PAUSE");
    return 0;
}
```

Output:

```
I am on number 1
I am on number 3
I am on number 5
```

This next for loop program repeats the same process but uses the increment value -1. The starting value in the variable declaration for this loop is 5 and the ending value is 1 because of the iCount > 0 expression. Therefore, the numbers 5 through 1 are displayed onscreen.

```
//Java example
public class For_Loop3
{
    public static void main(String[] args)
    {
        int iCount;

        for (iCount = 5; iCount > 0; iCount--)
```

```
            {
                System.out.println("I am on number " + iCount);

            }
        }
    }

    //C++ example
    #include <cstdlib>
    #include <iostream>

    using namespace std;

    int main()
    {
        int iCount;

        for (iCount = 5; iCount > 0; iCount--)
        {
            cout << "I am on number " << iCount << endl;
        }

        system("PAUSE");
        return 0;
    }
```

Output:

```
I am on number 5
I am on number 4
I am on number 3
I am on number 2
I am on number 1
```

Remember the post and pre operators for incrementing and decrementing? They're often used when updating the counter variable in the for loop. Be careful that you don't mistakenly update the counter variable in the looped statement, too. Updating the counter variable in the looped statement in addition to the increment/decrement part of the for statement affects the counter variable more than once and has serious consequences, as shown in these examples:

```
//Java example
    int iCount;

    for (iCount = 1; iCount <= 5; iCount++)
    {
      System.out.println("I am on number " + iCount++);
    }
```

```
//C++ example
    int iCount;

    for (iCount = 1; iCount <= 5; iCount++)
    {
        cout << "I am on number " << iCount++ << endl;
    }
```

Output:

```
I am on number 1
I am on number 3
I am on number 5
```

Instead of the expected 1 through 5 displayed as the output, the numbers 1, 3, and 5 are displayed because the looped statement is incrementing the counter variable and so is the increment/decrement part of the `for` statement.

`while` statement

If the looping is based on a condition or an expression that's checked before any statements are repeated, the `while` statement is used to process a group of statements a certain number of times, just like the `for` loop. The `for` and `while` loops are considered *precondition loops*, meaning the minimum number of times they execute is zero because the expression is checked before the source code in the loop is executed. In other words, the loop might not execute at all because the expression is evaluated before statements in the loop are executed. The *expression* part of the statement is a Boolean expression returning a true or false value. If the condition is true, the statements in the loop are executed, and processing continues until the expression returns false. Here's the syntax of the `while` statement:

```
while (expression)
{
    statements;
}
```

The difference between `while` and `for` is that the `while` statement doesn't provide a specified area for updating the counter, as in the increment/decrement part of the `for` statement's syntax. You're responsible for doing so, as shown in these examples:

```
//Java example
public class While_Loop
{
    public static void main(String[] args)
    {
        int iCount = 1;

        while (iCount <= 5)
```

precondition loop – *A loop that checks the expression before any source code in the loop is executed; might never be executed*

```
        {
          System.out.println("I am on number " + iCount);
          iCount++; //updates the counter
        }
      }
}

//C++ example
#include <cstdlib>
#include <iostream>

using namespace std;
int main()
{
      int iCount = 1;

      while (iCount <= 5)
      {
         cout << "I am on number " << iCount << endl;
         iCount++; //Updates the counter
      }
    system("PAUSE");
    return 0;
}
```

Output:

```
I am on number 1
I am on number 2
I am on number 3
I am on number 4
I am on number 5
```

endless loop – *A block of source code that repeats continuously and never stops*

The following source code is an example of an *endless loop*. Notice that the counter variable iCount is never updated (incremented). Its value always remains 1, which is always less than 5. Therefore, the expression that controls ending the loop is never satisfied, and the loop runs forever, as shown in these examples:

```
//Java example
    int iCount = 1;

    while (iCount <= 5)
    {
        System.out.println("I am on number " + iCount);
    }
```

```
//C++ example
    int iCount = 1;

    while (iCount <= 5)
    {
        cout << "I am on number " << iCount << endl;
    }
```

Output:

```
I am on number 1
I am on number 1
I am on number 1
I am on number 1
```

. . . and so on, until you kill the program.

do-while statement

If looping is based on an expression and statements are repeated before the expression is evaluated, the do-while statement is used. It's used mainly when processing a table. Its syntax is as follows:

```
do
{
    statement(s);
} while (expression);
```

postcondition loop – A loop that executes at least one time before the expression is evaluated

The do-while statement is considered a *postcondition loop*, meaning the loop executes at least one time before the expression is evaluated. The *expression* part of the statement is a Boolean expression returning a true or false value. If the condition is true, the statements between do and while are executed, and processing continues until the expression returns false.

```
//Java example
public class DoWhile_Loop
{
    public static void main(String[] args)
    {
      int iCount = 1;

      do
      {
        System.out.println("I am on number " + iCount);
      } while (iCount++ < 5);
    }
}
```

```
//C++ example
#include <cstdlib>
#include <iostream>

using namespace std;

int main()
{
    int iCount = 1;

    do
    {
        cout << "I am on number " << iCount << endl;
    } while (iCount++ < 5);

    system("PAUSE");
    return 0;
}
```

Output:

```
I am on number 1
I am on number 2
I am on number 3
I am on number 4
I am on number 5
```

The execution of the loop begins by printing I am on number 1. The do-while expression is then evaluated to determine whether to repeat the loop, and the iCount variable is incremented. Notice that the expression no longer checks to see whether the iCount variable is <= to 5. Instead, it checks to see whether the variable is < 5 and prints I am on number 5 before determining that iCount is indeed no longer < 5 and exiting the loop.

An important point is whether you use the pre or post operator. Look at the same program, using the preincrement operator instead of the postincrement:

```
//Java example
public class DoWhile_Loop2
{
    public static void main(String[] args)
    {
        int iCount = 1;

        do
        {
            System.out.println("I am on number " + iCount);
        } while (++iCount < 5);
    }
}
```

```cpp
//C++ example
#include <cstdlib>
#include <iostream>

using namespace std;

int main()
{
    int iCount = 1;

    do
    {
        cout << "I am on number " << iCount << endl;
    } while (++iCount < 5);

    system("PAUSE");
    return 0;
}
```

Output:

```
I am on number 1
I am on number 2
I am on number 3
I am on number 4
```

The loop repeats one less time because the variable was incremented to 5 before the expression was checked, which ended the loop after the fourth output line.

one last thought

No matter which programming language you choose, typically you use the four major control structures discussed in this chapter. Organizations usually select a programming language based on the application's needs. Sometimes programmers need to update their skills and learn new languages, but knowing C++ and Java is a good start because these object-oriented languages are widely used in both academia and industry.

To become proficient in any programming language, you must be dedicated to practicing writing code and troubleshooting errors. Becoming familiar with the basic control structures and common programming mistakes helps you become a better software engineer.

Software engineers have a responsibility to write structured programs that are easy to read and maintain. One way to do this is by including helpful comments in your source code. Remember to code unto others as you would have others code unto you.

chapter summary

- Java is a high-level programming language designed for the Internet.
- C++ is also a high-level programming language; it's based on the C language but incorporates object-oriented principles.
- Variables are of different data types, including integer (int), character (char), floating point, Boolean, and string. Assigning a value to a variable is called variable initialization, or "initializing a variable."
- Four types of control structures are used in high-level programming languages: top down, invocation, selection, and repetition.
- Java uses methods for the invocation control structure, and C++ uses methods and functions.
- Java uses the System.out statement to output data. In C++, the cout statement is used with the << redirection symbols.
- The Java Scanner class is used to gather input. In C++, the cin statement is used to gather input.
- C++ and Java use the if, if-else, if-else-if, and switch statements for selection control structures.
- In C++ and Java, the switch statement is used only with scalar variables, such as integers and characters. String variables can't be used with the switch statement.
- C++ and Java use the for, while, and do-while loops for repetition.
- To become a good programmer, you must practice, practice, and practice some more.
- Code unto others as you would have them code unto you.

key terms

concatenation (*517*)

declaration (*513*)

endless loop (*549*)

function (*520*)

Hungarian notation (*518*)

insertion point (*525*)

nesting (*537*)

parameters (*521*)

postcondition loop (*550*)

precondition loop (*548*)

reserved words (*513*)

scope (*521*)

variable initialization (*518*)

test yourself

1. Describe when to use integer variables in Java or C++. Explain the situation, provide a suggested variable name, and support your recommendation.

2. Describe when to use floating-point variables in Java or C++. Explain the situation, provide a suggested variable name, and support your recommendation.

3. Describe when to use character variables in Java or C++. Explain the situation, provide a suggested variable name, and support your recommendation.

4. Describe when to use string variables in Java or C++. Explain the situation, provide a suggested variable name, and support your recommendation.

5. Write a Java or C++ program that displays truth tables for the and (&&) logical operator and the or (||) logical operator. (Refer to Chapter 14 to review logical operators, if needed.)

6. Write a Java or C++ program that uses the addition, subtraction, division, multiplication, and modulus mathematical operators. (Refer to Chapter 14 to review these operators, if needed.)

7. Write a Java or C++ program that displays five names, using the `for`, `while`, and `do-while` statements.

8. Write a Java or C++ program that uses an `if-else-if` statement to determine your final grade in a course.

9. Repeat exercise 8 but use a `switch` statement.

10. Describe when you would use `do-while`, `for`, and `while` statements.

practice exercises

1. Java and C++ are case-sensitive languages.

   a. True
   b. False

2. @JT%name is a valid Java and C++ variable identifier.

   a. True
   b. False

3. Which Java data type do you use for the value 14?

   a. Int
   b. Long
   c. Byte
   d. Char
   e. None of the above

4. Which Java/C++ data type do you use for the value 14.9?

   a. Int
   b. Float
   c. Byte
   d. Short
   e. None of the above

5. Which Java/C++ data type do you use for the value `'e'`?

   a. Int
   b. Long
   c. Byte
   d. Char
   e. None of the above

6. Which Java/C++ data type do you use for the value `"Joe"`?

   a. Int
   b. Long
   c. String
   d. Char
   e. None of the above

7. In a precondition loop, the statements inside the loop might never execute.

   a. True
   b. False

8. In a postcondition loop, the statements in the loop are always executed at least once because the expression is checked after entering the loop.

   a. True
   b. False

9. Which C++ statement is used to gather input?

   a. `cout`
   b. `cin`
   c. `Scanner`
   d. `sConsole.Next()`

10. Which Java class is used to gather input?

   a. `cout`
   b. `cin`
   c. `Scanner`
   d. `sConsole.Next()`

11. Using the following statements, what value is displayed?

```
public class test
{
    public static void main(String[] args)
      {
      int iCount;
```

```
                        iCount = 0;
                        System.out.print("iCount has a value of " + ++iCount);
                    }
            }
```

    a. 0
    b. 1
    c. 2
    d. Unknown

12. Using the following statements, what value is displayed?

```
    #include <cstdlib>
    #include <iostream>

    using namespace std;
    int main()
        {
            int iCount;
            iCount = 0;
            cout << "iCount has a value of " << ++iCount;
        }
```

    a. 0
    b. 1
    c. 2
    d. Unknown

13. Using the following statements, what value is displayed?

```
public class test
{
    public static void main(String[] args)
    {
    int iCount;

        iCount = 0;
        System.out.print("iCount has a value of " + iCount++);
    }
}
```

    a. 0
    b. 1
    c. 2
    d. Unknown

14. Using the following statements, what value is displayed?

```
#include <cstdlib>
#include <iostream>

using namespace std;
int main()
    {
            int iCount;
            iCount = 0;
            cout << "iCount has a value of " << iCount++;
    }
```

   a. 0
   b. 1
   c. 2
   d. Unknown

digging deeper

1. Create for, while, and do-while loops. Make sure the same statements are performed in each loop. Which looping construct is more efficient time-wise? Prove it by writing source code.

2. Besides what was mentioned in the chapter, what other Java integrated development environments can you use, and where can you download them? Which one is considered the best to use?

3. Besides what was mentioned in the chapter, what other C++ integrated development environments can you use, and where can you download them? Which one is considered the best to use?

4. Create a list of some common Java classes, and describe when each class is used.

5. Create a list of some common C++ classes, and describe when each class is used.

discussion topics

1. What do you think the next great programming language will be? How will it work, and how will software engineers use it?

2. Many companies allow employees to work remotely via e-mail, cell phones, online chats, and so forth. What are the advantages and disadvantages of allowing remote work on software engineering projects?

3. Writing comments is time consuming, so convincing programmers they're important is difficult when deadlines are looming. Why is spending extra time writing comments worthwhile, even when deadlines are tight?

4. What is the difference between C++ and C#? What are the strengths and weaknesses of each? When would you use one instead of the other?

5. "Open source" is an important term in software engineering. What does it mean? What are the advantages and disadvantages of open-source code?

6. Compare Java with C++, and summarize their strengths and weaknesses.

Internet research

1. List some Web sites that offer free tutorials in C++ programming.

2. List some Web sites that offer free tutorials in Java programming.

3. Is C++ a "dead" language now that C# is being used? Base your opinion on information you find on the Internet, such as job search sites, course offerings from universities, and so forth.

4. Which language is best for beginners who are learning to program? Support your opinion with articles you find on the Internet.

5. What types of applications are written in C++ and Java? When might you use one language instead of the other? Give examples.

answers to test yourself
questions

chapter 1

1. Measuring resources, land, dimensions for construction, navigation, understanding the cycle of the year, and so forth

2. Probably the Chinese abacus. Although clay tablets and other counting mechanisms predate it, it was likely the first object with moving parts for doing calculations.

3. Both used stored information from a card (or roll of paper in the piano's case) with holes in it.

4. He borrowed the idea of stored information on cards with holes.

5. Ada Lovelace is considered the first programmer for her work with Babbage's Analytical Engine.

6. The program loop

7. Using vacuum tubes

8. The Mark I in the United States, the Colossus in Britain, and the Z1 in Germany

9. Machine code is difficult for humans to read. Assembly-language code makes it easier to program machine code.

10. Big Blue refers to IBM and its successful blue-suited salesforce.

11. The transistor and magnetic core RAM

12. Hard drives or any kind of magnetic disk storage device

13. The first UNIX OS was written in B. The C programming language was developed to create the second UNIX version.

14. It was written on a minicomputer, a Digital Equipment Corporation PDP-7.

15. Calculators

16. The Microsoft BASIC programming language

17. Steve Wozniak and Steve Jobs; VisiCalc, the first spreadsheet program

18. Apple launched the Apple Macintosh in 1984. Microsoft later came out with Windows.

19. It was originally conceived for the telephone system but never adopted.

20. Vannevar Bush

chapter 2

1. Clifford Stoll is most famous for writing the 1989 book *The Cuckoo's Egg: Tracking a Spy Through the Maze of Computer Espionage*, in which he describes his year-long effort to track the cracker who intruded on many government and private systems.

2. They have been called "phreaks" or "phone phreaks." They engaged in "phreaking," or finding ways to use AT&T phone lines free.

3. The term originated in the 1960s to describe a programmer with a high skill level. The name took on a negative connotation in the 1980s, with widespread viruses and costly intrusions of computer systems. The term "cracker" can be used to describe an unwelcome outsider, compared with a welcome insider. The common use of "hacker" might have made the distinction irrelevant to the general public. It's a good distinction to know, however, because many system security professionals make this distinction.

4. A directed hacker directs the attack at particular machines for purposes of theft or damage. An undirected hacker is motivated by the desire to break into any system.

5. One intruder is the worm or virus that doesn't target a particular machine but makes use of security holes in operating systems and applications to wreak havoc. Another is the general user who, if not denied entry to parts of the system, might damage the system, even without intending to.

6. The "Hacker's Manifesto" can be found on the Web easily. Among other things, it justifies breaking into systems just because they can be broken into.

7. Good system configuration, developing security rules and communicating them to users, updating operating systems and virus definitions regularly, making users aware of the dangers of seemingly innocent communication

8. The rlogin command allowed an administrator to log on to one system and then log on to other machines remotely without needing a password.

9. Many online shopping sites kept information about customers' purchases in the URL string. A clever thief could change the price in the URL if the server side of the program didn't verify the item and price.

10. In a buffer overflow, a program tries to place more information in a memory location than that location can handle, and it overflows into other areas. Crackers aim to overflow a buffer to get to memory that's critical to the machine's operation and insert their own code into this area.

11. Identification is a technique or mechanism for knowing who someone is. Authentication is the proof that people are who they say they are. Your name or Social Security number is your identification. Your fingerprint is proof that you are who you say you are.

12. A worm can actively search for vulnerable systems and replicate itself across systems. A virus must depend on some other mechanism (such as a person moving a file) to infect other systems.

13. A denial-of-service attack prevents legitimate users from using resources.

14. A repudiation attack seeks to create a false impression that an event that didn't occur did or an event that actually did occur did not. Attacking a system so that a credit card transaction that occurred appears as though it did not is an example.

15. Confidentiality, integrity, availability, accountability

16. Some ways to safeguard your data:

    Have a security policy, communicate it, and follow it.

    Have physical safeguards against intrusion: locks, secure trash disposal, ID badges, security guards, and so forth.

    Password-protect everything and make passwords difficult to discover.

    Make backup copies of everything and physically secure backups.

    Protect against system failures.

    Use up-to-date antivirus programs and antispyware and anticookie programs to protect privacy.

    In case the worst happens, have a disaster recovery plan.

    Use encryption.

    Use firewalls.

    Use secure system setups and programs with frequent security updates.

17. A virus signature (virus definition)

18. The 1968 law outlawing wiretapping would cover a network sniffer.

    The 1984 law on computer fraud and abuse would cover unauthorized use of a computer.

    The 1986 law on electronic communications privacy would cover unwanted viewing of e-mail contents.

    Many laws could be used, depending on what occurred. For example, intellectual property violations, consumer protection, threats to national defense, avoiding taxation, and fraud might be used.

19. $5000. This amount seems like a lot, but an argument can be made for not just lost computer time, but also lost processing time and its effect on business operations.

20. Avoid having a record of your purchases when possible.

    Have an unlisted phone number.

    Write to all companies you do business with and request removal of your name from mailing lists.

    Install antispyware software.

chapter 3

1. A main board provides a physical location for the CPU and supporting circuitry. It also allows attaching additional devices via expansion slots and ports.

2. Central processing unit

3. Adding, decoding, shifting, and storing

4. A decoder is used to select memory addresses and I/O devices.

5. Collector, base, and emitter

6. AND, OR, and NOT

7. Truth table

8. Decoder

9. 0

10. NOT

11. Plus symbol (+)

12. Flip-flop

13. SRAM

14. Binary instructions are processed sequentially by fetching an instruction from memory, and then executing that instruction.

   Both instructions and data are stored in the main memory system.

   Instruction execution is carried out by a CPU that contains a control unit (CU), an arithmetic logic unit (ALU), and registers (small storage areas).

   The CPU has the capability to accept input from and provide output to external devices.

15. A bus is a set of wires and protocols designed to facilitate communication between computer devices.

16. Address, data, and control

17. Cache memory is used to speed processing in a computer.

18. Polling is the process of the CPU interrogating each I/O device to see whether it needs servicing.

19. Interrupt handling

20. Resolution is normally measured in number of pixels in a horizontal and vertical direction.

chapter 4

1. Guided and unguided

2. Bandwidth, signal-to-noise ratio, bit error rate, and attenuation

3. Coaxial and twisted pair

4. 100 MHz

5. TCP/IP, FTP, HTTP

6. Seven

7. Wide area network

8. Bus, star, and ring

9. The bus topology has been the most popular in the past, but the advent of home networking has made the star topology increasingly popular.

10. Network interface card

11. Gateway

12. A switch can examine an input port's packet header and switch a point-to-point connection to the output port addressed by the packet.

13. Firewall

14. 300 to 3300 Hz

15. 256 Kbps to 1.5 Mbps

16. The speed a transmission medium is capable of handling, measured in bits per second

17. A WLAN is a LAN that uses wireless transmission instead of guided media.

18. AM places information on a carrier by modulating the amplitude. FM places information by modulating the carrier's frequency.

19. 24

20. FDM

chapter 5

1. LANs and WANs

2. Internet service provider

3. National backbone provider. NBPs provide high-speed communication lines to ISPs.

4. Sending e-mail

5. TCP

6. TCP

7. TCP

8. 32

9. Class C

10. Network broadcasts to every computer on the network.

11. ARIN (American Registry of Internet Numbers)

12. It automates the assignment of IP addresses in a network.

13. A hardware device or software that determines the next network point to which a packet should be forwarded

14. The time to live (TTL) field in the IP header

15. To provide reliable file transfer between devices

16. DNS server

17. `ipconfig`
18. HTML (Hypertext Markup Language)
19. Bots (or spiders)

chapter 6

1. Data that has been organized and logically related into a file or set of files to allow access and use

   A wide variety of answers are possible for examples of the database currently being used. Some possibilities are as follows:

   Registration

   Student transcripts

   Grocery store checkout

   Grading

   Library

   Health insurance

2. Record #

3. ```
   select *
   from teams
   order by wins desc;
   ```

   The table name can vary because it's not provided in the documentation. Letter case doesn't matter.

   You might be tempted to leave out the desc keyword. End users looking at the results probably want to see the team with the most wins at the top.

4. ```
   select *
   from teams
   order by wins desc, team;
   ```

   You might be tempted to put the desc keyword after team, but descending order applies only to the wins column, *not* the team column. You can also list each field instead of using the * wildcard.

5. ```
   insert into teams
   values (6, 'Bears', 3, 9);
   ```

   OR

   ```
   insert into teams (record_num, team, wins, losses)
   values (6, 'Bears', 3, 9);
   ```

6. ```
   insert into teams
   values (7, 'Lions', 9, 3);
   ```

   OR

```
insert into teams (record_num, team, wins, losses)
values (7, 'Lions', 9, 3);
```

The record number could be different, depending on whether question #5 was done.

7.
```
select *
from teams;
```

OR

```
select record_num, team, wins, losses
from teams
```

8. Normalization is the process of structuring tables to eliminate duplication and inconsistencies in data.

   The first problem is that if a database isn't normalized correctly, it can't represent certain real-world information items.

   The second problem occurs when the database contains redundancies (repetitions) in data, which simply wastes time and storage space.

   The third problem occurs when important information has been excluded during design of the data structures.

9. first normal form (1NF): Eliminate repeating fields or groups of fields from the table, and confirm that every column has only one value by creating a new record in the table.

   second normal form (2NF): First normal form has already been applied to the table, and every column that isn't part of the primary key is fully dependent on the primary key.

   third normal form (3NF): Eliminate columns that aren't dependent on only the primary key.

10. Step 1: Investigate and define
    Investigate and research the information you plan to model. Define the purpose of the database and how it will be used.

    Step 2: Make a master column list
    Create a list of all fields where you need to store information along with their properties.

    Step 3: Create the tables
    Logically group fields into tables.

    Step 4: Work on relationships
    Define the relationships showing how one table works with another.

    Step 5: Analyze the design
    Analyze the work completed by searching for design errors, refining tables as needed, and correcting any normalization violations.

    Step 6: Reevaluate
    Reevaluate database performance and ensure that it meets all your reporting and form needs.

11. Answers can vary.

12. Answers can vary.

13. Answers can vary.

14. The NOT NULL statement can vary, as shown:

```
CREATE TABLE ErrorDesc
(Error_Code char(4) NOT NULL,
Error_Code_Desc char(40) NOT NULL
);
CREATE TABLE Errors
(Error_Log_Date Date NOT NULL,
Error_Log_Time Time NOT NULL,
User_Code char(8) NOT NULL,
Error_Code char(4) NOT NULL,
Error_Log_Desc char(80),
Error_Status_Code char(1),
Error_Priority_Code number
);
CREATE TABLE Users
(User_Code char(8) NOT NULL,
User_First char(15) NOT NULL,
User_Last char(25) NOT NULL,
User_Password char(10) NOT NULL
);
```

15. The answer is an example of what you might use for the Users table. Be aware that values will be different.

```
insert into users
values ('mrooney', 'mickey', 'rooney', 'dance');
insert into users
values ('bboop', 'betty', 'boop', 'cartoon');
insert into users
values ('bbunny', 'bugs', 'bunny', 'rabbit');
```

16.
```
select User_Code, User_First, User_Last
from Users
order by User_Last, User_First;
```

17.
```
select Error_Log_Date, Error_Log_Time, Errors.Error_Code,
Error_Status_Code, Error_Priority_Code, Error_Code_Desc,
Error_Log_Desc
from Errors, ErrorDesc
order by Error_Log_Date, Error_Log_Time;
```

If you're using Access and specified the Error_Code column, you might have seen an error message stating that this field could refer to more than one table listed in the FROM clause. If you have more than one field with the same name used in two different tables, it's correct to precede the field name with the table name, followed by a period and then the field name (for example, Errors.Error_Code).

18.
```
select Error_Log_Date, Error_Log_Time, Errors.Error_Code,
Error_Status_Code, Error_Priority_Code, Error_Log_Desc,
Errors.User_Code, User_Last, User_First
from Errors, Users
order by Error_Log_Date, Error_Log_Time;
```

If you're using Access and specified the Error_Code and User_Code columns, you might have seen an error message stating that these fields could refer to more than one table listed in the FROM clause. If you have more than one field with the same name used in two different tables, it's correct to precede the field name with the table name, followed by a period and then the field name (for example, Errors.Error_Code and Errors.User_Code).

19.
```
CREATE TABLE ErrorStatus
(Error_Status_Code char(1) NOT NULL,
Error_Status_Desc char(50) NOT NULL
);
```

20.
```
CREATE TABLE PriorityDesc
(Error_Priority_Code number NOT NULL,
Error_Priority_Desc char(50) NOT NULL
);
```

chapter 7

1. The number is a base 10 number.
2. The number 2 is raised to the 10th power.
3. 256
4. 16
5. 16
6. 256
7. 170
8. 101011001
9. 7243
10. A10
11. BEAD
12. 1100010000111010

13. 11000

14. 10001010

15. 256

16. 786,432

17. 41

18. 2^{24} (more than 16 million)

19. BMP

20. 1

chapter 8

1. Arrays can be used any time you need to store information that should or can be accessed in sequential order.

2. `int[ ][ ] aiGrades = new int[5][2];`

3. Values can vary:

```
aiGrades[0][0] = 1234;
aiGrades[0][1] = 100;

aiGrades[1][0] = 4321;
aiGrades[1][1] = 90;

aiGrades[2][0] = 2212;
aiGrades[2][1] = 85;

aiGrades[3][0] = 8374;
aiGrades[3][1] = 75;

aiGrades[4][0] = 7758;
aiGrades[4][1] = 92;
```

4. A stack allows you to push (add) items on to the list and pop (remove) them from the list. Items are added to or removed from the top of the list. This means the last item added is the first item removed.

5. A queue allows you to push (add) items on to the list and pop (remove) them from the list. New items are added at the bottom of the list. Items are removed from the top of the list.

6. A binary tree represents hierarchical storage of data. Each position in a tree is called a node, and nodes have values associated with them. A node may or may not have child nodes. In a binary search tree, the left child's value is less than the parent node's, and the right child's value is greater than the parent node's. As you proceed through the search tree, you should compare to see whether the value you're searching for is in the current node. If not, check to see whether your value is greater than the current node value. If so, you move to the node on the right. Otherwise, you move to the node on the left and begin the comparison process again.

7. See the following two diagrams.

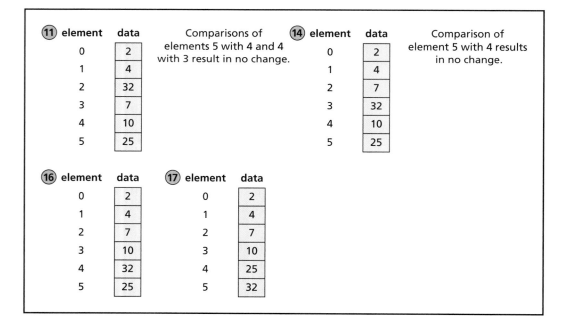

8. See the following diagram.

① element	data		② element	no changed data		③ element	no changed data
0	2		0	2		0	2
1	4		1	4		1	4
2	7		2	7		2	7
3	32		3	32		3	32
4	25		4	25		4	25
5	10		5	10		5	10

④ element	data
0	2
1	4
2	7
3	10
4	25
5	32

no more changes

9. See the following two diagrams.

① element	data		④ element	data		⑤ element	data
0	5		0	5		0	5
1	32		1	32		1	1
2	30		2	1		2	32
3	1		3	30		3	30
4	2		4	2		4	2
5	20		5	20		5	20

Comparisons of elements 5 with 4 and 4 with 3 result in no movement.

⑥ element	data		⑧ element	data		⑨ element	data
0	1		0	1		0	1
1	5		1	5		1	5
2	32		2	32		2	2
3	30		3	2		3	32
4	2		4	30		4	30
5	20		5	20		5	20

Comparison of element 5 with 4 results in no change.

⑩ element	data		⑪ element	no changed data		⑫ element	no changed data
0	1		0	1		0	1
1	2		1	2		1	2
2	5		2	5		2	5
3	32		3	32		3	20
4	30		4	20		4	32
5	20		5	30		5	30

⑬ element	data
0	1
1	2
2	5
3	20
4	30
5	32

10. See the following diagram.

① element	data		② element	data		③ element	data
0	5		0	1		0	1
1	32		1	32		1	2
2	30		2	30		2	30
3	1		3	5		3	5
4	2		4	2		4	32
5	20		5	20		5	20

④ element	data		⑤ element	data		⑥ element	data
0	1		0	1		0	1
1	2		1	2		1	2
2	5		2	5		2	5
3	30		3	20		3	20
4	32		4	32		4	30
5	20		5	30		5	32

11. See the following diagram.

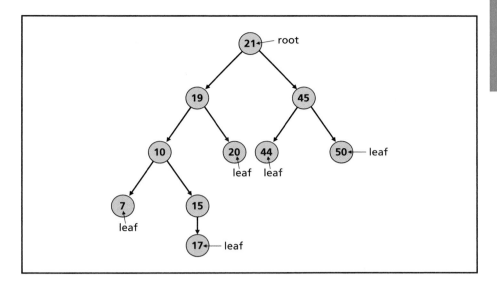

12. Four (21, 19, 10, 15, 17)

13. Three

14. Seven comparisons:
    1. 7 = 21? No.
    2. 7 > 21? No. Go left.
    3. 7 = 19? No.
    4. 7 > 19? No. Go left.
    5. 7 = 10? No.
    6. 7 > 10? No. Go left.
    7. 7 = 7? Yes.

15. Nine comparisons:
    1. 17 = 21? No.
    2. 17 > 21? No. Go left.
    3. 17 = 19? No.
    4. 17 > 19? No. Go left.
    5. 17 = 10? No.
    6. 17 > 10? Yes. Go right.
    7. 17 = 15? No.
    8. 17 > 15? Yes. Go right.
    9. 17 = 17? Yes.

chapter 9

1. Operating system

2. Device drivers, or just drivers

3. Kernel

4. An operating system's capability to support more than one process running at a time

5. The coordinated execution of a process, using two or more CPUs at the same time

6. Provide a user interface, manage processes, manage resources, provide security

7. Command-line interface and graphical user interface

8. A small program running on a computer that can be part of a larger program

9. Time slicing

10. To allow processes and hardware I/O devices to interrupt the processor's normal executing so that it can handle specific tasks

11. Tree structure

12. By using the `man` command

13. The process of formatting arranges the disk surface into addressable areas and sets up the basic directory tree structure on the disk. It can also be used to place a copy of the OS on the disk so that it can be used as a boot disk.

14. UNIX, Linux

15. `mkdir`

16. `ls`

17. A special character used to find matching patterns in filenames

18. The F2 key

19. To allow the OS and hardware to work together to detect and configure I/O devices automatically

20. Yes

chapter 10

1. A file system is responsible for creating, manipulating, renaming, copying, and moving files to and from a stored device.

2. The file management system organizes the hard drive into several different areas. FAT uses a table to keep track of which files are using which clusters. It also keeps track of which clusters are good and bad. FAT is implemented as a linked list. A file's clusters are linked until the last cluster (indicated with a special code) is stored.

3. As more files are stored on the hard drive, clusters become less contiguous. The system tries to recover open disk space. As time goes by, a file could have clusters stored all over the disk drive.

4. Disk defragmentation reorganizes clusters on a hard drive so that files are contiguous. Having contiguous clusters for a stored file improves performance because the read head doesn't have to move as much. Therefore, system speed is increased when working with files.

5. FAT uses a file allocation table, meaning that large files don't have to be stored contiguously. They can be placed wherever they fit on the drive. NTFS uses a Master File Table that stores information about files and folders. The MFT acts as a database table that keeps track of file and folder information. FAT is used on small drives (less than 10 GB), whereas NTFS is geared toward larger hard drives.

6. Using FAT can result in fragmentation on the hard drive, causing system performance to degrade. System performance also degrades just by the number of files being stored on the system. FAT lacks many security features found in NTFS. It can also have integrity problems with clusters.

7. NTFS is implemented with a Master File Table (MFT). The MFT resembles a database table that holds information on each file and volume. As new files or folders are created, new entries are added to the MFT. NTFS is a journaling system that keeps track of all transactions performed when working with files and folders. That way, if there's a problem, the system can "roll back" to a secure state.

8. NTFS is fast and reliable and can recover from problems without losing a lot of data. NTFS also improves security by adding file and folder permissions, and it supports file compression and encryption. One disadvantage of NTFS is that it's feasible for use only on large hard drives. In addition, you can't access NTFS volumes from DOS, Windows 9x, and some Linux distributions.

9. The MFT is similar to a database table that stores entries for each file and folder on a volume. It contains attributes about files and resembles a table of contents for files and folders in a volume. When a file or folder is created, a new record is created in the MFT.

10. The advantages of file compression are that you can save disk space and compressing and uncompressing are handled by the system. The disadvantage is that it can slow down performance because the system has to compress and uncompress files.

11. All files are stored as binary information, but a text file consists of ASCII or Unicode characters, and a binary file contains 1s and 0s. Text files are in human language and are more readable. Binary files can't be read by humans but are more compact and faster to access because the system already understands binary.

12. Sequential file access starts at the beginning of a file and processes it line by line until it reaches the end. The stored data can be thought of as one long row of information. Random file access allows you to access a particular record in a file without having to process all the information stored before it.

13. The writing process used in sequential file access is very fast because all information is added at the end of the file. Retrieving or reading the information can be very slow because you have to start at the beginning of the file and process through all the data until you find the specified information. Inserting, deleting, and modifying existing records require rewriting the file's contents to a new file. Random file access is useful for accessing records quickly because you don't have to process all the file information. You can also update records without having to rewrite the file's contents.

You can see that speed is an advantage of random file access. The disadvantage is that it can waste disk space if the data doesn't fill the entire record area or if a record doesn't have data associated with it.

14. Hashing creates and uses a hash key value that acts as an identifier for data. The process of hashing involves creating an algorithm that calculates a hash value suitable for identifying records yet avoids as many collisions or duplicates as possible. The goal is to make data searches, updates, deletions, and modifications more efficient.

15. Many different algorithms could be used to solve this problem. If you follow the example in the book, the algorithm is based on determining the maximum number of records you might have. The records should have a key value of 0 to the highest number minus 1. You need to identify how many students you might have in the system. This number will vary. For this example, say there are 2000 students. Divide 9999999 by 2000 to come up with approximately 5000 as the key. If the first student number is 1002394, you divide that number by 5000 to create the key of 200 for this record. There's no right or wrong algorithm for this question. It's intended to make you think creatively and get some hands-on practice in designing an algorithm.

chapter 11

1. The trouble that users have with technology can often be blamed on poor design.

2. Development teams might not have expertise in interface design; companies might have established development procedures that are difficult to change; companies might perceive the extra steps in user-centric design as resulting in increased costs.

3. Psychology, sociology, computer science, marketing, visual design

4. Infrared sensors

5. Superstitious behavior

6. Sensory storage, short-term memory, long-term memory

7. Repetition, chunking

8. When they've become familiar with an application

9. Quality of the experience, an understanding of users, an effective design process, learnability, an aesthetic experience, changeability, manageability

10. Users have some control over the interface; the application might run on many different platforms.

chapter 12

1. Approaches involving intuition and emotion

2. Boasting aloud or visualizing positive results, thinking about the problem-solving process positively, being patient

3. Architecture bug

4. Coding bug

5. Expecting data input to be consistently correct isn't logical.

6. Different platforms vary in architecture and, therefore, might require different coding.

7. Straw man arguments, rules of thumb (heuristics), following a procedure

8. Observe what's happening, propose a theory for why it's happening, test the theory, and repeat Steps 1 to 3 until you're satisfied with the theory.

9. The first place to look when debugging a program is your code. Most likely, the bug you find is your own doing, so *you're* responsible for fixing it.

10. Iterative program development means building a program up from small components; in other words, write a program component and debug it, write another component and debug it, and so forth. This approach is different from writing the entire program and then testing it. Iterative development can save you a lot of debugging time and gives you a baseline for debugging because you can ask, "What have I changed since the last time the program worked?"

11. Having multiple versions is useful for experimentation, such as testing different variables or components, and for isolating changes in a separate version without worrying about causing problems in the main program. You can also run two versions side by side to compare them.

12. Breakpoints

13. Help pages for the programming language, reference Web sites, documentation for borrowed code, online discussion boards, blogs, wiki posts

14. Changes you have made, program versions, results of your changes, and even details such as date, time, filename, and so on

15. To make sure you're fixing the underlying cause of the problem, not just the symptoms, and to prevent the problem from happening again in the current program or in future programs

chapter 13

1. Software engineering is the process of producing software applications. It involves not just the program's source code but also associated documentation, including UML diagrams, screen prototypes, reports, software requirements, future development issues, and data needed to make programs operate correctly. It's the heart of computer science and incorporates everything a software developer might encounter, including hardware components, networking, databases, Web development, software applications, and so forth.

2. A design document details all the application's design issues and includes its functionality, appearance, and distribution. Without a well-defined design document, a project is doomed to failure. Creating a design document is based on good communication with end users in determining the application's needs and requirements.

3. Prompt for card

    When card is entered, read card

    Ask for PIN

    Confirm that PIN matches card

    If there is a match, continue with transaction.
    Otherwise, display an error message.

    Ask for dollar amount to add to savings

    Add dollar amount to savings and update account

    Ask if they would like to make another transaction

    If so, continue by going back to Step 6. Otherwise,
    display a thank you message and quit.

    Eject card

4. Prompt for card

    When card is entered, read card

    Ask for PIN

    Confirm that PIN matches card

    If there is a match, continue with transaction.
    Otherwise, display an error message.

    Ask for dollar amount to remove from account

    Subtract dollar amount from account and update the
    account

    Ask if they would like to make another transaction

    If so, continue by going back to Step 6. Otherwise,
    display a thank you message and quit.

    Eject card

5. UML is a software modeling process that enables developers to create a blueprint showing the overall functionality of the program being engineered and provides a way for clients and developers to communicate. Better communication results in a better project.

6. A data dictionary is a document defining the structure of the database, describing the type of data used in the program, and showing table definitions, indexes, and other data relationships. Developers use it to clarify the data available for use in reports, screens, file transfers, and other data operations. Developers or end users can also use it during the report creation process. The document acts as a master guide for making sure all data is consistent.

7. A prototype is a typical example that gives end users a good idea of what they'll see when their application is completed. It's *not* the final product, ready to go. A software engineer can design all the screens and reports before any lines of source code are written and should get end users' input on factors such as color, position of fields, and so forth. The result should be a

product agreed on by both the user and the developer, thus promoting good communication throughout the process.

8. Not including the end user in the design process

    Writing your application without getting user approval for the prototype

    Not testing the application

    Using poor coding procedures

    Not creating a design document

    Thinking that end users don't know what they want, so you tell them what they're going to get

    This list shows just a few examples; you could add more examples.

9. The waterfall SDLC model represents the fundamental processes in creating a program as phases. The output from each phase is used as the input for the next phase. The first step is gathering all the requirements for the project. The second step is designing the system and software. After all the requirements have been defined and the project has been designed, it's time to build and implement the application. After the application is finished, it must be tested and then finally put into operation and maintained to meet users' needs. If you encounter a problem in the design, you must return to the first step and continue repeating the process until the final product has met all the users' functional requirements.

10. Project manager: Leader of the team, responsible for choosing the right players for the right positions, determining the project's risks, costs, and schedule of tasks, and keeping the project on schedule.

    Database administrator (DBA): Person assigned the role of creating and maintaining the database.

    Software developer (or programmer): Person responsible for writing source code to meet end users' functional requirements.

    Client: Person who has a need that can be met through the process of software engineering. Clients are the ones who know what they really want and why.

    Tester: Person responsible for making sure the program functions correctly and meets all the functional requirements specified in the design document.

    Customer relations representative (or support technician): Person responsible for interacting with testers, developers, and end users during the product's creation and early release and on an ongoing basis with end users as long as the product is being used.

11. See the following diagram.

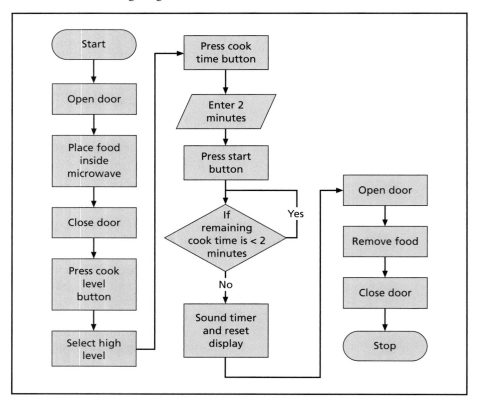

Answers can vary.

12. ```
Open microwave door
Place food inside microwave
Close microwave door
Press the cook level button
Select High
Press the cook time button
Enter 2 minutes
Press the start button
When timer goes off, open door
Remove food
Close door
```

Answers can vary.
```

13. See the following diagram.

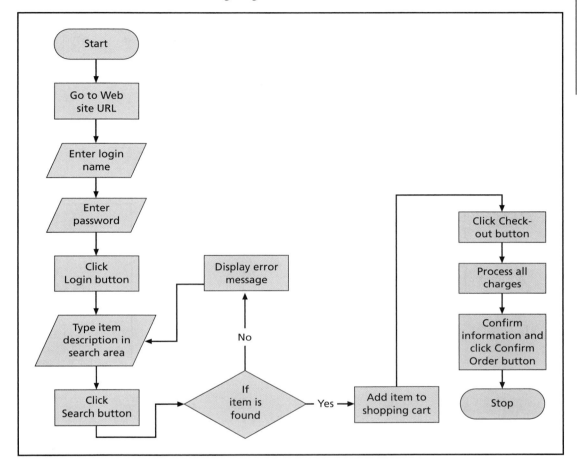

Answers can vary.

14.
```
Go to Web site URL
Enter login name
Enter password
Click the Login button
Type item description in search area
Click the Search button
If found, enter quantity and click "Add item to
shopping cart"
If not found, display error message and return to screen
Click the Checkout button
Confirm information and click the Confirm Order button
Click the Logout button
```

Answers can vary.

15. See the following diagram.

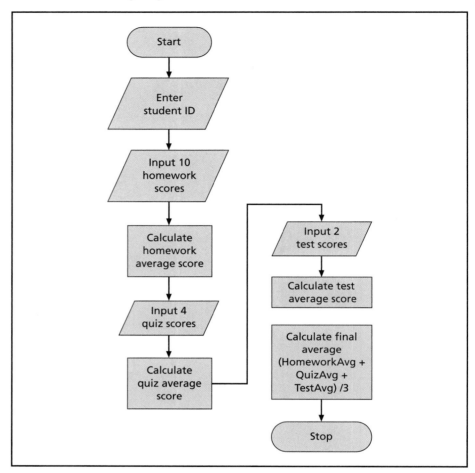

```
Enter student ID
Input 10 homework scores
Calculate the homework average score
Input 4 quiz scores
Calculate the quiz average score
Input 2 test scores
Calculate the test average score
Calculate the final average (HomeworkAvg + QuizAvg +
TestAvg)/ 3
```

Answers can vary.

chapter 14

1. A logically ordered set of statements used to solve a problem

2. If the amount is to be deposited, add it to the current balance. If the amount is to be withdrawn, subtract it from the current balance.

3. Pseudocode for calculating your checkbook balance:

```
Ask for the current balance of checking account
Ask if deposit or withdrawal (check written)
Ask for amount
Ask for date
If Deposit
    Current balance = Current balance + amount
Else if Withdrawal (check written)
    Current balance = Current balance - amount
Store information
```

4. When the gas pump lever is lifted up and the gas grade is selected, reset the dollar amount and the amount of gas pumped and display the price per gallon. When the pump handle lever is lifted, begin pumping gas and updating the display areas showing the dollar amount and amount of gas pumped. Continue pumping gas until the sensor clicks off the gas pump handle or until the user releases the handle. Turn off the pump when the gas lever is pushed down.

5. Pseudocode for maintaining a gas pump's operation:

```
System is idle
Continue checking to see if gas lever is lifted
While gas lever is lifted
    If gas grade selected = Unleaded
      Begin pumping unleaded gas
    Else if gas grade selected = Premium
      Begin pumping premium gas
    Update gas pump display area
End while
Put system back in idle state
```

6. Answers will vary, depending on the course. The algorithm should be a general description of accepting input in the form of scores for assignments, tests, quizzes, projects, and a final exam. It should then show the formula for calculating the final grade and assigning a letter grade to the resulting percentage.

7. The pseudocode will vary, depending on the course. It should be a step-by-step description of a professor entering grades into a system to calculate the scores for students based on a course syllabus.

8. Pseudocode for playing tic-tac-toe:

```
Declare a 2x2 array of char (or string)
LOOP: Stay in this loop until the game is won or all
positions have been used and there's no winner
Prompt for an X or an O
Store response in a variable
Prompt for a row
Prompt for a column
Check to see whether the location is available
    If not, prompt that the position has already been used
and go back to the LOOP
```

>   Else store the variable's contents in the array position using the row and column
> See whether the player has tic-tac-toe by evaluating the array's contents
>   If a player wins, display a prompt and set a value to terminate the loop
>   Else allow the loop to return back to LOOP

9. Pseudocode for getting to school (answers can vary):

```
Turn off alarm
Get out of bed
Shower and take care of bathroom necessities (BRUSH YOUR
TEETH)
Eat breakfast
Grab books and keys
Get in car
Drive to school
Park car
Run to class to avoid being late
```

10. Pseudocode for completing a 3 × 3 sudoku puzzles (answers can vary):

```
Select the next available cell in the grid
    If there are no available cells, display a message
that the sudoku is filled out and exit the loop
Select the lowest number for the cell (1 through 9)
Check that number is used in the row, the column, or the
3x3 cell
Repeat until you find an available number
    If there's no available number, display a message that
the sudoku can't be completed and exit the loop
After you find an available number, store it in the cell
Repeat until there are no available cells
Add up all values in each row and see if the sum is 45
    If not, display an error message and exit the loop
Add up all values in the columns and see if the sum is 45
    If not, display an error message and exit the loop
Display a message that the sudoku is completed
```

chapter 15

1. Integer variables are used for positive and negative whole numbers. Some examples are storing inventory counts, miles driven, points scored in a sporting event, and so on. Variable name for these examples could be iCount, iMilesDriven, and iPoints. Placing the letter "i" in front of the variable name improves readability of the source code because a person debugging the program can assume that any variables starting with "i" contain an integer value. Here's an example of declaring an integer variable:

```
int iMilesDriven;
```

2. Floating-point variables are used for positive and negative numbers that can also have decimals. Some examples are storing a student's grade percentage, the cost of an item, averages, and so on. Variable names for these examples could be fPercent, fCost, and fAverage. Placing the letter "f" in front of the variable name improves readability of the source code because a person debugging the program can assume that any variables starting with "f" contain a floating-point value. Here's an example of declaring a floating-point variable:

```
float fCost;
```

3. Character variables are used for storing only one character. Some examples are storing a student's middle initial, a letter grade that doesn't include a minus or plus, gender, and so on. Variable names for these examples could be cMiddleInit, cGrade, and cGender. Placing the letter "c" in front of the variable name improves readability of the source code because a person debugging the program can assume that any variables starting with "c" contain a character value. Here's an example of declaring a character variable:

```
char cGender;
```

4. String variables are used to store more than one character. Some examples are storing a student's first name, a letter grade that does include a minus or a plus, a street address, and so on. Variable names for these examples could be sFirstName, sGrade, and sAddress1. Placing the letter "s" in front of the variable name improves readability of the source code because a person debugging the program can assume that any variables starting with "s" contain a string value. Here's an example of declaring a string variable in Java and C++:

```
String sFirstName; //Java example
string sGrade; //C++ example
```

5.
```
//Java example
public class chap15
{
public static void main(String[] args)
    {
    boolean bFirst = true;
    boolean bSecond = true;
    if((bFirst) && (bSecond))
       System.out.print("T");
    else if((bFirst) && (! bSecond))
       System.out.print("F");
    else if((! bFirst) && (bSecond))
       System.out.print("F");
    else if((! bFirst) && (! bSecond))
       System.out.print("F");
    }
}
```

```cpp
//C++ example
#include <cstdlib>
#include <iostream>

using namespace std;

int main()
{
    bool bFirst = true;
    bool bSecond = true;

    if ((bFirst) && (bSecond))
        cout << "T\n";
    else if ((bFirst) && (!bSecond))
        cout << "F\n";
    else if ((!bFirst) && (bSecond))
        cout << "F\n";
    else if ((!bFirst) && (!bSecond))
        cout << "F\n";

    system("PAUSE");
    return 0;
}
```

Try changing the values for the bFirst and bSecond variables and see the results, as in this example:

```java
//Java example
public class chap15
{
public static void main(String[] args)
    {
    boolean bFirst = false;
    boolean bSecond = true;
    if((bFirst) && (bSecond))
      System.out.print("T");
    else if((bFirst) && (! bSecond))
      System.out.print("F");
    else if((! bFirst) && (bSecond))
      System.out.print("F");
    else if((! bFirst) && (! bSecond))
      System.out.print("F");
    }
}
```

```cpp
//C++ example
#include <cstdlib>
#include <iostream>

using namespace std;

int main()
{
    bool bFirst = false;
    bool bSecond = true;
```

```
        if ((bFirst) && (bSecond))
            cout << "T\n";
        else if ((bFirst) && (!bSecond))
            cout << "F\n";
        else if ((!bFirst) && (bSecond))
            cout << "F\n";
        else if ((!bFirst) && (!bSecond))
            cout << "F\n";

        system("PAUSE");
        return 0;
}
```

6.

```
//Java example
public class Arithmetic
{
public static void main(String[] args)
    {
    int iFirstNum = 15;
    int iSecondNum = 10;
    int iResult;
    System.out.print("Addition: ");
    iResult = iFirstNum + iSecondNum;
    System.out.print("15 + 10 = ");
    System.out.println(iResult);
    System.out.print("Subtraction: ");
    iResult = iFirstNum - iSecondNum;
    System.out.print("15 - 10 = ");
    System.out.println(iResult);
    System.out.print("Multiplication: ");
    iResult = iFirstNum * iSecondNum;
    System.out.print("15 * 10 = ");
    System.out.println(iResult);
    System.out.print("Division: ");
    iResult = iFirstNum/iSecondNum;
    System.out.print("15/10 = ");
    System.out.println(iResult);
    System.out.print("Modulus: ");
    iResult = iFirstNum%iSecondNum;
    System.out.print("15%10 = ");
    System.out.println(iResult);
    }
}

//C++ example
#include <cstdlib>
#include <iostream>

using namespace std;

int main()
{
```

```cpp
      int iFirstNum = 15;
      int iSecondNum = 10;
      int iResult;

      iResult = iFirstNum + iSecondNum;
      cout << "Addition: 15 + 10 = " << iResult << "\n";

      iResult = iFirstNum - iSecondNum;
      cout << "Subtraction: 15 - 10 = " << iResult << "\n";

      iResult = iFirstNum * iSecondNum;
      cout << "Multiplication: 15 * 10 = " << iResult << "\n";

      iResult = iFirstNum / iSecondNum;
      cout << "Subtraction: 15 / 10 = " << iResult << "\n";

      iResult = iFirstNum % iSecondNum;
      cout << "Modulus: 15 % 10 = " << iResult << "\n";

      system("PAUSE");
      return 0;
}
```

7.

```java
//Java example
public class Looping
{
public static void main(String[] args)
    {
    int iCount = 1;
    for (iCount = 1; iCount <= 5; iCount++)
    {
    System.out.println("For Loop - Dr. Doolittle # " + iCount);
    }
    iCount = 1;
    while (iCount <= 5)
    {
    System.out.println("While Loop - Dr. Doolittle # " + iCount);
    iCount++;
    }
    iCount = 1;
    do
    {
    System.out.println("Do While Loop - Dr. Doolittle # " + iCount);
    } while (iCount++<5);
    }
}
```

```cpp
//C++ example
#include <cstdlib>
#include <iostream>

using namespace std;

int main()
{
    int iCount = 1;

    for (iCount = 1; iCount <= 5; iCount++)
    {
    cout << "For Loop - Dr. Doolittle # " << iCount << "\n";
    }

    iCount = 1;

    while (iCount <= 5)
    {
    cout << "While Loop - Dr. Doolittle # " << iCount << "\n";
    iCount++;
    }

    iCount = 1;

    do
    {
    cout << "Do While Loop - Dr. Doolittle # " << iCount << "\n";
    } while (iCount++ < 5);

    system("PAUSE");
    return 0;
}
```

8. Answers can vary.

```java
//Java example
public class Grade_If
{
public static void main(String[] args)
    {
    int iGrade = 72;
    if (iGrade >= 90)
      System.out.println("You get an A");
    else if ((iGrade >= 80) && (iGrade < 90))
      System.out.println("You get a B");
    else if ((iGrade >= 70) && (iGrade < 80))
      System.out.println("You get a C");
    else if ((iGrade >= 60) && (iGrade < 70))
      System.out.println("You get a D");
    else
      System.out.println("See you next semester!");
    }
}
```

```
//C++ example
#include <cstdlib>
#include <iostream>

using namespace std;

int main()
{
    int iGrade = 72;

    if (iGrade >= 90)
        cout << "You get an A\n";
    else if (iGrade >= 80)
        cout << "You get a B\n";
    else if (iGrade >= 70)
        cout << "You get a C\n";
    else if (iGrade >= 60)
        cout << "You get a D\n";
    else
        cout << "See you next semester!";

    system("PAUSE");
    return 0;
}
```

9.

```
//Java example
public class Grade_Switch
{
public static void main(String[] args)
    {
    int iGrade = 82;
    switch (iGrade)
    {
      case 100 :
      case 99 :
      case 98 :
      case 97 :
      case 96 :
      case 95 :
      case 94 :
      case 93 :
      case 92 :
      case 91 :
      case 90 :
         System.out.println("You get an A");
    break;
      case 89 :
      case 88 :
      case 87 :
      case 86 :
      case 85 :
      case 84 :
```

```
          case 83 :
          case 82 :
          case 81 :
          case 80 :
             System.out.println("You get a B");
       break;
          case 79 :
          case 78 :
          case 77 :
          case 76 :
          case 75 :
          case 74 :
          case 73 :
          case 72 :
          case 71 :
          case 70 :
             System.out.println("You get a C");
       break;
          case 69 :
          case 68 :
          case 67 :
          case 66 :
          case 65 :
          case 64 :
          case 63 :
          case 62 :
          case 61 :
          case 60 :
             System.out.println("You get a D");
       break;
       default :
          System.out.println("See you next semester!");
       }
       }
}

//C++ example
#include <cstdlib>
#include <iostream>

using namespace std;

int main()
{
    int iGrade = 72;

    switch (iGrade)
    {
       case 100:
       case 99:
       case 98:
       case 97:
       case 96:
```

```
      case 95:
      case 94:
      case 93:
      case 92:
      case 91:
      case 90:
        cout << "You get an A\n";
  break;
      case 89:
      case 88:
      case 87:
      case 86:
      case 85:
      case 84:
      case 83:
      case 82:
      case 81:
      case 80:
        cout << "You get a B\n";
  break;
      case 79:
      case 78:
      case 77:
      case 76:
      case 75:
      case 74:
      case 73:
      case 72:
      case 71:
      case 70:
        cout << "You get a C\n";
  break;
      case 69:
      case 68:
      case 67:
      case 66:
      case 65:
      case 64:
      case 63:
      case 62:
      case 61:
      case 60:
        cout << "You get a D\n";
  break;
  default:
    cout << "See you next semester!\n";

  }
  system("PAUSE");
  return 0;

}
```

10. A `do-while` statement is used when you want to execute a loop at least one time before the expression is evaluated; the loop executes as long as the expression evaluates to true. The `while` and `for` statements are precondition loops, meaning the expression is evaluated before statements in the loop are executed. Therefore, the loop might never execute. A `for` statement is used when you want to repeat a group of statements a known number of times. Like a `for` statement, a `while` statement is used to repeat a group of statements a certain number of times or for a certain condition, but `while` doesn't provide a specified area for updating the counter variable, as the increment/decrement part of the `for` statement does.

B

appendix

ASCII (American Standard
Code for Information
Interchange) table

The following table shows the ASCII character set.

ASCII code	character	ASCII code	character	ASCII code	character	ASCII code	character
000	NUL	032	space	064	@	096	`
001	SOH	033	!	065	A	097	a
002	STX	034	"	066	B	098	b
003	ETX	035	#	067	C	099	c
004	EOT	036	$	068	D	100	d
005	ENQ	037	%	069	E	101	e
006	ACK	038	&	070	F	102	f
007	BEL	039	'	071	G	103	g
008	BS	040	(	072	H	104	h
009	HT	041	)	073	I	105	i
010	LF	042	*	074	J	106	j
011	VT	043	+	075	K	107	k
012	FF	044	,	076	L	108	l
013	CR	045	–	077	M	109	m
014	SO	046	.	078	N	110	n
015	SI	047	/	079	O	111	o
016	DLE	048	0	080	P	112	p
017	DC1	049	1	081	Q	113	q
018	DC2	050	2	082	R	114	r
019	DC3	051	3	083	S	115	s
020	DC4	052	4	084	T	116	t
021	NAK	053	5	085	U	117	u
022	SYN	054	6	086	V	118	v
023	ETB	055	7	087	W	119	w
024	CAN	056	8	088	X	120	x
025	EM	057	9	089	Y	121	y
026	SUB	058	:	090	Z	122	z
027	ESC	059	;	091	[	123	{

ASCII code	character	ASCII code	character	ASCII code	character	ASCII code	character
028	FS	060	<	092	\	124	|
029	GS	061	=	093	]	125	}
030	RS	062	>	094	^	126	~
031	US	063	?	095	_	127	delete

ASCII values are given as decimal numbers.
Control characters are listed with their abbreviations.

C

Java and C++ reserved words

reserved word	Java or C++	description
abstract	Java	declares that a class or method is abstract
assert	both	declares a Boolean variable
bool	C++	declares a Boolean variable
boolean	Java	declares a Boolean variable
break	both	stops processing `case` statements
byte	Java	declares a byte variable
case	both	declares a `case` statement in a `switch` statement
catch	both	handles an exception
char	both	declares a character variable
class	both	signals the beginning of a class definition
const	C++	specifies an object or variable that can't be modified
continue	both	returns to the beginning of a loop prematurely
default	both	default action in a `switch` statement; signals that no match was found
do	both	begins a `do-while` loop
double	both	declares a double variable
else	both	signals the code to execute when an `if` statement is not true
extends	both	specifies that a class is a subclass of another class
final	both	declares that a class can't be subclassed or a field or method can't be overridden
finally	both	declares a block of code that's guaranteed to be executed
float	both	declares a floating-point variable
for	both	begins a `for` loop
if	both	declares a block of code to be executed if a condition is true
implements	Java	declares that the class uses a given interface

reserved word	Java or C++	description
import	Java	permits access to a class or group of classes in a software package
#include	C++	tells the compiler to treat the included file as part of the source code
instanceof	Java	tests whether a class is an instance of another class
int	both	declares an integer variable
interface	both	signals the beginning of an interface definition
long	both	declares a long integer variable
native	Java	declares that a method is implemented in native code
new	both	declares and allocates memory for a new object
package	Java	defines the package in which the source code file belongs
private	both	declares a method or member variable to be private
protected	both	declares a class, method, or member variable to be protected
public	both	declares a class, method, or member variable to be visible to all classes
return	both	returns a value from a method
short	both	declares a short integer variable
signed	C++	allows a variable to be positive or negative
static	both	declares that a field or a method belongs to a class rather than an object
string	C++	declares a string variable
String	Java	declares a string variable
super	Java	references the parent of an object
switch	both	tests a true condition in the possible cases
synchronized	Java	indicates that a section of code is not thread-safe
this	both	references the current object

reserved word	Java or C++	description
throw	both	raises an exception
throws	Java	declares the exceptions thrown by a method
transient	Java	declares that the field shouldn't be serialized
try	both	attempts an operation that might throw or raise an exception
unsigned	C++	indicates that a variable can have only a positive value
void	both	declares that a method or function doesn't return a value
volatile	both	warns the compiler that a variable changes asynchronously
while	both	begins a `while` loop

glossary

10BaseT A twisted pair Ethernet networking cable capable of transmitting at rates up to 10 Mbps (megabits per second)

10GBaseT The fastest Ethernet networking cable, capable of transmitting at 10 Gbps (gigabits per second) over twisted pairs of wires

100BaseT A fast Ethernet networking cable made up of four twisted pairs of wire and capable of transmitting at 100 Mbps

802.11 A family of specifications for WLANs developed by IEEE; currently includes 802.11, 802.11a, 802.11b, 802.11g, and 802.11n

abacus A counting device with sliding beads, used from ancient times to the present; useful mainly for addition and subtraction

acceptable use policy (AUP) An organizational policy that defines who can use company computers and networks, when, and how

access attacks Attacks on a system that can include snooping, eavesdropping, and interception; more commonly known as spying or illicitly gaining access to protected information

accountability Making sure a system is as secure as feasible and a record of activities exists for reconstructing a break-in

adder The circuit in the CPU responsible for adding binary numbers

affect system How emotions, and potentially aesthetics, play a role in decision making

algorithm A logically ordered set of statements used to solve a problem

AM (amplitude modulation) A technique of placing data on an alternating carrier wave by varying the signal's amplitude; this technique is often used in modems

American National Standards Institute (ANSI) An organization that works with industry groups to formulate and publish standards

American Standard Code for Information Interchange (ASCII) A standard for storing text characters in computers; the ASCII standard allows representing 128 possible characters with 7 bits

AND Boolean operator that returns a true value only if both operands are true

antivirus software A program designed to detect and block computer viruses

ARIN (American Registry of Internet Numbers) The U.S. organization that assigns IP address numbers for the country and its territories

arithmetic logic unit (ALU) The portion of the CPU responsible for mathematical operations, specifically addition

array   A set of contiguous memory cells used for storing the same type of data

ASP (Active Server Pages)   A Web server technology that combines features of HTML and JavaScript or VBScript programming code; used on a Web server to create Web pages dynamically

assembler   A program that reads assembly-language code and converts it into machine language

assembly language   A human-readable language used to represent numeric computer instructions (binary code)

asymmetric encryption   Encryption using both a public key and a private key

ATM (Asynchronous Transfer Mode)   A network technology based on transferring data in cells or packets of a fixed size at speeds up to 2.488 Gbps

attenuation   A reduction in the strength of an electrical signal as it travels along a medium

attitude   A measure of how much users enjoy their experience with the technology

authentication   A technique for verifying that someone is who he or she claims to be; a password is one type of authentication

availability   Accessibility of information and services on a normal basis

backdoors   Shortcuts into programs created by system designers to facilitate system maintenance but used and abused by crackers

bandwidth   A measurement of how much information can be carried in a given time period over a wired or wireless communication medium, usually measured in bits per second (bps)

base (or parent) class   A general class from which other classes can be created via inheritance

behavioral thinking   Thinking about how something works

binary   Numbering system with two digits, 0 and 1, also known as base 2; the basis for modern computer systems

binary code or machine code   The numeric language of the computer based on the binary number system of 1s and 0s

binary search tree (BST)   A binary tree in which the left child's data value is less than the parent node's, and the right child's data value is greater than the parent node's

biometrics   Biological identification, such as fingerprints, voice dynamics, or retinal scans; considered more secure than password authentication

BIOS (basic input/output system) A ROM (or programmable ROM) chip on the motherboard; the BIOS provides the startup (boot) program for the computer as well as basic interrupt routines for I/O processing

bit The abbreviation for "binary digit"; a bit is a 1 or a 0 and is the smallest unit of representation in a computer system

bit error rate The percentage of bits that have errors in relation to the total number of bits received in a transmission; a measure of the quality of a communication line

Bluetooth A specification for short-range radio frequency (RF) links between mobile computers, mobile phones, digital cameras, and other portable devices

Boolean algebra or Boolean logic A logical system developed by George Boole that uses truth tables to indicate true/false output based on all possible true/false inputs; the computer owes a lot to this concept because at its most basic level, the computer is manipulating 1s and 0s—in other words, true or false

Boolean basic identities A set of laws that apply to Boolean expressions and define ways in which expressions can be simplified; they're similar to algebraic laws

Boolean operator A word used in Boolean algebra expressions to test two values logically; the main Boolean operators are AND, OR, and NOT

booting The process of starting a computer system

bot A small program, also called a spider or crawler, that accesses Web sites to gather their content for search engine indexes

breakpoint A stop command inserted in a program to prevent it from executing past that point

bridge A special type of network switch that can be configured to allow only specific network traffic through, based on the destination address

browser A program that accesses and displays files and other information or hypermedia available on a network or on the Internet

bubble sort A sorting routine that compares each item in the list with the item next to it; if the first item is greater than the second, it swaps them, and then repeats this process until it makes a pass all the way through the list without swapping any items

buffer overflow A program tries to place more information into a memory location than that location can handle

bus A collection of conductors, connectors, and protocols that facilitates communication between the CPU, memory, and I/O devices

bus protocol   The set of rules governing the timing and transfer of data on a computer bus

byte   A group of 8 bits considered as one unit and used as the basic unit of measurement in a computer system; memory is measured in number of bytes, for example

cable modem   A type of digital modem that connects to a local cable TV line to provide a continuous connection to the Internet

cache memory   High-speed memory used to hold frequently accessed instructions and data in a computer to avoid having to retrieve them from slower system DRAM

callback   A method that allows users to connect only by having the network initiate a call to a specified number

cardinality   Shows the numeric occurrences between entities in an ER model

Cat 5   A popular Ethernet twisted pair communication cable capable of carrying data at rates up to 100 Mbps

CCITT (Comité Consultatif International Téléphonique et Télégraphique or International Telegraph and Telephone Consultative Committee)   A standards group involved in the development of the ISO OSI reference model

CD-ROM   A 120-mm disc used to store data, music, and video in a computer system by using laser technology; CD-ROMs are capable of holding up to 850 MB of information

central processing unit (CPU)   The central controlling device inside a computer that makes decisions at a very low level, such as what math functions or computer resources are to be used and when

CGI (Common Gateway Interface)   An older Web server technology used for dynamic Web page creation

checksum   A mathematical means to check the content of a file or value (such as a credit card number) to ensure that it has not been tampered with or re-created illicitly

chip   A piece of encased silicon, usually somewhere between the size of your fingernail and the palm of your hand, that holds integrated circuits (ICs)

class   A template for defining new object types and their properties (characteristics or attributes) and behaviors

cluster   Area of the hard drive containing a group of the smallest units that can be accessed on a disk (sectors)

coaxial   Communication cable that consists of a center wire surrounded by insulation and then a grounded foil shield wrapped in steel or copper braid

collision   In hashing, what happens when the hashing algorithm generates the same relative key for more than one original key value

column, field, or attribute   A specific piece of information in a table row

command prompt   Words and symbols displayed onscreen that indicate the OS is waiting for user input

command-line interface   A method of communicating with the OS by typing commands and receiving responses in text format

compiler   An application that reads all the program's statements, converts them into computer language, and produces an executable file that doesn't need an interpreter

composite key   A primary key made up of more than one column

concatenation   The process of combining or joining strings into one value

confidentiality   Ensuring that only those authorized to access information can do so

constructor   A special method for instantiating an object

control structure   An instruction that dictates the order in which statements in a program are executed

control unit (CU)   The part of the CPU that controls the flow of data and instructions into and out of the CPU

cookie   A program that can gather information about a user and store it on the user's machine

copyright   The legal right granted to an author, a composer, an artist, a publisher, a playwright, or a distributor to exclusive sale, publication, production, or distribution of literary, artistic, musical, or dramatic works

cracker   An unwelcome system intruder with malicious intent

CRT (cathode ray tube)   The technology used in a conventional computer monitor; CRTs use electron beams to light up phosphor displays on the screen

customer relations representative (or support technician)   Person responsible for interacting with testers, developers, and end users during the product's creation and early release and on an ongoing basis with end users as long as the product is being used

data dictionary   A document describing the type of data being used in the program, showing table definitions, indexes, and other data relationships

data structure   A way of organizing data in memory, such as arrays, lists, stacks, queues, and trees

database   Data that has been logically related and organized into a file or set of files to allow access and use

database administrator (DBA)   Person assigned the role of creating and maintaining the database structure

database management system (DBMS)   A program for managing storage, access, and modifications to a database

datagram   A packet of information used in a connectionless network service that's routed to its destination by using an address included in the datagram's header

deadlock   A rare situation in which I/O devices and/or processes are waiting for each other for use of resources; this situation would continue indefinitely without intervention by the OS

debugging   The process of finding and fixing problems in program code

declaration   A statement that associates an identifier with a variable (or an action or another programming element)

decoder   A digital circuit used in computers to select memory addresses and I/O devices

demilitarized zone (DMZ)   A location outside the firewall (or between firewalls) that's more vulnerable to attack from outside

denial-of-service (DoS) attacks   Attacks that prevent legitimate users from using the system or accessing information

depth or level   The distance from the node to the root node; the root's depth or level is 0

dequeue   To remove an item from a queue

design criteria   Factors to consider in creating a good design, including users' needs and experiences and what's appropriate given the design's constraints

design document   A document that details all the design issues for an application

determinant   In a database, any column you can use to determine the value assigned to another column in the same row

DHCP (Dynamic Host Configuration Protocol)   A communication protocol that automates assigning IP addresses in an organization's network

DHTML (Dynamic HTML)   An extension to HTML tags and options for producing Web pages that are responsive to user interaction

digital certificate   The digital equivalent of an ID card; used with encryption and issued by a third-party certification authority

directed (targeted) hacker   Generally, a cracker motivated by greed and/or politics

directory   Same as folder; "folder" is often used in Windows, and "directory/subdirectory" is more often used in DOS and Linux

disaster recovery plan (DRP)   A written plan for responding to natural or other disasters, intended to minimize downtime and damage to systems and data

disk fragmentation   Occurs when files' clusters are scattered in different locations on the storage medium instead of being in contiguous locations

DNS (Domain Name System)   A method of translating Internet domain names into IP addresses; DNS servers are servers used in this process

domain   Set of possible values for a column

domain name   A name used to locate the IP address of an organization or other entity on the Internet, such as www.cengage.com

DOS (Disk Operating System)   A single-user, single-tasking, command-line operating system; the Microsoft predecessor to Windows

DRAM   Dynamic RAM, a generic term for a type of RAM that requires constant refreshing to maintain its information; various types of DRAM are used for the system main memory

driver   A special program that provides an interface to a specific I/O device

DSL (digital subscriber line)   A method of sending and receiving data over regular phone lines, using a combination of FDM and TDM

dumpster diving   Picking through people's trash to find things of value; although often innocent, it has been used by thieves to glean potentially damaging information

DVD   A technology that uses laser and layering technology to store data, music, and video on 120-mm discs; DVDs are capable of holding up to 9 GB of information

effectiveness   A measure of how well the technology helps users perform their tasks; often expressed as how quickly, how easily, how safely, and so forth

element   A memory cell in an array

embedded computers   Computers embedded into other devices: a phone, car, or thermometer, for example

encapsulation   The process of hiding an object's operations from other objects

Encrypting File System (EFS)   An encryption technology that converts data in a file to unreadable information by using an encryption algorithm and key value; to make the information readable again, you must decrypt it with another key value

encryption Transforming original data (plaintext) into coded or encrypted data (ciphertext) so that only authorized parties can interpret it

encryption key A string of bits used in an encryption algorithm to encrypt or decrypt data; the longer the key, the more secure the encryption

end user Someone or something that needs the program to perform a function or meet a need and determines the program's required functionality

endless loop A block of source code that repeats continuously and never stops

enqueue To insert an item into a queue

entity relationship (ER) model A data model that represents how all tables interact and relate to each other in the database

ergonomics Science of the relationship between people and machines; designing work areas to facilitate both productivity and human ease and comfort

Ethernet A common method of networking computers in a LAN, using copper cabling at speeds up to 100 Mbps

ethics Principles for judging right and wrong, held by a person or group

event An action or occurrence recognized by a class

event handler How a class responds to an event

exponent In scientific notation, it's the power of the base and is multiplied by the mantissa to give the actual number

expression A statement containing a combination of values that's interpreted and computed to produce another value

Extended ASCII A method for storing characters with an 8-bit code; adds 128 more characters to the original 7-bit ASCII code

FAT (File Allocation Table) File management system used to locate files on a storage medium

FDDI (Fibre Distributed Data Interface) A token-passing, fiber-optic cable protocol with support for data rates up to 100 Mbps; FDDI networks are typically used as the main lines for WANs

FDM (frequency-division multiplexing) A technique for combining many signals on a single circuit by dividing available transmission bandwidth by frequency into narrower bands, each used for a separate communication channel

fiber optic Guided network cable consisting of bundles of thin glass strands surrounded by a protective plastic sheath

file compression The process of reducing file size and, therefore, taking up less disk space

file system   The part of the OS responsible for creating, manipulating, renaming, copying, and moving files to and from a storage device

firewall   A software or hardware network device that protects a network by filtering out potentially harmful incoming and outgoing traffic

first in, first out (FIFO)   The last item placed on the queue is the last item removed, and the first item removed from the queue is the first item placed onto it

first normal form (1NF)   Eliminating repeating fields or groups of fields from the table and confirming that every column has only one value by creating a new record in the table

flash drive   A small, thumb-sized memory device that functions as though it were a disk drive; flash drives normally plug into a PC's USB port

flip-flop or latch   A digital circuit that can retain the binary value it was set to after the input is removed; static RAM is constructed by using flip-flop circuits

floating-point or scientific notation   A method of representing numbers containing fractional values consistently; uses a mantissa and an exponent, such as 3.144543E+8

flowchart   A combination of symbols and text that provides a visual description of a process

FM (frequency modulation)   A technique of placing data on an alternating carrier wave by varying the signal's frequency; this technique is often used in modems

folder   Structure on a formatted disk that enables storing and organizing files; also known as a directory or subdirectory

foreign key (FK)   A column in one table that relates to a primary key in another table

format   Organizing the disk's surface in a way that allows writing folders and files to it

FTP (File Transfer Protocol)   A protocol designed to exchange text and binary files via the Internet

function   A block of code that performs a task and can return a value

functional dependency   A column's value is dependent on another column's value

gate   A transistor-based circuit in the computer that implements Boolean logic by creating a single output value for a given set of input values

gateway   A network component, similar to a bridge, that allows connecting networks of different types

gaze system   A system that uses users' eye movements as input

gold plating   Adding unnecessary features to the project design

graphical user interface (GUI)   A method of interacting with the OS, in which information is displayed in a graphical format, and the user can select items by using a pointing device, such as a mouse

guided media   Physical transmission media, such as wire or cable

hacker   A technically proficient person who breaks into a computer system; originally denoted good intent, but general usage today is similar to "cracker"

Hacker's Manifesto   A document, written anonymously, that justifies cracking into systems as an ethical exercise

hacktivism   Cracking into a system as a political act; one political notion is that cracking itself is useful for society

haptics technologies   Technologies that allow users to feel a response from a system, not just see or hear a response; optimally, can replicate the sensation of feeling an object in real life to create a virtual tactile experience

hardware   The physical device on which software runs

hash key   A unique value used in hashing algorithms and identifying records

hashing   A common method for accessing data in a file or database table with a unique value called the hash key

hashing algorithm   A routine of logic used for determining how hash values are created

head pointer   A pointer indicating the beginning of the first element in a data structure

height   The longest path length in the tree

heuristics   In virus detection, a set of rules predicting how a virus might act; for example, anticipating that the virus will affect certain critical system files

hexadecimal (hex)   Numbering system with 16 digits, 0–9 and A–F; also known as base 16 and often used as shorthand for binary (one hex digit = four binary digits)

high-level language   A programming language written in a more natural language that humans can read and understand

honeypot   A trap (program or system) laid by a system administrator to catch and track intruders

HTML (Hypertext Markup Language)   Markup symbols or codes inserted in a file that specify how the material is displayed on a Web page

HTTP (Hypertext Transfer Protocol)   A protocol designed for transferring files (primarily content files) on the World Wide Web

hub   A network device that functions as a multiport repeater; signals received on any port are immediately retransmitted to all other ports on the hub

Hungarian notation   A variable-naming method that adds a letter at the beginning of a variable name to indicate its data type

hyperlink   A link that allows users to select a connection from one word, picture, or information object to another

hypermedia   Different sorts of information (text, sound, pictures, video) that are linked in such a way that a user can move and see content easily from one link to another

hypertext   Hypermedia that is specifically text

IANA (Internet Assigned Numbers Authority)   The organization under contract with the U.S. government to oversee allocating IP addresses to ISPs

identification   A technique for knowing who someone is; for example, a Social Security number can be identification

identifier   Name of a variable

IEEE (Institute of Electrical and Electronics Engineers)   An organization involved in formulating networking standards

IEEE-754   A standard for the binary representation of floating-point numbers; it's the 754th standard proposed by the IEEE

IMAP (Internet Message Access Protocol)   A standard protocol for accessing e-mail from a mail server

impedance   The opposition a transmission medium has toward the flow of alternating electrical currents

index (subscript)   How an array accesses each element stored in its data structure

index   A special file that occupies its own space and specifies one or more columns that determine how information stored in the table can be accessed more efficiently

inductance   The magnetic field around a conductor that opposes changes in current flow

inductive reasoning or scientific method   A basic approach to problem solving, consisting of four steps: observe, theorize, test, and repeat

inheritance   The process of creating more specific classes based on generic classes

insertion point   Where the cursor is placed

instantiation   The process of creating an object based on a class and assigning memory to it

integrated circuit (IC)   A collection of transistors on a single piece of hardware (called a "chip") that reduces the circuit's size and physical complexity

integrated development environment (IDE)   An interface provided with software development languages that incorporates all the tools needed to write, compile, and distribute programs; these tools often include an editor, a compiler, a graphical designer, and more

integrity   Assurance that information is what you think it is and hasn't been modified

intellectual property   An idea or product based on an idea that has commercial value, such as literary or artistic works, patents, business methods, industrial processes, and trade secrets

interpreter   An application that converts each program statement into a language the computer understands

interrupt handling   A computer process in which a signal is placed on the bus to interrupt normal processing of instructions and transfer control to a special program designed to deal with events such as I/O requests

IP (Internet Protocol)   The protocol that provides for addressing and routing Internet packets from one computer to another

IP address   A unique 32-bit number assigned to network devices that use Internet Protocol

IPCONFIG   A Windows command-line utility that can be used to display currently assigned network settings

IPv4   Version 4 of Internet Protocol, the most widely used version of IP

IPv6   Version 6 of Internet Protocol has more capabilities than IPv4, including providing for far more IP addresses

ISO (International Organization for Standardization)   An organization that coordinates worldwide standards development

ISO OSI reference model   A data communication model consisting of seven functional layers

ISP (Internet service provider)   A company that provides access to the Internet and other related services, such as Web site building and virtual hosting

JavaScript   An interpreted programming or script language from Netscape; somewhat similar in capability to Microsoft VBScript

JSP (Java Server Pages)   Comparable with Microsoft's ASP technology, except that it runs only programs written in Java

kernel   The core of an operating system; controls processor, disk, memory, and other central functions

killer app   A software program that becomes so popular that it drives the popularity of the hardware it runs on

LAN (local area network)   A network of computers in a single building or in close proximity

last in, first out (LIFO)   The last item placed on the stack is the first item removed from the stack

LCD (liquid crystal display)   A type of electronic device used as a computer monitor; popular in notebook computers and PDA devices and now used widely for desktop monitors

leaf node   A node that has no child nodes

learnability   A measure of how quickly users can learn to use the technology to perform their tasks

left child   The child node to the left of the parent node

linked list   A data structure that uses noncontiguous memory locations to store data; each element in the linked list points to the next element in line and doesn't have to be contiguous with the previous element

Linux   A multitasking, multiuser, open-source variation of the UNIX OS

long-term memory   Where information is stored on a semipermanent basis; can store a potentially limitless amount, but retrieving information can be more difficult

lower bound   The lowest position in an array

low-level language   A programming language that uses binary code for instructions

machine language   The lowest-level programming language, which consists of binary bit patterns

main board or motherboard   The physical circuit board in a computer that contains the CPU and other basic circuitry and components

mainframe   A large, expensive computer, often serving many terminals and used by large organizations; all first-generation computers were mainframes

malicious code   Code designed to breach system security and threaten digital information; often called a virus, although technically a virus is only one kind of malicious code

mantissa   In scientific notation, it contains the number's significant digits and is placed before the exponent

many-to-many (M:M) relationship   Many instances of one entity or table (parent table) are associated with many instances of another entity (child table)

Master File Table (MFT)   A table used in NTFS to store data about every file and directory on the volume

metadata   In XML and in database systems, information about characteristics of the data in a file; sometimes called "data about data"

method   The work performed by an object; a function defined in a class

microcomputer   A desktop-sized computer with a microprocessor CPU designed to be used by one person at a time

microprocessor   A CPU on a single chip used in microcomputers

minicomputer   Mid-sized computer introduced in the mid to late 1960s; it typically cost tens of thousands of dollars versus hundreds of thousands of dollars for a mainframe

modem   A device that converts binary signals into audio signals for transmission over standard voice-grade telephone lines and converts the audio signals back into binary

modification attacks   Attacks on a system that alter information illicitly

MP3 (MPEG-1 Audio Layer-3)   A standard technology and format for compressing a sound sequence into a small file, compared with an uncompressed sound file, such as a WAV file

multidimensional array   An array consisting of two or more single-dimensional arrays

multiprocessing   Coordinated execution of a process, using two or more CPUs at the same time

multitasking   An OS's capability to effectively support more than one process running at a time

NAND   A logical AND followed by a logical NOT that returns a false value only if both operands are true

NAT (Network Address Translation)   Used to translate an inside IP address to an outside IP address; NAT is often used to allow multiple computers to share one Internet connection

natural-language processing   A system that recognizes the natural way in which humans communicate verbally (by speech or text) and can discern meaning from this communication

NBP (national backbone provider)   A provider of high-speed network communication lines for use by ISPs

nesting   Putting one control structure inside another

network interface card (NIC)   A circuit board that connects a network medium to the system bus and converts a computer's binary information into a format suitable for the transmission medium; each NIC has a unique, 48-bit address

network operating system   An OS designed to provide strong network services

network topology   A schematic description of the arrangement of a network, including its nodes and connecting lines

nibble   A term sometimes used to refer to 4 bits (half a byte)

node   Any addressable device attached to a network that can recognize, process, or forward data transmissions

node or vertex   A position in a tree data structure

NOR   A logical OR followed by a logical NOT that returns a true value only if both operands are false

normalization   A database design process that structures tables to eliminate duplication and inconsistencies in the data structure

NOT   Boolean operator that returns a false value if the operand is true and a true value if the operand is false

NTFS (New Technology File System)   File management system introduced in Windows NT and incorporated into all desktop and server Windows OSs since then; used to locate files on a storage medium

null value   The absence of a value, meaning there's no value stored; null is not the same as blank or zero

object   A self-contained entity consisting of both data and procedures

object-oriented programming (OOP)   A style of programming that involves representing items, things, and people as objects instead of basing program logic on actions

offset   Used to specify the distance between memory locations

one-to-many (1:M) relationship   One instance of an entity (parent table) is associated with zero to many instances of another table (child table)

one-to-one (1:1) relationship   One instance of an entity (parent table) is associated with only one instance of another entity (child table)

open architecture   Computer hardware that's accessible for modification and sometimes even documented

open source   Computer programs, including operating systems, developed as a public collaboration and made available free for use or modification

operating system (OS)   Software that allows applications to access hardware resources, such as printers or hard drives, and provides tools for managing and administering system resources, processes, and security

operators   Symbols used to indicate data-manipulation operations

OR   Boolean operator that returns a true value if either operand is true

overflow area   Area in a file that's used in case a collision occurs during the hashing algorithm

packet-filtering firewall   A firewall that inspects each packet and moves it along an established link to its destination; usually faster but less secure than a proxy firewall

parallel computing   The use of multiple computers or CPUs to process a single task simultaneously

parameter   A received value assigned to a variable; used by a block of source code

partition   An area of a hard disk reserved to hold files of a particular OS type

patent   A government grant that gives the sole right to make, use, and sell an invention for a specified period of time

PCI   A system bus to connect a microprocessor with memory and I/O devices; PCI is widely used in personal computers

PDU (protocol data unit)   A data communication packet containing protocol information in addition to a data payload

peeking   Looking at the top item in the stack without removing it from the stack

Perl   A script programming language similar in syntax to the C language; often used to develop CGI dynamic Web pages

personal computer (PC)   Originally an IBM microcomputer; now generally refers to any microcomputer

PHP   In Web programming, a free script language and interpreter used primarily on Linux Web servers

phreaking   Subverting the phone system to get free service

pixel (picture element)   The basic unit of programmable color on a computer display or in a computer image; its physical size depends on the display device's resolution

platform   The OS running on a computer

Plug and Play (PnP)   A technology that allows the OS and hardware to work together to detect and configure I/O devices automatically

PM (phase modulation)   A technique of placing data on an alternating carrier wave by varying the signal's phase; the most common modulation type in modems

pointer   A memory variable containing the address of a memory cell as its data

polling   A technique in which the CPU periodically interrogates I/O devices to see whether they require attention; polling requires many more CPU resources than interrupt handling

polymorphism   An object's capability to use the same expression to denote different operations

POP (point of presence)   An access point to the Internet

pop   Remove an item from the stack

POP3 (Post Office Protocol version 3)   The most recent version of a standard protocol for receiving e-mail from a mail server

port   In the context of I/O devices, the physical connection on the computer that allows an I/O device to be plugged in

port number   An addressing mechanism used in TCP/IP as a way for a client program to specify a particular server program on a network computer and to facilitate Network Address Translation

positional value   The numerical value each position in a number has; calculated by raising the base of the number to the power of the position

POST (power-on self test)   A procedure performed by the computer boot routine to check hardware devices

postcondition loop   A loop that executes at least one time before the expression is evaluated

precedence   The order in which something is executed; symbols with a higher precedence are executed before those with a lower precedence

precondition loop   A loop that checks the expression before any source code in the loop is executed; might never be executed

primary key (PK)   A column or combination of columns that uniquely identifies a row in a table

privacy   Freedom from unwanted access to or intrusion into a person's private life or information; the Internet and computerized databases have made invasion of privacy much easier and are an increasing cause for concern

procedure   A group of one or more related commands that perform a task

process   A small program running on a computer; can be part of a larger program

program   A collection of statements or steps that solves a problem and needs to be converted into a language the computer understands to perform tasks

program loop   The capability of a program to "loop back" and repeat commands

project manager   Leader of the software development team; responsible for choosing the right players for the right positions and making sure the project is on schedule

property or attribute   Characteristic of an object

protocol   A set of rules designed to facilitate communication; protocols are heavily used in networking

prototype   A standard or typical example that gives end users a good idea of what they will see when their application is completed

proxy firewall   A firewall that establishes a new link between each packet of information and its destination; slower but more secure than a packet-filtering firewall

pseudocode   A readable description of an algorithm written in human language

push   Place an item on the stack

Python   An interpreted, object-oriented programming language similar to Perl that has gained popularity in recent years

queue   A list in which the next item to be removed is the item that has been in the list the longest

radix point   The point that divides the fractional portion from the whole portion of a number; in the decimal numbering system, it's referred to as a decimal point

RAID (redundant array of independent disks)   A collection of connected hard drives arranged for increased access speed or high reliability

RAM (random access memory)   A generic term for volatile memory in a computer; RAM is fast and can be accessed randomly but requires power to retain its information

random access   Reading data from or writing data to anywhere on a disk

recursion   The process of a routine calling itself

reflective thinking   Thinking about how something reflects on the user and his or her relationship to others

refresh rate   The number of times per second an image is renewed onscreen; a higher refresh rate results in less flickering in the display

register   A small unit of very high-speed memory located on the CPU; used to store data and instructions for the CPU

relationship   How one entity or table works with another

repeater   A network device used to amplify signals on long cables between nodes

repudiation attacks   Attacks on a system that injure the information's reliability; for example, a repudiation attack might remove evidence that an event (such as a bank transaction) actually did occur

reserved word   A keyword with a specific instructional meaning; the name can't be used for a variable because the programming language is already using it as an instruction

resolution   A measurement of the granularity of a computer monitor or printer; usually given as a pair of numbers indicating the number of dots in a horizontal and vertical direction or the number of dots per inch

resources   Devices connected to the CPU, such as the main memory, hard disk, and CD/DVD-ROM drive; all running processes have to share these devices

reverse-engineer   To figure out the design of a program or device by taking it apart and analyzing its components; for example, source code can be reverse-engineered to determine a design model

RGB (red, green, and blue)   A type of computer monitor that displays color as a function of these three colors

RGB encoding   A method of defining a pixel's color and brightness in terms of intensity of the colors red, green, and blue

right child   The child node to the right of the parent node

risk   The relationship between vulnerability and threat; total risk also includes the potential effect of existing countermeasures

ROM (read-only memory)   A type of memory that retains its information without power; some types of ROM can be reprogrammed

root   The node that begins the tree

root level   The main folder/directory level on a drive

router   A network device, similar to a gateway, that directs network traffic, based on its logical address

row, record, or tuple   A collection of columns

SATA (Serial AT Attachment)   A popular bus used to connect hard drives and other mass storage devices to the computer

scope   Where source code can be seen and whether other programs can see and use it

scope creep   Occurs when new changes are added to a project constantly, thus changing the proposed deadline so that the project is never completed; instead, it's in a constant improvement mode

script kiddie   An amateur hacker who simply uses the hacking tools developed by others

SCSI   A high-speed bus designed to allow computers to communicate with peripheral hardware, such as disk drives, CD/DVD-ROM drives, printers, and scanners

search engine   A program, usually accessed on the Web, that gathers and reports information available on the Internet

second normal form (2NF)   First normal form has already been applied to the table, and every column that isn't part of the primary key is fully dependent on the primary key

selection sort   A sorting routine that selects the smallest unsorted item remaining in the list, and then swaps it with the item in the next position to be filled

semiconductor   A medium that's neither a good insulator nor a good conductor of electricity, used to construct transistors

sensory storage   Where sensory information is first processed by the human brain before passing it to short-term memory; can handle a lot of information simultaneously but can't store it for long

sequential access   Reading and writing data in order from the beginning

SGML (Standard Generalized Markup Language)   A standard for how to specify a document markup language or tag set

shifter   A circuit that converts a fixed number of inputs to outputs that have bits shifted to the left or right, often used with adders to perform multiplication and division

short-term memory   Where information is sent after the sensory system receives it; limited to storing five to nine items temporarily

signal-to-noise ratio   A measure of the quality of a communication channel

single-tasking   An OS that allows running only one process (task) at a time

slide rule   A device that can perform complicated math by using sliding guides on a rulerlike device; popular with engineers until the advent of the cheap electronic calculator

SMTP (Simple Mail Transfer Protocol)   A TCP/IP-related, high-level protocol used in sending e-mail

sniffer   A software program, such as Wireshark, that allows the user to listen in on network traffic

social engineering   Social interaction that preys on human gullibility, sympathy, or fear to take advantage of the target, for example, to steal money, information, or other valuables—basically, a con

software   The instructions that operate the hardware

software developer (or programmer)   Person responsible for writing source code to meet the end user's functional requirements

software development life cycle (SDLC)   A model that describes the life of the application, including all stages involved in developing, testing, installing, and maintaining a program

software engineering   The process of producing software applications, involving not just the program's source code but also associated documentation, including UML diagrams, screen prototypes, reports, software requirements, future development issues, and data needed to make programs operate correctly

software piracy   Illegal copying of software; a problem in the United States and Europe, but rampant in the rest of the world

sort key   In a database table, one or more columns used to determine the data's sort order

spam   Unsolicited (and almost always unwanted) e-mail; usually trying to sell something

spider   Also called a bot or crawler, a program that visits Web sites and reads their pages and other information to create entries for a search engine index

spyware   Software that can track, collect, and transmit to a third party or Web site certain information about a user's computer habits

SRAM   Static RAM, a type of high-speed memory constructed with flip-flop circuits

SSH (Secure Shell)   A network protocol for secure data exchange between two networked devices, usually in a Linux environment.

stack   A list in which the next item to be removed is the item most recently stored

stack pointer   A pointer that keeps track of where to remove or add an item in a data structure

stored program concept   The idea that a computer can be operated by a program loaded into the machine's memory; also implies that programs can be stored somewhere and repeatedly loaded into memory, and the program itself, just like other data, can be modified

Structured Query Language (SQL)   A special language used to maintain database structure and modify, query, and extract information

subclass   A more specific class based on a parent class and created via inheritance

subnet   A portion of a network that shares part of an address with other portions of the network and is distinguished by a subnet number

supercomputer   The fastest and usually most expensive computer available; often used in scientific and engineering research

superstitious behavior   Users with incomplete information on how to use a technology create an incorrect model of the way a technology works

switch   A network repeater with multiple inputs and outputs; each input can be switched to any of the outputs, creating a point-to-point circuit

symmetric encryption   Encryption using a private key to both encrypt and decrypt

syntax   Rules for how a programming language's statements must be constructed

system bus   The main bus used by the CPU to transfer data and instructions to and from memory and I/O devices

system clock   A crystal oscillator circuit on a main board that provides timing and synchronization for operating the CPU and other circuitry

T1 line   A digital transmission link with a capacity of 1.544 Mbps; T1 uses two pairs of normal twisted wires, the same twisted wire used in most homes

table or entity   Data arranged in rows and columns, much like a spreadsheet

tail pointer   Keeps track of the end or rear position of the data structure

TCP (Transmission Control Protocol)   An OSI Transport layer, connection-oriented protocol designed to exchange messages between network devices

TCP/IP (Transmission Control Protocol/Internet Protocol)   The suite of communication protocols used to connect hosts on the Internet

TDM (time-division multiplexing)   A technique for combining many signals on a single circuit by allocating each signal a fixed amount of time but allowing each signal the full bandwidth during an allotted time

tester   Person responsible for making sure the program functions correctly and meets all the functional requirements specified in the design document

third normal form (3NF)   Eliminate columns that are not dependent on only the primary key

threat   The likely agent of a possible attack, the event that would occur as a result of an attack, and the target of the attack

time slicing   A method of allocating fixed time units to running processes so that it appears to users that all processes are running simultaneously

time-sharing   A computer's capability to share its computing time with many users at the same time

time to live (TTL)   A field in the IP header that enables routers to discard packets that have been traversing the network for too long

token ring   A LAN technology that has stations wired in a ring, in which each station constantly passes a special message token on to the next; whichever station has the token can send a message

trade secret   A method, formula, device, or piece of information that a company keeps secret and that gives the company a competitive advantage

transistor   A signal amplifier much smaller than a vacuum tube used to represent a 1 (on) or a 0 (off), which are the rudiments of computer calculation; often used as part of an integrated circuit (IC)

transitive dependency   One column is dependent on another column that isn't a primary key

transmission medium   A material with the capability to conduct electrical and/or electromagnetic signals

tree   A data structure that represents a hierarchical structure, similar to that of organizational or genealogical charts

Trojan program   A program that poses as an innocent program; some action or the passage of time triggers the program to do its dirty work

truth table   A table representing the inputs and outputs of a logic circuit; truth tables can represent basic logic circuits as well as complex ones

twisted pair   A pair (sometimes pairs) of insulated wires twisted together and used as a transmission medium in networking

twos complement   A method of representing negative numbers in a computer system; a binary number is converted to twos complement format by flipping, or reversing, the state of each bit and then adding 1 to the entire word

ubiquitous computing   The possibility of computers being embedded into almost everything and potentially able to communicate

undirected (untargeted) hacker   A cracker motivated by the challenge of breaking into a system

unguided media   Transmission media you can't see, such as air or space, that carry radio or light signals

Unicode   A 16-bit standard for storing text or script information; defines 34,168 unique characters and control codes

Unified Modeling Language (UML)   A software modeling process for creating a blueprint that shows the progam's overall functionality and provides a way for the client and developer to communicate

UNIX   A multitasking, multiuser, command-line operating system known for its stability and reliability

upper bound   The highest position in an array

URL (Uniform Resource Locator)   The English-like address of a file accessible on the Internet

USB (universal serial bus)   A high-speed interface between a computer and I/O devices; multiple USB devices can be plugged into a computer without having to power off the computer

usefulness   A measure of how many of the intended tasks users can perform with the technology

user environment   Where users perform their tasks

user interface   The component that handles interaction between a technology and the user; consists of what the user's senses can perceive and what the user can manipulate to operate the technology

user profiles   Written descriptions of who the users are, including backgrounds, skills, and so forth

user requirements   What users want and need to do

user scenarios   Examples of user activities, written to show the steps users go through in using a technology

user tasks   What users do and how they do it

user-centric design   Designing by focusing on users' needs before considering other constraints of the system

vacuum tube   A signal amplifier that preceded the transistor; like a transistor, it can be integrated into a circuit, but it takes more power, is larger, and burns out more quickly

variable   A name used to identify a certain location and value in the computer's memory

variable initialization   Supplying a value when a variable is first declared

VBScript An interpreted script language from Microsoft that's a subset of the Visual Basic programming language; often used by Web browsers and Active Server Pages (ASP) servers

Very Large-Scale Integration (VLSI) The current point of evolution in the development of the integrated circuit; VLSI chips typically have more than 100,000 transistors

virtual private network (VPN) A private network connection that "tunnels" through a larger, public network and is restricted to authorized users

virus An uninvited guest program with the potential to damage files and the operating system; this term is sometimes used generically to denote a virus, worm, or Trojan program

virus hoax E-mail that contains a phony virus warning; started as a prank to upset people or to get them to delete legitimate system files

virus signature (or virus definition) Bits of code that uniquely identify a particular virus

visceral thinking Immediate, instinctive thinking; an object's look and feel play a role in how it's perceived

voice-recognition technology A technology that can recognize human speech and process instructions

Von Neumann machine A computer architecture developed by John Von Neumann and others in the 1940s that allows for input, output, processing, and memory; it also includes the stored program concept

vulnerability The sensitivity of information combined with the skill level an attacker needs to threaten that information

WAN (wide area network) A network in which computer devices are physically distant from each other, typically spanning cities, states, or even continents

waterfall model An SDLC approach involving sequential application development with processes organized into phases; after a phase is completed, a new one starts, and you can't return to the previous phase

WAV An audio file format that has become a standard for everything from PC system and game sounds to CD-quality audio

Web server A program running on a computer that responds to HTTP requests for Web pages and returns the pages to the requesting client

Web service Programming and data on a Web server designed to make data available to other Web programs

whole (integer) number A number (positive, zero, or negative) that has no fractional portion

wildcard   A symbol that stands for one or more characters, used in selecting files or directories

Windows   A popular Microsoft GUI operating system for Intel-based systems

WLAN (wireless LAN)   A local network that uses wireless transmission instead of wires; the IEEE 802.11 protocol family is often used in WLANs

word   A group of bits in a computer system; the number of bits in a word depends on the machine, but common word sizes are 16, 32, and 64 bits; a typical computer system manipulates bits in word increments

worm   A type of bot that can roam a network looking for vulnerable systems and replicate itself on those systems; the new copies look for still more vulnerable systems

XML (Extensible Markup Language)   A markup language designed to create common information formats and share the format and data on the World Wide Web

XOR   A logical operator that returns a true value if one, but not both, of its operands is true

index